The Ultimate Windows 2000 System Administrator's Guide

Robert Williams

Mark Walla

 Addison-Wesley

An imprint of Addison Wesley Longman, Inc.

READING, MASSACHUSETTS   HARLOW, ENGLAND   MENLO PARK, CALIFORNIA
BERKELEY, CALIFORNIA   DON MILLS, ONTARIO   SYDNEY
BONN   AMSTERDAM   TOKYO   MEXICO CITY

The publisher offers discounts on this book when ordered in quantity for special sales. For more information, please contact:

AWL Direct Sales
Addison Wesley Longman, Inc.
One Jacob Way
Reading, Massachusetts 01867

Visit AW on the Web: *www.awl.com/cseng/*

Library of Congress Cataloging-in-Publication Data
Williams, G. Robert, 1948–
    The ultimate Windows 2000 system administrator's guide / Robert Williams and Mark Walla.
        p. cm.
    ISBN 0-201-61580-0 (alk. paper)
    1. Microsoft Windows (Computer file)   2. Operating systems (Computers)   I. Walla, Mark.   II. Title.
    QA76.76.O63 W55467 2000
    005.4′4769—dc21   00-022163

Acquisitions Editor: Gary Clarke
Editorial Assistant: Rebecca Bence
Production Coordinator: Marilyn Rash
Compositor: Publishers' Design and Production Services, Inc.

ISBN 0-201-61580-0
Text printed on recycled and acid-free paper.
1 2 3 4 5 6 7 8 9 10–DOC–04 03 02 01 00
First printing, April 2000.

Contents

Chapter 4   **Getting Started**   **93**

Chapter 5   **The Active Directory**   **113**

Chapter 9   Permissions Security, Folder Sharing, and Dfs   315

x   Contents

Chapter 11   Additional Security Issues and Solutions   451

Preface

Windows 2000 is a complex, feature-rich operating system product family whose deployment in an enterprise requires highly skilled individuals to support its installation, maintenance, and optimization. These individuals are aided by the abundance of tools and wizards for effective operating system management that Microsoft has provided. Indeed, many of the enhanced tools should shift the traditional role of administrator to that of proactive manager of computing environments. Thus, the depth of function, flexibility, and granularity of Windows 2000 ultimately represents both opportunity and challenge for system administration.

This book is written to help you succeed in the administration of the Windows 2000 Server family. Much of the information it provides is also applicable to the desktop Windows 2000 Professional version. While the use and management of Windows 2000 Professional is incorporated, the Server side is clearly our primary focus. In this preface we provide a framework for the primary topics covered, define the target audience and describe how to use this book.

THE ROLE OF THE ADMINISTRATOR

Windows 2000 will not eliminate the system administrator. To the contrary, features such as the Active Directory and the Microsoft Management Console will vastly broaden this role. Rather than spend time on mundane tasks and the management of dozens of disjointed tools, and consolidated approach provided by Windows 2000 will free the administrator to concentrate on more mission critical activities.

The functions of the Windows 2000 system administrator are generally those that support the user population and those that support the system. The following list summarizes some of the most common responsibilities:

USER-ORIENTED TASKS

- Adding and removing users
- Group management
- User application support
- End-user customer service, education, and communication
- Management of basic services like mail and printing

SYSTEM-ORIENTED TASKS

- Booting, shutdown, and everything in between
- Backups and restoration
- Hardware maintenance, additions, and removal
- System accounting and monitoring
- System administration logs
- System security and password aging
- Network support
- General troubleshooting

Obviously this list only scratches the surface of system administration and IT management. However, as a means of setting the reader's expectations, it does underscore the types of activities for which this book can be used as a guide.

BASIS OF OUR RESEARCH

In preparing this book we utilized three primary sources of information. First, we relied heavily on our combined professional experience in application development, system administration, and IT management. Unlike so many books written in theory by technical writers, our recommendations did not emerge from a vacuum but are based on reality and experiences. We hope the experience we bring to this book will assist our fellow IT professionals to better manage an enterprise.

Second, we used observations from system administrators in the field to provide "reality checks" to our conclusions. Theoretical understanding of Windows 2000 is a nice beginning, but it is no substitute for the actual experience of system administrators. Because Windows 2000 is a new product, one of our primary sources was participants in Microsoft's Rapid Deployment Program and their experience with final beta and final release versions of the operating system.

Finally, we performed extensive tests and simulated real-world environments in an extensive laboratory environment. The tests centered primarily on the Server and Advance Server versions; however, Windows 2000 Professional was also tested and is periodically referenced as client software within the broader enterprise framework. Windows 2000 DataCenter was not available for testing at the time this book was written, and so references to it are based on published Microsoft specifications. Where differences exist in the version levels, we call attention to them.

AUDIENCE

This book was written for system administrators and other IT professionals who manage a Windows 2000 environment. Administrators coming from other operating system environments like UNIX will find many significant conceptual differences and numerous familiar technologies. Seasoned Windows NT administrators will find many familiar aspects but many significant differences as well that will require a general updating of their technical skills. The addition of the Active Directory, a new domain model, advanced authentication technologies, and the enhanced Microsoft Management Console are just a few examples of entirely new or expanded operating system features.

Our aim was to produce an intermediate reference guide for administrators, leaving out specialized architectural or programming topics. Thus, this book should be used for an understanding of key concepts and for common "how-to" walkthrough support. Experienced professionals should find the discussions on operating system migration and the use of the new enhanced tools valuable. Those with moderate system administration experience can also benefit, but we assume these readers already have hands-on operating system experience. Novices will need to learn network and operating system fundamentals.

Attempting to provide useful information to an audience of system administrators was a challenge. Inevitably, some of the book's material may appear either overly basic or too advanced, and depending on a reader's level of experience, some discussions will be more helpful than others. To accommodate this wide variance in prior knowledge, we first cover each major topic from a conceptual basis and then expand this foundation with discussions on applying specific advanced Windows 2000 functions.

System administrators coming from UNIX might find helpful our sister publication *Windows NT & UNIX: Administration, Coexistence, Integration, & Migration* (Addison-Wesley 1998). There will be updates of that book focusing on Windows 2000 in the future.

ORGANIZATION

The book is organized into three sections and an appendix:

- The first four chapters focus on Windows 2000 concepts, deployment, and installation. They cover the role of the system administrator, Windows 2000 features, operating system structure, and deployment and actual installation. Chapter 4 discusses getting started with tools such as the Microsoft Management Console (MMC).

- The heart of the book, chapters 5 through 14, is a discussion of fundamental administration topics. In a series of very technical chapters, we cover the Active Directory, user management, group policies, security, printer and file services, networking, and other topics essential to Windows 2000 system administration.

- The last part of the book covers advanced tools and concepts. It examines the Internet Information Service and optional components such as Terminal Services, System Management Server, Indexing Services, Message Queuing Services, Cluster Services, and other topics applicable to enterprise-level system administration.

- The Appendix, Windows 2000 Commands and Utilities, is a quick reference for the most significant commands in the operating system and in the Windows 2000 Resource Kit.

A Glossary of common terms is also provided.

OTHER REFERENCES

A wealth of information should be utilized by system administrators to supplement this book. The Windows 2000 operating system provides extensive online help available from the **Start → Help** facility. Microsoft also regularly posts white papers on its website, which should be regularly checked for updated information.

At the time of publication, Microsoft had not released some anticipated Windows 2000 auxiliary tool kits. In the interim, we suggest at least two Windows NT downloadable components. The Zero Administration Toolkit (ZAK) facilitates administration of Windows NT. Its current tools are available from *http://www.microsoft.com/windows/zak*. Operating system interoperability is increasingly an important issue with Windows 2000 deployment. Microsoft provides a number of helpful applications for the management of such environments. Also, Microsoft Services for UNIX provides a number of tools and applications for enterprises that must interoperate with Windows 2000 and UNIX. For information on it see the Microsoft Web page *http://www.microsoft.com/Windows/server/Deploy/interoperability*.

Trade magazines can also be an excellent source of information. We recommend *Computer World, Windows 2000 Magazine* (formerly *Windows NT*), *Platform Decisions, ENT, MS Journal,* and *Dr. Dobb's Journal.* As for online services, we strongly recommend Microsoft's security and patch e-mail service at *www. microsoft.com/security/.* Other Web-based services are *Windows 2000 Advantage.com, Lyris nt-administration tools, Bug Track, Brainbuzz.com,* and *San NT.*

Finally, we will be posting updated information on Windows 2000 on our website at *http://www.EnterpriseCertified.com/w2kbook.htm.*

Acknowledgments

This book is a result of the efforts of many individuals, whose support the co-authors would like to acknowledge.

The special effort of contributors Byron Bielman and Ellen Beck Gardner in the development of this book deserve our thanks. Thanks also to our very supportive editor Gary Clarke and his editorial assistant Rebecca Bence, as well as executive editor J. Carter Shanklin, marketing director Robin Bruce, production coordinator Marilyn Rash, and the entire Addison Wesley Longman production team. The extremely valuable insights of AWL reviewers John Holmwood, Martin Sjoelin, Bryan E. Helvey, and Michael P. Deignan (president, Ideamation, Inc.) are also greatly appreciated. Production coordinator Diane Freed and copy editor Dianne Wood provided superior assistance.

Microsoft's Rapid Deployment Program (RDP) team provided firsthand information on the use of the Windows 2000 operating system, and we greatly appreciate the Microsoft engineers who managed the RDP newsgroups and those RDP participants who provided data. Several RDP members clearly went an extra mile in reviewing early drafts of the book. Thus, we cannot overstate the value of contributions made by Andrew van der Stock, James Edelen and James Morris of the University of Washington, Michael Brown and Rick Kingslan of MSCE+I, Tom Gutnick, and Uwe Mundry. They are truly unsung heroes.

Microsoft was extremely cooperative in the development of the book. We thank Ed Muth and Michael Emanuel, who, despite their heavy schedules, made themselves and members of the Windows 2000 team available, and group vice president Jeff Raikes, who made resources available when needed. Our thanks also go to John Ford, who continually extended himself by providing friendly support and road maps into the Microsoft organizational maze; Marsha Kabakov and Dean

Murray, who provided early educational information; and Donna Senko and Anne Marie McSweeny, who gave insight into the Windows 2000 certification programs. We thank Nancy Lewis and the longtime support of her excellent team, and we acknowledge the support and insight of Ian Rogoff, Gary Schare, Chris Ray, Andy Forsberg, Douglas Miller, Liz Brackett, and Stephen Walli. In our Rocky mountain region, we acknowledge Chris Munger, Gene Cornfield, and Kent Sarff.

Special thanks to executive editor Charlie Simpson of *Enterprise Systems* and *Platform Decision* magazines and to the *Windows NT 2000* magazine team, especially managing editor Karen Forster, senior acquisition editor Amy Eisenberg and news editor (and my partner in crime on other book projects) Barrie Sosinsky. *Computer World*'s Bruce Hoard, Ellen Fanning, and Stefanie McCann also warrant a special thanks.

Bob Williams has special personal and professional acknowledgments. Thanks to family members Flora Williams and Sue and Mike Montgomery. Great appreciation for years of support to friends Bill Kuehl, Deb Murray, Ed Nichols, Ellen and Kevin Gardner, Ivory Curtis, Jim Fry, Dr. James and Wanda Riviere, Karen Bircher, Margaret Krawczck, Mark and Toni Sehnert, Martha McGavin, Mike and Mary Glynn, Roger Ayan, Roger Caauwe, and Scott Woodland. Finally, to my goddaughter, Emily, and her brother, Alex.

Mark Walla expresses personal thanks to a number of people who have provided support and encouragement. Special thanks to his parents Gary Walla and Sandy Minter and their respective spouses Kay and Jules, and to brother Tom Walla and Brittany. Professional and personal thanks also to Dave and Anne Peterson, Troy Love, Jim Welch, Byron Beilman, Peter Shen, John LaPorte, Dem Pilafian, Darrel Ritchie, Dave Kovsky, Carl Castillo, Diane Horn, Kent Tang, Nancy Robins, Glen Sater, Joseph Chen, Dan Chinon, Kevin Greenfield, Jim Fitzgerald, and Mark Malinowski.

About the Authors

G. Robert Williams, Ph.D., is the managing partner for Enterprise Certified Corporation, a consulting services, training, and IT professional certification organization. His experience includes positions as president of the professional services organization PDS Advanced Technologies; president and founder of the UNIX applications developer Decathlon Data Systems; senior executive at UNISYS and System Development Corporation; and dean of research at both the University of California, Los Angeles, and California State Polytechnic University. Dr. Williams keynoted at the Windows NT and UNIX Summit with Microsoft's Bill Gates. He was also the featured speaker at the international road shows sponsored by Microsoft, Hewlett-Packard, Compaq, and Tech Data on UNIX and Windows NT interoperability. He is the co-author of *Windows NT & UNIX: Administration, Coexistence, Integration, & Migration* (Addison-Wesley 1998) and other books, and is a regular contributor to *Computer World, Platform Decisions,* and *Windows NT/2000* magazines.

    Mark Walla is a senior partner for Enterprise Certified Corporation. Prior to this he served as director of professional services at PDS Advanced Technologies. He has consulted for Microsoft Corporation and Hewlett-Packard, where he helped develop integration strategy and materials for the national tour Integration97/98. While consulting for US West, he evaluated network management tools, and at Bay Networks he was the technical lead for sustaining released software and customer hot site issues. He was also a software engineer at Motorola with software design and testing responsibilities and an embedded software engineer at Storage Technology. Mr. Walla has written a number of technical articles for *Computer World, Platform Decisions,* & *Windows NT/2000* magazines and was a contributor and technical editor for the book *Windows NT & UNIX: Administration, Coexistence, Integration, & Migration* (Addison-Wesley 1998).

Contributors

Byron Beilman is a senior consultant for Collective Technologies, a consulting firm specializing in operating system administration. He has worked in the system administration field for 10 years, supporting highly complex distributed computer environments. As a consultant, he has assisted a number of companies in both the Silicon Valley and New England areas in leveraging UNIX and Windows NT with a focus on project management and enterprise system security. Before his consulting work, Mr. Beilman developed IT Infrastructures at Teknowledge, NOAA, and Storage Tek.

Ellen Beck Gardner is an authority and consultant on UNIX and Windows NT operating systems. Her UNIX experience began at NCR Corporation, where she managed technical support services for field locations throughout the United States. She further refined her UNIX expertise as a senior vice president at Decathlon Data Systems, Inc., a pioneer in UNIX office automation and groupware applications. Ms. Gardner is the co-author of *Windows NT & UNIX: Administration, Coexistence, Integration, & Migration* (Addison-Wesley 1998) and has written a number of articles with others. In 1997, she contributed to the *Microsoft BackOffice Bible* published by IDG Books.

Administrative Overview

This chapter is an overview of the major Windows 2000 components from an administrative perspective. The pure breadth and depth of Windows 2000 suggests that a concise view from 30,000 feet will be valuable to those with little knowledge of the operating system. For those with a baseline knowledge of Windows 2000, subsequent chapters will have greater value. This chapter explores several topics:

- Windows 2000 from an historical perspective
- The Windows 2000 product family
- The implications of key features to system administration

WINDOWS 2000—AN HISTORICAL PERSPECTIVE

Microsoft has carefully crafted a computing environment that borrows heavily from legacy operating systems while adding a familiar front-end, advanced features, and numerous administrative tools. The operating system incorporates some of the best of UNIX, NetWare, VMS, DOS, and OS/2, and adds a Windows 98 look and feel. To a very large extent, Microsoft has succeeded in producing a robust environment that captures the best of the old technology while leveraging much of the new.

The history of Windows 2000 is relatively short, but its lineage can be traced back over two decades. The formal history of Windows NT/2000 began in 1993. At that time, Microsoft had recently parted company with IBM on OS/2 and decided to change directions. The first released version of Windows NT was widely viewed as a curious little network operating system (NOS) designed as an alternative to

IBM's OS/2 LAN Manager. However, Microsoft had bigger plans than what was perceived by early industry naysayers. The first upgrade came a year later as version 3.5 and offered many significant improvements in performance and functionality. Microsoft then upstaged itself with the release of Windows 95, and Windows NT was relegated to the back burner. The 1995 release of Windows NT 3.51 added to the networking functionality and offered a greatly enhanced suite of server products known as BackOffice. With this release, Microsoft became a serious threat to NOS vendors like Novell.

Since its release in late 1996, Windows NT 4.0 has experienced significant market acceptance. The single most important advancement made with the release of Windows NT 4.0 is the incorporation of the Windows 95 user interface. In fact, Microsoft internally referred to NT 4.0 as the Shell Update Release (SUR), referring to the Windows 95 front-end. Windows NT 4.0 added the Distributed Common Object Model (DCOM) and enhanced Domain Name Server (DNS) support for its TCP/IP transport. Moreover, a great number of components to the optional BackOffice suite were added—in particular, the Exchange Server.

Despite its many enhancements, Windows NT 4.0 experienced a number of real and perceived shortfalls, especially within larger enterprise environments. Windows 2000 is designed to overcome these shortfalls with a product family that meets the needs of environments ranging from workgroups to the largest enterprises.

The history of and influences on Windows 2000 are illustrated in Figure 1.1.

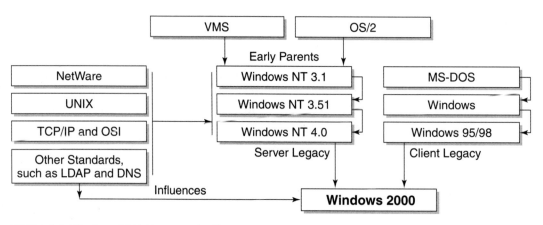

FIGURE 1.1 Windows 2000 History and Influences

WHAT'S IN A NAME—THE WINDOWS 2000 FAMILY

What's in a name? Apparently Microsoft believes that there is much to be gained from shifting the name of its flagship operating system from *Windows NT* to *Windows 2000*. As *NT* stood for "new technology," the *2000* moniker seemingly heralds a new millennium of computing. In the renaming, the company has created a family of operating system products that addresses the entire market spectrum from desktop to the largest enterprise. Understanding Windows 2000 for a system administrator begins with a review of this product family, outlined in Table 1.1.

Windows 2000 Professional

Originally slated as Windows NT 5.0 Workstation, Windows 2000 Professional is the desktop and small workgroup version of the operating system. It is also commonly viewed as the replacement for Windows 95/98 on the business desktop. This incarnation of Microsoft's workstation software makes significant leaps in security, general system stability, and Help functions. However, its most dramatic improvements are in system management—it is generally easy enough for a semi-sophisticated user and sufficiently robust for a seasoned administrator.

Windows 2000 Server

Windows 2000 Server is designed for smaller client/server environments, but can manage a moderately complex organization. In system administrator terms, this is best for an extended LAN and small WAN infrastructure, such as an enterprise that comprises a central office of modest size and several remote branch offices. Windows 2000 Server supports four-way symmetric multi-processing (SMP).

TABLE 1.1 The Windows 2000 Product Family

Windows 2000	Windows NT Equivalent
Windows 2000 Professional	Windows NT Workstation
Windows 2000 Server	Windows NT Server
Windows 2000 Advanced Server	Windows NT Server—Enterprise Edition
Windows 2000 DataCenter Server	No equivalent Windows NT product

Windows 2000 Advanced Server

Windows 2000 Advanced Server expands the core of networking and Internet functionality. Specifically designed for multi-department use, it is equally well suited as an applications server. Windows 2000 Advanced Server supports up to 8 GB of main memory via Intel's AWE API—a significant advance over early versions of Windows NT. Because of its expanded main memory capability and eight-way SMP, this operating system becomes a real challenger for large database work like data warehouse implementations. Windows 2000 also includes Microsoft's clustering and load-balancing applications.

Windows 2000 DataCenter Server

Windows 2000 DataCenter is targeted as the enterprise UNIX killer. While it will not strike a deathblow, it will erode some of the traditional UNIX marketplace. Windows 2000 DataCenter expands on the Advanced Server version primarily in its 32-way SMP support. Its Process Control Manager and four-node back-end clustering are also important features. Obviously, this version is best suited for large-scale operations that require intensive processing and fail-safe reliability, such as on-line transactions, large data warehouses, scientific simulations, and financial service operations. (See Table 1.2.)

BackOffice Suite

BackOffice suite comprises high-end support and management applications built on the Windows NT/Windows 2000 foundation. These products are optional to the

TABLE 1.2 Windows 2000 Products Differences

Option	Professional	Server	Advanced Server	DataCenter Server
Processor limit	2	4	8	32
Memory Support	4 GB	4 GB	8 GB (PAE)	64 GB (PAE)
Server Clustering	No	No	Yes (2 node max)	Yes (4 node max)
Job Object	Job Object API	Job Object API	Job Object API	Process Control Manager
WinSock Direct	No	No	No	Yes
Hardware Comparability List	Yes	Yes	Yes	Gold HCL
Network load balancing	No	No	Yes (32 node max)	Yes (32 node max)

standard Windows 2000 operating system, but are still members of its total product family. Several are examined in greater length in subsequent chapters, but we summarize them here:

- *The Commercial Internet System* expands on the base Internet Information Server (IIS) included with the Windows 2000 operating system. It is specifically designed for Internet server providers, telecommunications companies, and large commercial sites.
- *The Exchange Server* is Microsoft's answer to Lotus Notes and other groupware suites. It is first and foremost an e-mail engine, but it also provides extensions for rich messaging and collaboration.
- *The Proxy Server* is an Internet security program providing firewall and Web cache server capabilities.
- *The Site Server* is an intranet deployment tool primarily for e-commerce.
- *The System Management Server,* version 2.0, emerges as a world-class suite for managing local and remote computer systems, software distribution, and diagnostics. Chapter 11 examines SMS in greater depth.
- *The SNA Server* is a communications server for connectivity with legacy mainframe systems through the Internet and intranets.
- *The SQL Server,* version 7.0, is being positioned as a high-end database for mission-critical activities. It is challenging the market space dominated by Oracle, Sybase, and Informix. While technically a part of the BackOffice suite, SQL Server is rapidly becoming a "front office" application similar to Office 2000.

BackOffice server software programs are packaged in different forms to meet the needs of both large and small organizations. There is, for example, the BackOffice for Small Business and the BackOffice Enterprise Server. These programs can be purchased to stand alone or to be part of the integrated BackOffice suite. The naming of the BackOffice suite software will undoubtedly change to reflect its Windows 2000 namesake. Also, users of BackOffice 4.5 or earlier will need to download patches to assure that the software components work with Windows 2000.

WINDOWS 2000 ADMINISTRATION ROLES

Windows 2000 defines a universe of system administration responsibilities. Yet only a few system administrators have the broad enterprise-level view. Instead, they have specialized responsibility for planning and deployment of such things as domain controller servers, domain models, the Active Directory, sites, security policies, and network infrastructures. At this level they may also oversee all other tasks within the enterprise.

Because the majority of administrators perform these more specialized functions, Windows 2000 allows the assignment and delegation of both broad and function-specific roles (Figure 1.2). An administrator could have all or a portion of these management responsibilities:

- *Operating system maintenance*—the health of the operating system processes and services. The Monitoring and logging tools help tune individual computers, domain controllers, and specialized server performance. In this work, many administrators find both standard tools and custom scripts handy.

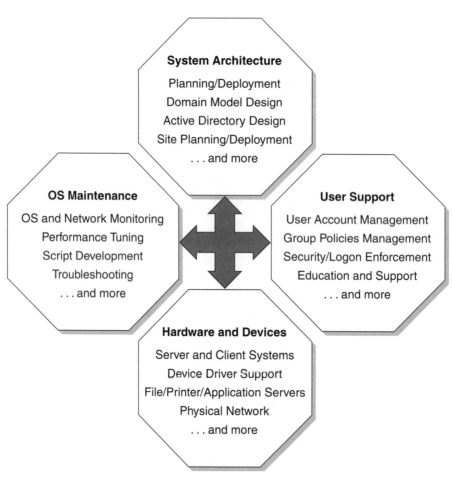

FIGURE 1.2 Windows 2000 Administrative Roles

- *User and group management*—adding, modifying, and deleting user accounts and group policies. Windows 2000 security groups are used to establish the rights and privileges of individuals and groups of users. Underlying group policies is the establishment and enforcement of security and user behavior. The Active Directory services manage the distribution of group policies. This includes such activities as logon and password management, and granting permissions and restrictions access.

- *Hardware and device management*—the health of the physical network devices, computers, and peripherals. Microsoft provides a Hardware Compatibility List (HCL) to assess the viability of a given item of hardware in a Windows 2000 environment. This also permits the system administrator to ensure that the most recent device drivers for the hardware components have been utilized. This involves not only traditional network hardwired connections but also such items as wireless devices and assessment of Internet and intranet bandwidth.

Scope of Responsibility

Windows 2000 provides for different levels of administrative authority, for which there exists a relative *hierarchy*. An administrator gains authority by becoming a member of one or more built-in or default security groups, *inheriting* the rights, privileges, and restrictions associated with each (Figure 1.3). In Chapter 7 we explore group policies in depth. However, for the sake of this discussion of administrative roles, we note that responsibilities are assigned through the accumulation of group memberships.

Another important concept is *specialized function versus broad responsibility*. Members of different groups have broad-based authority to manage domain activities. These include Administrators, Domain Admins, and Enterprise Admins. The scope of authority can be granted to other users with specialized functions— for example, printer support or backup operations. The specialized security groups are Account Operators, Backup Operators, Printer Operators, Replicators, and System Operators. Membership in these groups can be applied individually or in any combination.

The final major concept is *granularity*. The organizational unit (OU) is a structural mechanism (also viewed as a container object) by which domains can be divided into smaller elements such as a sales department. In turn, this OU can be divided into other units that involve users, devices such as printers, and network components. Each parent and child OU can then be assigned specific system administrators to manage the allotted functions.

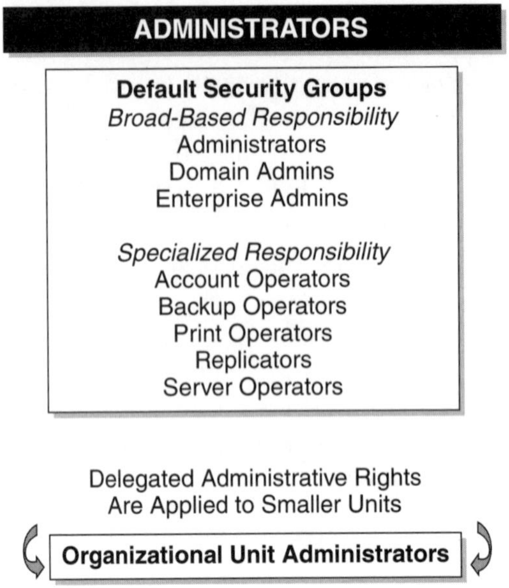

```
┌──────────────────────────────────────────┐
│              ADMINISTRATORS                │
├──────────────────────────────────────────┤
│        Default Security Groups             │
│       Broad-Based Responsibility           │
│             Administrators                 │
│             Domain Admins                  │
│            Enterprise Admins               │
│                                            │
│        Specialized Responsibility          │
│            Account Operators               │
│            Backup Operators                │
│             Print Operators                │
│               Replicators                  │
│             Server Operators               │
└──────────────────────────────────────────┘

        Delegated Administrative Rights
        Are Applied to Smaller Units
    ┌──────────────────────────────────────┐
    │   Organizational Unit Administrators   │
    └──────────────────────────────────────┘
```

FIGURE 1.3 Levels of Administrator Responsibility

WINDOWS 2000 FEATURES AND THEIR ADMINISTRATION IMPLICATIONS

Windows 2000 enhances Windows NT features and adds many new functions, each of which has a direct impact on system administration. Rather than merely outline the major new features and enhancements, we will look at them from the administrator's perspective.

The Active Directory

In Windows 2000, everything is treated as an object, including users, computers, files, and network elements. One of its core innovations is the Active Directory, which manages all domain objects in a hierarchical and replicated structure, thus allowing a significant difference in the way an administrator can conduct business. From a central location, administrators with appropriate permissions can add, delete, modify, and view objects and services anywhere in the domain, domain tree, or forest.

Among the highlights of the Active Directory detailed in Chapters 5 and 6 are

- *Advanced data query functions.* The Active Directory's Global Catalog of objects on the network permits the system administrator and authorized users to drill down to the object attribute level.

- *Directory Replication.* The Windows NT structure of a primary and a backup domain controller is replaced by a multi-master arrangement in which directory replication occurs across peer domain controllers. In theory, this provides greater redundant operations and higher availability.

- *Adherence to standards.* System name resolution in the Active Directory is dependent on the Domain Name System (DNS) over TCP/IP. System administrators with network knowledge of TCP/IP and DNS can easily manage the Directory.

- *Extensible schema.* The Active Directory can be dynamically altered to include new objects and even to modify existing object attributes. This means that the administrator can dynamically change the object definitions and associated attributes to meet enterprise requirements.

- *Interoperability.* Working with different operating systems and directory services is always a constant challenge. The goal of the Active Directory is greater interoperability. Consequently, for example, the Directory allows integration with the Lightweight Directory Access Protocol (LDAP v3) to resolve objects in Windows 2000 and heterogeneous environments. The Name Service Provider Interface (NSPI) provides directory services interplay with Microsoft's Exchange Server.

The Interface

The interface to the operating system is much more than how windows are displayed and the pull-down menus function. Yes, a clean and familiar user interface makes user training and support easier. With regard to system management, it also dictates how easily administrative tasks can be accomplished locally, through a network, or over the Internet. Equally important is the flexibility of the interface to accommodate both standard tools and custom scripts.

THE USER INTERFACE

The default user interface mirrors the familiar Windows 98 look and feel, reducing the administrative requirement to retrain an army of current Windows users. However, a few variances should be noted. The basic Windows 2000 look and feel is one of an advanced Internet browser. As windows are opened, browser functions become available from the top tool bar, including Back and Forward buttons and favorites lists. This Active Desktop was first introduced with Internet Explorer 4.0 and applied to Windows 98. Windows 2000 users experienced only with Windows 3.x and Windows 95 may need the same type of instruction that would have been required in updating to Windows 98.

Easy navigation through the operating system is basic to overall usability. The Adaptive Start function, for example, tracks the most commonly utilized features and promotes them on the menu while temporarily hiding other items until they are required. This reduces the clutter in older menus. Even so, system administrators can count on receiving calls from users about "missing" functions until the users become familiar with the Adaptive Start feature.

The enhanced search functions should lighten the system administrator's load. Working with the Active Directory, users can locate objects anywhere in the domain. All persons or resources are treated as objects with specific attributes. Searches can be conducted based on the name of the object (or a part thereof) or its attributes. In the case of a document, one attribute would be its contents.

Personal settings established by users can be mirrored in a central store that permits easy retrieval. Thus, users can log on to any computer on the network and have their personal preferences reflected in that environment. A comfortable user is generally a happy user.

In global enterprises internationalization becomes an important end-user support issue for the administrator. Windows 2000's multi-lingual support makes it possible to edit in any supported language or combination of languages.

THE ADMINISTRATOR INTERFACE AND TOOLS

Most system administrators seek simplicity but demand power in their interface. For that reason administrative tools—in particular, those that hide the background process, like Windows 2000 Wizards—must be rock solid, stable, and reliable. Many administrators distrust automated tools they cannot directly control at all stages. Those coming from largely character-based environments such as UNIX should alter this view, as much of Windows 2000 administration is based on Wizards. Fortunately, our testing shows that the stability and reliability of Wizards have been largely achieved.

System administrators also rely on facilities that support character-based command-line interfaces and a wide variety of scripts. The Windows Scripting Host provides a direct interface to VBScript and Jscript facilities. The user can write and execute scripts to these engines in the same way a UNIX user might write a *Perl* or Korn shell script.

Underlying the management of Windows 2000 is Microsoft's Zero Administration Windows (ZAW) Initiative. While the term "zero administration" is at best an oxymoron because all operating systems require some level of management, Microsoft's goal was to provide a more intelligent approach to system management. Many of the tools under the ZAW umbrella go a long way toward it. ZAW is divided into several initiative areas that deserve mention here.

- *Central policy administration*. User and group policies can be effectively managed by a centralized system administration function. These policies can be applied by a site, domain, or organizational unit. The most common types of centralized policy administration involve security, file use, software publishing/distribution, and scripting.

- *Web-Based Enterprise Management (WBEM)*. Windows 2000 embraces Web Based Enterprise Management using the industry standard Common Information Model (CIM) for application and system management as adopted by the Desktop Management Task Force (DMTF). WBEM is designed to provide consistency across operations and configuration management. Scripts can be written to interface with it, through the Windows Scripting Host, and to query enterprise systems. The Common Object Model (COM) API is employed with WBEM, ensuring greater extensibility for both system administrators and third-party software and hardware vendors.

- *System management tools*. As discussed throughout this book, administrators are provided a wide range of graphical tools for both local system and domain administration. For example, with the Computer Management tool a local user can assume an administrative role (providing Administrator rights are granted) to fine-tune the performance of a local machine. For the system administrator, this tool also supports troubleshooting for remote systems on the same network. The Task Scheduler allows the user and the system administrator to establish specific parameters for the execution of programs and events. Windows 2000 system backup is now integrated with the Task Scheduler, giving automatic system backup without direct human intervention to hard drives, tape, recordable CD-ROM, robotic changer tape banks, and the like. The Removable Storage Manager can administer tape or disk mounting at the appointed scheduled time. However, file shares, system sessions, and connections are more effectively managed with the Files Service Manager. The foregoing represents only a small portion of the tools available to the system administrator.

- *Software management*. The software management infrastructure permits the assignment of applications to specific users and computers. Applications can also be "published" to a server and then added, upgraded, or removed as the user requires. The concept of publishing applications to the enterprise reduces traditional system administrator support of common applications installation. Users who must roam between systems can get access to those applications in which they have assignment through the IntelliMirror technology. Finally, as

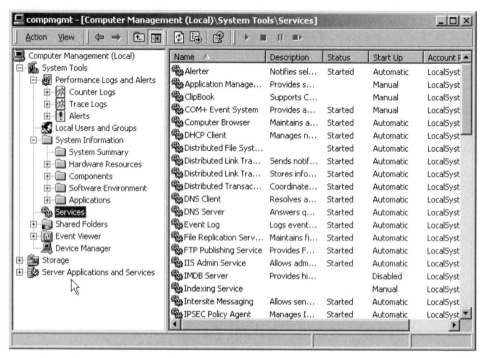

FIGURE 1.4 The Microsoft Management Console

systems are replaced, the need for individualized application installation is
greatly reduced.

• *Microsoft Management Console (MMC).* A common frustration in computer
management is attempting to learn and manage a variety of disjointed tools.
To alleviate it, Windows 2000 permits the consolidation of tools into one or
more Microsoft Management Console(s) (MMC), illustrated in Figure 1.4.
Because the MMC is extensible, "snap-in" application tools can be included as
Windows 2000 evolves and as third-party management software becomes
available. Microsoft publishes an API to facilitate the development of management tools with a common look and feel. Thus, administrators can now go to
a single point and use tools that have the same interface. The MMC can be
shared with other administrators and used to delegate selected tasks.

Networking and Communications

Network connectivity and other forms of communication represent another area
of system administration concern. Windows 2000 has designed a number of

Wizards that facilitate connectivity and reduce some of the more mundane system administrator activities. The tools and support for protocols they provide aid the management of Internets and intranets.

Windows 2000 supports a Network Connections Wizard that walks the end user and system administrator through network, dial-up, virtual private network, and serial connections. This facility controls configuration setup and management, allowing protocols and services to be set for each connection. From a user's perspective, offline browsing that permits review of a Web page after disconnection and subscription support for automatic Web page updates is a valuable addition.

In addition to the more standard forms of connectivity, Windows 2000 also provides administrator tools to support advanced communications—for example, the creation, viewing, and management of virtual private networks (VPN). Windows 2000 embraces both PPTP and L2TP tunneling protocols, and IPSec can be employed as an alternative approach. VPNs permit a sales office to connect "virtually" through the Internet to corporate headquarters in a secure tunnel.

The final Windows 2000 user feature is a Microsoft Telephony application with which both voice and data can be sent over the network. These built-in facilities permit the administrator to implement functions that would otherwise require third-party applications.

Windows 2000 Servers have added many enhancements in the communications and networking arena. These include

- Enhanced support for the TCP/IP suite, including a Telnet server and SMTP native support.
- Reliance on dynamic Domain Name Services (dynamic DNS).
- Multiple protocol routing through the Routing and Remote Access Service (RRAS) that enables IP, IPX, and AppleTalk routing.
- The Point-to-Point Tunneling Protocol (PPTP) and the Layer 2 Tunneling Protocol (L2TP).
- The Routing Information Protocol (RIPv2).
- Asynchronous Transfer Model (ATM) support.
- Fibre Channel 1-GB-per-second data transfer.

Hardware Support

Hardware management can be a nightmare. However, Windows 2000 is based solely on Intel-compatible systems, so the requirement to support dozens of proprietary architectures is reduced. Even so, hardware support will continue to be an important administrative task.

The Win32 Driver Model (WDM) theoretically establishes binary driver compatibility and I/O services with earlier Windows environments and Windows 2000. Windows NT system administrators frequently complained about the lack of support for certain devices supported by Windows 95/98. Windows 2000 is working to overcome this limitation, which should greatly reduce administrative headaches over hardware incompatibility. However, given the thousands of possible devices available, we can be sure that the updating process will continue for many years.

Windows 2000 provides a more robust Plug and Play facility with a significantly larger set of device drives. Support for the Universal Serial Bus (USB) permits the operating system to dynamically detect both connected hardware and automatic driver installation. Printer device improvements are particularly significant. Users can send documents (including those utilizing the Image Color Management 2.0 API) to printers connected to an intranet or the Internet. The Advanced Configuration and Power Interface helps to streamline both Plug and Play and power management. Also supported is fibre channel technology for the transmission of data at 1 GB per second. Smart Cards (for secure transmission of online banking, for example) and flash memory can also be utilized in connection with Windows 2000. Finally, Windows 2000 supports such graphics and multimedia standards as DirectX 6.0, Direct3D, and DirectSound acceleration technology.

Windows 2000 provides an assortment of utilities that make life easier on the desktop. The Hardware Wizard attempts to find and configure attached devices, although we found this to be a mixed blessing because it is difficult to turn off. The *Device Manager,* however, is a handy application designed to configure devices and resources interactively. Also useful are the *Windows Installer* service, which manages application installation, and the *OnNow* applet, which places the system in hibernation when not in use, thereby reducing wear on hard disks and other mechanical devices.

File and Storage Systems

Disk management and storage and backup are another headache for system administrators. A number of Windows 2000 automated tools greatly reduce these manual burdens while enhancing utilization. They include

- *Windows 95/98 and Windows NT File System compatibility.* Windows 2000 maintains base-level compatibility with earlier Windows environments. Its native file system is NTFS version 5, enhancements to which include file encryption using public keys and tracking of distributed links. With respect to

Windows 98, Windows 2000 fully supports the FAT32 file system; disk defragmentation is supported for FAT, FAT32, and NTFS volumes.

- *Disk quota utility.* The Windows 2000 Server now supports disk quotas to limit user storage and to monitor the status of such limits.

- *Universal Disk Format.* This format permits the exchange of data with DVD and compact disk media.

- *Removable Storage Management (RSM).* RSM supports tape and disk libraries through a common interface.

- *Remote Storage Service (RSS).* RSS intelligently monitors frequently used files and periodically sends the most commonly used items to backup. In conjunction with RSM, RSS sends infrequently used files to the library, where they can be retrieved as needed. All directory information on the files is retained so that retrieval becomes seamless. RSS greatly reduces the need to add local hard disk capacity.

- *Distributed File System (DFS).* With this distributed model, a single directory tree can be created and maintained across several file systems or even the entire enterprise. This permits a more global view of resources and data across the network.

Security and Authentication

Windows 2000 comes of age as a greatly enhanced security-aware enterprise operating system. As discussed in detail in Chapters 9 through 11, it fully embraces a wide variety of technologies to protect the enterprise. For example, the MIT Kerberos security standard is used by the Active Directory for single-point enterprise logons. Public key certification is based on the X.509 standard and is integrated with the Active Directory. To facilitate easier administration, the *Security Configuration Editor* permits fine-tuning of security-sensitive registries, files, and system services.

Microsoft has adopted the Internet Protocol Security (IPSec) model in its *IP Security* management tools. The *Encrypted File System* extends the NTFS with the ability to provide public key encryption of disk-based files. Finally, a Smart Card infrastructure permits secured transmission of sensitive data between systems and in mobile situations.

The enhancement of Windows 2000's support of new security technologies represents a real opportunity for system administrators. Through the proper development and deployment of security policies, better protection from unwanted breaches can be achieved. For example, the administrator can monitor potential attacks and close possible security leaks before damage is done. In essence, the administrator becomes a proactive agent for security rather than a reactive defender of the realm.

POSTSCRIPT

Windows 2000 is a powerful enterprise operating system, particularly in its management tools and security features. The consolidation of many system administrator activities under the Microsoft Management Console streamlines the administrative burden, and the Web-based interface provides the consistency that was missing in earlier versions of Windows NT. Moreover, the addition of scripting should make life for system administrators grounded in other operating systems, such as UNIX, more controllable. The addition of tools makes management of Microsoft Windows 2000 both easier and more complex. This is the reality of modern enterprise system administration.

Chapter 2

Windows 2000 Structure and Architecture

The underlying operating system structure and the relationship of component parts are fundamental to deploying and managing Windows 2000 environments. By understanding the operating system architecture, the system administrator should be in a position to better install, configure, optimize, and troubleshoot the Windows 2000 enterprise. This chapter is an architectural overview of Windows 2000. After reading it, you should understand the following:

- An understanding of the operating system structural layers, subsystems, and managers, including the Executive kernel mode and User mode structures, subsystems, and managers.
- A working knowledge of Windows 2000 process management, including multi-tasking, the interplay of processes and threads, process viewing, and management tools.
- A perspective on physical and virtual memory management.
- A basic understanding of the boot process.
- A working grasp of the Registry function and structure.
- An understanding of application dependencies and software compatibility with Windows 2000 through the use of its tools.

STRUCTURAL MODES, SUBSYSTEMS, AND MANAGERS

A surface view of the Windows 2000 structure reveals an eloquently simple arrangement of functions that separates system-related events from user-related events. As you move deeper into the component parts of Windows 2000, you will see that Microsoft has designed a very compartmentalized operating system. In this section we will review:

- The structural layers of the kernel mode, the Hardware Abstraction Layer (HAL), and the User mode
- The role of the Windows 2000 Executive and its managers
- The role of the Windows 2000 User mode and its subsystems

Structural Layer Modes

Windows 2000 functions in two primary modes: the privileged *kernel,* or *executive mode* and the open nonprivileged *User mode* (Figure 2.1). Low-level operating system services, system data, and interfaces to hardware are controlled by the kernel mode. The User mode handles everything else that is subject to user interface or intervention, including the default Win32 subsystem, optional subsystems, and applications. The User mode interacts with system data and hardware through a tightly integrated API.

The Windows 2000 Executive Mode

The Windows 2000 Executive (Figure 2.2) is alternately known as the kernel mode and the privileged Executive mode. Windows 2000 breaks down its operations into five segments that run within the kernel or privileged mode.

- Hardware Abstraction Layer (HAL)
- Microkernel
- Device drivers
- Executive managers
- Executive Services buffer

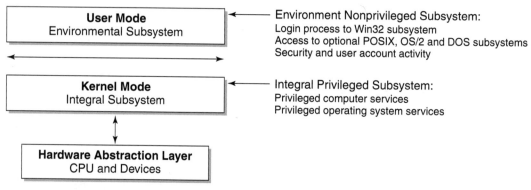

FIGURE 2.1 Relationship of the User and Kernel Modes

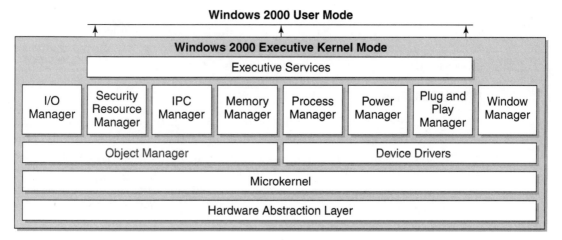

FIGURE 2.2 The Windows 2000 Executive

Collectively, these elements handle the system responsibilities that are hidden from the user. In Windows 2000, the Executive controls essential operating system functions. Other functions are pushed into the nonprivileged area or into protected subsystems, as discussed in the next section. The elements of the Windows 2000 Executive are discretely independent and exchange data through defined interfaces. In theory, any component can be deleted and replaced with a technologically updated version. Assuming adherence to the interface APIs, the operating system should function without difficulty after swapping Executive components.

Each element of the Executive provides two discrete functions. The *system services* are available within both User and kernel mode operations. By contrast, the *internal routines* are used only to communicate with other managers or components within the Executive itself.

THE HARDWARE ABSTRACTION LAYER

At the base of the Windows 2000 Executive is the Hardware Abstraction Layer (HAL). Microsoft originally placed hardware-related interfaces in a discrete segment of code as a means of ensuring greater portability across platforms. Early Windows NT was to be a cross-platform operating system in which HAL provided a layer of code that accounted for system differences. This design criterion has been eliminated under Windows 2000. HAL now deals with Intel-compatible CPU and related device-dependent issues.

Concentrating on a single architecture makes the writing of device drivers considerably more straightforward. With a published API, instructions can be written by application developers for a device that is optimized for Windows 2000. Whenever possible, system administrators should utilize such enhanced device drivers.

In multi-processor systems, HAL serves an additional function of automatically synchronizing hardware-related threads with the next available CPU. Priorities range from real-time processes (with the highest priority) to variable, or dynamic, processes (lower priority), as discussed in a subsequent section.

THE MICROKERNEL

In operating systems such as Windows 2000 and UNIX, the base-level functions in operating system operations are managed by a kernel. In Windows 2000 this component takes the form of a nonconfigurable and nonpageable microkernel. By nonconfigurable, we mean that the microkernel is never modified and never recompiled; by nonpageable we mean that the 4KB memory pages associated with the microkernel are fixed and not referred to the PAGEFILE.SYS file, where dynamic paging activities are retained.

The microkernel *dispatches* and *controls* threads. (Where multiprocessors are involved, it also synchronizes that workload.) Dispatcher objects implement and synchronize events, semaphores, timers, threads, and mutants (defined by mutually exclusive resource access). Control objects regulate virtual address processes, system interrupts, thread profiles, and asynchronous procedure calls.

DEVICE DRIVERS

A device driver is a set of instructions that coordinates the operating system with hardware such as printers, storage units, modems, network equipment, fax machines, scanners, and digital cameras. The Windows Device Model (WDM) theoretically allows a common set of device drivers for both Windows 2000 and Windows 98. In theory, the WDM should greatly reduce the system administration burden of maintaining multiple device driver versions. With the release of Windows 2000, this objective has been largely achieved.

In the case of streaming media software, the WDM has shifted the processing from the User mode to WDM Kernel Streaming. The objective was to improve overall speed and performance. An application must be specifically written for WDM to take advantage of this architecture. The same principle applies to the new WDM Still Image Architecture for specific support of digital camera and scanners.

EXECUTIVE MANAGERS

The fourth segment of the Executive is a collection of tightly coupled applications, known collectively as the *Executive managers,* that allow the subsystems and user applications to access system resources. They are the following:

- *The Object Manager.* The Object Manager is responsible for the creation, deletion, and interim management of object resources: files, directories, threads, processes, ports, semaphores, events, symbolic links, and shared memory.

- *The Virtual Memory Manager (VMM).* The Virtual Memory Manager in Windows 2000 Professional, Server, and Advanced Server versions regulates the allocation of 32-bit linear memory. Windows 2000 supports 4 GB of virtual addressable memory—by default, half is allocated to system tasks and half for the application workload. (Windows 2000 Advanced Server and DataCenter Server in certain configurations permit the shifting of this memory allocation to allow additional dedicated memory for application support (up to 32 GB for DataCenter). Applications must be coded to use the Very Large Memory (VLM) APIs.) As required, the Virtual Memory Manager pages information to disk or physical memory. It also regulates *demand paging,* which uses the physical hard drive to effectively expand total memory availability.

- *The Process Manager.* Windows 2000 support for program processes is controlled by threading. A thread is a logical sequence of instructions that is executed to completion or until a thread with a higher priority temporarily preempts it. The Process Manager specifically monitors thread and related process objects. Later discussion will clarify the role of threads and processes.

- *The Interprocess Communication Manager.* This Executive manager regulates both Local Process Calls (LPCs) and Remote Process Calls (RPCs). The *Local Process Call Facility* manages client and server communications within the computer. As a local procedure that impacts system resources is launched from the User mode, the server elements in the kernel mode are called. The *Remote Process Call Facility* manages client/server communication across different computers.

- *Security Reference Monitor (SRM).* To create or gain access to an object, a request must first flow through the Security Reference Monitor (Figure 2.3). Unlike some of the other Executive managers, the SRM operates in both kernel and User modes. As discussed later, each Windows 2000 object has a descriptor known as the Access Control List (ACL). Each user and group with object rights is provided an individual Access Control Entry (ACE) containing its security ID (SID). Upon logging in, users are assigned an access token that operates as a passkey to objects that match their entry levels. For greater detail, refer to Chapter 9, Permissions.

- *I/O Manager.* All input and output functions are controlled by the I/O Manager. These activities are broken into several components that regulate the input/output of the system cache, file system, network drivers, and specified devices (Figure 2.4).

- *Windows Manager and Graphics Device Drivers.* The Windows Manager and Graphics Device Drivers (GDDs) were moved from the User mode, where they resided under Windows NT 3.5 and earlier versions, to the kernel mode

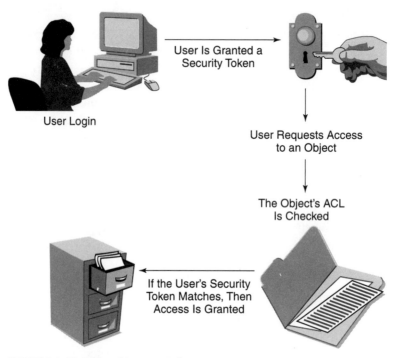

FIGURE 2.3 The Flow of Security Reference Monitoring

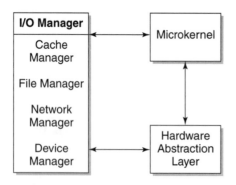

FIGURE 2.4 The I/O Manager

in Windows 2000. Applications can address the WIN32K.SYS interface; the GDD talks directly to HAL.

- *Plug and Play Manager.* The new Plug and Play Manager reduces the mundane system administration burden of identifying and configuring devices on the network. It activates existing devices and adds new devices via automatic discovery or with the assistance of the Hardware Wizard.

- *Power Manager.* Power Manager regulates the power to computers and devices. In system with power management client interfaces, Windows 2000 can automatically and remotely order a system to boot, shut down, or go into temporary hibernation.

THE EXECUTIVE SERVICES BUFFER

The Executive Services buffer consists of a relatively small layer of code that sits on top of the other Executive components. It separates the kernel and User modes and acts as the medium for passing API and system calls.

The Windows 2000 User Mode

The User mode comprises components that work together to facilitate user and application integrity. It has two parts:

- *Protected environmental subsystems.* Windows 2000 supports User mode subsystems that maintain specific requirements for native Windows (16/32-bit and legacy MS-DOS), POSIX, and OS/2 applications as well as user-related system calls. An examination of protected subsystems follows this introduction.
- *Dynamic integral user intervention.* This part oversees the unprotected actions of individual users. We discuss the impact of this dynamic intervention in the Process section, to come.

THE PROTECTED USER MODE SYSTEM

The subsystem structure can be viewed as a buffer between user applications and the kernel mode services structure. The term *protected* refers to these subsystems because they are not directly changed or modified by the administrator or the user but merely pass and manage API calls. They are configurable only through APIs and built-in utilities.

Windows 2000 supports two protected subsystems:

- The *integral subsystem* performs underlying operating system tasks—for example, security management.
- The *environmental subsystem* establishes the foundation for applications and user interfaces.

Integral Subsystems

The integral subsystems overlay and interact with the environmental subsystems. For example, the API that provides access to the network is either the Workstation

Services or the Server Services subsystem, depending on the version of Windows 2000 installed. As another example, the integral Security subsystem acknowledges login requests, authenticates logins, monitors the use of resources by a user, and manages user rights and permissions.

Environmental Subsystems

The User mode supports three environmental subsystems, as shown in Figure 2.5. The intent behind this was to provide support for applications originally written for other operating systems or to make porting of applications easier. This "support," depending on the environmental subsystem, ranges from executing shrink-wrapped applications to merely providing programming APIs.

Environmental subsystems may be thought of as operating system "multiple personalities." The Win32 subsystem provides native support for applications written to support Microsoft's 16- and 32-bit APIs. The other subsystems are a set of APIs that emulate other operating system calls.

- *Win32 Subsystem.* Win32 is the mother of all subsystems. It supports standard Windows 2000 input and display output. Specifically, it controls the graphical user interface. All Win32 applications are run directly inside this subsystem.

  Win32 also takes on a type of arm's length relationship with the other subsystems by switching personalities when necessary. For example, when a POSIX application is invoked, Win32 is not directly involved in the execution. Instead, it detects the type of executable and then invokes the appropriate subsystem.

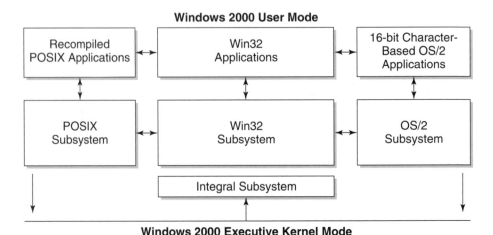

FIGURE 2.5 Windows 2000 Subsystem Relationships

MS-DOS and 16-bit applications utilize both the Virtual DOS Machine (VDM) and the Win32 system. The VDM is created automatically when these programs are launched. The application process technically runs as a VDM process, but its display handling is offloaded to Win32. Because API "stubs" support the old graphical drivers and dynamic linked libraries (DLLs), Win16 applications generally operate without impacting other operating system activities. It should be remembered that Windows 2000 is a preemptively multi-tasking operating system that supports numerous single processes simultaneously. In the case of Win16 applications, *WOW,* or *Windows on Windows,* defines the interplay between VDM and Win32.

- *OS/2 Subsystem.* The OS/2 subsystem is actually very limited in function and supports only the older, character-based version of OS/2, 1.x. Users wanting to load Presentation Manager or IBM OS/2 Warp applications are out of luck. Furthermore, it supports only x86 computers.

- *POSIX Subsystem.* For those involved with multiple platforms, the Portable Operating System Interface Computing Environment (POSIX) subsystem is a great point of interest. It is embraced by a number of operating systems such as VMS and CTOS. However, its greatest potential is in the interface of UNIX and Windows 2000.

Within Windows 2000 only the NTFS file system supports the POSIX subsystem. By *subsystem* we mean solely the implementation of a small portion of the total POSIX specification set. The IEEE 1003.1 standard for the C-language API is supported in the standard Microsoft distribution.

In order to broaden its support of POSIX, Microsoft has made available its Services for UNIX under Windows NT 4.0. The latest version of Services for UNIX also supports Windows 2000. This offers an assortment of third-party UNIX applications and utilities, including Korn and C shell support and NFS. By adding these features, it is possible to utilize many scripts written within a UNIX environment and move them directly across to Windows 2000.

Microsoft recently purchased Interix (formerly Softway Systems), whose product includes additional layers of POSIX-compatible code. This is to be offered as part of an optional Service Package known as Microsoft Services for UNIX. The Interix code actually replaces Microsoft's POSIX subsystem and overlays a complete UNIX 95 environment within Windows 2000. In this configuration, true operating system interoperability is achieved. It is also possible to migrate existing UNIX applications to Windows 2000 with comparative ease. Among the common UNIX features that Interix provides are the following:

- Over 300 UNIX commands and utilities
- Shell support for the Korn shell, Bourne shell, and C shell

- Scripting languages—*awk, Perl, sed, Tcl/Tk*—with full shell job control
- POSIX.1, POSIX.2, and ANSI C interfaces
- BSD sockets implemented with Winsock
- SVID IPC (message queues, semaphores)
- Shared memory, memory-mapped files
- ODBC and OpenGL application library support
- X11R5 Windowing System clients and libraries
- The X11R6.3 Windowing System display server
- X11R6 fonts and font management
- The OSF/Motif® 1.2.4 Window Manager and libraries
- Execution of Win32 applications from Interix
- Full tty semantics mapped to console windows and pseudo-terminal support
- Full integration with the Windows NT security model, administration, file systems, networking, and printers
- *Telnetd & rlogind* services (multi-user login support)
- Berkeley r-utilities (servers and clients)

MKS and its DataFocus division's NutCRACKER development product also provide POSIX utilities and application porting directly to the Win32 API, bypassing the POSIX subsystem.

WINDOWS 2000 PROCESSES

Windows 2000 processes are viewable through a surprisingly simple yet informative set of graphical utilities. Utilizing the *Task Manager* (with three equally helpful screens), the *Event Viewer,* the *Services Manager,* and the Resource-Kit-based *Process Viewer,* a system administrator can review and govern many of the process-oriented activities of the local server. The Task Manager can also rapidly address many performance issues. These tools effectively manage a robust process-oriented, multi-tasking, and multi-threading operating system.

After reviewing this section, a system administrator should have sufficient baseline information to

- Understand Windows 2000 processes, threads, pipes, and handles
- Use the Task Manager and Services Manager to identify, start, and kill processes
- Use the Event Viewer to diagnose process success and failure
- Employ the Process Viewer to ascertain priorities
- Schedule processes

Processes, Threads, and Handles

A Windows 2000 *process* is an executable that flows through a logical sequence of events until the appointed action is complete. Technically, an executable program is composed of the base code and related data, a dedicated memory address space, defined system resources, and at least one thread. A *thread* is the portion of the process being executed. It has a unique identification, its *client ID,* and a register that defines its microprocessor state. Every thread maintains reserved memory stacks for the execution within the user and kernel mode. It also has storage memory for interaction with other applications, dynamic linked libraries (DLLs), runtime libraries, and environmental subsystems.

Processes use threads to invoke an action with a reaction, pipes to connect threads, and semaphores to synchronize activities. Unlike UNIX processes, which involve exec/fork replication and parent/child relationships, Windows 2000 utilizes *handles*. Handles are assigned to threads and identify resources such as a Registry key used for access by a program. (They are also applied to events, semaphores, pipes, processes, and communications.)

A Windows 2000 process is treated as an object. As such it has a number of characteristics, including a virtual memory address, defined resources, and a security profile. Each process has one or more thread objects associated with its execution. As an object, the thread also has its own unique memory stack and system state. The thread is an agent that does the bidding of the process. The Object Manager controls both process and thread objects.

When a new process is created, the CreateProcess() and CreateThread() calls are made. As additional threads are required to support a given process, other CreateThread() calls are invoked. The thread should be thought of as a unit of execution. Between the ends of the thread is a pipe, both ends of which must be open. If either end is broken, the process data is lost.

Windows 2000 also utilizes *named pipes* to transmit information. These are viewed similarly to file objects and operate within the same security framework. A named pipe retains information in memory and dispenses the data as requested by a process. It acts like a regular data file, except that the information is in resident memory, not physically archived on disk. Figure 2.6 illustrates the hierarchy of processes.

Windows 2000 is a multi-tasking and multi-threaded operating system. One of its strengths is its ability to manage and synchronize multiple threads. On a single processor system, only one thread can execute at a time, but, as a result of *context* switching, it appears to the user that multiple threads are running. In this scheme (Figure 2.7), a thread executes until it has completed its task, is interrupted by a thread with a higher priority, or waits for system resources. During an interruption, Windows 2000 saves the "context" of the thread and reloads it when the CPU is free to continue.

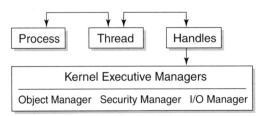

FIGURE 2.6 Process Hierarchy

Windows 2000 provides a robust process and thread priority facility. The programming API permits the setting of application process priorities, or states, that include idle, normal, high, and real time, and within each of these states two subpriorities can be established. It is important for a programmer to consider the impact of this facility on the entire system. There are 32 priority levels numbered 0 to 31. The first 16 (0–15) are reserved for the User mode, and the remainder are reserved for the kernel mode. After a base priority level is set for a process or a thread, the kernel may dynamically raise it in the event of user interaction. By the same token, the kernel can lower the priority rating for strictly computer-associated operations.

How long a thread is allowed to execute is controlled by a property known as a quantum. A quantum type can be of fixed or variable length. By default, Windows 2000 Server versions give priority to fixed-quanta background services, although Windows 2000 Professional gives higher priority to applications that generally use variable-length quanta. In theory, these priorities provide greater smoothness to key multi-tasking functions of the respective environments.

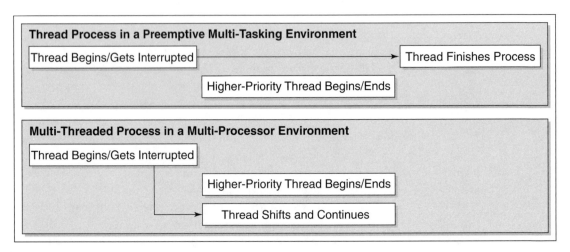

FIGURE 2.7 Single and Multi-Processor Preemptive Multi-Tasking

MULTI-PROCESSOR SUPPORT

Where processing load is significant, systems with more than one CPU can reduce thread executing wait times. Windows 2000 uses symmetric multi-processing (SMP), which allows User and kernel mode activities to utilize any available processor. Symmetric multi-processor systems have identical processors and functions. (By contrast, an asymmetric multi-processor system allocates resources to a specific processor even if that CPU is overloaded and others are relatively free.) The clear advantage is the balancing of the processing load across all available resources.

Process Accounting and CPU Throttling

With its Internet Information Services, Windows 2000 adds two features that make multi-user environments more efficient. The first is *processor accounting,* which measures the number of processor cycles consumed by Web requests. The second is *CPU throttling,* which restricts Web applications from overwhelming CPU time. Both are enabled by *job objects,* which allow the operating system to manage groups of processes as a single unit. The use and administration of process accounting and CPU throttling are discussed in Chapter 16.

INTER-PROCESS COMMUNICATION

Inter-Process Communication (IPC) and Remote Procedure Call (RPC) are basic to Windows 2000. (At the risk of being overly simplistic, RPC can be regarded as the distributed network version of IPC.) Microsoft claims that its implementation of RPC is compliant with DCE.

Windows 2000 employs a direct relationship between processes and threads. At any given time, there is a producer and a consumer (similar to BSD socket library calls). The objective is to achieve a very scalable operating system that permits easy load balancing of discrete measured threads. Windows 2000 also employs a FIFO (first in first out) message model.

WINDOWS 2000 COMPONENT SERVICES

A Windows 2000 service is a special class of process with fixed characteristics. The Windows 2000 Component Services are similar to the UNIX daemon in that they perform tasks defined as in either the foreground or the background. They can be managed either locally or remotely (Figure 2.8).

The Windows 2000 Component Services provide the list of all defined services, their current status, and their status at startup. These services can be started, stopped, paused, continued, or defined for system startup with a simple mouse click.

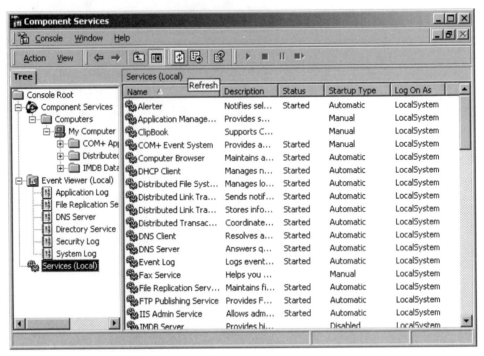

FIGURE 2.8 Windows 2000 Component Service Manager

To view or change the status of a service, press the **Start** menu → select **Programs** → select **Administrative Tools** → select **Computer Services**. From the left panel click **Services**. All defined services on the system will appear on the right-hand panel. Double-click on a target service to view its properties. Four tabs are available in which you can make changes or simply view the current status: General, Logon, Recovery, and Dependencies.

The Task Manager

The Task Manager is a handy system administration tool that provides a quick snapshot of computer system activity. It is readily available to an administrator at any point during a logon session. These are the two most common methods of executing the Task Manager:

1. Click the right mouse button on the Task bar and select **Task Manager**.

2. Press **Ctrl-Alt-Del** and select **Task Manager** from the Windows 2000 Security window.

The Task Manager provides three window tabs for three very different views of the Windows 2000 process schema:

- The *Applications window* permits the view and control of all User mode applications. Applications may be responsible for one or more processes (Figure 2.9).

- The *Processes window* provides in-depth information about individual processes, including resource utilization.

- The *Performance window* provides a graphical and numeric view of the system based on the current application and process load.

A simple dissection of the **Applications** window shows the application name in the first column followed by the current status. The bottom set of buttons permits the administrator to **End Task**, **Switch** to another task, or invoke a **New Task**. At the bottom of the screen is a system summary status that includes a number of open processes, CPU usage, and memory utilization.

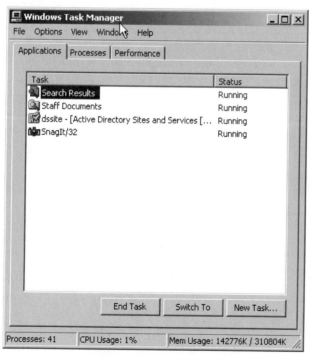

FIGURE 2.9 The Task Manager Applications Window

STARTING AND KILLING PROCESSES

Invoking an application from an icon or command-line instruction ordinarily starts processes. As discussed in a later section, processes can also be initiated through scheduling services like *at*. The **Task Manager** can start a **New Task** as well if this option is selected at the bottom of the screen. When selected, a new dialog box, such as that shown in Figure 2.10, appears.

Ordinarily, processes are terminated by the graceful exit of the application through its own kill signals. However, from time to time more radical solutions are required. Processes can be easily killed using the Task Manager. When in the Applications window, simply highlight the offending process and select the **End Task** option at the bottom of the screen. When in the Processes window, select the **End Process** option, also at the bottom of the screen. In both cases, a confirming message will appear before final termination. At this point, all handles, threads, and pipes are destroyed and any data being transmitted is lost.

NOTE   Another way to kill processes is the Resource Kit's support tool called the **Process Viewer** (Figure 2.11), which provides detailed information about a given process, its priority status, and the amount of memory being utilized. Simply highlight the given process and press the **Kill Process** button.

The Resource Kit also includes a command-line utility called **kill.exe**. To force the end of a process, load the **Command Prompt**, type *kill –f (process identification number or PID)* → press **ENTER**.

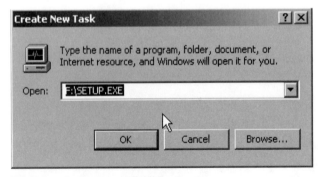

FIGURE 2.10 The New Task Dialog Box

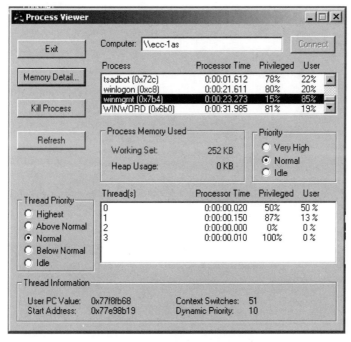

FIGURE 2.11 Resource Kit Support Tool—Process Viewer

NOTE   Administrators coming from the UNIX environment occasionally face a runaway
process known as a *zombie*. Microsoft claims that zombies will not occur in Windows 2000 because its processes do not utilize the child and parent relationship
inherent in UNIX. Each Windows 2000 process is discrete and independent of the
presence or health of a parent. While this may be technically true, certainly some
processes (generated by either Microsoft or third-party software) begin sapping
very large amounts of memory and become very difficult to kill. Use the **Task
Manager** or the **Process Viewer** to kill such processes. On rare occasions, you
may have to invoke the action more than once.

SCHEDULING TASKS

Early versions of Windows NT supported the UNIX-like utility known as the ***at***
command. This command is still supported, but its functions are greatly enhanced
by the **Task Scheduler**. The Task Scheduler and the **at** command can work

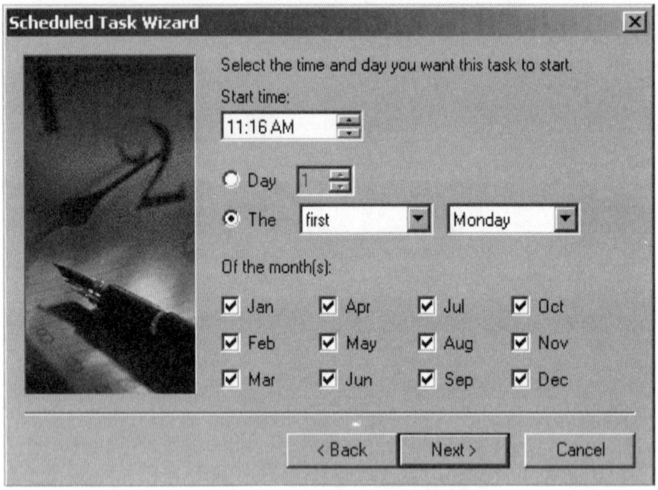

FIGURE 2.12 The Scheduled Tasks Wizard Window

together, which is important for older scripts that rely on **at**. When a task is invoked by the **at** command, it appears in the list in the Scheduled Tasks window. The Task Scheduler also can use **at** to run tasks automatically.

The *at* program is invoked from the Virtual DOS Machine command line for single event scheduling. **Scheduled tasks** are accessible from the Control Panel. The Scheduled Tasks Wizard (Figure 2.12) is invoked when double-clicking on this icon. Tasks are added by dragging scripts, programs, or documents from Windows Explorer or the desktop to the Scheduled Tasks window. They can also be deleted or modified this way.

VIEWING PROCESSES

The Processes window provides system administrators with a very good snapshot of system activity. Its default screen has five process checkpoints: image name, process identification number (PID), CPU utilization, CPU time, and memory usage (Figure 2.13). A total of 22 items may be selected for analysis by changing **Select Columns** under the **View** menu bar command. When the dialog box appears, use the mouse to click on the additional reporting parameters. If all options are selected, the system administrator has a reasonably comprehensive view of active processes and their impact on the overall system, as shown in Figure 2.14.

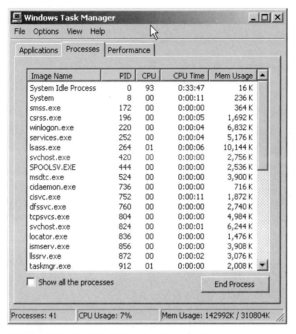

FIGURE 2.13 The Task Manager Process List

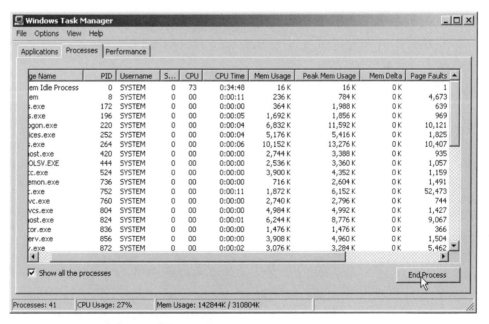

FIGURE 2.14 Expanded View of Process Activity

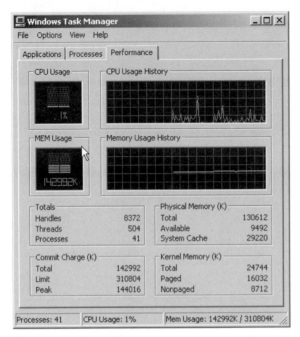

FIGURE 2.15 The Task Manager Performance Window

The Windows 2000 Task Manager Performance screen (Figure 2.15) displays four graphical representations and four numeric boxes of data for the entire system:

- *CPU Usage* shows current CPU utilization (in this example, the CPU has reached a critical utilization state).

- *CPU Usage History* is a longer-term view generally showing CPU usage over time. Unfortunately, in this window there is no ability to change time intervals or to save or print this information. A tool to further refine this view can be accessed by pressing **Start** → **Programs** → **Administrative Tools** → **Performance.**

- *MEM Usage* shows current memory utilization.

- *Memory Usage History* shows fluctuation of real memory over time. Again, there is no way to change time intervals or to save or print this information. You can refine this view by pressing **Start** → **Programs** → **Administrative Tools** → **Performance.**

- *Totals* shows the number of currently open handles, threads, and processes.

- *Physical Memory* summarizes the system memory defined as a total, currently available, and cache available in kilobytes.

- *Commit Charge* shows the total memory allocated to programs, the system limit, and peak memory, including swap memory.
- *Kernel Memory* defines the total memory allocated to kernel mode activities, broken down by paged and nonpaged events.

Command-Line Process Views

The **pmon.exe** character-based, command-line utility monitors process resource, CPU, and memory usage. It measures *paged* and *nonpaged* pool usage, and it creates a snapshot of process utilization that is particularly useful for identifying kernel mode memory leaks. A memory leak is the result of an executable allocating memory and not freeing it when the process is complete. If a process or application is displayed using pmon.exe when it is known that the activity should have completed, a memory leak is probably being created. The item will need to be killed as described earlier.

The Event Viewer

The Event Viewer provides a defined log for both normal and abnormal system event occurrences. It can be one of the most valuable system administrative tools for troubleshooting problems. A regular analysis of these logs should be undertaken if system problems are suspected.

In Windows 2000 an event is any system occurrence that requires notification. One type of event that is recorded in the Event Viewer system log is a dysfunctional driver or load failure (Figure 2.16). The Source column identifies the application that initiated the message. The Category classifies the event as being related to security, object access, logon/logoff, detail tracking, system, policy changes, account management, and miscellaneous (none). The level of importance of an event message is shown as an icon in the extreme left-hand column: Error, Informational, Warning, Success Audit, and Failure Audit. This application can be launched from the Event Viewer for the local system by clicking the **Start** menu → select **Run** → type **eventvwr** → press **ENTER**. Alternately, the **Event Viewer** is available from **Administrative Tools**.

The Event Viewer has a very flexible set of options that permits long-term tracking of potential system, security, and application problems. These are listed in Table 2.1.

To review detail information, highlight the item in the right-hand detail panel and double-click. The appropriate event properties window will then be displayed for analysis and action. As seen in Figure 2.17, a significant amount of information is provided to permit zeroing in on the precise location of the event. If a warning or error occurs, appropriate action can then be taken.

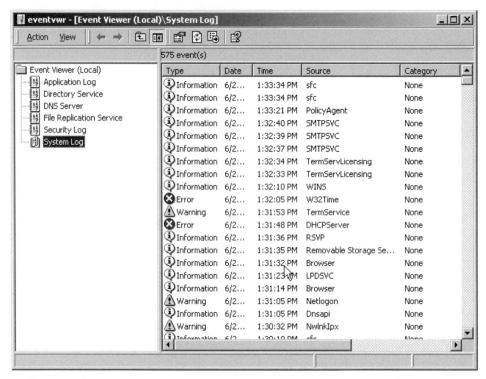

FIGURE 2.16 The Event Viewer Screen

TABLE 2.1 Event Viewer Options

Option	Description
Logging	Rolls events as needed, removes events after a defined number of days; prohibits overwriting of events (requires manual event removal).
Sorting	Sorts events based on categories, sources, user, or machine.
Archiving	Saves event records in native Event format (*.EVT) or in normal or comma-delimited ASCII text (*.TXT) format.
Details	Provides additional information on the event.
Filtering	Filters desired events or characteristics.
Find	Locates events based on type, category, source, computer, or other criteria.

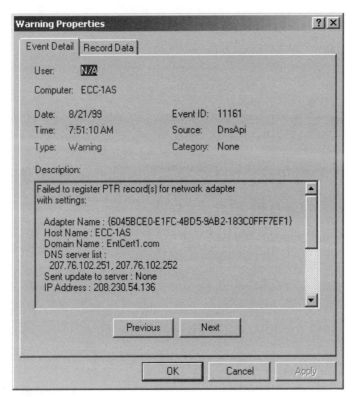

FIGURE 2.17 Event Log Properties

STORED AND VIRTUAL MEMORY

Stored memory is the storage of data bits on devices such as a hard drive. Its management is predicated on the type of file system being utilized. The role and dynamics of storage for Windows 2000 vary radically between the native NT File System (NTFS), the File Allocation Table (FAT), and FAT32. In general, stored memory is designated as "storable" and "retrievable archival."

Virtual memory is defined as dynamic or temporary. Physical memory, known as Random Access Memory (RAM), combines with temporary disk storage. For example, if a process requires more memory than is available from the system's RAM, the hard drive is used to temporarily store process data. It utilizes a set of temporary registers where information about processes is stored during execution. This is known as paging.

Stored Memory and File System Basics

Windows 2000 supports three file systems, NTFS, FAT, and FAT32, all of which have unique characteristics. For base-level security we have already established the clear advantage of native NTFS. However, under some circumstances, such as a need to switch between older Windows versions and Windows 2000, the FAT file system is necessary. FAT32 is an expanded version of FAT that allows larger disk partitions and is primarily used in the Windows 98 operating system. The relative merits of the three file systems are examined in detail in Chapter 14, but a brief review is appropriate at this stage.

THE FILE ALLOCATION TABLE—FAT AND FAT32

For the sake of this discussion, FAT and FAT32 are viewed as the same system except where specifically noted.

FAT is a simple file system that dates back to the days when the $5\frac{1}{4}$-inch floppy drive was the default medium and a 10MB hard drive was an expensive luxury. In many cases, a system administrator may install Windows 2000 using FAT because of the preexistence of legacy MS-DOS and/or Windows 3.x applications that simply have not been updated to take advantage of Win32 functionality. Fat 32, introduced to support Windows 98, is simply an extension of FAT with additional 32-bit application support.

A number of limitations are inherent in FAT and FAT32 such as reduced security. Even so, it provides an acceptable file system for legacy environments. One very nice feature Microsoft has included is the ability to convert the file system from FAT to NTFS (but not vice versa) when appropriate. This is accomplished by invoking the CONVERT command from the Virtual Dos Machine with the following syntax:

```
CONVERT [drive:] /fs:ntfs [/nametable:filename]
    Where filename is the name of file that is created during the conversion
process that contains a name translation table for unusual filenames.
```

The File Allocation Table includes the following basic information about a file:

- The name of the file or directory (folder) with a structured maximum eight-character name and a three-character mandatory extension known as the 8.3 format
- A pointer to the physical location of the first byte of data associated with the file
- The size of the file in bytes
- The designation of the file's attributes as hidden, read-only, archive, or system based

Within the context of file storage on a disk or partition, the FAT hierarchy is very simple (Figure 2.18). The first sector contains the machine BIOS block

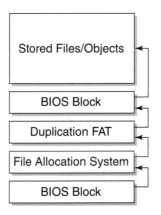

FIGURE 2.18 Disk Structure for the FAT File System

followed by the File Allocation Table and a duplicate image. The root directory is the first set of information visible to a user. Individual files are stored in the root directory or in created subdirectories.

THE NTFS FILE SYSTEM

NTFS was first introduced with Windows NT 3.1 as an outgrowth of the original OS/2 High Performance File System (HPFS). With the introduction of Windows NT Server 4.0, the NTFS file system has taken a giant leap forward in terms of stability and flexibility. It boasts numerous advantages over the FAT file system, including

- *Superior security,* which extends to files, processes, and user access protection.
- *Fault tolerance,* using Redundant Array of Inexpensive Disks (RAID 1-5) to create duplicate copies of all files on servers. If a bad partition is detected, for example, Windows 2000 can use these copies to create a new sector.
- *Unicode,* which supports file names dedicating 16 bits per character with a maximum of 255 characters. This facilitates easy internationalization. FAT supports only 8 characters using 7- or 8-bit ASCII and ANSI standards.
- *Master File Table redundancy,* which ensures recovery of system data in the case of corruption.
- *32-bit virtual memory* support with 2 GB allocated to system requirements and 2 GB to applications.
- *File name length,* which is 255 characters but also automatically generates the shorter DOS files names for backward compatibility

The NTFS file system maintains a number of key files that should not be removed or unnecessarily modified. Table 2.2 summarizes several of the most important.

TABLE 2.2 NTFS Files

File	Description
$	Root directory name
$Bitmap	Bitmap representation used by MFT for tracking volume contents
$Boot	Boot file listing bootable volumes
$Mft	Master File Table (MFT)
$MftMirr	MFT mirror
$Volume	Volume name and version information

NTFS Version 5 Differences

The Windows 2000 implementation of NTFS is version 5, which differs in a number of ways from the NTFS used in Windows NT for versions before Service Package 4. It is not backward compatible. Rather, during installation, if NTFS 4.0 is detected on a disk, it is upgraded to version 5.

One of the principal differences with NTFS 5 is that it can undertake something akin to symbolic linking through the use of *reparse points*. The reparse point is 16 KB of data that takes the form of a tag that identifies the device driver. When a Windows 2000 NTFS process sees a reparse point tag, it redirects the action to the defined device driver. A symbolic link is a special type of reparse point used to redirect the NTFS process to a specified file or directory.

NTFS 5 has a useful link tracking facility. Anytime a linked item is moved anywhere within the same domain, the link is tracked and remains intact.

NTFS 5 also supports disk quotas. These are important in that they permit regulation of disk usage. The specific management of disk quotas is discussed in Chapter 14.

Another important enhancement with NTFS 5 is support for the Encrypting File System (EFS). When a user wants to encrypt a file, a file encryption key (FEK) is generated. The Windows 2000 EFS uses an extended variant of the Data Encryption Standard algorithm (DESX).

NTFS 5 expands support of the CD-ROM File System (CDFS) that was based on a read-only principle. It now supports the Universal Data Format (UDF), which is emerging as the DVD-ROM format.

Finally, NTFS 5 supports FAT32 drives. Windows NT should not interpret FAT32 partitions or drives, nor can it boot from a FAT32 partition. Windows 2000 NTFS overcomes both of these limitations.

FILE OBJECTS WITHIN THE NTFS FILE SYSTEM

NTFS boasts a relational database structure that uses B-trees to organize and stream file object management. Microsoft publishes precious little information about the internal structure of this database, known as the Master File Table (MFT), although it is the first line in an NTFS partition. The MFT is in a mirrored format for redundancy. Pointers from the boot sector describe the location of the MFT and its mirror.

Think of the MFT as the trunk of the B-tree in which small files and directory data are stored in *residence* (Figure 2.19). Large files and directories are stored as *nonresident* in *extents* (branch extensions) or *runs* (runners). Nonresident data can cross multiple extents or runs.

File and directory objects are similar in structure and utilize the same form for defining information sometimes known as metadata; however, they differ in their back-ends. The NTFS treats directory objects as a special form of file object. Both files and directories contain *standard attributes,* a *file name,* and *security descriptors* (Figure 2.20). Files also include raw data content that is otherwise not managed by the operating system. The directory object holds indexes of the relative location and size of the directory, plus a bitmap representation of the directory structure. The term *bitmap* does not refer to the kind of bitmap graphic com-

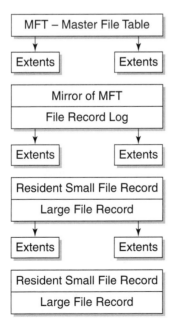

FIGURE 2.19 A Simplified View of the MFT Structure

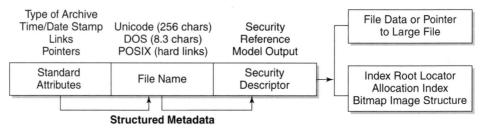

FIGURE 2.20 The NTFS View of Files and Directories

monly known to any PC user; here the bitmap is utilized by the database as a kind of road map depiction of the structure.

File names follow a specific convention depending on the file system utilized (FAT having an 8-character maximum with a 3-character extension (8.3), NTFS having a maximum of 255 characters). Directories are separated in all cases with the backslash (\). Windows NT directories are similar to UNIX directories in that they are a special form of file object that merely maintains information about the files they manage.

The NTFS database structure facilitates system recovery, which is not available with the File Allocation Table. NTFS's transaction database methodology employs a logging process to initiate disk writing instructions. Data enters cache memory, where it is then directed to the Virtual Memory Manager (VMM) for background or lazy writing to disk. The VMM sends the data to the fault-tolerant driver (assuming the existence of a RAID structure), which then attempts to physically write to the drive. If it is successful, the transaction in the database is released. If not successful, the record of the logged process is retained in the transaction table until restoration.

The Virtual Memory Manager and Paging

Windows 2000 utilizes a flat 32-bit virtual and linear memory scheme, reserving half of the capacity for system resources and half for applications. It allows tuning of addressable memory for applications that was unavailable to Windows NT. For information on how this is accomplished for your version of the operating system, examine the Help files. The Virtual Memory Manager (VMM) allocates each process an address space, which is then mapped to physical memory in 4-KB-size pages (Figure 2.21). As memory is required, the system swaps between physical memory (hardware RAM) and pageable memory stored on the hard drive.

Windows 2000 Professional and Server memory management is limited to 2^{32}. Windows 2000 DataCenter supports 2^{64}. Whereas 2^{32} sustains 4 GB of real mem-

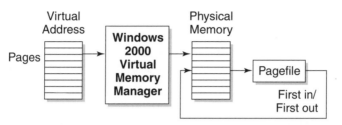

FIGURE 2.21 Virtual Memory and Paging

ory, 2^{64} allows 16 exabytes (or 18,446,744,073,709,551,616 bytes). In most computing environments, 4 GB is more than sufficient.

The VMM provides memory mapping through a table that defines virtual addresses. It also regulates the paging process—the movement from physical to disk memory. The area on a disk drive where paging occurs is known as the *pagefile*, the proper sizing of which can be critical to overall system performance. By default, Windows 2000 sets up a pagefile equal to the amount of installed RAM plus 12 MB (unless the available disk space is less than that formula). The minimum pagefile size is 2 MB. Given that hard drive space is relatively inexpensive, we recommend an expansion of the pagefile if system performance becomes an issue.

Pagefile size is changed in the following steps after you log on as the administrator: Open the **Control Panel** → double-click on the **System** icon → select **Advanced System Properties** → click **Performance** → click **Change** → if multiple drives are listed within the Drive box, select the drive containing the pagefile → within the **Initial Size** box increase or decrease the amount shown → click **Set** → click **OK** to close the Virtual Memory box → click **OK** on the Performance Options box → click **OK** on the Systems Property box. The computer must be restarted for the change to take effect.

THE BOOT PROCESS

The Windows 2000 booting sequence involves a series of system configuration checks, hardware activation, and application loading. The following lists the Windows 2000 boot process:

- *Power On Self-Test (POST)* checks whether key hardware elements are present, such as sufficient memory, keyboard, video card, and so forth.

- *Startup initialization* checks the hard drive's first sector for the Master Boot Record (MBR) and Partition Table. If either is missing or corrupted, the process terminates.

- *Memory switch and system driver load.* Ntldr instructs the microprocessor to convert from real mode to the FAT32 memory mode used by Windows 2000. Ntldr is an operating system load driver. Appropriate system drivers are then started that are actually built into Ntldr and that identify the type(s) of file system(s) present.

- *The boot loader* permits the selection of the desired environment where multiple operating systems are present on the system. The system looks for Ntldr in the root directory (by reading Boot.ini and invoking Ntdetect.com and Bootsect.dos). A typical boot loader screen (for a dual-boot environment) is shown below. (A single boot screen would show only Windows 2000.)

```
Please select the operating system to start:
        Windows 2000 Server (or Professional, Advanced Server,
DataCenter)
        Windows 98
Use ↑ and ↓ to move the highlight to your choice.
Press Enter to choose
Seconds until highlighted choice will be started automatically is: 23
```

Boot.ini is divided into two sections: boot loader and operating systems. The *[boot loader]* defines the number of seconds before an automatic load of the default operating system (whose path is defined in the next line). The *[operating system]* lists the environments available for initiation. In this case, two modes of Windows 2000 Server and Windows 98 are available.

The Boot.ini file is set as read-only, system, and hidden to prevent unwanted editing. To change the Boot.ini timeout and default settings, use the **System** option available in the **Control Panel** from the **Advanced** tab and select **Start-Up** (Figure 2.22).

NOTE   If Windows 98 rather than Windows 2000 is selected at this stage, Ntldr executes Bootsect.dos. This file contains an image of the boot sector as it existed prior to installing Windows 2000. At this stage, the boot processes inherent in Windows 98 take control.

CAUTION   Dual booting, while obviously possible, is generally not recommended. A number of security issues arise in a dual-boot environment. The dual boot is generally used only if a legacy application is not supported by Windows 2000.

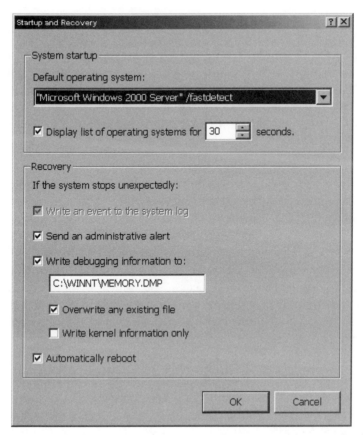

FIGURE 2.22 The System Option Screen to Change Boot.INI Timing and Default

- *The hardware configuration review.* At this stage, information about the system and attached devices is gathered by Ntdetect.com. This information is later included in the Windows 2000 Registry as HKEY_LOCAL_MACHINE\ HARDWARE.

- *Kernel load and preliminary initialization.* As dots are drawn across the computer screen, Windows 2000 loads the kernel with Ntoskrnl.exe and the Hardware Abstraction Layer's Hal.dll. The Windows 2000 Registry HKEY-LOCAL_MACHINE\SYSTEM is then loaded. Ntldr loads device drivers with a value of 0x0 and as specified in the Registry as HKEY_LOCAL_MACHINE\ SYSTEM.

- *Kernel initialization.* The actual initialization of the kernel occurs when the blue screen appears and identifies the Windows 2000 version and build number and your system configuration. Behind the scenes several activities occur. First, a Registry key for hardware is created from the gathered information as HKEY_LOCAL_MACHINE\HARDWARE. This is where hardware system specs and device interrupts are stored. A clone set of system references is created and remains unchanged within the Registry HKEY_LOCAL_MACHINE\ SYSTEM\Select subkey. The kernel initializes devices after scanning the Registry for HKEY_LOCAL_MACHINE\SYSTEM\CurrentControlSet\Services.

NOTE   Depending on severity, the boot process may continue or fail if errors are detected in the initialization of devices. There are four levels of error control values. With an ErrorValue of 0x0, the boot process continues uninterrupted. An ErrorValue of 0x1 is not sufficiently critical to halt the boot process, but warning messages are displayed. A severe ErrorValue of 0x3 causes a failure in the boot process. At this stage, the system automatically restarts and uses the LastKnownGood control set, and then continues the boot process. The critical ErrorValue of 0x4 halts the process and attempts to restart, as with 0x3. A 0x4 message will then be displayed if the LastKnownGood control set also is defective.

- *Starting of services.* The Session Manager (smss.exe) launches the subsystems and those services defined to start immediately.
- *User logon.* The Win32 subsystem starts the Winlogon.exe and then the Local Security Authority (lsass.exe). The Service Controller scans the HKEY_LOCAL_MACHINE\SYSTEM\Set\Services subkey for all service start entries. Two additional subkeys are scanned: **DependOnGroup** and **DependOnService.** The system is ready to use when the Begin Logon box appears with instructions to press **Ctrl-Alt-Delete** *to log on.* Windows 2000 does not consider the startup procedure complete until the first user has logged on.

NOTE   During the initial boot phase, it is possible to enter an alternative boot sequence and invoke the Advanced Menu system. When F8 is pressed during the initial sequences, the Advanced Menu is displayed, which is used strictly for repair and maintenance activities. It permits you to invoke the system in Safe Mode, Enable Boot Logging, Enable VGA Mode, or Last Known Good configurations. In the Disaster Recovery section of Chapter 14, we discuss how these options are applied. We also discuss other system recovery methods.

THE WINDOWS 2000 REGISTRY

The Windows 2000 Registry contains operating system, hardware, and software information for the local computer system. It is used by many programs, including the Windows 2000 kernel, device drivers, setup, and detection executables. One example of the type of information stored in the Registry is a listing of all properly installed applications. Therefore, when you double-click on a file with the Windows 2000 Explorer, its extension is matched with a list of installed applications and launches the appropriate software. Other items stored in the Registry include:

- Hardware configuration data
- Program group and desktop settings for each user
- User profile data
- Local language and time settings
- Network configuration data
- Security information for users and groups
- ActiveX and OLE server data

NOTE   The relationship between the Registry and the Active Directory is very close. The Registry maintains information for the local system, and the Active Directory provides object information about the domain network as a whole.

The Registry Structure

The Registry is based on a logical hierarchy of information, beginning with five subtrees known as keys. The concept of *keys* and *subkeys* follows the same principle as folders and subfolders within a directory tree. Every key or subkey has at least one entry that contains its name, data type, and configuration value (Table 2.3).

The keys and subkeys are stored in collections known as *hives*. Hive files are stored in *%systemroot%\System32\Config* or for user data in *\%systemroot%\Profile\username*. When changes are made to the Registry data, the data is compared to the logs before it is written. The log file is written first in a type of data streaming mechanism. When it is saved to disk, changes are then updated to the hive key components. In this way, hive information is coupled with associated log files in an effort to minimize corruption.

If the Registry is lost or damaged, Windows 2000 cannot function. Therefore, its care and feeding is a critical system administrator responsibility. The first rule is to retain an emergency copy of the Registry in case of damage or loss. As stated

TABLE 2.3 Registry Keys

Key	Description
HKEY_LOCAL_MACHINE	Information about the local system such as hardware and operating system data. Major keys are hardware, SAM, security, software, and system.
HKEY_CLASSES_ROOT	File allocation and OLE/ActiveX data; includes association of extensions to applications.
HKEY_CURRENT_CONFIG	System startup configuration that permits changes to device settings.
HKEY_CURRENT_USER	Profile for currently active user as well as console, Control Panel, environment, printer, and software data.
HKEY_USERS	Profiles for all currently active users as well as default profile.

before, the Registry information is found in *%systemroot%\System32\Config*, where *%systemroot%* is the root directory for a system, such as *\winnt*. For system recovery, the Windows 2000 Setup program also creates a *%systemroot%\Repair* folder containing the following files:

- *Autoexec.nt*—a copy of %systemroot%\System32\Autoexec.nt used to initialize the MS-DOS environment.

- *Config.nt*—a copy of %systemroot%\System32\Config.nt used to initialize the MS-DOS environment.

- *Default.*—the Registry key HKEY_USERS\DEFAULT in compressed format.

- *Ntuser.DA_*—a compressed version of *%systemroot%*\Profiles\Default User\ Ntuser.dat. The process uses Ntuser.da_ if this area needs repair.

- *Sam._*—the Registry key HKEY_LOCAL_MACHINE\SAM in compressed format.

- *Security._*—the Registry key HKEY_LOCAL_MACHINE\SECURITY in compressed format.

- *Setup.log*—the log of installed files with cyclic redundancy check (CRC) data. This file is Read-Only, System, and Hidden by default.

- *Software._*—the Registry key HKEY_LOCAL_MACHINE\SOFTWARE in compressed format.

- *System._*—the Registry key HKEY_LOCAL_MACHINE\SYSTEM in compressed format.

During system startup, the Windows 2000 kernel extracts information from the Registry, such as which device drivers to load and their load order. The Ntoskrnl.exe program also passes other information to the registry, including its version number.

The Registry Editor

System administrators may find it necessary to regularly view and edit the Registry. The **Registry Editor** tool (regedt32.exe) is located in the \System32 directory. Generally speaking, it is best to use the Windows 2000 Administrative tools to resolve system issues prior to directly editing the Registry. However, from time to time, it is necessary to go to the source of system data. That is when the Registry Editor (Figure 2.23) comes into play.

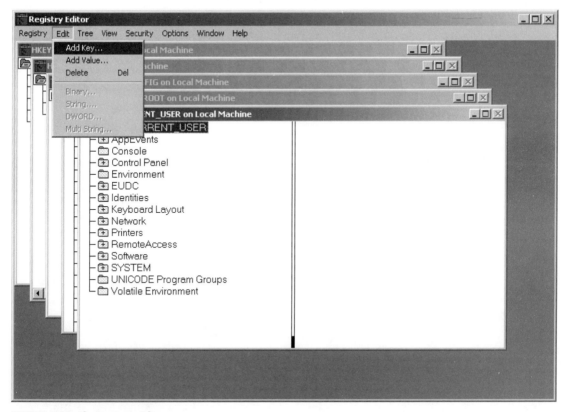

FIGURE 2.23 The Registry Editor

CAUTION   The Registry Editor is not a toy. Its improper use can result in fatal system behavior. When viewing and copying the Registry always turn the Editor to Read-Only mode. When directly editing, always think twice before entering information. The Registry Editor automatically saves all changes, so once they are entered you must live with the consequences. Changes are reflected automatically.

VIEWING APPLICATION DEPENDENCIES

Anytime an application fails to properly execute or fails to load, a Resource Kit's Support Tool, called the Dependency Walker, can be an excellent analytical utility. It shows what minimum set of files is required to run an application or load a DLL, and it also shows which functions are exposed by a particular module and which ones are called by other modules. Moreover it illustrates the full path of all modules being loaded by an application plus their base addresses. Where application fails, the Dependency Walker provides an error message about the problem components.

The Dependency Walker operates by recursively scanning all dependent modules required by an application. Missing files are detected first; corrected or invalid files are then identified. For example, a 16-bit version of a DLL might be present when a 32-bit version is required. Circular redundancy problems and CPU mismatches are also detected during the recursive scans.

The Dependency Walker (Figure 2.24) identifies different types of dependencies between modules, which are briefly described in Table 2.4.

To review an application's dependencies, load the **Dependency Walker** from the **Start** → **Programs** → **Windows 2000 Support Services** → **Tools**. From the **Files Menu** select **Open** and browse to the desired application or DLL.

The Dependency Walker can also be used for application profiling. This technique permits it to detect dynamically loaded modules in a running application that may not be reported in the static import tables. The profiler is also used to detect when a module fails to initialize. This activity is initiated once an application is loaded into the Dependency Walker. From the **Profile** menu, select **Start Profiling**. You will then need to select the options from the **Profile Module** dialog box. Continue the process until the desired information is obtained. Then select the **Profile** menu → **Stop Profiling** to terminate the analysis.

NOTE   The Windows 2000 Resource Kit also supplies a command-line method of launching the Dependency Walker through the **depend.exe** command-line utility.

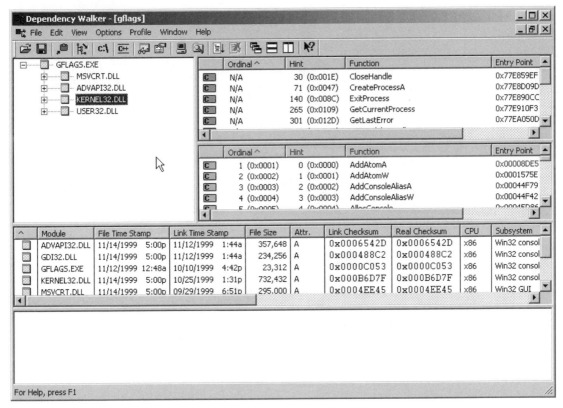

FIGURE 2.24 The Resource Kit's Dependency Walker

TABLE 2.4 Dependency Types Between Modules

Type	Description
Implicit	A load-time dependency in which one module calls functions in another module. Even if no direct calls are made to the second module, that module is still loaded into memory.
Delay-Load	A dynamic dependency in which a module is loaded only when a specific call is made to it by the application.
Forward	A dependency in which an application calls a function in a dependent module that is actually available from another module. The call is forwarded from the second module to the third module.
Explicit	A runtime dependency, i.e., a dynamic load of library functions common to OCXs, COM objects, and Visual Basic applications.
System Hook	A dependency that occurs when a specific application action is undertaken, e.g., the use of a mouse will result in a new process.

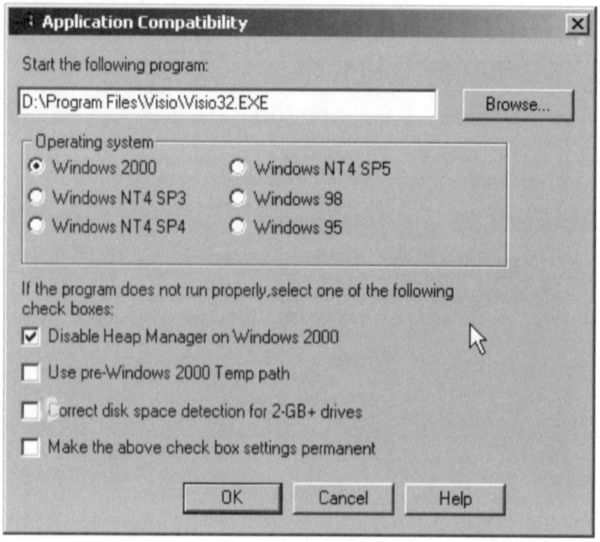

FIGURE 2.25 The Resource Kit's Application Compatibility Tool

REVIEWING APPLICATION COMPATIBILITY

Application incompatibility is always an issue when upgrading operating systems or attempting to run legacy software. The Windows 2000 Resource Kit provides a utility to help resolve operating system incompatibility, available via **Start → Programs → Windows 2000 Support Services → Tools → Application Compatibility** (Figure 2.25). If an application does not run properly, try to install and run it using the Application Compatibility utility. Select the operating system in which the application was originally designed. If it properly executes, the compatibility issue has been resolved. If it fails, the application must be assumed incompatible with Windows 2000.

NOTE   The Windows 2000 Resource Kit supplies a command-line method of launching **Application Compatibility** via the **apcompat.exe** command-line utility.

INTELLIMIRROR AND OTHER INNOVATIONS

Prior to moving into installation of Windows 2000, there are several other innovations that should be highlighted. Specifically, the manner in which IntelliMirror, Remote OS Installation, and System Management Server interplay may have an effect on how Windows 2000 is installed and administered.

IntelliMirror technology should be regarded as a collection of functions rather than a specific application. Microsoft simply calls IntelliMirror the "follow me" function. Within an Active Directory environment, system settings, applications, and data will move with the user regardless on which physical computer system the logon occurs. IntelliMirror was built upon the original Zero Administration Initiative in order to minimize management costs associated with user frustration in moving between computers or coping with system failures. For example, if a user accidentally removes a critical dynamic link library (.DLL), IntelliMirror can be configured to seek out that component and automatically reinstall it when the application is launched. Yet another example is a user that moves between physical locations as is common for consulting, sales, or technical support personnel. When such a user logs on to a computer in a different location, IntelliMirror will launch the same desktop environment and data access as would be available in the home office. In the broadest terms, IntelliMirror provides three basic functions:

1. Management of desktop settings including any customizations and restrictions

2. Software maintenance and installation including configuration, repair, and application removal known as the Software Installation and Maintenance Feature

3. User data access and management including policies that define properties and the location of user folders

Remote OS Installation is a set of technologies that supports administration of Windows 2000 client installation and configuration. It supports the new Pre-Boot eXecution Environment (PXE) remote boot technology that requests an installation of Windows 2000 Professional from a delegated server. (Using Remote OS Installation is not recommended for Windows 2000 Server because of the number of configuration issues involved.) The specific application of these technologies is discussed in the next chapter. When coupled with IntelliMirror, Remote OS Installation helps facilitate the rollout of the Windows 2000 operating system and then automatically creates and maintains end-user applications and settings.

The final ingredient in the scenario is the utilization of the optional System Management Server (SMS version 2.0 with Service Pack 2 or higher), which is discussed in greater detail in Chapter 17. SMS can be utilized to perform enterprise-wide inventory and troubleshooting. This includes management of non-Windows 2000 systems.

Each of these technologies offers the system administrator different advantages. The Remote OS Installation permits automatic installation and repair of Windows 2000 Professional client systems. IntelliMirror provides a "just in time" approach to software installation and user environment management. SMS provides an advanced set of "just in time" applications for application deployment and system management. A system administrator should take a careful look at each of these technologies and apply them to more efficient management of client environments.

POSTSCRIPT

In this chapter we provided a view of Windows 2000 basic architecture. The chapter did not attempt to view Windows 2000 in a networked or enterprise environment. Instead, we examined the basic operating system internals and provided information about several useful system administration tools. System administrators need this high-level perspective to manage more demanding system issues. Subsequent chapters will expand on the topics reviewed here.

Chapter 3

Planning and Installation

This chapter provides baseline planning guidelines and Windows 2000 installation instructions. The first part is primarily for system administrators who have more global responsibility for the design and maintenance of the enterprise. However, an administrator with a smaller scope of responsibility, such as the management of an organizational unit, might also find this material helpful, as it puts into perspective some of the considerations that go into planning Windows 2000 installations. Most of these considerations have equal applicability in an enterprise-wide and an organizational unit deployment scheme. The second part of the chapter walks through the Windows 2000 operating system installation process.

This chapter provides information that enables a system administrator to

- Understand the critical difference between the logical and physical structures inherent in Windows 2000 enterprises.
- Construct a checklist of baseline considerations that must go into the planning of a Windows 2000 implementation, by first evaluating the current computing environment and then addressing anticipated changes.
- Utilize a series of underlying planning tips.
- Prepare a checklist of information that must be gathered in the preinstallation phase of Windows 2000 deployment.
- Formulate decisions on key Windows NT upgrade issues.
- Perform a standard Windows 2000 Server (or above) installation.
- Design and perform remote Windows 2000 installation procedures.
- Design and perform automated or ghost Windows 2000 installations.

NOTE   The creation of a Windows 2000 enterprise is not trivial. While Microsoft has given the system administrator a number of Wizards and other tools, planning based on a solid understanding of Windows 2000's strengths and potential pitfalls is critical to successful deployment. A misstep during the early stages can be very costly. Therefore, we strongly encourage an early investment in the creation of a planning and deployment team. This team should be empowered to consult with system administrators and operational managers. They should gather all appropriate information discussed in this chapter as well as data unique to the environment. To translate this information into a working structure, the team must have a credible knowledge of Windows 2000 and its underlying technologies. The cost in time and money for a lead team of internal professionals and/or external expert consultants should be factored into a Windows 2000 deployment budget, as Microsoft's much promoted reduction in total cost of ownership (TCO) is predicated on making the correct decisions during the planning phase.

LOGICAL AND PHYSICAL STRUCTURES

Windows 2000 is designed to take into account both *logical* and *physical* structural parameters. The *logical structure* can be described as how an organization breaks down into a hierarchy of units and subunits. These units may be business groups, product lines, geographic locations, and the like. As discussed in Chapters 5 and 6, the Windows 2000 enterprise model relies on the concepts of forests, domain trees, domains, and organizational units to formulate the logical structure. These divisions are based on an assortment of criteria, including domain names, security boundaries, resource availability, and administrative authority. Users, computers, devices, applications, and other system objects are grouped together into organizational units where function and responsibility are logically assembled. The logical structure of most organizations is very dynamic, and the Windows 2000 logical structure can effectively accommodate change.

The *physical structure* is defined in Windows 2000 primarily by network connectivity. Windows 2000 assumes that reliable and cost-effective connectivity achieves optimal performance. A *site* is the Windows 2000 base unit of the physical structure and is defined by well-connected TCP/IP subnets. The planning process will determine how sites are linked together to best facilitate directory service replication, user logons, and data flow.

Independent accounting for both logical and physical structural paradigms adds levels of complexity. However, through careful planning and deployment, administration of the enterprise can be greatly enhanced. The demands of the logical organizational structure coupled with the potential limitations of the physical structure require careful review. When planning a Windows 2000 enterprise, both sides of the equation require attention.

In this chapter, we look at the logical and physical structures from a more homogeneous vantage point. That is, we do not distinguish between them at this stage of this discussion, for a reason that can be classically defined as the "chicken and the egg" dilemma. To fully appreciate the distinction between Windows 2000's treatment of logical and physical structures, it is necessary to better understand the topics covered in the next several chapters (specifically those dealing with the Active Directory and networking). Unfortunately, to get to those topics, it is vital that foundations of information be laid. In the real world, attention must be paid to both the logical and the physical enterprise. While the two can be independently administered, their interplay is vital to effective Windows 2000 deployment. For this reason we recommend that you utilize the information outlined in this chapter after at least a minimal review of the Active Directory (Chapters 5 and 6), user management (Chapter 7), group policies (Chapter 8), and networking (Chapters 12 and 13).

UNDERSTANDING THE CURRENT ENTERPRISE

There is no such thing as a "one size fits all" computing environment. Thus, the IT infrastructure design for one enterprise will not be appropriate to all other enterprises. Complicating the underlying uniqueness of enterprise infrastructures is the element of change. Organizations are dynamic, with constant shifts in mission, personnel, and technology affecting responsibilities. Enterprises also have inherent limitations that include the political and the budgetary. Finally, legacy hardware, applications, and data stores influence any migration plan. For all these reasons, the first step in deploying Windows 2000 in the enterprise is to take very careful stock of the organization, its strengths and limitations, and its future. With this baseline of data, it is then possible to determine how best to utilize Windows 2000 for current and future computing needs.

Taking Stock: First Inventory, Then Document

The first step is to carefully inventory the enterprise and document the results from several perspectives. We understand that nothing is probably less thrilling, but the potential pain associated with failing to take this important step can be crippling.

The meaning of *inventory* is much broader than a simple list of all existing computing equipment. An IT inventory involves a very analytical look at how and where this equipment is utilized, underscored by the need to ask how Windows

2000 will positively affect existing infrastructures. A decision on equipment and network retention begins at this stage.

Throughout this process there is one clear message: You must document, document, and then document some more. Table 3.1 is a partial checklist of IT-specific information that should be minimally inventoried and reduced to quick reference documentation. Note that since some of the items are covered in greater detail in other sections of the book, some cross-referencing may be required.

TABLE 3.1 Inventory Checklist of the Enterprise

Document Item	Description
IT Organization Itself	Understand the number, location, and skills of existing IT talent. Review current available skills and required training at the site or organizational unit level.
Network Operating Systems	Identify the NOS environments currently in place along with those that will continue to be utilized. Also determine any protocols that will enhance interoperability with Windows 2000. For example, what directory services are in use for existing Windows NT, UNIX, or Novell-based networks? If DNS is employed, what is the level and does it support Dynamic DNS and SRV record (BIND 8.1.2 or better, RFC 2052- and RFC 2136-compliant) functionality? Networking upgrades and operating system interoperability will be predicated on this data.
Physical Network Structure and Traffic Patterns	Document the existing network structure, specifically end nodes, hubs, switches, and routers. Also determine network traffic patterns, bandwidth availability, and overall reliability, and extrapolate future network requirements. This information will define Windows 2000 domains, trees, forests, and sites.
Addressing Scheme	As discussed in Chapter 5, Windows 2000 supports a number of industry standard naming conventions. The default network protocol is TCP/IP. Windows 2000 directory services Active Directory utilizes Dynamic DNS, DHCP, and LDAP. Active Directory also embraces a hierarchical domain scheme. In most enterprises, a new naming scheme for nodes and servers may be required. Careful consideration of domain naming must begin prior to installing Windows 2000 and when adding nodes. Computer names must be unique across the forest.
Internal and External Connectivity	Inventory internal LANs, WANs, and Internet connectivity. Also look at phone lines, dial-up networking, fax services, ftp services, etc.
Software Licensing	Look at current licensing operating system software and determine if it is the most appropriate. Make a decision on licensing based on this evaluation.

Document Item	Description
File Storage Policies (especially with other operating systems)	If you anticipate using UNIX, Novell, or other environments with Windows 2000, assess how technologies such as NFS, Samba, and SMB are utilized. Also look at File server connectivity.
Backup and Restoration Policies	Make sure that the backup and restoration routines and scripts currently used will be compatible with Windows 2000, including encryption or compression methodologies. Also compare current devices to Microsoft's Hardware Compatibility List (HCL).
Applications Services	The issue of managing applications either in a distributed or centralized fashion will play in the planning process. Review how application servers are currently used.
Network Applications and Management Tools	Although operating system network tools will probably be sufficient for smaller organizations, larger enterprises will probably need to invest in tools that support Simple Network Management Protocol (SNMP) and other protocols. Network equipment vendors typically provide SNMP tools. Third-party products such as Hewlett-Packard's OpenView or Microsoft's own System Management Server can prove invaluable in very large networks. The important message is to evaluate your needs during the early stages and make appropriate provisions for network management tools.

LEGACY ENTERPRISE ANALYSIS

Reviewing the current configuration of hardware and software will reveal issues that must be addressed as part of the migration. The following issues will influence a successful deployment:

- *Windows NT upgrades.* For existing Windows NT environments, you will need to identify the domain model in use and rethink the current network topology. This topic is explored in the section on upgrading.

- *Operating system interoperability.* In many environments heterogeneous operating systems such as UNIX and NetWare will continue to be used. It is important to understand that Windows 2000 needs to simply coexist or be fully integrated. Pay particular attention to network connectivity and directory service interoperability. Mapping the total enterprise and understanding how heterogeneous operating systems will interplay is an important planning step. A number of excellent reference books discuss related topics, including *Windows NT & UNIX: Administration, Coexistence, Integration, and Migration* (Addison-Wesley 1998).

- *Legacy system life cycle.* A life-cycle analysis of legacy systems should be undertaken to determine realistic migration schedules. You must determine how much of the enterprise you are going to migrate. A decision to migrate, coexist, or integrate presents both opportunities and costs. Most organizations do not have the luxury to abandon existing equipment, software, and, most important, staff with older skills.

- *Personnel training.* Legacy system evaluation is only one aspect of the equation; "retrofitting;" staff to use the new operating system must enter into the scheme. Ultimately, technology is only as good as the people using it.

ORGANIZATIONAL STRUCTURE ANALYSIS

Analysis of the organization is a key component in defining the logical structure of a Windows 2000 enterprise. As discussed in Chapter 6, Windows 2000 offers a hierarchical domain structure that accommodates very granular administration. A domain tree comprises a root domain and one or more child domains that share a common security boundary and namespace. A domain can be divided easily into components known as organizational units (OUs), the administration of which can be delegated to individuals or groups. At the other end of the spectrum, domain trees can be joined to form a forest. Trust is established between these structures that permits users with permission to access any resource in the OU, domain tree, or forest. The inherent Windows 2000 design accommodates very complex organizations of virtually any size. It also takes change into account by permitting the movement of organizational units as well as their pruning from the tree when they disappear.

   With this type of facility in mind, it is obvious that the initial design of the Windows 2000 enterprise must take into account the structure of the organization. How an organization is structured affects the type of computing environment that should be put into place. The planning process should begin with an understanding of both the formal management structure and the physical sites to be served. In some cases, a separate child domain might be created for the sales, engineering, and manufacturing organizations. In other cases an enterprise may be organized around product lines, and a product line child domain might be in order: OUs would then be formed to separate the internal sales, engineering, and manufacturing resources.

Centralized versus Decentralized Models

A key question is the administrative model to be used. This will determine Active Directory hierarchies, administrative delegation schemes, and many security parameters. Generally, three classic administrative models are applied in the planning processes:

- *Centralized Administrative Model.* Under this scenario, all administrative responsibilities are controlled by a central authority. This model works well for relatively small organizations, but can prove unwieldy for very large enter-prises.

- *Decentralized Administrative Model.* In this model, multiple organization units have full responsibility for the management of their IT resources. While it provides extensive grassroots autonomy, decentralization raises the issue of incompatibility and nonstandard policies. It is preferred by many organiza-tions, but can lead to conflict where communication between units is neces-sary. Fortunately, the Windows 2000 domain and OU model can overcome some inherent conflict, especially if careful planning occurs at the outset.

- *Mixed Administrative Model.* The most common for larger enterprises, the combined centralized/decentralized model delegates authority to organiza-tional units. Responsibilities are defined by the centralized authority. The decentralized authority granted to the organizational units may vary signifi-cantly, obviously resulting in a new level of complexity. The Windows 2000 domain model is particularly useful in creating more complex mixed models.

ORGANIZATIONAL PROCESSES AND DYNAMICS ANALYSIS

The type of access to network resources required between organizational units, domains, trees, and forests becomes a significant planning issue. Every organiza-tion has its own dynamics. The computing requirements for a manufacturer are radically different from those of a finance house. Information can be very struc-tured or completely ad hoc.

Access to resources is typically granted on the basis of need. Process manage-ment breaks apart a business's functions, tasks, and responsibilities to determine the relative needs of each. The identification of computing needs is vastly enhanced by an understanding of how data flows through the entire organization. For example, the accounting, marketing, and manufacturing departments need access to customer information, but the human resources department may not. By the same token, human resources departments have many data files that are processed and stored on a confidential basis. Understanding the business rela-tionships between departments and their processes makes it easier to configure and implement the relative group policies. It also provides a road map for manag-ing permissions to avoid unauthorized use of network resources.

Potential Change and Growth

It may not always be possible to predict the future of any organization. However, effective planning involves breaking out the crystal ball to make reasonable pro-jections. While Windows 2000 is designed to facilitate unexpected changes, the more that can be anticipated in advance, the better the deployment. This requires that the planning team engage key executives and operational managers in sometimes very confidential discussions regarding potential growth and downsizing. Since the job of the professional system administrator is to handle sensitive information pertaining to many security issues, this is a good place to gain additional respect within the organization.

Plans should attempt to reflect organizational change for a period of three to five years. The checklist of growth and change items to be integrated into the plan includes the following questions:

- What are the projections for growth and reduction both on an enterprise level and within each organizational unit?
- How are shifts going to be distributed both organizationally and geographically?
- Where are reorganizations most likely to occur and what will be the overall impact?
- What is the impact of mergers, acquisitions, and business unit spinoffs?
- What new or emerging technologies are most likely to affect the plan?

SECURITY REQUIREMENTS ANALYSIS

Windows 2000 offers a vastly enhanced set of security technologies and implementation policies. A careful review of current security mechanisms and policies should be undertaken very early. User and group policies and permissions may be the first issue to consider. Thereafter, issues involving Windows 2000 Kerberos authentication and public key infrastructure, as discussed in Chapter 11, can be examined for their impact on how business is currently conducted. Start with a baseline of current policies and how they interrelate. In a move from a Windows NT environment, these policies should translate rather transparently. However, greater functionality can be added through an early security assessment and plan.

USER PROFILES ANALYSIS

When it comes time to define user and group profiles, having an understanding of inherent commonalities and differences will greatly facilitate the deployment and management process.

The size of the user base on an enterprise-wide and organizational-unit basis must be identified. Users' geographical distribution and need for multi-lingual support should then be assessed, as should likely movement within and between organizational units. In addition, many users may belong to matrix organizations where reporting relationships and responsibility cross boundaries, so there must be plans to apply policies to them.

Mobile or roaming user requirements must also be addressed. For example, will the user need to maintain the same set of data on home and field office computer systems? These requirements, once defined, can be translated into policies that will permit transparent Windows 2000 synchronization of files. Issues of remote access connectivity will also be resolved based upon this planning data.

PHYSICAL STRUCTURES ANALYSIS

Windows 2000 establishes the concept of a site to better help the management of physical connectivity to resources. Microsoft defines a site as one or more well-connected TPC/IP subnets. A "well-connected" operating system usually is defined by the administrator, but ideally is based on transmission speeds that do not negatively impact network performance. One of the early tasks is to review the definition of logical sites based on Windows 2000 criteria. For example, each remote office might be defined as an individual site and intersite communication can then be managed. With such information, it is possible to better plan and schedule information flow between sites.

Physical site structures are often defined as a specific building. However, they can be as small as a couple of adjoining offices or as large as network segments or even entire cities. Again, the key is reliable connectivity. Geography is usually a defining method of establishing sites and domains in a large enterprise. The planning process involves site definition, domain controller and Global Catalog requirements, and Active Directory replication schedules.

The checklist of information that is generally required in the early assessment of the physical structure includes

- The number of physical locations that must be served.
- The geographic location of all remote sites, both domestic and international.
- The number of buildings, floors, square footage, and other factors that could impact networking for each geographic location.
- The business function of each potential site, which determines the level of bandwidth and networking support required.

Bandwidth and Network Speeds

An assessment of current network activity provides a baseline for Windows 2000 deployment, but you must assume that network activity will increase with Windows 2000, especially in connection with Active Directory replication and Global Catalog inquiries. LAN speed requirements within a site can generally be accommodated by the addition of domain controllers to handle the internal target. Intersite traffic, however, is more complex. Two primary areas must be assessed when planning intersite network requirements:

- *Intersite link speeds.* Link speeds are defined by how rapidly packets of data can be transmitted between network segments or geographical locations. Unfortunately, speed and reliability between links can vary radically. Therefore, control of Active Directory replication and other data transmission may be required. It is important to identify the weak links and plan on applying appropriate properties to them.

- *Bandwidth requirements.* Network bandwidth is the space available for the flow of traffic. It is important to assess when the maximum amount of bandwidth is available for transmission and replication, including the conditions that exist during normal, busy, and off-peak hours. Again, this information will be used to set intersite link properties for controlling reliable communication.

Physical Structure Design

Planning the physical structure includes the early design of site topology, server placement, domain controller requirements, and replication policies. The specific requirements associated with each of these demand an underlying understanding of the Active Directory and networking, so we recommend a review of these technologies first. However, it is important to then return to the planning process in order to clearly define the intersite and intrasite connectivity requirements well before deployment.

Common Sense Planning and Deployment Tips

There are a number of commonsense tips for implementing Windows 2000. Here are ten of them:

1. *Make the plan available for review and comment.* The biggest mistake that any IT organization can make is to force change and do so from an ivory tower. Publishing a set of policies and procedures can help promote an early buy-in by both managers and end users. Everyone should understand that the planning document is dynamic and subject to input, as feedback is very healthy during all phases of migration or implementation. Contributions made by teams of users or individuals can often prove invaluable and also prevent being blindsided by hidden agendas. User input reflects the true nature of a group and thus greatly helps in the creation of child domains and organizational units.

2. *Think carefully about leveraging current investments.* The conventional wisdom of utilizing current assets whenever possible was true when the cost of personal computers regularly exceeded $2,500 and access to reliable, inexpensive networks was a rarity. However, significant changes have occurred in the last year. Sub-$500 personal computers may become increasingly commonplace even within corporate environments, and DSL (or greater) connectivity between sites is readily available and becoming less expensive. What this possibly means is that legacy environments may eventually prove more costly than simple replacements. There are times, however, when it is possible to "recycle" the systems in one department to another department as needs change. A valid plan must include buy-versus-retention analysis.

3. *Think early about personnel needs.* Windows 2000 is a complex enterprise-level operating system that will require support by senior system administration talent. You should conduct a skill set survey early in the process, and count on providing additional training.

4. *Determine hardware, software, and funding availability.* A plan to migrate or integrate operating systems must be cost justified via a series of subjective questions. Will organization performance be enhanced? Will productivity be increased? Will lower-cost network connectivity and equipment demonstrably impact cash flow? What is the anticipated cost of system administration? Can legacy mission-critical applications be supported in the new environments? A TCO analysis underscores this part of the planning process.

5. *Use test environments.* Create a test lab environment, particularly for the introduction of the Windows 2000 Active Directory into the environment. Within existing Windows NT enterprises, take a current Backup Domain Controller (BDC) offline to a test environment. By upgrading the BDC and promoting it with the Active Directory as a Windows 2000 domain controller, you will retain all of the current security and configuration information. Add other systems and commonly used devices to test the environment, and invite some of your users to play in the test bed to get further feedback. After testing, the promoted domain controller can then serve as the root for the new Windows 2000 enterprise. These pilot and test environments will also help with staging the implementation, as discussed in the next tip.

6. *Consider deployment staging.* Any deployment must occur with minimal impact on the user and mission-critical business activities. To that end a number of questions must be resolved in advance. For example, do you unpack the equipment at the user's workstation or preload the software? Because of the time required to upgrade or install Windows 2000, we recommend using a staging area whenever possible to preload and configure. As a part of this strategy, consider the use of remote automated or ghost installations to decrease direct user impact.

7. *Enlist the support of others in the rollout.* The best way to create a supportive environment is to enlist as many users as possible in the process. To gain their confidence, it is equally important that all IT professionals involved be fully equipped to handle common questions. Remember, deployments without some level of crisis are rare. Buffer these crises with knowledgeable people who will support temporary shortfalls.

8. *Get operational management early.* An operational management plan complete with clear policies and procedures must be in place. Because Windows 2000 permits very granular administration, this may result in an increased early burden. If people are being assigned as printer administrators, they must be fully equipped from the beginning to react to system management issues. This is where documentation proves extremely valuable to the management team. Standard operational procedures and policies normally evolve from this type of documentation.

9. *Begin training and support early.* Two primary levels of training are generally required. Clearly, the first in line are system administrators and support personnel, which is where most of the training budget should be focused. However, do not overlook the end user. While Windows 2000 should feel comfortable to most users of Windows 95/98 systems, some differences may require explanation. Fortunately, much end user training can be accomplished with computer aided training or Web-based tools.

10. *Audit use and perform monitoring.* Determine the nature and level of event auditing and performance monitoring. Establish baselines early and build metrics into your processes to help you identify and correct performance bottlenecks proactively.

A FINAL THOUGHT

Regardless of the relative perfection of your plan, there will always be issues that mar otherwise exceptional performance. As an IT manager or system administrator, you must realize that your profession is often thankless. However, if everything goes well, your reward will be fewer trouble calls, and you can kick back and congratulate yourself for a job well done. Remember, though, that the job is just beginning. A system administrator must always strive to be proactive, not reactive.

PLANNING FOR WINDOWS NT UPGRADES

The issues discussed in previous sections all apply to planning an upgrade for a Windows NT enterprise. However, a number of additional issues must be taken into account that do not exist when creating a Windows 2000 enterprise from scratch.

Upgrades to Windows 2000 Server can occur directly from Windows NT Server 3.51 or 4.0. Windows NT Server 3.1 versions must first be upgraded to version 3.51 prior to moving to Windows 2000. Windows 2000 Professional upgrades can occur directly from Windows NT Workstation 3.51 or 4.0, Windows 95, and Windows 98. Windows 3.x must first be upgraded to Windows 9x prior to a Windows 2000 Professional installation.

NOTE   This discussion assumes that those involved with the upgrade from Windows NT have full working knowledge of that operating system. If you do not have administrative knowledge of Windows NT, please seek additional reference information on it. While it is possible to perform an upgrade from Windows NT to Windows 2000 without knowing Windows NT, doing so could result in problems.

Native versus Mixed Mode Installations

Windows 2000 can exist in one of two primary modes. The first is the *native mode.* Here all domain controllers with a domain or forest utilize Windows 2000 exclusively, although down-level clients and servers can still run using other versions of Windows NT, Windows 3.x, and Windows 9x. The second is the *mixed mode,* in which both Windows 2000 and Windows NT domain controllers are accommodated. The two modes are compared in Figure 3.1.

One of the most significant planning decisions to be made is which mode Windows 2000 will operate under, native or mixed. As discussed in later chapters, there are a number of advantages to working in native mode. For quick reference, Table 3.2 provides a comparison of native versus mixed mode functions and features.

As described in the Active Directory installation section in Chapter 6, advancing to native mode involves a single command. However, in practical terms many enterprises will need to phase their migration to Windows 2000 and therefore will operate in mixed mode for some prescribed period of time. Therefore, for the purpose of this initial planning discussion we will assume that the deployment will initially involve a mixed mode environment.

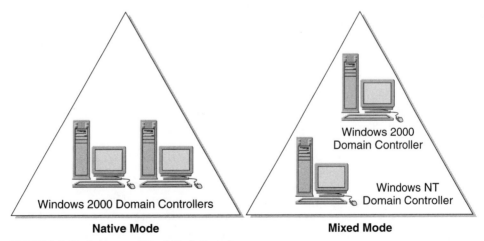

Native Mode   **Mixed Mode**

FIGURE 3.1 Native versus Mixed Mode Domains

TABLE 3.2 Native and Mixed Mode Function and Feature Comparison

Function and Feature	Native Mode	Mixed Mode
Administration across Domains	Full	Limited
Configuration Management with Desktop Queries	Full	Limited
Group Types Support	Universal, Global, Domain Local, Local	Global, Local
Multi-Master Replication	Yes	Yes
Password Filters	Automatically on all domain controllers	Must be individually installed on each domain controller
Scalability	1 terabyte or more	40 MB
Security Group Nesting	Yes	No
Transitive Trusts	Yes	No (not automatic to Windows NT)

THE PDC EMULATOR

Since the Windows 2000 domain model is based on a multi-master domain scheme in which all domain controllers replicate information as peers, the Windows NT Primary Domain Controller (PDC) and Backup Domain Controller (BDC) model is replaced. However, in mixed mode, Windows 2000 must also fill the role of the PDC. Therefore, it includes a PDC Emulator that permits continued interaction with Windows NT BDC and member servers.

A Windows 2000 domain controller is selected to serve as the PDC Emulator. When requests for changes in the Windows NT Security Account Management database occur, the PDC Emulator maintains the security account manager (SAM) and replicates that information using NTLM to the BDC. It also supports authentication logon requests for LAN Manager (LANMAN), but this activity is transparent to down-level clients. The PDC Emulator communicates any changes to the Active Directory so that normal replication can occur between domain controllers. While all Windows 2000 objects are maintained by Active Directory, this data is exposed to down-level clients as a flat Windows NT data store.

NOTE   The scalability of the Active Directory in a mixed environment is limited to 40 MB as a result of the size limitation that existed on Windows NT domain controllers. This limitation can only be overcome and full scalability provided to the Active Directory by moving to native mode.

MIXED MODE SECURITY

Mixed mode environments involve a number of security-related concerns. These are briefly outlined here.

- *Object security and relative identifiers.* The relative identifier (RID) identifies the domain controller that creates objects and limitations and is always unique. Every domain controller can create objects and assign a RID in a native environment. However, in Windows NT domains only the PDC assigns identifiers based on sequential numbers. This situation creates an obvious conflict potential. Therefore, in a mixed environment every domain assigns a Windows 2000 domain controller (usually the upgraded PDC) to act as a RID operations master. The RID operations master creates the security identifiers (also known as security principals) for down-level domain controllers. Each domain controller is assigned a set of relative IDs (RIDs) within a domain by the RID Operations Master. The domain controllers then use RIDs in conjunction with their unique domain ID to issue security IDs (SIDs) for new groups, user accounts, and computer accounts.

- *SAM database.* When a PDC is upgraded, all information stored in the Security Account Manager (SAM) is moved to the Active Directory. In mixed environments, the PDC Emulator communicates down-level changes to the SAM databases in the remaining BDC. Table 3.3 illustrates how a SAM database is migrated to the Active Directory.

- *System security application.* Windows NT group policies used by clients and servers are processed by Windows 2000, but once an upgrade occurs, only Windows 2000 group policies will be recognized. Older Windows NT policies can still be used on an upgraded system via an option that can be set to enable them. However, this should be done with great caution. A better approach is to

TABLE 3.3 Migration of SAM Database Information to the Active Directory

SAM Database Component	Moved to Active Directory
User Accounts	→ User container
Computer Accounts	→ Computer container
Built-in Local/Global Groups	→ Built-in container
Non–Built-In Groups	→ User container
PDC Computer Account	→ Domain controller organizational unit
NTFS File and Folder Permissions, Local Groups, Shared Folders, and Registry Key	→ Retained, not changed

create Windows 2000 policies that mimic the Windows NT policies desired and apply them as part of the Windows 2000 deployment.

- *Trust relationships.* As discussed in Chapter 6, Windows 2000 utilizes two-way transitive trust relationships between domain controllers. These are not automatically supported by Windows NT down-level domain controllers. To permit authentication between domains in a mixed environment, Windows NT domain controllers must establish an explicit trust.

MIXED MODE VARIATIONS

The mixed mode environment limits some of the available Windows 2000 services. A partial list of mixed mode environment limits includes the following:

- *Logon services.* When Windows 2000 clients attempt to log on, they first use the DNS to find a Windows 2000 domain controller and use Kerberos for authentication. In the event that a Windows 2000 domain controller cannot be located, the client uses the NTLM protocol and logs on to a Windows NT domain controller. In this case no Windows 2000 group policies and scripts are processed. A minimum of one Windows 2000 domain controller per site should be installed to prevent this rollover.

- *Replication services.* Windows 2000 uses the File Replication Service (FRS). FRS replaces the Windows NT LAN Manager Replication (LMRepl) service, which Windows 2000 does not support. Therefore, these services in mixed environments must be bridged. The Windows NT export directory server should be upgraded last and those containing the import directory first. Add the export list on Windows 2000 by use of the Server Manager. The Windows NT scripts directory should be copied to the Windows 2000 domain controller system volume.

Domain Models

Windows 2000 is designed under a multi-master replication domain model, which is much less complex than the four models available under Windows NT. The transitive trust relationships between domains in Windows 2000 permit flexible configurations that greatly simplify the older models. Note that it may be appropriate to go directly to the Chapter 6 discussion of the Windows 2000 domain model after reading this section.

In the upgrading of Windows NT domain models, it is important to understand how the current model will be used in Windows 2000. The following is a brief summary of how the Windows 2000 domain model relates to existing Windows NT domains.

- *Windows NT single domain model.* The Windows NT single domain model converts directly to the Windows 2000 domain model. It provides the added value of being able to break the existing domain into organizational units in which administrative delegation can occur.

- *Windows NT master domain model.* In Windows NT, the master domain model provided a hierarchy in which child domains were used as resource domains. One-way trust relationships went from the resource domains to the master domain. This model can remain in place under Windows 2000 with the added value of two-way transitive trusts between domains. The master domain should be upgraded first and will become the root domain for the Windows 2000 domain tree. Alternately, the Windows NT resource domains can be included in a sir.gle Windows 2000 domain and treated as administrative organizational units.

- *Multi-master domain model.* The Windows NT multi-master domain model provides two-way trusts between two or more master domains. It was used primarily in large enterprises where decentralized account management was desired. To move this model across, you will need to create a domain tree. The root domain should initially be created and remain empty. The master domains should then be upgraded as child domains in the domain tree.

- *Complete trust domain model.* The complete trust model provided two-way trusts between all the domains. The upgrade can take the form of a single forest with multiple domains or the creation of multiple forests with explicit trust.

Figure 3.2 illustrates how existing Windows NT domains can be adapted to Windows 2000. In the cases of existing Windows NT multi-master domain model and the complete trust domain model, two alternative migration paths are illustrated.

Upgrade Steps

Six primary steps should be taken during the upgrading a Windows NT enterprise to Windows 2000. The objective of these steps is to preserve account information and other data from the Windows NT environment.

1. *Review the domain structure and determine the DNS name.* As suggested in the previous section, changes to the domain structure may be required. At this stage you will need to understand the current trust relationships that exist and how they will be implemented under Windows 2000, as well as determine the number of domain controllers per domain. Also, you must assign DNS-compliant names during the upgrade process. If you do not already have a DNS name, we

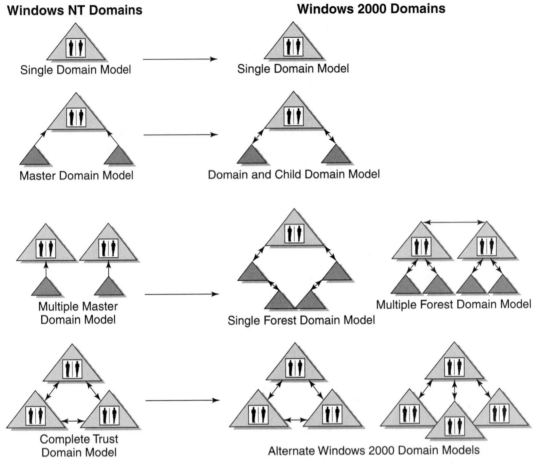

FIGURE 3.2 Changing Domain Models

recommend that you select one and register it through one of the Internet name registration authorities.

   2. *Establish a backup and recovery plan.* Guarding against accidents or improper upgrade installations should be very important. First, back up all services running on the PDC, and test the backup media prior to continuing. Second, make sure that the PDC and all BDCs are fully synchronized. Third, remove a BDC from the network, promote it as a standalone PDC, and demote it back to BDC status. Make sure that no data corruption occurs and that the system is fully operational. The system should remain apart from the network until the upgrade to Windows 2000 has been carried out and fully tested. This BDC is your lifeline if Windows 2000 fails and it is necessary to revert to Windows NT. In such a case, the Windows 2000 domain controllers would be removed and this system would go back online and be promoted as the PDC.

3. *Upgrade the Primary Domain Controller.* The PDC is always the first domain controller to be upgraded. If the current PDC is older, slower, and lacking sufficient disk and memory, consider replacing it before upgrading. The root Windows 2000 domain controller initially serves many functions, including the schema operations master and Global Catalog server functions. To make this upgrade, install a new system as a BDC and then promote it to the PDC. Now Windows 2000 Server, Advanced Server, or DataCenter can be installed. After the basic installation is completed, install the Active Directory. The Windows NT SAM database security components, including user accounts, local and global groups, and computer accounts, are moved into the Active Directory. If additional domains exist, they should be upgraded after the root Windows 2000 domain controller with the Active Directory fully operational. (The initial upgrade should be done off-line in a test environment.)

4. *Upgrade the secondary domain controllers.* BDCs should be upgraded as soon as possible to prevent continued use of a mixed mode. When the existing BDCs join the domain, they are automatically promoted to peer-level domain controllers, and should then be added to the replication topology. (Retain a BDC until the Windows 2000 installation has been judged to be successful.)

5. *Upgrade workstations and member servers.* Workstations and member servers can be upgraded in any order. If upgrades won't be done immediately, Active Directory client software should be added to Windows NT or Windows 9.x systems. We suggest installing the Active Directory client so that organizational units are visible. Systems without Active Directory client software, or down-level systems, view objects as flat stores without any information about which organizational unit they reside in.

6. *Verify and test the upgrade.* Verification and testing should take place from both the domain controller and the user client vantage point. From the root domain controller, review the *dcpromo.log* file. In addition, run two scripts available with the Windows 2000 Resource Kit: *listdc.vbs* to list all the domain controllers, and *listdomains.vbs* to list domain names within a tree. From the client perspective, attempt several user logons to help verify if logon authentication is operational, user and group accounts have been applied, and logon scripts are being run.

INSTALLATION

Installing Windows 2000 is fairly straightforward, but it requires advance information and the exercise of caution. Like the installation of Windows NT, a series of blue character-based screens begins a fresh installation of Windows 2000. Once the basic configuration is complete and system files have been copied to the server's hard drive, the graphical Windows 2000 Wizard completes the process.

The administrator is led through the installation process in a logical fashion, but some very important questions are asked that require knowledge of both Windows 2000 and the enterprise. Preparing for the installation is a critical first step that will save both time and frustration. This section helps in that preparation and then goes through the entire process. The discussion assumes that the installation is being conducted for an Intel Pentium-class server.

NOTE   The reference to "Intel Pentium-class servers" or "CPU" is very generic. In addition to Intel processors, we conducted tests on processors manufactured by Advanced Micro Devices (AMD). While extensive benchmarking of these processors was outside our scope, we can report that they all fared well in supporting base-level Windows 2000 functions.

For specific questions on CPU and other component compatibilities, refer to the latest version of the Hardware Compatibility List available on the Microsoft website. This type of reference comparison should also be made with regard to support of other system component equipment.

Preparation

If you are in the installation phase, it is assumed that you have a fundamental plan for deployment. If not, one message cannot be overstated: Windows 2000 is a very complex operating system that requires careful consideration and planning. If so, you now must take five additional steps:

1. Gather critical system information.
2. Have ready answers to the questions that will be asked during actual installation.
3. Determine when optional components will be installed.
4. Determine the order in which to migrate existing servers.
5. Determine the DNS-compliant names for the domain or workgroup.
6. Create domain computer accounts and administrative passwords.
7. Perform a final review of the installation checklist provided.

NOTE   All release notes should be reviewed in advance. In addition, be prepared to download operating system patches from the Microsoft website. If Windows NT 4.0 provided any indication of the type of evolution that will occur with Windows 2000, regularly checking Microsoft's site for tips, technical updates, and system patches will be required. As a company, Microsoft is very aggressive in providing this level of technical support. It is an excellent resource and it should be used regularly.

GATHERING CRITICAL SYSTEM INFORMATION

The installation process requires critical data. This is true for both fresh installs and upgrades. This section provides information that will prove very helpful and may prevent aborted installations. Take the time to gather this data and make sure that system requirements are fully available.

System Requirements

Prior to any installation, the system administrator should compare minimum Windows 2000 hardware requirements and compatibilities with those available on target systems. Microsoft freely publishes minimum system requirements that can change over time. The requirements in Table 3.4 were those recommended at the time this book was written. Note that there is a major difference between minimum requirements and those for optimal performance. With the declining cost of computer hardware, it may be better to purchase new equipment than to retrofit existing systems for Windows 2000 Server and Advanced Server use. Older systems with at least a 133MHz CPU can be used with Windows 2000 Professional; other systems with less power can be used as Window 98 clients during the migration phase.

TABLE 3.4 System Requirements

Component	Server or Advanced Server Requirement
CPU	Intel Pentium class with a minimum clock speed of 166 MHz minimally required. In practical terms, we would not recommend an installation on a system with less than 300 MHz.
RAM	A minimum 64 MB is required for installation. A member server should have a minimum of 128 MB; a domain controller should have at least 256 MB. Specialized functions (e.g., an applications server) require another 128 MB at minimum.
Hard Disk	A 1GB hard drive partition is the minimum for system files and basic swapping but inadequate for more use. A bare minimum for network use is 4 GB. More is recommended.
Network	Standard network adapter card(s). A second interface card is recommended for domain controllers.
Display	Monitor and adapter with minimum resolution of the VGA (video graphic adapter) standard.
Other	CD-ROM (12X or higher recommended) for installation, keyboard, mouse, or other pointing devices.

Gathering Adapter Information

The Windows 2000 installer attempts to identify the devices and hardware adapters. If a device does not respond in a normal fashion, it may be necessary to supply additional drivers or remove it for installation at a later time. As a backup, the following data should be gathered about a system prior to installation. Not all adapters or settings are applicable to all computer systems.

- Advanced Configuration and Power Interface—settings enabled or disabled
- BIOS—revision level and date
- External/internal modem—COM port connection (i.e., COM1); IRQ and I/O address for the internal modem
- I/O port—IRQ, I/O address, DMA (if used) for each I/O port
- Mouse—type (serial, bus, USB) and port
- Network—IRQ and I/O address, DMA (if used), and bus type
- PC card—Optional PC card information
- SCSI controller—Model or chipset, IRQ, bus type
- Sound adapter—IRQ, I/O address, DMA (if used)
- Universal Serial Bus—devices and hubs attached
- Video—adapter or chipset and number of adapters

Maintain this list for quick reference, as it greatly facilitates finding proper device drivers. Check the Microsoft and device manufacturer's websites to download the latest device drivers for Windows 2000.

KEY QUESTIONS

During the installation process of Windows 2000 server versions, the system administrator is prompted for a series of important decisions. An incorrect decision could result in the requirement to re-install.

Disk Partitions

Windows 2000 must be installed on a single disk partition. You have four choices to make with regard to partition creation or use:

- Create a new partition on a nonpartitioned portion of a hard disk.
- Create a new partition on a partitioned hard disk.
- Install Windows 2000 on an existing partition.
- Remove an existing partition and create a new one for installation.

Several other partition-related decisions must be made. One is the file system in which to format the partition (as described in the next section). Another involves size. While it is possible to install the operating system in a 600MB partition, doing so is not practical. The Windows 2000 partition should be well over 1 GB. As a general rule, we recommend that applications and data files be placed on separate disks to assure better performance.

When installing a new system, it is recommended that a multi-gigabit partition be created. If additional unpartitioned space remains on the hard drive, the Disk Administration tool can be used after the initial installation to partition the remaining space.

On systems with preexisting partitions, you will have two alternatives. You can delete the current partitions and properly size and format a new one. Or, if the size of the existing partition is adequate, you can install Windows 2000 without modification.

File System Choice: FAT, FAT32, or NTFS

During the install process, you will need to determine what file system partition will be used for Windows 2000. FAT or FAT32 should be selected only in environments where security is not an issue and where legacy applications reside that do not support NTFS. FAT can support up to a 2GB partition; FAT32 supports partitions greater than 2 GB. In the event that FAT or FAT32 is initially selected for Windows 2000 installation, it is possible to later migrate to NTFS with the *convert* command.

As a general rule, NTFS should be selected because it supports the full Windows 2000 suite of security features, file compression, disk quotas, and file encryption. For a server to support the Active Directory as a domain controller, NTFS is a prerequisite.

It is also possible to create a dual-boot environment in which multiple operating systems can be launched—for example, Windows 98 on one partition and Windows 2000 on a second one. When booting the computer, the user can select between the two. A dual-boot system is not recommended, however, as it causes a number of potential security and performance problems.

Licensing Modes

Windows 2000 Advanced Server offers two distinctly different types of licensing. When installing the operating system you will be required to define the type that will be used. Each of the licensing modes has advantages depending on the nature of the environment (Figure 3.3):

- *Per seat mode.* The per seat mode permits an unlimited number of concurrent clients to connect to the server, providing each has its own Client Access

License (CAL), which permits the client to connect to any Windows 2000 Advanced Server in the domain. This method is very practical for large organizations with multiple Windows 2000 Advanced Servers or a great number of roaming users.

- *Per server mode.* The per server mode sets the number of concurrent users or clients that can log on to a specific server. It is ordinarily used for organizations with a relatively fixed environment in which extra client utilization can be predicted. In a 24-hour customer service environment, for example, it is possible to predict the maximum number of users using the server at any given time. It is more economical to invoke a per server license than to purchase individual licenses for every client computer system.

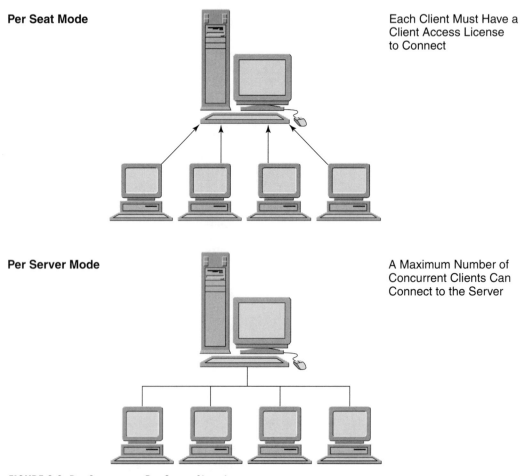

Per Seat Mode

Each Client Must Have a Client Access License to Connect

Per Server Mode

A Maximum Number of Concurrent Clients Can Connect to the Server

FIGURE 3.3 Per Seat versus Per Server Licensing

NOTE   CALs are not required for anonymous or authenticated access to Windows 2000 Internet Information Services (IIS) or other Web server access. Telnet and FTP connections also do not require CALs.

Workgroups versus Domains

A decision must be made as to whether the computer will join a workgroup or a domain. A brief explanation of the two environments is appropriate here:

- *Windows 2000 Workgroup.* The workgroup is a logical peer-to-peer connection of computers. The systems do not share a common security database. All security databases are stored locally, which means that user accounts must be created on each workstation. This is a decentralized model most commonly utilized by small organizations. In this type of environment, a workgroup name must be assigned to the computer.

- *Windows 2000 Domain.* The Windows 2000 domain is a grouping of network resources that share a common security database and namespace. (A namespace is the domain name used in the DNS naming convention, like EntCert.com.) As described in Chapters 5 and 6, the domain model uses a directory service known as the Active Directory. The Active Directory is replicated among servers known as domain controllers. Rather than the Primary and Backup Domain Controller technology used in Windows NT, Windows 2000 maintains peer relationships between its Active Directory domain controllers. This model supports a single source for user logon and a central focal point for system administration.

NOTE   To join a domain, an existing domain controller must be available for connection. This assumes that the Active Directory and the DNS are fully operational. In our enterprise, we give our users our domain name, EntCert.com. A computer account within the domain must also be created before the client computer can join the domain. If the domain system administrator has not created the computer account, access to the domain may be denied during the installation process, but will be granted later when the basic installation is completed.

NOTE   If this is the first Windows 2000 installation, it really doesn't matter whether you join a workgroup or a domain. You will automatically be the first domain controller when you promote the server by installing the Active Directory. See Chapters 5 and 6 for related information.

OPTIONAL SERVICES AND COMPONENTS

The system administrator can install a number of optional components, but as a general rule this should be avoided in the initial installation. Don't install options unless it is clear that they are required.

Several optional components, such as Certificate Service, also require technical sophistication. Moreover, Cluster Services and Terminal Services on the same server are mutually exclusive. Since these optional services and components can be installed at a later time, it may be best to do so when the base-level installation and configuration are completed. Once the system administrator becomes familiar with each of the desired service components, the basic procedures can be modified for future installs.

Table 3.5 lists the optional components that can be selected during the initial installation process. Unless otherwise noted, these services are described in later chapters. Specific installation requirements and methods are included in those discussions.

SERVER MIGRATION ORDER

Since each system in a workgroup maintains discrete security databases, the selection of which system to upgrade first is moot. This is not true of a domain model. Upgrading of domain member workstations and servers can be done in any order as well. The biggest consideration comes when promoting a server to a domain controller, since the first domain controller becomes the root of the domain tree. In existing Windows NT environments, the PDC or a reliable BDC is usually selected as the first to have Windows 2000 with the Active Directory installed. Another consideration when dealing with existing domains is the possible conversion of a multi-domain model to a single domain with multiple organizational units (OUs). Prior to installing the Active Directory and placing a Windows 2000 domain controller into service, review Chapters 5 and 6 for specific planning and installation instructions.

Installation Steps

Now it is time to begin the installation process, but first review the installation checklist. With this information readily available, the Windows 2000 install should go very smoothly. Depending on your system, the installaton should take at least two hours.

TABLE 3.5 Optional Services or Applications

Component	Description
Accessories/Utilities	Include familiar Windows applications like WordPad, Paint, games, CD player. Generally safe to install. Select individual components from the **Details** button.
Certificate Authority	Advanced X.509 digital certificate authentication support for secure e-mail, Web access, dial-up accounts, and Smart Cards (see Chapter 11).
Cluster Services (Advanced Server and Data Center Only)	Failover of two or more servers that mirror each other. If one fails, the other continues to provide resources (see Chapter 17).
Indexing Services	Indexes documents for user search of document properties. Generally safe to install without prior system knowledge.
Internet Information Services (IIS)	Suite of Web-based applications for site creation and administration, plus FTP, NNTP, and SMTP (see Chapter 16).
Management and Monitoring Tools	Communication monitoring and management tools, including SNMP. Recommended option for network environments.
Message Queuing	Infrastructure for messaging across heterogeneous environments (see Chapter 17).
Microsoft Scripting Debugger	The script development module, valuable to system administrators seeking to customize the environment.
Network Services	An essential suite that includes DNS, COM Internet Service Proxy, DHCP, IAS, TCP/IP, and WINS (see Chapter 12).
Other Network File and Print Services	Used for environments where UNIX printer services or Macintosh file or printer services are required.
Remote Installation Services	Provides server-based remote installation (see the Network Installations section).
Remote Storage	Extends the local disk storage system to remote or auxiliary storage devices (see Chapter 14).
Terminal Services	Allows client machines to run applications on the server in a "thin" client environment (see Chapter 15).
Terminal Services Licensing	Provides licenses for Terminal Services; must be installed with them (see Chapter 15).
Windows Media Services	Multi-media Internet extensions for the Advanced Streaming Format.

INSTALLATION CHECKLIST

The checklist for an upgrade installation is slightly different than that for a fresh install. Use Table 3.6 as a baseline for all installations.

TABLE 3.6 Decisions Common to All Domain Installations

System requirements are sufficient	Yes → Proceed
Hardware is on Microsoft's HCL	Yes → Proceed
Sufficient hard disk partition exists	Yes → Proceed
Partition/file system has been selected	Yes → Proceed
Licensing method has been determined	Yes → Proceed
Domain or workgroup name has been obtained	Yes → Proceed
Computer Account exists for joining a domain	Yes → Proceed, if not → Proceed and join later
Optional components have been selected	Yes → Proceed
Administrative password has been selected	Yes → Proceed to completion

To upgrade existing systems to Windows 2000, take these additional steps:

- Back up files as a precaution.
- Disable disk mirroring.
- Uncompress existing volumes.
- Determine if existing FAT or FAT32 file systems are to be upgraded.
- Disconnect the server from UPS and clustering environments.

Basic Installation

The first phase in the actual installation involves working through a series of blue character-based screens, after which the computer will reboot to the graphical setup Wizard. This supports the base-level installation. The network installation process then follows. Finally, optional components are configured. For example, if the system is to become a domain controller, Active Directory installation, as described in Chapter 6, is undertaken after the basic installation is complete.

INSTALLATION OF WINDOWS 2000 SERVER VERSIONS

Since the installation screens are reasonably self-explanatory, we have not listed every possible option. However, the following steps should be observed to install the Intel Pentium class version of Windows 2000 Server or Advanced Server:

1. Insert the Windows 2000 Server or Advanced Server CD:

    a. For a system that is currently powered off, turn the power **ON** and press **ENTER** when prompted to boot off the CD.

    b. For a system that is live and running Windows NT or Windows 95/98, press **Start** → select **Run** → **Browse** to the **CD** → select **Setup**.

NOTE

Some systems do not support booting from a CD drive. In this event, use Setup Diskette 1 in Floppy Drive A to start the boot installation process. To create the Setup Diskette set it is necessary to run the *makeboot.exe* located on the Windows 2000 compact disk *bootdisk* folder. Four formatted diskettes must be available. With the first diskette inserts → invoke the **Command Prompt** → change directory to the *bootdisk* on the CD containing Windows 2000 → type **makeboot a:**.

---

2. The installation loads a minimal version of Windows 2000 into memory and starts the setup program.

3. Select the type of installation. For new systems, the only choice is the **Clean Install** option. If you select Clean Install for an upgrade, all files, settings, and applications will be deleted and replaced with a fresh copy of the operating system. For existing systems, the Upgrade option preserves system settings and installed applications.

4. You are prompted to read the Windows 2000 license. Accept it to continue.

5. You are prompted to make decisions on the disk partition. See the previous discussion on disk partitions for additional information.

6. You are prompted to select the file system on which Windows 2000 will be installed. See the previous discussion on file system selection for additional information.

7. Select the location of the operating system program files. The default location is *%systemroot\%winnt*. If this is a dual-boot environment in which an earlier version of Windows NT exists on the specified partition, you should move the Windows 2000 program files to another location like winnt2. Otherwise, it is generally recommended that the default setting be accepted.

8. Files are now loaded onto the hard drive. Once complete, the computer will restart with the Windows 2000 Setup Wizard.

9. The Windows 2000 Setup Wizard goes through a series of screens as follows:

- *Regional settings.* This provides an opportunity to change the language, locale, and keyboard settings for international or special use.

- *Name and organization.* Enter the user's name and organization. In most cases, the default Administrator should be the user name.
- *Licensing mode.* See the previous discussion on the per site and per server license options. This is an important decision, as it will determine all Windows 2000 licensing for the server.
- *Computer name.* The computer name can be up to 15 characters to reflect the constraints of NetBIOS naming conventions. It cannot be the same as those for existing network computers, workgroups, or domains. A default name is displayed. It can be accepted or modified.
- *Password for administrator account.* Enter the administrative password for the administrator.
- *Windows 2000 optional components.* See the previous discussion on optional components.
- *Display setting.* Set and test screen resolution, refresh frequencies, and display colors now, or perform this fine-tuning after the initial installation.
- *Time and date.* Make adjustments to the time zone, time, and date.

The network component phase of the Windows 2000 installation is now initiated. The Wizard detects system components, permits the selection of network protocols, and allows the choice of joining a workgroup or domain. During this process, you will be asked to interact at several stages:

1. The detected network adapter card must be verified.
2. Selection of network protocols must be confirmed. The default or typical installation will include (1) Client for Microsoft Networks; (2) File and Printer Sharing for Microsoft Networks; and (3) the standard Windows 2000 networking environment, TCP/IP. See Chapters 12 and 13, Networking, for additional information.
3. The opportunity to join an existing workgroup or domain is presented. See the previous discussion.

The process of confirmation and installation takes 15 to 45 minutes depending on the system. Relax as the install copies files, saves configurations, removes temporary files, and restarts the system for use.

INSTALLATION OF WINDOWS 2000 SERVER ACROSS A NETWORK

Rather than run the installation for each machine from individual CD-ROMs, it is possible to store a copy of the operating system on a network server and permit downloading across the network. The first prerequisite is that the target machine must have installed the network client to a point where it can connect to the distribution server. The second prerequisite is that the distribution server must be configured to share out the directory in which the operating system Windows 2000 installation files reside. An archive distribution server is created either by sharing out the CD-ROM containing Windows 2000 or by copying over the /i386 folder from the CD to a shared folder on the server.

The steps that must be taken to install over a network follow:

1. Boot the target system with the network client.
2. Connect to the archive distribution server and move to the Windows 2000 shared folder.
3. Run the Winnt.exe command from the shared folder. Winnt.exe performs a series of functions:
   a. Creating the four Windows 2000 boot disks on Drive A of the target machine (be prepared to swap diskettes).
   b. Creating a temporary folder on the target machine called Win_nt.~ls.
   c. Copying all the Windows 2000 files from the archive distribution server's shared folder to the temporary folder on the target system.
4. Disconnect and reboot the target system with Setup Diskette 1 in Drive A.
5. Install Windows 2000 in the same fashion as described in the previous section.

System Configuration

During the first logon, a screen will prompt you to complete the specific configuration tasks. These installation and configurations are specifically covered in other chapters of the book. To retrieve this menu at any time in the future, press **Start → Programs → Administrative Tools → Configure Your Server**. Table 3.7 outlines the system configuration options.

Changing the Basic Setup

When a large number of installations are anticipated that require changes to the default settings, it may be advisable to modify the basic setup installation process. From the Command Prompt or Run Prompt, it is possible to set switches as described in Table 3.8. For repeated use, modify the autoexe.com file line containing Winnt.exe on Setup Diskette A.

Automated or Unattended Installations

The Setup Manager Wizard, available from the Resource Kit, can be used to create scripts to facilitate unattended installations. The key is to create or modify an

TABLE 3.7 Server Configuration Options

Option	Brief Description
Active Directory	Installs the Active Directory on systems that will serve as domain controllers.
File Server	Facilitates creation and maintenance of shared folders and the Distributed File System (DFS).
Print Server	Manages network printers, queues, and related elements.
Web/Media Server	Supports the creation and management of websites, FTP, news groups, multi-media sites, Internet Information Services, and other selected components. A requirement of Windows 2000 Advanced Server.
Networking	Supports and manages network protocols, DNS, DHCP, remote access, and routing services.
Application Server	Supports distribution of applications across the network. Also contains the facility to install and manage Terminal Server.
Advanced	Provides an assortment of server functions including clustering (Advanced Server and Data Center Server only), remote installation services, message queuing, and components of the Windows 2000 Resource Kit.

answer file that is queried during the installation process. An answer file will bypass the questions that would be otherwise asked interactively of the installer. A sample answer file is shipped on the Windows 2000 compact disk.

When the Setup Manager Wizard is invoked, you will first need to determine whether to create a new answer file or one based on the current machine's configuration, or to modify an existing one. The Setup Manager Wizard can create the following types of answer files:

- Windows 2000 Professional *unattend.txt* setup file
- Windows 2000 Server (all levels) *unattend.txt* setup file
- Remote Installation Services (RIS) *remboot.sif* file
- System Preparation tool *sysprep.inf* file (used with disk duplication, discussed in the next section)

The Wizard will walk you through other questions that permit the setting of user interaction levels. Simply enter the level you desire.

Automated installation is particularly useful when creating domain controllers. As part of the setup script, the command to complete the basic setup, *dcpromo/ answer:<answer file>*, should be invoked.

TABLE 3.8 Switch Options for Customizing Setup Winnt.exe

Switch	Description
/a	Turns on accessibility options
/e	Identifies any additional commands to be run after the Wizard setup
/I[:]infile	Sets the name of the setup information file; the default is DOSNET.INF
/r	Identifies optional directory/folder to be installed
/rx	Identifies optional directory/folder to be copied
/s[:]sourcepath	Identifies the source path of the Windows 2000 installation files
/t[:]tempdrive	Designated temporary setup file location; overrides default location
/u	Used for unattended operation or optional script file (also requires /s)
/copydir:folder	Creates additional folders
/cmd:command	Executes the specified command prior to the final setup action
/cmdcons	Installs files for the recovery and repair console
/debug level:file	Creates a debug log for the level specified
/s:source_path	Sets the locations for the installation files
/syspart:drive	Copies the setup files to a drive that can later be moved
/tempdrive:drive	Establishes which drive to use for the temporary setup files
/unattend num:file	Uses the optional answer file to perform unattended installations
/udf:id,udf_file	Installs the Unique Database File

Disk Duplication

On systems with *identical* hardware, the most efficient method for installation is to duplicate hard drives. The master image of Windows 2000 can be copied to many disks with comparatively little effort via the System Preparation tool (sysprep.exe).

STEPS FOR SUPPORTING DISK DUPLICATION

Disk duplication involves a series of steps as outlined:

1. Windows 2000 should be installed and fully configured on a master computer.
2. Other installation and application software should also be installed on the master computer.

3. From the **Command Prompt** → run ***sysprep.exe***. Alternately, the **Setup Manager** Wizard can inactively create a *sysprep.inf* file. This method creates a *Sysprep* folder on the root of the drive, which the Mini-setup program checks for.

4. Restart the master computer.

5. Utilize a third-party image copying tool to create a master image.

6. Utilize a third-party image copying tool to make multiple images on destination drives.

Once the destination disks are installed in the computers and booted for the first time, the Mini-setup program prompts for computer-specific variables, including the administrator password and computer name. However, if the *sysprep.inf* file is present, all invention by the user will be bypassed if the settings so designate.

CONFIGURING THE SYSTEM PREPARATION TOOL

The System Preparation tool (sysprep.exe) used for master hard disk duplication primarily deletes security identifiers (SIDs) and other user- and system-specific data. The new SID and related information are regenerated when the system reboots from the loaded disk image. The syntax used when running sysprep.exe follows. Sysprep.exe switches are listed in Table 3.9.

```
Sysprep.exe /-option
```

Remote OS Installation

The Remote OS Installation provides the use of the new Pre-Boot eXecution Environment (PXE) remote boot technology. PXE is based on Dynamic Host Configuration Protocol (DHCP). PXE combines with server-based distribution software to support client installation of Windows 2000 Professional. This permits administrators to remotely install Windows 2000 and desktop images without on-site support. Once the client operating system is installed, IntelliMirror can be utilized to manage user desktops, data, settings, and application software.

TABLE 3.9 System Preparation Tool Switches

Switch	Task
-quiet	Runs the mini-setup without user invention
-pnp	Forces the detection of Plug and Play devices on the destination system
-reboot	Invokes the reboot rather than shutdown option
-nosidgen	Forbids automatic generation of the SID on the destination system

The Remote OS Installation supports Remote Installation Services (RIS) in which a server hosts an equivalent to the CD copy of Windows 2000 Professional. The implementation of a CD-type RIS installation is discussed in the next subsection. Alternately, a preconfigured Remote Installation Preparation (RIPrep) can be used to provide a desktop image. In this case, administrators can clone desktop configurations and applications across identical computer systems. Once the first system is properly configured, an image can be created and then replicated using the RIS Wizard.

Client remote boot is initiated either by the computer's BIOS or through use of a remote boot floppy disk-based program. DHCP provides an IP address for client system when the service boot is requested. When connection to the RIS server is made, the user initiates the download by pressing the F12 key. Depending on the level of automation that was established by the RIS administrator, the user may have to input a few configuration settings or none at all. The Active Directory will then determine what installation options and other rights for a particular user are to be used based upon those established in Group Policies.

RIS INSTALLATION OF WINDOWS 2000 PROFESSIONAL

The *Remote Installation Services (RIS)* permit the installation of Windows 2000 Professional clients located anywhere on the network from a central location. RIS can be run from either a domain controller or a member server. DNS, DHCP, and Active Directory services must be fully operational.

The RIS server must be installed on a volume shared over the network. This volume must be of sufficient size to contain both the RIS software and a complete image of Windows 2000 Professional. Moreover, it must be formatted with NTFS, and it cannot run on the same drive that is running Windows 2000 Server.

The *Remote Installation Services Setup* Wizard installs the RIS software and copies Windows 2000 professional installation files to the server. It adds a variation of the Unattend.txt file that has a .sif ending. As a final step it sets up the Client Installation Wizard screens that appear during the actual remote installation.

The RIS component is added as follows: Invoke the **Windows Components Wizard** → select **Add/Remove Programs** → select **Start** and **Run** → type *risetup* → select **OK**. RIS is configured via the **Active Directory Users and Computers** snap-in tool discussed in Chapter 6.

Troubleshooting the Installation

Countless issues can create problems during the installation process, and it would be impossible to outline every one. However, to provide a basis for troubleshooting, Table 3.10 lists the most common points of failure.

TABLE 3.10 Potential Points of Failure

Failure	Possible Remedy
CD-ROM or Media Error	Contact Microsoft or your computer manufacturer (in the case of OEM versions) for a replacement CD. If the physical CD-ROM is incompatible, it will be necessary to replace it.
Insufficient Memory	Add a minimum of 64 MB.
Insufficient Disk Space	Run the setup program to check on the partitioning. It may be necessary to create new partitions and perhaps delete existing partitions. Replacement of the hard drive may also be necessary.
Services Fail to Start	Could occur if service dependencies are not met, most commonly with networks. Return to the Network Settings and check what network adapter(s) and protocols are installed. Also, in the case of clients, make sure the computer account is established and unique within the domain forest.
Failure to Connect to the Domain Controller	Verify that the domain controller is running, the DNS service is running, the domain name is correct, and protocol and adapter settings are properly set.
Windows 2000 Refuses to Install or Start	Could be a hardware compatibility issue. Make sure that Windows 2000 is detecting the hardware and that it is on the Hardware Compatibility List.

POSTSCRIPT

Planning is always advised when performing any Windows 2000 system adminis-trator task. However, during initial installation and deployment it is absolutely crit-ical. This chapter provided an overview of planning concepts that should be implemented when deploying a Windows 2000 enterprise. It also provided core instructions on installing the basic operating system. Subsequent chapters will explore planning and installation issues relevant to other topics such as the Active Directory.

Chapter 4

Getting Started

This chapter reviews items that are essential to the use and administration of Windows 2000. Some of the discussion will be elementary to those already familiar with Windows environments. However, since certain topics, like the Microsoft Management Console (MMC), are new or greatly enhanced, we suggest that you selectively examine the topics that fit your current knowledge level. Having read this chapter, the system administrator should have the following:

- An understanding of the Windows 2000 user and administrative interfaces
- A working knowledge of the Microsoft Management Console
- The ability to work with other administrative tools
- The ability to use the Help facility
- The skills to find objects—Search

INTERFACE BASICS

The Windows 2000 user interface should be familiar to anyone who has used Windows 98 or Windows NT with Internet Explorer 4.0 or later. However, in the unlikely event that you have not used these products, this section will provide a view of the user interface from 30,000 feet. Even for experienced users, there may be a few tips worthy of brief review. While the options available to an administrator are different from those of the typical user, the underlying interface is the same.

The Windows Management Services interface is based on the industry initiative Web-Based Enterprise Management (WBEM) that attempts to establish infrastructure management across heterogeneous environments. It identifies the underlying methods for accessing data on a variety of platforms. WBEM is derived from the Common Information Model (CIM) as defined by the Distribution Management Task Force (DMTF).

Microsoft's implementation of WBEM is called the Windows Management Instrumentation (WMI). WMI supports traditional administration that uses scripts that kick off other applications. It also goes further by permitting the use of scripts at the object level. WMI can be thought of as the method in which things get done. The Windows Scripting Host, discussed in Chapter 17, automates the action. Finally, the Microsoft Management Console (MMC) discussed in this chapter determines how the administrative tools are to be presented. The MMC user interface creates linkages to the WMI.

The Windows 2000 interface is basically a desktop comprising a customizable tool bar and a group of icons that serve as shortcuts to applications, folders, files, or other objects. As menus or iconic items are opened, Microsoft Explorer windows are launched and objects are displayed with a Web browser look and feel.

In Chapter 8, Group Policies, we discuss how the system administrator can standardize the desktop to add or restrict the menu and desktop items available to a user or group.

The Tool Bar and Cascading Menu System

All Microsoft Windows environments provide a Start tool bar and cascading pulldown menus (Figure 4.1). If you have not already played with tool bar and menu setups, take a few moments to get fully acquainted. Also, take the time to customize the Start tool bar and menus by pressing **Start** → select **Settings** → select **Task Bar and Start Menu**. The Start tool bar can be customized by right-clicking on it and selecting **Properties**. At this stage, any item can be added to the tool bar by clicking on it in the dialog box. Other modifications are possible, including the location of the Start tool bar itself. (Its default location is at the bottom of the screen rather than at the top, which is how it appears in Figure 4.1. The figure simply illustrates a customized setting.)

DESKTOP ICONS

The desktop displays default icons and others added by the user or system administrator. They are mere representations of the programs, folders, or files themselves. The default desktop icons for new users (Figure 4.2) include

- *My Documents*—a shortcut to the user's default directory that displays files and folders resident in the folder.

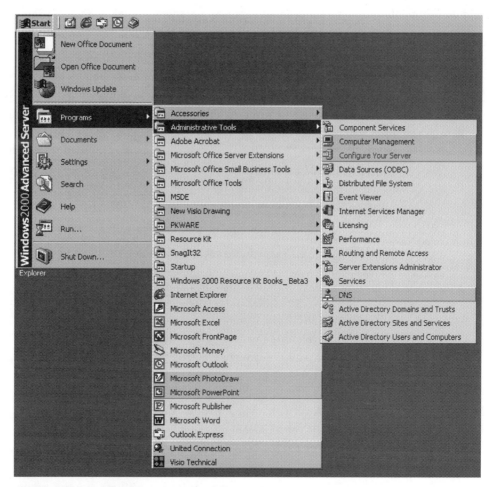

FIGURE 4.1 Start Menu Bar and Pull-Down Menu System

FIGURE 4.2 Default Desktop Icons

- *My Computer*—a shortcut to resources available on the local computer, including disk drives, CD drives, removable media, and the like.

- *My Network Places*—a display of connected network resources that provides access to resources the user has permission to use.

- *Recycle Bin*—a temporary storage area for documents marked for removal. This is basically a safety measure that permits the retrieval of documents deleted by mistake. Users should be instructed to empty the recycle bin periodically and thereby free disk space and permanently remove the files.

- *Internet Explorer*—access to Microsoft's Web browser. If connected to the Internet, it will permit surfing to sites on the World Wide Web. It will also permit viewing objects on the local system or internal network to which the user has permission.

A number of actions can be taken to manage desktop icons, including

- *Moving icons to the desktop.* When a file, folder, or application is in common use, it should be added to the desktop. You can move it there directly simply by holding the right mouse button down on it and "dragging" it across the screen to where you want it.

- *Creating shortcuts from the desktop.* Another method of gaining access to a commonly used object is to create a pointer, known as a shortcut, to it. This duplicate iconic representation can then be dragged to the desktop. A shortcut is created by selecting the target object → right-click on the object → select **Create Shortcut**.

- *Reorganizing the desktop icons.* Icons can be dragged to any location on the desktop.

- *Adding desktop icons to the Start tool bar.* It is sometimes convenient to list desktop icons on the Start tool bar. Selecting the target icon and dragging it to the Start tool bar accomplishes this action.

- *Deleting icons from the desktop.* Deleting the actual object deletes the access to the application, folder, or file. However, shortcut icons can be deleted and the actual program, folder or file remains. The deletion is accomplished by clicking the icon, pressing the **Delete** key, and confirming by pressing **YES** when prompted.

THE MY COMPUTER TOOL

Double-clicking the desktop **My Computer** icon provides a view of the resources available on the local computer system. Alternately, the Microsoft Explorer view provides a default two-panel view: On the right is an icon view of objects and folders, and on the left is the cascading menu view. The Microsoft Explorer view is

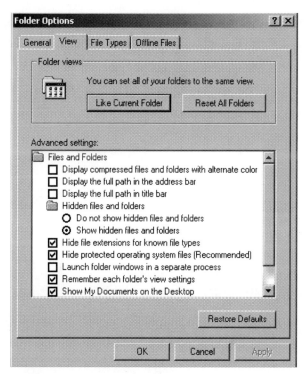

FIGURE 4.3 Viewing Hidden Files

obtained by a **right mouse button** click on **My Computers** → select **Explorer**. To drill down to either panel, simply select the folder and double-click. Alternately, the cascading menu can be opened or closed by selecting either the + or – sign, respectively.

Expanding the View of Folders and Files

Windows 2000 presents default files that are generally visible to the user or system administrator. The view can be expanded to include hidden (Figure 4.3) and operating system files. To view such files from the Tools menu, select **Folder Options** from the tool bar of the **My Computer** or other Explorer Windows, select the **View** tab, and select the items to be modified. (This dialog box is also available from the **Control Panel** under **Folder Options**.)

My Computer Customization

The **Tool** pull-down menu on **My Computer** (Figure 4.4) and any **Explorer** window permits three important local system views and accessibility:

- *Map Network Drive.* This option permits the local "mounting" of a remote disk drive. From a user's perspective, the remote drive looks local.

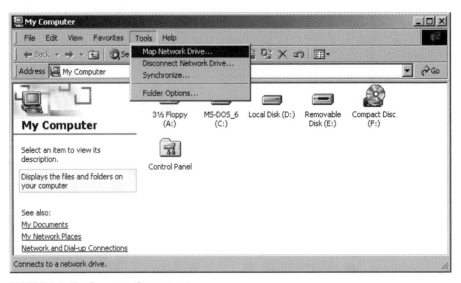

FIGURE 4.4 My Computer Customization

- *Disconnect Network Drive.* This option disconnects a previously mapped drive.
- *Synchronize.* This option permits the synchronization of data that was changed while working offline with information on the server. It is possible to define the data to be synchronized and schedule the process.

MY NETWORK PLACES

Known in previous Windows versions as the Network Neighborhood, this is an improved network interface. When **My Network Places** is opened, it typically reveals several icons. One of them is **Entire Network**, with which you can drill down to lower levels of the present network. To view resources within the **Microsoft Windows Network**, double-click on that icon. This will reflect all of the Microsoft-based workgroups and domains that are currently connected (Figure 4.5).

Network Directory Search

By selecting the Directory icon, the system administrator is shown the domain user and Computers folders (Figure 4.6). You can drill down any of the folders to view and manage associated users, groups, computers, and other objects. As discussed later, this method can be used for some remote administration.

The Directory icon can also be used to find resources within the domain. For example, to find a printer, follow these steps (Figure 4.7):

1. Right-click on any Directory icon (and domain name) → select **Find**.
2. Select **Advanced Tab** from the Find dialog box.

3. Select **Printer** from the **Find** pull-down menu → complete whatever data is known in the three tabs.

4. Press the **Find Now** button.

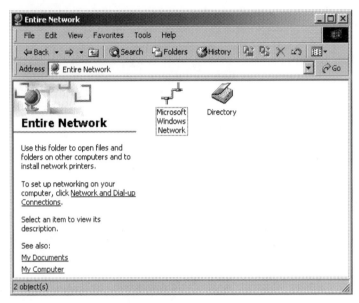

FIGURE 4.5 Entire Network Selection

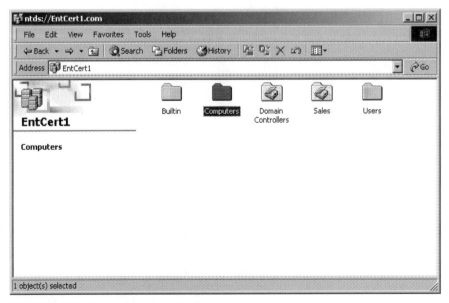

FIGURE 4.6 The Network Directory Option

Another option for finding network resources from the **My Network Places** interface is the **Search** button on the tool bar. Complete the information in the left-hand panel and press **Search Now** (Figure 4.8).

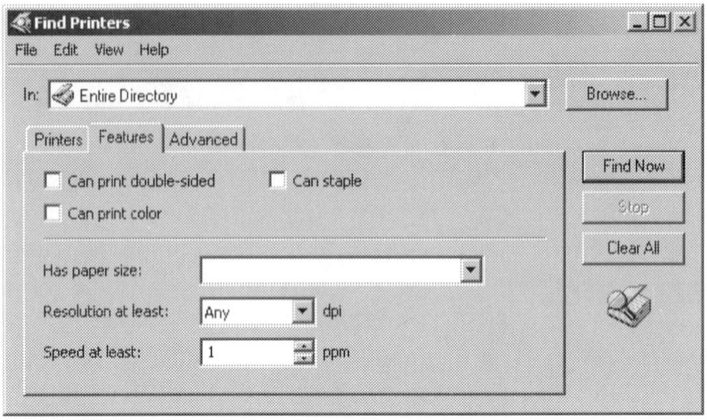

FIGURE 4.7 Finding a Network Printer

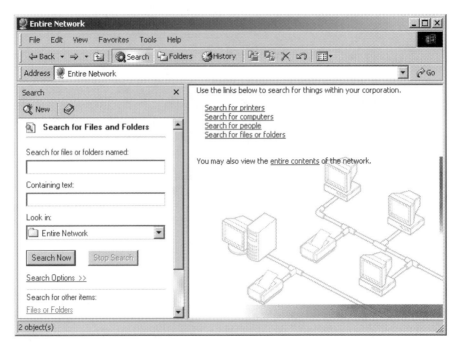

FIGURE 4.8 The Network Find Dialog

MICROSOFT MANAGEMENT CONSOLE

One of the strengths of Windows 2000 is its consolidation of many administrative tools into a single interface. The Microsoft Management Console (MMC) has the familiar look and feel of the Microsoft Explorer. By default, it is divided into two panels: On the left side is a listing of the tools that have been added to the console; on the right are details for the selected administrative tool.

Administrative tools are called *snap-ins* that are simply hosted within the MMC framework. All components in an MMC snap-in are organized hierarchically in order to view relationships and provide a logical structure for administration. Each MMC can contain one or more administrative tools. It is also possible to create multiple MMCs and cluster similar snap-in functions together. The decision to add or remove snap-ins is the system administrator's. The snap-ins include both those bundled with Windows 2000 and others from third-party vendor applications that adhere to API guidelines.

The MMC also facilitates the delegation of administrative responsibility. As discussed in later chapters, Windows 2000 permits the creation of smaller administrative components known as organizational units (OUs), in which specific and granular responsibility can be assigned. An MMC can be created for a specific set of responsibilities and provided to the administrator of the OU.

Creating and Using MMC

MMCs provide a consistent and single point of access for administrating Windows 2000. The initial step is to create the first Microsoft Management Console (Figure 4.9) by simply pressing **Start** → select **Run** → type **MMC** → press **OK**. This procedure can be used to create additional consoles, or you can create a new MMC from within an existing console.

The MMC permits a number of methods to interact with snap-ins. The tool bar is used to selected the following options:

- *Console*, used in the Author mode, primarily adds or removes snap-ins and provides other customizations.
- *Action* lists the possible actions that can be taken for each snap-in. The options are different for each one.
- *View* provides a list of methods to customize the view of each administrative task. Each snap-in has a different view.
- *Favorites* are used in much the same way as Web browser favorite links for rapid maneuvering to snap-in components.

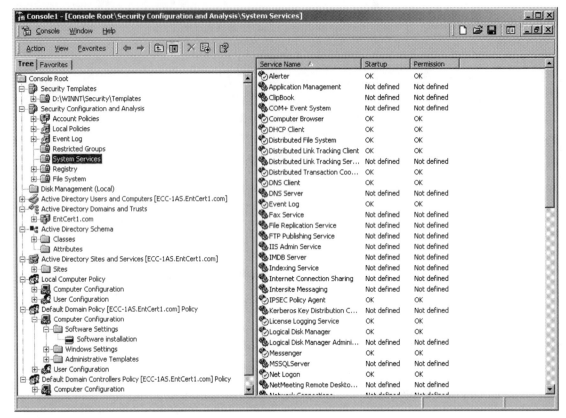

FIGURE 4.9 View of the Microsoft Management Console

ADDING A SNAP-IN

As shown in Figure 4.10, the Microsoft Management Console snap-ins are added by following these steps:

1. Open a new or existing **MMC** while in the Author mode.
2. Click on the **Console** button → select **Add/Remove Snap-in**.
3. From the Dialog box listing the current snap-ins (Figure 4.11) press the **Add** button.
4. Select the target snap-in → press **Add**.
5. Repeat this for all additional snap-ins → press **Close**.
6. Press **OK** to complete the addition of snap-ins.

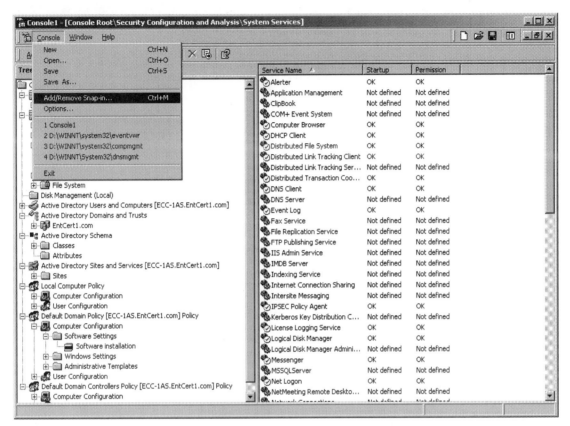

FIGURE 4.10 Adding Snap-Ins

MMC MODES

The Microsoft Management Console operates in two primary modes. **Author** is used for the creation of an MMC and the setting of options, and offers full control over the MMC and all related snap-ins. **User** comprises three levels ranging from internal full access to strictly delegated utilization; its purpose is to restrict the addition, removal, or modification of snap-ins. The three levels of the User mode assign the following rights:

- *Full Access.* The user can customize the MMC with the snap-ins provided. The only Console option is to exit, so this user cannot add or remove other snap-ins.

- *Delegated Access.* The Console, Window menu, Help menu, and main toolbar are not displayed.

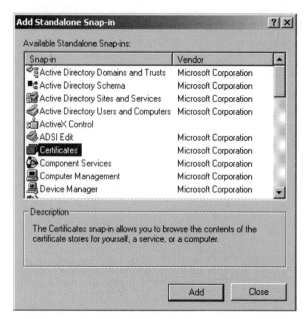

FIGURE 4.11 The Snap-In Dialog

- *SDI Delegated Access.* The user is provided one view or window to administrative tasks. SDI has the same restrictions as its non-SDI delegated counterpart; plus, it removes the Console System menu controls.

Setting MMC Modes

Modes can be set only by an individual with Author mode control. They are set in a very straightforward fashion. Once the **MMC** is open → select **Options** → select the desired level from the **Console Mode** pull-down (Figure 4.12).

SAVING MMC LOCALLY OR TO DELEGATED ADMINISTRATORS

Once the console has been created with the mode set, it can be saved to the system administrator's desktop or to a delegated administrator. If the MMC is to be saved on the author's desktop, **Save** is the only action necessary. To save the MMC to another administrator's desktop, select **Save As** → change the name of the console if desired → select the drive location → select **Documents and Settings** → select the user's folder → select **Desktop** → press **OK**.

When creating an MCC for another user, the use of **Taskpads** is helpful to provide a restricted or simplified view of a selected number of tasks. In order to create console Taskpads, the following procedures should be followed using the target tool (in this example, we will use **Computer Management**):

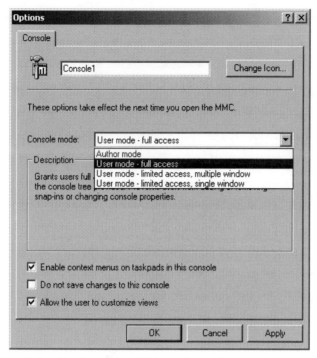

FIGURE 4.12 The Options Dialog to Change the MMC Mode

- Launch the MMC and select the target management tools (in this case, select **Computer Management**)
- From **Computer Management** → open **System Tools** → open **System** → select **Event Viewer** → right-click **System** → select **New Taskpad**
- Utilize the Wizard to set the properties and other configuration items.

Working with Individual Administrative Tools

Windows 2000 administrative tools can be used as standalone applications or as snap-ins to Microsoft's Management Console. In most cases, they are presented in the same console format as the MMC, which guarantees a consistent and familiar interface. Other administrative tools are also available from the Control Panel and through character-based command-line utilities.

THE CONTROL PANEL

The **Control Panel**, shown in Figure 4.13, is familiar to any user of Windows products. The tools available in the Windows 2000 Professional version are differ-

FIGURE 4.13 The Control Panel

ent from those in the Server and Advanced Server versions. For Windows 2000 Professional, the most important tools are available individually from the **Control Panel**. Server versions of Windows 2000 can access major applications by double-clicking on the Control Panel **Administrative Tools** icon.

To gain access, press **Start** → select **Settings** → select **Control Panel**. Then double-click the **Control Panel** item you want to open.

Administrative Tools

There are a number of ways for an administrator to access **Administrative Tools**. As discussed before, these tools can be launched from the **Start** → **Programs** → **Administrative Tools** menu or as MMC snap-ins. They can also be launched from the **Command Prompt** or through the **Control Panel** (Figure 4.14). As

FIGURE 4.14 Administrative Tools Available from the Control Panel

shown in Figure 4.13, double-clicking the **Administrative Tools** icon will display
a secondary window containing the available management applications. (In Windows 2000 Professional the **Control Panel** is the primary method for accessing
Administrative Tools.) To launch an administrative tool, simply double-click on
the target icon.

Add Hardware Example
A good example of **Control Panel** tools operation is the **Add/Remove Hardware Wizard**. One of the first things to notice about this tool is its automatic
detection of hardware. With this feature, Windows 2000 can determine both the
presence and the health of attached system devices and components. Once the
detection process is complete, the system administrator can further analyze the
hardware device or subcomponent. If a new device is found, the Wizard will
prompt the system administrator to have it automatically added to the found
device drivers (Figure 4.15). Alternately, the administrator can manually select dri-

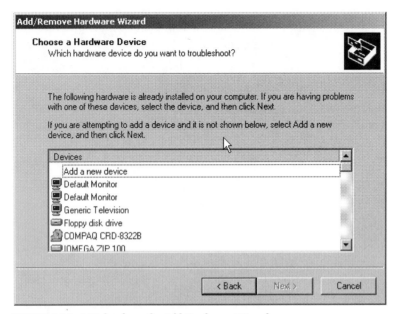

FIGURE 4.15 A Dialog from the Add Hardware Wizard

vers, if, say, they are not fully Plug and Play compatible. One of the nice aspects of this Wizard is that it always attempts to load the most current drivers for a given device.

Computer Management Example

To illustrate the use of individual administrative tools, we briefly review the Computer Management application, which looks at the health of the local computer or member server and performs appropriate management actions (Figure 4.16). This chapter is designed as an overview, so we will not walk through each of the powerful management options available.

Character-Based Administrative Interface

Windows 2000 provides a primary graphical user interface, but it is also possible to perform most administrative activities through a character-based interface. For seasoned UNIX system administrators, this will be a much more familiar approach. The text interface is required for some administrative tasks, as illustrated in the appendix, Windows 2000 Commands and Utilities.

The **Command Prompt** is the interface to the character-based world (Figure 4.17). It opens an MS-DOS-like window in which commands and flags can be set.

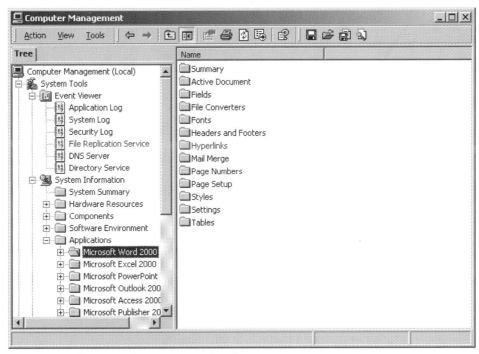

FIGURE 4.16 The Computer Management Console

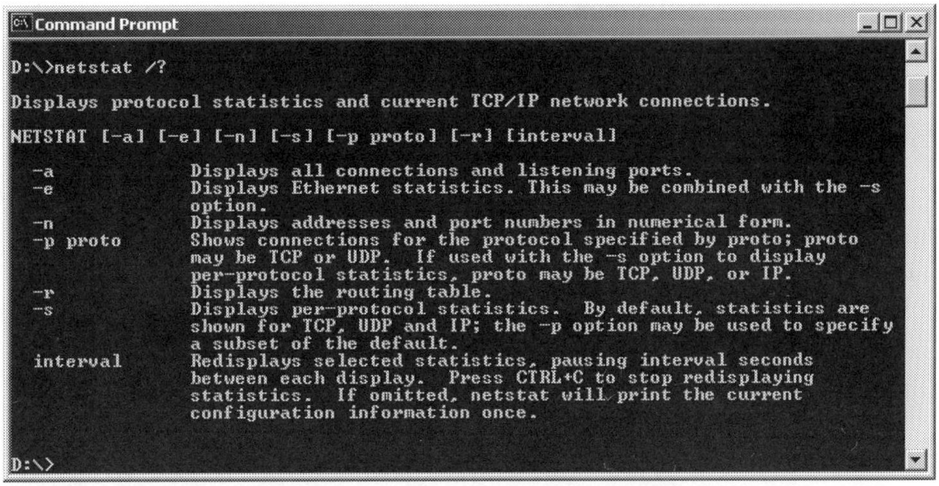

FIGURE 4.17 The Command Prompt Character-Based/DOS-Like Interface

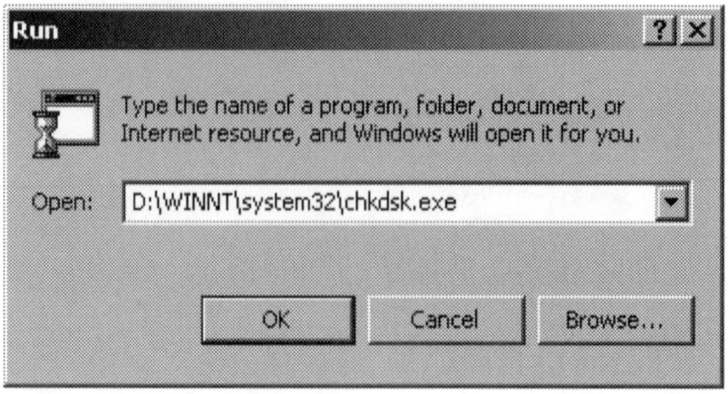

FIGURE 4.18 Run Dialog Box

The **Command Prompt** is available by pressing **Start** → select **Program** → select **Accessories** → select **Command Prompt**.

The appendix provides a review of the most common graphical and character-based administrative tools. Chapter 17 also reviews aspects of the Windows Scripting Host environment.

LAUNCHING TOOLS FROM THE RUN MENU

The Run dialog is provided specifically to launch applications, including administrative tools (Figure 4.18). Located from the **Start** menu, it is generally very straightforward and reliable. If you know the location of the application, it is very easy to type from path to executable in the text box and press **OK**. If you do not know the location, the **Browser** option will permit you to move between locations until you find the executable file.

HELP

If you are a system administrator coming from a UNIX environment, the Windows 2000 Help facility (Figure 4.19) makes the UNIX man(ual) pages pale in comparison. Topics are hyper-linked to related topics, making it very easy to drill down into a subject or move laterally to related information. Within any Windows 2000 system console it is possible to jump to the Help facility by pressing the Help button. Alternately, press **Start** → select **Help**. Basic Help topics will be displayed on the left-hand panel, or you can seek more specific information by selecting the **Index** or **Search** tabs. The Help facility is very valuable and should be used on a regular basis.

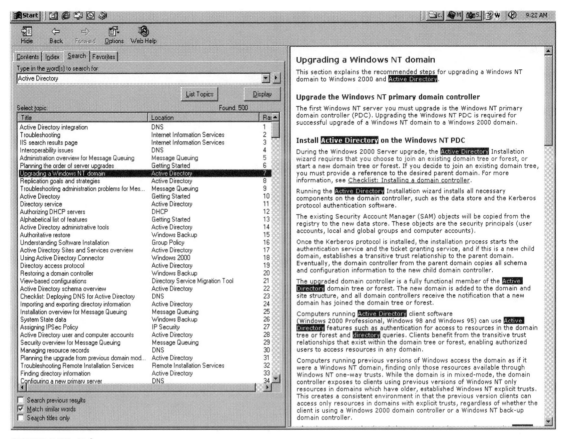

FIGURE 4.19 Help

SEARCH

The extremely powerful search function in Windows 2000 is valuable to both the system administrator and the regular user. If you are not exactly sure about the name of the object, general attributes can be supplied to locate the network resource. To launch this function select **Start** → select **Search** → select the search category. This is shown in Figure 4.20.

The Search dialog box provides a number of options to fine-tune the action. For example, if you are looking for files or a folder, you can search by name or content (Figure 4.21). Take the opportunity to use this facility. It is something that will be regularly used by the system administrator and user alike.

FIGURE 4.20 Search Menu Options

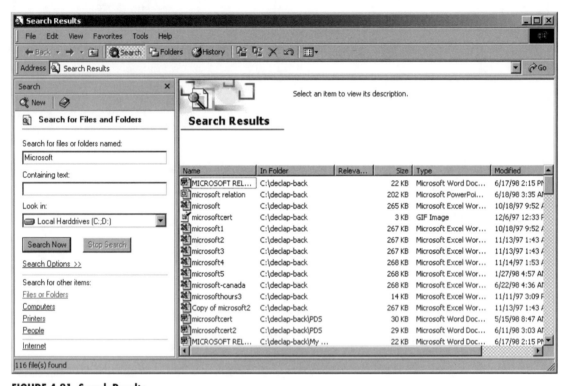

FIGURE 4.21 Search Results

POSTSCRIPT

This chapter provided a view from 30,000 feet of the Windows 2000 user interface and its administrative management tools. Subsequent chapters will explore how to properly apply these tools to real-world environments.

Chapter 5

The Active Directory

The next two chapters examine the Windows 2000 directory services, known collectively as the Active Directory. This is one of the new breed of metadirectories, and so it is integral to the Windows 2000 Server operating system's infrastructure, security, and maintenance. Because of the pure volume of information that must be covered to properly explain the Active Directory technology, our review spans this chapter and Chapter 6, Active Directory Management and Use. An understanding of the conceptual underpinning of the Active Directory and how it can be managed is fundamental to Windows 2000 system administration.

After reading this chapter, you should have a working knowledge of the following Active Directory concepts:

- *The role of directory services*—the function of the Active Directory and an identification of some of its important features for system administrators.
- *Active Directory logical structure components*—the role of domains, domain trees, forests, and organizational units.
- *Active Directory physical structure components*—the role of sites and domain controllers.
- *Active Directory schema*—how the Active Directory schema defines object classes and attributes.
- *Open standards support and naming conventions*—the Active Directory's use of open standards like DNS and LDAP together with its employment of the most common naming conventions to ensure interoperability.
- *Migration and Application Programming Interfaces*—the support provided for the migration and/or integration of the Active Directory with other direc-

tory services such as Novell's NDS and API options available for both third-party application development and administrative scripting.

- *The Global Catalog and replication services*—the new Global Catalog feature and the directory replication services.
- *Security and trust relationships*—the role played by domains, trees, and forests with respect to security and trust relationships.
- *Administrative Delegation*—how the Active Directory structure lends itself to very granular resource management and the delegation of system administration authority.

DIRECTORY SERVICES

The Windows 2000 Active Directory is Microsoft's consolidation of the major enterprise-wide directory services within a single, replicable data store and administrative interface.

A directory is a listing that helps organize and locate things. The index of this book is one example. As the reader of the index, you become the *directory service* provider that scans the entries, locates the page number(s) for a given topic, and turns to the identified page.

In computing terms, the two components of a directory are the data store and the services that act on that data. In Windows 2000, a *directory* is simply a store of objects, within which those objects can be located anywhere in the enterprise and can include applications, databases, printers, users, and other workstations or servers. A *directory service* performs many functions that act on that store: replication, security rule enforcement, data distribution, and much more.

NOTE   An *object* is a representation of real things such as a user, a data file, a printer, or a software application. All objects have *named attributes* that describe the item. Thus an attribute of a printer might be its location, its manufacturer, or its type. A *container* is a special class that has both a namespace and attributes. It does not represent anything real or concrete but instead holds one or more objects. A *tree* is simply a hierarchy of objects and containers. As discussed later, the domain tree is a special form of tree that defines a domain directory hierarchy. The endpoint of any tree branch is an object; the branch is typically viewed as a container for multiple objects. Think of a tree as the relationship of objects and their path from the root. For example, the user container holds the objects associated with all users on a computer system. Subbranches hold the objects associated with an individual user.

What Is the Active Directory?

Stated very simply, the Active Directory is a network-based object store and service that locates and manages resources, and makes these resources available to authorized users and groups. An underlying principle of the Active Directory is that everything is considered an *object*—people, servers, workstations, printers, documents, and devices. Each object also has certain *attributes* and its own security *Access Control List (ACL)*. Objects can be organized within the Active Directory in a special kind of object known as a *container,* which can be used on a very granular level. Specifically, the Active Directory plays several very important roles within a Windows 2000 enterprise, which include but are not limited to the following:

- A store for information about every network object and its attributes
- A security conduit for ACL authentication and domain trusts
- A focal point for system administration
- A mechanism for operating system interoperability
- A means of consolidating divergent directory services
- A system for replication of object data

The Active Directory, as illustrated in Figure 5.1, is a distributed, hierarchical, replicated, and secure directory service designed for Windows 2000 that is theoretically capable of interoperability within heterogeneous directory service environments.

The Active Directory catalogs file objects with their attributes in a hierarchical arrangement, fully embracing naming resolution services like DNS. It also organizes users and groups with their associated attributes. The Active Directory plays an important role in identifying security policies across the network, integrating e-mail, Internet addressing, and groupware applications. In essence, the Windows 2000 Active Directory merges all of these directory services within an extensible system environment.

A user inquiry about an object is passed through the *Global Catalog (GC),* which, as we will discuss later, is an abstraction of object information contained in the Active Directory data store. The GC resolves the most common object inquiries. It is created and refreshed with updated information for the Active Directory. The *schema* residing within the Active Directory presents object definitions. The Active Directory manages the store of data through an *Extensible Storage Engine (ESE).* The upper functions of the directory services themselves are separated from the ESE by APIs through the *Directory System Agent (DSA)* layer. No direct calls are made to the ESE.

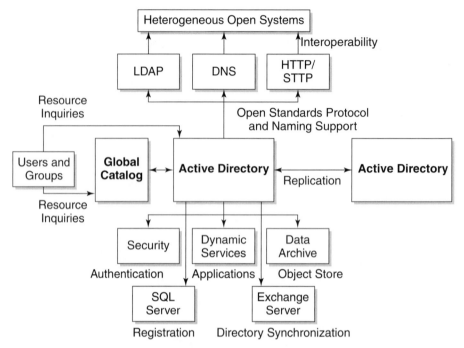

FIGURE 5.1 A View of the Active Directory Relative to Other Elements

Figure 5.2 illustrates the structural relationship of the data store and extensible storage engine to the Directory system agent. Queries made by a user are passed through the Global Catalog. If the object cannot be resolved by the GC, it is passed to the data store via the ESE database API.

FILE STRUCTURE

The Active Directory stores *database* and *log* files. It is important to understand the nature of these files in order to facilitate a backup and restoration policy in the event of system corruption.

The Active Directory database file is *Ntds.dit* and is stored in the *%system/NTDS* folder. Every domain controller has a copy of it. Ntds.dit stores all domain objects together with their attribute data organized into several tables. The *schema table* contains the definitions of the possible objects that can be created. The *object table* organizes a single object per role, with a column provided for every attribute that contains data. Finally, the *link table* contains the relationship data between the object itself and the object table.

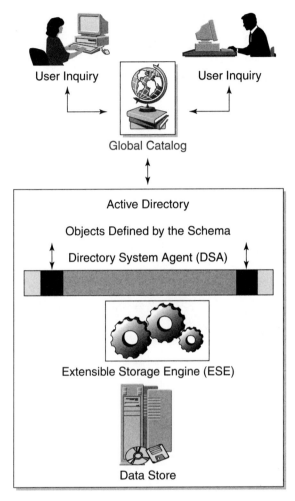

User Inquiry   Global Catalog   User Inquiry

Active Directory

Objects Defined by the Schema

Directory System Agent (DSA)

Extensible Storage Engine (ESE)

Data Store

FIGURE 5.2 A Structural Overview

The Active Directory creates and stores four types of log files on the maintenance and management of transactions. These files are stored in *%system/NTDS*
and include

- *Transaction log files.* The *current transaction* file is *Edb.log,* which by default
  contains information about recent transactions and is limited to 10 MB. When
  this limit is reached, transaction files are automatically created with the name
  edbxxxxx.log (*x* is a sequential number). They are retained until the transactions are committed to the Active Directory. Once every 12 hours, old previ-

ous transaction files are purged during a process known as garbage collection. If you do not want previous transaction files created, it is possible to set circular logging, where the current file is overridden when it is filled. This action is not recommended because it could limit your ability to recover recent transactions.

- *Checkpoint files.* The checkpoint is *Edb.chk,* and it used to list transactions that have been committed to the Active Directory and those that remain uncommitted. Each time a transaction is committed, it advances to the next entry. If all transactions are not committed at the time of shutdown, the checkpoint file is read when the system is rebooted and all remaining transactions are then committed to the Active Directory.

- *Reserved log files.* The reserved log file can be a number sequence of logs, with a maximum size of 10 MB, named res1.log, res2.log, and so on. These logs are used in place of the transaction log when the creation of a new log file is attempted but insufficient disk space is available. When this occurs, the system will automatically shut down.

- *Patch files.* Patch files (with a .pat suffix) are used during the backup and restore process of the Active Directory. Database entries are sometimes divided during backup into what is known as split transactions. The patch files are used to record these splits and "patch" the transaction back together during restoration.

DATA STORES AND PARTITIONS

To facilitate information storage and replications, the Active Directory uses three types of data store for directory partitions, each of which is discretely replicated as a separate unit according to its own schedule. The three Active Directory partitions are

- *Schema data.* Schema information comprises definitions of the objects that are available or can be created within the Active Directory. It also includes the required and optional object attributes.

- *Configuration data.* The logical structure of the domain is reflected in configuration data. Common to all domain trees and forests is a strategy for replicating all three Active Directory partitions between domain controllers. This replication topology is stored in the configuration data partition.

- *Domain data.* All objects within the tree are stored as domain data. This information relates strictly to the objects within the domain and is not replicated to other domains. Instead of total replication of all domain object information, a subset is derived for the Global Catalog. In addition to this subset, the Global

Catalog server contains the schema and configuration data. It becomes the index for locating data within a domain or across a tree or forest.

An Administrative View of the Active Directory

From a system administrator's perspective, the Active Directory provides many keys for success.

- Since the Active Directory network is organized hierarchically, it is possible to more finitely organize the infrastructure for better management.
- The ability to assign and delegate the administration of Windows 2000 to manageable elements is one of its major strengths. The Active Directory is responsible for managing the hierarchical structure of the domain, the child domain, and the organizational units with logical administrative boundaries.
- The Active Directory provides a consolidated, single point for administration and system replication services.
- The Active Directory includes support for a number of open standards (DNS and LDAP), rich APIs (using C/C++, Java, Visual Basic GUIs, and scripts), extensible schema, and streamlined object lookup and network login via the new Global Catalog.
- The Active Directory provides easy migration and backward compatibility with earlier Windows NT versions and theoretical interoperability with NetWare and UNIX.

Based upon the use of objects and attributes, as shown in Figure 5.3, Active Directory forms associations.

The scope of the Active Directory can be as small or as large as required, and can contain every object and container within the domain tree. In essence, the Active Directory can scale from a single server to an extremely large enterprise network. The primary constraints are fast connectivity and security, discussed later.

ACTIVE DIRECTORY STRUCTURAL COMPONENTS

The two primary Active Directory components are its *logical* and *physical* structures, which respectively involve the organization and communication of objects. A third component, known as the *schema,* defines objects that make up the Active Directory. The discussion of the schema is included in the logical structure section for the sake of convenience.

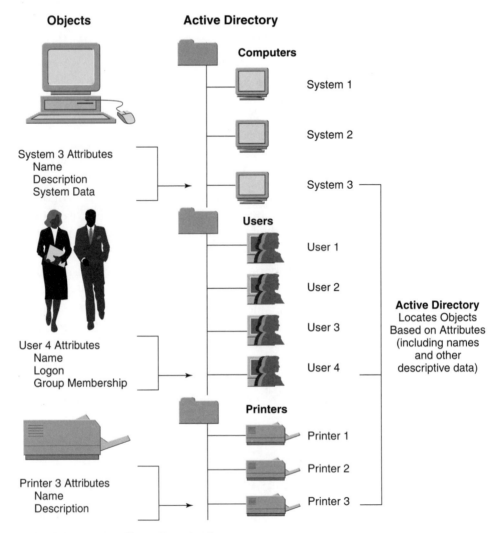

FIGURE 5.3 **Locating Objects Using Attributes**

Logical Structure

The base logical components of the Active Directory are *objects* and their associated *attributes*. *Object classes* are merely definitions of the object types that can be created in the Active Directory. The *schema* is the Active Directory mechanism for storing object classes. It also permits the addition of other object classes and associated attributes.

Active Directory objects are organized around a hierarchical domain model. This model is a design facility that permits the logical arrangement of objects within administrative, security, and organizational boundaries. Each domain has its own security permissions and unique security relationships with other domains. The Active Directory utilizes *multi-master replication* to communicate information and changes between domains.

The following sections provide an overview of domain model building blocks: domains, domain trees, forests, organizational units, and the schema.

DOMAINS

The Active Directory manages a hierarchical infrastructure of networked computers with the domain as the foundation. A *domain* comprises computer systems and network resources that share a common logical security boundary. It can store over 17 terabytes within the Active Directory database store. While a domain can cross physical locations, all domains maintain their own security policies and security relationships with other domains. They are sometimes created to define functional boundaries such as an administrative unit (e.g., marketing versus engineering). They are also viewed as groupings of resources or servers that utilize a common domain name, known as a namespace. For example, all servers or resources in the EntCert.com namespace belong to a single domain.

In very simple terms, every domain controller has the following information as part of its Active Directory:

- Data on every object and container object within the particular domain
- Metadata about other domains in the tree (or forest) to provide directory service location
- A listing of all domains in the tree and forest
- The location of the server with the Global Catalog

DOMAIN TREES

When multiple domains share a common schema, security trust relationships, and a Global Catalog, a *domain tree* is created, defined by a common and contiguous namespace (Figure 5.4). Thus, for example, all domains with the ending namespace of EntCert.com belong to the *EntCert* domain tree. A domain tree is formed through the expansion of child domains like Sales.EntCert.com or Research.EntCert.com. In this example, the *root domain* is EntCert.com.

The first created domain is known as the root domain, and it contains the configuration and schema data for the tree and (as we shall see) the forest. A tree structure is formed by adding child domains. There are a number of reasons for creating multiple domains in a tree—for example, some are the following:

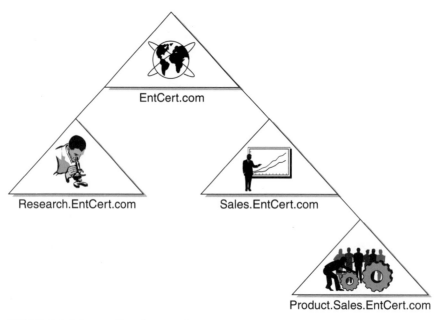

FIGURE 5.4 A Domain Tree Common Namespace

- Discretely managing different organizations or providing unit identities
- Enforcing different security boundaries and password policies
- Requiring a better method of controlling Active Directory replication
- Better handling a very large number of managed objects
- Decentralizing administration

A single domain contains a complete Active Directory partition for all of its objects. It is also, by definition, a complete domain tree. As child domains are added to the domain tree, Active Directory partitions are replicated to one or more domain controllers within each of the domains.

DOMAIN FORESTS

Trust relationships can be formed between domain trees with different name-spaces. When this occurs, a domain forest is created, which allows the enterprise to have different domain names, such as "entcert.com" and "unint.com."

All trees within the forest share a number of common attributes, including a Global Catalog, configuration, and schema. A forest is simply a reference point

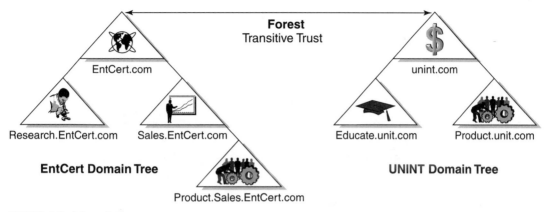

FIGURE 5.5 A Domain Forest

between trees and does not have its own name. As discussed later, forests utilize the Kerberos security technology to create transitive trust relationships between trees. Figure 5.5 illustrates how two domain trees form a forest.

ORGANIZATIONAL UNITS

Domains and child domains can be internally divided into administrative substructures known as *organizational units* (OUs), each of which can compartmentalize over 10 million objects. As container objects, OUs can be nested within other OUs. For example, the marketing division may be defined as an organizational unit and product groups within this division as suborganizational units. A domain usually comprises one or more organizational units arranged hierarchically. Objects can be organized within organizational units for administrative purposes. The OU acts as a container that lists the object contents, including users, computer systems, and devices such as printers.

An organizational unit is a logical subset defined by security or administrative parameters. In this administrative arrangement, the specific functions of the system administrator can also be easily segmented or delegated with the organizational unit level. From a system administrator's vantage point, this is very important to understand. It is possible to delegate system management responsibility solely to certain activities within a domain, OU, or child subsidiary OU. For example, a person within an organizational unit can be granted authority to manage print and file server functions but be denied authority to add, modify, or delete user accounts.

Figure 5.6 illustrates the relationship of an organizational unit to a domain tree. Organizational units are subunits with a domain or child domain.

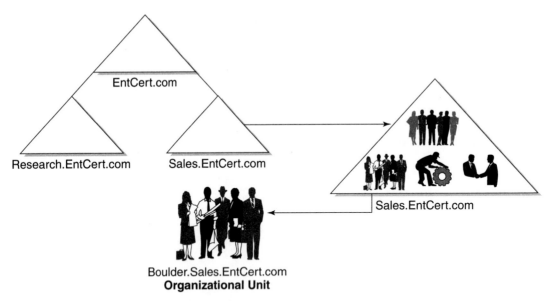

FIGURE 5.6 A Domain Tree and Organizational Units

TREES AND FOREST SCALING AND EXTENSIBILITY

The Active Directory scales across environments ranging from a single server to a domain of one million users or more. The basis of this scaling is the peer-to-peer directory service relationship that is established between domains. Every domain server (known as a domain controller) is provided updated information on Active Directory objects. Consistency across domains is ensured through the automatic replication services. To avoid extremely large and unwieldy directories, the Active Directory creates tree partitions that comprise small portions of the entire enterprise directory. However, every directory tree has sufficient information to locate other objects in the enterprise. In addition to greater efficiency, objects that are more frequently used are placed in the local store for more rapid access. A trust relationship is automatically established between the domains in the same tree, so it is possible to transparently locate resources anywhere in the tree or forest enterprise where the Active Directory resides.

SCHEMA

The *schema* is simply a framework of definitions that establishes the type of objects available to the Active Directory. These definitions are divided into *object classes,* and the information that describes the object is known as its *attributes*. There are two types of attributes: those that *must* exist and those that *may* exist. For example,

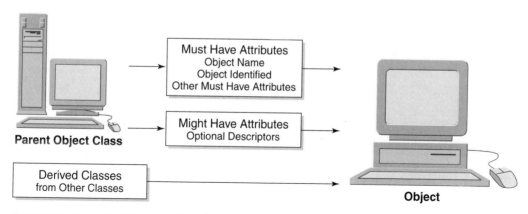

FIGURE 5.7 The Active Directory Schema Object Relationship

the schema defines a user object class as having the user's name as a required attribute; the user's physical location or job description is optional. Attributes are used to further help distinguish one object from another. They include Object Name, Object Identifier (OID), Syntax, and optional information, as shown in Figure 5.7.

The schema is stored within the Active Directory database file Ntds.dit. Object definitions are stored as individual objects, so the Directory can treat schema definitions in the same way it treats other objects. The default schema is created with the first installation of the Active Directory. It contains common objects and properties for such items as users, groups, computers, printers, and network devices. It also establishes the default Active Directory structure that is used internally.

As an extensible component, new object classes may be dynamically added to the current schema and old object classes can be modified. It is not possible to modify or deactivate system classes and attributes.

NOTE   *Schema data* should not be confused with *configuration data,* which provides the structural information for the Active Directory. The schema provides information on what objects and attributes are available to the Directory. Configuration information maintains the Directory structure that represents the relationship between the actual objects and indicates how to replicate this structure between domain controllers.

The schema is accessible only to the Administrators and Schema Admins user groups by default. It is managed through the **Active Directory Schema** snap-in tool. (The Active Directory Schema snap-in becomes available only after the *adminpak* application is installed from the Windows 2000 Server CD within the I386 folder.) Active Directory schema elements are dynamic and available to applications after the initial startup of the system. New attributes and classes can be added to the schema to provide dynamic extensibility to the Active Directory.

The *Schema Active Directory Service* Interface (SADS) is another method to facilitate the browsing and extending of functions and relationships of a schema object or attribute. The four SADS objects and schema object containers are listed in Table 5.1.

The schema object container attaches definitions to the directory tree. It is typically represented as a child of the directory root. In turn, each instance has its own individual schema.

The Schema operations master domain controller (as discussed in greater detail in Chapter 6) manages the structure and content of the schema. It replicates schema information to the other domain controllers in the forest. Every domain controller loads a copy of the schema in a RAM-based cache, ensuring rapid access to currently used object and attribute definitions. If changes occur in the schema, the cache is refreshed.

TABLE 5.1 Schema ADSI Objects

Object	Description
Schema	Contains all the information involved in a particular Active Directory schema.
Object Class	Establishes the classification of the object. Examples are computers, users, and groups. Object classes include • Name • Object Identifier (OID) • "May Contain" optional attributes • "Must Contain" required attributes • Parent object classes • Derived classes from secondary or auxiliary classes
Property	Describes the defined properties (a device type, screen color, etc.). Properties are not subdivided into functional sets as occurs with directory service objects, like a Group object.
Syntax	Describes first how the properties are defined and then specific options.

Physical Structure

The second component of the Active Directory is the physical structure, which holds the mechanisms for data communication and replication. This section covers two physical structure topics: the definition of the IP subnet network structural component that constitutes Active Directory *sites;* and the physical server that stores and replicates Active Directory data known as the *domain controller* and the related *Global Catalog.*

SITES

In an ideal world, network communication would always be rapid and reliable. Unfortunately, geographic and other limitations result in the need to create smaller networks, known as subnets, to facilitate communication within and between locations. Although rapid and reliable network communication can be achieved within the larger unit, that between subnets can vary radically. Therefore, to ensure the most effective network communication by Windows 2000, the Active Directory offers methods of regulating inter-subnet traffic.

The physical network structure of the Active Directory is based on a unit known as a *site*. The role of the administrator is to design sites that ensure the greatest network performance. A *site* comprises one or more Internet Protocol (IP) subnets that are tied together by high-speed, reliable connections. What speed is considered sufficient is really arbitrary. For example, in small networks a 128KBps connection could be sufficient, whereas the bandwidth for a large network might need 3 MBps or more. The administrator must determine what speed best accomplishes the goal of minimum performance loss due to network traffic and establish sites accordingly. While many subnets can belong to a single site, a single subnet cannot span multiple sites.

The primary goal of a site is rapid and economical data transmission. An important part of that is efficient directory services replication. The Active Directory physical structure governs when and how replication takes place. This is true of both intersite and intrasite replication. Network site performance also impacts the location of objects and logon authentication. As users log on to the network, they are able to reach the closest domain controller site through the previous assignment of subnet information. The system administrator uses the Active Directory Sites and Services snap-in to manage the topology of replication services. With intrasite replication, the defined high-speed connection normally ensures rapid deployment. With intersite replication, the WAN bandwidth may be considerably slower. The site structure permits the management of Active Directory replication scheduling between sites.

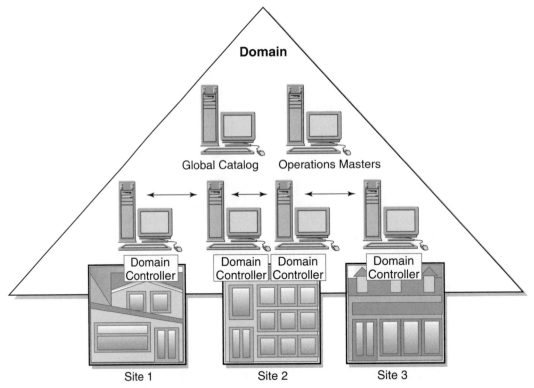

FIGURE 5.8 A View of Multiple Sites in the Same Domain

Administrative granularity is significantly enhanced through the concept of the site and its relationship to domain and organizational units. In many cases, sites have the same boundaries as a domain or an organizational unit; thus, delegation of site responsibility might be mirrored in OU or domain administration.

Sites and Domain Relationships

No formal relationship exists between the boundaries of a site or domain. A site can have multiple domains, as a domain can have a number of sites (Figures 5.8 and 5.9). In addition, sites and domains do not have to maintain the same namespace.

DOMAIN CONTROLLER

A domain controller is a server containing a copy of the Active Directory. All domain controllers are peers and maintain replicated versions of the Active Direc-

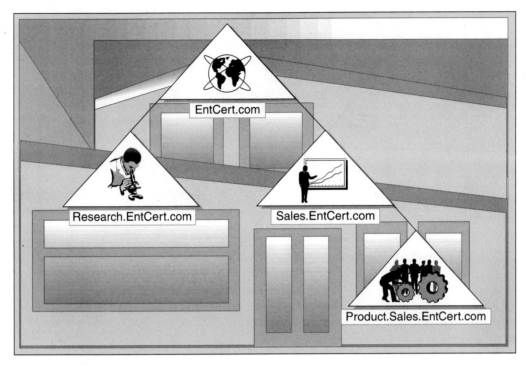

FIGURE 5.9 A View of Multiple Domains in the Same Site

tory for their domains. The domain controller plays an important role in both the logical and physical structure of the Active Directory. It organizes all the domain's object data in a logical and hierarchical data store. It also authenticates users, provides responses to queries about network objects, and replicates directory services. The physical structure provides the means to transmit this data through well-connected sites.

The Active Directory replaces the Windows NT Primary Domain Controller (PDC) and its Backup Domain Controller (BDC) counterparts. Now all domain controllers share a multi-master peer-to-peer relationship that hosts copies of the Active Directory. Another big difference from Windows NT is that all domain controllers in Windows 2000 have read and write capability to the Active Directory. In previous versions only the PDC was read/write capable and initiated replication. Now any Active Directory domain controller can initiate the replication process when new data is added.

Figure 5.10 illustrates that multiple domain controllers can exist within each domain or child domain.

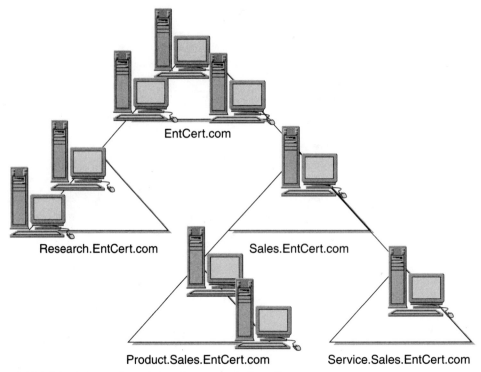

EntCert.com

Research.EntCert.com

Sales.EntCert.com

Product.Sales.EntCert.com

Service.Sales.EntCert.com

FIGURE 5.10 Domains Have One or More Domain Controllers

Reasons for Creating Multiple Domain Controllers

An Active Directory domain may have one or more *domain controllers* that replicate the directory partition. Among the reasons for having multiple domain controllers within a domain are:

- Better user connectivity
- High-volume user activity
- Greater failover and redundancy of information

When creating multiple domain controllers, the system administrator must
take into account the added network load that will occur as a result of replication
traffic. Still, it is recommended that each domain and each site have more than one
domain controller so as to provide logical and physical structure redundancy and
fault tolerance. It is important to protect both key domain information and geographical site connectivity.

Domain Controller Site Membership

A domain controller is assigned to a site during installation of the Active Directory and stays there unless the administrator manually intervenes to relocate it to another site. The site location of a domain controller is part of the Active Directory replication topology and other system requests.

Whereas assignment of a domain controller is a specific site, client systems may change. When a client computer boots and a IP address is assigned by DHCP, site membership may shift to a different subnet.

Replication

Active Directory replication between domain controllers is managed by the system administrator on a site-by-site basis. As domain controllers are added, a replication path must be established. This is done by the Knowledge Consistency Checker (KCC) coupled with Active Directory replication components. The KCC is a dynamic process that runs on all domain controllers to create and modify the replication topology (Figure 5.11). If a domain controller fails, the KCC automatically creates

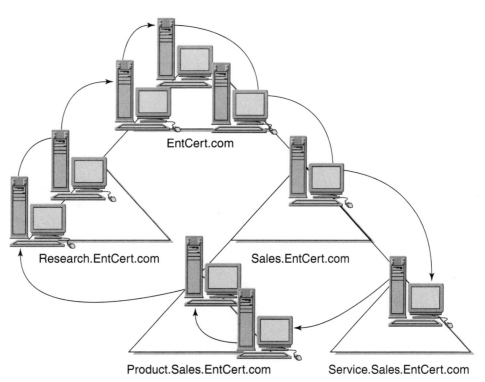

FIGURE 5.11 Active Directory Replication

new paths to the remaining domain controllers. Manual intervention with the KCC will also force a new path.

The Active Directory replaces PDCs and BDCs with multi-master replication services. Each domain controller retains a copy of the entire directory for that particular domain. As changes are made in one domain controller, the originator communicates these changes to the peer domain controllers. The directory data itself is stored in the *ntds.dit* file.

Active Directory replication uses the Remote Procedure Call (RPC) over IP to conduct replication within a site. Replication between sites can utilize either RPC or the Simple Mail Transfer Protocol (SMTP) for data transmission. The default intersite replication protocol is RPC.

INTERSITE AND INTRASITE REPLICATION

There are distinct differences in internal and intersite domain controller replication. In theory, the network bandwidth within a site is sufficient to handle all network traffic associated with replication and other Active Directory activities. By the definition of a site, the network must be reliable and fast. A change notification process is initiated when modifications occur on a domain controller. The domain controller waits for a configurable period (by default, five minutes) before it forwards a message to its replication partners. During this interval, it continues to accept changes. Upon receiving a message, the partner domain controllers copy the modification from the original domain controller. In the event that no changes were noted during a configurable period (by default, six hours), a replication sequence ensures that all possible modifications are communicated. Replication within a site involves the transmission of uncompressed data.

NOTE   Security-related modifications are replicated within a site immediately. These changes include account and individual user lockout policies, changes to password policies, changes to computer account passwords, and modifications to the Local Security Authority (LSA).

Replication between sites assumes that there are network connectivity problems, including insufficient bandwidth, reliability, and increased cost. Therefore, the Active Directory permits the system to make decisions on the type, frequency, and timing of intersite replication. All replication objects transmitted between sites are compressed, which may reduce traffic by 10 to 25 percent, but since this is not sufficient to guarantee proper replication, the system administrator has the responsibility of scheduling intersite replication, as described in Chapter 6.

REPLICATION COMPONENT OBJECTS

Whereas the KCC represents the process elements associated with replication, the following comprise the Active Directory object components:

- *Connection object.* Domain controllers become replication "partners" when linked by a connection object. This is represented by a one-way path between two domain controller server objects. Connection objects are created by the KCC by default. They can also be manually created by the system administrator.
- *NTDS settings object.* The *NTDS* settings object is a container automatically created by the Active Directory. It contains all of the connection objects and is a child of the server object.
- *Server object.* The Active Directory represents every computer as a computer object. The domain controller is also represented by a computer object, plus a specially created server object. The server object's parent is the site object that defines its IP subnet. However, in the event that the domain controller server object was created prior to site creation, it will be necessary to manually define the IP subnet to properly assign the domain controller a site.

When it is necessary to link multiple sites, two additional objects are created to manage the replication topology.

- *Site link.* The *site link* object specifies a series of values (cost, interval, and schedule) that define the connection between sites. The KCC uses these values to manage replication and to modify the replication path if it detects a more efficient one. The Active Directory DEFAULTIPSITELINK is used by default until the system administrator intervenes. The cost value, ranging from 1 to 32767, is an arbitrary estimate of the actual cost of data transmission as defined bandwidth. The interval value sets the number of times replication will occur: Fifteen minutes to a maximum of once a week (or 10080 minutes) is the minimum; three hours is the default. The schedule interval establishes the time when replication should occur. While replication can be at any time by default, the system administrator may want to schedule it only during off-peak network hours.
- *Site link bridges.* The site link bridge object defines a set of links that communicate via the same protocol. By default, all site links use the same protocol and are transitive. Moreover, they belong to a single site link bridge. No configuration is necessary to the site link bridge if the IP network is fully routed. Otherwise, manual configuration may be necessary.

PREVENTING DATA REPLICATION COLLISION

The Active Directory issues a unique identifier known as the *Update Sequence Number* (USN), which is given to every change made to an object. This number is incrementally changed whenever the object is modified. Each property of an object is also issued a USN. A source domain regularly communicates USN sequence changes to the peer domain controller. The latest USN is then registered in each domain controller to ensure the freshness of an object's current state. The Active Directory uses a timestamp only when changes are made at approximately the same time to the same object. At this point, in order to avoid data collisions, the change with the latest timestamp will be replicated by default. In all other cases, the Active Directory disregards the timestamping process.

Special Domain Controller Roles

Some domain controllers are assigned specific roles to facilitate better performance and to reduce conflict. While the principle of multi-master replication of services across all domain controllers is the underpinning of the Active Directory, certain specialized functions are best performed by a single domain controller. Therefore, Windows 2000 supports two forms of specialized functions: the *Global Catalog* and *operations masters*. Forests share a common Global Catalog and some common operations masters.

THE GLOBAL CATALOG

The *Global Catalog* (GC) has two primary functions. First, it acts as a domain controller that stores object data and manages queries about objects and their most common attributes. Second, it provides data that permits network logon. In single domain controller environments, the Active Directory and GC reside on the same server. Where multiple domain controllers exist, as we discuss later, it is often advisable to move the GC to its own dedicated domain controller. All domain trees have a GC and must reside on a domain controller.

NOTE   In the absence of a GC, a user can log on only to the local system. However, a member of the Domain Administrators group can log on to the network without a GC.

The Global Catalog server stores and replicates an assortment of information, including the domain forest schema data and configuration data. It can also be seen as a data repository and engine for rapid object searches. The GC lists all the objects within a domain tree or forest. However, it differs from the Active Directory in that it is comprised of a partial list of object *attributes*. A list of the most requested or common object attributes is contained in the GC in an abbreviated format that results from partial replication of domain data. By cataloging domain objects, locating objects can be faster without the need to search the entire source domain. Clearly, the reason for a dedicated GC is to separate the inquiry process from the updating and management processes within a directory service, as shown in Figure 5.12.

An object's distinguished name typically provides sufficient data to identify the partition that holds it. The GC contains a partial copy of every distinguished name namespace on the Active Directory.

The Global Catalog supports a set of default object attributes that are considered the most common or the most frequently queried—for example, a user's first and last names. However, for greater control over the defined attributes for a particular domain, Windows 2000 provides a means to modify the default settings. The system administrator can utilize the Schema Manager snap-in to update the attributes included in the Global Catalog replication.

When the first Active Directory is installed, it creates a default Global Catalog. More than one Global Catalog server can exist depending on the size of the enterprise, the number of physical sites, and the quality of network connectivity. Global Catalog servers are added through the Sites and Servers Management snap-in of

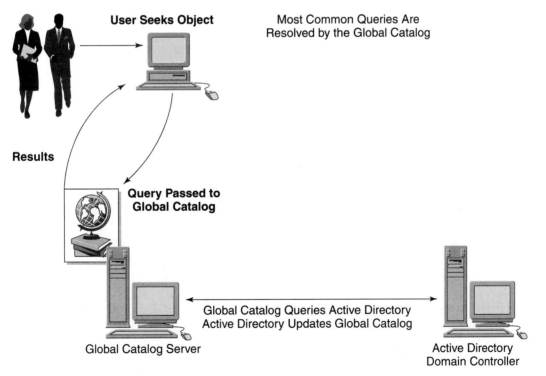

FIGURE 5.12 Global Catalog Relationship

the Microsoft Management Console (MMC). Moving the GC to another domain controller is accomplished by modifying the NTDS Setting Properties in the Sites and Server Management snap-in.

In selecting a system to become the Global Catalog server, it is important that both capacity and network connectivity be considered. The system should have sufficient storage capability to support the management of a million or more objects. The CPU system speed should be sufficient to permit the processing of a steady flow of queries.

GCs and Sites

Network connectivity to the Global Catalog server must be fast and of high quality, since access to a GC is required for successful network logon. Given that a site is bounded by rapid and reliable network connectivity, at least one GC domain controller per site is recommended.

MASTER OPERATION ROLES

Multi-master domain replication assumes that all domain controllers eventually receive synchronized Active Directory information. However, there are master domain controller relationships to handle certain Active Directory information within a domain or forest. The master roles are defined below:

- *Domain naming master.* This domain controller manages the addition and removal of domains in the forest. A forest can have only one domain naming master, which can be transferred to another domain controller through the Active Directory Domains and Trusts snap-in.

- *Infrastructure master.* The infrastructure master is responsible for managing group and user references. Expect a delay in changes to user group membership when they are made across domains. Updates to other domains are made by the infrastructure master domain controller via a process called multi-master replication. This master role can be transferred to another domain controller through the Active Directory Users and Computers snap-in.

- *PDC Emulator master.* In a mixed Windows 2000 and Windows NT environment, the PDC Emulator master supports the BDCs. Thus, it manages user account and password changes and forwards that information to the Windows NT BDC. In a native mode Windows 2000 environment, the PDC Emulator master receives preference in the replication of user account passwords. Before a logon fails, it is checked for updated information. This master role can be transferred to another domain controller through the Active Directory Users and Computers snap-in.

- *Relative ID master.* A single relative ID master in each domain of a tree manages the allocation of sequential relative IDs (RIDs) to each of the domain controllers. This makes all security IDs (SIDs) created in a domain relative to the domain controller. This master role can be transferred to another domain controller through the Active Directory Users and Computers snap-in.
- *Schema master.* The schema master controls updates to the domain schema data. There is one schema master in the entire forest. It can be transferred to another domain controller through the Active Directory Schema Master snap-in.

CAUTION   Microsoft issues a word of caution regarding potential conflicts between the infrastructure master and the Global Catalog. In environments where more than one domain controller exists, the Global Catalog should not be hosted on a controller that also hosts the infrastructure master. Since the infrastructure master compares its data with the Global Catalog, there may be significant replication impacts and full replication may fail. In particular, outdated information will not be seen. The exception to this rule about separating the Global Catalog and the infrastructure master is an environment where every domain controller retains a copy of the GC.

OPEN STANDARDS SUPPORT AND NAMING CONVENTIONS

One of the strengths of the Active Directory is its conformity to several important industry standards and conventions, permitting greater interoperability of Windows 2000 within a heterogeneous environment. While the interplay of the Active Directory with non-Windows 2000 directory services is far from seamless, it does provide the potential for greater multi-operating-system information exchange. The Active Directory embraces the Domain Name System (DNS) and supports the Lightweight Directory Access Protocol (LDAP). DNS resolves domain names to IP addresses in the Internet and within closed intranets. LDAP extends directory service interoperability by providing directory access across heterogeneous networks. In addition to its support for these protocols, the Active Directory also utilizes industry standard naming conventions, which are listed in Table 5.2.

NOTE   The Active Directory also supports the Hypertext Transfer Protocol (HTTP), which defines the methods of displaying information on a Web browser. Objects within the Active Directory can be displayed as HTTP pages.

TABLE 5.2 Industry Standards Used by the Active Directory

Standard	Reference	Description
DNS Dynamic Update	RFCs 2052, 2163	Dynamic host name management
Dynamic Host Configuration Protocol (DHCP)	RFC 2131	Network IP address management
Kerberos, v5	RFC 1510	Authentication
Lightweight Directory Access Protocol (LDAP) v3	RFC 2251	Directory access
LDAP 'C'	RFC 1823	Directory API
LDAP Schema	RFCs 2247, 2252, 2256	Directory schema
Simple Network Time Protocol (SNTP)	RFC 1769	Distributed time services for networks
Simple Mail Transfer Protocol (SMTP)	RFC 821	Message transfer
Transfer Control Protocol/ Internet Protocol (TCP/IP)	RFCs 791, 793	Network transport protocols
X.509 v3 certificates	ISO X.509	Authentication

The Active Directory and DNS

The DNS resolves names within a TCP/IP network. That is, it translates a domain name such as EntCert.com into an IP address and vice versa. All Active Directory domain names follow the DNS naming convention, allowing easy access to the IP address of Active Directory objects that use DNS names. Windows 2000 DNS is a Microsoft-developed implementation and not a port of public domain software, but does follow the RFC and BIND standards.

In spite of its long-time use in UNIX and other operating systems, DNS is a long way from being an automated or self-managed service. Maintenance of DNS is often viewed as a system administration burden. In most legacy environments, the system administrator labors with manual manipulation of flat text files. Most recently, the advent of the Dynamic DNS protocol has emerged to streamline the use and maintenance of this popular name locator. Windows 2000 bundles its own version of Dynamic DNS that tests and updates DNS registration across defined intranets and the Internet.

While Microsoft bundles its own version of Dynamic DNS, other third-party versions with base-level functionality are also supported by Active Directory. By "base-level functionality" we refer to the requirement for the third-party DNS to support both Dynamic DNS and Service Resource Records (SRV RR) technology as defined by RFC 2052 and 2136 and BIND 8.1.2. Active Directory with Dynamic DNS installed will check TCP/IP addresses across the network to make data correction and appropriate deletions. Local services are published through the Service Resource Records (SRV RR) in DNS with the following structure <service>. <Protocol>. <Domain>. For example, if a commercial version of sendmail were used to support the EntCert.com domain, the SRV RR would then look like <sendmail>. <Tcp>. <EntCert.com>. Since Active Directory can support other third-party DNS programs, the actual infrastructure can take one of three basic forms:

- Microsoft's own Dynamic DNS is installed and utilized by the Active Directory.
- A third-party Dynamic DNS that supports SRV RR is used by the Active Directory.
- Microsoft's Dynamic DNS installed as a back-end via a delegated zone from the older server, thereby providing new support for SRV RR and Dynamic DNS technology features.

In addition to interoperability with DNS servers in other operating systems, the Active Directory's Dynamic DNS reduces other administrative burdens. With the release of Windows NT 4.0, Microsoft integrated DNS with its own Windows Internet Naming Service (WINS). Within a Windows NT environment, clients may have fixed IP addresses or can be assigned an address at startup that employs the Dynamic Host Configuration Protocol (DHCP).

INTEROPERABILITY ISSUES

In many cases, UNIX-based DNS servers will exist within an enterprise. A desire to maintain DNS on UNIX will often prevail due to established investment and maintenance of these servers. While Windows 2000 supports this approach, Microsoft contends that there are a number of compelling reasons for the utilization of Windows 2000 DNS server in heterogeneous environments. The basis of their argument is the support of the latest RFC standards that may not be available with older versions of UNIX. The UNIX system can meet Active Directory DNS requirements by upgrading the BIND DNS server to version 8.1.2 or later. Support for SRV resource records is also required. Dynamic updates are desirable, but are not compulsory.

Where non-Windows 2000 DNS servers are to be used for the root zone, Windows 2000 DNS services should also be employed to support Active Directory registration and updates. This may require modification of the other DNS namespace design. Under one scenario, you can establish a new subdomain to root the first Active Directory domain. For example, if the established root domain name is

EntCert.com, the Active Directory subdomain might become win2k.EntCert.com. Another approach is to create multiple subdomains based on the second-level domain that support Active Directory registration. Both scenarios involve the delegation of the DNS namespace into additional zones.

Namespace and Naming Conventions

The Active Directory's naming conventions serve a number of important purposes. First, all directories are based on the concept of a *namespace*, that is, a name is used to resolve the location of an object; when name resolution occurs, it converts the namespace locator to the specific object, such as a printer on the third floor. Everything hangs off the Active Directory using the namespace to identify and locate persons, places, and things within an enterprise.

NAMING CONVENTIONS

In keeping with the namespace concept, the Active Directory uses four name types to recognize every object:

- The *distinguished name* (DN) defines the domain and related container(s) in which an object resides. It matches several defined attributes to the description—the basic ones are DomainComponent (DC), OrganizationalUnit (OU), and CommonName (CN). For example, a representation of a printer within the EntCert.com domain and sales organizational unit, physically located on the third floor, would have the distinguished name DC=COM,DC=EntCert, OU=sales,CN=Printer,CN=3rdfloorprinter

- The *relative distinguished name* (RDN) is really an attribute of the object itself. In the above example, CN=3rdfloorprinter is relative to its parent, CN=printer. The RDN is compared to the DN in Figure 5.13.

- The *Globally Unique Identifier* (GUID) avoids duplication of objects and ensures uniqueness. It is a 128-bit number assigned to an object at the time of creation and stored with it. This permits applications—for example, a word processor file with embedded graphical objects—to retrieve an updated version of a drawing by use of the GUID that is stored within the document.

- The *user principal name* (UPN) is considered a "friendly" naming convention. It combines the user account name with the DNS domain name where the account exists. The name bob@EntCert.com is the UPN for user account bob within the EntCert.com domain tree.

ADDITIONAL USE OF INDUSTRY NAMING STANDARDS

The Active Directory supports a number of industry standard formats to facilitate greater interoperability with other directory services. Microsoft's own Universal

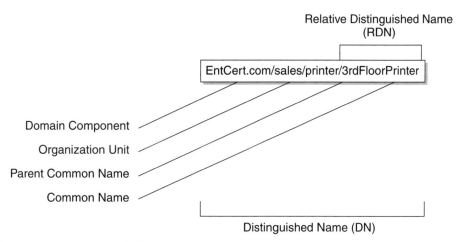

FIGURE 5.13 Distinguished versus Relative Distinguished Names

Naming Convention (UNC), which takes the form *EntCert.com**Administration*\
budget.doc, is the base naming convention. The Active Directory also incorporates
RFC 822, which defines the common Internet e-mail naming structure of
user@domainname.com. It supports the familiar HTTP Uniform Resource Locator (URL), which takes the form *http://EntCert.com/specific page*, as well. Finally,
borrowing from the X.500 communication protocol, the Active Directory incorporates the LDAP URL as defined in the draft of RFC 1779, which breaks the name
into very specific subunits that might look like: //EntCert.com/CN=myname,
OU=mybranch,OU=myproduct,DN=divisionarea. The initials provide greater
object specification. CN is the user's first and last name. The two hierarchical OUs
distinguish the branch of the company and the specific product area. Finally, DN
defines the work area, such as engineering, accounting, or marketing.

Active Directory Use of LDAP

The Lightweight Directory Access Protocol (LDAP), defined by the Internet Engineering Task Force RFC 2251, is a simplified version of the X.500 DAP. Microsoft's
Windows 2000 utilizes LDAP versions 2 and 3. LDAP permits the exchange of directory data between services. For example, since Novell Directory Services data is
LDAP compliant, it can be passed to and from the Active Directory.

   LDAP is utilized to access information from compliant directory services such
as the Active Directory. LDAP searches the Active Directory for information about
stored objects and their attributes. It uses both distinguished and relative distinguished names to locate the object and works closely with DNS throughout this
process (Figure 5.14). DNS provides resolution to locate the appropriate Active

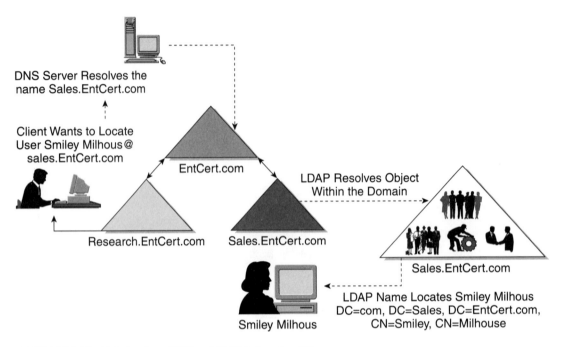

FIGURE 5.14 The Relationship of DNS and LDAP in Locating Objects

Directory domain controller; LDAP resolves the object itself. The process follows these basic steps:

1. A client queries DNS for an LDAP server (Active Directory domain controller).

2. The client queries the domain controller for information about the object.

3. If the requested object is not in the domain but the domain controller knows there are child domains or a forest domain, it issues a *referral* to contact the other domain controllers until object resolution is achieved.

4. The client is returned the object information.

LDAP's C language API (RFC 1823) permits the development of application enhancements and the building of related applications. Developing interfaces using the LDAP C API is perhaps the easiest way to provide interoperability between LDAP directory-compliant services. Existing LDAP directory service auxiliary applications migrated to communicate with Windows 2000 Active Directory may not need modification. If API code changes are required as well, they are typically for the identification of objects unique to the Active Directory.

NOTE   An extension of LDAP is its replication technology protocol LDUP (LDAP Duplication/Update Protocol), an open standards specification that is not embraced by the Active Directory. LDUP does a complete real-time replication of directory elements that requires that compliant directory services adhere to very specific rules and data structures. Violation of any of the rules such that a directory entry is not understood can lead to cascading errors throughout the directory. Rather than LDUP, the Active Directory utilizes a synchronization methodology to populate and update directories.

NOTE   Microsoft decided not to include major portions of the X.500 protocol in the Active Directory primarily because of its dependence on an OSI networking layer and a general lack of public interest. The excluded elements are the Directory Access Protocol, the Directory System Protocol, the Directory Information Shadowing Protocol, and the Directory Operational Binding Management Protocol. LDAP is the most significant element of X.500 incorporated in Windows 2000.

MIGRATION AND BACKWARD COMPATIBILITY

Many operating system upgrades of the past can best be described as nightmares. Microsoft has provided solid upgrading solutions, especially for those migrating from early versions of Windows NT. Chapter 3 discussed the mixed Windows 2000 and Windows 2000 native mode environment, but a further review in the context of the Active Directory is appropriate here.

The Active Directory is designed with backward compatibility as its cornerstone. Thus, a layer of code in Windows 2000 fully emulates the directory services of Windows NT 3.51 and 4.0. In fact, the Active Directory is designed to operate either in a native Windows 2000 environment or in a mixed enterprise with Windows NT.

Migration can take one of two forms: a rapid and systematic upgrade of Windows NT to Windows 2000, or coexistence of Windows 2000 and Windows NT for an undefined period. In the first instance, the existing Primary Domain Controller (PDC) should be the first server upgraded as a Windows 2000 Active Directory domain controller. User and group accounts are automatically loaded into the Active Directory during the installation process. Backup Domain Controllers (BDCs) are then upgraded to Windows 2000 Server with the Active Directory, and copies of the Active Directory are then automatically promoted as peer domain controllers.

NOTE   Group information is migrated only from Windows NT domain controllers to Windows 2000. Group policy, security, and other data that was created in a workgroup environment will remain local and is not migrated. The local security database remains discrete from the Active Directory.

Once the first Windows 2000 Active Directory domain controller is in place, the enterprise can start taking advantage of greater functionality. This is true even if the Windows NT BDCs are maintained for some protracted period. BDCs and associated Windows NT workstations will operate in the same manner as before. In environments where BDCs exist downstream, the same PDC/BDC relationship will continue to function. The older installations will immediately gain the added value of the Global Catalog to improve object resolution. At the same time, the Active Directory domain controller will still act as a peer with other Windows 2000 domain controllers. Over time, the older BDCs may be upgraded as needed and become peer domain controllers.

Client systems can be easily added in either case. The Windows NT Workstation is upgraded simply by installing Windows 2000 Professional. Existing Windows 95 and Windows 98 clients can take advantage of Active Directory awareness by installing a downloadable patch from Microsoft's website. This will permit downlevel clients to use Kerberos security and to fully support Active Directory-compliant and -aware applications.

For organizations with a heavy investment in Exchange Server, it will be good news that this popular groupware suite will also utilize the Windows 2000 Active Directory, eliminating the need to maintain two sets of user accounts and other data.

ADMINISTRATIVE INTERFACE SNAP-INS

The Active Directory offers system administrators consolidated management of all objects in a network. This is through the administrative user interface, which is based on the Microsoft Management Console (MMC) and its snap-in applications. The MMC is visible only to system administrators, not to the end user. The four primary MMC snap-ins associated with the Active Directory (Figure 5.15) are

- Active Directory Domains and Trusts Manager
- Active Directory Users and Computers
- Microsoft Site and Services
- Active Directory Schema Manager (available from the *adminpak* on the Windows 2000 CD under the I386 folder)

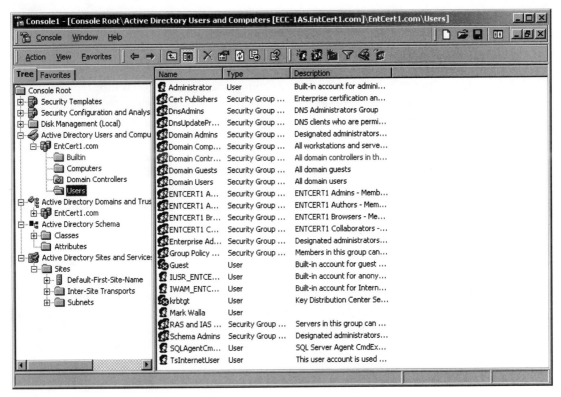

FIGURE 5.15 MMC Active Directory Snap-Ins

Specific utilization of these managers is discussed in other chapters of this book.

API OPTIONS

The Active Directory supports development of additional snap-in administrative tools through its Active Directory Services Interface (ADSI) API. The primary purposes of this API are to permit third-party software vendors to develop additional tools, to allow system administrators to write related scripts, and to afford more open interfaces with other directory services.

ADSI Resources

ADSI is perfect for automating administrative tasks such as changing passwords, creating users complete with Exchange mailboxes, working with file shares, and creating computer accounts.

The ADSI is based on the common object model (COM). Since it is a set of COM-based interfaces on the Active Directory, as well as to Win9x and Windows NT, it permits the administrator or software developer to work with the Active Directory without worrying about its internals. As is true with all COM development, a number of programming languages can be utilized, including C, C++, Java, and Visual Basic. Associated APIs that can be modified within the context of the Active Directory are the LDAP API (RFC 1823 for the C language) and MAPI.

ADSI is part of the Windows Open Services Architecture (WOSA) and the Open Directory Service Interfaces (ODSI). A discussion of these models, architectures, and interfaces is outside the scope of this book, but system administrators desiring additional information can download an assortment of white papers directly from the Microsoft website.

The architecture of the Active Directory employs a number of service interfaces that manage the object mode, schema, caching, namespace, navigation, and searching. It is based on an object model consisting of ADSI *host objects* and *dependent objects*. The host and dependent object relationship is different from the container/contents relationship that is part of the Active Directory itself, in that it acts as a parent and child relationship for the directory service objects only.

The ADSI provider implements requests made to the host and dependent objects. The objects can be one of two types. *Directory service container objects* can hold other ADSI objects. They include Namespace, Country, Locality, Organization, Organizational Unit, Domain, and Computer. *Directory service leaf objects* cannot be used as containers of other objects. They include User, Group, Alias, Service, Print Queue, Print Device, Print Job, File Job, File Service, File Share, Session, and Resources.

ADSI, currently at version 2.5, is available from the Microsoft website at *http://www.microsoft.com/adsi*. For development work, both the ADSI and ADSI SDK are necessary. The SDK contains a large variety of samples in C++, VB, and J++, as well as a sample ADSI provider and some tools to explore ADSI.

SAMPLE ADSI SCRIPTS

James Morris, a member of the Microsoft Windows 2000 rapid deployment program and a software engineer for the University of Washington, kindly offered the following two example scripts that can be used in connection with ADSI.

```
***
Sample1: VB code for adding full name and description to a user:
Private Sub Form_Load()
' Define the user object
Dim user As IADsUser
```

```
' Set the Domain equal to your domain
domain = "DOMAIN"
'Bind to the user object Administrator using the WinNT provider
Set user = GetObject("WinNT://" & domain & "/Administrator")
' Set the properties
user.FullName = "Jane Doe"
user.Description = "Senior Accountant" & domain
'It's important to commit the changes!
user.SetInfo
End Sub
***

***
Sample 2: VBScript to enumerate objects on a computer
Dim ComputerName
'Set the name of the computer to work with
ComputerName = "computer1"
'Bind to computer object using the WinNT provider
Set compobj = GetObject("WinNT://" & ComputerName & ",computer" )
'Echo the objects to the screen
For each obj in compobj
   wscript.echo obj.Name
Next
***
```

The User Interface

Active Directory UI data is stored in a Display Specifier object, whose attributes define the UI elements. The property pages for the Active Directory can be a Component Object Model (COM) object or a Hypertext Markup Language (HTML) file. The Display Specifier object stores the URL of the HTML page or the universally unique identifier (UUID) of the COM object.

For system administrators, the properties associated with system management are stored in the Admin-Property-Pages. Those for end users are stored in the Shell-Property-Pages. Menus for end users are different from those for administrators. Thus, the context menu for users is Shell-Context-Menu; for administrators, Admin-Context-Menu.

ADMINISTRATIVE SECURITY AND TRUST RELATIONSHIPS

Domains are fundamental security boundaries, which by default restrict users in one domain from gaining access to objects in another domain. However, "trust" relationships can be created between domains to allow object accessibility across these secure borders.

Since administration can be delegated to domains and organizational units, Windows 2000 establishes certain administrative defaults. The Domain Administrator group can control activities only within that domain, which means that administrative privileges do not automatically flow down to other domains. Thus, a system administrator for the root domain must be explicitly allowed rights to administrator child domains.

Administrative rights on another domain can be either limited or full. To be granted full rights in another domain, the user must be specifically added to that domain's Administrator group. For more limited rights, that administrator must grant permissions to target objects or organizational units.

Remember that domains are organized into trees that share a common namespace and are composed of a single domain or a root domain with child domains. All domains in the tree share a common Active Directory. Active Directory objects are contained on domain controllers in each of the individual domains.

Users gain access across domains within the tree through trust relationships. The hierarchical structure of the domain tree (extending internally to the organizational units) permits the flow of permissions to an OU. With appropriate group and OU permissions, a user in one domain can use resources or gain access to objects in another domain.

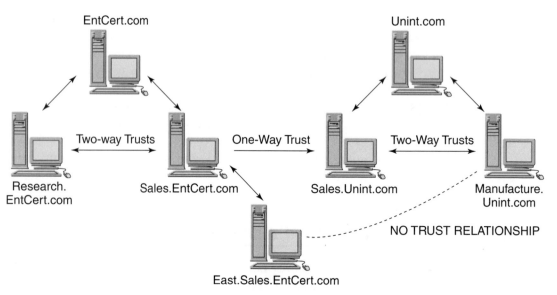

FIGURE 5.16 Trust Relationships

In trust relationships user logons are honored between trusted domains. When two trees are trusted at the root domain, users in one tree can log on to domains in the other tree. However, specific access to objects is based on specific permissions associated with that user and the object's ACL. The Active Directory supports two trust relationship models:

- A *two-way transitive trust* is automatically achieved between domains in the same tree or it can be established between root domains on different trees.
- *Explicit one-way trusts* are created between specific domains in two different forests and provide one-way, restricted permissions. As shown in Figure 5.16, the domain Sales.EntCert.com has granted logon authentication to users in Sales.unint.com; however, the relationship is not bidirectional, nor does it flow to any other domain in the tree or forest. (Note: Explicit trust can also be established with the same forest to provide short-cuts between domains.)

ADMINISTRATIVE DELEGATION

Each domain or domain tree has its own security boundaries. The system administrator can grant rights to individuals within organizational units with greater granularity. In fact, certain administrative responsibilities can be granted on an OU basis without endangering system security. As more users become "empowered" to manage aspects of their normal work within their environment, the mundane responsibilities of system administration are reduced.

If a system administrator considers a security boundary as a logical management segment, responsibility for each boundary or segment can then be delegated to other administrators. A system administrator in one domain is not automatically the administrator in another domain. Alternately, an administrator may want to extend his or her control over many domains. Administrative privileges can be delegated by organizational unit, domain, tree, or forest.

Another important aspect of this containerized OU and domain tree strategy is how it copes with organizational change. In many operating systems, changes or deletions usually equate to many hours of system administrator manual labor. The Active Directory permits OU changes to be accommodated by pruning, grafting, and merging branches from one domain tree to another. It also provides simple drag and drop functionality. For example, if the widget department in Ohio is to be consolidated with the super-widget department in Michigan, the system administrator need only drag that object to the domain tree of the merged organization.

POSTSCRIPT

In essence, the Active Directory should eliminate much of the drudgery of system administration while providing significantly more control. In Chapter 6 system administrator interaction and maintenance of the Active Directory are explored.

Active Directory Management and Use

The previous chapter defined base-level concepts surrounding the Active Directory core technology. This chapter explores its management and practical utilization.

Having read this chapter, you should be able to perform the following Active Directory system administrative tasks:

- Planning for the Active Directory
- Installing the Active Directory both on a fresh server and as part of a PDC or BDC promotion
- Using these primary Active Directory Administrative tools to carry out key management tasks:

  –Active Directory Domains and Trusts

  –Active Directory Schema Manager

  –Active Directory Sites and Services

  –Active Directory Users and Computers

  –Active Directory Replicator

- Creating a domain and performing basic domain controller management
- Creating organizational units
- Locating and managing objects
- Utilizing the Active Directory scripting functions
- Managing Active Directory object access
- Delegating Active Directory administration
- Managing the Global Catalog

PLANNING FOR THE ACTIVE DIRECTORY

The proper implementation of the Active Directory requires forethought and planning. Chapter 3 outlined many of the basic planning issues involved in the installation or upgrade of Windows 2000 generally. Since these issues apply equally to the Active Directory, we strongly advise you to review that chapter in conjunction with the discussions here. In this chapter, you will understand the importance of planning for the creation of namespaces, domains, sites, and organizational units. As discussed in Chapter 4, such planning is based on the system administrator's knowledge of the current IT infrastructure, business computing requirements, anticipated change or growth, and available connectivity and bandwidth.

The DNS Namespace

The Domain Name System (DNS) is an industry standard name resolution vehicle that the Internet uses to match IP addresses to specific namespaces, like ours, *EntCert.com*. Since domains and domain trees are defined by a common namespace based on DNS, the importance of establishing this strategy early is key. At the least a baseline understanding of DNS and domain name registration is required prior to the installation of the Active Directory. For additional information on DNS, including its installation, refer to Chapter 12, Networking and Naming Services.

DNS NAMES FOR CHILD DOMAINS AND FORESTS

Defining namespaces is based on an understanding of the organization's current and projected structure, growth, and relationship with related organizations. In most cases, a single domain name can accommodate even very large organizations. However, it can also be used to create child domain relationships where such division is necessary. The child name is a single descriptive text string that is added to the front of the domain name and separated from it by a period. Child domains can have children of their own. In this case the child name is added before the parent name, again separated by a period, giving the syntax *child2.child1.domain.com*. A child domain name should be fairly generic. Locations or broad, functional descriptive names are generally good choices. For example, for the domain *EntCert.com*, a location—*asia.EntCert.com*—or a function—*sales.EntCert.com*—is broad enough. The objective is to create child domain names that can survive over time.

Where multiple domain names are required or forced upon an administrator because of preexisting names (such as when two companies merge but maintain separate identities), forest relationships need to be established. The forest is created by joining in a two-way trust multiple domain trees with different DNS namespaces. Separate identities are maintained while transitive trusts to network resources are provided.

DOMAIN NAMES FOR INTERNAL AND EXTERNAL USE

Another important namespace issue is whether the domain name will be extended for both internal and external use. In the first case, the goal is a single user logon for all Internet and intranet communications. To achieve this end, the system administrator must create two DNS zones—the first resolves the name for internal resources; the second resolves names for external mail systems, Web services, TCP, news, and Telnet connectivity.

In the second case, an organization may choose different domain names for internal and external use. If so, two namespaces must be reserved and domain trees created to manage the respective resources, and transitive trust relationships must be formed by joining the trees together into a forest. This approach to domain naming increases administrative tasks. However, users should maintain a single login name.

The Physical Structure: Sites and Replication

The underlying objectives of the physical structure are easy Active Directory replication, rapid user logons, and efficient resolution of queries for network objects. When planning the physical structure and site topology in particular, remember that there is no direct relationship between sites and domains. A site can have multiple domains or portions of multiple domains, and vice versa. It is defined by fast and reliable connectivity, so the most critical issue in site planning is the bandwidth and other network constraints for related traffic. This means that site parameters should be dictated by the creation of subnets sharing cheap, fast, and reliable connections.

In some cases, two or more remote locations can still be treated as a single site. However, if they are in different area codes and connectivity is based on more expensive connection technologies, the creation of multiple sites is probably in order. Each site should have at least one domain controller that is configured for each location, with replication services set for times in which traffic is minimal and at the lowest rates.

Later in this chapter we will explore specific management of intrasite and multi-site network traffic and topology. Before that, however, it is important to understand site requirements and site replication and topology.

PREPARING FOR REPLICATION AND SYNCHRONIZATION

To best prepare for the creation of sites, it is important to understand data transfer and how it works within the Active Directory. There are two forms of data transfer. First, *replication* is used when Windows 2000 domain controllers communicate changes to each other. All domain controllers in a domain tree share a number of common traits, including the same schema and control models. When a modification is recorded by one domain controller, it is automatically "replicated" to all other domain controllers in the domain tree according to prescribed scheduling rules. The transitive trust relationships that exist between all domains ensure that new information is written to all domain controllers. This is transparent and fairly rapid within the same site. For intersite replication, the system administrator should determine the time and frequency of these updates based on an analysis of network traffic and cost.

Second, *synchronization* is used for communication between the Active Directory and other directory services such as Novell Directory Services (NDS). To share information, the two services must utilize an agent known as a security principle, which determines what schema information is common to both and selects the data to be shared. Since the structures of different directory services vary, the data must then be mapped. This can be streamlined by directory services that employ LDAP, which provides a common method of resolving object names.

Some large enterprises may currently have over a hundred different directory services in place, so planning consideration must be given to both Active Directory replication and heterogeneous synchronization. Clearly, the Active Directory does not have the ability to synchronize data with all third-party directory services. However, those services that employ both DNS and LDAP v3 are good candidates.

Planning the physical structure requires knowing where replication and synchronization might occur. Where possible, confine synchronization to intrasite topologies where internal traffic is the most reliable. Once the synchronization has taken place between the Active Directory and other directories' services within a site, the receiving domain controller can replicate the data to other domain controllers throughout the domain tree.

REPLICATION LATENCY

When updates occur on one domain controller, varying amounts of time can pass before they are replicated to others. This is known as *replication latency,* and within a site it typically resolves within a few minutes (every five minutes by default). Depending on how the system administrator has configured replication between sites, latency can be a few minutes or up to a week.

A part of intersite planning is determining how long a site can exist with latent data. In branch offices that perform well-defined activities and are not subject to regular change, latency is not much of an issue and replication can be safely set for a daily update. Since there is an acknowledged latency, the remote domain controller is in a state called *loose consistency* of Active Directory information. By the same token, a division headquarters site might demand replication from critical sites every half hour.

REPLICATION TOPOLOGY

The Active Directory's Knowledge Consistency Checker (KCC) automatically establishes the most efficient replication topology. To formulate connection rules, the system administrator must input information that is critical to the calculation of the best connectivity routes. The KCC also dynamically establishes alternative connectivity to other sites in the event that a site has one only domain controller and that system fails.

One-directional *connection objects* are created by the KCC (or manually by the system administrator). Contained in a domain controller's NTDS settings object, each connection object points in one direction to a replication partner. Two paired connection objects create a bidirectional relationship between the partners. Connection objects replicate the three Active Directory partitions of schema, configuration data, and domain data.

Within a site, the KCC uses the connection objects to establish a two-directional ring between intrasite domain controllers. It attempts to make connections such that there is a maximum of three hops between intersite domain controllers. When a domain controller receives a change, it notifies its partner domain controllers. Additional partners are then notified after a configurable delay that is 30 seconds by default. By design, intrasite replication of a change should be passed to all domain controllers within 15 minutes.

Typically, intrasite replication requires minimal system administration intervention. However, the system administrator must review the intersite topology and make manual changes where appropriate. As we shall illustrate later, topology links can be modified with the **Active Directory Sites and Services** administrative snap-in, but this requires that the connection objects be manually established. (If the KCC automatically creates the same connection object through its normal analysis of input data, no new manual connection objects are created.) Manual connection objects can never be deleted by the KCC. However, if they fail, the KCC automatically attempts to create a new connection to a domain controller.

The Active Directory Sites and Services administrative snap-in can also be employed to force replications or to execute the KCC manually. This is explained later in the chapter.

While the initial site topology is generally accomplished by the KCC, it is important to know the relative costs of connectivity between sites. It is also critical to define the minimum acceptable frequency of replication, as this information is required by the KCC. After Windows 2000 is in place, several tools will allow you to analyze those segments that require manual intervention. The typical basis for this review is network traffic. The *Network Monitor* measures RCP and SMTP traffic between domain controllers, the *Performance Monitor* measures traffic from a specific server, and the *Replication Monitor* provides a view of intrasite topology.

PLANNING FOR OPERATIONS MASTER LOCATIONS

As described in Chapter 5 and later in this chapter, each domain tree offloads important activities to selected domain controllers that perform up to five specialized activities. These *operations master* domain controllers perform all the activities of their peers plus one or more specialized functions. There can only be one schema, domain, PDC, RID, and infrastructure operations master in a domain tree.

Since all domain controllers rely on the information processed by the operations masters, it is important to carefully plan the location of the operations master domain controllers. As a general rule, they should be placed in a site with the best primary and secondary connectivity to the rest of the organization.

Logical Structure Planning

Planning for the Active Directory is predicated on an understanding of the organization itself. In centralized frameworks, a single domain may serve all requisite requirements and is obviously the easiest to administer. In larger and decentralized environments, multiple domains are often required. In both cases, it may be appropriate to divide the domain into organizational units to better manage user accounts and resources. In planning for the Active Directory, early mapping of domains and organizational units is highly recommended. In so doing, it is also important to determine where administrative authority is to be granted and delegated. Best practices in forming domains and organizational units include the following considerations:

- Providing users with authority to utilize appropriate network resources while restricting visibility to all other objects.
- Ensuring that administrators have rapid visibility to all resources.
- Accommodating current operational and business structures while providing for organizational changes.
- Organizing resources and accounts into OUs to permit delegation of administrative authority.
- Logically dividing organizational units into smaller, more manageable units.

SINGLE DOMAIN AND ORGANIZATIONAL UNITS

Even though Windows 2000 fully supports multiple domains and organizational units, the KISS principle (keep it simple, stupid) still applies. Complexity increases as the number of domains and OUs grows. Always weigh the trade-offs between administrative granularity and greater complexity. When creating organizational units, try to mirror the actual functionality of the business structure—for example, the sales group might logically be a single OU. Likewise, resources can be grouped into organizational units, say, all printers within a domain. In this way, it is possible to delegate one administrator to manage the printer OU and another to manage the sales group user account OU.

A common planning question is when to create a child domain versus an organizational unit. Unfortunately, there is no clear answer, although it is generally determined by scope and complexity. In the next section we list some of the reasons for forming child domains. Here we will say that when control of smaller user groups or resources can be logically delegated, organizational units are more appropriate. Also, where change is anticipated within the organizational structure, OUs can more easily accommodate such shifts.

DOMAIN TREES AND CHILD DOMAINS

While the single domain is the simplest to create and maintain, there are organizational and administrative situations in which multiple domains, trees, and forests must be created. Security, administrative, and connectivity borders exist between domains. When planning a domain tree or forest, it is important to understand how these components interact.

When Should Child Domains Be Created?

By default, a domain tree is created when the first domain controller is promoted with its own Windows 2000 Active Directory. When other domains are added they become *child* domains to this first, *root,* domain. In addition to automatic transitive trusts, all domains in the tree share a common schema, configuration, and Global Catalog. Beyond this point, however, domain characteristics within a tree can vary. This is important because it is at this level of setting specific characteristics that decisions must be made about child domains. If you answer yes to one or more of the following questions, a child domain could be in order:

- *Is decentralized administration desired?* If a requirement exists to manage assets or specific business activities, a decentralized model with separate child domains might be beneficial.

- *Does the organization need tight and/or localized administration?* For example, in global organizations it may be appropriate to localize administration within a given domain to account for differences such as language or time zone.

- *Do business activities or relationships dictate separate domains?* Competing business units or joint ventures may require autonomy, including the management of their own domain.

- *Do account policies need to differ?* Since account policies are applied at the domain level, it may be appropriate to logically group users into separate domains that have distinct policy requirements.

- *Does replication suggest a need for different domains?* While replication can be controlled on a per-site basis, it can also be controlled on a logical structure basis to reduce network traffic—for example, between international offices.

FORESTS

A forest is formed by joining two or more domain trees at the root. Transitive trusts are created by the forest relationship such that network resources become available to any tree and its associated domains. The resulting hierarchy permits the same Active Directory to resolve inquiries for objects within any of the trees in the forest. Each tree has its own DNS namespace, but shares a common schema, configuration, and Global Catalog. The forest itself is identified by the DNS name of the first tree created in it.

LDAP inquiries are conducted only within a tree and do not extend to the forest. The Global Catalog is used to resolve queries between trees; by default it is located on the first domain controller created in the forest. Part of the planning effort must be determining whether a dedicated domain controller should be used for Global Catalog activities. In addition, it must be decided if replica Global Catalog domain controllers will be created to offload heavy inter-tree query traffic. For these reasons, the placement of the Global Catalog within the network is a key administrative task. Make sure there is fast and reliable connectivity to it.

The creation of a forest involves three primary steps. First, a DNS name must be selected (and registered) for the domain trees. Second, the configuration of each domain tree as described earlier must be laid out. Finally, the new tree must be added to the forest while the first domain controller is promoted through the Active Directory installation process. You will need to select **Create New Domain Tree in an Existing Forest** from the Installation Wizard.

When Should a Forest Be Created?

Despite the fact that management of a forest is considerably more complex than that of singular trees, there still arise situations where distinct namespaces are required. If you answer affirmatively to one or more of the following questions, a forest may be necessary.

- *Are the business activities extremely different?* Organizations that operate on a radically different basis may require separate trees with distinct namespaces.

- *Are there reasons for maintaining separate identities?* Unique trade or brand names often give rise to separate DNS identities. This is particularly true when organizations merge or are acquired and naming continuity is desired.

- *Do joint venture or partner relationships exist that require tighter control over network resources?* Organizations often form partnerships and joint ventures. While access to common resources is desired, a separately defined tree can enforce more direct administrative and security restrictions.

MULTIPLE FORESTS

Relationships between forests are not based on transitive trusts. They are generally established to created limited access for one domain in one forest to one domain in another forest. The trust relationship is one-directional and must be explicitly set. It does not impact any of the other domains. If it is necessary to create multi-forest relationships, plan trust and resource management well in advance. Make sure that access is limited only to those resources required for the life of the relationship.

Planning for Upgrades to the Active Directory

Upgrades to the Active Directory from existing Windows NT Server environments are handled slightly differently depending on the domain structure that exists in the current enterprise. Remember, as was more completely discussed in Chapter 5, the multi-master replication model of the Active Directory supplants the four types of domain models employed by Windows NT. Consider the following issues when planning an Active Directory promotion:

- *Upgrading the Single Windows NT domain model.* When the single Windows NT domain model is upgraded to the Active Directory it remains a single domain. The primary change is in the added functionality afforded by the Active Directory and the optional use of organizational units.

- *Upgrading the master Windows NT domain model.* The Windows NT master domain model assumes a top-down hierarchy that is mirrored by the Active Directory, but since Windows NT did not support organizational units, additional domains were often formed to separate resources and users into more manageable components. One of the planning decisions when upgrading from a Windows NT master domain model is whether to collapse existing domains into a single Active Directory domain so that previously defined Windows NT domains can become organizational units. However, there is no requirement to convert an existing master domain model infrastructure to a single domain; the Active Directory will fully accommodate the existing structure. The root domain controller must be the first one upgraded to Windows 2000 and the Active Directory. Child domains can then be upgraded to form an Active Directory domain tree. They simply join the existing Windows 2000 domain during the promotion installation.

- *Upgrading the complete Windows NT trust model.* In this model, Windows NT provided trust between domains. The Active Directory provides upgrade options that allow for transitive trust between domain trees and/or forests. It also allows one-way trusts between selected domains in two nonrelated forests. The key issue when upgrading Windows NT from a complete trust model is the level of trust desired.

UPGRADING THE PDC AND BDC

Sound planning of an upgrade usually requires a conservative approach to full deployment. Therefore, we recommend that the initial Active Directory installation and domain tree formation be separate from the installation of the production environment. One way to accomplish this and preserve existing Windows NT domain data is to pull an existing BDC off production and then promote it to a PDC within a detached lab environment. At this stage, installation of Windows 2000 and the Active Directory can go forward on this domain controller while initial testing and fine-tuning are completed. When satisfactory testing is achieved, the domain controller can be returned to production as the root domain controller.

An alternative and less conservative approach is to install the Windows 2000 Active Directory in a production environment, first removing an existing Windows NT BDC from the network and production for safety purposes. In the unlikely event that the Windows 2000 deployment fails, you can remove Windows 2000 from production and restore the previous Windows NT environment. The offline BDC is put back in service and promoted to the PDC.

Planning for Domain Controllers

Every domain and child domain must have at least one domain controller. The addition of domain controllers generally improves reliability, speed, and flexibility. Since a user's network logon is predicated on access to a domain controller, fast and reliable connectivity is required. Therefore, we recommend that there be more than one domain controller for each domain and each site.

It is often wise to establish at least two domain controllers to serve as operations master domain controllers. The PDC Emulator and relative identifier master roles should be assigned to these mirrored domain controllers for redundancy.

The role of the standard domain controller and Global Catalog are also often divided between different domain controller servers. It is always advisable to separate the Global Catalog from the domain controller assigned to the infrastructure master role.

Sizing the Active Directory

Sizing the minimal requirements for the Active Directory server hardware involves a series of estimates. The process entails creating a sample population of Active Directory objects and then applying size factors to each. This should include a real-world collection of objects including users, computer accounts, groups, printers, and files. Objects that are security principals should be allocated 3,600 bytes each. Nonsecurity principal objects should be allocated 1,100 bytes. For each attribute of 10 or fewer characters, allocate an additional 100 bytes. Attributes that contain binary information should include the size of the data plus a 25 percent buffer.

We recommend a simple spreadsheet be used to calculate the size requirements of the sample population. The sample population's storage estimate is derived by adding the numbers together as illustrated in the example below for the objects and associated attributes. Make sure that every attribute associated with an object is included in the calculation.

The next step is to estimate the number of objects that must be managed by the Active Directory. This estimate should include all users, groups, printers, contacts, and files on the system and should then be doubled. The storage requirements can then be proportionately extrapolated by using the actual number of objects you estimate for your enterprise. For example, if the sample population represented 1/10 of 1 percent of all the Active Directory objects, you would multiply that amount by 1,000. If the sample population storage size estimate were 360,000 KB, then the actual requirements for the Active Directory size would be 360,000,000 KB, or 360 MB. It is generally recommended that the disk space be two to three times larger than the estimated size of the Active Directory to accommodate any miscalculation and future growth.

INSTALLING THE ACTIVE DIRECTORY

The installation of the Active Directory is remarkably straightforward. The Active Directory Wizard leads the system administrator through a series of decision points. Whether you are promoting an existing Windows NT PDC to Windows 2000 with the Active Directory or creating a new domain tree, the process is largely the same. Always begin with the server that is the root. Once the first Windows

2000 Active Directory server is running, all other domains within the tree are treated as its children.

A major prerequisite is that DNS be installed with Windows 2000 or an existing DNS server be designed prior to the completion of the Active Directory installation. Because of this dependence on DNS, this installation section will walk through the following:

- Use of the Active Directory Wizard to create a new domain and in so doing create the first domain tree
- Installation of Microsoft's DNS to support the Active Directory. (A third-party DNS server can also be utilized providing it supports service resource records (SRV) and dynamic DNS update functionality.)

Other dependencies must also be addressed prior to installation. The computer must have an installed version of Windows 2000 Server, Advanced Server, or DataCenter Server. The NTFS partition or volume must be sufficiently large to accommodate Active Directory requirements. Correct system time and zones should be set. Finally, TCP/IP should be installed. While DNS can be preconfigured or installed along with the Active Directory, it is absolutely required for the Active Directory to function.

Before installing the Active Directory, it is important to understand what happens during this process. Two primary sets of files are created: the directory store and log files, which are located in *systemroot*\Ntds; and a Shared System Volume, located in *systemroot*\Sysvol, which contains scripts and some group policy objects for the enterprise.

Active Directory Wizard Installation

The Active Directory is installed by following the steps outlined below. The Wizard provides a series of alternative choices from which the system administrator must make an educated selection.

If this is the first system to be configured with Windows 2000 and the Active Directory, it will become the root domain controller. During installation of Windows 2000, you will already have been prompted to determine whether this is a standalone server or part of a network. As the first domain controller, it is initially standalone, but during the installation process it is promoted to a domain controller.

If this system is being installed in an existing Windows 2000 domain or if it is being configured as a child domain, the Active Directory installation process will automatically make the appropriate connections and establish initial default trust relationships. The same process occurs when promoting a Windows NT PDC or BDC to Active Directory domain controller status. Replica versions of the Active Directory are then installed on the new domain controller.

ACTIVE DIRECTORY INSTALLATION EXAMPLE

The example of an installation here is based on the first domain controller to be promoted. The creation of child domains and forests is covered in subsequent sections and merely involves a decision to join an existing tree or forest; otherwise, the steps are generally the same.

The following steps should be observed when installing the Active Directory:

1. Launch the Active Directory Wizard (Figure 6.1) by invoking the **Command Prompt → dcpromo.exe → ENTER**. (Alternately, the **Configure Your System** dialog is launched as part of the logon process, or it is available under the **Start → Administrative Tools → Configure Your System → Active Directory → Install**.)

The text in the first Wizard screen is very explicit, stating that the installation of the Active Directory will make the server a domain controller. While you may repeat this process with other servers, this first domain controller becomes the root for the domain and the domain tree.

Select **Next>** to continue.

FIGURE 6.1 The Active Directory Wizard

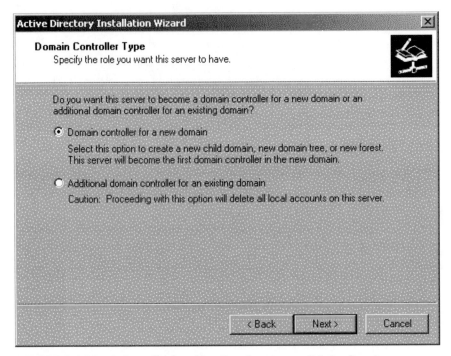

FIGURE 6.2 A Domain Controller for a New Domain versus an Existing Domain

2. The next dialog box provides the choice of making this a controller for a new domain or adding it to an existing domain (Figure 6.2). Since this example assumes a new domain, select the first option and press the **Next>** button. This option also creates a new child domain or domain tree. The second option is utilized only when creating additional domain controllers within the same domain.

Select **Next>** to continue.

3. At this stage you must be able to clearly see the forest for the trees. Therefore, in this example **Create a new forest of domain trees** should be selected, as shown in Figure 6.3. The first domain controller is automatically the root domain, tree, and forest. The second option in this dialog box is selected only if you are creating a new tree that is to have a trust relationship with a preexisting domain forest, and/or providing users in an existing forest access to the new domain.

Select **Next>** to continue.

4. This is a very important step, as the domain name selected at this stage will follow through the entire domain and domain tree. (If you have not already registered a domain name, obtain one from the registration service in your country.

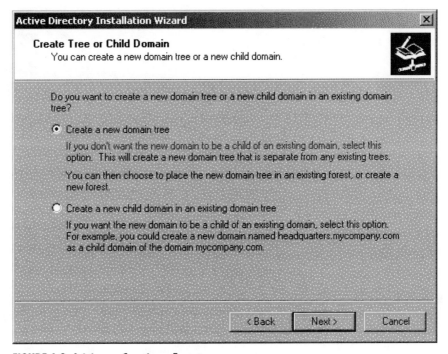

FIGURE 6.3 Joining or Creating a Forest

Also, if you do not understand DNS and naming conventions, please refer to Chapters 5 and 14 before completing this step.) In the text box shown in Figure 6.4, type the full name of the domain—in our example, this is *EntCert.com*.

Select **Next>** to continue.

5. The next dialog box identifies your NetBIOS name, which is used by Windows clients that employ WINS to resolve system names. In this case, the ENTCERT NetBIOS name was automatically inserted. Note that if your domain name is longer than 15 characters, it will be truncated to match the maximum length for NetBIOS names.

Select **Next>** to continue.

6. The next dialog box allows you to select the location of the Active Directory database and log. The default location for the database and log in which Windows 2000 is installed in \WINNT is *%systemroot%*\WINNT\NTDS. Ordinarily, the default location is recommended.

Select **Next>** to continue.

7. The next dialog box gives you the opportunity to select the location of the Shared System Volume, which stores all the shared information that is replicated

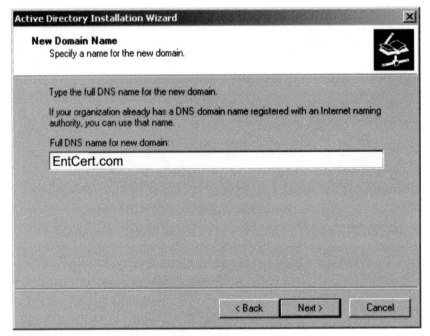

FIGURE 6.4 Designating the Name of the Domain

between domain controllers. The default is *%systemroot%*\WINNT\SYSVOL. If you choose to accept this, select **Next>** to continue.

8. The next Wizard screen provides a way for changing the permissions associated with the RAS Server. Unless you have a specific reason to make changes at this time, select **NO**.

Select **Next>** to continue.

9. The Active Directory review setting page should now appear. Take a moment to review this information. If anything is incorrect, use the Back button to return to the screen requiring a change and make the appropriate modifications. If everything appears correct, select **Next>** to continue.

10. The Active Directory is now being configured on your system, which can take a few minutes. The final Wizard screen in the basic installation process should then appear. Select the **Finish** button. You will see the prompt to **Restart** the computer. Select this option now if you have already configured DNS, but if you have not, proceed to DNS installation. The Active Directory cannot be successfully configured without DNS.

The Active Directory Wizard should automatically take you to the configure DNS screen (Figure 6.5). Select **YES**, then select **Next>** to continue. (If you select

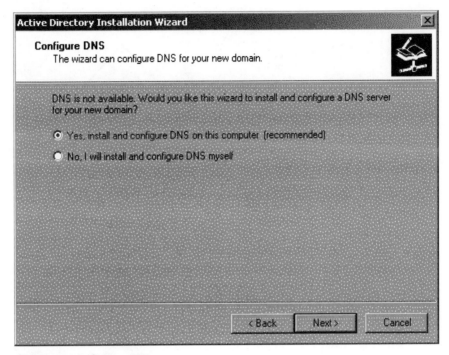

FIGURE 6.5 Configuring DNS

NO or if you want to configure DNS prior to installing the Active Directory, select **Start → Administrative Tools → Configure Your Server → Networking → DNS → Install**.)

Please turn to Chapter 12 for complete instructions on configuring the TCP/IP network with DNS.

INSTALLATION FOR DIFFERENT STRUCTURES

The example just completed assumed that the installation was being carried out on the first domain Active Directory. There are some variations when creating additional domain controllers, child domains, and trees within an existing forest (Figure 6.6). These are described in the following sections.

Adding Domain Controllers to Existing Domains

After the domain is created, additional domain controllers can be added by running *dcpromo.exe* from the new Windows 2000 Server. The Active Directory Installation Wizard will prompt you to determine the domain controller type. Select **Additional domain controller for an existing domain**. You will need to specify the user name, password, and domain name of a user account that has

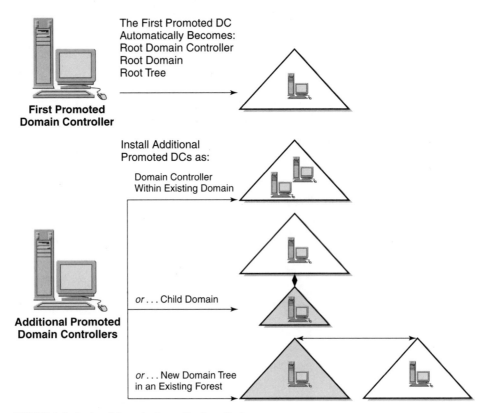

FIGURE 6.6 Optional Domain Controller Installations

rights to create domain controllers. The DNS name for the domain must also be provided. Finally, you will need to establish where database and log files, together with the Shared System Volume, are to be located. Generally, the default location will be used. All other installation questions will be the same as in the walk-through example.

Creating a Child Domain

The creation of a child domain also involves executing *dcpromo.exe* from the new Windows 2000 Server or installing Active Directory directly. The Active Directory Installation Wizard will prompt you to determine the domain controller type. Select **Domain controller for a new domain**. In the next screen, which allows you to create trees or child domains, select **Create a new child domain in an existing domain tree**. You will need to specify the user name, password, and domain name of a user account in the Enterprise Admins group that has rights to create domains. You will also need to supply the parent's DNS name and the name of the new child domain. Remember that the child name is added to the front of the parent DNS name, separated by a period. Also specified here is the NetBIOS name for the new domain. After the root domain has been created, child domains can be logically added. As before, you will need to establish where database and log files, together with the Shared System Volume, will reside. Generally, the default location will be used.

Finally, you will need to determine whether or not to weaken permissions in order to provide Windows NT 4.0 RAS access. This is generally not recommended unless you plan to continue using Windows NT for a substantial period. All other installation questions will be the same as in the walk-through example.

Creating a Tree in an Existing Forest

Once the root domain tree is created, it is possible to add a new tree to the forest by running *dcpromo.exe* from the new Windows 2000 Server. The Active Directory Installation Wizard will prompt you to determine the domain controller type. Select **Domain controller for a new domain**. In the next screen, where you can create trees or child domains, select **Create a new domain tree**. From the next screen, select **Place this new domain tree in an existing forest**. You will need to specify the user name, password, and domain name of a user account in the Enterprise Admins group that has rights to create domains. You will also need to supply the new tree's DNS name and specify the NetBIOS name for the new domain. After the root domain has been created, child domains can logically be added.

You will need to establish where database and log files, together with the Shared System Volume, are to be located—generally, the default location will be used. Finally, you will need to determine whether or not to weaken permissions in order to provide Windows NT 4.0 RAS access. This is generally not recommended unless you plan on using Windows NT for a substantial period. All other installation questions will be the same as in the walk-through example.

ACTIVE DIRECTORY MMC SNAP-IN TOOLS

The MMC snap-in tools handle most of the Active Directory management. This section examines how to use these tools to perform the most commonly used Active Directory functions. Excluded is the use of these tools in relation to user, group, and group policy management; that is covered in Chapter 7, User Accounts and Groups, and Chapter 8, Group Policies.

Three Active Directory snap-in administrative tools are made available as part of the standard installation; two optional tools are installed separately:

- Active Directory Domains and Trusts Manager
- Active Directory Schema Manager (optional, available from *adminpak*)

- Active Directory Sites and Services Manager
- Active Directory Users and Group Manager
- Active Directory Replication (optional, available from the Resource Kit)

The standard tools are obtained from the **Start → Administrative Tools** menu and the optional tools are obtained from **Start → Service Tools** (Figure 6.7). They may be added to the Microsoft Management Console (MMC) by following these steps:

1. Launch the MMC.
2. Select the **Console** (you must be in Author mode to select this option).

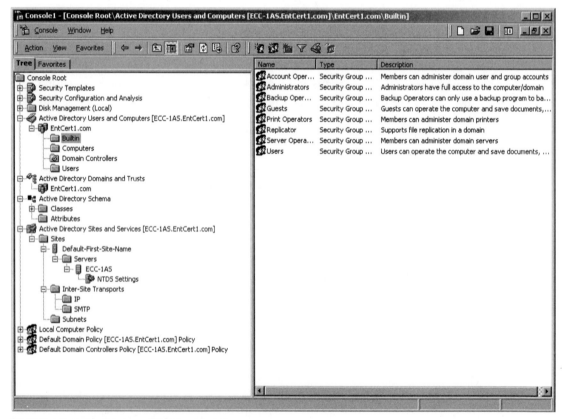

FIGURE 6.7 Active Directory MMC Standard Components

3. Select **Add/Remove Snap-In** → select **Add** from the Add/Remove Snap-In dialog → **highlight the Active Directory snap-in** from the Add Snap-In dialog box → select **Add**.

4. Repeat this process for each additional snap-in.

5. Select **Close** for the Add Snap-In dialog box → select **Close** for the Add/Remove Snap-In dialog.

These snap-in tools provide support for a wide assortment of Active Directory administrative functions.

The Active Directory Domain and Trust Manager

The Active Directory Domains and Trusts snap-in provides system administrator support for the management of trust relationships between domains, trees, and forests. It also provides assistance for managing mixed mode environments involving Windows 2000 and earlier Windows NT domains. In this section we will review how to use the Active Directory Domains and Trusts snap-in to perform the following tasks:

- Creating trust relationships, both transitive two-way and explicit one-way
- Changing from mixed to native Windows 2000 mode
- Adding UPN suffixes for alternate user logon
- Assigning a domain naming operations master domain controller
- Delegating domain controller administration

CREATING TRUST RELATIONSHIPS

The previous chapter described the types of trust relationship that can exist in a Windows 2000 enterprise. The Active Directory Domains and Trusts MMC snap-in tool is the easiest method for managing these relationships.

The default relationship between domains in the same tree or forest is transitive. Users have access to resources within the same tree or forest, assuming they have access permission to a requested object.

Explicit one-way trusts are created only between otherwise nonrelated forests. The trusting domain permits access to resources by a trusted domain in a one-directional interaction. The one-way trust is limited and does not create a permanent link. Nor does it automatically provide access to other domains in the tree. To extend the one-way relationship to other domains, additional explicit relationships are required.

Explicit Transitive Two-Way Domain Trusts (Short-Cut)

Two-way transitive trusts are established by following these steps:

1. Open the **Active Directory Domains and Trusts** MMC snap-in.

2. Right-click the domain you want to administer → select **Properties** → click the **Trusts** tab.

3. Click the **Domains trusted by this domain**, select the **Add** button, type in the target domain name, and supply the password information; then select the **Domains that trust this domain** and follow the same procedure as above. (For Windows 2000, the domain name is the DNS name for the domain. For legacy Windows NT domains, type the name of that domain.)

4. If the domain to be added is a Windows 2000 domain, type its DNS name. Or, if the domain is running an earlier version of Windows, type the domain name.

5. Gain Administrative logon to the target trust domain and repeat steps 1 through 4.

Explicit One-Way Domain Trusts

Explicit one-way domain trusts are created by following these steps (Figure 6.8):

1. Open the **Active Directory Domains and Trusts** MMC snap-in.

2. Right-click the domain you want to administer → select **Properties** → click the **Trusts** tab.

3. Click **Domains trusted by this domain**, select the **Add** button, and type in the target domain name and password information. (For Windows 2000, the domain name is the DNS name for the domain. For legacy Windows NT domains, type the name of that domain.)

Verifying a Trust

Once the process of establishing a trust is completed or during the normal course of auditing a domain, the trust relationship can be verified. To do so, take the following steps:

1. Open the **Active Directory Domains and Trusts** MMC snap-in.

2. Right-click the domain you want to administer → select **Properties** → click the **Trusts** tab.

3. In either the **Domains trusted by this domain** or the **Domains that trust this domain** list, click the trust to be verified, then click **Edit**.

4. Click **Verify/Reset**.

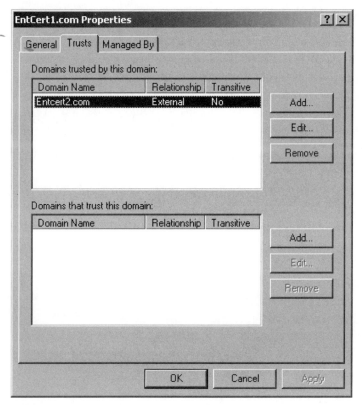

FIGURE 6.8 Creating a One-Way Explicit Trust

Removing a Trust

As organizational relationships change, trust relationships between domains may need to be removed. To do this, perform the following steps:

1. Open the **Active Directory Domains and Trusts** MMC snap-in.

2. Right-click the domain you want to administer → select **Properties** → click the **Trusts** tab.

3. In either the **Domains trusted by this domain** or the **Domains that trust this domain** list, click the trust to be revoked, then click **Edit**.

4. Click **Remove**.

5. Repeat the process for the corresponding trusted domain.

CHANGING FROM MIXED TO NATIVE MODE

Most enterprises initially operate in a mixed Windows 2000 and Windows NT mode. In this case, the Active Directory supports the existing Windows NT BDCs. Remember, these modes impact domain controllers, not down-level member servers or client systems. However, at some stage the migration will be complete and the Windows 2000 Active Directory should be moved to native mode. This task, illustrated in Figure 6.9, is accomplished by the following steps:

1. Open the **Active Directory Domain and Trusts** MMC snap-in (the **Active Directory Users and Computers** snap-in can also perform this task).

2. Select the domain to be upgraded to native mode, right-click, and select **Properties**.

3. From the **General tab** select **Change Mode** and choose **YES** from the confirming dialog window.

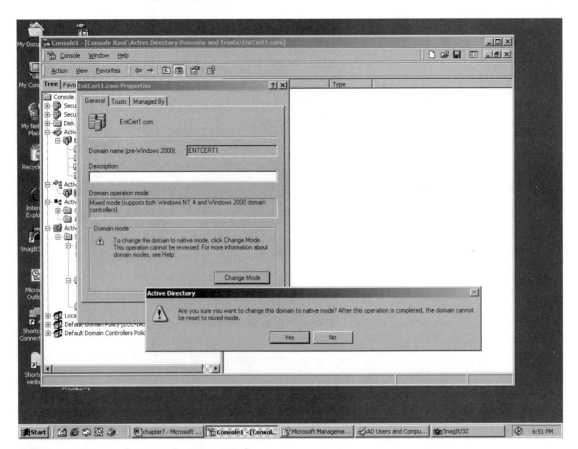

FIGURE 6.9 Changing from Mixed to Native Mode

CAUTION   It is impossible to reverse the upgrading of a domain to native mode. Therefore, if any Windows NT domain controllers exist within the domain, they must be upgraded to Windows 2000 and the Active Directory in order to be properly recognized.

ADDING UPN SUFFIXES FOR USER LOGON

Alias domain names can be applied to a user account, perhaps to provide a user account with a different identity by shortening long domain or child domain names. The user principal name (UPN) suffix is the portion of the DNS name that identifies a user's domain of origin. For example, *@EntCert.com* is the UPN suffix of the e-mail address *bob@EntCert.com*. For administrative and security reasons, alternate UPN suffixes can also be assigned to a user login name (the UPN prefix).

To add user principal name suffixes (Figure 6.10), follow these steps:

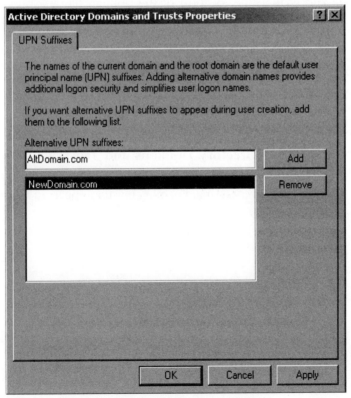

FIGURE 6.10 Adding Alternative Domain Name Aliases

1. Open the **Active Directory Domains and Trusts** MMC snap-in.

2. Right-click **Active Directory Domains and Trusts** and then click **Properties**.

3. From the **UPN Suffixes** tab, type an additional or alternate UPN for the domain and then click **Add**.

4. Repeat the previous step to add more alternative UPN suffixes.

When creating a new user account (as discussed later in this chapter), you can select which of the alternative domain UPN suffixes will be assigned to that user, as shown in Figure 6.11. In this example, three alternates can be applied to user bob.

ASSIGNING A DOMAIN NAMING OPERATIONS MASTER

Within a multi-domain controller environment, certain operation management tasks should be delegated to particular domain controller servers. The **Active Directory Domains and Trusts** snap-in permits the system administrator to identify and change the location of the domain naming operations master domain controller. The original location of the domain naming master is the root domain controller.

Identifying the Domain Naming Operations Master

The current location of the domain naming operations master is identified by the following steps:

1. Open the **Active Directory Domains and Trusts** MMC snap-in.

2. Right-click **Active Directory Domains and Trusts** → and select **Operations Masters**.

3. The name of the current domain naming master appears in **Domain naming operations master**.

User logon name:

| bob | @NewDomain.com ▼ |

@NewDomain.com
@AltDomain.com
@EntCert1.com

User logon name (pre-Windows 2000): | ENTCERT1\ | bob |

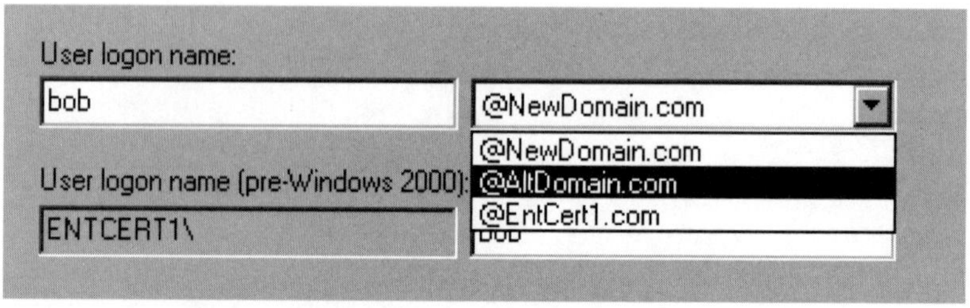

FIGURE 6.11 Selecting Domain Identities When Adding Users

Changing the Domain Naming Operations Master Location

The location of the domain naming operations master is changed from one domain controller to another by following these steps:

1. Open the **Active Directory Domains and Trusts** MMC snap-in.

2. Right-click **Active Directory Domains and Trusts**, select the **Connect to Domain Controller**, choose the target domain controller, and press **OK**.

3. Right-click **Active Directory Domains and Trusts**, select the **Operations Masters**, and make sure the target domain controller is listed in the second dialog text window. Press **Change**.

DELEGATING DOMAIN CONTROLLER ADMINISTRATION

System administrative responsibility can be delegated to specific user groups, but this should be done with great care. Remember, when authority is delegated to a domain controller or the entire domain, the rights to create or demote other domain controllers are vested in others. Granting such authority might be appropriate when a designated group of IT professionals shares system administration responsibility for the domain. It also makes sense when an alternate administrator needs temporary authority while the primary system administrator is on leave or on vacation.

Authority is delegated to a domain or domain controller (Figure 6.12) as follows:

1. Open the **Active Directory Domains and Trusts** MMC snap-in.

2. Right-click on the domain or domain controller and select **Properties**.

3. From the **Manage By** tab, select **Change** and **Add** the desired user or group.

4. Press **OK** to confirm the new setting.

The Active Directory Schema Manager Snap-In

The Active Directory Schema Manager is not loaded as part of the default Active Directory installation. Presumably, Microsoft made it an extra step because schema changes should be treated with great care. If a system administrator truly has a need and the knowledge to make modifications to the schema, he or she must deliberately install this tool. Installation is from the *adminpak* application suite available on the Windows 2000 Server or higher CD within the I386 folder. The following steps should be followed:

1. Load the **adminpak** from the Windows 2000 installation CD in the I386 folder, double-click **Support**, double-click **adminpak**, select **Setup**, and follow the instructions for **Typical** installation.

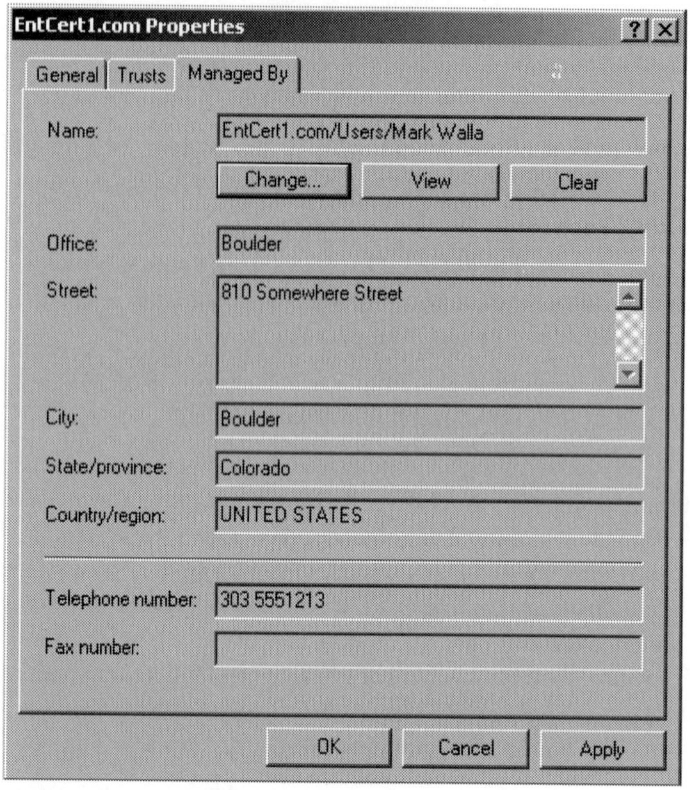

FIGURE 6.12 Delegating Domain Authority

2. Launch the **Microsoft Management Console** (MMC), select the **Console** menu, click **Add/Remove Snap-In**, and select **Add** from this dialog box. In the **Add Snap-In** dialog box double-click on **Active Directory Schema** and select **Close**. Press **OK** in the **Add/Remove Snap-In** dialog box.

Active Directory objects represent resources within the network. The most common domain objects include user accounts, groups, printers, computers, domain controllers, organizational units, and shared folders. The Active Directory schema defines the structure, the classes, and the attributes of allowable objects. These definitions can be viewed as the framework of the Active Directory.

Object classes inherit characteristics of parent objects. This creates a ripple effect in that changes can both positively and negatively affect objects down the line. The schema can be extended dynamically to modify and add to the objects stored by the Active Directory. In addition to the Admin group, the Schema Management group is the default system administrator group with full control to make schema changes. While other groups can be added, great caution is advised. If the Active Directory schema were inappropriately changed or damaged, your domain could be brought to its knees.

In this section, we will explore how to use the Active Directory Schema snap-in for the following:

- Identifying and modifying object classes
- Identifying and changing attributes
- Changing the schema operations master domain controller
- Ensuring schema availability and restoration

CAUTION   Changes to the Active Directory schema should be made only after full consideration of their impacts. It should be noted that the schema operations master by default cannot accept modifications. Modifications must be manually enabled by checking **the schema may be modified on this server** in the **Active Directory Schema** snap-in's **Operations Master** dialog. However, while this protects the enterprise from accidental changes, other actions should be taken. If the system administrator makes modifications, the domain controller that functions as the Schema Operations Manager should first be removed from the network. This will allow for recovery if those modifications prove inappropriate or harmful. Alternately, changes in the schema can be tested in an isolated network environment and moved over for replication *only* after full testing and troubleshooting are completed.

IDENTIFYING AND MODIFYING OBJECT CLASSES

To view the attributes associated with a schema object class, simply click on the target class in **Active Directory Schema** snap-in → **Classes**. As shown in Figure 6.13, the right-hand panel displays the attributes for the classSchema. If you look closely, you will note that both optional and mandatory attributes are identified. That is because all object attributes are either "must have" or "may have." Changing the mandatory setting will significantly impact the class's function and integrity.

To view additional information about a class or to make specific changes, right-click on the desired object and select Properties. The Properties dialog box displays four tabs:

- *General* provides the class common name, description, X.500 OID number, and class type. (Most Active Directory default classes have a type of Structural class type, but a few, like Country, are of the class type Abstract.) The class

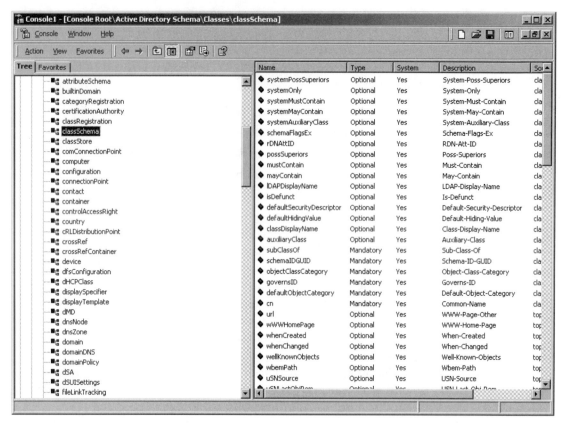

FIGURE 6.13 Classes and Associated Attributes

category is also shown with an option to change a class to one of the other classes available. An option to display classes of the same type and to deactivate the class is provided as well. Obvious caution should be used in making any changes to the schema's Structural classes.

- *Relationships* provides information on how a class fits within the class hierarchy. For example, the "group" class is identified as a "top"-level **Parent class**. It lists several **Auxiliary classes,** including mailRecipient, so it is logical to assume that a group member also can receive mail. Other **Auxiliary classes** can be associated with the group class by selecting **Add** and choosing among those listed. This tab also lists classes that have a **Possible Superior** position, such as organizationalUnit, domainDNS, builtinDomain, and container classes. You can use the **Add** button to select other classes.

- *Attributes* provides a list of both **Mandatory** and **Optional** attributes. While no option can increase or change the mandatory attributes, the **Add** button can be used to add more optional attributes, which can also be deleted by selecting the **Remove** button.

- *Security* provides the list of permissions granted to different groups for each class. By default, **Authenticated Users** have Read permission for most objects. The **Domain Administrator Group** and the **SYSTEM Group** generally have Read, Write, and Full Control. These two groups are also authorized to create and delete child classes for some of the classes. Other groups or specific users can be added to the permissions lists.

Class Types

In creating or modifying objects, it is necessary to identify their class type. The full-fledged object will be a member of the *Structural* class. The *Abstract* and *Auxiliary* types are used in the formation of the Structural type. The Active Directory schema recognizes four types of object class:

- *Structural class.* The Structural class is important to the system administrator in that it is the only type from which new Active Directory objects are created. Structural classes are developed from either the modification of an existing Structural type or the utilization of one or more Abstract classes.

- *Abstract class.* Abstract classes are so named because they take the form of templates that actually create other templates (abstracts) and Structural and Auxiliary classes. Think of Abstract classes as frameworks for the defining objects.

- *Auxiliary class.* The Auxiliary class is a list of attributes. Rather than apply numerous attributes when creating a Structural class, it provides a streamlined alternative by applying a combination of attributes with a single include action.

- *88 class.* The 88 class includes object classes defined prior to 1993, when the 1988 X.500 specification was adopted. This type does not utilize the Structural, Abstract, or Auxiliary definitions, nor is it in common use for the development of objects in Windows 2000 environments.

NOTE It should be remembered that the schema is loaded in the domain controller cache for easy access. To ensure cache consistency, there is a five-minute delay after changes are written to disk until they are moved to the cache. Threads that might have been running prior to the cache rebuild will continue to use the previous definitions. New threads utilize the definitions associated with the rebuilt cache.

IDENTIFYING AND CHANGING ATTRIBUTES

Attributes are defined only once but may be applied to multiple classes. As discussed above, the attributes associated with a specific class can be identified through the **Class Properties** dialog or directly from the Active Directory Schema snap-in.

A list of available attributes is found in the **Active Directory Schema** snap-in → **Attributes**. The right-hand panel of the MMC lists the attributes alphabetically. By right-clicking on any attribute, you can select the Properties option to learn more about its features and configuration (Figure 6.14). The information provided includes the description, common name, X.500 OID, syntax (such as integer, octet string, text, etc.), and range. Other options are also provided, such as deactivation and indexing within the Active Directory. It is important to note that attributes can never be deleted once they are created. Their use can be prevented only through deactivation.

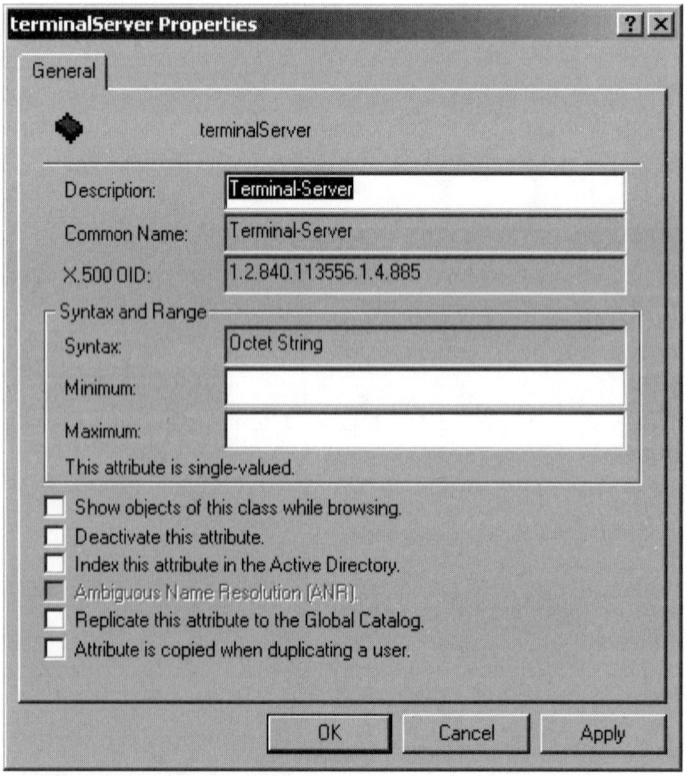

FIGURE 6.14 Attribute Properties

CREATING A NEW OBJECT CLASS OR ATTRIBUTE

When a new object class or attribute is created, it becomes a permanent part of the enterprise. It cannot be removed, only disabled. The following steps create a new object class or attribute:

1. Open the **Active Directory Schema** MMC snap-in.
2. Right-click **Active Directory Schema** → right-click either **Classes** or **Attributes** → select **New** → select **Class** or **Attribute**.
3. Press the **Continue** button in the message box (or **Cancel** to discontinue).
4. In the supplied dialog box, enter a **Common Name**, the **LDAP Display Name**, and a valid **OID** number, and identify the **Parent Class** and the **Class** type → press **Next**.
5. In the next dialog box, use the **Add** button to include **Mandatory** and **Optional** attributes.
6. Press **Finish** to complete the process.

For the creation of attributes, the process eliminates the need to set the Parent class with **Syntax** and appropriate ranges.

NOTE   One of the requirements in creating a new object class or attribute is the use of a valid OID number, which, like DNS numbers and IP addresses, is assigned on a national basis. For example, in the United States an OID number can be requested from the ANSI website at *http://www.web.ansi.org/public/services/reg_org.html*.

NOTE   Whenever possible, adding an attribute to an existing class is generally cleaner than creating a new class. Remember, classes cannot be removed but only disabled. However, if it is necessary to create a class, much time can be saved by utilizing a parent class that provides generic definitions. Attributes can then be added and the new class inherits the characteristics of its parent.

CHANGING THE DOMAIN SCHEMA OPERATIONS MASTER

Within a multi-domain controller environment, certain operation management tasks should be delegated to different domain controller servers. From the Active Directory Schema snap-in, it is possible to identify and change the location only of the schema operations master manager. The Active Directory Schema snap-in separates the definitions of classes and attributes.

Identifying the Schema Operations Master

The schema operations master domain controller can be identified by following these steps:

1. Open the **Active Directory Schema** MMC snap-in.

2. Right-click **Active Directory Schema** and select **Operations Masters**.

3. The name of the current schema master appears in **Domain Schema operations master**.

Changing the Schema Operations Master Location

The schema operations master domain controller can be moved to another domain controller by the following steps:

1. Open the **Active Directory Schema** MMC snap-in.

2. Right-click **Active Directory Schema**, select the **Connect** to Domain Controller, choose the target domain controller, and press **OK**.

3. Right-click **Active Directory Schema**, select **Operations Masters**, and make sure the target domain controller is listed in the second dialog text window. Press **Change**.

ENSURING SCHEMA AVAILABILITY AND RESTORATION

The schema master domain controller must be available to perform modifications or extensions. While the Active Directory will not cease functioning if the schema master is not available, it will remain static until connectivity is achieved. When this occurs, the first action of a system administrator is to check the network and also the system health of the domain controller that is serving as the schema master. It may be necessary to resize the resources available on the schema master domain controller to accommodate increases in the number of objects, classes, and attributes being stored. If it becomes necessary to pull the schema master domain controller offline, it is highly recommended that its function be transferred to another domain controller.

In the event that the schema becomes damaged or otherwise corrupted, the restoration of a default schema or a backup version will become necessary. The process of simply reloading the schema from backup is done by opening the **Active Directory Schema** snap-in → right-click on **Active Directory Schema** → **select Reload Schema**.

The Active Directory Sites and Services Snap-In

The Active Directory Sites and Services snap-in tool ensures efficient user logon authentication, the locating of directory services and objects, and more effective control of Active Directory replication. Specifically, it is used to create sites and subnets, move servers between sites, and formulate site links and bridges.

As discussed previously, three Active Directory partitions must be replicated within and between sites. The *schema* data and *configuration* data partitions are replicated to all domain controllers in the tree or forest; the *domain* data partition is replicated solely to domain controllers within the domain. Replication within a site is based on a bidirectional circular topology created automatically by the KCC service. Replication of all three partitions can use the same topology ring if the site supports a single domain. In the event that two or more domains share the same site, a topology ring for the schema and configuration partitions is established and separate domain topology rings are created for each domain using the site. The system administrator manually defines intersite replication. Figure 6.15 illustrates the relationship between intrasite and intersite replication.

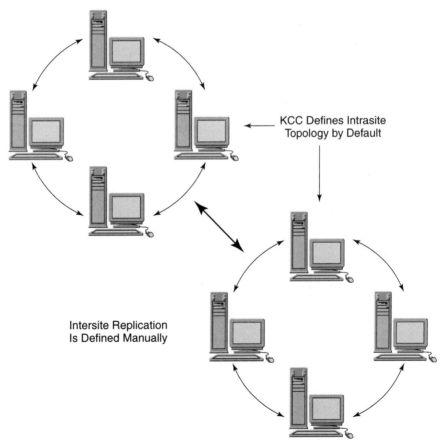

FIGURE 6.15 Intrasite versus Intersite Replication Topology

The physical structure is created by the KCC based upon information provided using the Active Directory Sites and Services snap-in. The Active Directory uses this information to determine how to replicate directory information and handle service requests. As an administrator, you can manually override the topology created by the KCC of the Active Directory. This is particularly true with respect to intersite communication and replication. The basis of intersite communication is the use of *site links,* which comprise three components.

- Cost—the cost is a representation of a path's relative priority. The higher its cost, the lower a path will be regarded in the utilization of a link.
- Replication frequency—where latency is an issue, the interval between replications should be fairly short.
- Transport mechanism—intersite links can use either RPC over TCP/IP or to end replicated data as e-mail using SMTP.
- Scheduling—when the frequency of replication can be deferred, the system administrator can determine specific offpeak times when replication should be scheduled.

The Active Directory Sites and Services snap-in manages the replication of Active Directory information both within and between sites. The system administrator can balance the timing of Active Directory data synchronization against the availability of network bandwidth and costs associated with remote connectivity. This is accomplished by customizing the site link connectivity properties.

When a user logs on or makes an inquiry of the Active Directory, an attempt is first made to contact the domain controllers within that defined site. In most cases, the authentication is resolved by a domain controller on the local site. The local workstation, as part of a subnet, will seek out authentication in that subnet (which is typically a local site). By not having to transmit information to a remote domain controller, network traffic is reduced, so domain controller placement must also be taken into consideration.

This section examines how to use the Active Directory Sites and Services snap-in to perform the following tasks:

- Creating new sites
- Creating site subnets
- Creating intersite links
- Establishing an intersite replication schedule
- Selecting an application licensing server

- Moving domain controllers between sites
- Repairing a domain controller
- Removing a domain controller from a site

NOTE   Site links are required before domain controllers can replicate information outside their own site. They are not automatic but require an explicit action by the system administrator to exchange Active Directory data. As new sites are created, the domain controllers are assigned to the specified site. This is accomplished when a domain controller is assigned a subnet address associated with a specific site. Links must then be established between sites in order to guarantee domain controller replication throughout the domain.

NOTE   When creating links between sites where replication activity is high, consider dedicating a single domain controller to the intersite synchronization. Known as bridgehead servers, these domain controllers accept changes made to the Active Directory within a site and transmit them to other sites. Once this information is posted, internal domain controller synchronization can occur with reduced impact on remote network connections.

CREATING NEW SITES

The topology of intersite replication spans the entire tree or forest. When all sites can find a replication route, the topology is considered functional. As the system administrator, you can create site links from any domain controller in any site to any other domain controller in any site throughout the enterprise.

The process for creating a new site is very straightforward. Launch the **Active Directory Sites and Services** snap-in, right-click on **Sites**, and select **New Site**. In the upper text box enter the name of the new site and highlight the site container. Press **OK**. You will receive a confirmation message stating that the site has been created together with a list of the following tasks that should be carried out:

- Making sure that the new site is appropriately linked to other sites.
- Adding the subnet addresses to the subnet container listed in the snap-in.
- Installing one or more domain controllers within the site.
- Selecting a licensing server for the site.

CREATING SITE SUBNETS

Site subnets are created from within the **Active Directory Sites and Services** snap-in by right-clicking on the **Subnet** menu and then selecting **New Subnet**. The Subnet dialog box now appears as shown in Figure 6.16. Each site typically gets its own subnet and mask. First highlight the target site name from the list provided in the **Select a site object for this subnet list box**; then insert the network address and subnet mask. Press **OK**.

CREATING INTERSITE LINKS AND TRANSPORTS

By default, the Active Directory Sites and Services snap-in provides transport link options for IP (Internet Protocol) and SMTP (Simple Mail Transport Protocol). To create site links for either or both, right-click on either **IP** or **SMTP** from within the **Active Directory Sites and Services** snap-in and select **New Site Link**. The

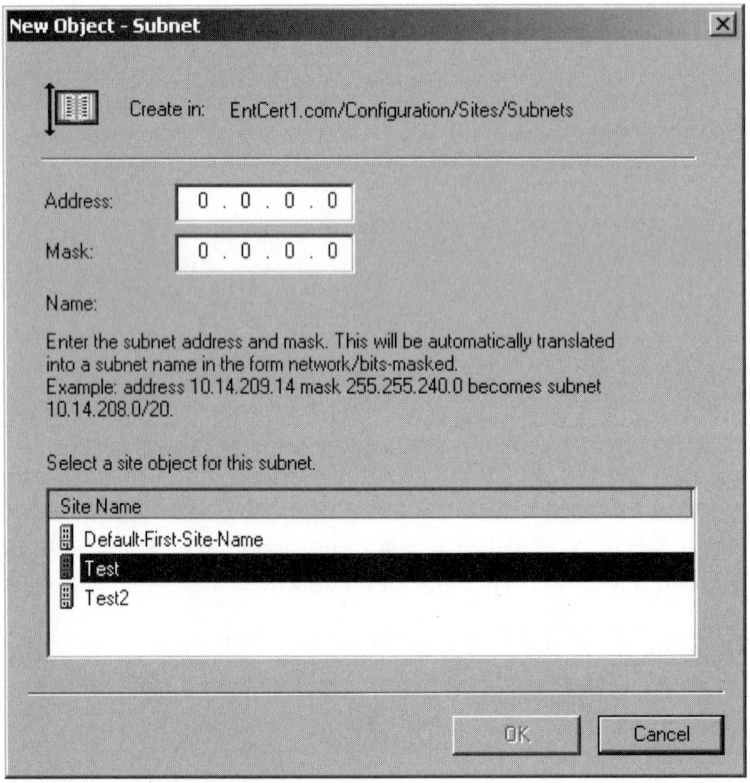

FIGURE 6.16 Subnet Creation

New Object—New Site Link Dialog box now appears. To link the sites, simply highlight the site(s) in the first column entitled **Sites Not in this Site Link**, press the **Add** button, and press **OK**. Repeat this procedure for all sites in which links are desired.

THE INTERSITE REPLICATION SCHEDULE

The Active Directory Sites and Services snap-in provides a nice graphical interface to schedule directory data synchronization between sites. From the **Active Directory Sites and Services** snap-in → select the target intersite transport folder requiring a schedule adjustment → right-click on the target site shown in the details panel and select **Properties** → click on **Change Schedule** → in the dialog box shown in Figure 6.17, make the appropriate schedule changes.

SELECTING AN APPLICATION LICENSING SERVER

The Active Directory creates services for application licensing when it is created. For every site, there should be an application licensing server installed. Unlike many other important services, the license server does not have to be a domain controller. However, it must have installed a copy of Windows 2000 Server or Windows 2000 Advanced Server. To move or select the licensing server, follow the steps on the following page:

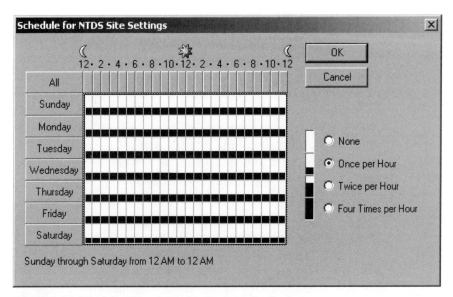

FIGURE 6.17 Scheduling Intersite Active Directory Replication

1. Open the **Active Directory Sites and Services** snap-in.
2. Open **Sites** and select the target site.
3. From the right panel, click on **Licensing Site Setting** to open the **Licensing Site Settings Properties** dialog box.
4. Select **Change** and then choose the server to be the licensing server.

MOVING DOMAIN CONTROLLERS BETWEEN SITES

The movement of domain controllers provides more effective load balancing and accommodates change or redundancy within a site. Rather than install additional domain controllers, it is easy to move a domain controller from a site with fewer Active Directory demands. The following procedure should be followed:

1. Open the **Active Directory Sites and Services** snap-in.
2. Open the **Sites folder**, then **domain controller sites**, then **Servers**.
3. Right-click on the target domain controller and select **Move**.
4. Select the new site from the dialog box and click **OK**.

DOMAIN CONTROLLER BACKUP AND RESTORATION

Periodic backup of the Active Directory (discussed in Chapter 14) should be a regular part of system administration. Of particular interest when backing up a domain controller is *System State* data, which constitutes the Active Directory, the Sysvol, and the Registry. There are several forms of restoration:

- *Nonauthoritative.* The entire replica of the Active Directory is transferred under a nonauthoritative restore. Assuming that other domain controllers exist, once the replica is installed the normal replication services will update the system with any changes since the last backup. To perform this type of restoration the server must be restarted in Safe mode (press F8 during the reboot to initialize the Safe mode). After the files have been restored, a flag is set in the Registry indicating that the Active Directory must be re-indexed at the next reboot. When the system is rebooted, it communicates with the Active Directory and is updated with changes.

- *Authoritative.* The authoritative restore permits the tagging of certain database information to prevent it being overwritten during a restoration. This will avoid its inadvertent destruction. When a restoration occurs, the tagged information will not be touched. It will, however, become part of the normal Active Directory database when the system is brought back online. This can apply to a single object, an OU, or an entire domain. To conduct an authoritative restore, the system must be restarted in Safe mode. From the **Command Prompt**, run the **Ntdsutil.exe** and type **restore subtree** *OU=name of unit, D C=domain, D C=.com*. Insert the appropriate information in the italicized portion of the command. Restart the system once the Ntdsutil has confirmed its completion. The authoritative information is then replicated to the other domain controllers.

The Ntdsutil command-line utility can be run from the Command Prompt. Help for the Ntdsutil utility can also be found at the Command Prompt by typing **ntdsutil/?**.

FORCED REPLICATION CHECK

Repairing an Active Directory domain controller can be accomplished by forcing a check of the replication.

NOTE The need to repair a domain controller is not a normal system administration event. Repair should be undertaken only when it is obvious that fundamental Active Directory databases or functions are corrupted.

The domain controller replication check is accomplished by these steps:

1. Open the **Active Directory Sites and Services** snap-in.
2. Open the **Sites folder** → the folder of the target domain controller.
3. Right-click on **NTDS Setting** → select **All Tasks** → select **Replication Check**.
4. Select the specific items to be repaired → press **OK**.

REMOVING A DOMAIN CONTROLLER SERVER FROM A SITE

A domain controller may need to be removed from a given site periodically for a variety of reasons. This can be done by following these steps:

1. Open the **Active Directory Sites and Services** snap-in.
2. Open the **Sites folder** → the folder of the site of the target domain controller.
3. Open the **Server** folder → right-click on the target domain controller.
4. Move to the **Action** menu → click **Delete**, and confirm with **OK**.

NOTE   If this is the only domain controller in the domain, be sure to promote another member server prior to removing the Active Directory. If this is not done, all information will be lost and users will not be able to log on to the network.

The Active Directory Users and Computers Snap-In

The Active Directory Users and Computers snap-in is possibly the most important and most often used system administrative tool. It supports the ability to add, modify, delete, and organize users, computer accounts, security groups, distribution groups, and resource publications. Because of the importance of user administration and group policies, we have broken their treatment into other chapters: Chapter 7, Users and Groups; Chapter 8, Group Policies; and Chapter 9, Files and Objects Permissions.

This section examines how to use the Active Directory Users and Computers snap-in to perform the following administrative tasks:

- Computer Account Management
  - Adding computer accounts
  - Removing computer accounts
  - Locating computer accounts
  - Moving computer accounts
- Managing local computer accounts
- RID, PDC, and infrastructure operations master management

COMPUTER ACCOUNT MANAGEMENT

The Active Directory Users and Computers snap-in facilitates the addition, removal, location, movement, and management of computers within the domain and tree. Remember that a computer account must be created in the Active Directory before a new computer can join the domain. This is generally before Windows 2000 is installed.

Computer systems are treated as objects within the Active Directory, much like user accounts. To identify a computer account or change components, use the **Active Directory Users and Computers** snap-in → select **Computers** → highlight the desired computer → right-click on **Properties**. From this dialog box, identification can be made of the computer's general attributes such as names and role, installed operating system, group and domain membership, physical location, and system management data (Figure 6.18). As the next section suggests, the

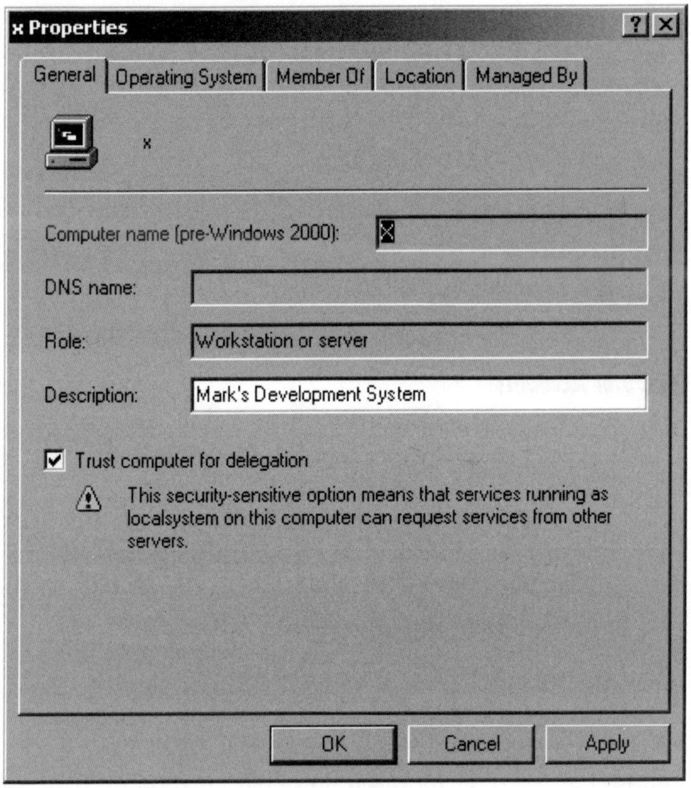

FIGURE 6.18 Computer Account Properties

Active Directory can track even those computer accounts that are not based on the Windows 2000 operating system.

Adding Computer Accounts

Adding a computer account to the Active Directory is required before member computers and servers can join the domain. This is an easy and straightforward process, as follows:

1. Open the **Active Directory Users and Computers** snap-in.
2. Open the target **Domain → Computers** (or **OU** folder).
3. Right-click **Computers** → select **New → Computers**.
4. Enter the computer's name, (optionally) change user groups authorized to use this computer account, check the box if pre–Windows 2000 computers are to use this account → press **OK**.

Removing Computer Accounts

When systems are taken out of service, they should be removed from the Active Directory. Consider this merely a housekeeping activity. To remove computer accounts, follow these steps:

1. Open the **Active Directory Users and Computers** snap-in.
2. Open the target **Domain** → **Computers** (or **OU** folder).
3. From the right panel, right-click on the target **Computer** → select **Delete**.
4. Confirm **YES** to remove this object.

Locating Computer Accounts

To perform any function on a computer account, the account must first be located. Manual identification within a very large enterprise can be time consuming, but an alternative method is as follows:

1. Open the **Active Directory Users and Computers** snap-in.
2. Right-click on the **Domain** → select **Find**.
3. Enter the appropriate information in the dialog.
4. Press the **Find Now** button.

Moving Computer Accounts

As organizations change or IT requirements shift, the computer account should be transferred to the appropriate domain or organizational unit as follows:

1. Open the **Active Directory Users and Computers** snap-in.
2. Open the target **Domain** → **Computers** (or **OU** folder).
3. From the right panel, right-click on the target **Computer** and select **Move**.
4. From the **Move Dialog box**, highlight the target container → then press **Enter**.

Managing Local Computer Accounts

From within the Active Directory Users and Computers snap-in, it is possible to launch the Computer Management MMC applications for the listed computer systems (Figure 6.19). The method is outlined as follows:

1. Open the **Active Directory Users and Computers** snap-in.
2. Open the target **Domain** → **Computers** (or **OU** folder).
3. From the right panel, right-click on the target **Computer** → select **Manage**.
4. The **Computer Management** MMC appears.

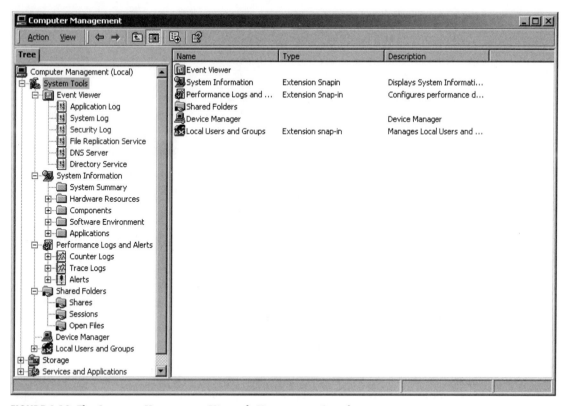

FIGURE 6.19 The Computer Management Microsoft Management Console

RID, PDC, OR INFRASTRUCTURE OPERATIONS MASTERS

Three of the domain operations masters are managed from the Active Directory User and Computers snap-in. The **RID operations master** establishes object IDs with numbers relative to a specific domain; the **PDC operations master** manages the PDC Emulator functions; and the **infrastructure operations master** manages group and user references. From the Active Directory Users and Computers snap-in, it is possible to identify and change the location of the RID, PDC, and infrastructure operations master managers. Their original location is the root domain controller.

Identifying the RID, PDC, or Infrastructure Operations Master

In larger enterprises where many domain controllers exist, it may not be obvious which one is serving as the RID, PDC, or infrastructure operations master. To find this out, use the steps that follow:

1. Open the **Active Directory Users and Computers** MMC snap-in.

2. Right-click **Active Users and Computers**, then select **Operations Masters**.

3. The name of the master appears in the respective **Domain Master** tab.

Changing the RID, PDC, or Infrastructure Operations Master

When an operations manager is taken offline, another domain controller must be promoted to perform this function. Promotion of a domain controller to a RID, PDC, or infrastructure operations master is accomplished as follows:

1. Open the **Active Directory Users and Computers** MMC snap-in.

2. Right-click **Active Users and Computers**, select the **Connect to Domain Controller**, and choose the target domain controller. Press **OK**.

3. Right-click **Active Users and Computers**, select **Operations Masters**, and make sure the target domain controller is listed in the second dialog text window → Press **Change**.

The Active Directory Replication Monitor

The Active Directory Replication Monitor is not loaded as part of the default installation but as part of the Windows 2000 Resource Kit located on the Windows 2000 Server or higher CD in the */support/tools* folder. This tool does exactly what its name implies—monitor Active Directory replication—and can be very useful. It is used specifically to view replication topologies, identify replication partners, and map transitive replication partners.

CREATING ORGANIZATIONAL UNITS

The organizational unit (OU) provides both flexibility and greater control. It is really an administrative container in which a logical grouping of network resources can be collected and their management delegated. Its form is hierarchical; that is, parent and child relationships exist between top- and lower-level OUs. The objects that constitute an OU are strictly up to the domain administrator. For example, the third floor of a large building can be defined as an OU, and since the sales staff occupies the third floor each of these users can be regarded as an OU as well. An organizational unit can contain other OUs. Thus, the printer OU can be placed inside the sales staff OU and the administration printer support can be delegated to an individual on the third floor.

This section reviews basic organizational unit management.

Creating, Deleting, Modifying, and Moving an Organizational Unit

The creation, deletion, modification, and moving of organizational units is a simple process. However, the ease of these activities belies the importance of proper planning.

CREATING AN ORGANIZATIONAL UNIT

The following steps should be followed to create an organizational unit within a domain or child domain:

1. Open the **Active Directory Users and Computers** MMC snap-in.
2. Right-click on **Domain** → select **New** → select **Organizational Unit**.
3. Within the OU dialog box enter the **Name** for the organizational unit. Press **OK**.

DELETING AN ORGANIZATIONAL UNIT

An organizational unit can be deleted as easily as it was created. However, great caution should be used in such deletion since objects within the OU will also be removed (Figure 6.20). For example, deleting the sales OU deletes all its users and resources. The following steps are invoked to delete an OU:

1. Open the **Active Directory Users and Computers** MMC snap-in.
2. Right-click on **Organizational Unit** → select **Delete**.
3. Confirm the deletion by pushing the **YES** button.

MODIFYING ORGANIZATIONAL UNIT PROPERTIES

The properties of an organizational unit are modified like any other Active Directory object. A discussion on standard object modification appeared earlier in this chapter. The steps to modify OU properties are listed on the next page.

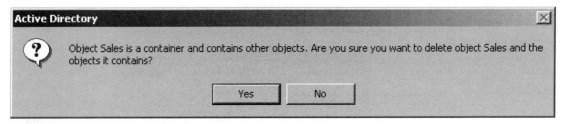

FIGURE 6.20 Deletion of an OU and Its Objects

1. Open the **Active Directory Users and Computers** MMC snap-in.
2. Right-click on the target **OU** → select **Properties**.
3. Make changes within the **General**, **Managed By**, and/or **Group Policy** tabs.
4. Press **OK**.

MOVING ORGANIZATIONAL UNITS

One of the major innovations of Windows 2000 is the ability to easily move or relocate an organizational unit to another domain or child domain to reflect the changes that regularly occur within an enterprise. The steps are as follows:

1. Open the **Active Directory Users and Computers** MMC snap-in.
2. Expand the target **Domain** or **OU** → right-click on the **OU** → select **Move**.
3. Highlight the new location of the OU in the **Move Dialog** → Press **OK**.

RENAMING ORGANIZATIONAL UNITS

To accommodate shifts in names or functions, the OU renaming function is handy. It requires the following steps:

1. Open the **Active Directory Users and Computers** MMC snap-in.
2. Expand the target **Domain** or **OU** → right-click on the **OU** → select **Rename**.
3. Enter the new name → Press **OK**.

LOCATING OBJECTS

Finding Active Directory objects in an enterprise is accomplished through the Microsoft Management Console. If Find is invoked from within a specific snap-in, as shown in Figure 6.21, the items managed by the snap-in will appear in the **Find** window and searches will center on that branch of the Active Directory. If it is not clear where the object is located, the **Directory Management** snap-in is utilized. The interface for finding an object is straightforward and requires no further explanation.

ACTIVE DIRECTORY OBJECT ACCESS

The security model used for the Active Directory mirrors to a very large extent Windows 2000 NTFS. A security descriptor defines which users and groups are assigned specific permissions to an object. Every object has an Access Control List (ACL) that contains information about who has access to it and what they can do with it. For every user or group, specific levels of permission can be assigned. As a

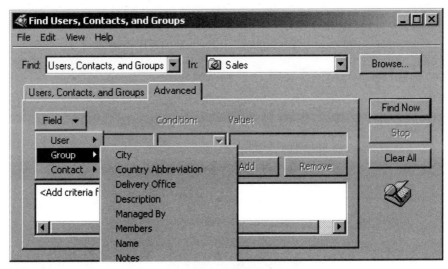

FIGURE 6.21 Finding an Object with Advanced Definitions

general rule, at least one user will have full control over an object, but full control for all users is seldom recommended. Where no permission is granted, that object becomes unavailable to the user or group. Also, when permission is specifically denied, all other rights are overridden. For example, a user can belong to a group that has permission to use a network resource, but if that user is specifically denied permission, any rights to that resource granted to him as a member of the group are canceled.

By default, an object inherits the permission rights of its parent. One use of the organizational unit is to group together objects with the same permissions.

STANDARD AND SPECIAL PERMISSIONS

The Active Directory supports two types of permission: standard and special. The five standard permissions, which may be applied in any combination to a user or group, are

- **Read.** The user can see the object and attributes, can identify its owner, and has other permissions where applicable.
- **Write.** The user can change the object's attributes.
- **Create Child Objects.** The user can create child objects in an OU.
- **Delete Child Objects.** The user can remove child objects.
- **Full Control.** The user can perform any action on the object, including taking full control.

Special permissions are extensions to the standard permissions and vary for each object.

Setting and Viewing Object Permissions

The security permission settings can be viewed for every object from its Properties dialog. The properties for all objects can be retrieved from the Active Directory Schema snap-in. To retrieve and set object permissions, the following steps should be taken (Figure 6.22):

1. Open the **Active Directory Schema** snap-in.
2. Open the **Classes** folder.
3. Right-click on the **target object class**.
4. With the **Properties** dialog, select the user or group for which permissions are to be set or **Add** or **Remove** a user or group to provide new permissions.

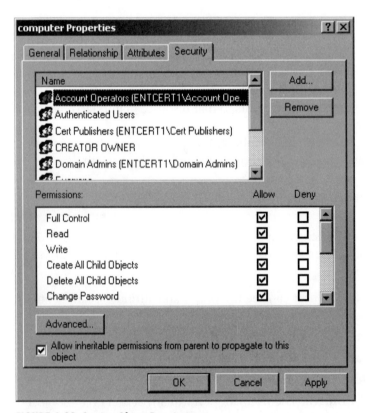

FIGURE 6.22 Setting Object Permissions

5. Click on the desired **Permission**.

6. Repeat for each user or group for which permissions are to be modified.

7. Press **OK** to complete.

To simply view the special permissions assigned to an object, press the **Advanced** button and double-click on the Permissions item (Figure 6.23). Changes in this list can then be applied by clicking (or unclicking) the special permission.

Permission Inheritance and Preventing Inheritance

By default, permissions are inherited from parent objects, which means that rather than have to set all permissions for every object, the system administrator can rely on the fact that permissions set on a parent object will filter down the object tree. There are times in which this facility needs to be short-circuited, which can be accomplished by following the steps listed on the next page.

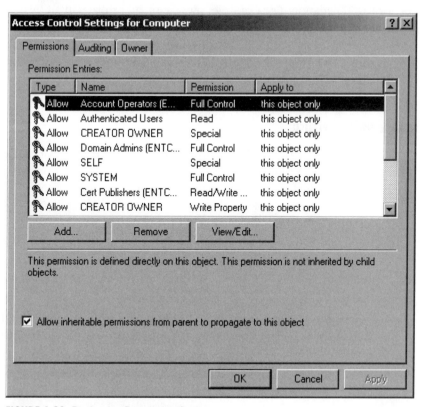

FIGURE 6.23 Reviewing Permission Settings

1. Open the **Active Directory Schema** snap-in.

2. Right-click **Active Directory Schema** and click **Permissions**.

3. On the **Security** tab, click the group whose permissions you want to change.

4. In **Permissions**, select **Allow** or **Deny** for the permissions you want to change.

5. Alternately, remove the checkmark at the bottom of the Permissions dialog that states, "Allow inheritance permissions from the parent to propagate to this object."

ACTIVE DIRECTORY ADMINISTRATIVE DELEGATION

The ability to delegate administrative responsibility is a major strength of Windows 2000. This delegation can be set at the domain, organizational unit, or object level and involves the assignment of appropriate permissions ranging from Read-Only to Full Control. As a general rule, objects should be placed in organizational units prior to delegation. For example, by placing all printers in an OU, it is possible to provide permissions to a group of users to manage these devices. All users in the Sales department might be in another organizational unit. A trusted administrator can then be delegated to manage the user accounts. Obviously, delegation must be granted with care.

The Delegation Wizard

Two best practices should be utilized when delegating authority: Delegate at the organizational unit level whenever possible for ease of permission tracking; and utilize the Delegation Wizard described as follows:

1. Open the **Active Directory Users and Computers** snap-in.

2. Right-click on the predefined organizational unit → select **Delegate Control** (Figure 6.24).

3. Select the user(s) or group(s) to whom authority is to be delegated (Figure 6.25).

4. For common tasks select from the items listed or, for expanded and specialized authority, click on the **Create a custom task to delegate** button (Figure 6.26).

5. If Custom Tasks was selected, mark those items to which delegated authority is to be granted (Figure 6.27).

6. Select the permission level that is to be delegated (Figure 6.28).

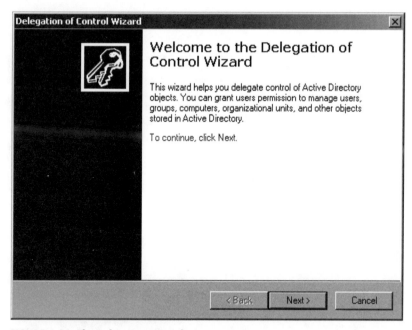

FIGURE 6.24 The Delegation Wizard

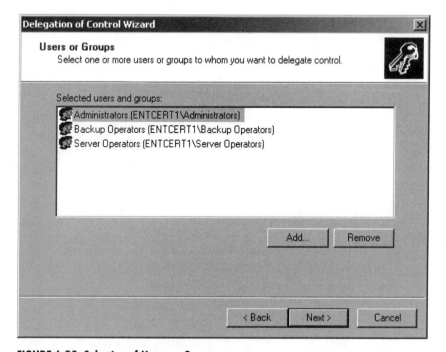

FIGURE 6.25 Selection of Users or Groups

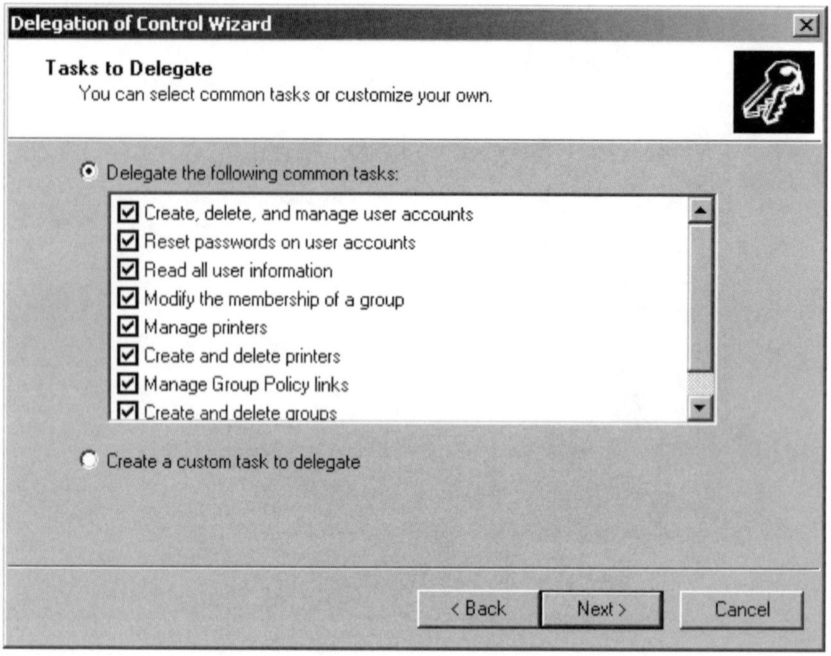

FIGURE 6.26 Common Task Delegation

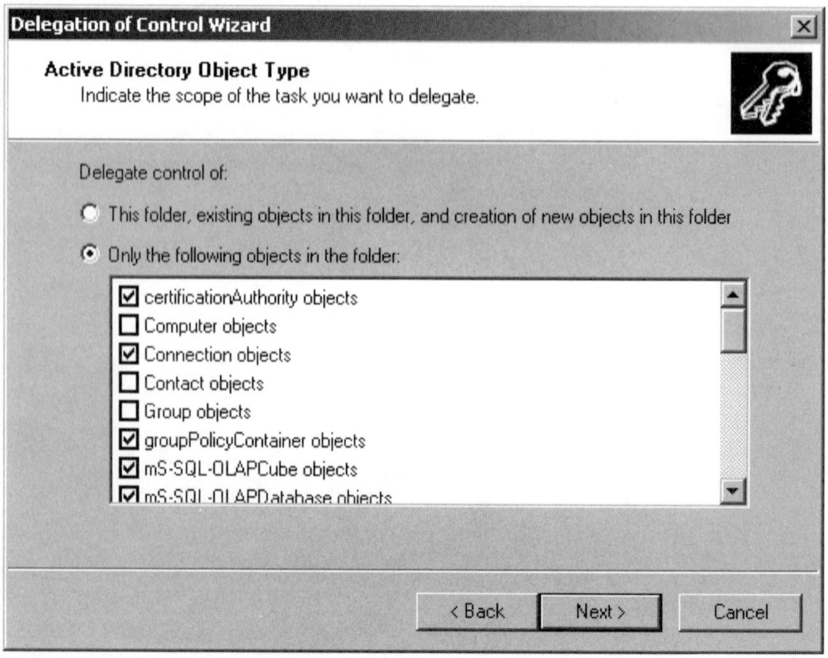

FIGURE 6.27 Custom Task Delegation

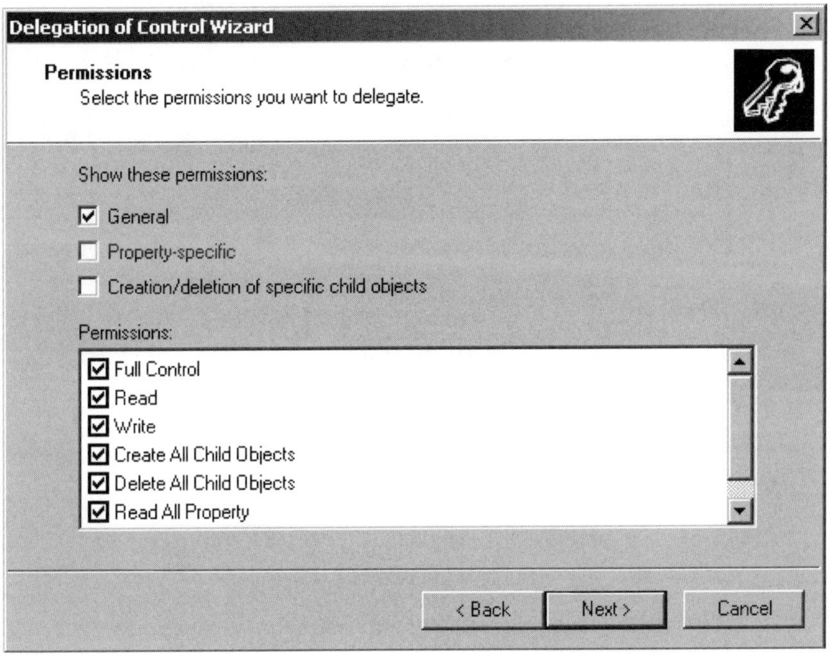

FIGURE 6.28 Level of Permission

GLOBAL CATALOG REFINEMENT

The Global Catalog authenticates network user logons and fields inquiries about objects across a forest or tree. Every domain has at least one GC that is hosted on a domain controller, and there is typically one on every site. While the Active Directory creates the initial Global Catalog during initial installation, there are a number of additional interactions that a system administrator may invoke to improve performance.

Enabling a Global Catalog

A domain controller must be taken offline or out of service sometimes. If this domain controller is also the sole GC for the domain, it is critical that another GC domain controller be placed into service first. Remember, with the exception of the Domain Administrator group, no user can log on to the network without an operative Global Catalog. Therefore prior to running dcpromo.exe to demote the GC domain controller, enable a new Global Catalog by following these steps:

1. Create at least a second domain controller.

2. Open the **Active Directory Sites and Services** snap-in.

3. Open the **Site** → **Server** → target the domain controller.

4. Right-click on **NTDS Settings** → select **Properties** → click **Global Catalog** at the bottom of the **General** tab.

Moving, Removing, and Duplicating the Global Catalog

In larger enterprises, it is recommended that the Global Catalog be moved to a separate domain controller. As noted in Chapter 5, this new location should not be the infrastructure master domain controller. Moving the domain controller is accomplished by following these steps:

1. Create at least a second domain controller.

2. Open the **Active Directory Sites and Services** snap-in.

3. Open the **Site** → **Server** → target the domain controller.

4. Right-click on **NTDS Settings** → select **Properties** → and click **Global Catalog** at the bottom of the **General** tab.

5. To remove the original GC, repeat the above process, but in step 3 return to the domain controller that originally contained the GC and during step 4 remove the checkmark next to **Global Catalog** at the bottom of the **General** tab.

To create multiple copies of the Global Catalog, simply follow steps 1 through 4 on several domain controllers.

Indexing and Adding Attributes to the Global Catalog

The Global Catalog is used to more rapidly locate domain objects. In some cases, users query more commonly used attributes to locate network resources. So that the GC recognizes these attributes, the system administrator can force it to both add and index them. To force the addition and/or indexing of an attribute, follow these steps:

1. Open the **Active Directory Schema** snap-in.

2. Open the **Attributes** folder.

3. In the right panel, right-click on the target attribute that should be added or indexed to the Global Catalog → then click **Properties**.

4. Click **Index this attribute in the Active Directory**.

5. Click **Replicate this attribute to the Global Catalog**.

6. Press **OK**.

THE ACTIVE DIRECTORY CONNECTOR

The Active Directory connector technology helps to synchronize information with other directory services. This section discusses synchronization with Microsoft Exchange Server's directory services as a matter of example. Connectors to other directory services will be made available through Windows 2000 Service Packs and third-party vendors.

The Active Directory Connector (ADC) is not installed as part of the standard Active Directory setup process. Instead, ADC setup is available on the Windows 2000 CD in the *\Valueadd\MSFT\MGMT\ADC* folder, and the only decisions it requires are where to store the installed software and what to name the service account and password for the group authorized for Connector use. The Exchange Server must be available to complete the configuration.

ADC utilizes LDAP v3 to resolve information about objects to be synchronized. *Connection agreements* synchronize information between directory services. Synchronization is achieved when the services' respective databases have equivalent information, but it need not be identical. Connection agreements must identify servers, target objects, selected containers, and the schedule for data transfer.

Configuring Connection Agreements

The ADC must be configured to ensure proper synchronization. The Active Directory Connector snap-in is used to define the configuration properties, via the primary configuration tabs described here:

- **General** establishes the direction of synchronization as two-way directions or one-way from/to the Active Directory or Exchange Server.
- **Connections** establishes the method of authentication for both the Active Directory and the Exchange Server for bridgehead servers.
- **Schedule** sets the time in which changes are to be synchronized (by default the systems are polled every 5 seconds for modifications during this scheduled period).
- **From Windows** and **From Exchange** respectively define which containers are polled, which changes are to be written, and the type of objects for synchronization.
- **Deletion** defines where deleted objects from one directory service are stored in the corresponding directory. By default, deleted objects are not removed. However, if you select deletion, it occurs on both sides.
- **Advanced Settings** establishes the number of entries per page of synchronization, known as *paged results*. It also defines the connector as primary.

POSTSCRIPT

This chapter and the last one provided a framework for Active Directory use. The chapters dealing with users (Chapter 7), group policies (Chapter 8), and security (Chapter 9) provide additional information on Active Directory utilization.

Chapter

7

User Accounts and Groups

User accounts and group management are core system administration responsibilities. Indeed, it is impossible to introduce the concept of user account management without a discussion of groups. All users belong to one or more groups. Rights and privileges are assigned to default "built-in" or customized groups, and the user receives rights by becoming a group member.

This chapter explores the nature of user accounts and groups and provides related management information. Upon completing it, you should be able to:

- Understand the concepts underlying Windows 2000 user accounts and groups
- Add, modify, and remove local and domain user accounts
- Add, modify, and remove local and domain groups
- Apply group membership to user accounts

USER ACCOUNTS

In order to gain access to Windows 2000 a user must have a valid user account. A user account determines three important factors: when a user may log on; where within the domain or workgroup the user may log on; and what privilege level he or she is assigned. Primary user account elements are login name, password, group membership, and allowable logon hours.

Privilege level and access permissions are assigned to a user account with security credentials. When an account is created it is given a unique access number known as a security identifier (SID). Every group to which the user belongs has an associated SID. The user and related group SIDs together form the user account's security token, which determines access levels to objects throughout the system and network. SIDs from the security token are mapped to the Access Control List (ACL) of any object the user attempts to access. (The ACL is discussed in Chapter 9.) The user is granted rights to the object based on the permissions or lack of permissions in the ACL has assigned to him and his groups (Figure 7.1).

NOTE   The security identifier is a unique number generated when a user account or group is created. If you delete a user account and attempt to recreate it with the same user name and password, the SID will be different. This means that all objects using the old SID to assign permissions are useless to the new user. Permissions must be reassigned to the new user account SID. The same principle applies to groups: Deleting a group and recreating a group with the same name will not generate the same group SID.

Any object trying to access a resource must do so through a user account. In this case an object can be a computer user or an application. For instance, the Internet

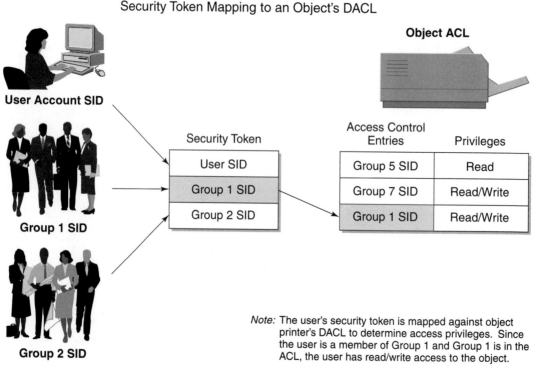

Security Token Mapping to an Object's DACL

Note: The user's security token is mapped against object printer's DACL to determine access privileges. Since the user is a member of Group 1 and Group 1 is in the ACL, the user has read/write access to the object.

FIGURE 7.1 Relationship of User and Group SIDs to Object ACLs

Information Services Web server creates the IUSR_*systemname* user account to provide anonymous Web users access to the local system.

Windows 2000 allows two types of user accounts: local and domain. Local accounts are supported on all Windows 2000 systems except domain controllers. They are maintained on the local system and are not distributed to other systems. The local security database manages the user account information. The domain user account permits access throughout a domain and provides centralized user account administration using Active Directory components. Let's take a closer look at these accounts.

Local User Accounts

Local user accounts are supported on member servers participating in domains and on standalone systems participating in workgroups. The local user account authenticates the user for local machine access *only*. This authentication is handled through a local security database (Figure 7.2). Local accounts do not support access to resources on other computers and require separate logins to access remote systems.

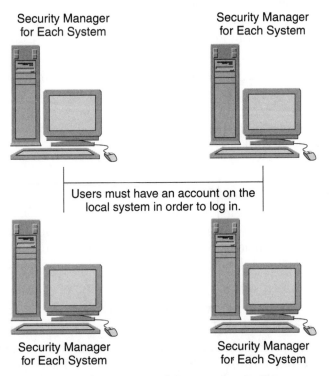

FIGURE 7.2 Local Computers with Separate Security Managers

NOTE   It is best not to create local user accounts on member servers, as they cannot be centrally administered and create added administrative headaches. However, they are useful when isolating applications from the rest of the domain. Local accounts on member servers or standalone servers may be added at any time.

At a minimum the Administrator and Guest accounts will already exist as local accounts. These are *built in* to the operating system. The Administrator account permits user account management, group management, and policies for the local systems. *The Guest account is designed for temporary users who require limited system access.*

CREATING A LOCAL USER ACCOUNT

User accounts comprise two mandatory pieces of information: user name and password. Other personal information is optionally tracked. Outlined below are some restrictions and suggestions on the creation of user names and passwords.

- User and logon names are interchangeable. Domain account names must be unique within the domain, although the same logon name can be used on several systems with local logon configurations. Logon names are not case sensitive, must not contain more then 20 characters, and must not contain the following characters: +, *, ?, <, >, /, \, [,], :, ;.

- Passwords should not contain such items as full words, family names, pop culture references, pets, or locations. They should contain both numeric and alphanumeric characters and should not be the same as the user name. The maximum number of characters is 128 and the minimum is determined by group policy. Password filtering is discussed in Chapter 11, Additional Issues and Solutions.

Local User Accounts on Windows 2000 Server

Creating a local user account involves the steps that follow. As noted before, local user accounts are available only on member servers and workstations. Domain controllers have no local accounts and creating them is not recommended on member servers. However, if there is a reason to provide temporary restricted user accounts, here is how:

1. Create a new user account on a workgroup server by selecting **Start** → **Programs** → **Administrative Tools** → **Computer Management** (Figure 7.3).

2. From the **Computer Management** snap-in open the **System Tools** → **Local Users and Groups** node. Right-click on the **Users** node and select **New Users...**. The **New User** dialog box should appear (Figure 7.4).

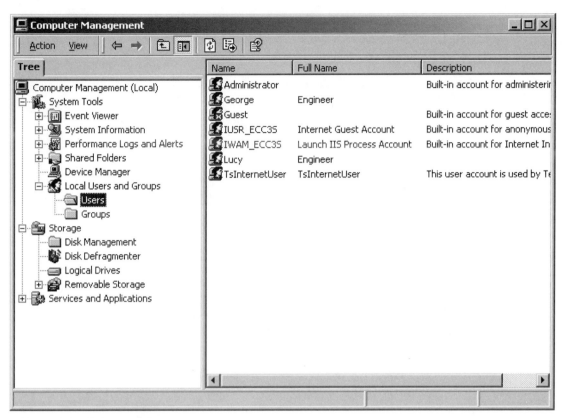

FIGURE 7.3 Local Users and Groups

The **User name** field will become the user's login name. The password properties are the same as those for the domain user discussed in the next section.
User accounts are viewed in the Details window of the **Computer Management**
tool under the **Users** node.

3. Enter the user's user name, full name, and description. Press the **Create** button.

Local User Accounts on Windows 2000 Professional

Windows 2000 Professional is designed either as a client system in a network environment or as a standalone workgroup computer. Domain and local accounts that
already exist may be assigned access to the local system using the following steps:

1. To permit existing user account access to the local system select **Start** → **Settings** → **Control Panel** (Figure 7.5). From the **Control Panel** double-click
the **Users and Passwords** icon.

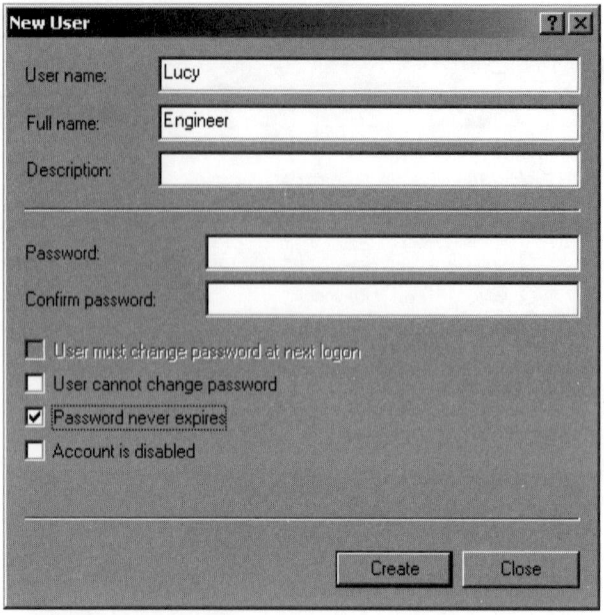

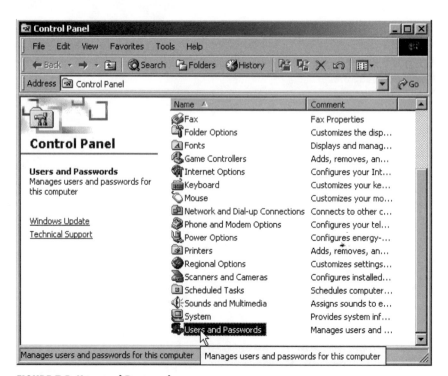

FIGURE 7.4 A New User

FIGURE 7.5 Users and Passwords

The **Users and Passwords** dialog box should now display all user accounts on the system (Figure 7.6).

2. To give another user access to the local system, press the **Add...** button.

3. Enter a domain or local user account name and choose a domain name for the **Domain:** field (Figure 7.7). If the account is a local one, enter the name of the local system. Press the **Next>** button to continue.

4. On the next screen enter a valid password for the user. Re-enter in the **Confirm password** field.

5. The next screen determines the permissions level for the user, as shown in Figure 7.8. There the **Standard user** radio button assigns the user to the **Power Users** Group; the **Restricted user** selection assigns the user to the **Users** Group. The user may become a member of any other security group using the **Other** option. These are only initial membership settings and may be easily modified later.

6. Press the **Finish** button.

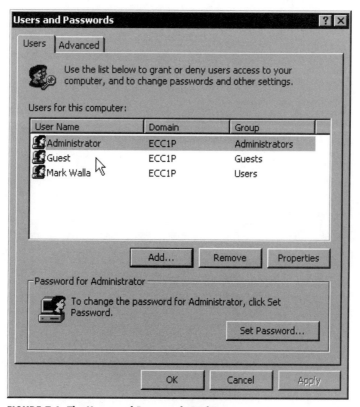

FIGURE 7.6 The Users and Passwords Dialog

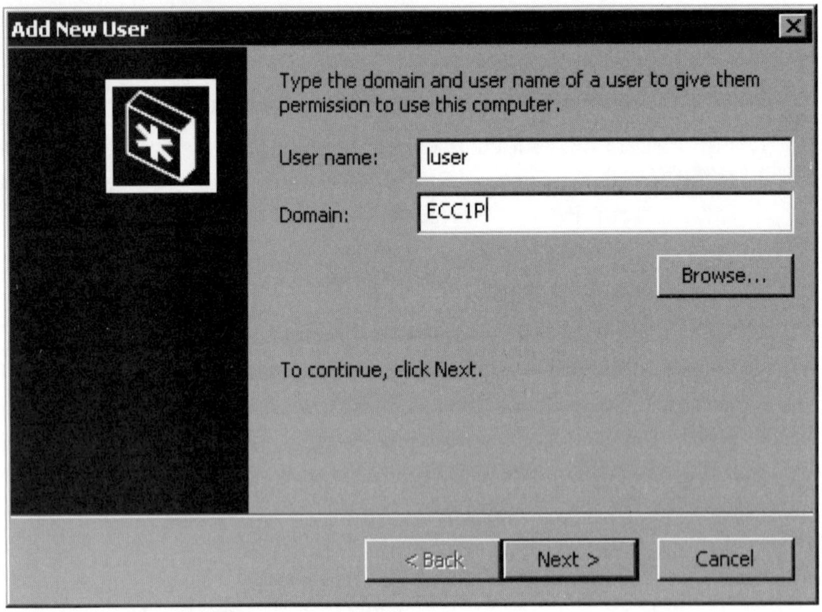

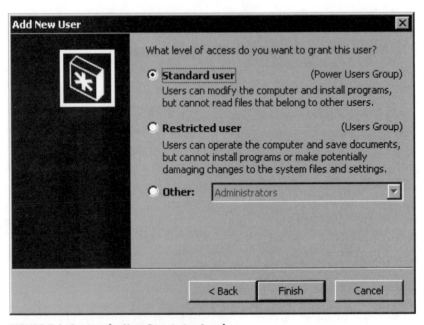

FIGURE 7.7 Assigning Permissions to a New User

FIGURE 7.8 Setting the User Permission Level

The account will have the access rights you have just assigned. Denying a user account access to the local system is accomplished by pressing the **Remove** button from the **Users and Passwords** dialog box (Figure 7.6).

Domain User Accounts

A domain user account allows access to resources in a domain or domain tree. It is created within a domain container in the Active Directory database and then propagated to all other domain controllers in the domain, permitting the user to log on to any of the domain's systems or resources. The domain model centralizes user account administration from any domain controller or member server in the domain.

Once the user has been authenticated against the Active Directory database using the Global Catalog, an access token is obtained. All resources in the domain will determine permissions based on the user's access token and Access Control List (ACL). The access token is dropped from the system when the user terminates the logon session.

CREATING A DOMAIN USER ACCOUNT

The creation of a domain user account involves the assignment of a logon name, a password, group membership, and several optional steps. Windows 2000 default settings dictate that only a member of the Administrators group (like Domain Admins or Enterprise Admins) can add users to a domain; however, administrative privileges may be delegated.

The following steps should be taken to add a domain user account:

1. Log in with administrative privileges.

2. Select from the **Start** menu **Programs → Administrative Tools → Active Directory Users and Computers** to bring up the **Active Directory Users and Computers** snap-in (Figure 7.9). Select the appropriate Active Directory container to house the new user account. This may be a domain or an Organizational Unit (OU).

3. Once an Active Directory container has been selected press the New User button to create the new user account. This will bring up the **New Object – User** window (Figure 7.10).

4. Enter the user's first and last names in the **First name:** and **Last name:** fields, respectively. Windows 2000 will then automatically fill in the **Full Name:** field for you. Fill in a user name in the **User logon name:** field. This name, along with the user's domain name (such as *jengineer@Entcert2.com*), uniquely identifies a user in a domain, tree, or forest. This is not to be confused with an

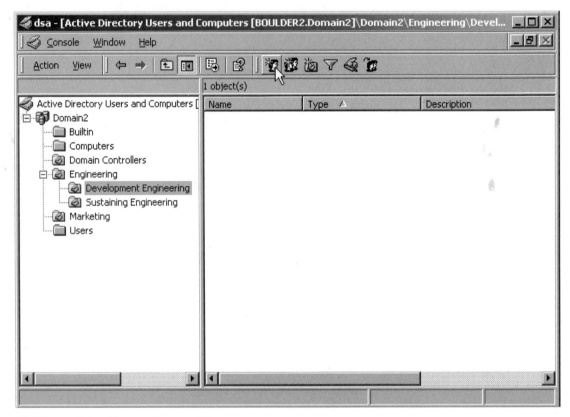

FIGURE 7.9 Active Directory Users and Computers

external Internet DNS domain name. The down-level pre–Windows 2000 logon name is the user account name to be used when accessing the domain from non-Windows 2000 clients such as Windows NT 4.0 and 3.51. Press the **Next>** button.

5. Enter a password for the user in the **Password:** field (Figure 7.11). Retype the password in the **Confirm password:** field. Check the appropriate boxes for the password options, as shown in Table 7.1.

6. Press the **Next>** button to bring up the user account confirmation screen (Figure 7.12). This verifies the restrictions and the account name assigned to the new domain user account. Press the **Finish** button to finalize the new account and view the new user within her Active Directory container from the **Active Directory Users and Computers** snap-in.

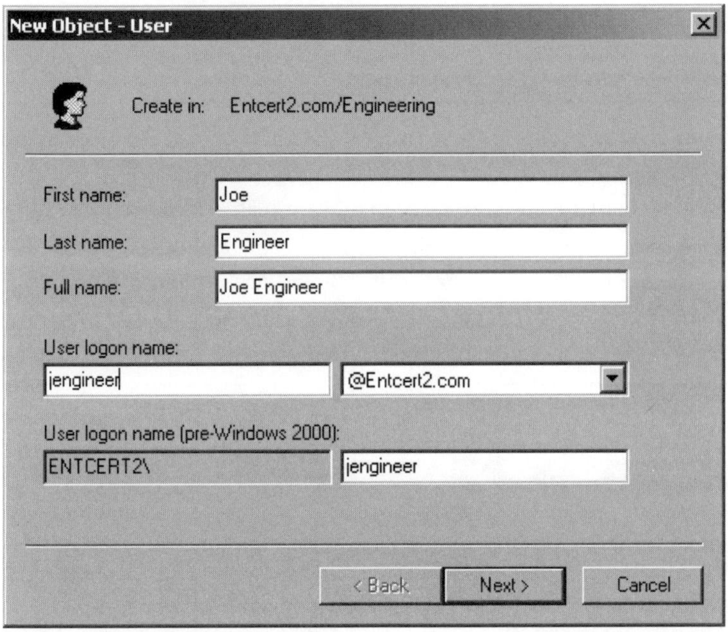

FIGURE 7.10 Creating a New User

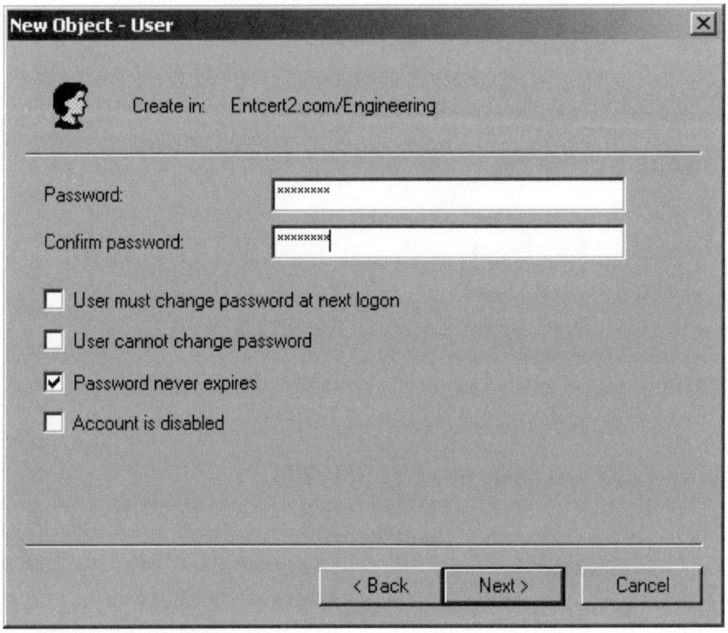

FIGURE 7.11 Password Properties

TABLE 7.1 Password Properties Options

Property	Description
User must change password at next logon	Password just assigned will be changed the first time the new user logs in.
User cannot change password	Account's password can be changed only with Administrator privileges.
Password never expires	User is not required to periodically change his password.
Account is disabled	Deactivate an account when user does not need it. May be useful for extended leaves or when planning future accounts.

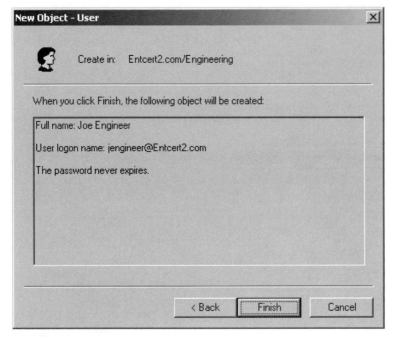

FIGURE 7.12 Finalizing a User Account

UNDERSTANDING USER ACCOUNT PROPERTIES

As with all Windows 2000 objects, the user account has a number of associated properties or attributes. Once the domain user account has been created, these properties may be modified from the **Active Directory Users and Computers** snap-in. Set the appropriate tabs by following the steps that follow. An explanation of each tab setting is provided in subsequent sections.

1. Select the **Start menu** → **Programs** → **Administrative Tools** → **Active Directory Users and Computers** snap-in.
2. Right-click the desired user → select **Properties**. Table 7.2 shows the tabs that are default to the basic Windows 2000 server installation (with Terminal Server).

User Account Properties General Tab

The **General** tab (Figure 7.13) contains the domain user's first and last name, description (usually a job title that will appear on the management console), office location, telephone number(s), e-mail address, and home page(s).

User Account Properties Address Tab

The **Address** tab (Figure 7.14) should contain a post office mailing address. This is helpful for mailing software upgrades, manuals, and other packages.

TABLE 7.2 User Account Properties Tabs

TABS	Description
Member Of	Groups user belongs to
Dial-in	Remote access and callback options
General	User's first name, last name, display name description, office location, telephone, e-mail, and web pages
Address	User's post office mailing address
Account	Logon name, domain, logon hours, logon to server name, account options, and account expiration date
Profile	User profile path, profile script, home directory path and server, shared document folder location.
Telephones/Notes	Home, pager, and mobile phone numbers and comments on where to contact user
Organization	Job title, company, department, manager, and people who report to user
Environment	Applications to run from Terminal server client
Sessions	Timeouts for Terminal Services
Remote Control	Permissions for monitoring Terminal Service sessions
Terminal Service Profile	Location for Terminal Service home directory

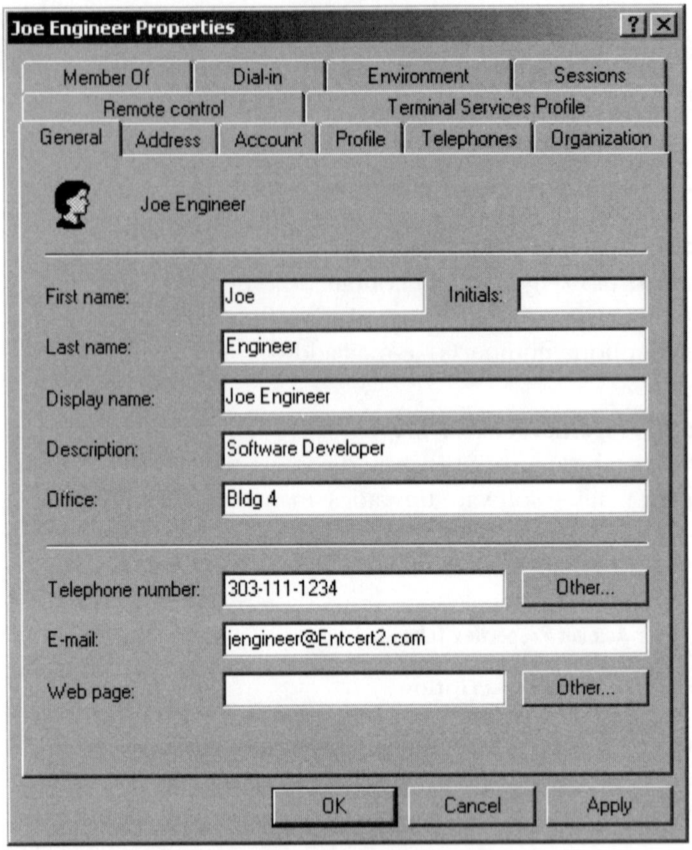

FIGURE 7.13 The User Properties General Tab

User Properties Account Tab

The **Account** tab (Figure 7.15) looks very similar to the screen used to create the domain user account. However, there are two new options here, shown in Table 7.3.

Pressing the **Logon Hours...** button displays the days and times of the week that the domain user is permitted to log on to the domain (Figure 7.16) (useful for preventing employees from logging on while backups are being performed). Current user sessions with backup targets must be terminated before backups begin to prevent sharing violations. Logon hour selections are made in two ways:

- Select day and hour region and select the **Logon Permitted** radio button to create a logon-permitted time zone.

- Select day and hour region and select the **Logon Denied** radio button to create a logon-denied time zone.

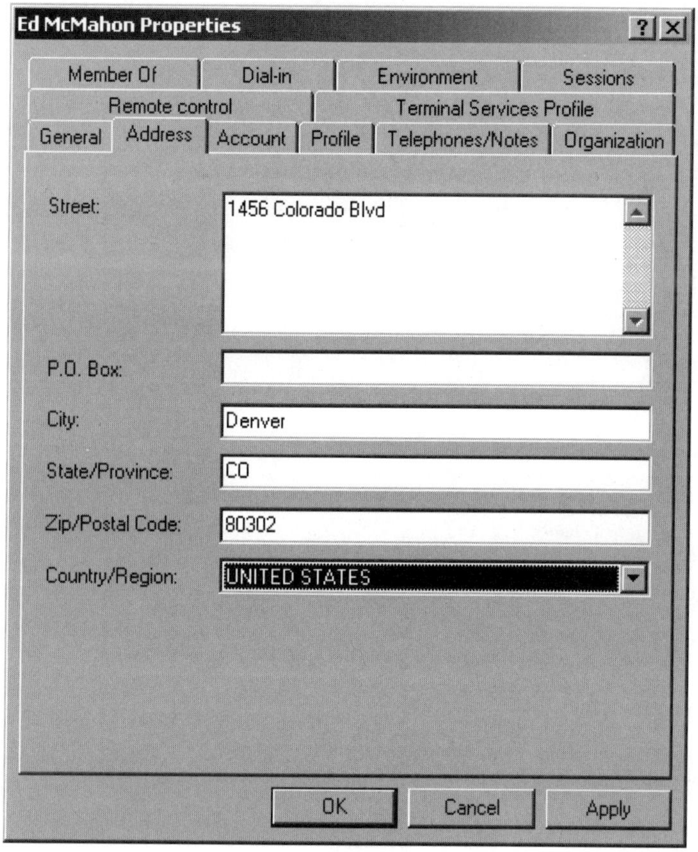

FIGURE 7.14 The User Properties Address Tab

NOTE   Changes to the user account will not affect a user who is currently logged on to the system. Nevertheless, the restrictions will apply during the next attempted connection.

Pressing the **Logon To...** button from the **Account** properties tab displays the **Logon Workstations** window (Figure 7.17). This facility allows the administrator to restrict the computers a user may log on to within the domain. The main issue here is that the computer name must be the NetBIOS name. Also, the NetBIOS protocol must be installed on all machines that use this account policy. Remember that a machine's NetBIOS name must be less then 16 characters in length.

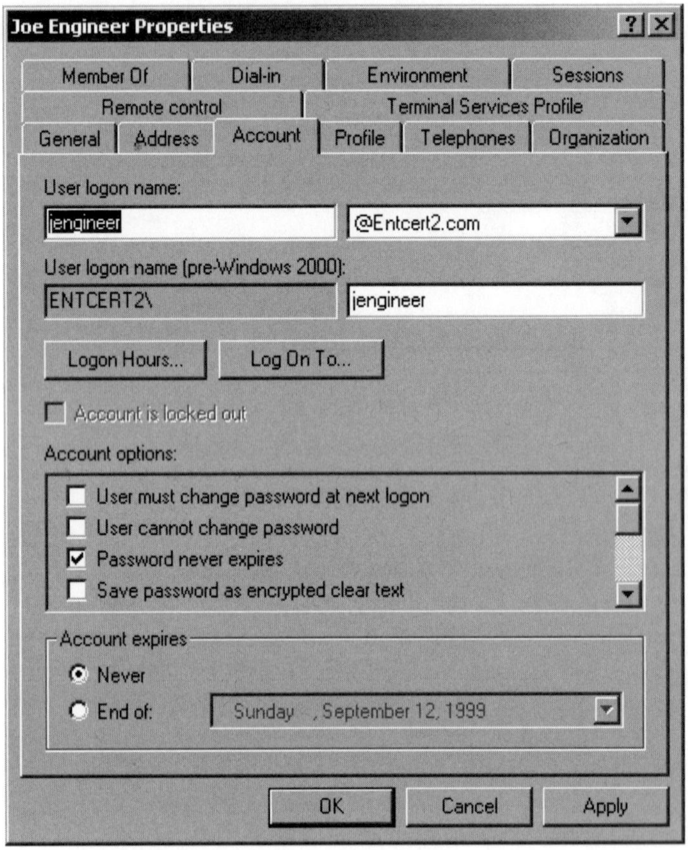

FIGURE 7.15 The User Properties Account Tab

TABLE 7.3 User Properties Account Tab Options

Definition	Description
Save password as encrypted clear text	Must be selected on Macintosh computers, which store passwords only in encrypted clear text.
Account expires	Takes precedence over the Password never expires selection. The Account disabled indicator is "checked" when an account expires. The Account expires date must be advanced to re-enable the user account.

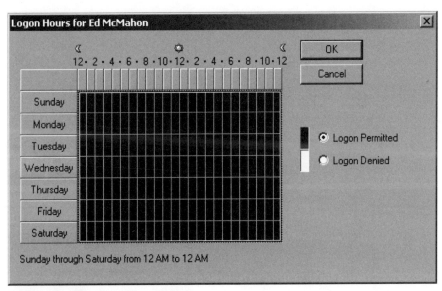

FIGURE 7.16 The Logon Hours Dialog

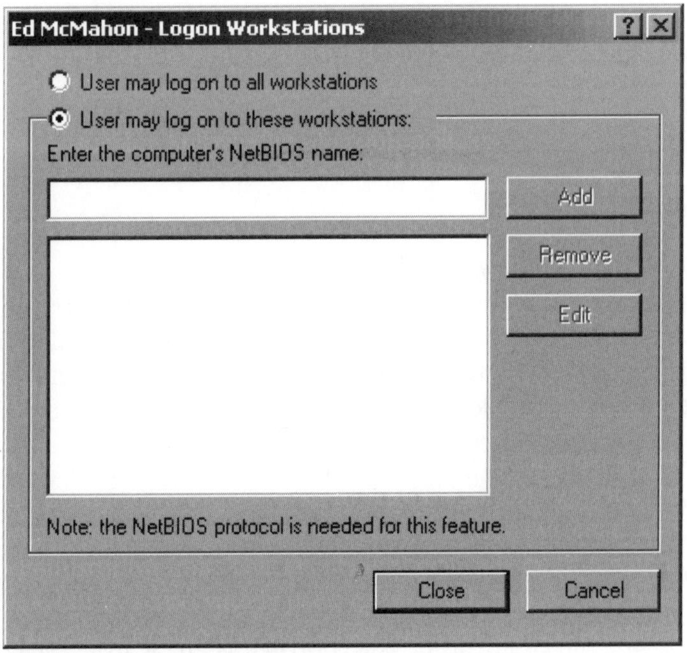

FIGURE 7.17 The Logon Workstations

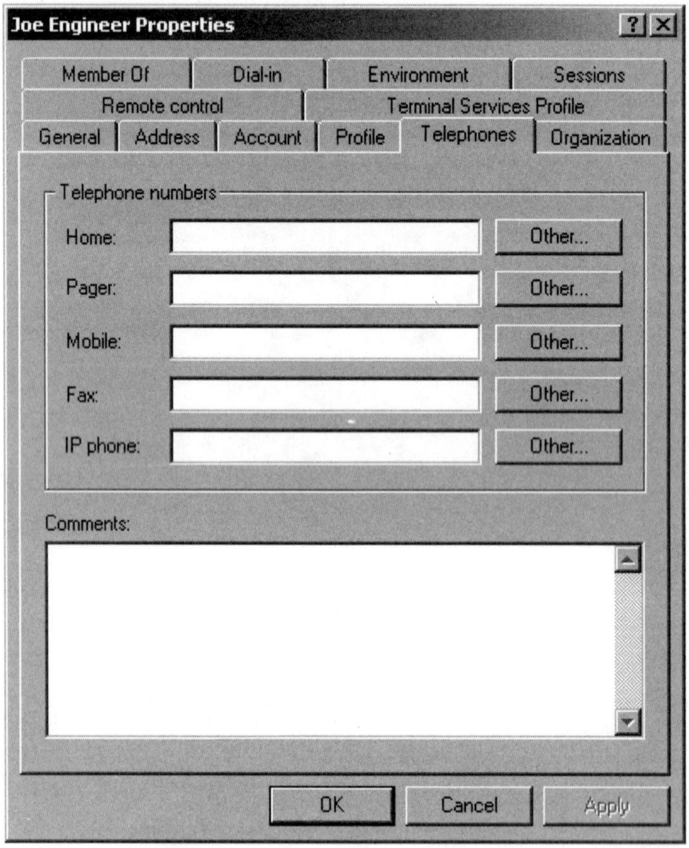

FIGURE 7.18 Telephones

User Account Properties Telephone Tab

The **Telephones** tab allows the storage of home, pager, mobile, fax, and IP phone numbers for quick reference (Figure 7.18). Entering information into this tab is optional. Pressing the **Other...** button allows alternative number entries. The **Comments** section provides room to track the user's schedule and availability at these numbers.

User Account Properties Member Of Tab

Member Of (Figure 7.19) is perhaps one of the most important user account properties tabs. Each domain user belongs by default to the domain users' group. To add the user to other security groups press the **Add...** button and choose a group from the directory. Group selection can be made from the current domain and trusted domains. As discussed in subsequent sections, the user inherits the appropriate permissions and rights associated with that group.

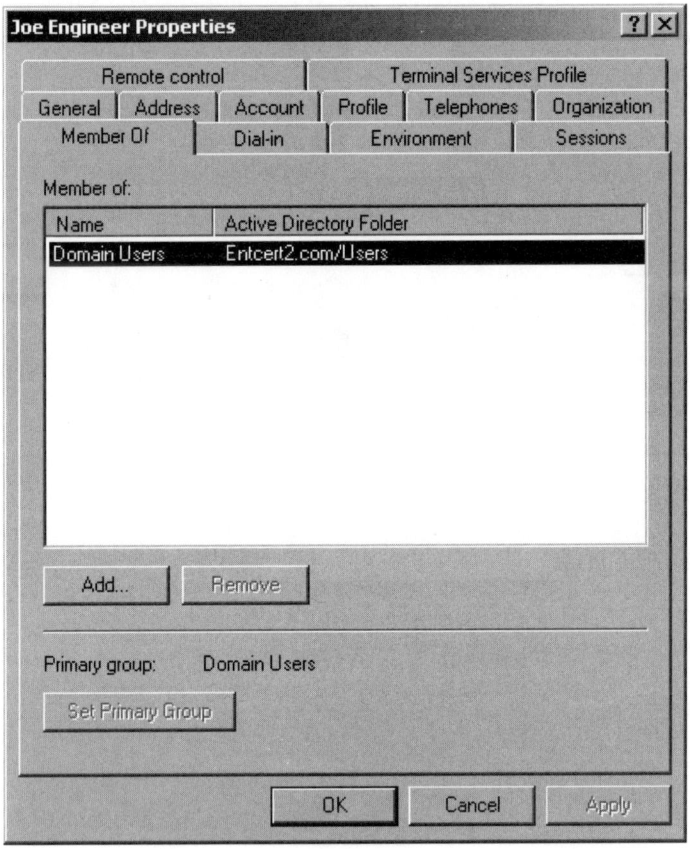

FIGURE 7.19 The Group Membership Tab

User Account Properties Dial-In Tab

A user can be granted access to the domain through a telephone dial-in or Virtual Private Network (VPN) connection only by selecting **Allow access** from the **Dial-in** tab (Figure 7.20). When the domain is switched to native mode the **Control Access through Remote Access Policy** option is displayed instead.

There are three options for the treatment of dial-in authority. The default is to permit no callbacks; the user can dial directly into the domain through a Remote Access Service (RAS) server to gain access to the network. The second option permits a defined callback; the user can specify a callback telephone number that RAS server will recognize in order to establish a remote session. This is good for traveling professionals and prevents large long-distance telephone bills. It also provides phone records of people who log in to the server. Finally, a single predefined number can be established for dial-in security. The RAS server will call back only

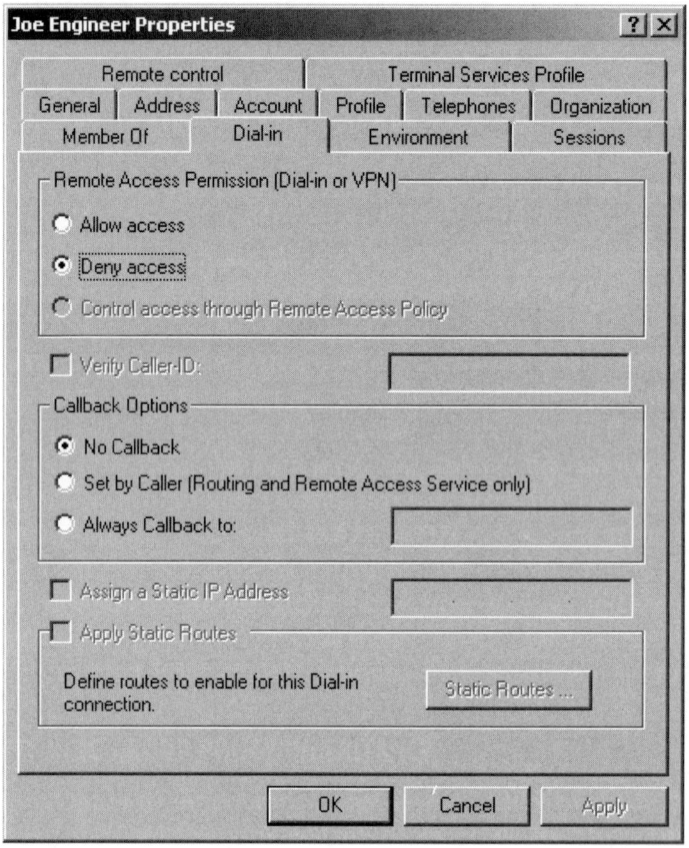

FIGURE 7.20 The Dial-in Tab

the number designated in the **Always Callback to:** field, so only someone at that telephone number can establish a RAS session.

User Profiles

A user's profile determines the desktop environment. This includes such items as the display type, applications available from the Start menu, shortcuts on the desktop, and desktop arrangement. Connections to remote computers are remembered and re-established from the last logon session. Profiles offer consistent desktop settings and document management regardless of which system the user logs on to in the domain.

USER PROFILE TYPES

Every user has a profile that defines how, when, and where a login is possible. The three types of user profile used with Windows 2000 are defined below:

- *Local user profiles* are maintained on each system the user logs on to in the user's profile directory. If the user logs on to another system in the domain, the local profile does not apply. The first time the user logs on to a system, a profile is created if one does not already exist. It is copied from the *\Document and Settings\Default User* profile. In other words, the *Default User* folder is a template for the creation of the new local user profile, which is created in the *Document and Settings\user id* directory (unless otherwise specified in the user account properties tab).

- *Roaming user profiles* allow domain users to move from system to system and maintain one profile. It is placed in a shared directory on a server in the domain, and whenever a user starts a session on a system within that domain, the profile is copied from the shared server folder to local disk space. All the documents and environmental settings for the roaming user are stored locally on the system, and, when the user logs off, all changes to the locally stored profile are copied back to the shared server folder. Therefore, the first time a roaming user logs on to a new system the logon process may take some time, depending on how large his profile folder is. A **My Documents** folder can be very large. However, the next time the user logs on to this particular system, the profile server will only update the local profile with files that have changed since the last session. If the current system a roaming user is attempting to log on to cannot establish a connection with the shared server folder, a new local profile is created based on the system's default profile. This new information is not copied back to the shared server profile folder.

- *Mandatory user profiles* are Read-Only and cannot be changed. Modifications made to the desktop are not saved to the user's profile once she logs out, so mandatory profiles are used when users must see the same desktop consistently. A user's profile is made mandatory by changing the file extension on the NTUSER.dat file to NTUSER.man.

User Profile Directory Structure

Regardless of whether the user's profile is roaming or local, there is a common folder structure for the profile directory. Table 7.4 describes the content and purpose of the standard Windows 2000 profile folders.

There are also some hidden profile directories (Figure 7.21 and Table 7.5) that can be viewed by selecting **Tools → Folder Options...** from Windows Explorer,

TABLE 7.4 Basic Contents of the Profile Directory

Sub-Profile Directory	Description
Cookies	Personalized data files stored on your system when visiting websites; must be disabled/enabled at the browser level.
Desktop	Shortcuts and files that comprise the user desktop.
Favorites	Files and folders used as Favorite pull-down options from My Computer, My Computer in Explore mode, and Internet Explorer.
My Documents	Default location for file storage of Microsoft Office products.
Start Menu	All applications the user will have access to from the Start menu.

clicking the **View** tab, and then selecting the **Show hidden files** radio button from the **View** tab advanced settings.

ALL USER AND INDIVIDUAL USER PROFILE SETTINGS

Besides understanding the contents of folders within a user's profile it is important to understand the *Document and Settings\All User* profiles. Two program groups are supported under Windows 2000 (Figure 7.22): common and personal.

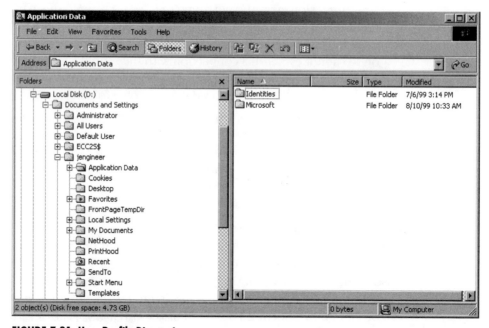

FIGURE 7.21 User Profile Directories

TABLE 7.5 Profile Files Hidden by Default

File	Description
Application Data	Application-specific data such as preferences and licensing.
Local Settings	Contains a history for all websites visited through the browser and all documents, applications, and Help pages accessed from My Computer, classified into today's, yesterday's, last week's, and two weeks' ago timeframes. Application data is also stored here, such as Outlook Express Inbox.
NetHood	Domains and file structures accessed from My Network Places. This is the system's current network neighborhood.
PrintHood	Printer data information and shortcuts.
Recent	Recently accessed files and folders.
SendTo	Shortcuts to common file storage areas.
Templates	Templates for Office applications.

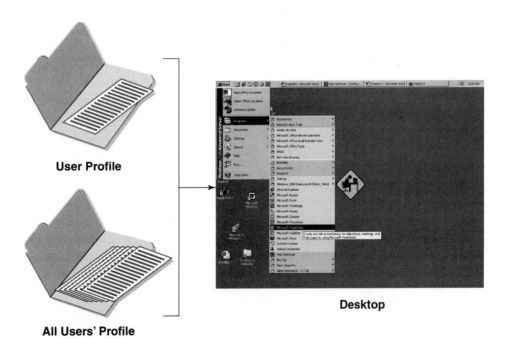

User Profile

All Users' Profile

Desktop

FIGURE 7.22 Combining All Users' and User Profiles—The Effective Profile Is the Individual User's Profile Combined with the "All Users' Profile"

Common program groups are applied to all users who log on to a system. Their profile is located in the *Document and Settings**All User* folder and includes a subset of the folder structure previously discussed. For instance, the *start menu* folder in the *Document and Settings**All User* directory dictates program availability from the **Start Menu** for all users who log in to the system. Each user's personal profile, locally located in *Document and Settings**Username*, is then overlaid on this common profile to provide additional Start menu application access and custom desktop setups. The user's personal profile, the same discussed in Table 7.5, can be either locally stored on each system in the domain or defined as roaming.

NOTE   The *Document and Settings**All Users* folder contains profile information that applies to all users. Say you wanted to restrict access to Microsoft Excel from the **Start menu**. The \\Document and Settings\\All Users\\Start Menu\\Program folder would contain the Microsoft Excel shortcut if installed for general access. Removing the shortcut from the *All Users* folder and placing it in select personal user profiles would restrict which users could view it from the **Start → Program** menu. Of course, the Microsoft Excel executable should be restricted only to users intended to run the application. Distributing applications to specific users could also be handled using the **assign** and **publish** group policies, to be discussed in the Group Policy section in Chapter 8.

CREATING USER PROFILES

Now that you have some background on it, we can apply the user profile to individual user accounts. The **Profile** tab (Figure 7.23) displays several fields in relation to a user's profile:

- *The profile path* dictates where a user's profile will be stored. If no directory is entered, the default location is *Documents and Settings**username*.
- *The login script* contains the path to an optional executable or batch file. Users logging in to Windows 2000 systems may take advantage of Jscript (*.JS) and Visual Basic Scripting (*.VBS) in addition to the traditional MS-DOS command scripts (*.BAT, *.COM, *.EXE). Stick with the MS-DOS scripts for down-level operating systems that may not support the Windows Scripting Host (WSH).

The home directory is specified on the local machine in the form *Drive label:\\directory path* or targeted on a shared folder accessible through the network. The network connection requires a network drive letter (available from the pull-down menu) which identifies how the remote connection will be referenced

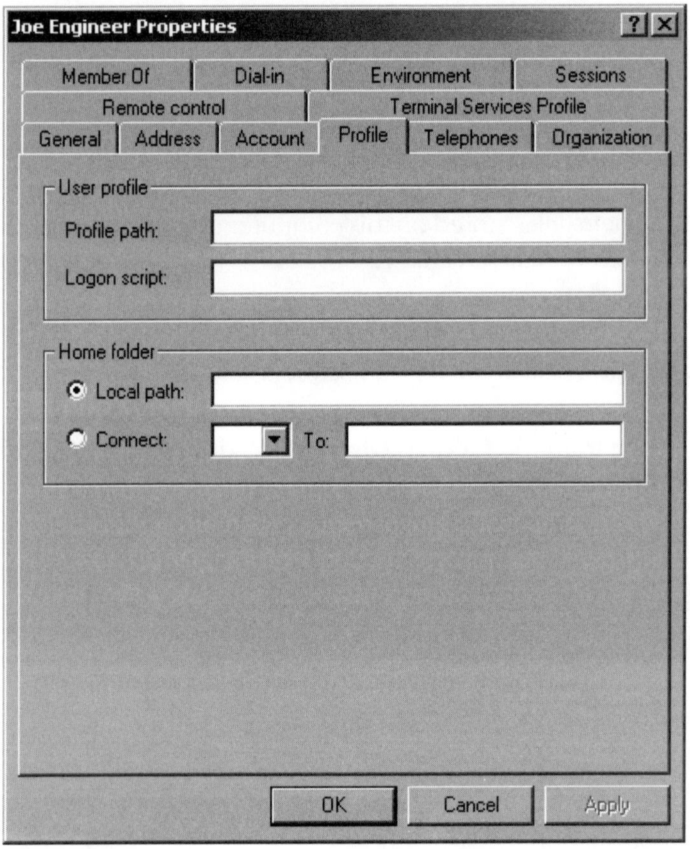

FIGURE 7.23 Profile

from the local machine; a machine name; and a directory path. The **To:** field should be in the form *system name\directory path*. The remote directory will be displayed from **My Computer** and will be the default directory within the Command Prompt. This is a good way to centralize your documents on a networked server for backup convenience and version control.

NOTE   The Command Prompt defaults to the home directory. However, if most administrative shell scripts, for example, are located in a directory called d:\scripts, you may want to make that directory your default instead. The home directory is also the default file storage directory for some applications such as Notepad. These applications will default to the home directory if there are other files that match the application's type already in existence there. Most Microsoft Office applications, however, default to the **My Documents** directory and ignore the home directory setting.

Local User Profile Setup Example

The following example illustrates how a user profile can be set up. Create a new user account with the user ID *luser*.

1. View existing user profiles by clicking **Start** → **Settings** → **Control Panel**. Double-click the **System** icon. Click the **User Profiles** tab (Figure 7.24).

2. Notice that profiles stored on this computer do not list a user profile for *luser*, since it has not been created yet.

3. Log off your system and log back on under the new account, *luser*. The profile for *luser* has now been created by copying *Document and Settings*\ *Default User* to *Document and Settings**luser*.

4. Right-click the desktop and select **Properties**. Choose a new background and select **Tile** from the **Picture Display** pull-down menu. Log off and log back on as Administrator.

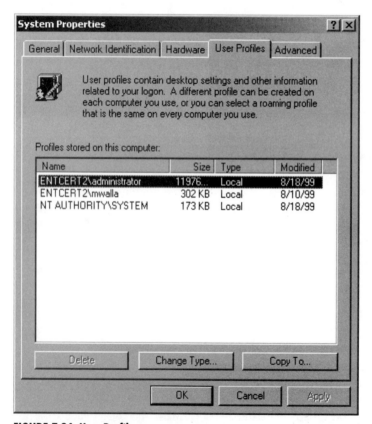

FIGURE 7.24 User Profiles

5. Repeat step 2 and view the current user profiles. The account *luser* should now exist as a local profile.

6. Log off and log back on as *luser*. Notice that the user's screen background is preserved.

Roaming User Profile Setup Example

The roaming user profile is set up by the steps described below:

1. Log in as Administrator and run **mmc** from the **Command Prompt**. Add the **Active Directory Users and Computers** snap-in and create a new domain user account named *ruser*.

2. Create a new share with **Full Control** permissions to the *Everyone* group on a network server called *profiles*. This will later be referenced as *server-name*\ *profiles*.

3. From the **Active Directory Users and Computers** snap-in for the domain, right-click *ruser* and select **Properties**. Select the **Profile** tab and enter the roaming user folder in the **Profile path:** entry (Figure 7.25). Use the form *servername*\ *profiles**ruser* to ensure that the correct network server path is accessed.

NOTE   When setting up a roaming user profile it is extremely important to follow these steps precisely. Any deviance will cause permission problems.

---

4. Before we log in to the new account, a profile must be copied to the roaming profiles directory (*servername*\ *profiles**ruser*) so that the roaming profile folder is used and a local one is not created. Open the **Control Panel** and double-click the **Systems** icon. Select the **User Profiles** tab.

5. Select the *luser* account created earlier and press the **Copy To...** button.

6. Enter the roaming profile folder directory in the form *servername*\ *profiles**ruser* (Figure 7.26).

7. Press the **Change...** button under the **Permitted to use** area.

8. Press the **Show Users** button and select *ruser* from the list (Figure 7.27).

9. Press the **Add** button to create the new directory *servername*\ *profiles*\ *ruser*, copy the *luser* profile to the new location, and permit the new remote user, *ruser*, to access to the directory and child directories. Press the **OK** button.

10. Press the **OK** button on the **Copy To** dialog box.

11. Press **OK** on the **Systems Properties** dialog box.

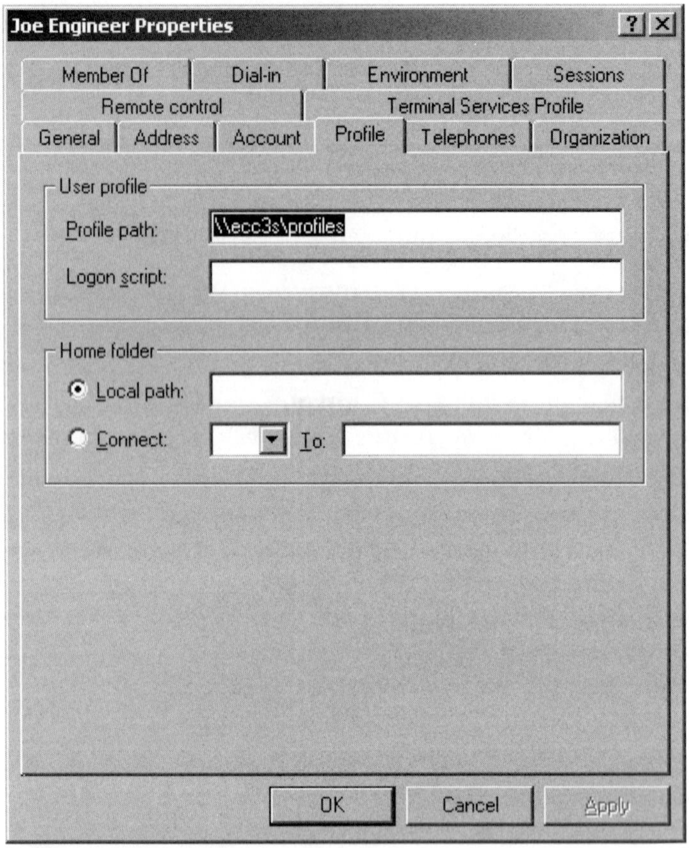

FIGURE 7.25 Roaming Profile Path

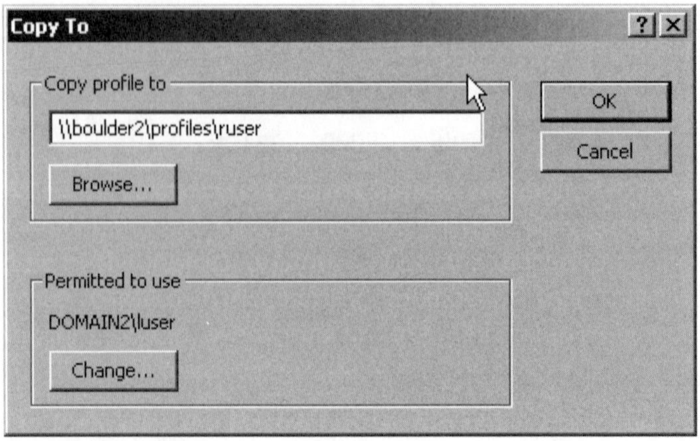

FIGURE 7.26 Copy To

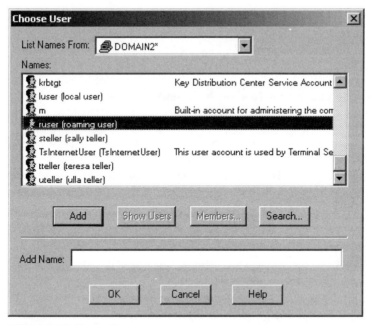

FIGURE 7.27 Choose User

12. Close all applications and log off.

13. Log in as *ruser*. Notice that the desktop environment is initially the same as *luser*. New changes to the *ruser* environment will be saved on the shared server/profiles directory. Try logging in from another domain member server. The *ruser*'s profile should follow the user throughout the domain.

GROUPS

A group is a collection of users, computers, and other entities. It can be a Windows 2000 built-in group or one created by the system administrator to conform to specific required attributes. Windows 2000 employs standard groups to reflect most common attributes and tasks. These are *built in* to the operating system with the idea that common tasks can be assigned to specific users. For instance, members of the Backup group will have access to tape drives, backup applications, and server folders requiring backup.

Groups enforce security permissions or carry out distribution functions. They perform three main tasks:

1. Security groups primarily assign limited permissions to groups that need access to certain folders, applications, and computers.

2. Security groups also filter out the effect of group policies assigned to their members through a Group Policy Object (GPO). (See Chapter 9, Group Policies.)

3. Distribution groups are used for e-mail and contact information.

Group-to-Group and Group-to-User Relationships

Rights and privileges are assigned at the group level. They represent an accumulation of the rights and privileges of all of the groups to which a user belongs. Typically a user belongs to more than one group and therefore is granted or denied rights on that basis. To complicate this relationship, groups can be nested, overlapped, or completely independent. Say, for example, that three groups exist for an organizational unit, and that *Group 3* members have been nested as automatic members of *Group 1*, while *Group 2* is independent. Thus, *User 1* has been assigned to *Group 1* and *Group 2*. Since *Group 3* is also a member of *Group 1*, *User 2* inherits any rights of *Group 1*. On the other hand, *User 2* is assigned to *Group 2* and *Group 3*. The relationship between *Groups 1* and *3* flows only one way. Therefore, *User 1* does not become a member of *Group 3* and so does not inherit any of that group's rights (Figure 7.28).

Let's take a look at the relationship from a slightly different perspective. A single user, computer, or group can belong to many groups. As shown in Figure 7.29, *User 4* belongs to both *Group 2* and *Group 3*. As *Group 1* is a member of *Group 2*, *User 2* and *User 5* have all rights associated with *Groups 1* and *2*. However, *User 3*, *User 4*, and *Computer 2* do not receive *Group 1* access rights.

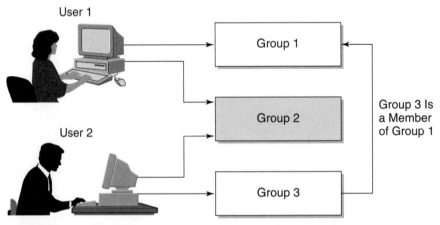

FIGURE 7.28 Relationship of Groups and Users—*User 2* Becomes a Member of the Group via Inheritance

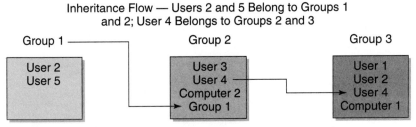

FIGURE 7.29 An Alternate View of Group Relationships

A user's rights and privileges are cumulative. If a user is a member of two groups, one having Read and Write privileges and the other having Modify privileges, then the user has Read/Write/Modify rights on an object. By the same token, if any of the groups are denied rights to that object, the user will inherit that denial. The **Deny** access permission has priority over **Allow** access permissions. Any member of a group that has been denied permission to an object may not reinstate or counteract rights with membership to another group. (For greater detail, see Chapter 9, Permissions Security, Folder Sharing and Dfs.)

NOTE   It is good practice to keep group nesting to a minimum. The reason is visibility—a complicated group membership and permission structure makes it difficult to determine a user's rights. The **Deny** access permission should also be used sparingly. Overriding permissions that another group has already established complicates the user's privilege level.

Group Scope

Proper planning of group structure affects maintainability in the future, especially in an enterprise environment where multiple domains are involved. Windows 2000 groups are classified into one of three group scopes. Each deserves careful examination. Group membership is predicated on a group's intended scope. Underscoring this entire discussion is the assumption that trust relationships exist between domains and the fact that access is determined by the ACL of the network resource. The three group scopes follow:

- *Domain local groups*—assign access permissions to global domain groups for local domain resources.

- *Global domain groups*—provide access to resources in other trusted domains.
- *Universal groups*—grant access to resources in all trusted domains.

NOTE   Participating domain member servers can view all directory groups. However, group scope is not visible from them. Determining whether a security group is domain local or global domain must be done at a domain controller. It can be made easier by choosing a group name that identifies the group's scope. Instead of calling a group **Engineering**, call it **Global Engineering** or **Local Engineering**. This may, however, prove potentially troublesome to users.

DOMAIN LOCAL GROUPS

Members of domain local groups can be from any domain, although group permissions are assigned only to resources in the local domain. These groups may contain users, computers, or groups from any domain in the enterprise (Figure 7.30), and they also may contain individual users from their own domain.

The domain local group may be assigned permissions to any object within its domain. For example, the *Printer Group* is the domain local group within *Domain C* and is assigned access rights to a printer within that domain only. The *Printer Group* may not be assigned permissions to objects outside of its own domain. When implementing domain local groups some additional guidelines should be followed. First, let's examine the global group definition.

NOTE   Although individual users may be assigned permissions to resources, this is not recommended. See the following sections for correct local domain usage.

GLOBAL GROUPS

Global domain group members may come only from the local domain, but they can be assigned permissions to resources in any trusted domain. They may also join any group within a trusted domain (Figure 7.31). For example, *User 1* and *Group 1,* created in *Domain A,* are members of the global *Accountants* group, which is then assigned membership to *Group 2* as well as permissions to a printer in *Domain C* and to a printer in its own *Domain A*. Again, this only

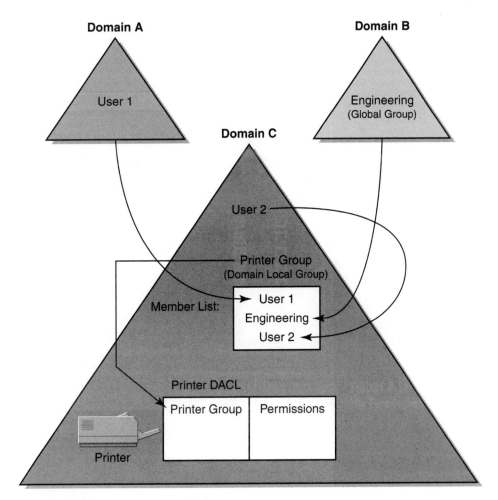

FIGURE 7.30 Domain Local Group Definition

demonstrates global group capabilities and does not reflect how they should be implemented.

NOTE   Although the Accountants' global domain group may be assigned permissions to resources, this is not recommended. See the following sections for correct global domain group usage.

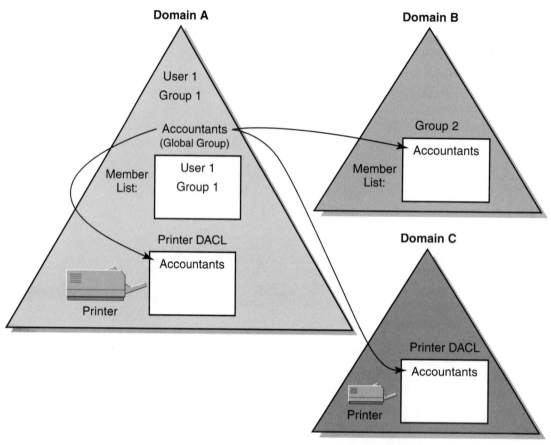

FIGURE 7.31 Global Group Definition

UNIVERSAL GROUPS

Universal group members are from any domain and may be assigned permissions to any resource in any trusted domain. The universal group has no restrictions on its member list and can be assigned to any object throughout the enterprise.

NOTE Universal groups are allowed only in native mode Windows 2000 environments. Native mode requires that all domain controllers are promoted to Windows 2000 Active Directory.

Group Types

In addition to proper group scope, the group type must be determined. The two group types are

- **Security.** These groups may be assigned to Discretionary Access Control Lists (DACLs) with associated permissions. They may also be used for e-mail distribution.
- **Distribution.** These groups cannot be assigned permissions through DACLs. They are intended only for e-mail distribution.

Since both **security** and **distribution** groups can be used for e-mail distribution, why do distribution groups exist? Optimization. When a user logs on to the domain, a security token is created consisting of the user's account security identifier (SID) and his group SIDs. This adds time to the user logon process. Additionally, the security token is presented to any system a user accesses throughout the enterprise, and if it is large, it creates more network traffic. **Distribution** groups do not participate with security credentials and are not included in the user's security token. Adding a user to multiple distribution groups will not increase the user's security token size.

Security groups may be converted to distribution groups and vice versa as long as the domain is operating in native mode. A mixed mode environment does not support such conversions.

Using Groups

There is no such thing as a perfect world when defining groups in a heterogeneous computing environment. Windows 2000 supports several group scopes, and the system administrator must understand how to use them.

The Windows 2000 group scopes may seem confusing at first. Group management might be less complex if universal groups could always be implemented. However, universal scope has some practical drawbacks, chiefly that it only works in native mode. Most enterprise networks require down-level compatibility. Because of the heterogeneity of a mixed Windows 2000 and Windows NT environment, the administrator must deal with global and domain local groups. Another consideration is that universal groups tax the network by passing group membership information between trusted domains and forests.

The Global Catalog stores domain local and global domain group names, and replicates changes made to group names to all Global Catalog servers. It maintains universal group membership on all Global Catalog servers as well. Whenever a member is added or removed from a universal group, the change is replicated throughout the trusted domain structure.

The recommended implementation for global and domain local groups involves further restrictions on group use. In general, object permissions should be assigned to domain local groups, whereas users and computer accounts should be placed in global groups. The global groups are then nested within domain local groups to gain access to network resources. To illustrate, we will look in depth at group implementation using default Windows 2000 groups.

DEFAULT USER ACCOUNT MEMBERSHIP

Consider the case of a user named *Joe Engineer* with a logon name of *jengineer*. Joe's user account is created in a Windows 2000 domain and added to the global group **Domain Users** by default (Figure 7.32). The **Domain Users** group is a member of the domain local group **Users**, and the **Users** group is used to assign permissions to local objects within a system or domain.

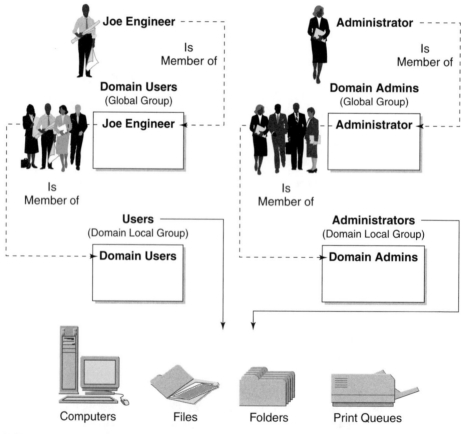

FIGURE 7.32 A Domain Membership Example

The **Administrator** account behaves in a similar fashion. The **Administrator** is a member of the **Domain Admins** global group by default. The **Domain Admins** group is a member of the domain local group **Administrators**, and the **Administrators** group is included in ACLs for objects throughout the system.

It is important to remember that these are default conditions and can be modified with the necessary authority. Newly created security groups should be implemented in the same way.

Built-In Local Groups

The **Built-in** folder contains predefined groups that reflect commonly employed functions. Figure 7.33 lists default domain local groups from the perspective of the **Active Directory Users and Computers** administration snap-in tool. Although the membership and permissions associated with these groups (Table 7.6) may be modified, they may not be deleted or removed from the system.

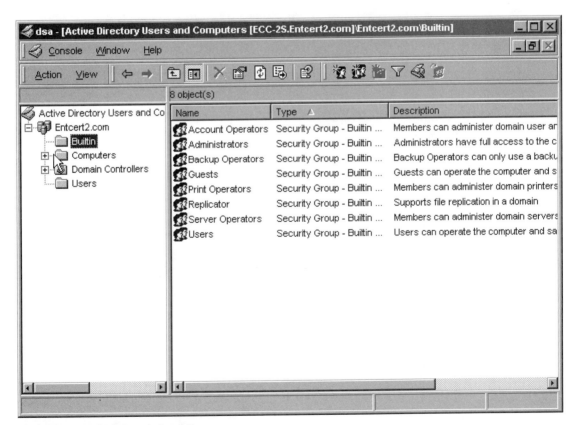

FIGURE 7.33 Default Domain Local Groups

TABLE 7.6 Domain Local Group Members

Group	Permissions/Access Level
Administrators	Default members include the Domain Admins, Enterprise Admins, and Administrator accounts; full control over the local computer system with all rights and capabilities.
Account Operators	Administrate Domain Users.
Backup Operators	Backup and restore Files on the local system regardless of permissions; also log on and shut down on the system. Group policies can restrict these permissions.
Guests	Limited logon/shutdown on the local system
Print Operators	Administrate the local printers.
Replicator	Allows Active Directory replication functions. Only persons supporting Replicator services should have membership.
Server Operators	Administrate the local system.
Users	Domain Users are members by default. Application execution, printer access, logon/shutdown/locking, and local group creation and modification.

Common Global Groups

The **Users** folder (Figure 7.34) contains the default global domain groups (Table 7.7), which grant domain-wide privileges through domain local group memberships. Default domain local group membership grants global domain groups sweeping access rights throughout the network.

ASSIGNING GROUPS

Three group scopes imply three implementation strategies. Thus, a system administrator must decide what type of group is required for a situation. Think about the resources the group needs to access. If you are assigning permission, a domain local group should be used. Users inside and outside your domain should be grouped together in global groups and added to domain local groups to provide access within your local domain.

Another way to choose a group type is to ask two questions:

- Is the purpose of the group to collect resources for user access?
- Is the purpose of the group to collect users for resource access?

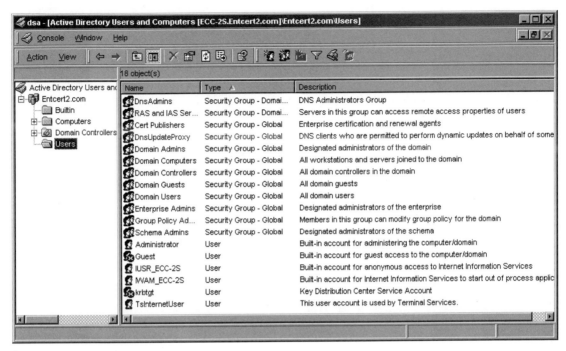

FIGURE 7.34 Global Groups

TABLE 7.7 Global Group Members

Group	Permissions/Access Level
Cert Publishers	Certificate Authorities for the domain
Domain Admins	Sweeping administrative privileges on all systems throughout the domain
Domain Computers	All domain computers
Domain Controllers	All domain controllers
Domain Guests	Membership to the Guests domain local group
Domain Users	Membership to the Users domain local group
Enterprise Admins	Membership to the Administrators domain local group
Group Policy Creators Owners	Members allowed to modify group policy
Schema Admins	Members permitted to modify the Active Directory schema

When collecting resources for user access, assign the same domain local group to each resource. Permissions are then assigned to an object by adding the domain local group to the object's ACL. When collecting users for resource access, put the common users in a global group, which is then given membership to the domain local group with access permissions. As a general rule, only add permissions to domain local groups or universal groups. This can best be illustrated by the following example.

GROUP SCOPE AND MEMBERSHIP EXAMPLE

A company maintaining two domains (Figure 7.35) called *Entcert1.com* and *Entcert2.com* is trying to permit engineers from both domains to access some folders and software configuration applications, all of which reside in the *Entcert2.com* domain. (This example assumes that a trust relationship exists between the two forests permitting *Entcert1.com* access to resources in *Entcert2.com*. If you only have one domain, simply drop the *Entcert1.com* domain and *Entcert1 Engineers* group from the example.) Two global groups must first be created to manage users in *Entcert1.com* and *Entcert2.com*. Membership in these groups should be based on common resource needs.

Create Global Groups
To create the two global groups, take the following steps:

1. Open the **Active Directory Users and Computers** snap-in.
2. Right-click the target domain node or, in this example, *Entcert2.com*. Select the **New → Group** option. (You can also select the target domain and press the **New Group** button instead.)
3. Enter a name for the new group—in this example, *Entcert2 Engineers* (Figure 7.36).
   - Set the **Group scope:** to **Global**.
   - Set the **Group type:** to **Security**.
   - Press the **OK** button.
4. The **Entcert2 Engineers Properties** window appears (Figure 7.37). Press the **Add...** button.
5. Select a user and press the **Add** button to include her in the new group (Figure 7.38). Put all engineers who need access to the same resource in the same group.
6. Create a new global group for engineers in the *Entcert1.com* domain, following the same procedure, and call it *Entcert1 Engineers*. (This is optional.)

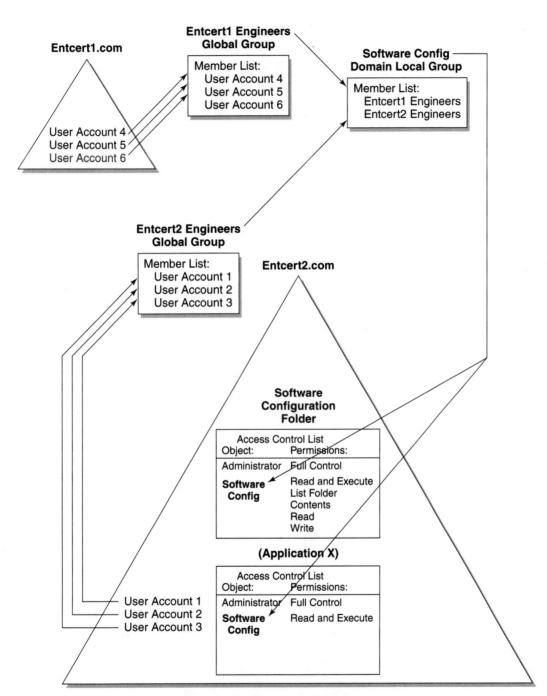

FIGURE 7.35 A Domain Local and Global Domain Group Usage Example

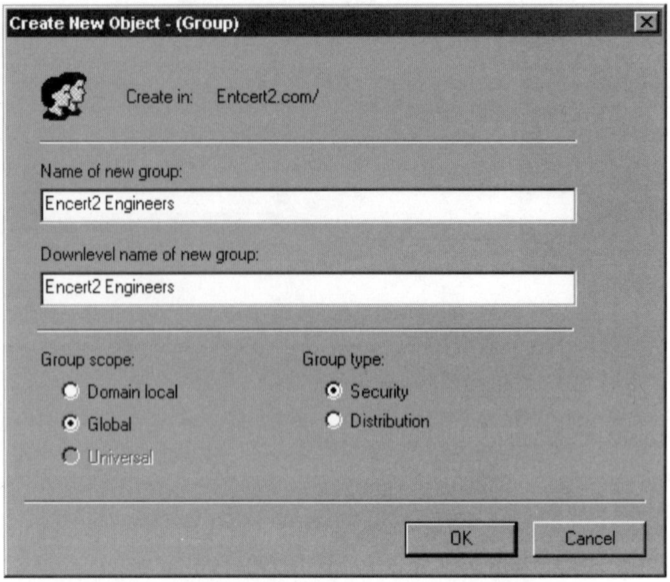

FIGURE 7.36 Creating a New Group

FIGURE 7.37 Group Membership in Entcert2

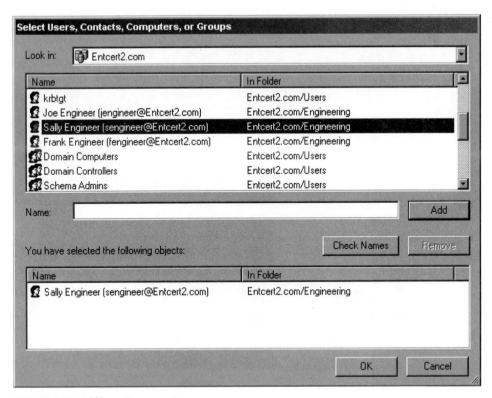

FIGURE 7.38 Adding a User to a Group

Two global groups have now been created. They can be used to assign administrative responsibilities, resource allocation, or resource denial.

Create New Domain Local Group

The *Software Config* domain local group will now be created and given permission to access the *Software Configuration* folder and a file, *Application X*.

1. From the **Active Directory Users and Computers** tool right-click your domain node or, in this example, *Entcert2.com*. Select the **New → Group** option. (You can also select the domain node (*Entcert2*) and press the **New Group** button instead.)

2. Enter the name *Software Config* for the group and select **Domain local** for the **Group scope:** field and **Security** for the **Group type:** field (Figure 7.39).

3. Double-click on the new group from the **Active Directory Users and Computers** snap-in and select the **Members** tab. Press the **Add...** button. The **Select Users, Computers, or Groups** dialog box appears (Figure 7.40).

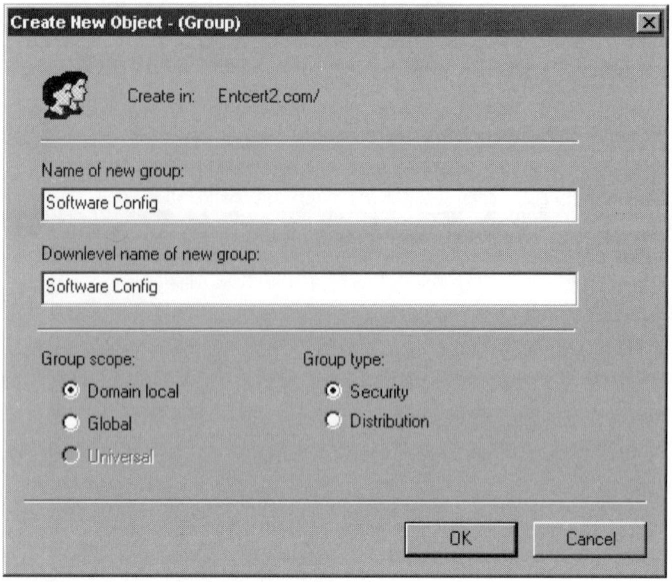

FIGURE 7.39 Creating a New Group

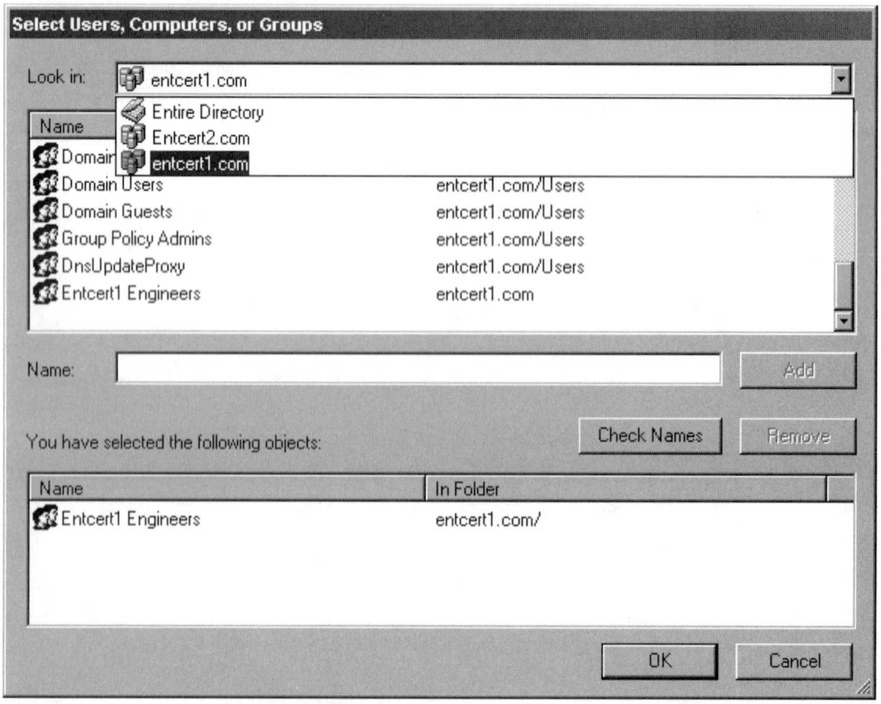

FIGURE 7.40 Selecting Security Groups from a Domain

4. Choose the **Entcert2 Engineers** group from the available domain groups and users. Press the **Add<...>** button.

5. From the **Look in:** pull-down box select the trusted *Encert1.com* domain.

6. Select the **Entcert1 Engineers** group and press the **Add<...>** button.

You have successfully added two global groups to a domain local group. The member list for the domain local group *Software Config* should look like the one shown in Figure 7.41.

Assign Permissions to Domain Local Group

To create folders on your server to simulate the folders and applications to which engineers from *Entcert1.com* and *Entcert2.com* require access, use the procedure that follows:

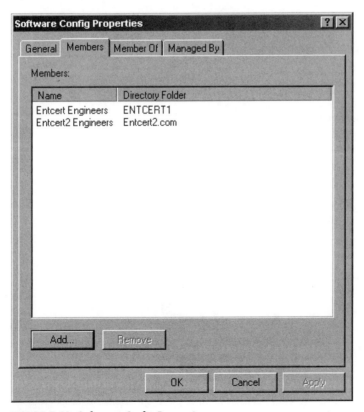

FIGURE 7.41 Software Config Properties

1. Right-click **My Computer** and select **Explorer**. On an NTFS volume create a folder called *Software Configuration* by selecting **File → New → Folder**.

2. Right-click properties on the **Software Configuration** folder. Select the **Sharing** tab and click the **Share this folder** radio button.

3. Press the **Security** tab and press the **Add...** button. Choose the **Software Config** group and press the **Add<...>** button.

4. Modify the **Permissions:** to allow and deny the appropriate permissions. In Figure 7.42, the engineers have been granted **Full Control**. The **Everyone** group has been removed from the ACL for the *Software Configuration* folder and replaced with the **Administrators** group.

5. The *Software Config* group could also be added to an application object and permissions could be set to allow **Read & Execute** privileges for the **Engineers** group.

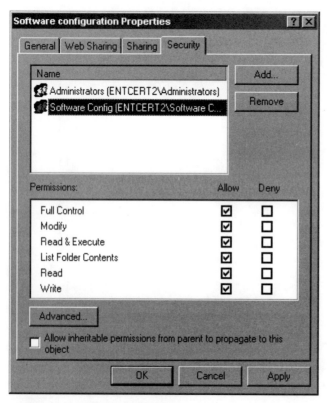

FIGURE 7.42 Software Config Security

POSTSCRIPT

This chapter addressed some of the basic issues and considerations in dealing with user accounts and Windows 2000 groups. Proper planning of domain user accounts and profiles can lead to effective centralized management and a familiar desktop for the user. The complexities involved with domain local and global domain security groups were also presented. Correctly implementing security groups can lead to a maintainable access control design that will grow and change with your network.

Chapter 8

Group Policies

Windows 2000 offers extensive control over system configuration and user environments through group policies. These policies may be applied to domain, site, and organizational unit (OU) Active Directory containers, giving the administrator more granular control over system configurations and user settings.

This chapter is divided into three main sections. The first reviews the concept of group policies; the second provides a number of implementation examples; and the third explores the underlying concepts of Microsoft's IntelliMirror. Upon completing this chapter, you should have

- A working knowledge of group policies
- The ability to establish and modify group policy properties
- The ability to apply group policies to user accounts
- An understanding of IntelliMirror technology and the ability to employ it effectively

UNDERSTANDING GROUP POLICIES

Since group policies are designed to apply to a great number of users, they have the potential to reduce system administration support. Once a group policy setting is established on a user account, it is then automatically applied to the desired administrative unit. This facility is specifically helpful when applying security policies, but it is also widely used to establish consistency in user environments. For example, through the use of group policies, an administrator can control the options available on users' desktops and the delivery of applications.

Group policies also implement the bulk of the Microsoft IntelliMirror technology. This strategy capitalizes on the centralized management of client/server systems while maintaining the flexibility and convenience of the distributed computing model. For example, users can log on from anywhere in the network and preserve user profiles, application data, security requirements, application access, and backup offline files. Microsoft's IntelliMirror, as discussed later in this chapter, provides more examples and details for this technology.

Group policies can be extended by third-party application vendors as well to manage desktop setting requirements for their applications.

NOTE   A user planning to modify group policies must have administrative privileges for the Active Directory and associated containers.

Group Policy Management and the Active Directory

Group Policy management is accomplished by assigning Group Policy Objects (GPOs) to specific machines, sites, domains, and OUs from the Active Directory. Applying GPOs involves determining which users and computers require policy settings so that selected Active Directory containers can group target users and computers accordingly. GPOs are then applied to the desired Active Directory containers and are inherited by child containers. Windows 2000 follows the LSDOU model in which inheritance flows in the order **Local Computer (L)** → **Site (S)** → **Domain (D)** → **Organizational Unit (OU)**.

The LSDOU inheritance model may seem unnatural at first (Figure 8.1). Local computer GPOs are the first applied to any user logging on to that particular system. They can be overridden by the GPOs assigned to the user's site, which are overridden by domain GPOs, which are overridden by relevant OU GPOs. This order gives the local administrator the first chance to set the computer's policies.

When GPO policies are enforced, any child GPO settings applied to a system are disabled. The local computer GPOs may not enforce policies. They are the first to be set, but may be nullified by further policy inheritance.

NOTE   The exception to the LSDOU model comes into play when using Windows NT 4.0 policies that are set with the Policy System Editor. These are applied before the Local GPO. In other words, if the NTConfig.pol file exists, it will be used to apply policies first. These policies may be overwritten by GPOs applied to the domain, site, and OU containers.

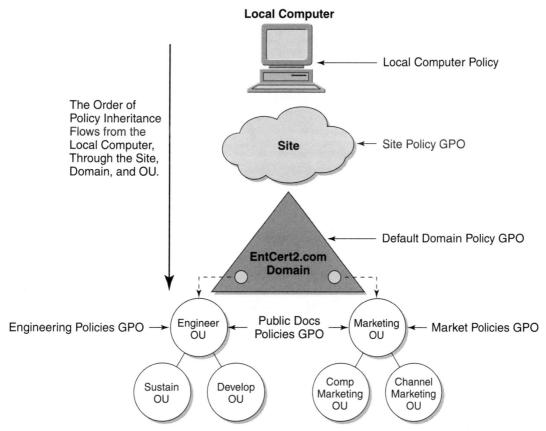

FIGURE 8.1 The Order of Policy Inheritance

The LSDOU model provides a reference point for determining the users and computers a GPO affects. A GPO can be applied to any of three container types: site, domain, and OU. In Figure 8.1, the *Default Domain Policy GPO* has been assigned to the *Entcert2.com* domain, so the users and computers in that domain as well as all OUs within it will receive these policy settings. The same GPO may also be applied to more than one Active Directory container. In the figure the *Public Docs Policies GPO* is applied to both the *Engineering OU* and the *Marketing OU*. This is referred to as linking.

GROUP POLICY OBJECT STORAGE

Before introducing the group policy feature set it is important to understand, on the local and domain level, group policy storage. Local computer policies are stored on the local system in the *%SystemRoot%System32\GroupPolicy* directory.

They are not replicated to other systems, nor do they cover the complete range of policies accessible to enterprise-wide GPOs applied to Active Directory containers.

Active Directory GPO storage is a little more complicated. These policies are stored in the **Group Policy Container** (GPC) and the **Group Policy Template** (GPT). The Group Policy Container includes version, status, and extensions for the GPO. As discussed earlier, it may be a site, domain, or OU Active Directory object, and is synchronized with other domain controllers on its own update schedule. Small amounts of information that are modified infrequently are stored in the GPC, which is assigned a *globally unique identifier (GUID),* such as {31B2F340-016D-11D2-945F-00C04FB984F9}, corresponding to a GPT. Data stored in the GPC is used to determine whether the GPO is enabled and to ensure that the correct GPT version is applied to user and computer accounts within the container.

The GPT is stored on domain controllers in the *%SystemRoot%\SYSVOL\ sysvol\domainname\Policies\GUID* folder for domain-wide replication and access. Standard folders in this directory are **Adm**, **USER**, and **MACHINE**. All user and computer policy settings for the GPO are stored in the GPT and synchronized on a different schedule from that of its sister GPC information. The GPT contains the raw policy settings, including security settings and software installation information. It can be thought of as the folder structure visible when modifying a group policy object from an MMC snap-in, such as is shown later in Figure 8.6.

REFINING GROUP POLICY INHERITANCE

In addition to inheritance order several other rules are used to control which users and computers are assigned group policies. These rules, listed below, allow the administrator to further refine policy application.

- Policy inheritance
- Blocking policy inheritance
- Enforcing policy inheritance
- Using security groups to filter group policies

Policy Inheritance

The LSDOU model discussed earlier generally describes how group policy inheritance is implemented in Windows 2000. A clear example may shed light on how it works. In Figure 8.1 the *Engineering Policies GPO* applied to the *Engineering OU* is also inherited by the *Sustaining* and *Development OU*s. This shows that whereas child Active Directory containers inherit group policies, group policy inheritance does not flow upward to parent containers.

Let's dissect the example in Figure 8.2 to illustrate this flow in greater detail. Policies inherited by the *Marketing OU* from its parents are applied to members

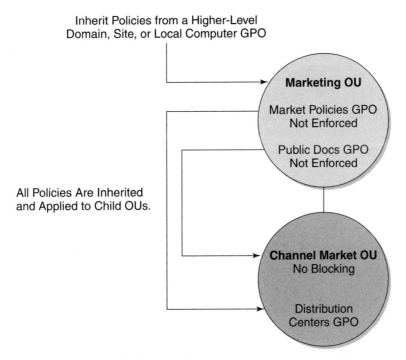

FIGURE 8.2 An Example of Policy Inheritance

of the *Channel Marketing OU*. Users and computers in the *Channel Marketing OU* also apply the *Marketing Policies GPO* and *Public Docs GPO* to their systems upon boot-up and logon. The *Distribution Centers GPO* is applied last and may override group policies previously applied to the *Channel Marketing OU*. Thus, *the lowest-level Active Directory container has the last opportunity to override inherited policies.*

NOTE   As levels are added to the Active Directory hierarchy, more GPOs are applied to a user account when a user logs on to the network. A vertical domain container structure generally results in additional policies are applied to the user and it will take longer to log on. Also, more GPOs result in more complexity when determining which policies apply to the user. A very horizontal Active Directory structure may eliminate some of this complexity and logon delay, illustrated in Figure 8.3.

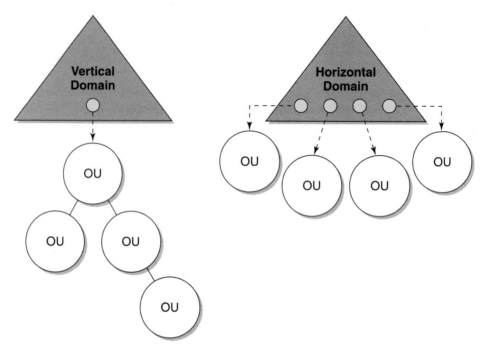

FIGURE 8.3 Horizontal versus Vertical Domain Structure—Horizontal Domain Structures Decrease Logon Time

Blocking Policy Inheritance and Enforcement

The inheritance hierarchy can be modified by use of the Override or Enforce function, which blocks inherited features associated with parent GPOs. The *Engineering OU* (Figure 8.4) has enforced the *Design Access GPO* policies and not the *Engineering GPO* policies. The *Sustaining OU* has elected to block inheritance and so it does not inherit the *Engineering GPO* policies since they are not enforced. However, the *Design Access GPO* policies are enforced at the *Engineering OU* level and thus override the *Sustaining OU*'s desire to block inheritance. In other words, *the enforcement of parent group policies takes precedence over policy blocking on child containers.*

NOTE   Both policy blocking and policy enforcement should be kept to a minimum. This capability makes it difficult to track policies that affect the user.

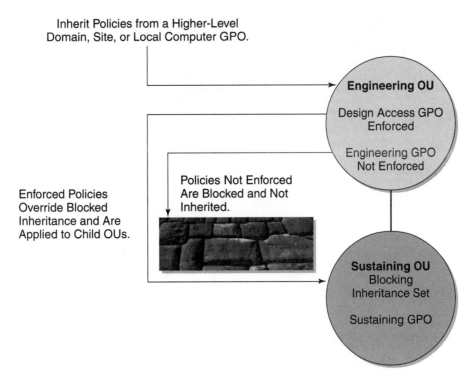

Inherit Policies from a Higher-Level
Domain, Site, or Local Computer GPO.

Engineering OU

Design Access GPO
Enforced

Engineering GPO
Not Enforced

Policies Not Enforced
Are Blocked and Not
Inherited.

Enforced Policies
Override Blocked
Inheritance and Are
Applied to Child OUs.

Sustaining OU
Blocking
Inheritance Set

Sustaining GPO

FIGURE 8.4 An Example of Blocking Policy Inheritance

Security Group Filtering

As with files and other objects in Windows 2000, the Discretionary Access Control List (DACL) determines permission levels for users and computers accessing a GPO. Each GPO has its own security settings determined by a DACL and associated permissions. Access Control Entries (ACEs) usually take the form of security groups, rather than individual users, and assign sweeping privileges to many users at once. Each ACE can be assigned **Allow** and **Deny** permissions through the GPO security settings (Figure 10.5).

The **Authenticated Users** group (Figure 8.5) is one of the default security groups assigned to a newly created GPO. **Read** and **Apply Group Policy** permissions are set to **Allow**, which means that all newly authenticated users mapped to this GPO will apply its policies. Consistent with other Windows 2000 permissions, **Deny** takes precedence over **Allow**. Members of a security group may "filter" group policies by denying the **Apply Group Policy** permission. A filtered security group will not accumulate logon delays due to the GPO. Group policy access permissions can also be used to delegate administrative authority to secu-

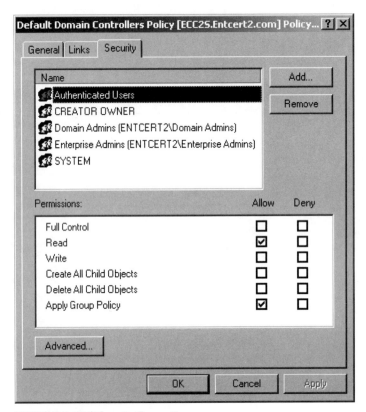

FIGURE 8.5 GPO Security Properties

rity groups and users. A user must have Read and Write access to make GPO changes.

CAUTION Security group filtering should be used sparingly, as determining which policies affect a user may become quite complex. As with all security permissions, use of the **Deny** setting to override **Allow** should be used with caution as well.

Group Policy Settings

Group policies are broken into five areas, each of which is discussed in the following sections. Example implementations are provided at the end of the chapter. Keep in mind that individual policies affect all aspects of system operation.

Following are the five policy categories defined in the **Group Policy** snap-in.

- *Administrative templates (Registry-based)*. These policies primarily impact the user interface and available tools and desktop settings.
- *Security settings*. These settings limit user access to systems and user account policies.
- *Software installation*. These policies allow the publishing and assignment of available software.
- *Scripts*. These configure scripts for logon, logoff, startup, and shutdown.
- *Folder redirection*. These settings permit the relocation of user profile folders (My Documents, Application Data, Start Menu) to other system network shares.

USER AND COMPUTER POLICIES

A GPO divides policies into two major sections, **User Configuration** and **Computer Configuration** (Figure 8.6). Policies within **Computer Configuration** are applied during the boot sequence and affect all sessions that follow on that system. **User Configuration** policies are applied when the user first logs on. *User policies follow the user; computer policies apply to the system.*

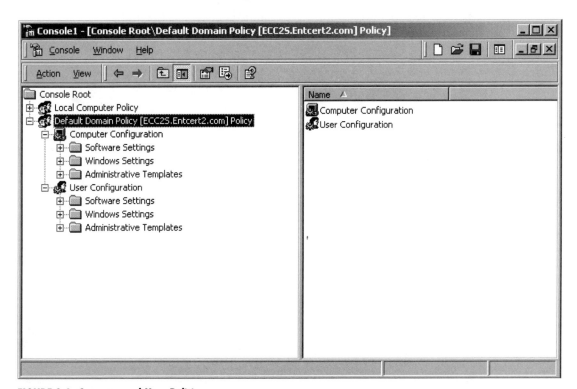

FIGURE 8.6 Computer and User Policies

Either the **User Configuration** or the **Computer Configuration** portion of a GPO may be disabled to save time and processing. For instance, if a GPO does not enable any computer policy settings, the **Computer Configuration** portion of the GPO should be disabled. This is demonstrated in the following sections.

ADMINISTRATIVE TEMPLATES

Both user- and computer-related **Administrative Template** nodes are used to modify Registry settings. The related Registry database settings are located in the HKEY_CURRENT_USER (HKCU) and HKEY_LOCAL_MACHINE (HKLM) Registry keys. Whenever policy changes are made to the **Administrative Template** portion of the GPO, the Registry keys HKCU and HKLM are also updated. If there is a conflict between user and computer settings, the computer settings take priority. A Registry.pol file in the %systemroot%\SYSVOL\sysvol\domainname\Policies\ GUID\MACHINE and USER directories maintains group policy changes to the Registry. Any changes made through administrative template policies are made in the Registry.pol file and then mapped onto the Registry.

The policies available under the **Administrative Templates** node take the form of the ASCII files system.adm and inetres.adm by default (Figure 8.7). The default Windows 2000 installation includes other administrative templates that may be loaded in order to modify policies for specific applications or network architectures (Table 8.1).

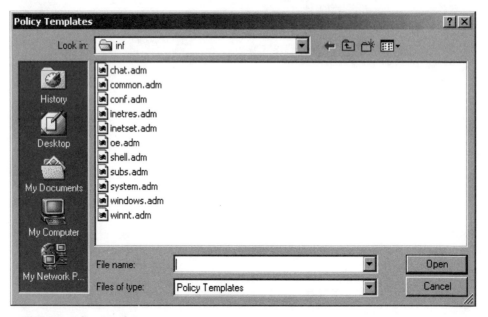

FIGURE 8.7 Policy Templates

TABLE 8.1 Administrative Template Options

Template	Purpose
Chat.adm	Microsoft Chat policies
Common.adm	Windows NT 4.0, 98, and 95 policies
Conf.adm	Microsoft NetMeeting policies
Inetres.adm	Internet policies
Inetset.adm	Internet restriction policies
Oe.adm	Microsoft Outlook Express
Shell.adm	Desktop settings—Wallpaper, tool bars, and Active Desktop
Subs.adm	Restrictions on channel subscriptions—size, update interval depth
System.adm	Default template with Windows 2000-specific policies
Windows.adm	Windows 98 and 95 policies
Winnt.adm	Windows NT 4.0 policies

In addition to these templates, located physically in the *%systemroot%\inf* directory, custom **.ADM** files may be created for specific application needs. Guidelines for doing this can be found in the Windows 2000 Help tool under **Creating Custom .Adm Files**. Application developers can also customize group policies by creating an MMC extension snap-in.

NOTE   In enterprises that implement the Windows 2000 remote installation, several group policies can be used to govern what installation options are available to the client. For instance, the administrator may choose to restrict which users may install an Active Directory domain controller. The policy to control this setting, located under ***gponame*** → **User Configuration** → **Windows Settings** → **Remote Installation Services** → **Choice Options**, can dictate an automatic installation setup preventing user control over installation options.

SECURITY SETTINGS

Group security policies apply to nine different areas within the Windows 2000 Group Policy Editor. The **Security Configuration Editor** can be used to compare the system's security policy settings with suggested settings. Security templates located in the *%systemroot%\Security\Templates* directory can be modified using the **Security Templates** snap-in tool. They can then be imported to the

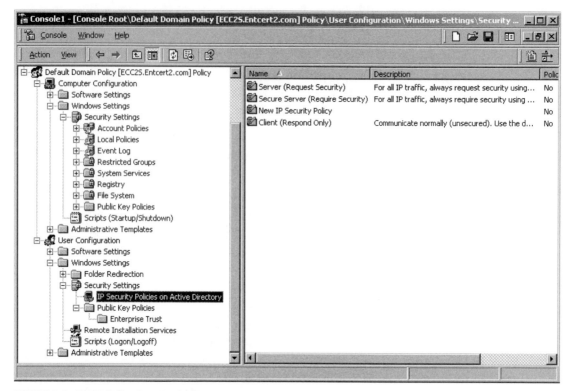

FIGURE 8.8 Group Policy Security Settings

Security Settings portion of the group policy tree. The security group policy settings, illustrated in Figure 8.8, include those listed in Table 8.2.

An understanding of security policies would not be complete without a review of Restricted Groups, Registry, and Files System settings. The sections that follow discuss each of these items.

Restricted Groups

When the **Restricted Groups** settings are applied to a system, the current group memberships are modified to match them. Only groups listed in the Details window of the Restricted Groups node are affected. Any group added to restricted groups has its own member and "member of" lists. These lists are then enforced on the local system, overwriting group membership assigned by the Active Directory.

To add a restricted group:

1. Right-click the **Restricted Group** policy node and select **Add Group...**.
2. Press the **Browse...** button and select a group from your directory (Figure 8.9).

TABLE 8.2 Group Policy Settings

Security Setting Node	Description
Account Policies	Password policies—uniqueness, maximum age, minimum length.
	Account lockout—invalid logon attempt.
	Kerberos policy—ticket lifetime, synchronization.
Local Policies	Audit policy—user rights, local machine security such as shutdown privileges and auto-disconnect.
Event Log	Size and time limits for event logs.
Restricted Groups	Designates some security groups to allow only designated members to participate in the group for any length of time; if a non-designated member is added to the group, the user will be removed.
System Services	System service startup mode (Automatic, Manual, Disabled) modification for the next system boot.
Registry	Security access permissions on portions of the registry; permissions for the CLASSES_ROOT, MACHINE, and USERS Registry keys may be assigned using security groups or user IDs.
File System	Security permissions for files and folders set and applied when user logs on to the system.
Public Key Policies	Designate trusted root Certificate Authorities and recovery agents for file encryption.
IP Security Policies on Active Directory	IP security level for the system; set software Authenticode, user authentication, and encrypted communication methods.

FIGURE 8.9 Add Group

3. Press the **OK** Button and right-click on the new group. Select **Security…**.

4. Add **Members of this Group:** and **this group is a member of:** entries as desired (Figure 8.10).

If you were to add the Power Users group to the **Restricted Groups** setting and not include any of its users in the member list, the policy would remove any current users from that group. Oddly enough, if the "member of" list is empty, no modifications are made to other group memberships. In other words, it is additive only. The restricted groups will be added to the groups listed in the **This group is a member of:** field. This policy setting is good for controlling membership to some select groups, but it should be used sparingly.

File System and Registry Policy

Group policies can be used to set permissions on files and Registry keys. The **File System** and **Registry** settings allow the administrator to configure the ACLs on a per file/folder/Registry directory basis.

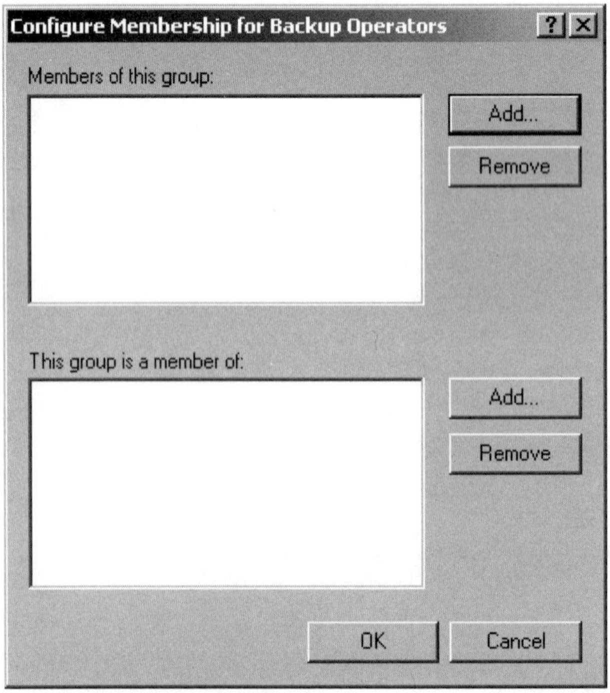

FIGURE 8.10 Group Membership

NOTE   When applied at the domain level these settings can lock down all system Registries, protecting against meddling users and ensuring uniform permission settings throughout an OU or domain.

Right-click the **GPO name** → **User** → **Security Settings** → **Registry** node and select **Add Key…**. This produces the **Select Registry Key** dialog box (Figure 8.11). Three Registry keys can be explored, and permissions may be selectively applied to the key structure.

Right-click the **GPO name** → **User** → **Security Settings** → **File System** node and select **Add File…**. This produces the **Add a file or folder** dialog box (Figure 8.12). The entire directory structure can be explored and selectively assigned permissions.

After an item is selected, security permission (Figure 8.13) can be assigned as covered in Chapter 10, Kerberos and the Public Key Infrastructure.

Once permissions have been assigned, inheritance properties are requested (Figure 8.14). Selecting the Configure option applies the permissions according to these subchoices:

- *Apply inheritable security to this file or folder and its subfolders.* This option applies the permissions set to the current object and all child folders and files. Any specific or explicit user or group that has been added to a child file or subfolder is not overwritten. In other words, all permissions that were inherited are replaced with the new permissions, but Joe Engineer, who was given Read privileges on a specific subfolder, still maintains his user right.

- *Replace existing security for this file or folder and its subfolders.* This option applies the new policy settings to all child folders and files, overwriting all existing permissions.

If the **Prevent the application of security policies to this file or folder and its subfolders** is selected, the current file or folder and its child file and folders are immune to permissions assigned in this particular GPO. This policy is needed only if a parent to this file or folder has been assigned new permissions within this GPO and you want this branch to keep its permissions and ignore the new settings.

SOFTWARE INSTALLATION: ASSIGNING AND PUBLISHING

The group policies for the **Software Installation** node provide two strategies for distributing applications throughout the network. The *assign* method places a shortcut to the application on the **Start** menu and loads the application advertisement into the Registry. Applications may be assigned with *user* or *computer* settings.

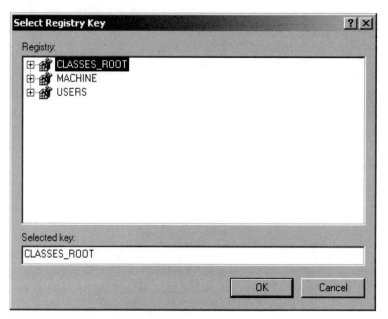

FIGURE 8.11 Registry Security Policies

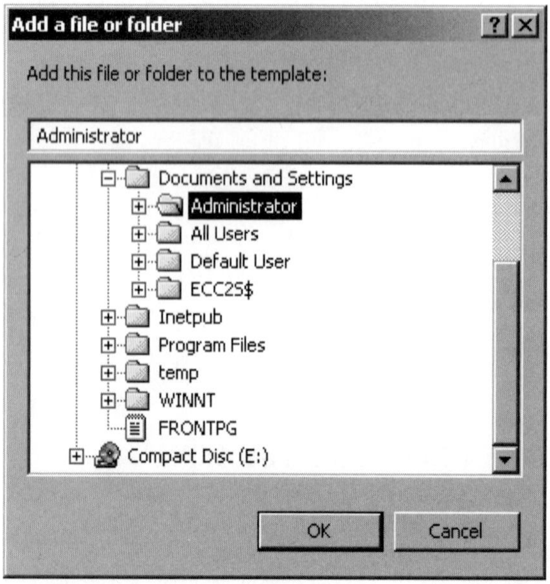

FIGURE 8.12 File Security Policies

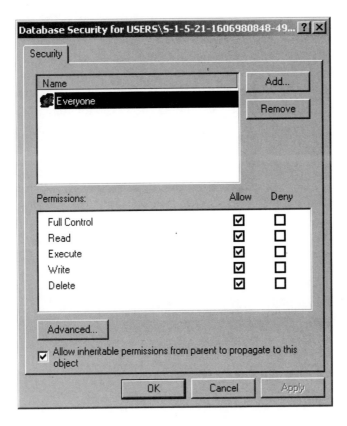

FIGURE 8.13 Registry and File Permissions

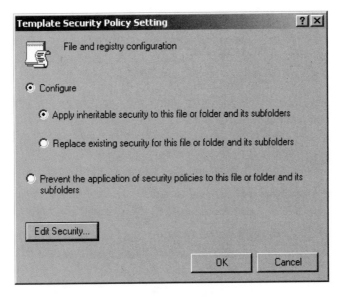

FIGURE 8.14 Permission Inheritance

Those assigned via user settings are installed on the local system the first time the application is executed. In this way they maintain consistent application availability for a set of users, who benefit from enhanced desktop usability since their **Start** menu will always appear the same regardless of where they log on. If the needed application is not already installed on the system the user is using, application installation may be invoked by selecting the application from the **Start** menu or by opening a file of the application's type. Applications assigned with computer settings will be installed on those systems when booted. Application availability is based on the computer system, not the user.

NOTE   The discussion of application installations involves elements of Microsoft's IntelliMirror that are discussed at the end of this chapter. The ability to set policies on applications that can be **intelli**gently **mirror**ed across the enterprise is one of the primary functions of IntelliMirror technology.

The second method for distributing software is to *publish* the application. A published application leaves the software installation up to the user without the aid of shortcuts and local Registry modifications. The user may install a published application by accessing the **Add/Remove Programs** icon from the **Control Panel** or by opening a file matching the published application type. An application must be published with user settings, so that its availability will follow the user, regardless of which system is used. Software may not be published using computer settings. Published software does not have the resilient quality of assigned software. If a library or file associated with the application is deleted, the software will not be repaired.

The software publish and assign capabilities for group policies rely on the Windows Installer to manage application installation. A software package with a *.MSI file name contains information necessary to install the application on different platforms, and to deal with previous versions and different configurations. The resiliency of the Windows Installer is a key new feature that rolls back application versions or repairs missing libraries when necessary. Assigned applications modify the Registry and persist on the system even when the user deletes an application or associated libraries. They will be reinstalled or repaired the next time the program is invoked.

Packaging Applications

For a software application to be assigned or published, a package for the software must be obtained in a couple of ways:

- Use an *.MSI package from the software vendor or repackaging software to generate *.MSI file.
- Use a *.ZAP file to guide software installation.

The *.MSI package and associated files are fairly straightforward. However, when *.MSI is not available a *.ZAP text file can be used to add applications using the Software Installer, rather than the Windows Installer, to *publish* (not assign) them. This of course means that the application will not be resilient or repair itself when damaged. The user instigating the Software Installer must also have the necessary access permissions to write to the required installation directories, since the Software Installer is not granted sweeping privileges to make system modifications, unlike the Windows Installer. The installation procedure will also probably involve user intervention and therefore lead to more handholding and user guidance.

A *.ZAP file requires an application section, designated by line 1, and two required tags on lines 2 and 3. The **Friendly Name** tag indicates the application name that will appear in the **Control Panel → Add/Remove Programs** utility, and the **Setup** command is the executable to instigate the application's installation. The following tags are optional and relate to parameters that are displayed in the **Add/Remove Programs** utility. The **Ext** marker on line 8 indicates the optional extension section. File extensions specified here will be stored in the Active Directory and linked to the newly installed application. The extension is listed without the period.

```
line 1: [Application]
line 2: FriendlyName = ECC W2K Starter
line 3: SetupCommand = setup.exe
line 4: DisplayVersion = 1.0
line 5: Publisher = Enterprise Certified
line 6: URL = http://www.EntCert.com/Software
line 7:
line 8: [Ext]
line 9: CUR=
```

Software Installation Example

The software installation component of the IntelliMirror technology allows the publishing or assigning of software applications to users and computers. As previously discussed, *assigning* software applications puts the software's icon on the Start menu. The application is then installed when invoked by the user and will "follow" the user wherever he goes within the network. Obviously, software application installation takes time and network resources. If the application is assigned to a computer, the software is installed at the system's leisure, which usually means that installation will occur when the system is booted. Publishing software requires the user to invoke the **Add/Remove Programs** tool from the Control Panel. Software components, published to the user or computer, are listed under the **Add New Programs** menu. They are then installed at the user's request.

In order to publish or assign software, an MSI package must be obtained for the application from the software vendor. In this example, the Office 2000 package is used to assign software to domain users. For more information on the MSI/MST formats see the Help pages.

NOTE   Repackaging tools, such as VERITAS WinInstall LE, are included on the Windows 2000 Server and Windows 2000 Advanced Server CDs. These tools examine the system before and after application installation and record system changes and package the final system state. The produced *.MSI package enables resilient application publish and assign capabilities.

1. Find an *.MSI software package and copy it to the *Network Docs and Settings* network share from the previous example.

2. Open the **Default Domain Policy** (or other GPO) and right-click on the **User Configuration → Software Settings → Software Installation** node and select the **New → Package...** option (Figure 8.15). Find the software package from the **Find File** window. BE SURE TO ENTER THE NETWORK PATH to the network share and software package. If it is on the local drive, reference the packet in the *servername**Network Docs and Settings*. Clients must be able to access the package from the network using the full file name given here. Press the **OK** button.

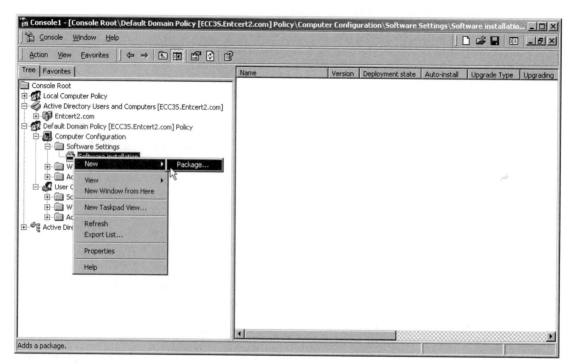

FIGURE 8.15 The Add Software Package

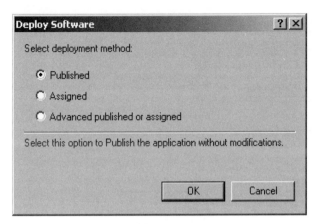

FIGURE 8.16 Select Deployment Method

3. Select whether the application is to be published or assigned (Figure 8.16). Press the **OK** button.

4. Once the application has been added to **Software Installation**, policy properties may be viewed. Right-click on the newly added package and select **Properties** (Figure 8.17). Configurable items (discussed further in the coming sections) include

   - *General*—name and product and support information.
   - *Deployment*—deployment type, options, and the allowed user interface during installation.
   - *Upgrades*—packages that upgrade this package and those that this package upgrades.
   - *Categories*—categories in which this application will be listed. New categories can be created to group software types. A category called Accounting might contain several accounting packages.
   - *Modifications*—*.MST files or transforms to customize software installations.
   - *Security*—users and groups with access to modify this package's GPO setting.

   Once the user logs on again, on any machine, the software will be installed once activated from the Start menu or by double-clicking a file of the application type from **My Computer**.

Modifying the Deployment Method

Once the package has been installed on a network share and added to a GPO, its deployment configuration may be further modified. Right-clicking the **Software installation** node for the GPO containing the new software package and select-

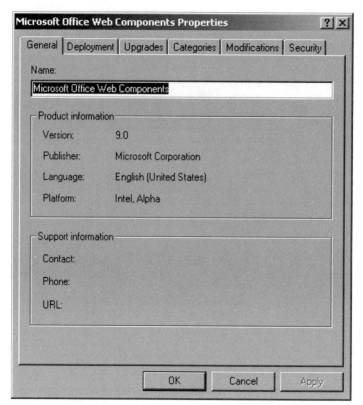

FIGURE 8.17 The Application Properties General Tab

ing **Properties** presents several configuration tabs. The **General** tab (Figure 8.17) presents product and support information for the application.

The **Deployment** tab (Figure 8.18) allows configuration of the deployment type, options, and user interaction. The **Deployment type** field allows you to change the current deployment method, published or assigned. The **Deployment options** field provides the following configuration options:

- *Auto-install this application by file extension activation.* This option applies only to published applications. It allows you to prevent or allow application installation when a user double-clicks a file with an extension matching the published application.

- *Uninstall this application when it falls out of the scope of management.* This option determines whether or not the application is uninstalled from a user or computer when leaving the scope of the current GPO. If a user no longer falls under the jurisdiction (scope) of this GPO, the application will be removed if this option is checked.

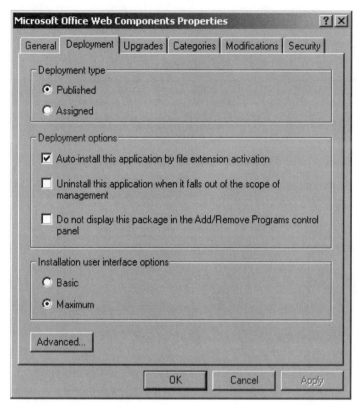

FIGURE 8.18 The Deployment Tab

- *Do not display this package in the Add/Remove Programs Control Panel.* If this option is checked, the user will not be able to browse for the application and install it from the Control Panel. If the user invokes or double-clicks a file of the application's extension type, the application will be installed.

The user interface options determine that the application will be installed using default values (**Basic**), or they prompt the user for installation configuration information (**Maximum**).

The **Advanced...** button allows removal of previous installations not governed by group policies. An option also exists to disregard language configuration during the install.

Upgrades

There are two ways to distribute software upgrades. A mandatory upgrade involves a checkmark in front of the **Required upgrade for existing packages** option

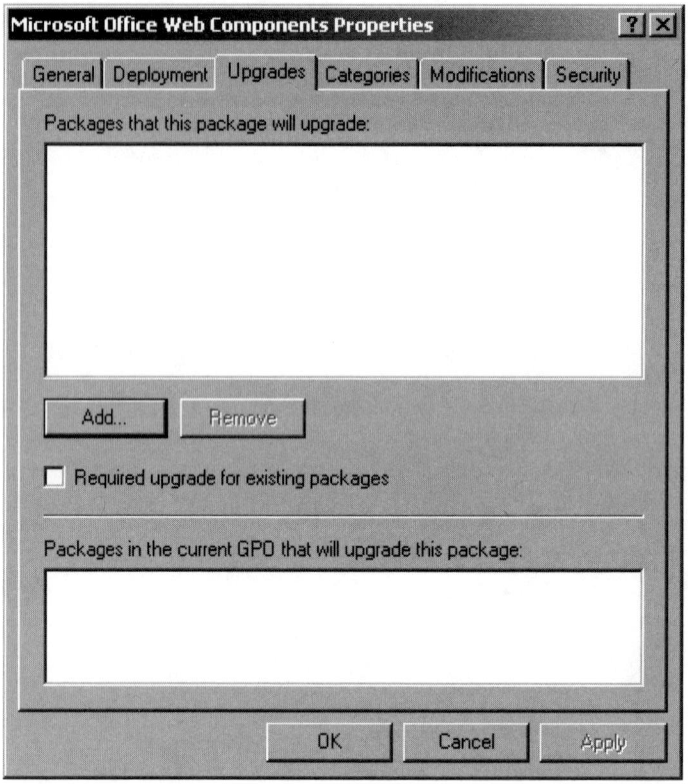

FIGURE 8.19 The Upgrade Tab

(Figure 8.19). This option requires the user to upgrade her current version of the application with the new package. The optional upgrade (clearing checkbox) allows the user to install the new application version or to continue using the current one. It also permits her to install the new version in addition to her current version and access both through old and new shortcuts.

To add an upgrade package, press the **Add** button from the **Upgrade** tab (Figure 8.20) and find the package to upgrade within the current GPO, or browse the directory by selecting the **A specific GPO** option and pressing the **Browse...** button. Once the correct GPO is located select the application package to upgrade from among those associated with that GPO. Then you may optionally **Uninstall the existing package**; then **Install the upgrade package** or select the **Package can upgrade over the existing package** option. The Uninstall option is used to replace an existing application with a new one; the upgrade option is used to upgrade a package with the same product.

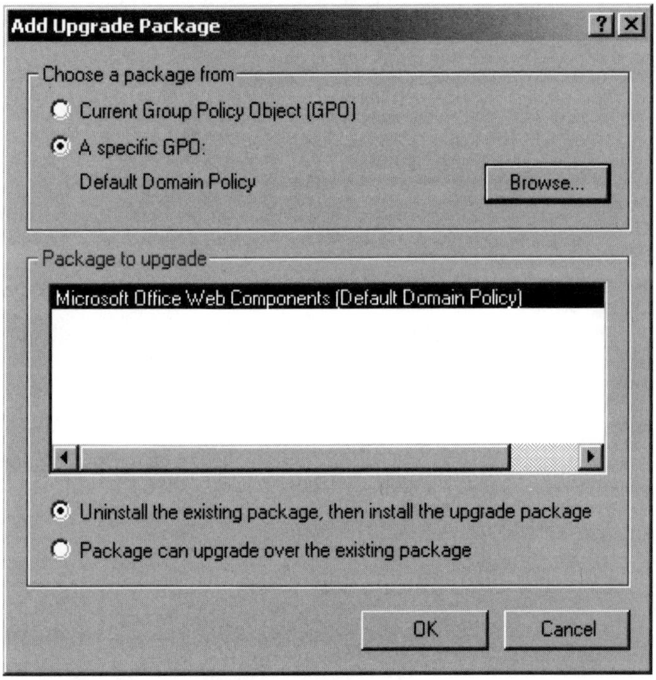

FIGURE 8.20 The Add Upgrade Package

Redeploying Software Patches

Once you obtain the new *.MSI package containing a software fix, replace the old *.MSI package and associated files with the new package and files on the network share. Select the **Software Installation** node from the GPO that originally deployed the software and right-click the software package in the Details window. Select the **All Tasks → Redeploy** application options and press the **Yes** button to redeploy the software fix. Regardless of whether the application was published or assigned, the first time it is started the patch will be installed.

Software Removal

Software may undergo either a forced or an optional removal. A forced removal will delete software installed through computer settings the next time the system is booted. The optional removal permits the current application installations to persist but will not allow new installations for the package.

To remove software, select the **Software installation** node from the corresponding GPO. In the Details window right-click the desired software package and select **All Tasks → Remove....**. The **Remove software** dialog appears and pre-

FIGURE 8.21 Software Removal Options

sents two software removal methods (Figure 8.21). These options correspond to the forced and optional removal strategies, respectively. Press the **OK** button.

File Extensions and Installation

Invoking application installation when a user selects a file of the application's file type is convenient. However, some organizations may have several applications associated with a given file extension. Suppose both Microsoft Office 2000 Premium and Microsoft Office 2000 Standard are deployed using group policies. Right-click the **Software installation** node for a given GPO and select **Properties**. From the **Extensions** tab select an extension and then assign application priority using the **Up** and **Down** buttons (Figure 8.22). The application at the top of the list for a selected extension will be installed first. In Figure 8.22, only one office product package has been added to group policies, so no priority decision need be made.

Categories

When the user accesses the **Control Panel** to **Add/Remove Programs**, the applications will be listed. Categories can be used to create a hierarchy of application folders to order the software more effectively. Three new categories, *Word Processors, Draw Tools,* and *Email Clients,* can classify available applications (Figure 8.23). To add categories right-click the **Software installation** node for a given GPO and select **Properties**. From the **Categories** tab press the **Add** button and type in a new category name. Press the **Apply** button and then press **OK**. The new category will be added to the Active Directory and become available from any GPO in it.

Once the new category name has been made available, software applications may be added to the new category. Add a package by right-clicking a software package in the Details window of the GPO **Software installation** node and selecting **Properties**. From the **Categories** tab choose a category from the **Available categories:** pane and press the **Select>** button to add the current package

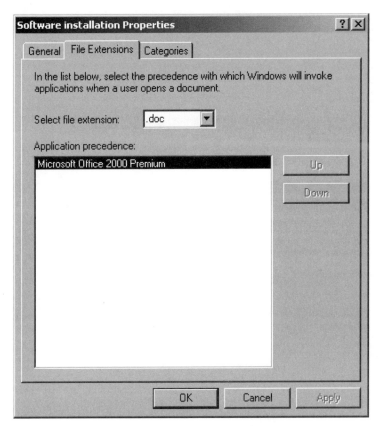

FIGURE 8.22 Associating File Extensions with Applications

to it (Figure 8.24). In this example, the Microsoft Office 2000 Premium package would be available under the *Word Processors* category from the **Control Panel** → **Add/Remove Programs** utility.

Application Modifications
Modifications may be made to customize a software application installation. Different GPOs may apply their own modifications to suit users who require additional features. A transform file or *.MST file is created to indicate application customizations. From the **Modifications** tab (Figure 8.25) press the **Add** button and browse for the desired *.MST file.

In order for modifications to be added, the application must be installed using the **Advanced published or assigned** option from the **Deploy Software** dialog

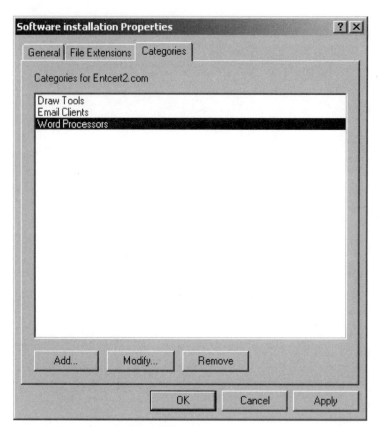

FIGURE 8.23 Add New Software Categories

(Figure 8.16). Once an application has been deployed, modifications may not be added or removed.

SCRIPTS

Group policies enable assigning scripts to entire domains or OUs rather than modifying each user account and tediously mapping logon scripts to it. The group policy scripts execute as follows:

- User Configuration
  - Logon scripts—executed when the user logs on to a system.
  - Logoff scripts—executed when the user logs off the system.

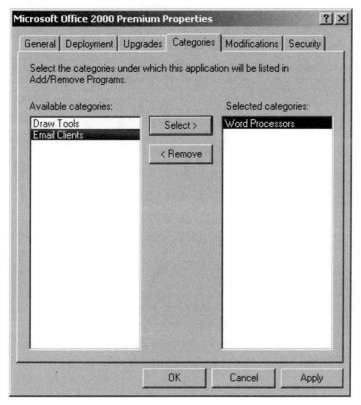

FIGURE 8.24 The Categories Tab

- Computer Configuration
  - Startup scripts—executed when the system boots.
  - Shutdown scripts—executed when the system is shut down.

NOTE   During the shutdown process, logoff scripts are executed before shutdown scripts. This allows for any gathering of log data, for example, to be written before the system terminates services and operations.

Scripting group policies for Windows 2000 can be found by highlighting the GPO and then → **Computer Configuration** → **Windows Settings** → **Scripts (Startup\Shutdown)** and *gponame* → **User Configuration** → **Windows Settings** → **Scripts (Logon\Logoff)** policy branches (Figure 8.26).

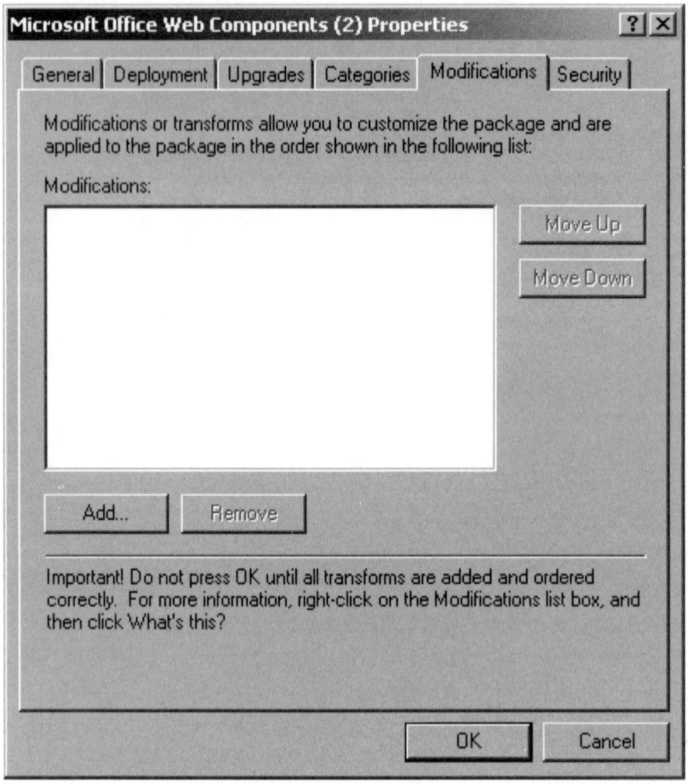

FIGURE 8.25 The Modifications Tab

Windows 2000 comes equipped with the Windows Scripting Host (WSH) 1.0, which currently supports Jscript (*.JS) and Visual Basic Scripting Edition (*.VBS) in addition to the MS-DOS command scripts (*.BAT, *.COM, *.EXE). The WSH may also be installed on Windows NT 4.0, 95, and 98 to support modern scripting languages on legacy systems. Scripts are accessed throughout the network by storing them in the server replication directory *%systemroot%\SYSVOL\sysvol\ domainname\Policies\scripts*. (A discussion of WSH 2.0 is found in Chapter 17.)

Additional policies that affect script performance can be found under the administrative templates (Figures 8.27 and 8.28). If the WSH is not installed on the legacy systems, scripts may need to run in the DOS Prompt window. The **Run legacy logon scripts hidden** option will minimize the script window or hide scripts from view.

The **Maximum wait time for group policy scripts** and asynchronous/synchronous settings are also helpful for centrally managing script behavior.

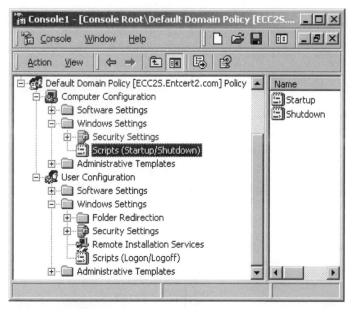

FIGURE 8.26 Shutdown

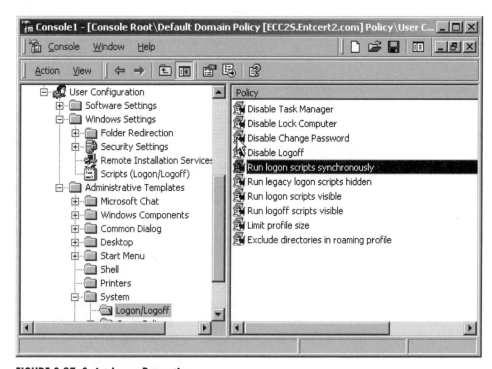

FIGURE 8.27 Script Logon Properties

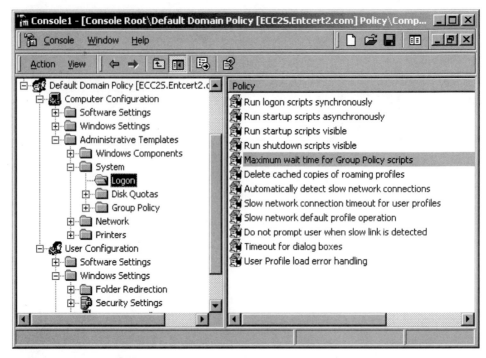

FIGURE 8.28 Script Policies

FOLDER REDIRECTION

The Folder Redirection policies allow the administrator to relocate several directories within the user's profile (Figure 8.29). Even with roaming user profiles, the profile directories are copied to the local system (*%SystemRoot%*\Documents and Settings\username) when the user logs on. This can be time consuming and can impact the network, especially for large **My Documents** folders.

NOTE   The discussion of redirection involves elements of Microsoft's IntelliMirror, which is discussed at the end of this chapter. As stated earlier, the ability to set policies on folder direction that can be **intelli**gently **mirror**ed across the enterprise is one of the primary features of IntelliMirror technology.

Redirection policies can relocate four user profile directories to a centrally managed network share so that they are not copied to the local system.

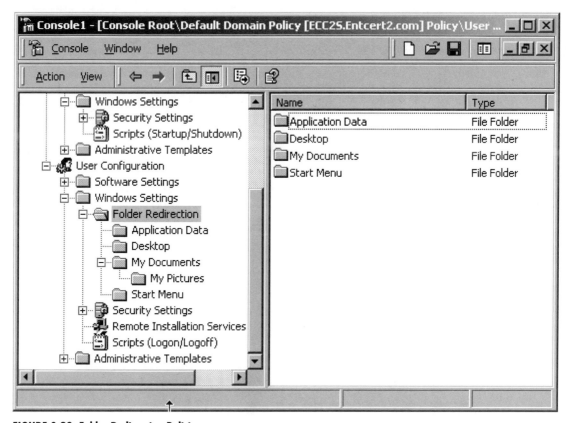

FIGURE 8.29 Folder Redirection Policies

The Offline Folder or Cache settings may be set on the network share to allow local system access to these network profile folders when the user's system cannot access the network. The profile information is cached locally and then updated on the network share when the user has access to the share at a later date.

GPO IMPLEMENTATION

The previous sections of this chapter provided some understanding of group policy application and usage. Before we discuss actually implementing GPO, there are a few systemic issues to address regarding group policy behavior.

Refreshing Policy Settings

Understanding the basic group policy refresh schedule is helpful when changing group policies on your local system. Once a group policy has been changed on a domain controller, the group policies on the local system must be refreshed in order to take effect. Non–domain-controller client computers receive policy refreshes every 90 minutes plus or minus a random time interval. The random time interval helps distribute client requests evenly so that they do not all come in at the same time. Change the interval using the **Computer Configuration** → **Administrative Templates** → **System** → **Group Policy** → **Group Policy refresh interval for computers** policy node within a GPO (Figure 8.30).

Domain controllers refresh group policies more frequently. The default group policy setting for the **Computer Configuration** → **Administrative Templates**

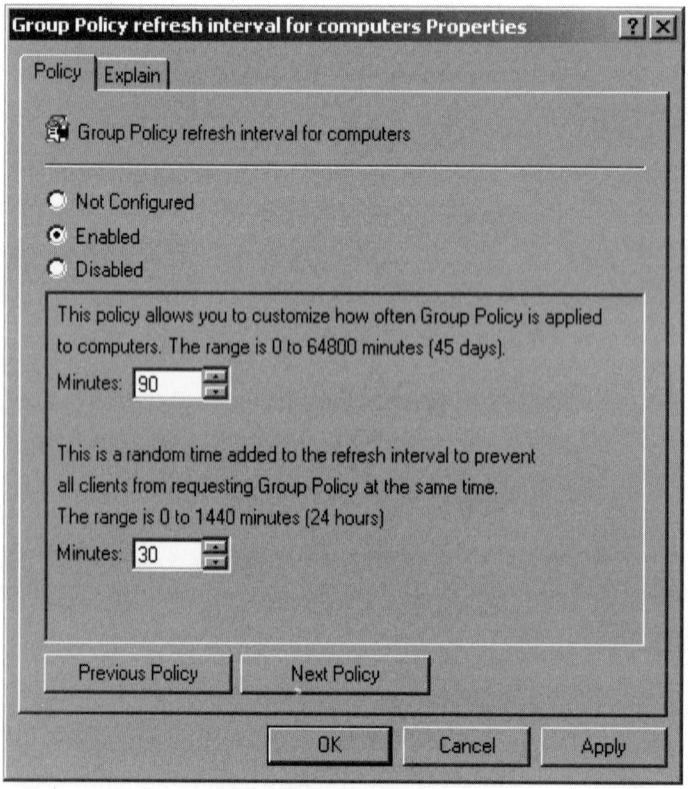

FIGURE 8.30 Client Group Policy Refresh Intervals

→ **System** → **Group Policy** → **Group Policy refresh interval for domain controllers** policy node sets the refresh interval for every 5 minutes (Figure 8.31). This is why succeeding examples should be executed on a domain controller.

NOTE The **secedit** command can also be used to instigate a policy refresh, although the actual refresh can still seem to take 2 or 3 minutes. This command is more fully discussed in the Appendix, but its two basic forms are:

```
secedit  /refreshpolicy  machine_policy  /enforce  (for computer settings)
secedit  /refreshpolicy  user_policy  /enforce  (for user settings)
```

Group policies are also refreshed when the system is started. Obviously, shutting down and booting a system could prove troublesome when simply trying to refresh policy settings.

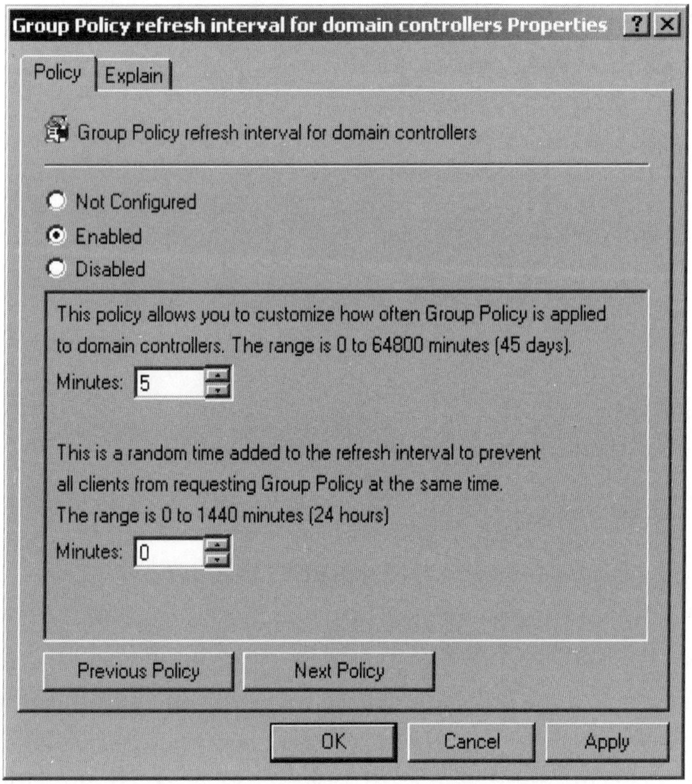

FIGURE 8.31 Domain Controller Group Policy Refresh Intervals

PDC Operations Manager

In addition to performing the functions of the primary domain controller (PDC) Emulator, the PDC Operations Manager is the default domain controller that handles group policy modifications. When the PDC Operations Manager is not available, an error message is displayed and the administrator may select another domain controller to handle changes. When you do this, be sure that all previous group policy changes have propagated throughout the domain and that no other administrator is currently making modifications.

IMPLEMENTING GROUP POLICY BY EXAMPLE

This section provides a number of examples of implementing group policies. These examples are representative of the type of group policy management available to the system administrator.

Local Computer Policy

The example that follows shows how to implement the **Local Computer Policy** snap-in and employ it to manage local GPOs. This is the easiest way to access this GPO; other GPOs can be reached through the Active Directory containers. Local computer policies are centrally managed on remote systems by adding the remote computer policies to the administrator's console. This example loads the local policies for the system the administrator is currently logged in to.

1. Log on as **Administrator**.
2. Go to the **Start** → **Programs** → **Accessories** → **Command Prompt** and type MMC and then Enter.
3. A **Console** window appears. Click the **Console** pull-down menu.
4. Select the **Add/Remove Snap-in...** selection.
5. The **Add/Remove Snap-in** dialog should appear (Figure 8.32).
6. Press the **Add...** button. The **Add Standalone Snap-in** should appear.
7. Select **Active Directory Users and Computers**.
8. Press the **Add** button.
9. Press the **Add...** button.
10. Select the **Group Policy** item from the **Available Standalone** snap-in (Figure 8.33).
11. Press the **Add** button. The **Group Policy Object:** should be the **Local Computer** (Figure 8.34).

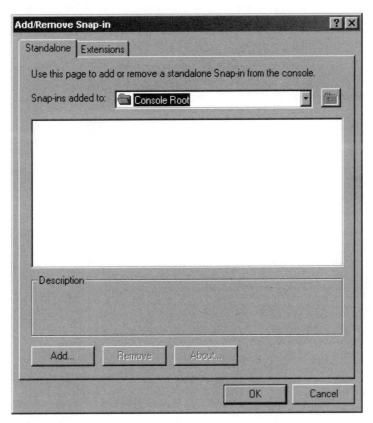

FIGURE 8.32 The Snap-In List

12. Press the **Browse...** button. The **Browse for a Group Policy Object** dialog appears (Figure 8.35).

13. There are four tabs associated with this dialog.

   • The **Domains/OUs** tab displays GPOs for the domain and OU containers.

   • The **Sites** tab displays current sites and their associated GPOs (Figure 8.36).

   • The **Computers** tab allows you to select the local GPO assigned to the current computer or to select another computer from the Active Directory. This provides remote administration of local computer policies (Figure 8.37).

   • The **All** tab displays all GPOs for the domain except for local computer policy (Figure 8.38).

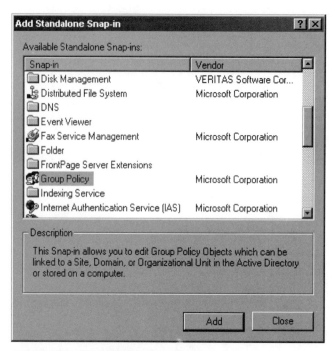

FIGURE 8.33 Add Standalone Snap-In

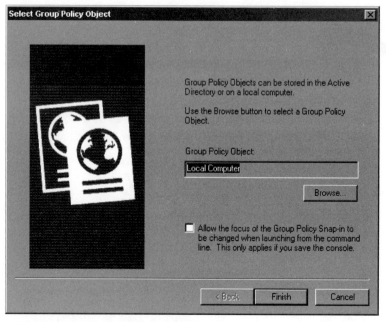

FIGURE 8.34 Select Group Policy Object

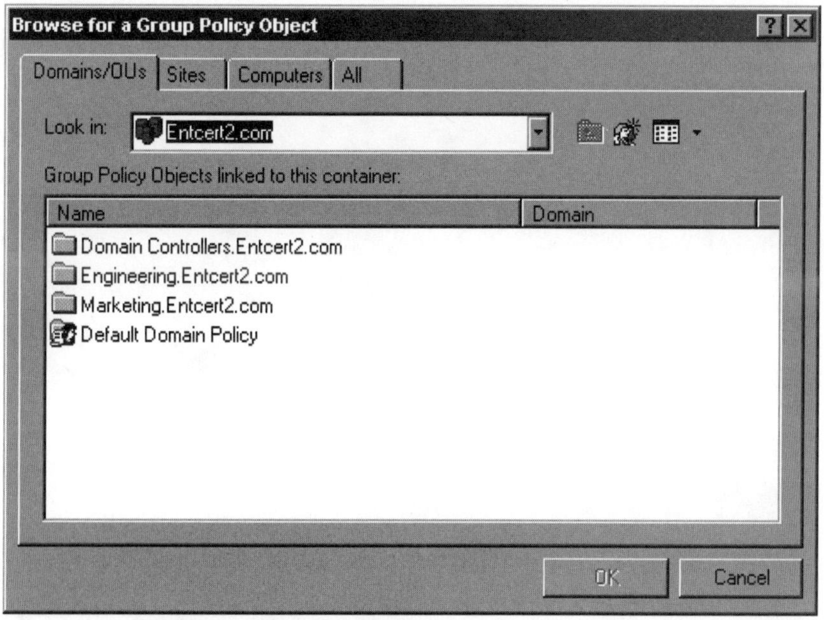

FIGURE 8.35 Available GPOs for a Domain

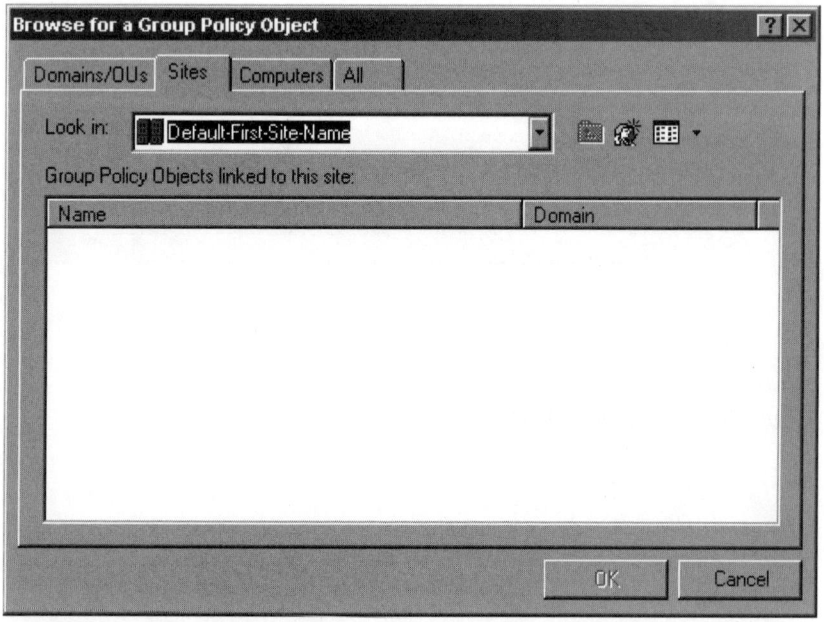

FIGURE 8.36 GPOs Linked to Sites

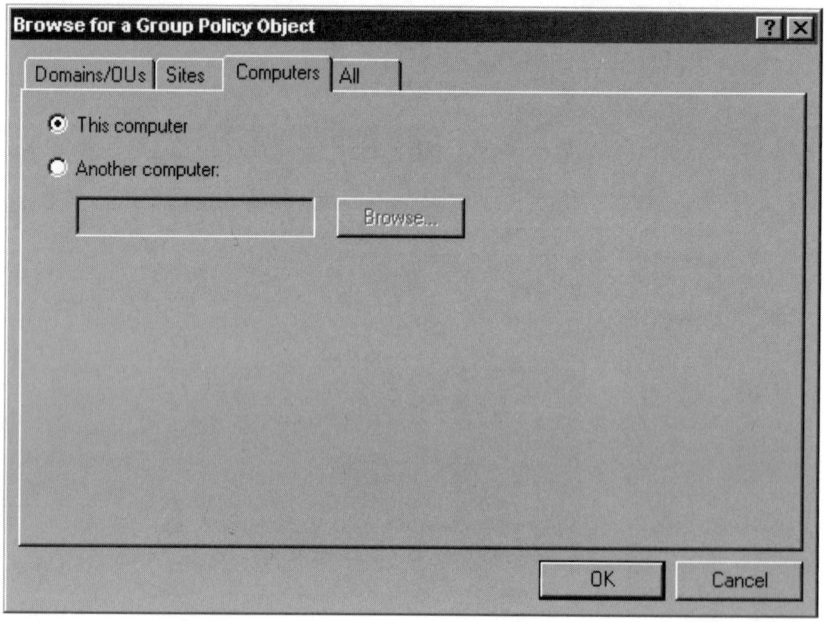

FIGURE 8.37 A Computer GPO

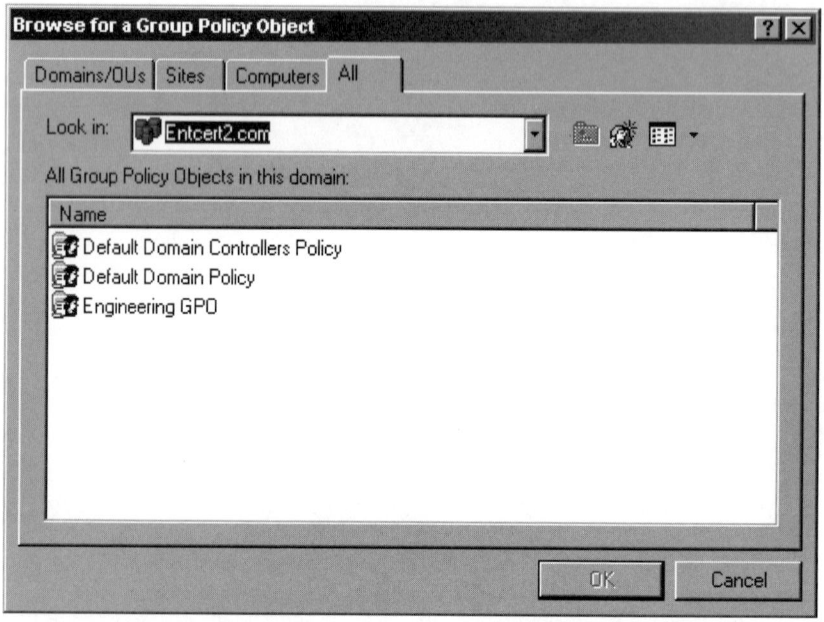

FIGURE 8.38 All GPOs in a Domain

14. For this example press the **Cancel** Button and select **Local Computer** as the **Group Policy Object**.

15. Press the **Finish** button. Press the **Close** button. Press the **OK** button.

The **Local Computer Policy** snap-in has now been added to your newly created console. Opening the policy node reveals available local policy settings. When you are finished, select the **Save As** option from the **Console** pull-down menu and save the console on the desktop or in a specific folder.

Creating a GPO and Linking to the Active Directory Container

This example illustrates how to create a GPO and apply it to an Active Directory container. In particular, a new organizational unit is created and then an Administrative Template group policy is enabled. Methods for blocking inheritances are also explored. As mentioned in the Implementation Considerations section of this chapter, the following examples should be implemented on a domain controller. In this way you will have to wait only five minutes for policies to be refreshed on your test system.

1. Start the custom console created earlier by double-clicking the console file from **My Computer** or the desktop.

2. Click the plus sign in front of **Active Directory Users and Computers** → *Your domain.com (Entcert2.com)*. Create a new OU called *Engineering* and add a user.

3. Create an OU within *Engineering* called *Sustaining* and add a user (Figure 8.39).

4. Right-click the *Engineering OU* and select **Properties**. The **Engineering Properties** dialog box appears (Figure 8.40). Select the **Group Policy** tab and press the **New** button. Name the new object *Engineering GPO* (Table 8.3).

5. Press the **Edit** button and select the plus sign in front of **User Configuration** → **Administrative Templates** → **System** → **Logon/Logoff**. In the Policy window double-click **Disable Lock Computer**.

6. The **Disable Lock Computer Properties** dialog window appears. Select the **Enabled** radio button. Notice that the **Previous Policy** and **Next Policy** buttons allow you to browse up and down the Policy window. The **Disable Lock Computer** policy has been enabled at the *Engineering OU* level (Figure 8.41).

7. Allow the group policy to refresh and log on as an *Engineering* user. Press **Ctrl-Alt-Del** and notice that the **Lock Computer** button is grayed out. Log on again as the **Administrator**.

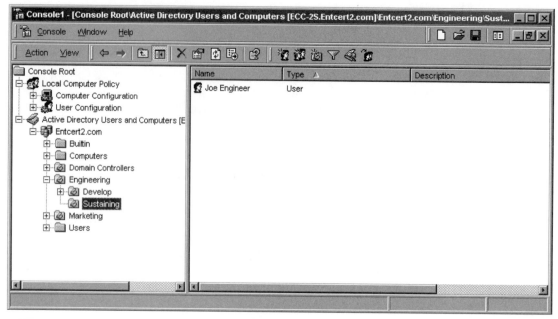

FIGURE 8.39 Creating New OUs

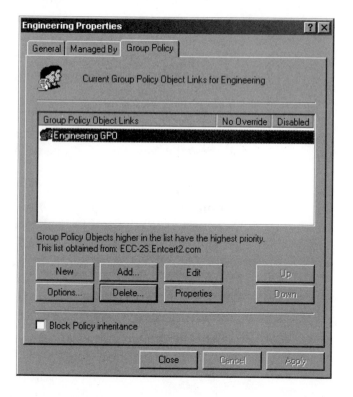

FIGURE 8.40 Create an Engineering GPO

TABLE 8.3 Group Policy Tab Option Buttons

Button	Function
New	Creates a new GPO and adds it to the Active Directory container.
Add...	Selects from a list of existing GPOs or creates a new GPO to add to the current container.
Edit	Displays the group policy tree for the selected GPO and allows policy modification.
Options...	Allows user to enforce this GPO on this container and child containers below it or to prevent this policy from acting on the container altogether.
Delete...	Removes the selected GPO from the container group policy list.
Properties	Allows the administrator to disable the user or computer portion of the GPO to enhance boot-up or user logon speed. Permits this GPO to be linked by other domains and allows access to security settings for the selected GPO.
Up	Promotes the selected GPO in the current GPO list. GPOs are applied from the top of the list to the bottom.
Down	Demotes the selected GPO in the current GPO list. GPOs are applied from the top of the list to the bottom.
Block inheritance	Blocks policy inheritance from a parent container.

DISABLING COMPUTER AND USER CONFIGURATION SETTINGS

As discussed earlier, it is helpful to disable the portions of a GPO that are not being used to save on processing time when applying group policies. Either user or computer settings may be disabled if no policies are enabled below the node in the policy hierarchy. In this example you have set a user policy and can therefore disable the computer portion of the GPO.

1. Right-click the *Engineering OU* and select **Properties**. Select the **Group Policy** tab. Press the **Edit** button.

2. Right-click the *Engineering GPO* root node and select **Properties**. From the **General** tab select **Disable Computer Configuration Settings** (Figure 8.42).

Users in the Engineering OU and its child OUs will also inherit this policy. For a child OU to disable a policy inherited from its parents it must counteract the policy setting using another GPO. Let's create a GPO at a lower level to override the **Disable Lock Computer** policy setting.

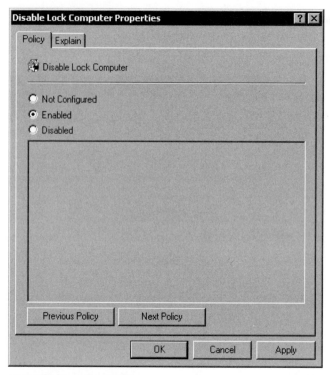

FIGURE 8.41 Policy Details

1. Click the plus sign in front of the **Active Directory Users and Computers** selection in the custom console. Open a domain → open the *Engineering OU* → open the *Sustaining OU*.

2. Right-click the *Sustaining OU* and select **Properties**. The **Sustaining Properties** dialog appears. Select the **Group Policy** tab.

3. Press the **New** button. Name the new object *Sustaining GPO*.

4. Highlight the new GPO and press the **Edit** button.

5. Click on the plus sign in front of **User Configuration → Administrative Templates → System → Logon/Logoff**. In the Policy window, double-click the **Disable Lock Computer** policy. Select the **Disabled** radio button. Press the **OK** button.

6. The **Disable Lock Computer** policy should be disabled at the *Sustaining OU* level.

7. Log off the system and log on again as a *Sustaining user*. Notice that the **Lock Workstation** button is no longer grayed out.

FIGURE 8.42 Disable Computer Configuration Settings

By disabling the **Disable Lock Computer** policy in the *Sustaining GPO,* users within the *Sustaining OU* will be able to lock their systems. Rather than directly override an inherited policy, try using the **Block Policy Inheritance** feature as demonstrated below:

- From the custom console open the *Sustaining OU* and right-click **Properties**. Select the **Group Policy** tab and select the *Sustaining GPO*. Press the **Edit** button. Proceed to the **Disable Lock Computer** policy - **User Configuration** → **Administrative Templates** → **System** → **Logon/Logoff**. In the Policy window double-click **Disable Lock Computer**. Select the **Not Configured** radio button. Press the **OK** button.

Now the **Disable Lock Computer** policy will again be inherited by the *Sustaining OU*.

Block policy inheritance from the *Engineering OU* as follows:

• Close the **Group Policy** window. From the **Sustaining Properties** dialog check the **Block Policy Inheritance** box (Figure 8.43). Close the custom console, log off, and log on as a *Sustaining user*. Notice that the **Lock Workstation** box is still accessible. Blocking policy inheritance prevents the *Engineering GPO* from being applied to the *Sustaining OU*.

Enforcing a GPO from the *Engineering OU* takes precedence over both the block policy inheritance and the policy override settings.

1. Open the custom console, right-click the *Engineering OU,* and select **Properties**.

2. Select the **Group Policy** tab and press the **New** button. Name the new GPO *Design Access GPO*. Press the **Options...** button and check the **No Override:** checkbox (Figure 8.44). Press the **OK** button. Notice that the **No Override** col-

FIGURE 8.43 Block Policy Inheritance at *Sustaining OU*

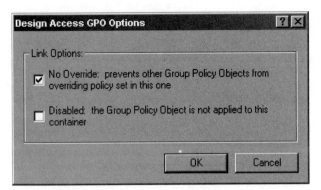

FIGURE 8.44 The No Override Group Policy Object Setting

umn is now checked. This feature can also be enabled/disabled by double-click-ing in the **No Override** column in the *Engineering OU*'s Properties dialog box.

3. The *Design Access GPO* is now enforced at the *Engineering OU* level.

4. Exit **Custom Console**, log off, and log on as a *Sustaining user*. Notice that the **Lock Workstation** button is grayed out once again.

The Sustaining group cannot override an enforced policy from a parent. The **Block Inheritance** feature is also unable to prevent enforced policy inheritance.

NOTE   One of the tasks an administrator should undertake is preventing users from "tat-tooing" the Registry. From the Administrative Templates node, the user can view user preferences in addition to policy settings. This is accomplished by selecting the *View* pull-down menu and deselecting the *Show Policies Only* option. The user can now view and modify user preferences that are not stored in maintained portions of the Registry. The user preference settings are coded red, the policies blue. If the group policy is removed or changed, the user preference will persist in the Registry. This is known as "tattooing," a prominent problem in earlier group policy implementations. Avoid letting users modify user preferences by enabling the **User Configuration** → **Administrative Templates** → **System** → **Group Policy** → **Enforce Show Policies Only** policy (Figure 8.45).

Security Group Filtering Example

GPOs that are linked to a given Active Directory container (site, domain, or OU) apply to all authenticated users within the container by default. However, Security permissions associated with a GPO also govern which users the GPO will apply to.

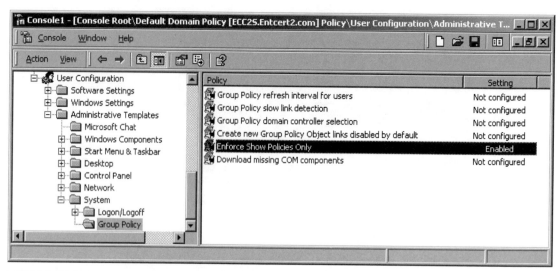

FIGURE 8.45 Limiting Registry Tattooing by Enabling a Policy

A security group may deny the GPO policy, making all users who are members of that group immune to it. Let's look at an example.

1. Create a domain local security group called *Software Config* and add an *Engineering OU* user to it.

2. Go to the *Engineering OU,* right-click **Properties**, and view the **Group Policy** tab. Select the *Engineering GPO* and press the **Properties** button.

3. Click the **Securities** tab (Figure 8.46) and press the **Add...** button. Select the *Software Config* security group and press the **Add** button.

4. Select the *Software Config* group and check the **Deny** box after the **Apply Group Policy** permissions line.

5. Press the **OK** button and answer *Yes* to the **Warning** dialog box.

6. Log off and log on as the *Engineering OU* user previously added to the *Software Config* security group. The **Lock Workstation** button should be accessible.

This new member of the *Software Config* group has filtered out the *Engineering GPO* by denying the **Apply Group Policy** permission. Even though this *Software Config* is also a member of the *Engineering OU,* the *Deny* permission from the *Software Config* group takes priority over all other security groups that may **Allow Apply Group Policy**. In the following steps the *Engineering GPO* will be rendered useless if neither the **Allow** box nor the **Deny** box is marked for the **Apply Group Policy** permission for all security groups associated with it.

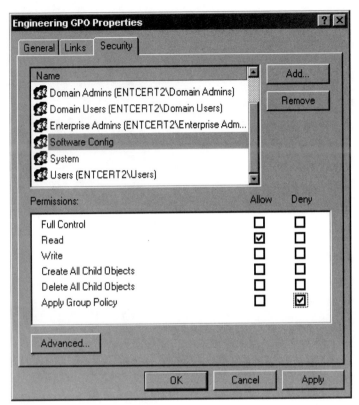

FIGURE 8.46 GPO Security for *Software Config*

1. Go to the *Engineering GPO* **Properties** dialog box. Remove all security groups except for **Domain Users**, **Domain Admins**, and *Software Config*. Select the **Domain Users** group and the *Software Config* group and ensure that the **Apply Group Policy** box is not checked under **Allow** or **Deny** for either group (Figure 8.47).

2. The Domain Admins group should allow Read/Write/Create All Child Objects/Delete All Child Objects so that administrative functions can still be performed on the GPO.

3. Log off and log on as the *Engineering* user. The **Lock Workstation** button should be accessible. The GPO is not applied to either the **Domain Users** or the *Software Config* group of which the user is a member.

If the **Domain Users** group allowed **Apply Group Policy**, then the user would have the group policy applied. A user must be a member of a security group that

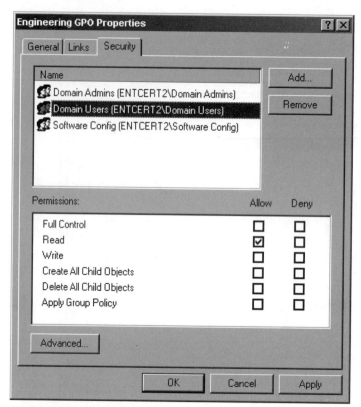

FIGURE 8.47 The Domain Users Security Group

applies the group policy in order to use the GPO. The default security settings for GPOs apply policies to the **Authenticated Users** group. This covers most users with interactive logon capability.

Scripts Example

In a previous section, we discussed the conceptual basis of scripts. For system administration, scripts can be used for numerous activities. A script can be executed in one of four time periods: startup, shutdown, logon, or logoff.

This example runs a test script when the user logs on to a system:

1. Create a very simple test Java script to run on login. Open **Notepad** and enter the following line:

```
Wscript.echo("You have run the logon script!");
```

2. Save the file as *testscript.js* on the local hard drive.

3. Open the custom console and find the *Engineering OU*. Open the group policies linked to this OU and edit the *Engineering GPO*.

4. Follow the **User Configuration** → **Windows Settings** → **Scripts** path and double-click the **Logon policy** (Figure 8.48).

5. Press the **Add...** button to expose the **Add a Script** dialog box (Figure 8.49). Press the **Browse** button and find *testscript.js*. Press the **OK** button.

The script should be available to the user at logon.

Scripts execute from top to bottom and may be rearranged by pressing the **Up** and **Down** buttons. The **Edit** button allows script path modification, name changing, and parameter editing. Scripts are removed by pressing the **Remove** button.

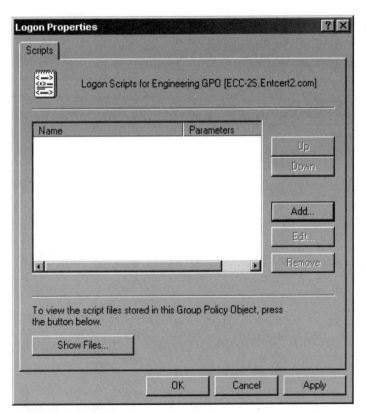

FIGURE 8.48 Logon Scripts

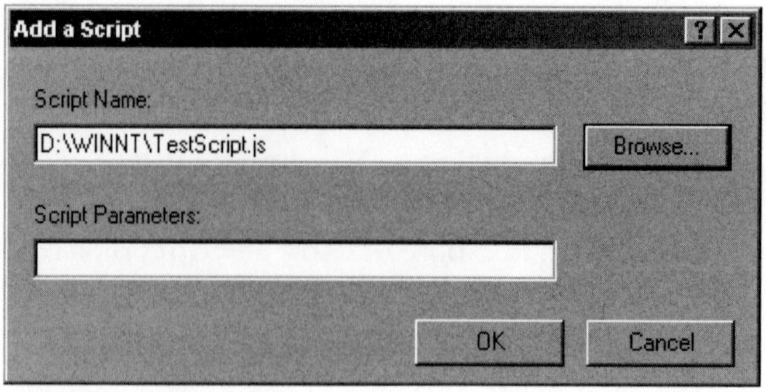

FIGURE 8.49 Add a Script

The **Show Files...** button displays the scripts stored in the default directory for this GPO. The startup and shutdown script policies may found in **Computer Configuration → Windows Settings → Scripts**.

Folder Redirection Example

This example will illustrate how to implement folder redirection. To redirect all **My Document** folders for the *Engineering OU* to a common shared server, follow these steps:

1. Edit the *Software Config GPO* applied to the *Engineering OU*. Go to **User Configuration → Windows Settings → Folder Redirection → My Documents**. Right-click **My Documents** and select **Properties**. The **My Document Properties** window appears. From the **Setting** pull-down menu select **Basic – Redirect everyone's folder to the same location**.
2. Press the **Browse** button and find a shared server folder for all *Engineering* users.
3. Press the **OK** button.

See the next section for more folder redirection examples.

INTELLIMIRROR

One of the more widely promoted aspects of Windows 2000, IntelliMirror simply brings together other Windows 2000 technologies to provide more intelligent user interfacing. In particular, it helps to reconcile desktop settings, applications, and stored files for users, particularly those who move between workstations or must periodically work offline. This section provides a highlight of IntelliMirror functionality.

Roaming Documents and Preferences

Together folder redirection and offline folders provide centralized management and storage of user documents. Additionally, the user is permitted to access and update documents when not connected to the network. This design is ideally suited to laptop users. Maintaining an offline folder on the network allows the administrator to perform backups on a scheduled basis without direct concern for backing up the laptop system.

REDIRECTING MY DOCUMENT FOLDERS

In this example the user's **My Documents** folder is redirected to a directory in his name under a shared network folder using group policies. The **My Documents** folder is designated as offline. A security group is used to determine which users and groups the folder redirection policy will affect.

1. Create a network share called *Network Docs and Settings*.
2. Create a global security group called *Engineers* and a new user account called *Joe Engineer*.
3. Add *Joe Engineer* to the *Engineers* group.

Redirect Joe Engineer's My Documents folder to the network share folder using the **Default Domain Policy**.

1. From the Default Domain Policy right-click the **User Configuration → Windows Settings → Folder Redirection → My Documents** node and select **Properties** (Figure 8.50).
2. Select the **Target** tab and select **Advanced – Specify locations for various user groups**. Press the **Add...** button to reveal the **Specify Group and Location** dialog (Figure 8.51) and browse for the *Engineering group*. Press the **Add** button. Press the **OK** button.
3. In the **Target Folder Location** field, press the **Browse** button and search for the *Network Docs and Settings* folder on the appropriate server. Complete the path name using the *servername\Network Docs and Settings\%username%*. The *%username%* environmental variable will be used to create a separate directory for each user. Press the **OK** button.
4. On the **Settings** tab make appropriate choices for policy removal and permissions. The default settings are fine for this example. Press the **OK** button.

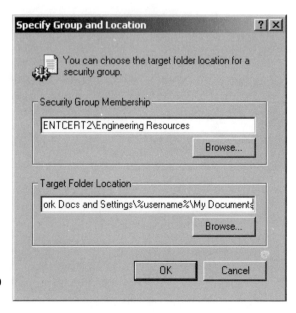

FIGURE 8.50 Folder Redirection

**FIGURE 8.51 Redirect Security Group
to Target Folder**

Now all users in the *Engineering* security group will have their folders redirected to the new network share and have their own **My Documents** subdirectory below their personal folder. Let's use offline folders to allow the engineering users access to their documents when they are offline.

1. Go to *Joe Engineer*'s laptop and select **My Computer** → **Tools** → **Folder Options**. From the **Offline Files** tab enable the **Enable Offline Files** option.
2. From **My Computer**, right-click the **My Documents** folder and select **Make Available Offline**. The **Offline Files Wizard** starts. Press the **Next>** button.
3. Select the **Automatically synchronize the Offline Files when I log on and log off my computer** option to instruct the **Synchronization Manager** to handle file updates between the remote system and the network share. Press the **Next>** button.
4. Select the **Create shortcut** option. Press the **Next>** button.
5. Select **Yes, make this folder and all its subfolders available offline**. Press the **OK** button.

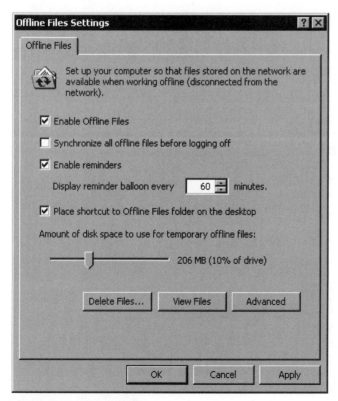

FIGURE 8.52 Offline Settings

Now when Joe Engineer logs on to his laptop when not connected to the network, an offline dialog warns that the system is offline. An icon on the Task bar appears. Right-clicking the icon gives the user four options:

- Status—indicates whether the folder is off- or online.
- Synchronize—allows manual synchronization of the offline files.
- View Files—displays all files that are available offline.
- Settings—set reminders, synchronization, and offline availability (Figure 8.52).

The **Synchronization Manager** may be manually started from either the **My Computer** or **My Network Places** desktop tools. From the **Tools** pull-down select **Synchronize...**. Manual synchronization may be started by selecting the desired directories and pressing the **Synchronize** button. Pressing the **Setup** button allows configuration via three tabs (Figure 8.53):

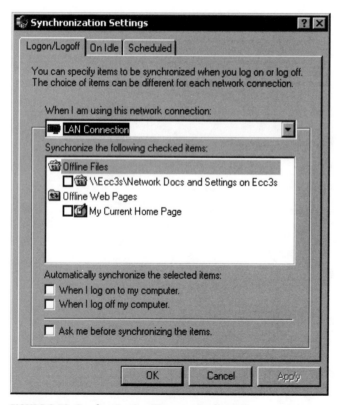

FIGURE 8.53 Synchronization Manager Configuration

- **Logon/Logoff**—logon, logoff, and prompting before synchronization configuration.
- **On Idle**—idle time before synchronization configuration.
- **Scheduled**—times and directories to synchronize.

POSTSCRIPT

Group policies are obviously a very powerful system administration tool. When applied cautiously, a GPO can streamline repetitive tasks such as individually setting the rights of every user in an OU. It can also be used to assign and publish common applications. Despite their many strengths, group policies can also cause real user and system problems. If a GPO is improperly constructed or assigned, it could have a ripple effect through all child objects and user accounts.

Our advice is to experiment with group policies in a very narrowly defined arena. Once you understand the impact of the GPO on your test environment, you can expand as required. Again, caution is important when using group policies.

Permissions Security, Folder Sharing, and Dfs

Permissions and remote folder sharing are mainstays of Windows 2000 security. NTFS-based permissions allow and deny access to files and folders both locally and across the network. By contrast, folder sharing provides or denies access to objects on a remote computer. The two can be combined to provide granular access and proper control.

FAT/FAT32 and NTFS exhibit different permission functionality. FAT and FAT32 provide no security over locally logged-on users. Only native NTFS provides extensive permission control on both remote and local files. All three file systems do support shared folder permissions that apply to remote users. However, to take advantage of Windows 2000's advanced security, NTFS volumes must be used.

This chapter provides both theoretical and hands-on examination of Windows 2000 NTFS permissions security and folder sharing. We also examine the use of the Distributed File System (Dfs) as another means of facilitating access to objects across the network. After completing this chapter, a system administrator should be able to

- Apply permissions on objects
- Utilize a working knowledge of ownership and how it can be changed
- Implement shared folders
- Manage Dfs

REVIEWING NTFS PERMISSIONS

To protect data from users in a Windows 2000 enterprise, the administrator should understand how NTFS employs permissions. NTFS permissions are divided into folder and file categories. Folder permissions control what files and subfolders a user or group may view and which folders a user may open. They also restrict what users and groups may create, delete, and change permissions on the contents of a folder.

Every file, folder, or other object has an owner. For example, every user owns his **My Documents** home directory, as well as all files he creates and saves in the **My Documents** folder. As the owner, the user has full control over his objects and can assign permissions for other users to access them. As we shall discuss later, this control ranges from total denial of access to granting ownership of a file or folder to another.

NOTE   As an administrator, you also have full control of a user's files and folders. This is particularly useful when the user requests intervention or leaves the organization. However, this privilege should not be abused. Direct administrative modification of a user's file and folder permissions is ordinarily on an "as needed" basis.

Windows 2000 utilizes Access Control Lists (ACLs) to track an object's permissions. All objects have ACLs, which control what users and groups can do with them. The specific user or group is defined as an Access Control Entry (ACE).

The ACL is composed of a System Access Control List (SACL) and a Discretionary Access Control List (DACL). The SACL configures auditing permissions and determines which file and folder operations will be written to the audit logs; the DACL contains security settings and permissions granted to specific users and groups. Each of the ACL's Access Control Entries (ACEs) has security settings and audit settings (Tables 9.1 and 9.2).

TABLE 9.1 DACL Elements

Type	Description
Access Allowed	Identifies users and groups having explicit permission to utilize the object.
Access Denied	Identifies the permission denied expressly to a user or group.

TABLE 9.2 SACL Elements

Type	Description
Audit Successful File/ Folder operation	Users and groups logged on when attempts to access and modify file/folder attributes and contents are successful.
Audit Failed File/ Folder operation	Users and groups logged when attempts to access and modify file/folder attributes and contents fail.

Standard and Special Permissions

Windows 2000 supports two overlapping categories of permissions: *special* and *standard*. Standard permissions are generally applied to objects; special permissions provide finer granularity to file- or folder-based security. The majority of this discussion centers on standard permissions. We will apply their use by example after we review the basic concepts.

PERMISSIONS LEVELS

Six types of permissions can be combined for different results: Read, Write, Execute, List Folder Contents, Modify, and Full Control. They are described in Table 9.3.

TABLE 9.3 Permissions

Abbreviation	Type	Description
R	Read	Provides the designated user or group the ability to read the file or the contents of the folder.
W	Write	Provides the designated user or group the ability to create or write files and folders.
RX	Read & Execute	Provides the designated user or group the ability to read file and folder attributes, view folder contents, and read files within the folder. If this permission is applied to a folder, files with inheritance set will inherit it (see the inheritance discussion).
L	List Folder Contents	Same as Read & Execute, but not inherited by files within a folder. However, newly created subfolders will inherit this permission.
M	Modify	Provides the ability to delete, write, read, and execute.
F	Full Control	Provides the ability to perform any action, including taking ownership and changing permissions. When applied to a folder the user or group may delete subfolders and files within a folder.

The Full Control permission level obviously is automatically provided to the object's creator/owner and to the Administrators group.

Working with Folder Permissions

Users may overwrite, delete, read, execute, and own NTFS files. It is important to understand that file permissions take precedence over folder permissions. If a user has permission to execute a file she may do so even if she does not have permissions to read and execute the file's folder.

NOTE   It is possible for a user to navigate to a file for which he does not have folder permission. This involves simply knowing the path of the file object. Even if the user can't drill down the file/folder tree using **My Computer**, he can still gain access to the file using the Universal Naming Convention (UNC). In this example, the user does not have permissions to do anything in the folder called Book. However, he does have full control over the file called Chapter10.doc that resides in the Book folder. If the user attempted to user Explorer to see the contents of the Book folder, it would not be displayed. However, if the user wanted to execute the file within Microsoft Word, he could do so by using either the **Start → Run** dialog or the **Start → Accessories → Command Prompt**, and provide the full path to the object as C:\Book\Chapter10.doc. The user must know the file's full path and name, but it is still possible to override the folder permissions.

SETTING PERMISSIONS

Permissions apply differently to files and folders. In addition, NTFS permissions to other objects like applications are accessed and managed in the same way. Setting permissions is accomplished by following these steps:

1. Right-click **My Computer** and select **Explore**.
2. Find a folder on an NTFS volume and right-click on **Properties**.
3. The **Program Files Properties** dialog box appears. Select the **Security Tab**.
4. Make changes by selecting **Allow** or **Deny** at each permissions category.

Permissions Properties

Folder permissions are listed with **Allow** and **Deny** checkbox columns. They are displayed for a user or group selected in the *Name* window, also known as the ACL. The example shown in Figure 9.1 includes two ACEs, Administrators, and Software Config.

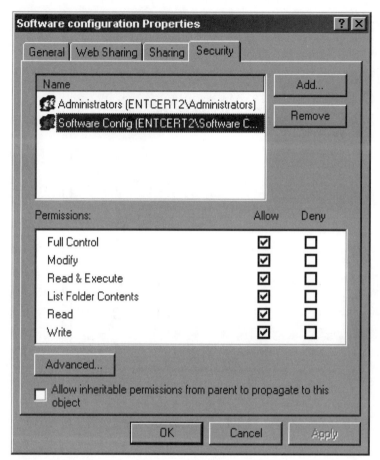

FIGURE 9.1 Software Configuration Properties

Permissions are cumulative. If a user belongs to more than one ACE (multiple group memberships), her permissions are an accumulation of those of each group.

To illustrate how permissions are applied, let's provide and deny permissions to a specific user. *Joe Engineer* is once again our user.

Allow Permissions Example

Joe Engineer is assigned Read privileges, and he also belongs to the *Software Config* group, which is assigned Write privileges. The ACE permissions for both *Joe Engineer* and *Software Config* are shown in Figures 9.2 and 9.3, respectively. *Joe Engineer* will have the effective rights of both ACEs, including Read and Write.

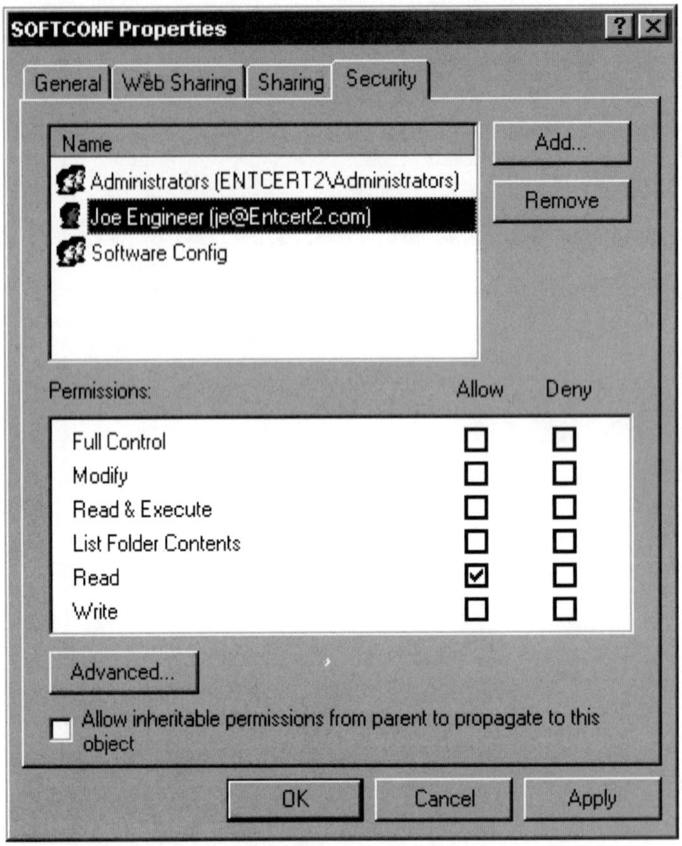

FIGURE 9.2 Joe Engineer Security Settings

Deny Permissions Example

The **Allow** permissions are cumulative, but the **Deny** permissions behave quite differently. **Deny** overrides **Allow**. For instance, *Joe Engineer* has been specifically allowed to read the *Software Config* folder. However, when he joins a new group called *Engineering Security,* he loses the previous permissions since this group has been denied access to the *SOFTCONF* folder.

Let's review how this is accomplished.

1. The new group is added to the ACL by pressing the **Add...** button and choosing the *Engineering Security* group from the **Select Users, Computers, or Groups** dialog box (Figure 9.4).

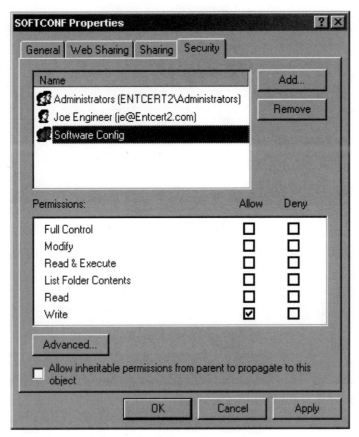

FIGURE 9.3 The Software Config Group Security Settings

2. From the **SOFTCONF Properties** box (Figure 9.5) select the *Engineering Security* group and check **Deny** in the **Read** permission row.

3. Press the **Apply** button to apply the new permission and display a warning (Figure 9.6).

4. Answer **Yes** to the warning. *Engineering Security* now denies all members Read access to the *SOFTCONF* folder.

No matter what group has granted *Joe Engineer* permission to read the folder, the Deny permission assigned to the *Engineering Security* group takes precedence.

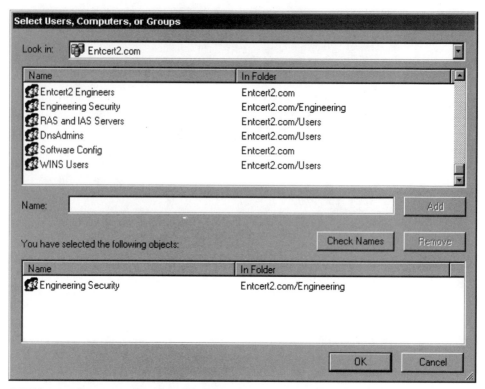

FIGURE 9.4 Select Users, Computers, or Groups

SPECIAL PERMISSIONS

The standard NTFS permissions just discussed provide general control over user and group access. However, on some occasions where greater granularity may be needed, the NTFS special permissions come into play. There are 14 special permissions. They are mapped to the standard permissions, as shown in Table 9.4.

Let's apply special permissions to our example of Joe Engineer:

1. Right-click on an object and select **Properties**.
2. From the **Subfolders Properties** dialog box add *Joe Engineer* to the ACL.
3. Assign **Write** permissions to the user by checking the **Allow** checkbox.
4. Press the **Advanced...** button. The **Access Control Settings for Subfolder** appears.
5. Select *Joe Engineer* and press the **View/Edit...** button. The **Permission Entry for Subfolder** dialog box appears (Figure 9.7).

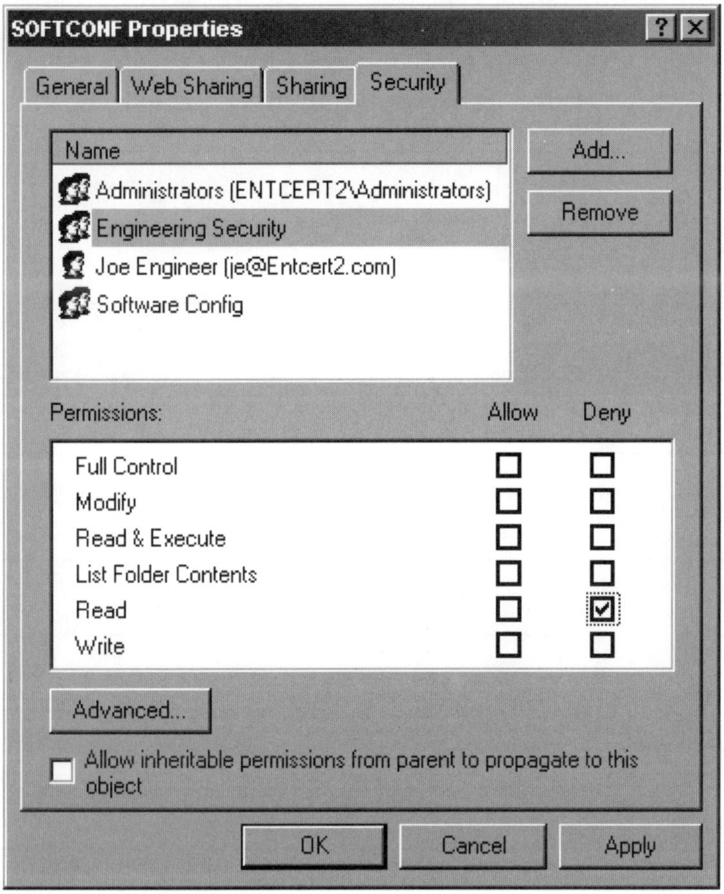

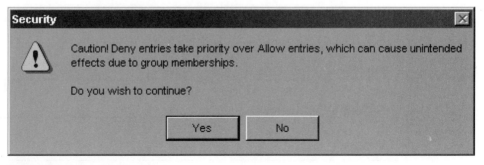

FIGURE 9.5 Software Config

FIGURE 9.6 A Security Warning

TABLE 9.4 Mapping Standard Permissions to Special Permissions

Types	Full Control	Modify	Read & Execute	List Folder Contents	Read	Write
Traverse Folder/ Execute File	X	X	X	X		
List Folder/ Read Data	X	X	X	X	X	
Read Attributes	X	X	X	X	X	
Read Extended Attributes	X	X	X	X	X	
Create Files/ Write Data	X	X				X
Create Folders/ Append Data	X	X				X
Write Attributes	X	X				X
Write Extended Attributes	X	X				X
Delete Subfolders and Files	X					
Delete	X	X				
Read Permissions	X	X	X	X	X	
Change Permissions	X					
Take Ownership	X					

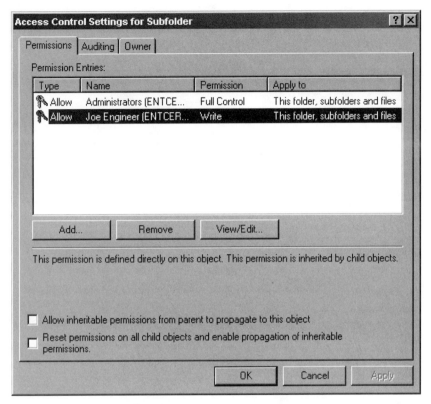

FIGURE 9.7 Access Control Settings

Notice that the allowed permissions, **Create Files**, **Create Folders**, **Write Attributes**, and **Write Extended Attributes**, correspond to the **Write** column of the previous table (Figure 9.8). They are associated with the standard *Write* NTFS permission. Each of the six standard permissions is mapped to a subset of the 14 special permissions. In fact, as you add special permissions, the standard permission level changes to include them.

1. From the **Subfolder Properties** window, select the **Security** tab. Select *Joe Engineer* and notice that only the **Write** permission is set to **Allowed**.

2. Press the **Advanced...** button.

3. Select *Joe Engineer* from the **Permission Entries** and press the **View/ Edit...** button.

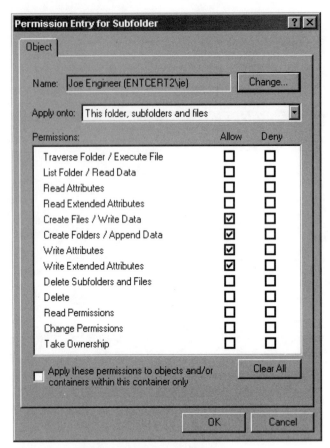

FIGURE 9.8 Permissions Entry for Subfolder

4. Check the **Allow** boxes next to the following four special permissions: **List Folder/Read Data**, **Read Attributes**, **Read Extended Attributes**, **Read Permissions** (Figure 9.9).

5. Press the **OK** button. Press the next **OK** button.

6. The **Subfolders Properties** window should now show the standard **Read** and **Write** permissions as allowed (Figure 9.10).

Permission Inheritance

All folders and subfolders inherit permissions from their parent folder by default. This is true of files within a folder as well. In other words, a folder with Read and

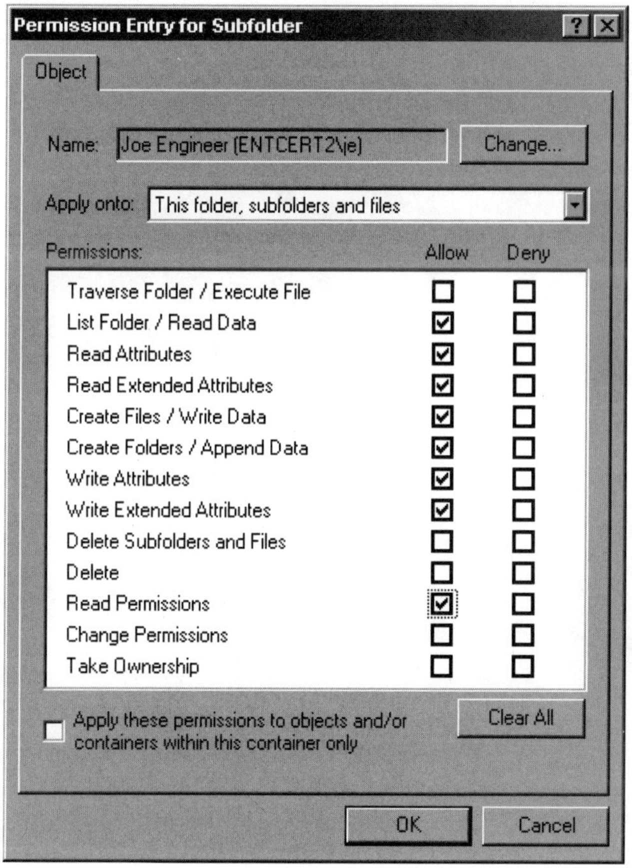

FIGURE 9.9 A Permissions Entry

Write permissions for the *Everybody* group will pass these characteristics to subfolders and files unless otherwise changed.

Inheriting NTFS permissions can be prevented at the child folder or file level by clearing the **Allow inheritable permissions from parent to propagate to this object** attribute on any file or folder. Once permission inheritance has been stopped, permissions may be assigned to the object by copying them from its parents or by clearing all permissions currently assigned. All children of the object will inherit its permissions rather than those of its grandparents. This point is illustrated with the following example:

1. Create a new subfolder within the *SOFTCONF* folder called *Subfolder*.
2. Right-click the new folder and select **Properties**. The **Subfolder Properties** dialog appears.

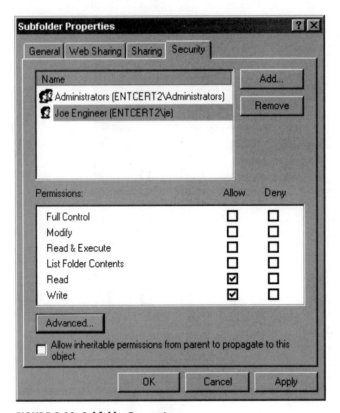

FIGURE 9.10 Subfolder Properties

3. Select the **Security** tab and uncheck the **Allow inheritable permissions from parent to propagate to this object** checkbox (Figure 9.11).

4. The **Security** dialog box (Figure 9.12) appears, presenting three options:

   • Copy parent permissions to the new object.

   • Remove all permissions on the new object.

   • Abort the block inheritance operation.

Selecting either the **Copy** or the **Remove** option will block the inheritance of parent NTFS permissions and allow this branch of the directory tree to propagate its own set of permissions.

1. Press the **Remove** button and notice that all permissions have been eliminated from *Subfolder*.

2. New groups and users can be added by pressing the **Add...** button and their associated permissions can be assigned.

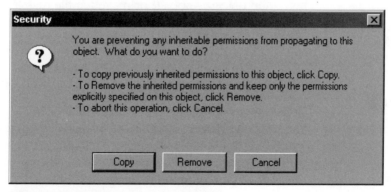

FIGURE 9.11 Subfolder Security Settings

FIGURE 9.12 Permission Inheritance Options

New files and folders created within *Subfolder* will receive the permissions assigned to *Subfolder* rather than those assigned to the *SOFTCONF* folder.

MOVING AND COPYING FILE AND FOLDER PERMISSIONS

Moving and copying files can affect their permissions, so it is important to understand the basic rules associated with these actions.

Copying Files and Folders

The copy procedure simply duplicates an existing file or folder to another location. To copy, the user must have at least **Read** permission for the source file or folder and **Write** permission for the destination parent folder. Once the new file or folder has been created, it inherits its permission settings from the *new* parent folder. Permissions are not retained since this is a new object.

Moving Files and Folders

The process of moving a file or folder simply involves removing it from its current location and placing it in a new location. To do this the user must have **Read/Modify** permission on the object and **Write** permission for the new parent folder. A file or folder moved within the same NTFS volume is not considered a new object and thus retains its permissions once in the new parent folder. However, a file or folder moved to another NTFS volume inherits permissions from the destination parent folder.

NOTE   Regardless of whether an object is copied or moved, a file or folder transferred from an NTFS volume to a FAT volume loses all permissions. Remember, FAT/FAT32 does not support permission assignment.

Ownership

Every file and folder has permissions along with an owner. The owner has full control over the object regardless of what other permissions are assigned to that object. Anyone with **Full Control** can assign the special NTFS permission **Take Ownership** to someone else. Note, however, that that right does not make them owner. Users with the **Take Ownership** permission must make themselves owner to obtain full control over a file or folder.

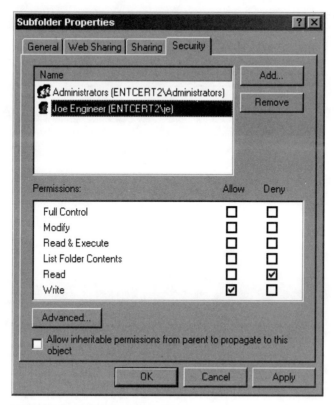

FIGURE 9.13 Subfolder Permissions

Denying Rights to a Subfolder—Example

In the following example we will test the principle of ownership and folder access. The first step is to deny *Joe Engineer* **Read** permission.

1. Deny *Joe Engineer* the right to read *Subfolder* (Figure 9.13).

2. Verify the **Deny** entry by pressing the **Advanced** button and viewing the ACL settings (Figure 9.14).

3. Select the **Allow** entry for Joe Engineer and press the **View/Edit** button.

Take Ownership Example

Transferring ownership involves two primary steps. The first is allowing another user to take ownership. The second is the other user actually accepting it. The following example walks through the steps required to allow Joe Engineer to take

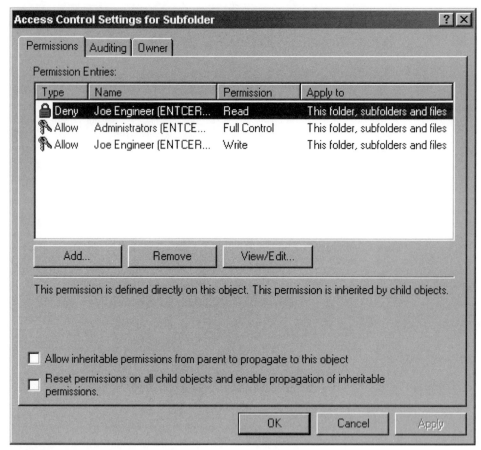

FIGURE 9.14 Access Control Settings

ownership. Once he accepts it he can change permissions to view and edit *Subfolder*'s contents. This example depends on settings from the preceding examples.

4. Set the allow **Take ownership** special permission (Figure 9.15).

5. Press the **OK** button. Notice that the modified permission entry for *Joe Engineer* is now **Special** in the **Permissions** column. Press **OK** again and log off the system.

6. Log back on as *Joe Engineer*.

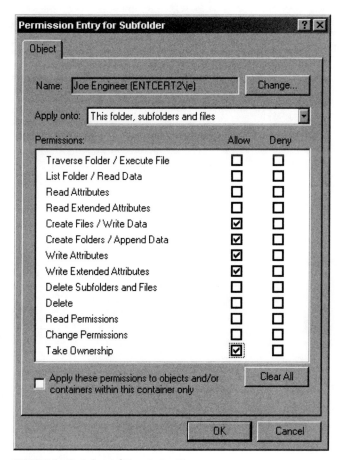

FIGURE 9.15 A Special Permission Entry

7. Try to access the *Subfolder* as *Joe Engineer*. Notice that it is not accessible.

8. Right-click *Subfolder* **Properties** and select **Security** Tab. No properties are visible. The **Read attributes** permission has been denied *Joe Engineer,* and security permissions are no longer readable (Figure 9.16).

9. From the **Subfolder Properties** window, select the **Security** tab.

10. Press the **Advanced...** button.

11. Select the **Owner** tab from the **Access Control Settings for Subfolder** window.

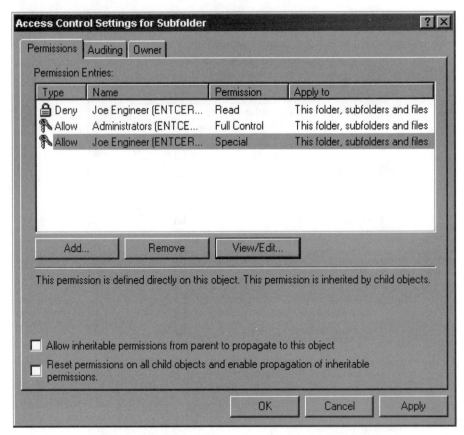

FIGURE 9.16 Access Control Settings

12. Select *Joe Engineer* and press the **Apply** button (Figure 9.17).

13. Press the **OK** button. Press the **OK** button again.

14. Re-open the **Subfolder Properties** window and select the **Security** tab. *Joe Engineer* can now view and change permissions (Figure 9.18).

Owner Sets Permissions

At this stage Joe Engineer has taken ownership of *Subfolder*. He must now assign himself the needed permissions to access it.

1. Uncheck the **Deny Read** permission and check the allow **Full Control** box (see Figure 9.19, page 337).

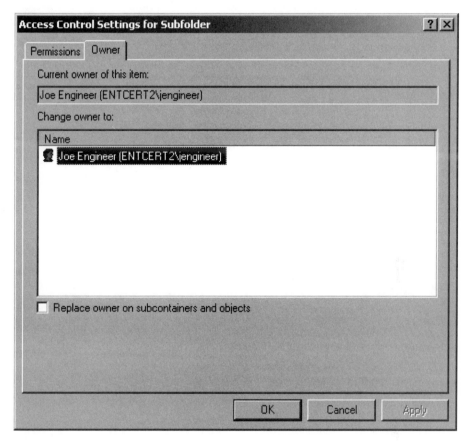

FIGURE 9.17 Ownership

2. Press the **OK** button.

3. Try to access *Subfolder*. Joe Engineer now has full control over the folder.

IMPLICIT GROUPS AND PERMISSIONS

Users, security groups, and implicit groups are assigned varying levels of permissions for files and folders. Implicit groups are local to all Windows 2000 systems but not available through the Active Directory or local account databases. They are accessible only when assigning file/folder permissions and reflect how the user accesses the resource. Membership in an implicit group is determined by the operating system, and their group SIDs are not passed with Kerberos authorization information.

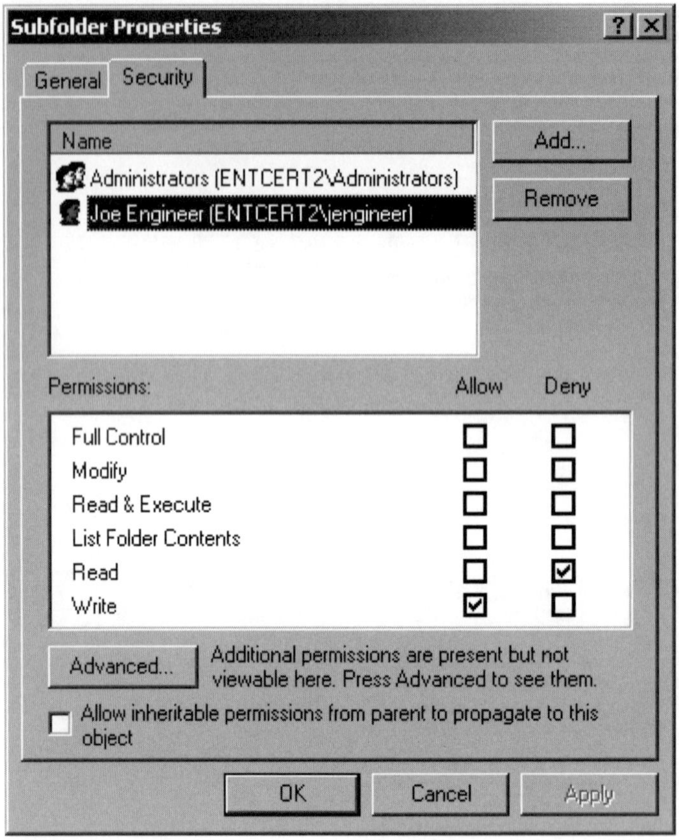

FIGURE 9.18 Security

Implicit groups can be used to assign permissions to folders and files. They are defined as shown in Table 9.5 on page 338.

FOLDER SHARING

Folder sharing is used whenever one computer user needs access to a file on another computer's file system. Once a folder is shared, all files and subfolders receive the same share permissions. Share permissions apply to the entire folder and not to specific files. Both NTFS and FAT volumes require that shared folder

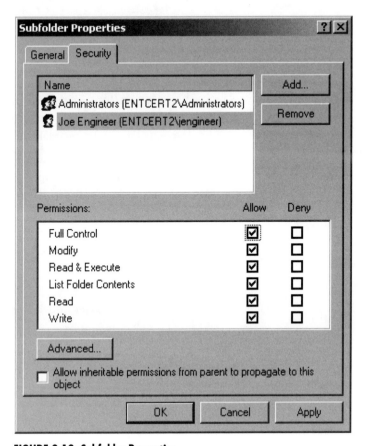

FIGURE 9.19 Subfolder Properties

permissions be set for network users to gain access. FAT volumes have no local user authentication, but share permissions provide security for remote users. Only NTFS volumes can apply file permissions to the objects in a shared folder.

Several additional user rules govern the use of shared folders:

- The effective permission is an accumulation of the user's individual and group membership rights.
- **Deny** permissions always cancel out corresponding **Allow** permissions.
- A copy of a shared folder does not retain the "shared" status.
- Shared folder status is discarded when a folder is moved.

TABLE 9.5 Implicit Groups

Group	Description
ANONYMOUS LOGON	User without system identifier (SID).
Authenticated Users	Same as Everyone but does not contain guests or anonymous users.
BATCH	Batch program (*.cmd and *.bat) rights.
CREATOR	Creator of the file/folder/print job.
CREATOR OWNER	Creator and owner of the file/folder/print job.
DIAL-UP	User accessing the system via the Remote Access Service (RAS).
ENTERPRISE DOMAIN CONTROLLERS	Enterprise domain controllers remotely accessing the system.
Everyone	Local and remotely logged-on users.
INTERACTIVE	Locally logged-on user.
NETWORK	User logged on to the system through the network.
RESTRICTED	Users cannot install programs or make changes to file system settings.
SYSTEM	Operating system, otherwise known as the local system.
TERMINAL SERVER USER	Terminal server client.

Creating Shared Folders

Shared folders work in the same manner for Windows 2000 domains and workgroups. The only measurable difference is in who can create them. In a Windows 2000 domain environment, the built-in **Administrators** and **Server Operators** groups can establish shared folders throughout the domain. In the workgroup, the **Administrators** and **Power Users** groups have authority to share folders on the individual server. These two groups can also share folders on standalone servers and on Windows 2000 Professional installations.

SHARING FOLDERS

The actual creation of a shared folder is similar to applying permissions to a file or folder. The following steps set shared permissions:

1. Log on with administrative privileges.
2. Open **Explorer** and right-click **Properties** on a folder you want to share.

3. Select the **Sharing** tab and click the **Share this folder** radio button, as shown in Figure 9.20.

4. Press the **Permissions** button. The **Permissions for Software Configuration** dialog appears as shown in Figure 9.21.

Three levels of available permissions are presented for each of the named users or groups. Select the **Allow** permission(s) that apply. While you can also **Deny** a specific right, it is generally advisable to use an affirmative approach.

- **Read** allows a user to open files and see subfolder names.
- **Change** allows all privileges offered by Read permissions and allows users to change file contents and delete and create files and subfolders.

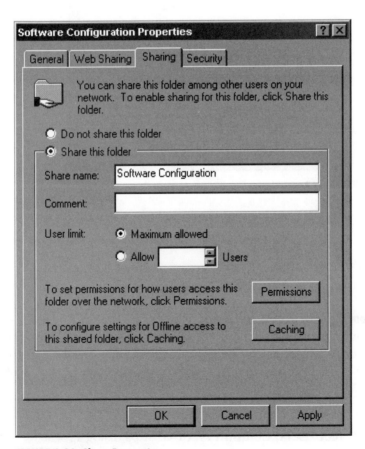

FIGURE 9.20 Share Properties

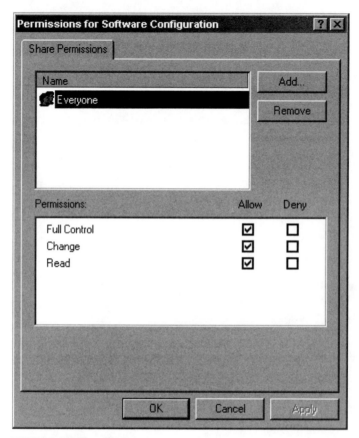

FIGURE 9.21 Share Permissions

- **Full Control** allows all privileges offered by **Change** and adds the ability to take ownership and modify permissions.

Adding and Deleting Groups and Users

The default share permissions give full control to *Everyone*. If you want to ensure folder security only to users and groups you add, remove the *Everyone* group by selecting the **Everyone** name and pressing the **Remove** button. To Add users or groups,

1. Press the **Add...** button.
2. The **Select Users, Computers, or Groups** dialog appears.

NOTE   The **Look in:** menu displays your domain and other trusted domains as shown in
Figure 9.22. You may add users or groups and then assign shared permissions.
Note that a user account in a trusted domain must be selected from its domain,
not the local domain.

3. Using the **Look in:** drop-down menu, select the domain where the user or
   group resides.
4. Select the user or group from the **Name** window and press the **Add** button.
5. Press the **OK** button.

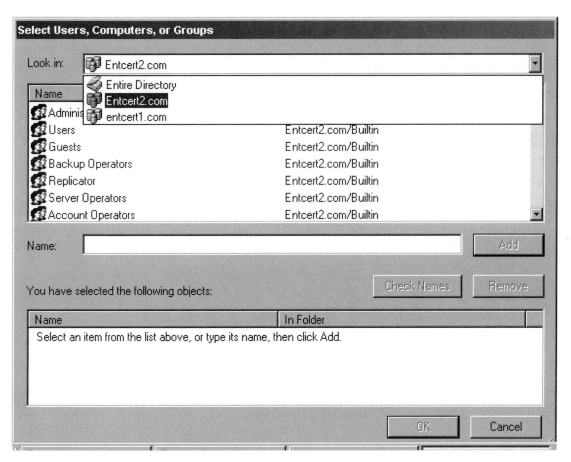

FIGURE 9.22 Select Users, Computers, and Groups

NOTE   In connecting to shared folders there are three common scenarios:

1. The user is accessing a shared folder within your own domain. In this case she can use her own user name and password in the standard form.

2. The user is accessing a shared folder from another untrusted domain. She must use a user name and account for the domain in which the share resides.

3. The user is accessing a shared folder from another trusted domain. *Important:* She must use a user name and password from her home domain. The user name should be in the form *domainname\username*.

Facilitating Shared Access

Once a share has been created, clients may connect to the folder using one of three methods: (1) map a network drive; (2) use **My Network Places**; and (3) use the **Run** menu option.

MAPPING A NETWORK DRIVE TO A SHARED FOLDER

Mapping a network drive makes a remote shared folder available to the local machine **Explorer** or **My Computer**. From all appearances, the remote shared folder looks local. Mapping follows these steps:

1. From **My Computer** select **Tools** → select **Map Network Drive...**.

2. Right-click **My Network Places** and select **Map Network Drive...**.

3. Select the drive letter to be associated with the remote share from the **Drive:** drop-down list (Figure 9.23).

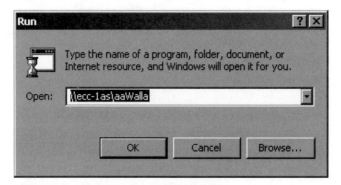

FIGURE 9.23 The Map Network Drive Wizard

4. Click **Browse**; then search for the desired network share. Ensure that the share is addressed in the form *servername**sharedfolder*.

5. From this dialog you may also log on to the share with another user name. (This is required for access to a share in a trusted domain.)

6. The new folder share will be accessible from **My Computer** as the **Drive:** letter.

THE MY NETWORK PLACES LINK TO A SHARED FOLDER

My Network Places can also facilitate access to a shared folder. To use it follow these steps:

1. From **My Network Places** find the computer containing the share. If you have trouble connecting to the desired computer, press the **Search** button, enter the computer name, and press the **Search Now** button.

2. Open the desired shared folder. If required, enter the appropriate user name according to the Note on page 342.

USING RUN COMMAND TO ACCESS SHARED FOLDERS

Another approach to gaining access to a shared folder is the **Run** command. To use the **Start Menu->Run**

1. **Start** → select **Run**. The Run window appears as shown in Figure 9.24.

2. Enter the name of the server with the path to the desired share in the form *servername**sharefolder*.

3. Press the **OK** button.

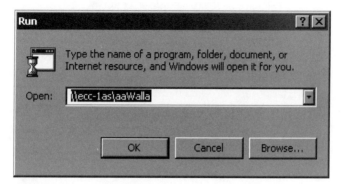

FIGURE 9.24 The Run Dialog Box

ACCESSING A SHARE FROM INTERNET EXPLORER

A share may be accessed from Internet Explorer using the share's Uniform Naming Convention (UNC) name. From the URL address field enter the share name in the form *servername**sharefolder*. A shared folder address may be added to the Favorites list for convenient access.

Special Hidden Shares

Windows 2000 special shares are system root folders accessible to the network but not necessarily visible to normal users. There are several types of administrative share folders, as shown in Table 9.6.

Additional shares may be added for different services. For instance, the Certificate Authority adds its own share when installed. The **Shared Folders** snap-in may be added to any management console to display all currently shared folders (Figure 9.25).

TABLE 9.6 Special Hidden Shares

Share Name	Description
Admin$	The root system folder is by default C:\Winnt, but may have been placed in a different volume or under a different name during installation. The Administrator group is granted full control and is the only group with any access to this shared folder for remote administration.
Drive$	Each volume is associated with a disk drive designation. A$ and B$ are reserved for floppy disk volumes. C$ through Z$ are designations for hard disks, CD-ROMs, and removable media. The Administrator group has full control over these volumes.
IPC$	Shared memory space for inter-process communication when accessing remote shares and remotely administering a computer.
NETLOGON	Space used by the Net Logon service during logon. Startup/logon scripts are accessed here.
print$	Used for shared printers and contains the device drivers. Administrators, Server Operators, and Print Operator group members have full control over this shared folder.
SYSVOL	Used by the net logon service and provides access to Active Directory information.

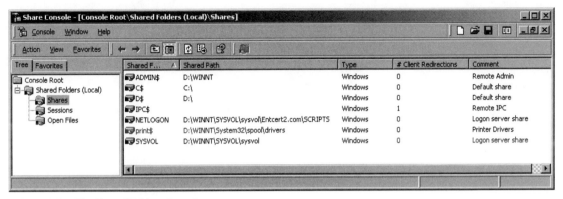

FIGURE 9.25 The Shared Folders Snap-In

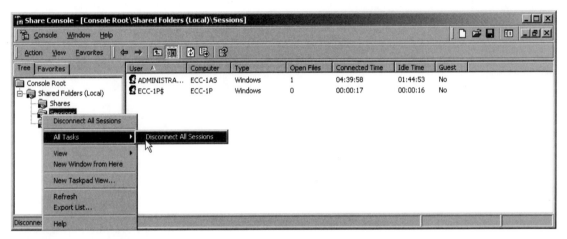

FIGURE 9.26 Current Share Sessions

The **Sessions** node displays users and systems currently accessing network shares. The administrator can selectively terminate connections or terminate all sessions at once (Figure 9.26).

The **Open Files** node displays the files currently being accessed from shares. Individual files may be closed or all files may be closed at once (Figure 9.27).

Using NTFS Permissions and Shared Folders

While the permissions associated with a shared folder are automatically inherited by the files and subfolders, it is possible to apply additional permissions to individual files on an NTFS volume. Doing so provides greater security over the

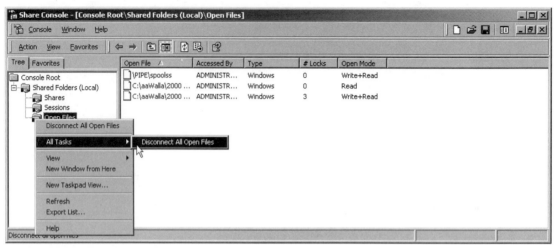

FIGURE 9.27 Open Files Being Accessed

contents of a shared folder. Both the NTFS permissions and shared folder permissions are applied to objects. Remember that the most restricted set of permissions is used. For example, if the shared folder permits a user only **Read**
permissions, **Read** will be the overriding permission level even if an individual file
delegates the user **Full Control** NTFS permissions.

Publishing Files and Folders to the Active Directory

Like users, computers, and printers, files and folders may be published to the
Active Directory. The Active Directory provides a way to locate published files and
folders and secures permissions on the resources. To publish a file or folder, share
out the folder and complete the following:

1. Open the **Active Directory Users and Computers** snap-in.
2. Right-click the desired domain node or Active Directory container and select
   the **New → Share Folder** option.
3. Enter a name for the share to publish in the **Shared Folder Name** field.
4. Enter a path to the network share in the **Network Path** field in the form
   *servername**sharedfolder*. Press the **OK** button.

The shared file or folder should now appear in the Active Directory and be available for lookup from the Global Catalog.

DISTRIBUTED FILE SYSTEM SHARING

The distributed file system (Dfs) allows several shared file systems to be mounted from one location. The shares may exist on separate machines, but users can reach them through one folder. This folder is called the root node and is accessible from the Dfs root server. Shared folders on other systems are linked to the root node (Figure 9.28).

Users maintain one connection to the root node on their desktop environment and connect to resources throughout the network without having to establish a connection with each server and folder. The Dfs root node contains link nodes that point to these shared folders and mimic the directory tree structure. The tree structure can be customized according to user needs.

Dfs centrally manages shared folders and maintains network permissions. Share and NTFS permissions still apply to individual users—creating the root Dfs share does not compromise previously assigned security permissions.

Standalone versus Fault-Tolerant Dfs

Root nodes can be configured as standalone or fault-tolerant (or domain-based). The standalone server stores the Dfs directory tree structure or topology locally. Thus, if a shared folder is inaccessible or if the Dfs root server is down, users are left with no link to the shared resources. A fault-tolerant root node stores the Dfs

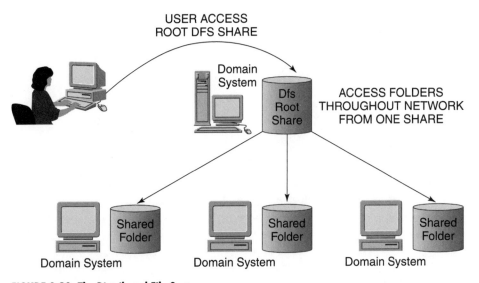

FIGURE 9.28 The Distributed File System

topology in the Active Directory, which is replicated to other domain controllers. Thus, redundant root nodes may include multiple connections to the same data residing in different shared folders.

A fault-tolerant link node can point to two or more shared folders on different servers containing the same files. This serves two purposes:

1. The network user requesting access from the fault-tolerant link node will receive address information for each redundant folder. The client then picks the folder closest to it, thereby saving network traffic and time.

2. Redundant shared folders can replicate automatically, providing data redundancy.

NOTE   Version control may be an issue depending on how users access the folders. A user may overwrite changes another user made to a file. In this case, automatic replication should be disabled and handled by a person or configuration management tool. It should be noted that replica folders must reside on NTFS v5 volumes running Windows 2000 Server. It should also be noted that client Dfs software is required to access Dfs shares. Windows 2000, Windows NT 4.0, and Windows 98 come preconfigured with such software. Client software must be downloaded and installed on systems running Windows 95. Currently, only Windows 2000 Dfs clients may access fault-tolerant Dfs root shares using the directory location services. Clients may still access fault-tolerant Dfs roots using the full UNC root path.

Creating Dfs

The Dfs is created using the Distributed File System snap-in. It primarily involves the creation of two components: the Dfs root and the Dfs child link.

THE Dfs ROOT

As previously discussed, the Dfs root may be created either as standalone or domain based. It centrally collects all links to folders throughout the network. A domain-based root can have multiple Dfs links and supports Dfs shares below the root folder. Thus, Dfs subfolder shares may be created in the Dfs root folder and be accessible to Dfs clients. The domain-based Dfs root stores topology information in the Active Directory, but if the server hosting the root Dfs folder is shut down, access to all child links is interrupted. A replica for the domain-based root share may be created on a separate server to support a redundant failover point

EXAMPLE OF DFS ROOT CHANGE REPLICATION

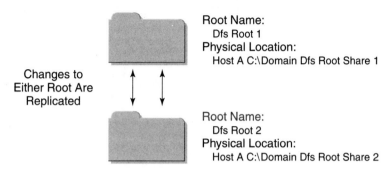

Changes to
Either Root Are
Replicated

Root Name:
  Dfs Root 1
Physical Location:
  Host A C:\Domain Dfs Root Share 1

Root Name:
  Dfs Root 2
Physical Location:
  Host A C:\Domain Dfs Root Share 2

FIGURE 9.29 Root Dfs Replication and Redundancy

(Figure 9.29). All child links are duplicated on the root replica and effectively function as an alternate for the original Dfs root. Standalone Dfs roots do not support
replicas at the root level or child level.

THE Dfs LINK

Dfs links maintain a mapping or a junction point between the root and individual
shared folders throughout the network. When the user accesses a link, the link
name resolves the destination shared folder path. The *link name* simply displays
the subfolder within the Dfs root folder; the link is responsible for pointing to the
folder's physical location using a full UNC path. A Dfs root may support up to 1,000
links (Figure 9.30).

Each link has a name and owns a replica set with at least one corresponding
shared physical folder identified by a fully qualified UNC path name. The replica
set may be associated with up to 32 shared folders. The folders within the replica
set are meant to contain identical information. To accomplish this, they may be
maintained manually or automatically using the Folder Replication Service (FRS).

NOTE   To host a domain-based Dfs root or fault-tolerant Dfs link replica folder, the host
most be running the Distributed File System service for Windows 2000 (and be
located on an NTFS volume). Windows 2000 Professional does not come pre-
installed with this service and therefore cannot be used to host Dfs roots or target
folders. Windows NT 4.0 running with Service Pack 3 may host standalone root
and target folders.

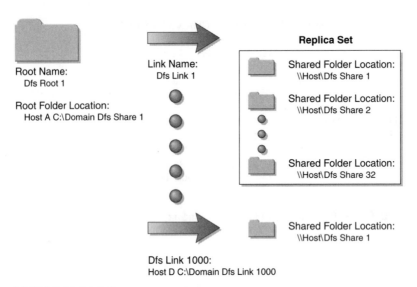

FIGURE 9.30 Dfs Links

Dfs TOPOLOGY

Dfs maps logical share volumes to physical disk space throughout the network. The main difference between standalone and fault-tolerant, or domain-based, Dfs roots is that domain-based Dfs roots store topology information in the Active Directory in the Partition Knowledge Table (PKT) object, which is distributed to all domain controllers throughout the domain. A standalone Dfs root does not store PKT information in the Active Directory and so relies solely on the Dfs root host to maintain topology information.

Dfs Client and Share Access

Since a domain-based Dfs root automatically publishes information to the Active Directory, a Dfs client running Dfs v5.0 client software (Windows 2000) may access a Dfs share in a couple of ways. The first method involves using the domain name and the root share name:

`\\domain name\fault tolerant root name\link name\path\file name`

The second method involves accessing the fault-tolerant root share name:

`\\fault tolerant root name\link name\file name`

The standalone Dfs share is accessed by Dfs v5.0 in the following UNC form. This form is also used by clients running Dfs 4.x accessing either domain-based roots or standalone Dfs shares.

`\\root host server name\root name\link name\path\file name`

NOTE	As of the writing of this book, both Dfs v4.x and v5.0 are available for Windows 95, Windows 98, and Windows NT 4.0.

Files in the replicas of Figure 9.30 are referenced from a Windows 2000 client system using

```
\\domain name\Dfs ROOT 1\Dfs LINK 1\subfolder name\file name
Dfs ROOT 1\Dfs LINK 1\subfolder name\file name
```

or

```
\\HOST A\Dfs ROOT 1\Dfs LINK 1\subfolder name\file name
```

More Dfs Advantages

In addition to the obvious advantages offered by Dfs sharing files, several others need to be highlighted.

BROWSE AND SEARCH DIRECTORIES

Dfs affords naming transparency that allows users to browse and search the network without concern for physical file location. Dfs share names can more accurately reflect logical meaning for data storage and can be limited to the file system naming structure, which is restricted only by a 260-character path name. File search tools available from the **Start → Search** menu may be used to search the logical Dfs structure. This more effectively limits extensive document searches to logical volumes rather than entire physical volumes, which are time consuming.

BRINGING SERVERS OFFLINE WITHOUT USER INTERRUPTION

The logical Dfs namespace allows network resource substitutions to be made without involving users or client system reconfiguration. A logical share can be redirected to another physical location without affecting the logical Dfs path to file resources. Additional disk space may be added in the form of new subdirectories under an existing Dfs share. Shortcuts and drive mappings on the user's desktop no longer need to be reconfigured as physical hardware changes occur.

EASE OF WEB SERVER MAINTENANCE

Internet Information Server runs on the Windows 2000 operating system and acknowledges the Dfs logical drive structure. Web page links within HTML documents do not require update when server names change, or when the underlying physical storage is reorganized, if Dfs logical share references are used.

Concerns Regarding Dfs Use

Although load balancing and high availability can be viewed as positive Dfs attributes, there are some basic concerns. First, since the Dfs client arbitrarily selects a Dfs share path, user access should be evenly distributed among fault-tolerant shares. However, if file and application access is not restricted to Read-Only, multiple versions of a file will be created on replica shares. Even though folder replicas distribute permission, folder, and file changes, file-locking attributes are *not* replicated. Thus, there is nothing to keep two users from opening the same file on separate Dfs link target folders, which can lead to lost data as a result of overwriting.

Pointing all Dfs clients to a primary share and directing them to an alternate share upon primary share failure should alleviate most problems. One share will function as the primary resource, relying on the other one for backup. This can be configured using the Active Directory sites container. Put all computers in the same site as the target host for one of the Dfs link folders. When the Dfs client resolves the link target folder UNC location, it will first attempt connection to the resource within its own site. If this server is down, the client will attempt to connect with the remaining target hosts. In this way, the host within the site container will be the first choice, with the backup being accessed only when the first host is down. This will help eliminate file duplication and data overwrites. Obviously, load balancing will no longer occur, but data loss will be kept to a minimum.

Setting Up a Standalone Dfs Share

Creating a Dfs share involves the following procedure:

1. Log on with administrative privileges.
2. Press **Start** → select **Programs** → choose **Administrative Tools** → select **Distributed File System**.
3. Select the **Action** pull-down window → select **New Dfs Root Volume...** as shown in Figure 9.31.
4. The **Create New Dfs Root Wizard** appears. Press the **Next>** button.
5. Select the **Create a standalone Dfs root** radio button (Figure 9.32).
6. Enter the server name on which the Dfs root will reside (Figure 9.33). Press the **Next>** button.
7. Select the **Use existing share:** or **Create new share** radio button. The **Create new share** option requires the **Path to share:** (*drivename:*

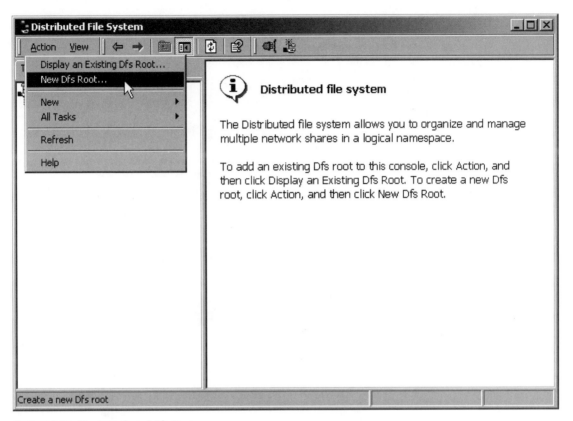

FIGURE 9.31 The Distributed File System

foldername) and the **Share name:**. Users will access the Dfs share using the share name. (Figure 9.34). Press the **Next>** button.

8. If you used an existing share, the name for the Dfs root will be grayed out (Figure 9.35). Otherwise, enter a name for the Dfs root. Press the **Next>** button.

9. The new Dfs root settings are displayed. Press the **Finish** button. The new Dfs has been created. Its status may be checked from the Dfs console by right-clicking the share and choosing the **Check Status** option (Figure 9.36, page 356). A green checkmark should appear. This can also be used to test child nodes throughout the Dfs structure.

Create a child node on the standalone Dfs root by following this procedure:

1. Highlight the new Dfs root share and press the **New Child** button.

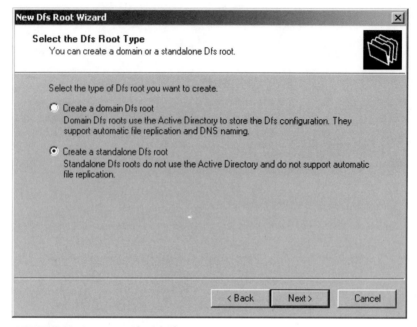

FIGURE 9.32 Creating a Shared Dfs

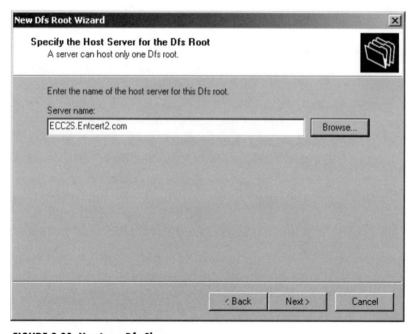

FIGURE 9.33 Naming a Dfs Share

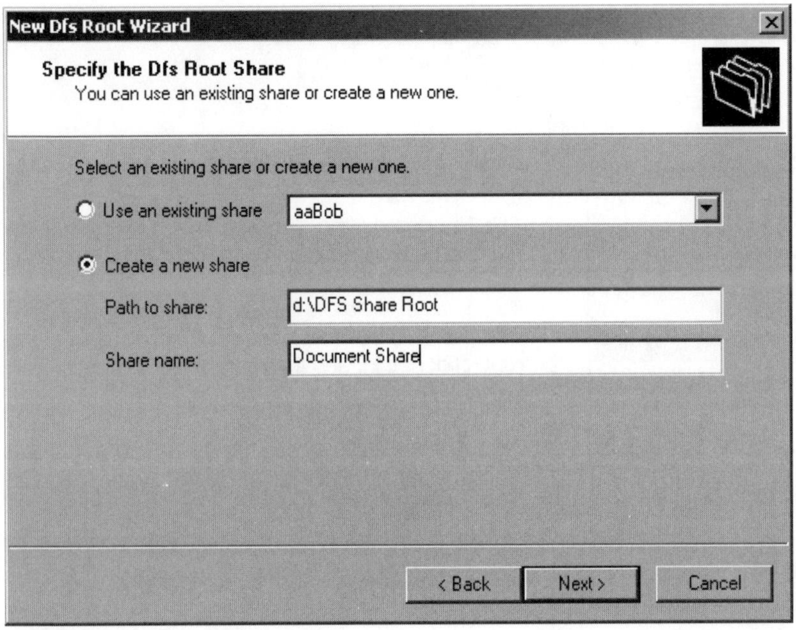

FIGURE 9.34 A Root Volume Share

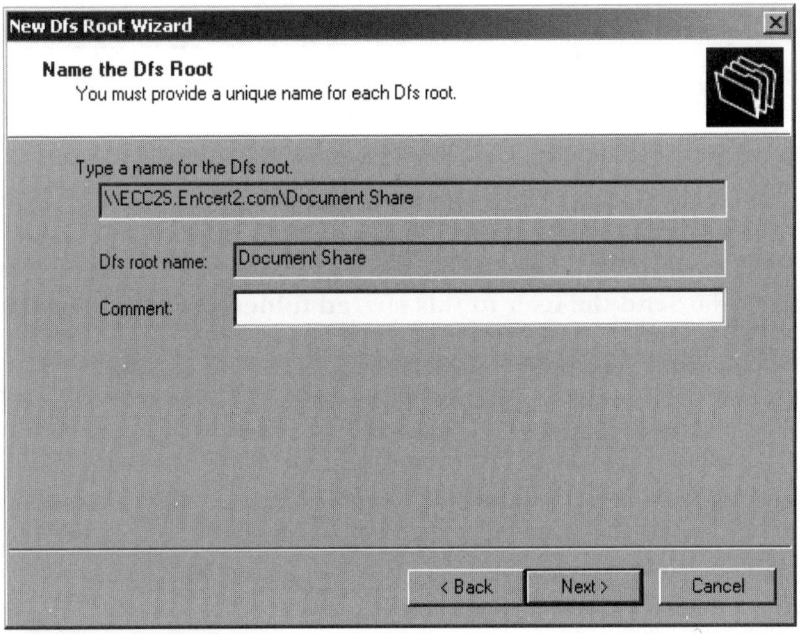

FIGURE 9.35 A Root Name

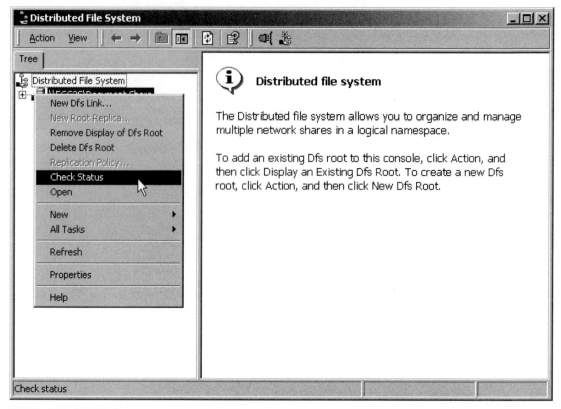

FIGURE 9.36 MCC Action

2. In the **Create a New Dfs Link** dialog window enter a name for the child
   node which will be seen by users in the **Link Name:** field (Figure 9.37).
   Enter the network path for the folder to be referenced from the Dfs root in
   the **Send the user to this shared folder:** field. Press the **OK** button.

The **Clients cache this referral** field defines the time period during which the
client may use the referral before needing to contact the Dfs root for renewal.
However, the Windows 2000 Dfs client software (Dfs client 5.0) will refresh its
cache's Time To Live (TTL) for the client cache after every successful share access.

   The new child node should now be visible from the Dfs console (Figure 9.38).
The Dfs share has been created and the child node connects to a remote machine.

It is important to understand that the Dfs root share is now seen as a local folder on the system with the Dfs root. Notice that the child folders are not accessible from the local drive but through **My Network Places**. Find the system with the root share and you will see the folder named after the "share name" configured earlier.

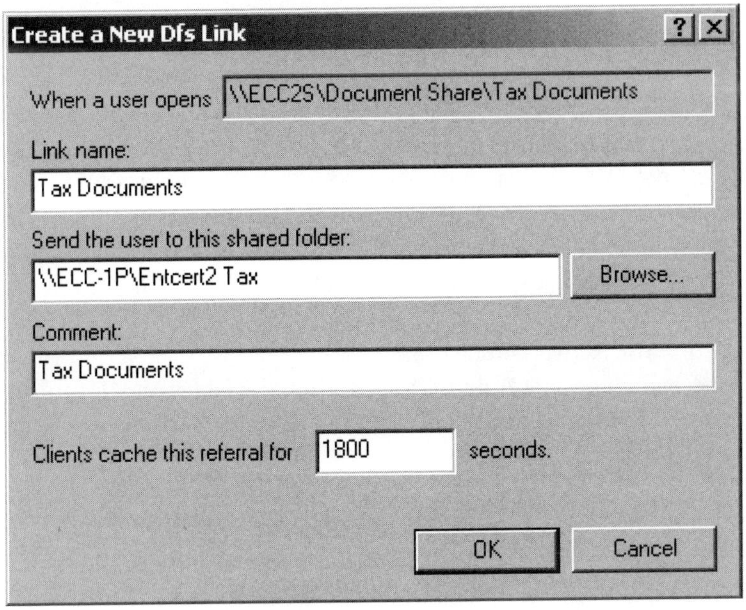

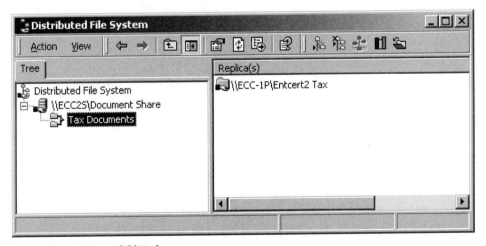

FIGURE 9.37 Create a New Dfs Link

FIGURE 9.38 A New Child Node

DELETING A DFS SHARE

Deleting a Dfs share is a straightforward process. Log on with administrative privileges. From the **Start Menu** → select **Programs** → select **Administrative Tools** → select **Distributed File System**. First remove the targeted share from the Dfs console. Then delete the shared folder from the local drive.

Setting Up a Fault-Tolerant Dfs Share

To set up a fault-tolerant Dfs share you must be in a domain environment with the Active Directory fully installed. The folders must reside on NTFS partitions and be within the same domain. The first step is creating a domain Dfs root. Then a Dfs root replica may be created. Both will be stored in the Active Directory and available for all Dfs client systems. If the system with the domain Dfs root system fails, the client may then redirect to a root replica using the Directory Service Store (located in the Active Directory).

The following example creates a domain Dfs root and a domain Dfs root replica. Dfs link replicas will be created in the next section of the example.

1. Log on with administrative privileges.
2. Press **Start** → select **Programs** → select **Administrative Tools** → select **Distributed File System**.

The standalone Dfs share created must be removed from the server or another server must be used to host the new domain Dfs root.

1. Right-click the standalone share **Document Share** and select **Remove Dfs root**.
2. Press the **Yes** button.

Now add the new domain Dfs root:

1. Right-click the **Distributed File System** node and select the **New Dfs Root...** option. The **New Dfs Root Wizard** appears. Press the **Next>** button.
2. Select the **Create a domain Dfs root** option and press the **Next>** button.
3. Select the domain where the Dfs will reside. Press the **Next>** button.
4. Browse for a system to host the Dfs root and press the **Next>** button.
5. Select the **Create a new share** radio button and enter *drivelabel:\ Domain Dfs Root Share 1* for the share path and *Dfs Root 1* for the share name. Press the **Next>** button. Answer yes to the following dialog and create the new root share.

6. Name the Dfs root *Dfs Root 1* and press the **Next>** button. Press the **Finish** button.

Create a new Dfs root replica for redundant root information.

NOTE   The second Dfs root has been added here only for continuity. It is recommended that it be added after links have been created and topology information has had time to propagate to all domain controllers.

---

1. Right-click the new *domainname**Dfs Root 1* node and select the **New Root Replica...** option.
2. Browse for another server to host the root replica and press the **Next>** button.
3. Create a new root share on this server with the path *drivename:\Domain Dfs Root Share 2* named *Dfs Root 2*. Press the **Finish** button.

Add two new child nodes to the Dfs root to create replicate shares. The Dfs root replicas previously created will enable fault-tolerant root access. Create a Dfs link or child node and a corresponding replica child node (on another server) to enable fault-tolerant shares for file and folder data. Before taking the following steps, create two new shares, *Dfs Share 1* and *Dfs Share 2,* on separate servers (make sure they are NTFS volumes).

1. Right-click the *DfsRoot1* node and select **New Child Link...**.
2. Enter *DfsLink1* in the **Link Name:** field.
3. Browse for the *Dfs Share 1* folder in the **Send the user to this shared folder:** field. See the previous standalone example for an explanation of the **Clients cache this referral for** field. Press the **OK** button.

Create a new Dfs link replica:

1. Right-click the *DfsLink1* node and select **New Replica...** (Figure 9.39).
2. The **Add a New Replica** dialog appears. Use the **Browse** button to find the *DfsLink2* folder that will contain a duplicate copy of the original child node folder *DfsLink1* (Figure 9.40). Select **Automatic replication** to invoke the Folder Replication Service (FRS). Press the **OK** button.

You will next be prompted to modify **Replication Policy** for the new replica set:

1. Select *Dfs Share 1* and press the **Enable** button (Figure 9.41).

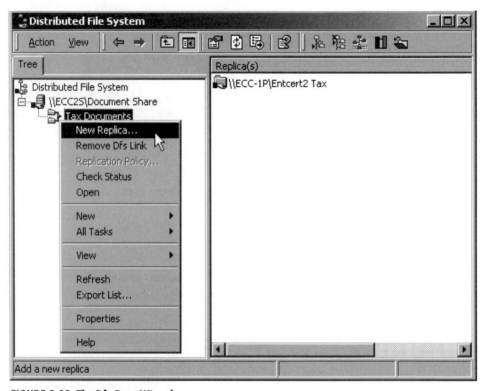

FIGURE 9.39 The Dfs Root Wizard

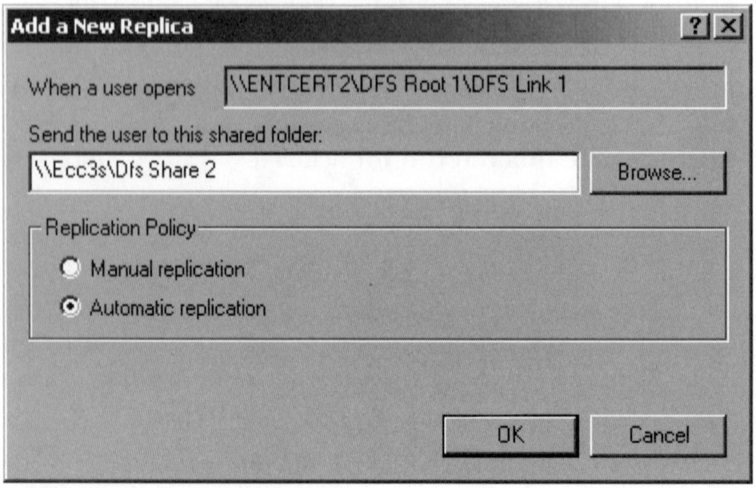

FIGURE 9.40 Replica Set Addition

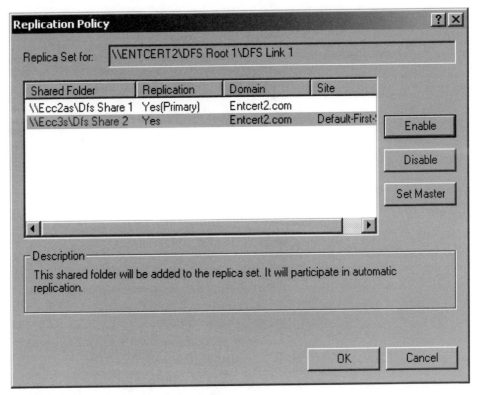

FIGURE 9.41 The Dfs Share Replication Policy

The first share enabled is set as **Primary**. Its contents are copied to all replica members to ensure that all folders start off with the same contents. After initialization, if there are modifications to any share's file permissions or contents, the changes are propagated to all other replica members.

1. Select *Dfs Share 2* and press the **Enable** button. Press the **OK** button.
2. Both fault-tolerant nodes should now be displayed in the Details window of the **Distributed File System** tool (Figure 9.42). Verify the shares by right-clicking the fault-tolerant nodes and selecting **Check Status**. Green check-marks should appear for both shares.

You may later modify replication policies by right-clicking the *Dfs Link 1* node and selecting **Replication Policy...** Once folder replication has commenced, the **Set Master** button will no longer be relevant and is not displayed.

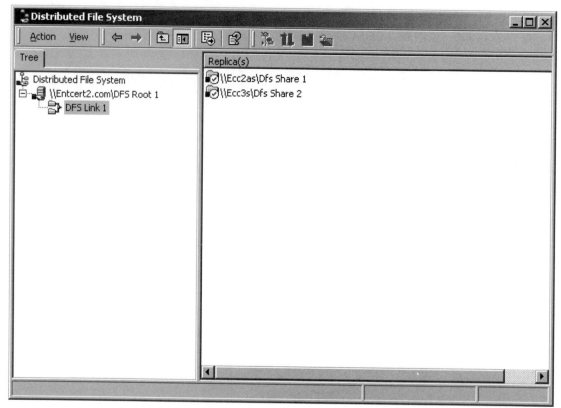

FIGURE 9.42 The Distributed File System Snap-In

Publishing the Dfs Root to the Active Directory

The Dfs root is published to the Active Directory like any other folder so that users may gain access. This is accomplished through **My Network Places** → **Entire Network** → **Directory** browse tool.

1. From the **Active Directory Users and Computers**, snap-in right-click the domain and select **New** → **Volume**.

2. Enter the Dfs root UNC path information.

NOTE   Currently only standalone Dfs roots may be used on systems running Microsoft Cluster Server. However, a domain-based Dfs root may *not* be used with the cluster product.

POSTSCRIPT

This chapter examined how to apply permissions to files and folders, and how to share folders and use the Distributed File System (Dfs). These facilities provide the baseline Windows 2000 security at the file and folder level. In the next two chapters we examine authentication, public key infrastructure, basic security lockdown, and related topics.

Chapter 10

Kerberos and the Public Key Infrastructure

Authenticating the identity of users during login is the first step in gaining system access. For local machines not actively participating in a domain, Windows NT LAN Manager (NTLM) protocol is still utilized to verify a user's name and password. However, in domain environments Microsoft has coupled the Active Directory very closely with the emerging industry standard for authentication from MIT known as Kerberos. Once access is granted, keys are exchanged that permit specific access to other system resources within the domain. This combines underlying Kerberos technology with the Public Key Infrastructure (PKI).

Concepts surrounding both Kerberos and PKI are relatively new in Microsoft environments, and they are important technologies for system administrators to understand. This chapter provides both theoretical and hands-on examination of their Windows 2000 implementation.

KERBEROS AUTHENTICATION

Underlying Windows 2000 security is user authentication. The centralized account management supported by Active Directory Services requires a corresponding authentication protocol for network logon. Based on RFC 1510, Kerberos version 5 provides enhanced authentication for the distributed computing environment and standardization to interoperate with other operating systems. However, while Kerberos is the centerpiece of Active Directory domain authentication, other schemes exist within a Windows 2000 environment to verify user logins. For example, Windows NT LAN Manager (NTLM) protocol is still supported for down-level systems and provides nondomain, local logon capability. In addition, secure channels are used to join domains, make password modifications, and access nontrusted domain resources. Finally, Windows 2000 supports methods of user authentication that depend on whether the connection is dial-up, over the Internet, or within the local network. The Kerberos protocol is the preferred method and first choice for authenticating users and services within a local intranet.

NOTE   Authentication verifies the user's identity to the Local Security Authority (LSA). User authentication merely ensures that the user name and password are verified against a highly secure database. As discussed in Chapter 9, the user's eventual ability to use network resources is determined by access permissions assigned to the resource. These permissions are checked after the authentication process completes.

NOTE   As stated previously, the NT LAN Manager (NTLM) authentication protocol is used in Windows NT and Windows 2000 workgroup environments. It is also employed in mixed Windows 2000 Active Directory domain environments that must authenticate Windows NT systems. When Windows 2000 is converted to native mode, where no down-level Windows NT domain controllers exist, NTLM is disabled. Kerberos then becomes the default for the enterprise.

Understanding Kerberos Concepts

Kerberos version 5 is standard on all versions of Windows 2000 and ensures the highest level of security to network resources. Its name comes from the three-headed dog of Greek mythology. Its three heads are the Key Distribution Center (KDC), the client user, and the server with the desired service. The KDC is installed as part of the domain controller and performs two services: authentication and ticket-granting. As exemplified in Figure 10.1, three exchanges are involved when the client initially accesses a server resource:

- Authentication Service (AS)
- Ticket-Granting Service (TGS)
- Client/Server (CS)

THE AUTHENTICATION SERVICE EXCHANGE

When initially logging on to a network, the user must negotiate access by providing a login name and password that is verified by the AS portion of a KDC within his domain. The KDC has access to Active Directory user account information.

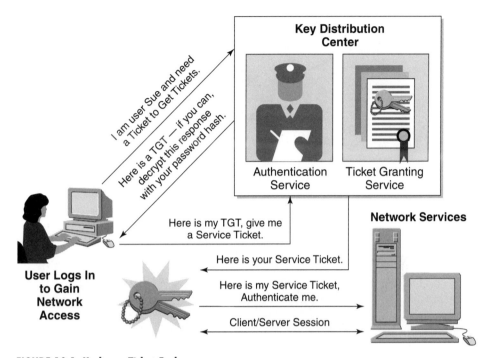

FIGURE 10.1 Kerberos Ticket Exchange

Once successfully authenticated, the user is granted a Ticket to Get Tickets (TGT) that is valid for the local domain. The TGT has a default lifetime of 10 hours and may be renewed throughout the user's logon session without the user having to re-enter his password. It is cached on the local machine in volatile memory space and used to request sessions with services throughout the network.

Authentication Service Exchange Details

The AS Request identifies the client to the KDC in plain text. If pre-authentication is enabled, a timestamp will be encrypted using the user's password hash as an encryption key. If the KDC reads a valid time when using the hash (stored in the Active Directory) to decrypt the timestamp, it knows that the request is not a replay of a previous one. This feature may be disabled for specific users in some applications that do not support pre-authentication. Access the user account from the **Active Directory Users and Computers** snap-in and select the **Account** tab. From the **Account options:** slide window, checkmark the **Do not require Kerberos preauthentication** option (Figure 10.2). Table 10.1 outlines the basic parameters contained within the client's AS Request to the KDC.

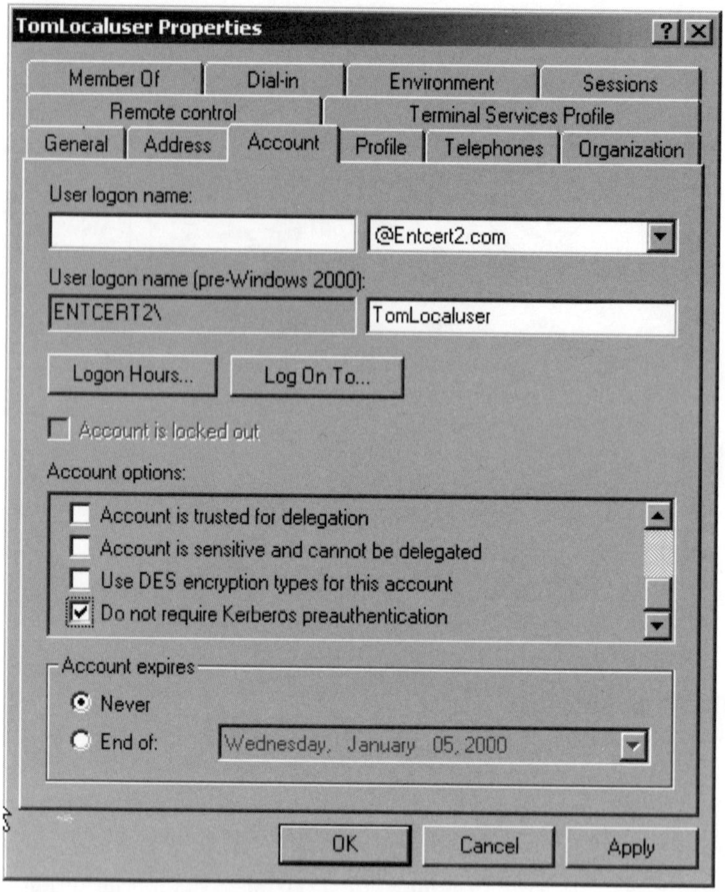

FIGURE 10.2 Disabling Kerberos Pre-Authentication

TABLE 10.1 Authentication Service Request (Client Request for a TGT from the KDC)

Field	Description
Client ID	Client user ID
Desired Flag Settings for the TGT	Flag settings specified below
Domain Name	Name of the Kerberos realm or Windows 2000 domain where client resides
TGS ID	Request for access to the TGS via a TGT
Expiration and TTL Times	Specified end-time and renew-till times for the ticket
Timestamp	Timestamp encrypted with user's password hash to prevent replays of this request

The TGT may be issued with many characteristics identified in the client's request, specified through flag settings. These settings will enable different authentication requirements discussed later in the chapter. Table 10.2 defines the TGT flag types.

If the KDC approves the client's request for a TGT, the reply (referred to as the *AS Reply*) will include two sections: a TGT encrypted with a key that only the KDC Ticket Granting Service (TGS) can decrypt and a session key encrypted with the user's password hash to handle future communications with the KDC. Since the client system cannot read the TGT, it must blindly present it to the TGS for Service Tickets. The TGT includes Time To Live parameters, authorization data, a session key to use when communicating with the client, and the client's name. The AS reply is composed of data identified in Table 10.3.

THE TICKET-GRANTING SERVICE EXCHANGE

The user presents the TGT to the TGS for access to a server service. The TGS authenticates the user's TGT and creates a ticket and session key for both the client and the remote server. This information, known as the *Service Ticket,* is then cached locally on the client machine.

The client sends its TGT and desired Service Ticket settings to the TGS, which reads it using its own key. If the TGS approves the client's request, a Service Ticket is generated for the client *and* the target server. The client reads its portion using the TGS session key retrieved earlier from the AS Reply (Table 10.3). It presents

TABLE 10.2 TGT Flag Types

Flag	Purpose
INITIAL	Identifies a TGT-type ticket
FORWARDABLE	Front-end server is permitted to use the TGT
FORWARDED	Server is using TGT on behalf of client
PROXIABLE	Service Ticket may be issued with a different address than TGT
PROXY	Service Ticket represents a client with a different address
RENEWABLE	Ticket's Time To Live (TTL) may be updated
PRE-AUTHENT	KDC authorized client before issuing ticket
HW-AUTHENT	Specific hardware is required for authentication
MAY POSTDATE	TGS may post-date the Service Ticket
POSTDATED	Ticket will be used on a future date
INVALID	Ticket is invalid

TABLE 10.3 Authentication Service Reply—KDC to Client

Field	Description
Section 1—Plain Text	
Client ID	Client identifier
Domain Name	Client's domain
Section 2—TGT Encrypted Portion (KDC Readable Only)	
Flags	Flag setting as identified in TGT Flag (Table 10.2)
TGS Session Key	Session key to be used when communicating with the TGS
Domain Name	Client's domain name
Client ID	Client identifier
Start Time/End Time	Ticket TTL parameters
Authorization Data	User SID and group membership SID info
Section 3—Encrypted Using Password Hash (Readable by Client)	
TGS Session Key	Session key to be used when communicating with the TGS
Start Time/End Time	Ticket TTL parameters
TGS Domain	Domain in which the TGS resides
TGS ID	TGS identifier
Timestamp	Timestamp encrypted with user's password hash

TABLE 10.4 Ticket Granting Service Request

Field	Description
Server ID	Server client wishes to access
Desired Flag Settings for Service Ticket	TGT flag (Table 10.2)
TGT Ticket	TGT encrypted (only readable by KDC)
Expiration and TTL Times	Specified end-time and renew-till times for the ticket
Timestamp	Prevents replays of this request

the server portion (Table 10.5, Section 2) of the TGS reply to the target server in the CS exchange, coming next.

THE CLIENT/SERVER EXCHANGE

Once the client has the Client Server Service Ticket, it can establish the session with the server service. The server can decrypt the information coming indirectly from the TGS using its own long-term key with the KDC. It can then use the

TABLE 10.5 Ticket-Granting Reply—TGS Reply to Client

Field	Description
Section 1—Plain Text	
Client ID	Client identifier
Domain Name	Client's domain
Section 2—Service Ticket Portion Encrypted Using Key Known Only to Target Server and KDC	
Flags	Flag setting as identified in TGT (Table 10.2)
Client/Server Session Key	Session key to be used when communicating between client and server with resource
Domain Name	Client's domain name
Client ID	Client identifier
Start Time/End Time	Ticket TTL parameters
Authorization Data	User SID and group membership SID info
Section 3—Encrypted Using TGS Session Key	
Client/Server Session Key	Session key to be used when communicating between client and server with resource
Start Time/End Time	Ticket TTL parameters
Server's Domain	Domain in which resource resides
Server ID	Server identifier
Nonce B/Timestamp	Prevent replay

Service Ticket to authenticate the client and establish a service session with it. When the ticket's lifetime is exceeded, it must be renewed to use the service.

Client/Server Exchange Detail

The client blindly passes the server portion of the Service Ticket to the server in the CS request to establish a client/server session (Table 10.6). If mutual authentication is enabled, the target server returns a timestamp encrypted by the Service Ticket session key (Table 10.7). If the timestamp decrypts correctly, not only has the client authenticated itself to the server, but the server has authenticated itself to the client.

NOTE   The target server and the KDC never have to communicate directly. This reduces down time and pressure on the KDC.

TABLE 10.6 Client/Server Exchange Request

Field	Description
Desired Flag Settings for the TGT	TGT flags (Table 10.2)
Service Ticket Encrypted with Key Known Only to Server and KDC	

TABLE 10.7 Client/Server Exchange Reply

Field	Description
Timestamp	Mutually authenticates client and server
Sequence Numbers	Maintains session through number sequence

FURTHER CLARIFICATION OF THE LOGIN PROCESS

A TGT and a Service Ticket are needed to access services on remote computers, but they are also required to successfully log on to a local system. When the logon window appears, password encryption using a one-way hash algorithm occurs immediately, and negotiations commence with the KDC for a valid TGT and Service Ticket. The process is the same as that for accessing a remote service. An access token is created for the user containing all security groups to which he belongs. It is attached to the user's logon session and subsequently inherited by any process or application the user starts.

REFERRAL TICKETS

The Authentication Service and Ticket Granting Service functions are separate within the KDC. This permits the TGT obtained from an AS in one domain to be used to obtain Service Tickets from a TGS in other domains. This is accomplished through referral tickets.

Once a trust has been established between two domains, referral tickets can be granted to clients requesting authorization for services in both. An interdomain key based on the trust password becomes available for authenticating KDC functions. As illustrated in Figure 10.3, a user client in Entcert1.com requests authority for a server in Entcert2.com utilizing referral tickets. The numbers in Figure 10.3 correspond to the following explanations:

1. The client contacts its domain KDC TGS using a TGT. The KDC recognizes a request for a session with a foreign domain server and responds by returning a referral ticket for the foreign domain KDC.

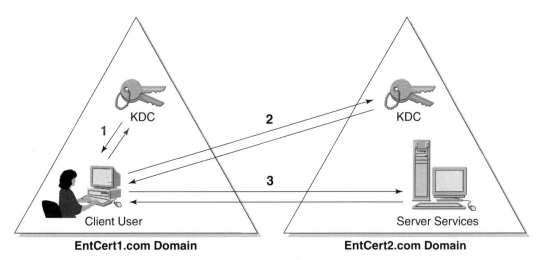

FIGURE 10.3 Key Referral between Trusted Domains

2. The client contacts the foreign trusted domain KDC with the referral ticket. This ticket is encrypted with the inter-domain key. If the decryption works, the TGS for the foreign domain returns a Service Ticket for the server service in Entcert2.com.

3. The client performs the CS Exchange with the server and begins the user session with the service.

When more domains are involved, the referral process extends and involves the transitive properties between Windows 2000 domains. Maintaining individual two-way trusts between Windows NT domains was an administrative nightmare, but Kerberos transitive domains cut down on inter-domain administration. This can best be explained as illustrated in Figure 10.4, where Entcert1.com has a trust relationship with Entcert2.com, which has a trust relationship with Entcert3.com. As there is no trust between Entcert1.com and Entcert3.com, an Entcert1.com client accessing a service on a server in Entcert3.com would obtain a Service Ticket through the following steps, numbered to correspond with those appearing in the figure.

1. Use the TGS in Entcert1.com to obtain a referral ticket for a KDC in Entcert2.com.

2. Use the referral ticket with the TGS on the KDC in Entcert2.com and obtain a referral for Entcert3.com.

3. Use the second referral ticket with the TGS on the KDC for Entcert3.com and obtain a Service Ticket for the server in that domain.

4. Use the CS Exchange to open a session with the service in Entcert3.com.

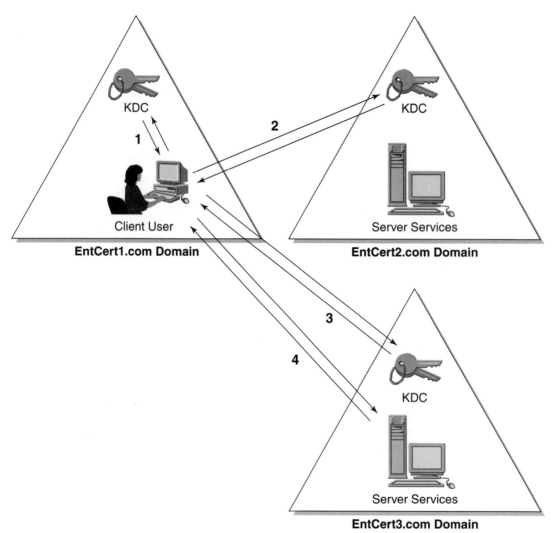

FIGURE 10.4 Key Referrals Enable Transitive Trusts

DELEGATION WITH FORWARDING AND PROXY

Some server services require access to a second server, such as backend database. In order to establish a session with the second server the primary server must be authenticated on behalf of the client's user account and authority level. This is common in a three-tier client/server model (Figure 10.5) and is usually accomplished with proxy or forwarding authentication.

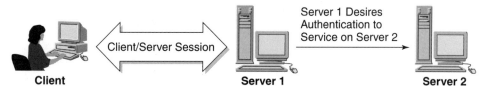

FIGURE 10.5 Proxy and Forwarding Authentication

Proxy Authentication

Proxy authentication requires the client to obtain a Service Ticket for the primary server to use with the secondary server on the client's behalf (Figure 10.6). The client must have the proxy policy enabled when its initial TGT is issued. Then the PROXIABLE flag will be set in the client's TGT. When the primary server requests access to the second server, the client must obtain the second server's name and request a Service Ticket using the proxy-enabled TGT. The KDC then issues a Service Ticket with the PROXY flag set, which the client returns to the primary server. The first server uses the new Service Ticket to establish a session with the desired service on the second server. This new session is based on the client's user ID and address.

NOTE   The client must learn the name and address of the secondary server. The client is acting on behalf of the primary server and is burdened with retrieving secondary server credentials.

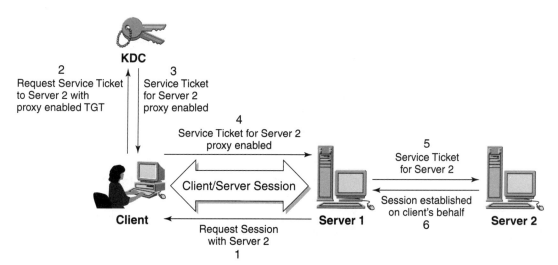

FIGURE 10.6 Proxy Authentication

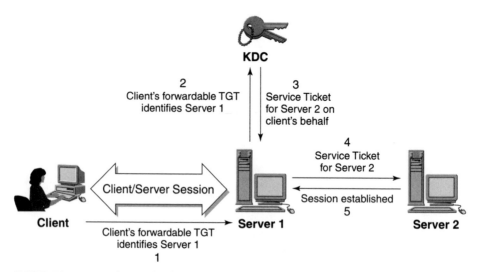

FIGURE 10.7 Forwarding Authentication

FORWARDING AUTHENTICATION

Forwarding allows the primary server to access the secondary server without requiring the client to participate when establishing a session (Figure 10.7). If the forwarding policy is enabled on the KDC, the client may request a forwarding TGT. When it retrieves the TGT, it must reveal the forwarding server's address (the server will soon act on the client's behalf) during the AS Exchange. The FOR-WARDABLE flag is set on the client's TGT. The client then sends the TGT directly to the server requiring access to a second server, after which the primary server requests Service Tickets on the client's behalf using the forward-enabled TGT given by the client. New Service Tickets requested by the first server from the KDC also have the FORWARDED flag set and allow the first server to use the Service Ticket with second server. The client is not required to know the second server's name, as in the proxy delegation method.

The Kerberos Process

The previous sections discussed ticket exchanges required for user authorization. We now take a look at how these exchanges are handled without compromising user information or causing security breaches.

SYMMETRICAL ENCRYPTION AND SHARED KEYS

The basis for Kerberos communication and authentication is symmetrical encryption algorithms using shared secret keys. These keys depend on fast and comparatively simple encryption, and their implementation does not require a public/private key infrastructure. Figure 10.8 demonstrates symmetrical encryption and how shared keys work.

Data is encrypted using a standard encryption algorithm such as Data Encryption Standard (DES) (discussed in Chapter 13). The algorithm takes in readable data and a key for producing encrypted data. Depending on the algorithm, this encrypted data is very difficult to decrypt without the corresponding decryption algorithm and key. Two parties can share a secret key using an out-of-band method and communicate with a strong degree of confidentiality. For example, they might transfer the secret key through a telephone call or "snail" mail; assuming the sender is the only one with the matching secret key, the receiver has some degree of authentication. This assumes that decrypted data is readable and meaningful to the receiver. There is the possibility that someone is replaying a previously sent message, a scenario addressed in the next section.

SHARED SECRET KEYS

In Kerberos, the shared secret key is generated from the user's password using a one-way hash function that is a combination of the Data Encryption Standard, Cipher Block Chaining (CBC), and Message Digest 5. All Kerberos version 5 implementations must minimally implement this hash function for interoperability. A hash function generally inputs the password text string and generates a 128-bit string that would appear meaningless to anyone without the original password—it is very difficult to obtain the original password string from the generated hash. For further explanation of this hash function, please see William Stallings' excellent book *Cryptography and Network Security: Principles and Practice,* 2nd ed. (Prentice Hall, 1999). The KDC and all clients are aware of the hash function and can produce the hash, given the user's password. When the user logs on to the client, the password is put through the hash function to produce a hash that is used as a shared secret key to communicate with the KDC.

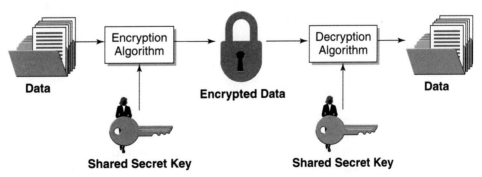

FIGURE 10.8 Encrypting Large Amounts of Data or for Continuous Connections

Preventing the Replay of Previous Communications

One security concern is that someone will intercept a communication and attempt to pass it off as his own and potentially gain authorization. To avoid this, a time-stamp is used to prevent someone from replaying a previous communication. Say a client desires to establish a session with a server. Both the client and the server share knowledge of a common key, based on the user's password. The client sends a request to log on containing its user ID and the current date/time encrypted using the symmetric key. The server reads the requesting user ID and retrieves the correct key for that user, whereupon the date/time is decrypted. If the date/time value is tolerably close to the server's local clock, the time must have been encrypted using the user's password hash and so the client's identity is ver-ified. Since the date/time is constantly changing, an intruder cannot simply resend the same data to the server. The server also saves all logon attempts from that user for the last several minutes and tests each logon to make sure it is later than the previous one. This obviously requires domain-wide clock synchronization within the tolerable settings.

Another option to prevent replay is using a *nonce,* which is a number ran-domly generated by the client and sent to the server. The server encrypts the nonce and sends it back to the client with the reply. It keeps track of previously sent nonces and rejects repeats for a given time period. The client can verify that the server has the shared key if it correctly encrypts the original nonce in the reply.

NOTE In addition to the client being authenticated to the server, the server is also authenticated to the client. When the client receives a correctly encrypted time-stamp from the server, it is certain that the server is who it claims to be. This is known as mutual authentication, another benefit of Kerberos.

NOTE Encryption and session keys function differently. Rather than repeatedly using the user's password hash as the encryption key, a session key can be distributed using the password hash for further communication. The session key is a randomly gen-erated key that is valid only for the length of the communication session.

Kerberos Policies

The system administrator manages Kerberos through **Group Policy** settings. Ker-beros policies are found under the **Security Settings → Account Policies → Kerberos Policy** node under all group policy objects (GPOs). Figure 10.9 displays the default settings for the Default Domain Policy GPO.

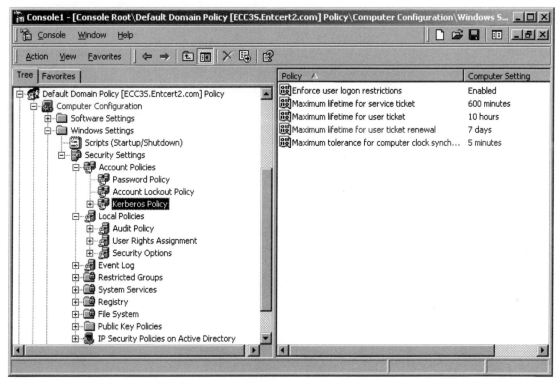

FIGURE 10.9 Kerberos Policies

To modify the current settings, double-click on the target policy and make the appropriate changes in the dialog box that appears. The **Enforce user logon restrictions** policy may be disabled to cut down on the user right verifications Kerberos must perform. The default lifetimes for the TGT (use ticket) and CS Service Tickets can be increased to lengthen the time between ticket renewals. All systems participating in a Kerberos realm must implement some sort of clock synchronization so that the timestamps are relatively accurate. The clock tolerance interval field can be increased from the default of five minutes to provide more time lag between systems.

The standard Kerberos policies that are manageable by system administrators are further explored in Table 10.8.

NOTE   The **Log on locally** policy and the **Access this computer from the network** policy are modified from a group policy snap-in in the **Computer Configuration** → **Windows Settings** → **Local Policies** → **User Rights Assignment** node.

TABLE 10.8 Standard Kerberos Policy Options

Policy	Purpose
Enforce User Logon Restrictions	If this policy is enabled: users requesting Service Tickets for the local machine must have the right to **Log on locally**; or users requesting Service Tickets for remote machines must have the right to **Access this computer from the network**.
Max Lifetime for Service Ticket	Maximum time until the CS Service Ticket expires.
Max Lifetime for User Ticket	Maximum time until the TGT expires without renewal (user ticket = TGT).
Max Lifetime for User Ticket Renewal	Maximum time until the TGT expires, even when client renews the ticket with KDC.
Max Tolerance for Comp Clock Sync	Maximum time skew between system clocks when verifying timestamps during Kerberos exchanges.

THE PUBLIC KEY INFRASTRUCTURE

The Windows 2000 Kerberos version 5 implementation affords a secure, central-ized, and efficient solution to domain-wide authentication. However, the need to communicate with the Internet represents additional security problems. Most companies today offer extranet and Internet access to a large number of clients beyond their own user database maintained with the Active Directory. This is when the Public Key Infrastructure (PKI) becomes necessary.

Maintaining passwords for the numbers of end users who communicate via e-mail or access an enterprise's Web server is a daunting task. In addition to authen-tication, users require confidentiality and integrity in Internet traffic, which is exposed to the world and can be read or monitored with common network sniff-ing tools available to any personal computer. External users need secure private connections to your network that ensure their identity and limit data tampering and snooping, but they should not have to remember myriad passwords or buy expensive Smart Card hardware. The PKI provided by Windows 2000 limits these problems through a couple of strategies. The first is *digital signatures,* which overcomes a number of potential problems, including

- *Impersonation*—sending an e-mail message to someone pretending to be someone else or logging on to Web server or other system under a false identity; also pretending to be the intended message recipient or Web server for a client.
- *Message replay*—replaying messages sent by another party in an attempt to gain access to resources authorized for her use.
- *Message data modification.*
- *Repudiation.*
  - –Let the receiver ensure that the sender sent a particular message.
  - –Let the sender prove that the receiver received message.

The second strategy used in Windows 2000 with respect to the Public Key Infrastructure is the use of *data encryption*. This provides confidentiality by transforming data into an unreadable form that is not reasonably possible to decipher without the corresponding key.

PKI Background

The PKI uses public and private keys to implement digital signatures and data encryption. It provides the basic components and foundation for implementing cryptographic techniques for secure network communications and authentication. Public keys are distributed via the X.509 version 3 certificate standard.

Any entity on the network desiring secure communication maintains a public key/private key combination. Both keys can be used for encryption but require the other key for decryption (Figures 10.10 and 10.11). Each key is considered *asymmetrical* and can produce encrypted data using an encryption algorithm. The asymmetrical matching key for the public/private key pair is required to decrypt the encrypted data and make it readable. By contrast, *symmetrical keys,* discussed in the Kerberos section, require only one key for both encryption and decryption (Figure 10.8).

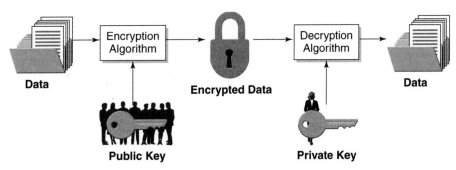

FIGURE 10.10 Encryption for Confidentiality

FIGURE 10.11 Digital Signatures for Authentication and Integrity

DATA ENCRYPTION

Each encryption client is responsible for securing a private key and preventing its exposure to the network. In contrast, the public key is given out to all parties with whom the entity wishes communication. For example, a Web server client wanting to retrieve information securely from a Web server sends the server its public key, which the server uses to encrypt sensitive data or a secret key and sends it back. The client then uses its private key to decrypt the message data or secret key.

The public/private model allows the two parties to set up a Secure Channel (Schannel) through the shared secret key using the industry standard Secure Sockets Layer (SSL) or Transport Layer Security (TLS) protocol. The PKI provides authentication and key exchange for small amounts of data. The public/private key encryption process is processor intensive and is best used to set up secret symmetrical encryption keys to handle bulk transfers.

THE DIGITAL SIGNATURE

A very useful aspect of PKI is the digital signature. Suppose a Web server needs to verify that a client is the owner of a public key. The client uses a hash algorithm on the entire message to generate a message hash, which will always be the same value as long as the message data remains unchanged. This hash value is then encrypted using the client's private key, producing a digital signature for the message.

NOTE   Some common hashing algorithms are RSA Data Security's Message Digest-5 (MD5), which produces a 128-bit hash, and the Secure Hash Algorithm 1 (SHA-1), which produces a 160-bit hash.

The message data may remain unencrypted and is sent along with the digital signature to the Web server (Figure 10.12). There the client's public key is used to decrypt the message hash from the digital signature. The server re-computes the message hash from the message data using the same hash algorithm as the client and compares the sent hash to the newly computed one. If they are the same, it can be concluded that the digital signature must have been encrypted using the

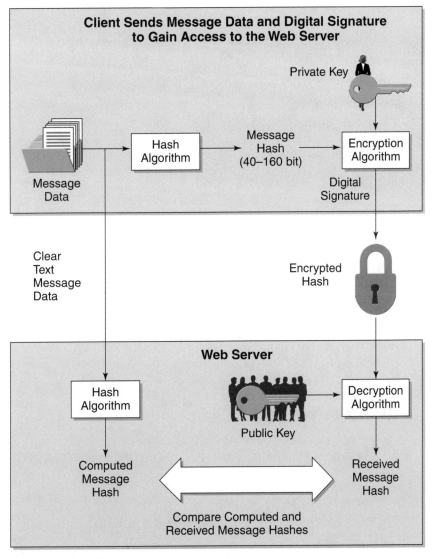

FIGURE 10.12 Using a Digital Signature

private key corresponding to the public key. It can also be concluded that the message content did not change en route to the server unless someone else had access to the private key. In this way the digital signature provides message authentication (i.e., it verifies who the data is from) and provides integrity (if the message content had been modified, the computed hash would not match the hash in the digital signature).

Understanding basic public/private key mechanics enables a grasp of the Windows 2000 PKI components. Let's examine these key components:

- Certification Authority (CA)
- Secure Channel (SSL/TLS/Server Gated Cryptography (SGC))
- Authenticode
- Encrypted File System (EFS)
- Microsoft Exchange Server Key Management Server
- IP Security (see Chapter 13, Networking)

The following sections will mainly address Certification Authority (CA) concepts and examples. The other PKI components are discussed after a lengthy introduction to the CA.

Certification Authority

The certificate authority server issues certificates to clients (also known as subjects) and assigns certificate policies based on the client. It also verifies the owner of previously issued certificates using a database that maps user identities to their public keys. It is possible to contact the CA and verify the owner of a public key. However, the digitally signed certificate eliminates the need to do this if the client trusts the CA. The digital signature validates the certificate, thus proving that the true owner has the corresponding private key and is the only one who can decrypt information that has been encrypted with the public key.

CERTIFICATE COMPONENTS

Certificates supported by Windows 2000 follow the X.509 version 3 standard established by the IETF. Among other things, a certificate contains the following information:

- The subject's public key value
- The subject's name (X.500 distinguished name (DN)) or certificate holder
- Serial number
- Valid from date/time to date/time

- CA that issued this certificate (X.500 DN)
- Digital signature and associated algorithm (protects the contents of the ticket with a hash code and includes the hash algorithm used to sign the certificate)

NOTE The digital signature contains a hash of the entire certificate, which is then encrypted with the issuing CA's private key. Someone can read the certificate, decrypt the hash using the CA's public key, generate his own hash using the specified hash algorithm, and compare the two. This validates the certificate contents and that the certificate was created using the CA's private key. If this is a trusted authority, the user can assume that the contents are correct. This is the standard method for interpreting X.509 certificates.

The certificate authority binds the public key to the subject, which usually takes the form of a person or computer. The subject must have a corresponding private key to validate the certificate for authentication and encryption. A certification authority (CA) is responsible for issuing the certificates to subjects requesting them, managing issued certificates, and mapping public keys to their corresponding owners.

An enterprise CA also manages policies or the intended uses for certificates. In this the Microsoft Certificate Management Services follows the guidelines established by the IETF Public Key Infrastructure X.509 (PKIX). Table 10.9 lists some uses for certificates issued by the Windows 2000 CA.

TRUSTED AUTHORITIES AND CERTIFICATE STORES

Now that we have some understanding of certificate components and their possible uses with Windows 2000, we can review the CA architecture. The first step is to establish a common trusted certificate authority for all users that intend to communicate with each other.

Clients establish an implicit trust with a certificate authority by retrieving a copy of the CA's certificate and storing it in their local trusted store (Figure 10.13). The user now has the CA's public key and can use it to verify signatures created by it. Windows 2000 allows a domain controller to import a CA certificate into **Public Key Policies** and distribute it to all domain members. An example of this is covered later in the Certificate Authority Administration section.

Once a user has established a trusted CA, she may generate her own public/private key pairs and request a certificate by presenting the CA with her public key and identity. The CA encrypts this key using its private key, thus authenticating the certificate. Once the CA issues the certificate, the user stores it in her

TABLE 10.9 Intended Uses for Certificates

Certificate Purposes	Intended Uses
Code Signing	Ensure software came from software publisher and protect software from tampering after publication.
Microsoft Trust List Signing	Signing for the Root CA list or certificate trust list (CTL) that domain administrator finds trustworthy for users.
Encrypting File System	Allow data on disk to be encrypted.
Secure E-Mail	Ensure that the content of e-mail cannot be viewed by others; protect e-mail from tampering; ensure that e-mail came from the sender; and
Client Authentication	Guarantee the client's identity to a server.
Server Authentication	Guarantee the identity of a server.
Certificate Request Agent	Allow an enrollment agent to request certificates on behalf of the client for Smart Card programming.
File Recovery	Allow trusted recovery agents to decrypt the EFS when an owner loses his key.

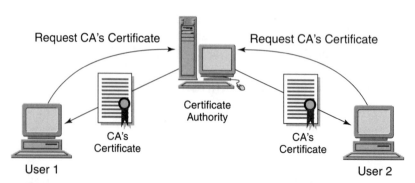

FIGURE 10.13 Storing a CA's Certificate in a Local Trusted Store

personal store. She can then exchange certificates with all others desiring secure communication and authentication.

Once users exchange certificates signed by commonly trusted authorities, they may set up services such as secure e-mail, IPsec, secure channels, and so forth (Figure 10.14). Certificates may be issued to users, computers, and services and are kept in several defined stores within Windows 2000.

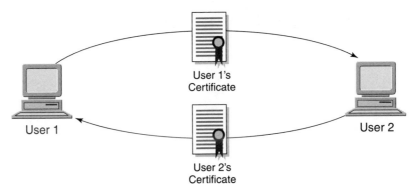

User 1's Certificate

User 1

User 2's Certificate

User 2

FIGURE 10.14 Certificate Exchange between Users

The **Certificates** snap-in can be used to view the contents of the local system's certificate stores. This is demonstrated in the Certificate Authority Administration section. Certificates can be viewed by store or by purpose (Table 10.10).

Certificates are imported and exported, in a variety of formats (to be discussed later), from the **Certificates** snap-in. This tool is designed to manage personal certificates, certificates for the operating system's service account, or computer certificates (Figure 10.15). Provided that a private key is available for export, the user may back up certificates for later retrieval.

TABLE 10.10 Purpose of Certificates Stores

Store	Purpose
Personal	Certificates with associated private keys, used to authenticate a user to other entities and secure inbound communications.
Trusted Root Certification Authorities	A certificate from a root CA in this store designates a trust between the user/computer account and the root CA. The user/computer account can then validate certificates issued by the CA.
Enterprise Trust	Store for Certificate Trust Lists (CTLs). A CTL may set policies for certificates and limit how a certificate may be used.
Intermediate Certification Authorities	Contains certificates belonging to intermediate CAs that verify other CAs through a chain.
Request	Pending certificate request.
Active Directory User Object	Store for user accounts published using the Active Directory.

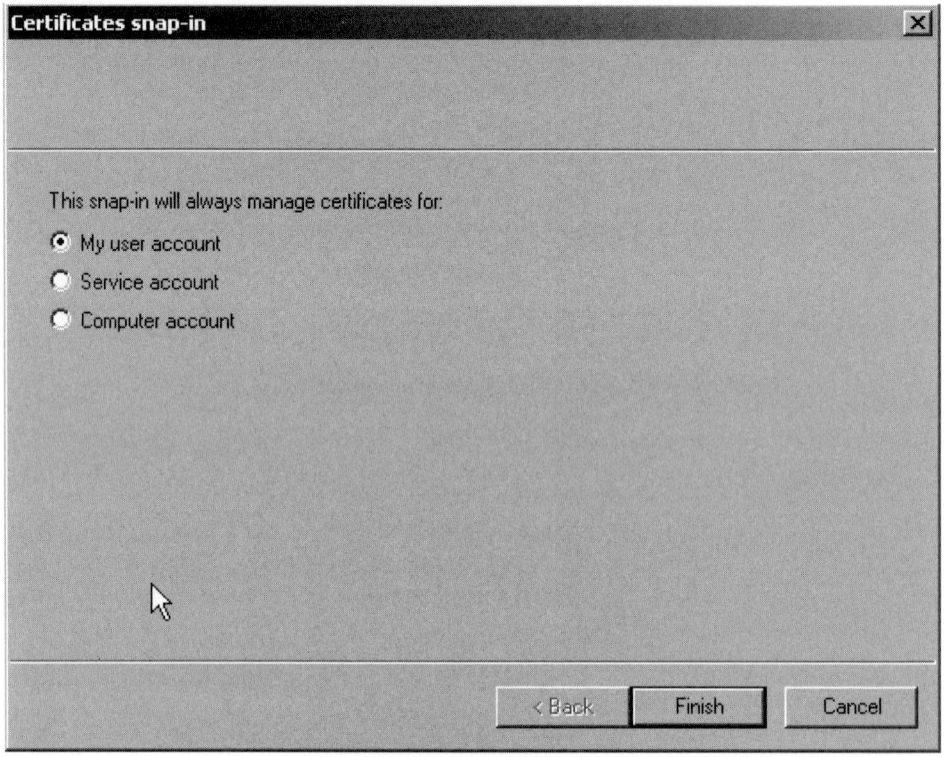

FIGURE 10.15 Account Types for the Certificate Snap-In

When the **Certificate** snap-in has been added, certificate stores for the user, computer, or service account may be perused. It can be used to view stores on any computer within the domain (Figure 10.16).

As discussed earlier, a trusted CA may be used to verify a user's identification based on his certificate and corresponding digital signature. Usually verifying the trusted CA's signature on the certificate with its public key provides enough proof that the certificate is valid. Once this is established, the user must prove that he has the corresponding private key for the certificate, which confirms his identity (Figure 10.17). For example, the Web server can establish secure communication with Joe User once it possesses a copy of his certificate. It uses the public key in the certificate to send information that may be decrypted only with Joe's private key. This enables the Web server to share a temporary secret with Joe and secure future session communications.

Certificate exchange is relatively simple when both users trust the same certificate authority. However, any time users communicate with someone or some

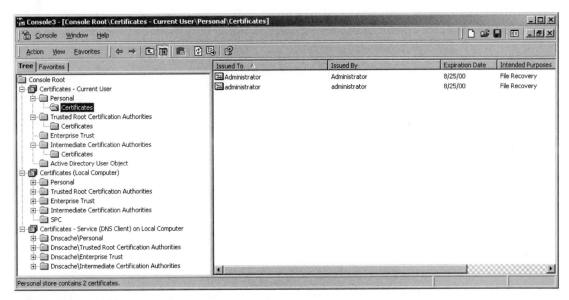

FIGURE 10.16 Local Stores

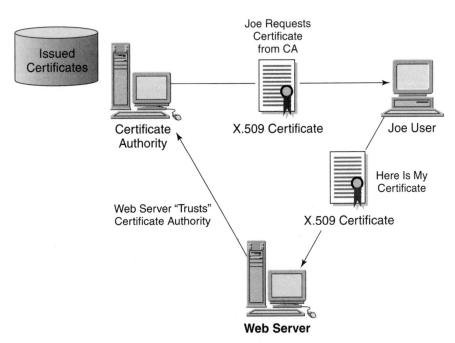

FIGURE 10.17 Verifying Identity by the CA's Signature

service outside of their Windows 2000 domain, a trusted CA must be established. This requires an extensible and universal strategy for certificate verification throughout the Internet.

Certificate Authority Hierarchies

Microsoft has adopted the hierarchical model for its simplicity, wide acceptance, and scalability. A CA hierarchy is composed of one or more CAs to form a tree-like structure. The parent CA is known as the *root* CA and connects to subordinate *intermediate* and *issuing* CAs. An *issuing* CA handles user requests for certificates and issues them accordingly. An *intermediate* CA basically maintains a link in the chain to validate other CAs. The relationship between CAs is established by exchanging each other's respective certificates. The root CA gives an issuing CA its certificate and vice versa.

Each CA stores the other's certificate in its Trusted Root Authority store. The certificate authority hierarchy is then built on these mutual trusts (Figure 10.18). It is important not to confuse CA trusts with Kerberos domain trusts. The Active Directory conveniently distributes certificates within the Windows 2000 domain, but many hierarchies involve CAs outside the corporate domain and must be manually established. Also, CA hierarchies are not modeled after the DNS hierarchy, which forms one large tree consisting of one root. Rather, they involve an unlimited number of separate and unconnected hierarchies.

With the hierarchy is in place, users import and store certificates from a CA that is conveniently accessible. A chaining process is used for validation when a certificate that has been signed by a CA not within their Trusted Root Authority store is received. If a certificate is validated by a CA within one of the user's trusted hierarchies, the user may contact the point of trust and work her way to the CA that validated the certificate.

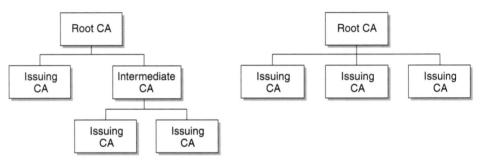

FIGURE 10.18 Certificate Authority Hierarchies May Vary

Let's look at this process through the example illustrated in Figure 10.19. *User 1* has received a certificate from *User 2*. *CA 5* issued that certificate, and to verify it, *User 1* must have a public key for CA 5's signature. A certification path is made between *User 1*'s trusted authority, CA 1, and *User 2*'s trusted certificate authority, CA 5. As shown by the hierarchy, we know that CA 1 has a certificate for CA 2, which has a certificate for CA 3. CA 3 owns a certificate for CA 4 who possesses a certificate for CA 5. From this chain of certificates, User 1's system can eventually unravel a public key for *User 2*'s signed certificate.

At first glance, multiple issuing certificate authorities may seem unduly complex. However, they have some advantages, including the following:

- Good network connectivity to an issuing CA relieves the burden on a slow connection to the root CA.
- Certificate policies can be set differently for each issuing CA. OUs and domains may require different intended uses for their certificates as well.
- Parts of a CA hierarchy can be turned off without affecting the rest of the tree.

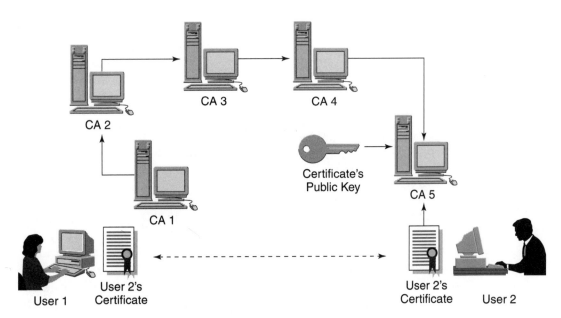

Note: In order for User 1 to utilize User 2's Certificate, User 2's Certificate must be verified using the Public Key from CA 5. User 1 obtains CA 5's Public Key through a trust relationship with other certificate authorities.

FIGURE 10.19 Chaining within a CA Hierarchy to Validate a Certificate

- Portions of the hierarchy can have shorter validation periods and require more frequent updates for higher security.
- Different cryptography may be chosen for each issuing CA.

THIRD-PARTY CERTIFICATE AUTHORITIES

In previous examples we demonstrated the extensibility of the certification hierarchy model. It is important to remember that the intention of PKI is not only to authenticate users and resources within the domain (this could be handled by Kerberos and the Active Directory) but also to authenticate users throughout the Internet. For that reason PKI is designed for broad Internet and extranet authentication situations. Two people in separate companies trying to authenticate and encrypt communications must both have an established trust with the same CA hierarchy. The two companies can trust a third-party certificate authority—for example, GTE CyberTrust, KeyWitness, and Verisign Inc.—which can generally be relied on to maintain the CA root. In this case, the third party becomes responsible for performing initial authentication when issuing certificates and then maintaining the CA. Now the two companies share a CA hierarchy trust and can use the PKI to establish secure communication.

NOTE   Windows 2000 uses the industry standard PKCS-10 certificate request and PKCS-7 certificate response to exchange CA certificates with third-party certificate authorities.

OTHER PKI FEATURES

The Windows 2000 PKI implementation has a number of other features that should be noted before moving to the next section:

- *Roaming*. Users logging in to a Windows 2000 domain can take advantage of roaming user profiles and access their installed personal certificates wherever they log on. Personal certificates are kept in the */Documents* and *Settings/Username/Application Data/Microsoft/Crypto* profile directory. The default location for private keys is in the */Documents* and *Settings/Username/Application Data/Microsoft/Protect/UserSid* directory. However, when third-party Certificate Service Providers (CSP) are employed, the certificate and associated private keys may not roam with the user since they are stored elsewhere.
- *Recovery*. The Windows 2000 CA supports the ability to back up and restore its certificate log. This is important for recovering all public/private key pairs and their associated user names.

Microsoft Certificate Authorities

The Microsoft Certificate Authority can be installed as an *enterprise CA* or as a *standalone CA*. The main difference is that the standalone CA does not interact with the Active Directory and is intended for use with extranets and the Internet. Both support certificates for secure Web services, secure e-mail, digital signatures, and so forth, but the enterprise CA supports Smart Card logon to a Windows 2000 domain. Also, both can publish and distribute user certificates and *Certification Revocation Lists (CRLs)* using the Active Directory. The Exit Module discussed in the Certification Authority Administration section demonstrates how this is done.

THE STANDALONE CERTIFICATE AUTHORITY

The standalone CA does not have access to user account information. Users must enter more information to authenticate themselves, specifically the type of certificate they need since certificate templates (to be discussed later) are not supported by this CA type. A standalone CA should follow the default request action and be set to "pending" so that certificate requests are not automatically fulfilled without the CA administrator's approval. If the request action is not set to "pending," users may request and receive a certificate without identity verification. Since Active Directory user account information is not accessible to the standalone server, the user's identity must be verified from the certificate request form, which involves verifying an address or social security number. Even this may not be enough for verification, and human interaction may be required.

A standalone authority will not issue certificates for Smart Cards, and the certificate must be distributed either manually to domain users or via the group policies to be discussed in the Public Key Policies section.

THE ENTERPRISE CERTIFICATE AUTHORITY

The enterprise CA automatically publishes certificates and Certificate Revocation Lists (CRLs) to the Active Directory for domain users and computers (Figure 10.20). Once installed, its certificate is also placed in all *Trusted Root Certification Authority* stores for all domain users and computers. The enterprise CA has more features and is more closely coupled with the Active Directory. However, it does not support users who are not a part of the Windows 2000 domain. Another consideration when installing an enterprise CA is the difficulty in changing its name because of its tie to the Active Directory and previously issued certificates. The enterprise CA uses certificate templates to control which users may retrieve a given certificate type.

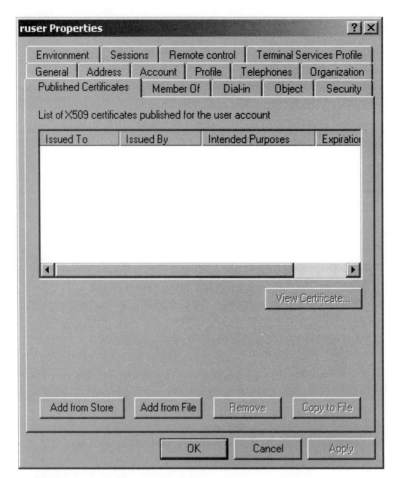

FIGURE 10.20 Publishing Certificate Using the Active Directory

Certificate Templates

Certificate templates are used with the Windows 2000 enterprise CA to help users choose the type of certificate to request. The administrator assigns certificate purposes to a template and the user simply chooses the template that matches his needs. The templates shown in Figure 10.21 are installed by default.

The Microsoft Windows 2000 Help pages have complete information on templates.

Public Key Policies

The **Group Policy** snap-in provides a means for distributing public key policies throughout an Active Directory site, domain, or OU. Enterprise CAs may not find

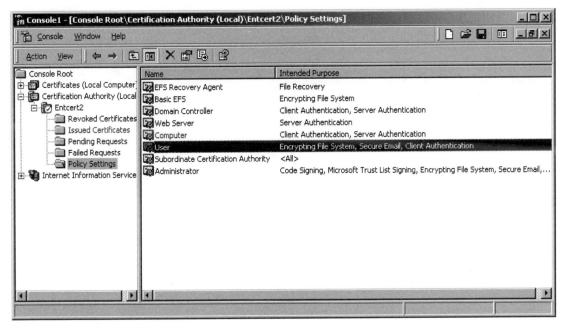

FIGURE 10.21 Default CA Templates

all of these policies useful, as they distribute and publish certificates directly through the Active Directory.

Group policy settings apply to standalone, enterprise, and external certificate authorities. Four main policy areas are set under the **Public Key Policies** node (Figure 10.22):

- *Encrypted Data Recovery Agents*. These specify recovery agents for EFS, which is discussed in more depth in the Encrypted File System section.

- *Automatic Certificate Request Settings*. These allow certificates to be automatically requested and distributed to computer accounts when systems boot. The certificate type may be selected from the certificate template list. This policy helps ensure that all systems have a certificate to implement IP security.

- *Trusted Root Certificate Authorities*. This policy is useful for establishing common root trusts throughout the domain or OU to which the policy applies. Certificates for standalone CAs or external CAs imported into this policy are distributed to policy participants. Enterprise CAs do not require this policy, as all domain users and computers trust the CA through the Active Directory.

- *Enterprise Trust*. These allow the administrator to create trust lists with a designated purpose and lifetime. Each trust list is composed of one or more CA

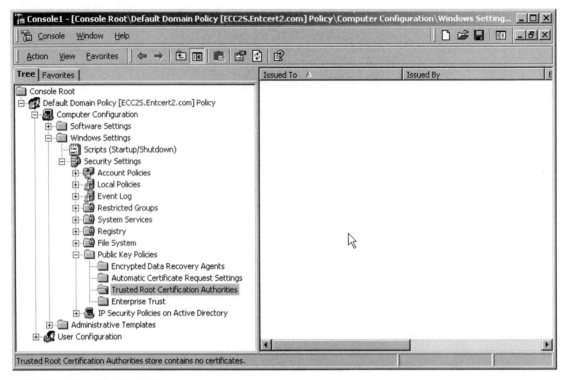

FIGURE 10.22 Public Key Policies

certificates signed by the administrator. In this way, the individual CAs may be limited in the type of certificate they issue to domain users. Since the group policy may be assigned to any Active Directory container, different users may be selectively restricted on the type of certificate they can obtain.

PKI and Other Components and Applications

Once certificates are made available, users may take advantage of services using PKI technology. In this section, we examine some components and applications that interface with PKI, including

- Web security
- E-mail
- Encrypted File System (EFS)

- Smart Cards
- Authenticode
- IP security (see Chapter 13)

WEB SECURITY

A number of technologies are commonly applied to Web security. The most common are the *Secure Sockets Layer (SSL), Transport Layer Security (TLS),* and *Secure channel (Schannel)* protocols. In this section, we summarize how these technologies interact with PKI.

Schannel generates a security token for users regardless of whether they are authenticated through PKI or Kerberos. Users can then access objects according to Access Control Lists (ACLs). The Schannel and the Active Directory integration permit this type of user authorization.

The CA is used together with issued certificates, digital signatures, and SSL/TLS to authenticate and establish a secure channel between an Internet Web client and server. For simplicity, assume that both the Web client and the Web server have deemed this particular CA a trusted root authority, as exemplified in the following (Figure 10.23):

1. The Web client and Web server have both requested and received a certificate from the CA. They put the certificate into their trusted root authority store, which enables them to trust the CA. All information issued or verified through a trusted root authority is assumed to be accurate and sound.

2. The Web client requests a user certificate from the CA, which is usually valid for about a year but is configurable. The certificate is stored in the Web client's personal store and will be used to authenticate the client to all Web servers, e-mail clients, and entities with whom it wants to communicate.

3. The Web server requests a Web server certificate when coming online. It uses this single certificate to authenticate itself to all future Web clients.

4. The basic PKI is now in place.

NOTE   Certificates may remain valid for years, so to revoke previously issued certificates, the CA distributes a Certificate Revocation List (CRL), which is retrieved by clients. Revoking a certificate may be required if a user's private key is discovered or if the user is no longer employed by an organization. The revocation process is demonstrated in examples at the end of this chapter.

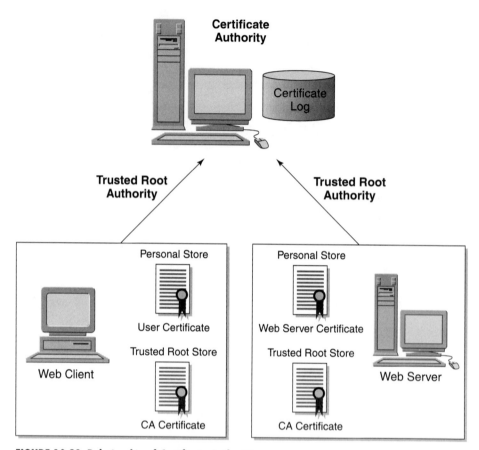

FIGURE 10.23 Relationship of Certificate Authorities

Certificates are used to authenticate and confidentially share a symmetrical encryption key between the Web client and server. The SSL and TLS protocols use the public key structure to implement a fast and secure channel.

As illustrated in Figure 10.24, the following steps outline how the SSL establishes a connection:

1. The Web client requests a secure connection with the Web server. The server authenticates itself by sending its Web server certificate to the Web client.

2. The Web client decrypts the digital signature with the CA's public key to recover the message hash. The client then generates its own message hash using the same hash algorithm and compares the two. If they are the same, the signature must belong to the trusted CA. The Web client trusts the CA and believes that the Web server is the subject name listed in its certificate.

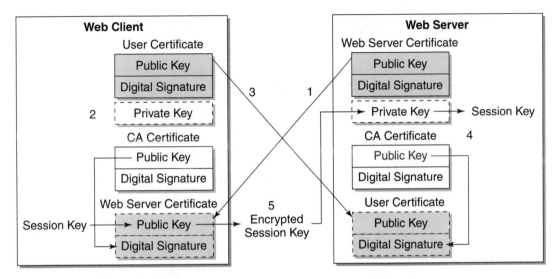

FIGURE 10.24 Public Key Exchange

3. The Web client sends its user certificate to the Web server.

4. The Web server performs the same signature verification using the CA's public key on the client's certificate. It has now identified the Web client. User ID and password authentication may be used optionally for additional user authentication.

5. The Web client generates a random symmetrical key for this session, encrypted using the Web server public key obtained from the Web server's certificate.

6. The Web server decrypts the symmetrical session key using its private key. The session key is then used for communication throughout the rest of the secure Web connection.

ELECTRONIC MAIL

Most e-mail clients support the two message formats of HTML and plain text. The Multipurpose Internet Mail Extensions (MIME), for example, supports HTML formatting, which allows graphics, hyperlinks, color, and text settings within e-mail text between mail clients that support it. More advanced systems now implement an extended secure version known as S/MIME.

PKI is used by S/MIME version 3-compliant applications to implement any combination of digital signatures and encryption desired by the sender. Certificates are easily exchanged between users employing digital signatures to set up secure communication.

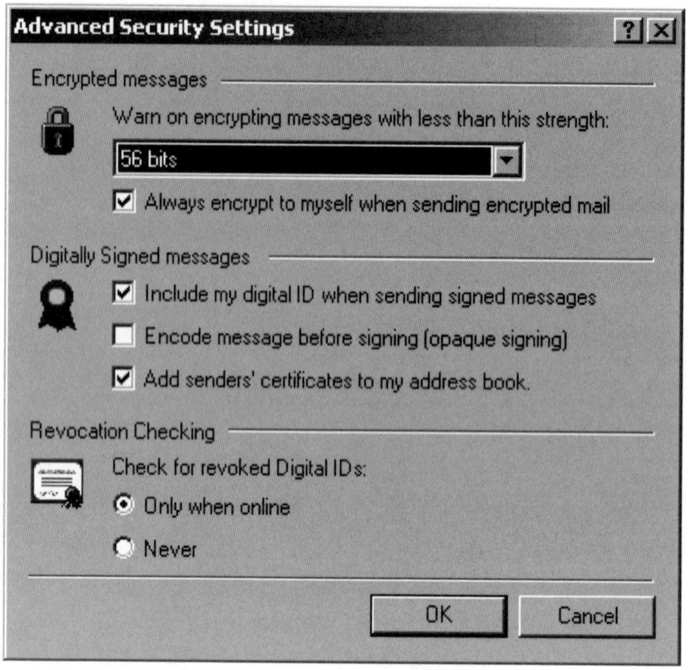

FIGURE 10.25 E-mail Settings for Certificate Exchange

Mail client settings such as **Add sender's certificates to my address book** and **Include my digital ID when sending signed messages** (Figure 10.25) permit the initial exchange of user certificates. Once certificates are obtained for all desired correspondents, the user may send encrypted messages. Microsoft Outlook 98 and Microsoft Outlook Express both support S/MIME version 3 and maintain certificates within the address book associated with each contact. Outlook Express uses only the SHA–1 hashing algorithm for digital signatures and the encryption algorithms shown in Table 10.11.

AUTHENTICODE

Authenticode uses digital signatures to verify software ownership and integrity upon retrieval. ActiveX, *.dll, Java applets, *.exe, and *.cab files can all have the Authenticode digital signature applied and verified before they are executed in the user's system environment. Trusted publishers are referenced from Internet Explorer 5.0 from the **Tools → Internet Options... → Content** tab → **Publishers...** button (Figure 10.26). The user simply retrieves Authenticode certifi-

TABLE 10.11 Outlook Express 5.0 Encryption Support

United States/Canada	Export Versions
RC2 40-bit and 128-bit	RC2 40-bit
DES (56-bit)	DES (56-bit)
3DES (168-bit)	Not allowed for export
Decrypt RC2 (64-bit) But Not Encrypt	Decrypt RC2 (64-bit) But Not Encrypt

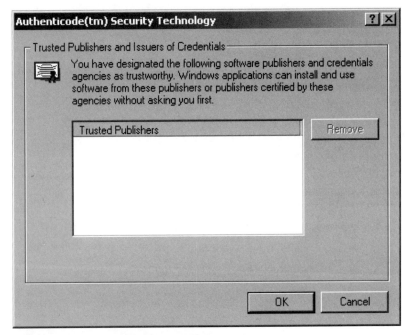

FIGURE 10.26 Trusted Component Publishers

cates from CAs that support them such as Verisign (*www.verisign.com*) and Thawte (*www.thawte.com*).

The Encrypted File System

Windows 2000 NTFS supports the Encrypted File System (EFS). The EFS process is transparent to the user and file handling requires no special treatment. A file can be opened and read just like any other file; however, other users will not be able to read, copy, rename, or move it.

A recommended method for maintaining encrypted files is to create an encryption folder to hold them. It is good practice to encrypt the entire folder to ensure that its files stay encrypted. Encrypting the **My Documents** folder will secure most personal user documents without the need to change the encryption on individual files. It is also a good idea to encrypt the **temp** directory so that the files you are editing or opening from your mail client are encrypted as well. Note that an encrypted file will become decrypted if it is moved to a folder with the drag and drop method. Instead, use the **Cut** and **Paste** options from the **Edit** pull-down menu.

System and compressed files may not be encrypted, and users with correct permissions may delete an encrypted file.

THE EFS PROCESS

The Microsoft Cryptographic Provider randomly produces a 128-bit (56-bit for the exported versions of Windows 2000) symmetrical File Encryption Key (FEK) to encrypt a file. EFS encrypts the FEK with the user's public key from an issued certificate and stores it in the file's Data Decryption Field (DDF). The user's private key is used to decrypt the FEK when accessing the file in the future; the FEK is then used to decrypt the file.

The user may lose her public/private key pair, so Windows 2000 designates the domain administrator as the default recovery agent. For each recovery agent, in addition to the DDF field stored with the encrypted file, a Data Recovery Field (DRF) is maintained. The FEK is encrypted using the recovery agent's certificate. In the event that users lose their encryption certificate, they may e-mail the folder/file to the recovery agent, who can decrypt the object and return it in a readable form.

NOTE   See the `cipher` command for encryption at the Command Prompt.

Although the behind-the-scenes activities may be somewhat complex, encryption from the user interface is quite simple. Simply right-click on a file or folder to encrypt and select **Properties**. Press the **Advanced...** button under the **General** tab (Figure 10.27) and check the **Encrypt contents to secure data** option.

A dialog appears when encrypting a folder (Figure 10.28) asking if encryption should be applied to subfolders and files. Select the **Apply changes to this folder, subfolders and files** option.

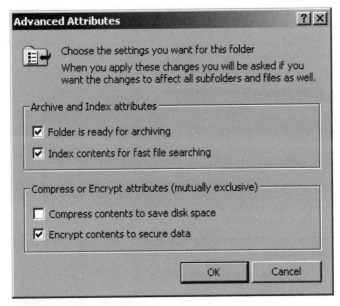

FIGURE 10.27 File Encryption

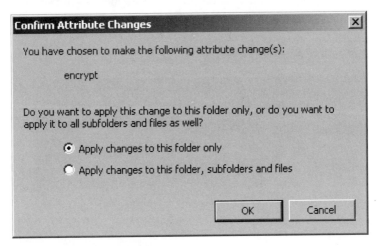

FIGURE 10.28 Encryption Inheritance

EFS ISSUES

A number of best practices apply when using EFS. Here are some of them:

- Both the user and the recovery agent should export certificates and make backups of them. These certificates can be restored later so that encrypted files may be recovered.

NOTE   Backing up a certificate with its corresponding private key has some obvious risks. If the backup file were compromised, the certificate would be as well.

- The first time a file/folder is encrypted the group policy for Encrypted Data Recovery Agents appoints recovery agent responsibility to the administrator. This may be modified with the **Group Policy** snap-in (Figure 10.29) by right-clicking **Encrypted Data Recovery Agent** policy and selecting **New → Encrypted Recovery Agent…**.

- The **Add Recovery Agent Wizard** starts up and allows new user agent designation. If certificates are published to the Active Directory (as in the enterprise CA), users may be added without importing certificates. Otherwise, new recovery agents must import new encryption certificates before they become recovery agents.

- A user with Delete permission on a file/folder may delete the object regardless of his decryption ability.

- Only files created on NTFS can be encrypted. Using the Backup utility on an encrypted file/folder and then moving that file to a FAT file system or tape

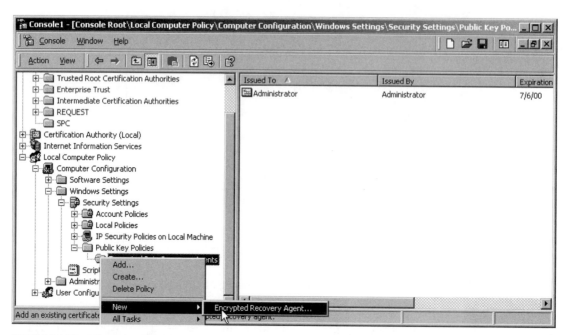

FIGURE 10.29 A Recovery Agent

backup will preserve encryption, but moving it directly to a FAT file system will not.

- Encrypted files may not be shared to the network. However, they may be stored to a remote server. This computer account must have the **Trusted for Delegation** checkbox set from the Active Directory before it is permitted to move the files (Figure 10.30). The delegation property is modified by right-clicking the destination Windows 2000 server from the Active Directory and selecting **Properties**. Note that the files are not encrypted while in transit to the destination server. IP security and SSL should be used for secure file transfers.

- Files must be manipulated using **Cut**, **Copy**, and **Paste** instead of drag and drop.

- Compressed and system files cannot be encrypted.

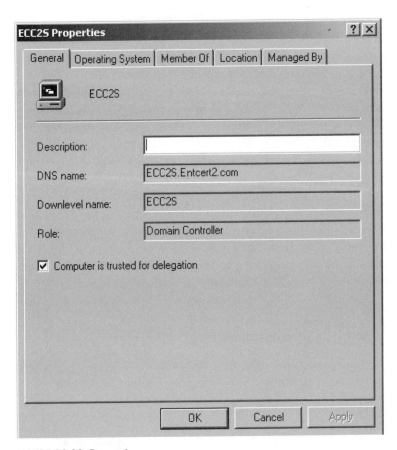

FIGURE 10.30 Properties

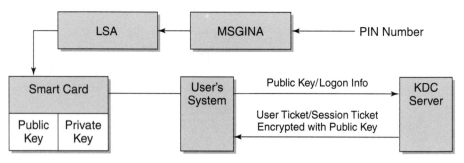

FIGURE 10.31 Smart Card Authentication

Smart Cards

Smart Cards are small storage devices that store the user's public and private keys. They can be used only by systems that support a card reader. Smart Cards modify Kerberos authentication, specifically the AS Exchange between a client trying to log on to the network and the KDC. (See the Kerberos section for elaboration on the AS Exchange.) Instead of the user's password hash as a key to encrypt the AS reply, the KDC uses the user's public key, obtained from the Smart Card, to encrypt portions of the reply. This offers stronger encryption and eliminates the need to remember complicated passwords. The Smart Card requires a PKI CA to obtain a certificate and load a public/private key pair. A certificate must be issued from a trusted CA so that a user may roam the domain and use his card to log on throughout the network.

When a user logs on to a system using a Smart Card, the *Microsoft Graphical Identification and Authentication (MSGINA)* dialog box starts and requests the usual logon information (Figure 10.31). However, the user needs to enter only his Smart Card PIN number. The *Local Security Authority (LSA)* will access the Smart Card with the PIN number and retrieves the X.509 v3 certificate for Kerberos authentication. The KDC authenticates the user based on the certificate and returns an encrypted TGT and session key for further communication.

Certificate Authority Administration

The following sections offer basic information on the installation and management of Certificate Authority. Several examples are provided.

INSTALLATION

Both the standalone and the enterprise CAs may reside on a domain controller or member server within the domain. The enterprise CA requires the domain to have Windows 2000 DNS and Active Directory services. The standalone CA may also be installed on a workstation and does not require these services, but does require administrative privileges on the server on which it will be installed. The following occurs with all enterprise and standalone CA installations when the person installing it is a member of the **Domain Administrators** group:

- A copy of the CA's certificate is stored in every user and computer's **Trusted Domain Root Authority** store.
- The CA becomes a member of the **Cert Publishers** global group, enabling it to publish to the Active Directory. The CA must be manually added to this group in other domains that desire this functionality.

NOTE   A standalone CA is used for Internet and extranet user access and for security reasons will probably be placed outside the firewall. It must be installed using Administrative authority and probably should not be installed with Domain Administrative authority. A workstation should be used for deployment.

NOTE   Be sure that IIS is already installed prior to installing Certificate Services. Terminal Server may not be installed concurrently with Certificate Services on the same server.

NOTE   If you install Certificate Services before IIS, the **CertServ** Web pages will not be available. To remedy the problem, de-install Certificate Services, install IIS, and then re-install Certificate Services. To de-install from the **Configure Your Computer** menu, remove the checkmark from the component and continue. To install a component, checkmark the component and continue.

The following steps should be taken to install Certificate Authority:

1. Start the installation process by selecting **Start → Programs → Administrative Tools → Configure Your Server**.
2. From the Windows 2000 Configure Your Server tool, select **Advanced → Optional Components**. The **Windows Components Wizard** should start (Figure 10.32). Select the **Certificate Services** checkbox.
3. Select the type of certificate authority you want to install (Figure 10.33).
4. Press the **Next>** button.
5. Enter the CA identifying information (Figure 10.34).
6. Confirm where the certificate's database will be stored (Figure 10.35). Remember, all issued and revoked certificate information will be stored here.

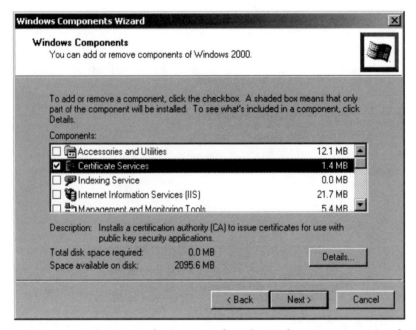

FIGURE 10.32 Selecting Certificate Services from the Windows Component Wizard

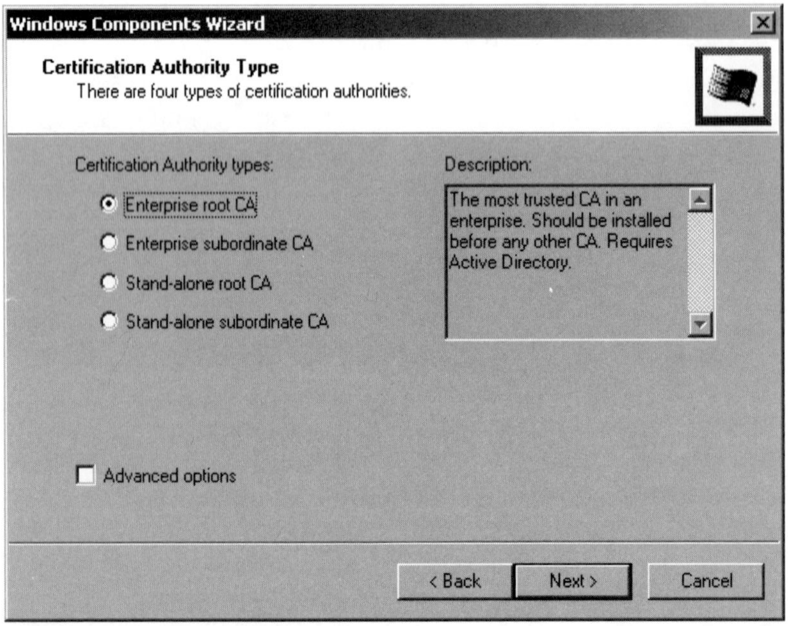

FIGURE 10.33 Certification Authority Type

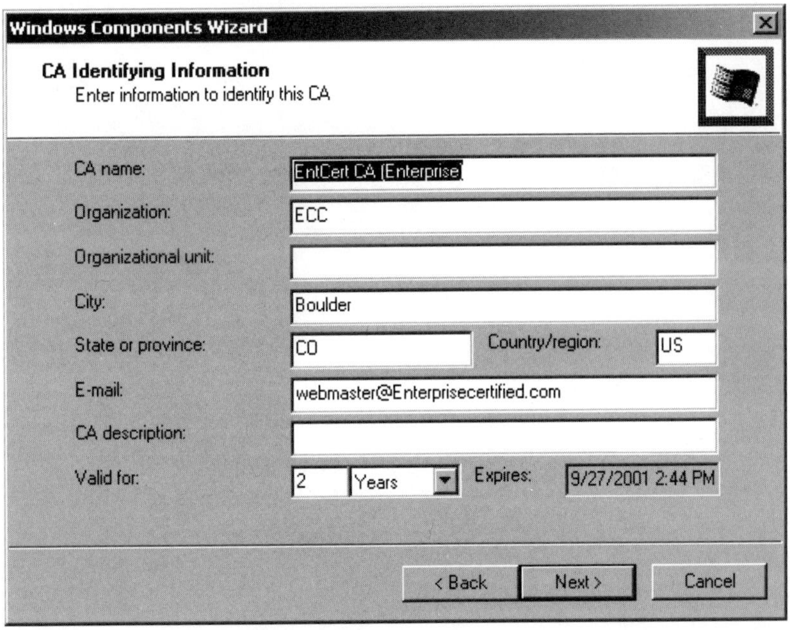

FIGURE 10.34 CA Identifying Information

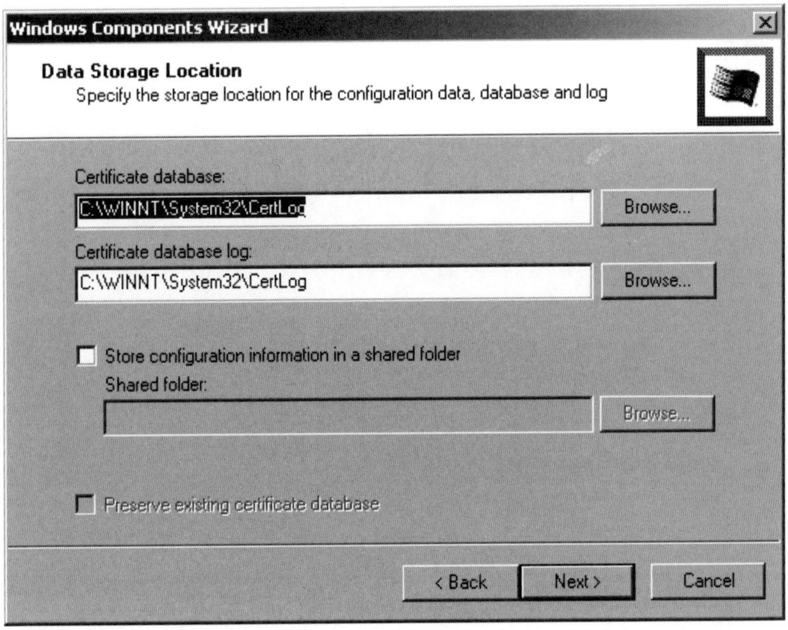

FIGURE 10.35 Data Storage

Management

Once Windows 2000 Certificate Authority is installed, the challenge becomes managing it. The first administrative issue is setting certificate group policies.

DISTRIBUTING CERTIFICATES USING GROUP POLICIES

Group policies are used to distribute certificates throughout a domain. The four group policy nodes under **Computer Configuration → Security Settings → Public Key Policies**, discussed earlier, that pertain here are

- *Encrypted Data Recovery Agents*
- *Automatic Certificate Request Settings*
- *Trusted Root Certificate Authorities*
- *Enterprise Trust*

The following examples demonstrate how these group policies are used.

Establishing Trusted Root Authorities

The first example demonstrates how to establish a trust with an external CA or standalone CA that cannot publish to the Active Directory upon installation. The CA's certificate needs to be placed in the local **Trusted Root Certification Authorities** store. A domain controller will import it and place it in the **Default Domain Policy** GPO to establish trust for all domain members.

1. Open a Microsoft Management Console and add the **Group Policy** snap-in for the **Default Domain Policy** object.

2. Open the **Computer Configuration → Windows Settings → Security Settings → Public Key Policies → Trusted Root Certificate Authorities** node.

3. Right-click **Trusted Root Certificate Authorities**. Select **All Tasks → Import...** (Figure 10.36)

4. The **Certificate Manager Import Wizard** starts. Press the **Next>** button.

5. When the standalone CA is installed, a root security certificate is put into the *\WINNT\system32\certsrv\CertEnroll\systemname.domainname* file. Import this certificate unless you have a third-party certificate you want to load onto your root CA (Figure 10.37). Like the Windows 2000 CA Web interface, a third-party CA certificate is usually retrieved using a Web browser and then stored locally to disk. Go to the third-party Website and request such a certificate. If you want to use the Web interface to retrieve the CA certificate from either an enterprise or standalone CA, see the Retrieving Certificates section. Press the **Next>** button.

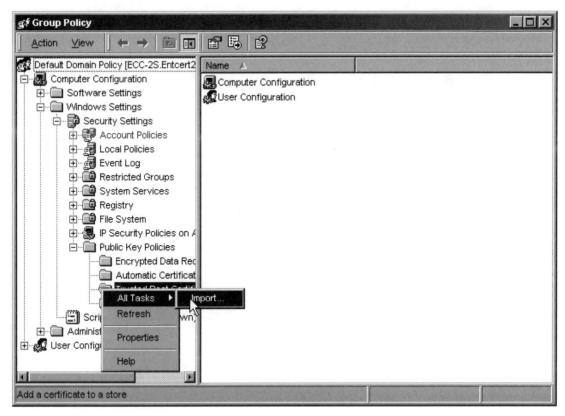

FIGURE 10.36 Group Policy

6. Store the CA certificate in all **Trusted Root Certificate Authority** stores (Figure 10.38). Press the **Next>** button.

7. Press the **Finish** button to complete the import process (Figure 10.39).

8. Press the **OK** button to acknowledge a successful import.

9. View local **Trusted Root Certification Authorities** stores throughout the domain to verify the domain CA trust. (Refer to the Viewing Certificate Stores section for directions.)

The **Default Domain Policy** GPO assigned your newly installed Certificate Authority as the trusted certificate root authority for the domain. A domain controller imported a certificate from the CA into the **Trusted Root Certification Authorities** policy to do this.

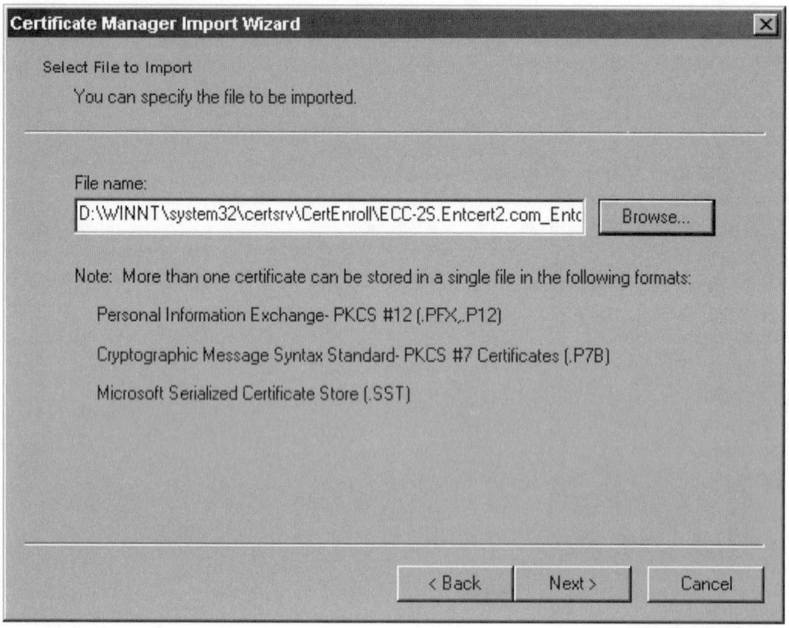

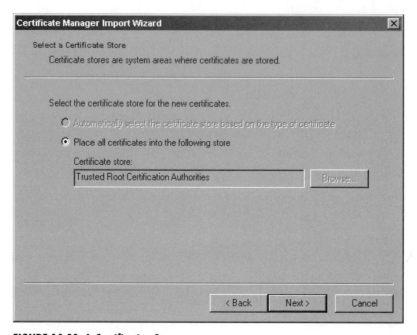

FIGURE 10.37 Import Selection

FIGURE 10.38 A Certification Store

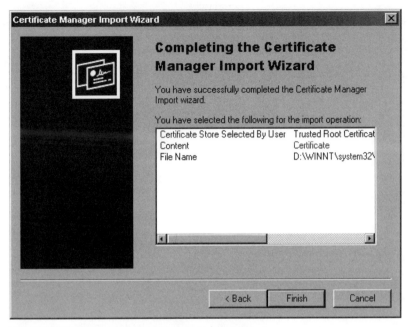

FIGURE 10.39 The Certificate Manager Import Wizard

Automatic Certificate Requests

Automatic certificate requests are generated whenever a user logs on or a computer boots. The group policy node **Computer Configuration → Windows Settings → Security Settings → Public Key Policies → Automatic Certificate Request Settings** specifies the type of certificate to be requested and the CA server to field the certificate request. The following steps demonstrate how to add an automatic certificate request to the **Default Domain Policy**:

1. Right-click the **Automatic Certificates Request Settings** node and select **New → Automatic Certificate Request...** (Figure 10.40).

2. The **Automatic Certificate Request** dialog appears. Press the **Next>** button.

3. Select the certificate type to request from the available certificate templates. Press the **Next>** button (Figure 10.41).

4. Select the CA server to which to send the certificate request (Figure 10.42). Press the **Next>** button.

5. Press the **Finish** button. The policy must be allowed to propagate to other domain controllers and clients.

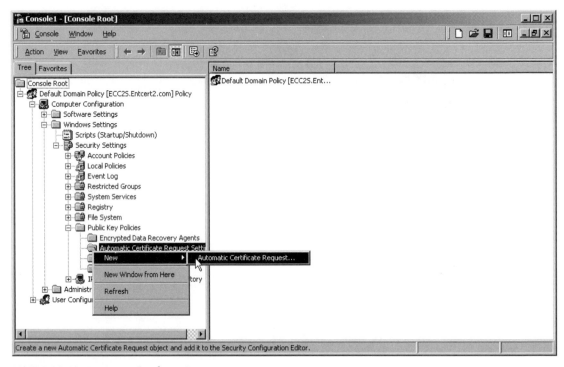

FIGURE 10.40 Automatic Certificate Request

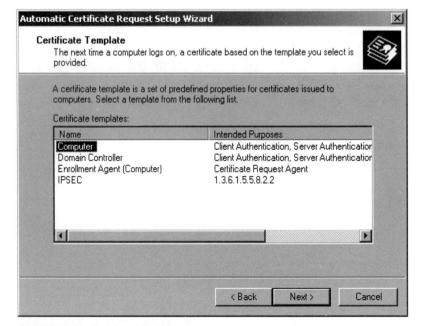

FIGURE 10.41 Certificate Templates

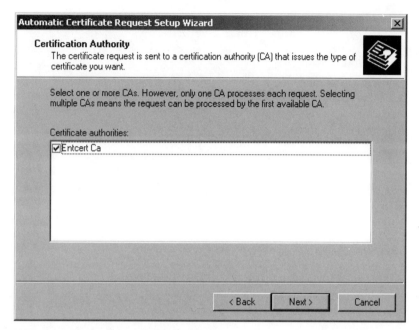

FIGURE 10.42 Certificate Authority Selection

Viewing Local Certificate Stores

Local certificate stores can be viewed through the Certificates MMC snap-in or through a variety of applications such as Outlook Express and Internet Explorer. Here is an introduction on viewing certificate stores using these tools.

Using the Certificate Snap-In

To view local certificate stores with the **Certificates** snap-in, use the following procedure:

1. Open a command window and type **MMC** to start a management console.
2. From the Console pull-down menu select **Add/Remove Snap-in…**.
3. Select the **Certificates** snap-in and press the **Add** button.
4. Select the **Computer account** radio button (Figure 10.43). Press the **Next>** button.

At this point you will notice that the Certificate snap-in can be installed to manage one of three types of accounts: user, service, or computer. A different local store will be engaged for each selection. The user account is self-explanatory; the service account deals with how the operating system interacts with the local com-

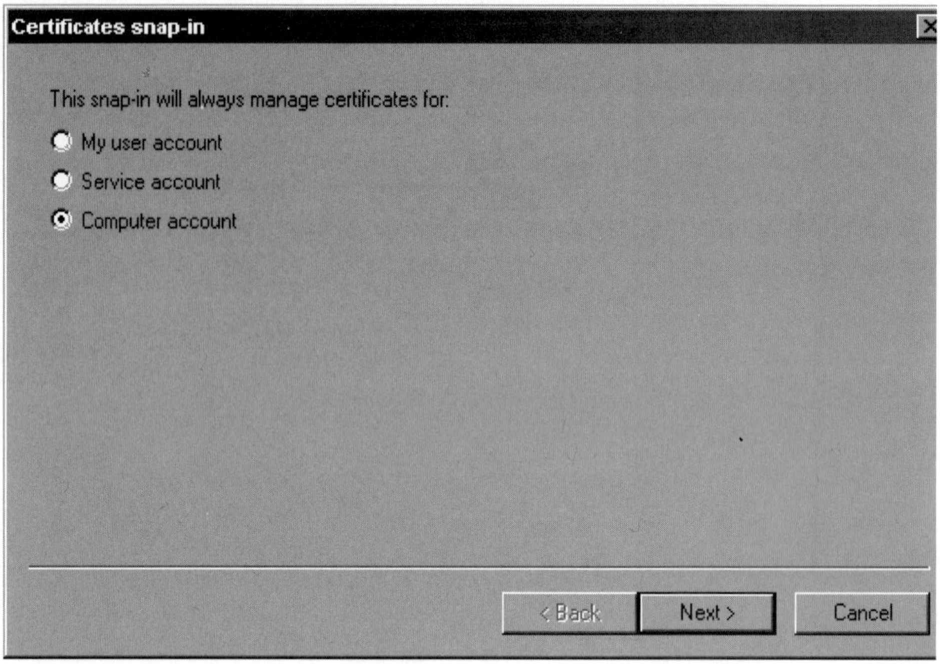

FIGURE 10.43 Choosing a Certificate Store

puter; and the computer account deals with how the computer interacts with the rest of the domain. To participate with IPSec, the computer account must be assigned a certificate. This will be addressed in Chapter 13.

5. Select the **Local computer:** radio button and press the **Finish** button (Figure 10.44).

6. The **Certificates (Local Computer)** should be added to your console.

7. From the Console open **Certificates** → **Trusted Root Certification Authority** → **Certificate** node.

8. Find a certificate and double-click. The **General** tab lists the intended uses for the certificate, the valid dates, and who issued the certificate to whom (Figure 10.45, page 418).

9. The **Details** tab displays all the certificate's characteristics in detail (Figure 10.46, page 419).

10. The **Certification Path** tab displays the root authority that granted the certificate.

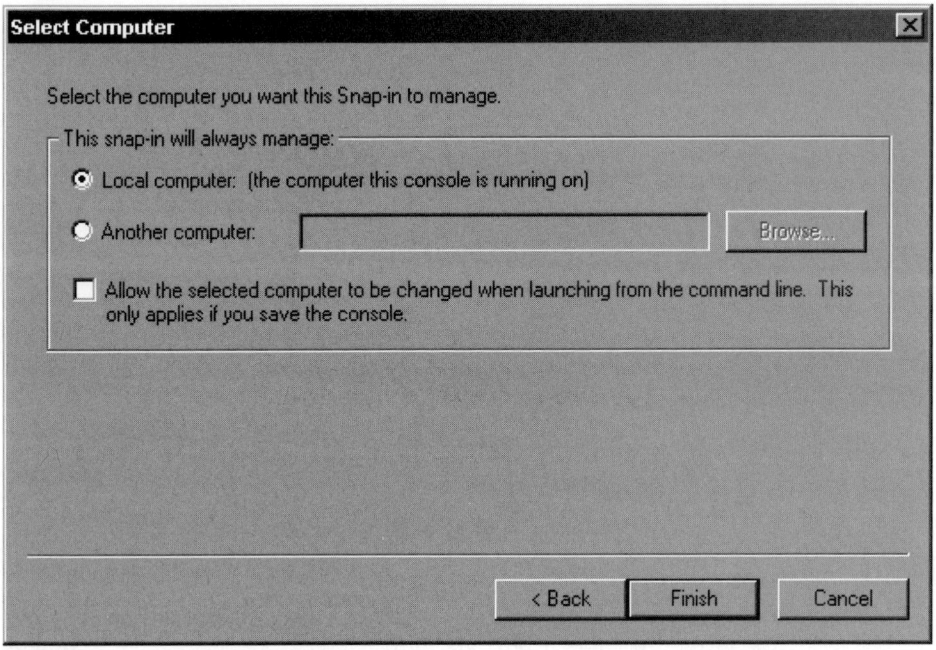

FIGURE 10.44 Selecting the Local Computer

Using Internet Explorer 5.0

To view local certificate stores from Internet Explorer 5.0:

1. From the Web browser you are using find the Internet Options menu (**Tools → Internet Options...**).

2. If you are using IE 5.0, select the **Content** tab and press the **Certificates...** button (Figure 10.47, page 420).

3. Local stores are displayed in tab form (Figure 10.48). Double-click on a certificate to view its properties.

A similar procedure enables local certificate store viewing from Outlook Express 5.0.

RETRIEVING CERTIFICATES

There are two basic methods to retrieve certificates from a Windows 2000 enterprise CA. One is with the **Certificate Request Wizard** using the **Certificates** snap-in; the other is with the Windows 2000 Certificate Services Web pages. The standalone CA requires the Web page retrieval method. Once a user retrieves a

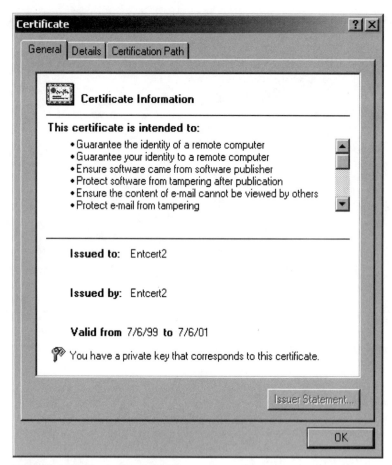

FIGURE 10.45 The Certificate Node

certificate, she may use it for secure e-mail, IPSec, secure Web transactions, and other services previously discussed.

Windows 2000 Certificate Services Web Pages

At this stage of the example, the Web server installed on the CA will be used to populate other systems in the domain with certificates. The Certificate Services Web page offers a few advantages over the **Certificate Request Wizard** in carrying this out. First, the Web page allows certificates to make their private keys exportable, which means that a certificate and its private key may be backed up. This is important since the private key is not part of the certificate and will proba-

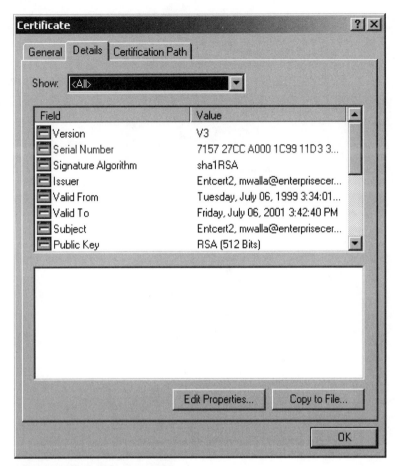

FIGURE 10.46 Certificate Details

bly not be saved when a system fails unless it is exported concurrently with its associated certificate (containing the public key) during routine backups. Second, the user may select the desired hash algorithm, key length, PKCS #7 request standard, and PKCS #10 reply standard when requesting certificates from the Certificate Services Web page.

An optional but recommended action is to review and confirm the installation. To ensure that the **CertSrv** directory and Web pages are installed and that Windows authentication security is in place for a standalone server on your CA, take these steps:

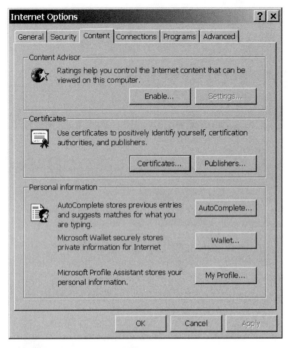

FIGURE 10.47 Internet Options

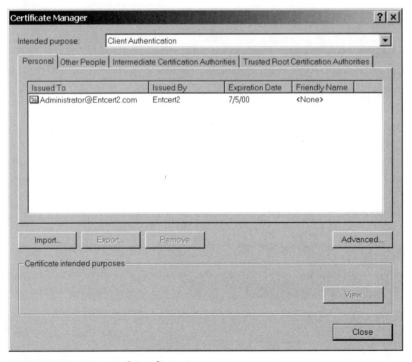

FIGURE 10.48 A Personal Certificate Store

1. Open a Microsoft Management Console or create a new one by typing **mmc** from the Command Prompt.

2. From the Console pull-down select **Add-Remove Snap-in...** and add the **Internet Information Server** snap-in to the console.

3. Open the snap-in by selecting **Internet Information Server** → *CAserver-name* → **Default Web Site**. Verify that the **CertSrv** directory exists so that Web-based certificate services are available (Figure 10.49).

4. Right-click the **Administration Web Site** node and select **Properties**. Select the **Directory Security** tab and press the **Edit...** button.

5. Be sure to check only the **Integrated Windows Authentication** checkbox (Figure 10.50) to ensure Windows authentication. Press **OK** and exit.

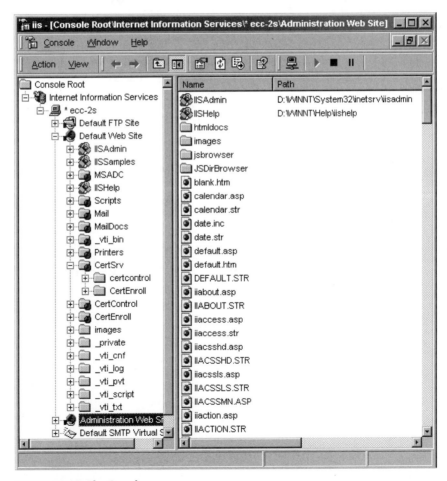

FIGURE 10.49 The Console

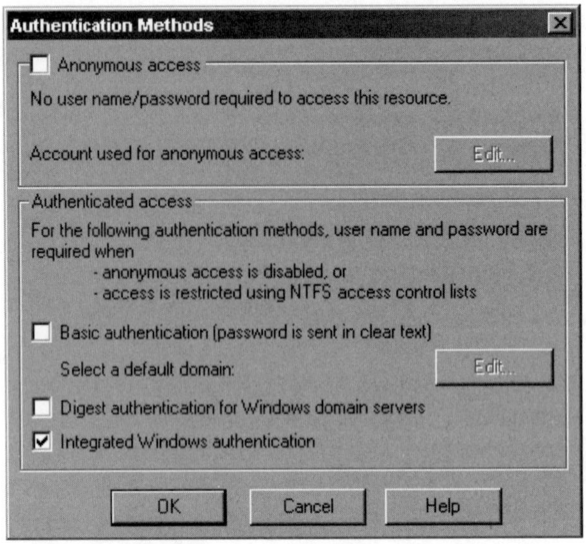

FIGURE 10.50 Authentication Methods

Retrieving a Root CA Certificate
The following steps outline basic certificate retrieval from Windows 2000 Certificate Services Web pages. The basic retrieval options are shown in Figure 10.51.

1. Go to a system requiring a CA certificate and start a Web browser using the URL *http://caservername/CertSrv*.

2. Select the **Retrieve a CA certificate or certificate revocation list** radio button. Press the **Next>** button.

3. Select the **Download CA Certificate** link (Figure 10.52).

4. From the **File Download** dialog select the **Open this file from its current location** radio button (Figure 10.53). Press the **OK** button.

5. Press the **Install Certificate…** button (Figure 10.54) and start the **Certificate Manager Import Wizard**. Press the **Next>** button.

6. Select the **Automatically select certificate store** radio button and press the **Next>** button (Figure 10.55). This will put the trusted root certificates in the trusted store. Press the **Finish** button.

7. A warning dialog is displayed since an addition is being made to the root store (Figure 10.56, page 425). Press the **Yes** button.

8. Press the **OK** button to complete the install.

The revocation list can be retrieved similarly.

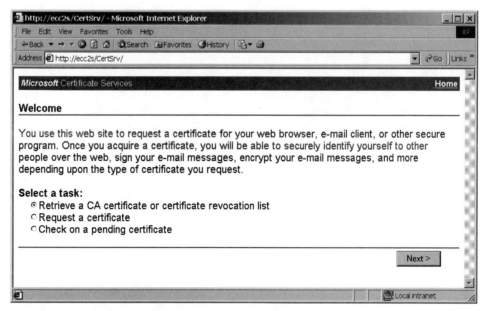

FIGURE 10.51 The Main CA Server Menu

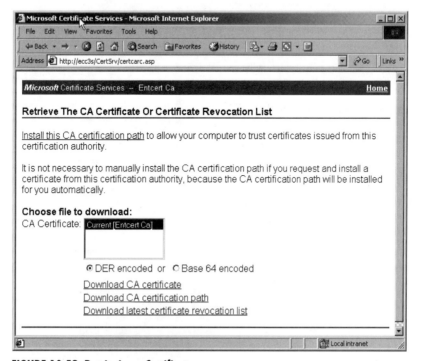

FIGURE 10.52 Retrieving a Certificate

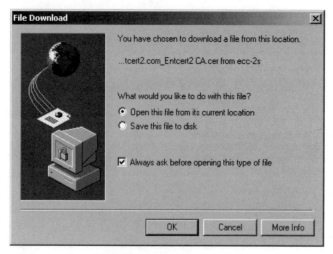

FIGURE 10.53 A Certificate Download

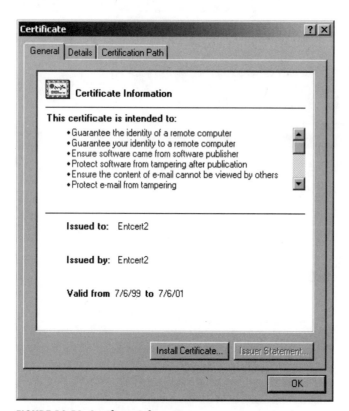

FIGURE 10.54 Certificate Information

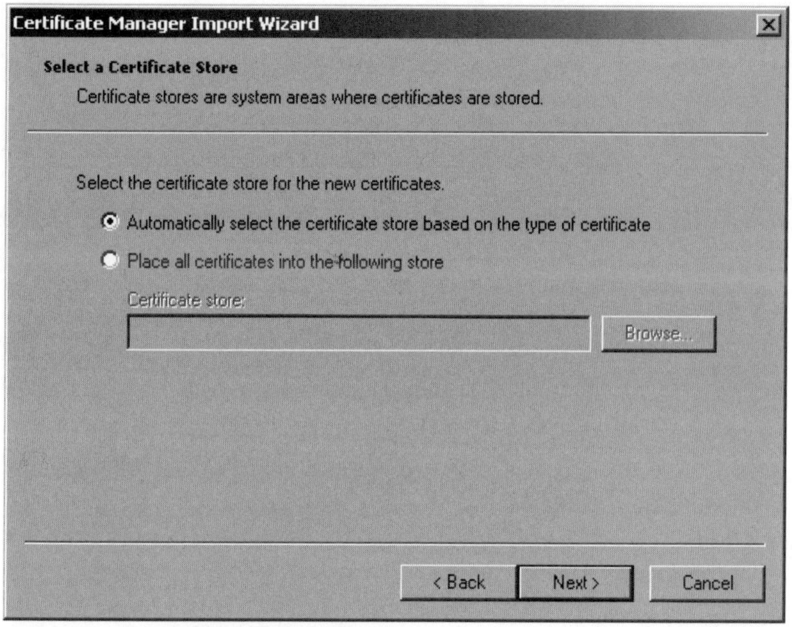

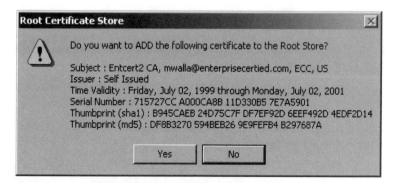

FIGURE 10.55 Selecting a Certificate Store

FIGURE 10.56 Confirmation of Certificate Selection

Retrieving a User Certificate

Now let's retrieve a certificate from the CA for uses other than establishing a root CA. By retrieving a user certificate from the Web server, we may access the Web server and communicate securely with other services.

1. Go to the CA certificate Web retrieval site (*http://caservername/CertServ*) and select **Request a certificate** (Figure 10.57).

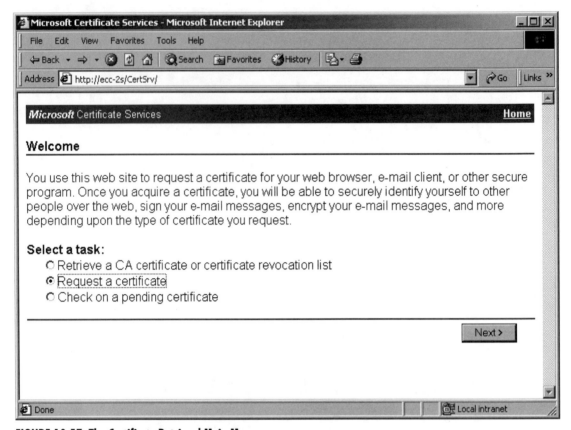

FIGURE 10.57 The Certificate Retrieval Main Menu

2. Select the **User certificate request:** to access resources as a client (Figure 10.58). Press the **Next>** button.

3. A standalone CA will require you to enter the User Certificate information if you haven't already done so. You may select another Cryptographic Service Provider for the certificate exchange, but sticking with the Microsoft Base Cryptographic Provider v.1.0 is recommended (Figure 10.59). Press the **Submit** button.

4. Press the **Install this certificate** option.

You have installed the certificate (Figure 10.60). However, it may not take effect until some time in the future. The timestamp is checked along with the date stamp. Sometimes certificates are issued to become valid an hour or so after they are issued.

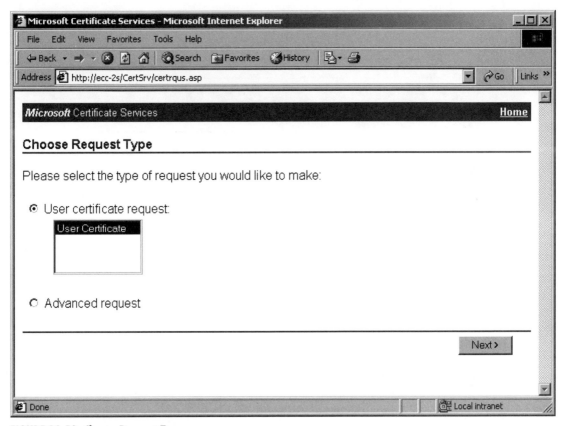

FIGURE 10.58 Choose Request Type

Checking Pending Certificates
As mentioned earlier, standalone CAs should implement the "pending" policy since they cannot authenticate users with the Active Directory.

1. Check on impending certificate requests by selecting the **Check on a pending certificate** option from the starting Web page (*http://caservername/ CertSrv*). Press the **Next>** button.

2. There may not be any pending requests (Figure 10.61).

Advanced Certificate Requests
An Advanced certificate request allows more options to be selected. Follow these steps to initiate Advanced certificate requests.

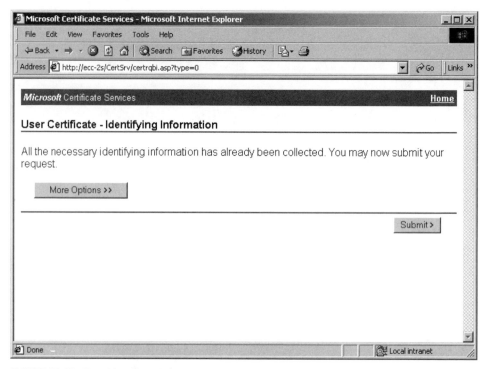

FIGURE 10.59 User Identifying Information

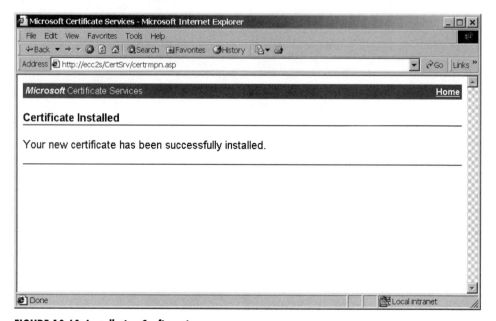

FIGURE 10.60 Installation Confirmation

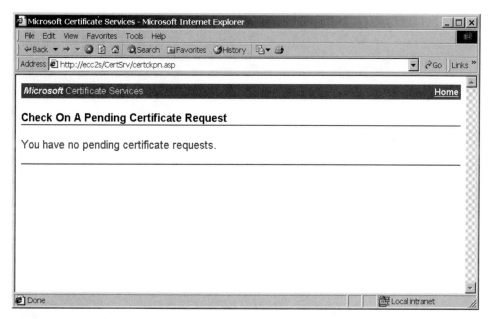

FIGURE 10.61 Pending Status

1. Go to the original Web site (*http://servername/CertServ*) and select **Request a certificate**. Press the **Next>** button.

2. Request a user certificate and select the **Advanced request** option (Figure 10.62).

3. The **Advanced Certificate Request** allows three types of request: form, PKCS #10 and #7 file, and certificate for Smart Card enrollment station. Select the **Using a form** option (Figure 10.63).

4. **Certificate Templates**, discussed earlier this chapter, defines the available certificate types. Pick a template corresponding to the intended use for the certificate (Figure 10.64).

5. Select the type of Cryptographic Service Provider (CSP) to be used for generating the local public/private key pair (Figure 10.65).

6. The hash algorithm, key size, key usage, and, most important, the **Mark Keys as exportable for backup purposes** options are all available from the Advanced Certificate Request form.

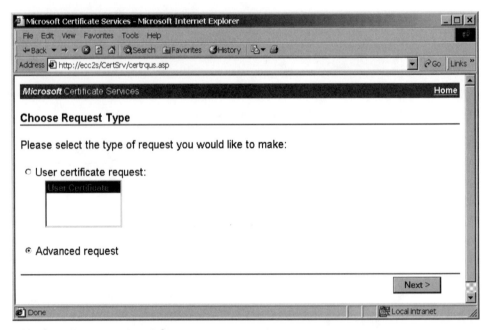

FIGURE 10.62 Request Type Selection

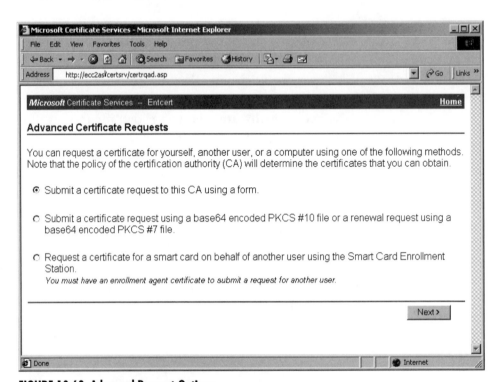

FIGURE 10.63 Advanced Request Options

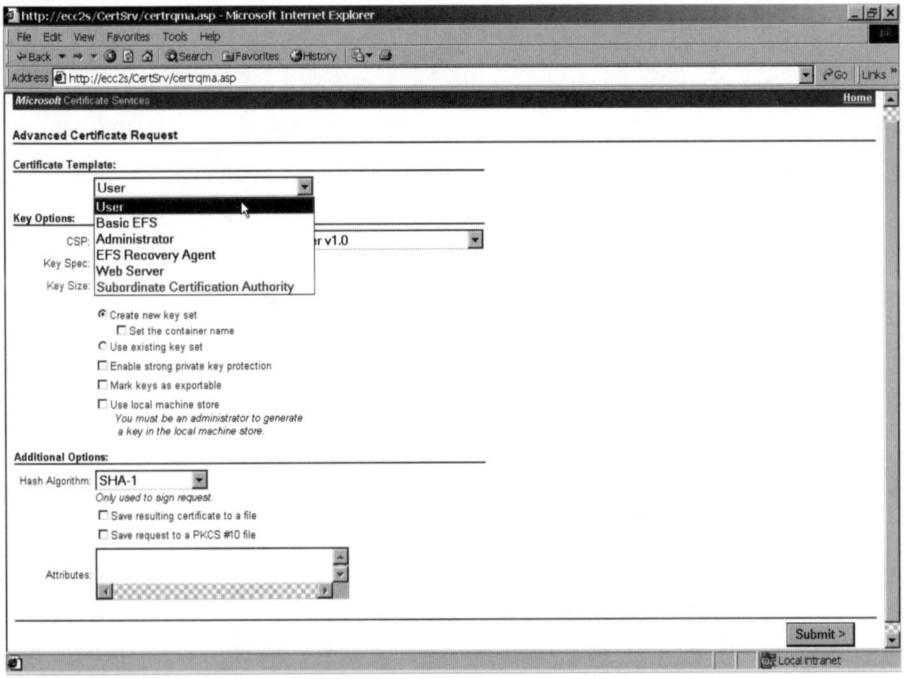

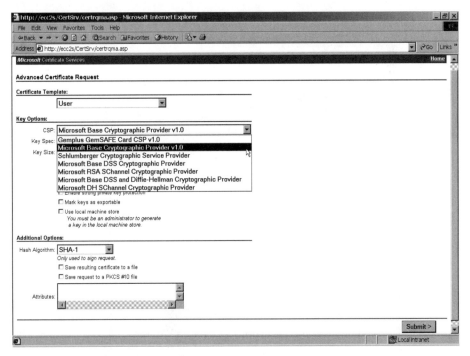

FIGURE 10.64 A Certificate Template

FIGURE 10.65 Cryptographic Provider Options

Active Directory Certificate Retrieval

Enterprise CAs support the **Certificates** snap-in with the **Certificate Request Wizard**. Certificates for EFS and EFS recovery agents may have their private keys marked for export. Follow these steps to allow Active Directory Certificate Retrieval.

1. Add the **Certificates** snap-in for a user account into a Microsoft Management Console.

2. Right-click a certificate store and select **All Tasks → Request New Certificate** (Figure 10.66).

3. The **Certificate Request Wizard** starts. Press the **Next>** button.

4. Select a certificate type from the available certificate templates. The advanced options will allow CSP selection (Figure 10.67). Press the **Next>** button.

5. Choose the enterprise CA to send the certificate request (Figure 10.68). Press the **Next>** button.

6. Type a name for the certificate. Press the **Next>** button (Figure 10.69).

7. Complete the request by pressing the **Finish** button.

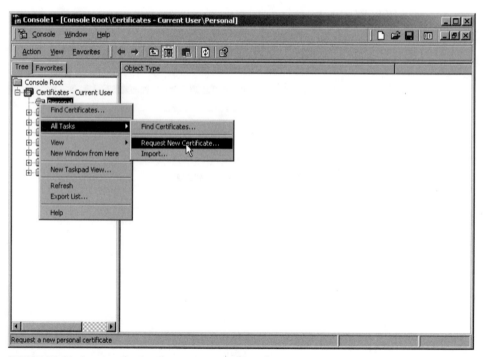

FIGURE 10.66 Starting the Certificates Request Wizard

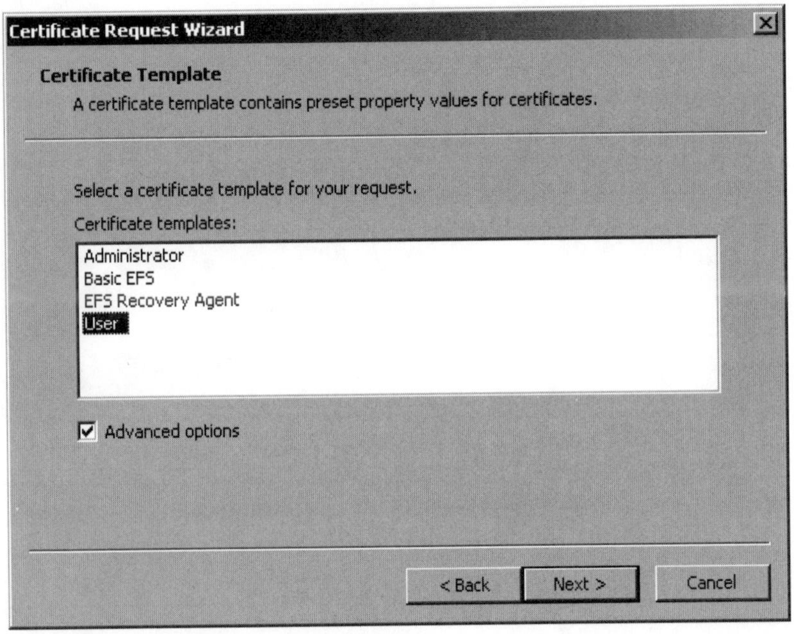

FIGURE 10.67 Selecting a Certificate Type

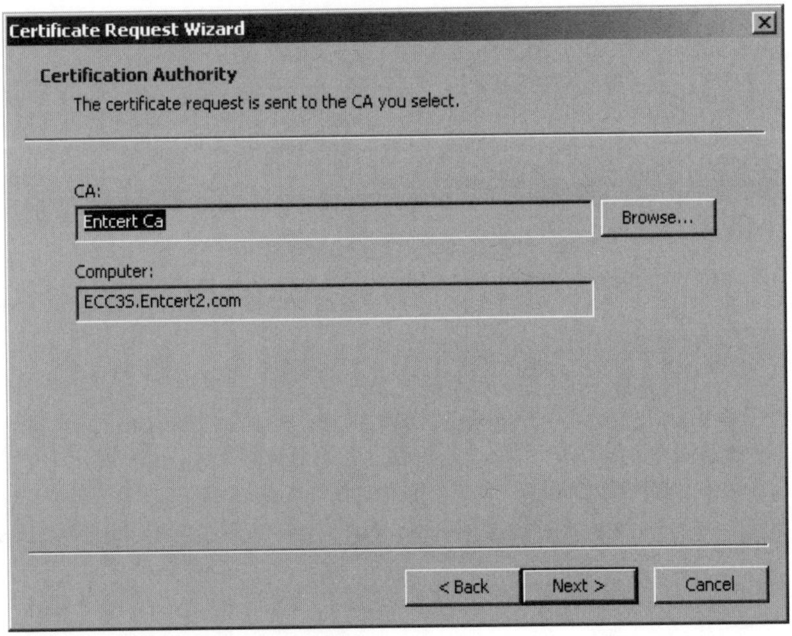

FIGURE 10.68 Enterprise CA Selection

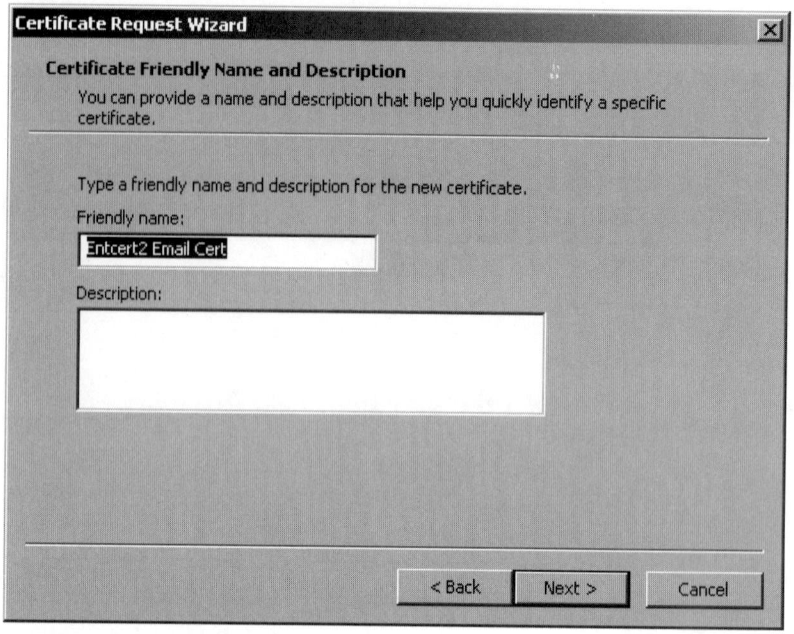

FIGURE 10.69 Entering Certificate Name

EXPORTING CERTIFICATES AND BACKUP

A certificate may be exported for backup purposes or simply for transport. It may be exported with its associated private key if it has been marked appropriately. Export is accomplished through the **Certificate Export Wizard**, which can be invoked from several locations.

1. Open the **Certificates** snap-in.
2. Right-click the certificate to export and select **All Tasks → Export...** (Figure 10.70).

To accomplish exporting from within Internet Explorer 5.x, follow these steps:

1. Select **Tools → Internet Options...**. Select the **Content** tab and press the **Certificates...** button. Select a certificate from one of the local stores and press the **Export...** button (Figure 10.71).
2. Once the **Certificate Export Wizard** appears, press the **Next>** button.
3. If the certificate is marked for export you may choose whether it will be accompanied by its associated private key (Figure 10.72).

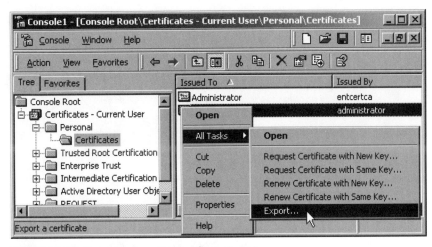

FIGURE 10.70 Exporting from the Certificate Snap-In

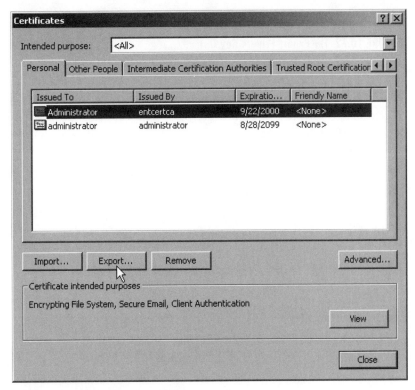

FIGURE 10.71 Exporting from IE 5.0

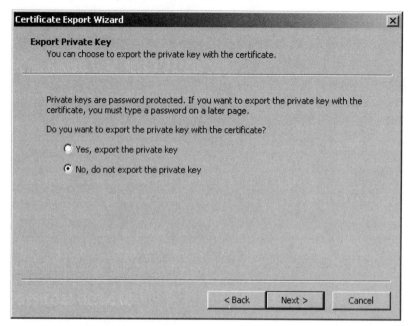

FIGURE 10.72 The Export Private Key Option

4. If the certificate is exported without the private key, three file formats are available as listed in Figure 10.73. For export with the private key, only the PKCS #12 file format is available. A password must be entered to protect the file only when exporting the private key.

5. Enter the destination directory and file name (Figure 10.74).

6. Press the **Finish** button to complete the export.

NOTE   Certificate exports with the private key are represented as icons showing a key and an envelope (Figure 10.75).

Importing Certificates

The import process is implemented from the **Certificate Import Wizard** in much the same way the **Certificate Export Wizard** is used.

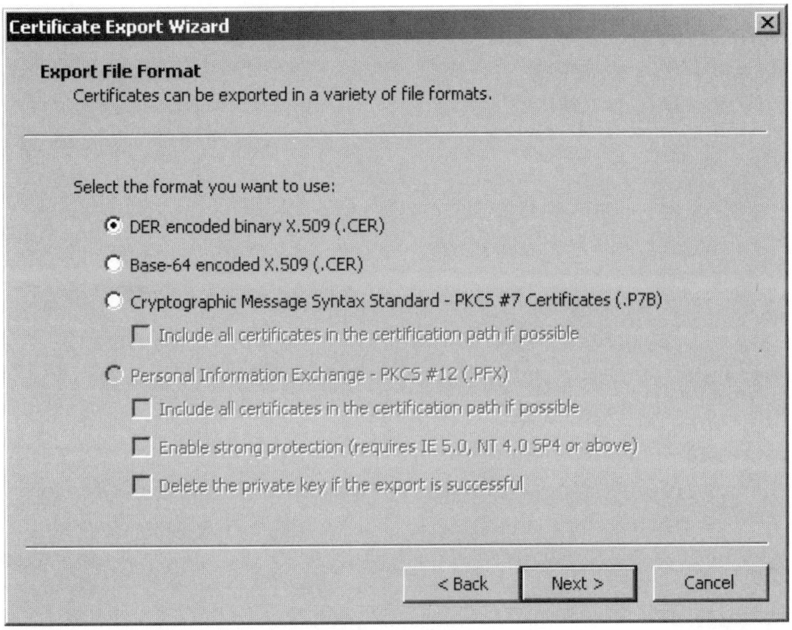

FIGURE 10.73 File Formats without a Private Key

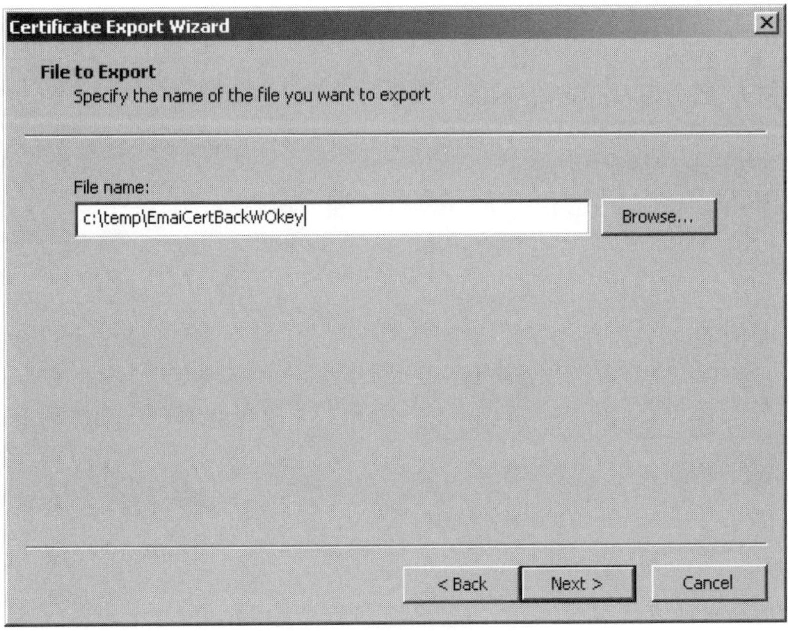

FIGURE 10.74 A Destination for an Exported Key

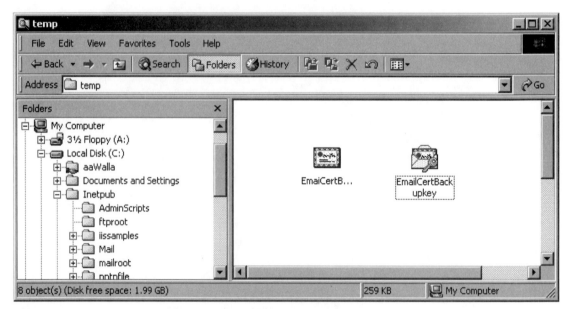

FIGURE 10.75 The Icon for a Certificate with and without a Private Key

CERTIFICATE AUTHORITY SERVICE MANAGEMENT

The Certificate Authority service management tool provides a number of functions, including administrative logs. Like all Windows 2000 logs, CA logs can be a valuable administrative tool.

Certificate Authority Logs

The certificate authority has five useful logs for managing a CA server, listed in Table 10.12. A number of column and filtering options are available to manage the certificates in the viewing window (Figure 10.76)

1. Right-clicking a certificate log and selecting **View → Choose Columns...** allows control over the columns displayed (Figure 10.77).

2. Right-clicking a certificate log and selecting **View → Filter...** allows the administrator to apply display restrictions or filters that determine what certificates are shown (Figure 10.78).

3. Add the **Certificate Authority** snap-in to a Microsoft Management Console and open the CA server's node. Right-click a certificate in the **Issued Certificates** log and select **All Tasks → Revoke Certificate**.

TABLE 10.12 Certificate Authority Logs

Certificate Store	Description
Revoked Certificates	Certificates issued by this CA that are invalid and members of the current CRL
Issued Certificates	Certificates issued by this CA server
Pending Requests	Certificate requests awaiting issue or rejection
Failed Requests	Rejected certificate requests
Policy Settings	Certificate types available for issue based on the **Certificate Templates** snap-in

4. Specify a reason code for revoking the certificate (Figure 10.79) and press the **Yes** button.

To add a certificate to a Revoked Certificates List:

5. Check the **Revoked Certificates** log and verify the new certificate status (Figure 10.80).

To display a CRL and properties:

1. Right-click the **Revoked Certificates** log and select **Properties** (Figure 10.81). The publication interval can be modified from the **CRL Publishing Parameters** tab. Press the **View Current CRL...** button.

2. Certificate revocation information is displayed.

3. Select the **Revocation List** tab to display the current CRL (Figure 10.82, page 442).

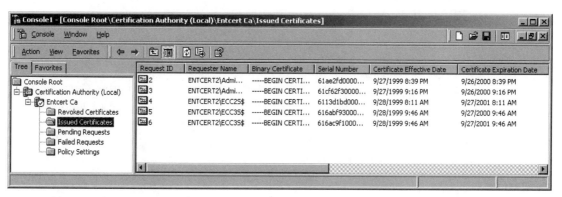

FIGURE 10.76 Certificate Authority Logs

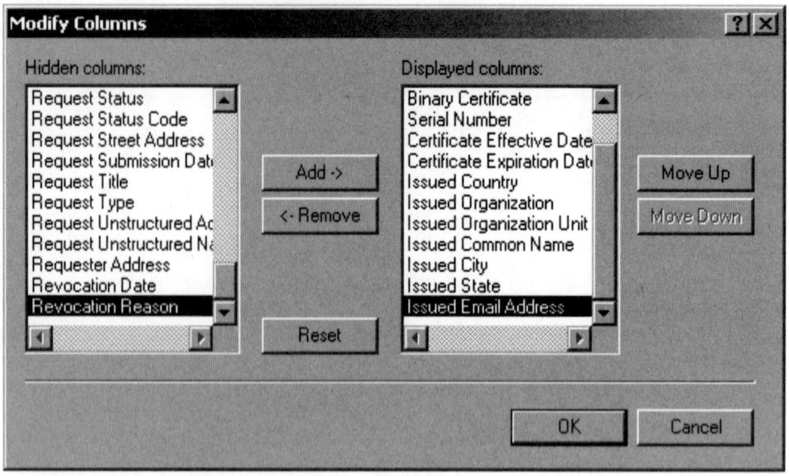

FIGURE 10.77 Columns Displayed

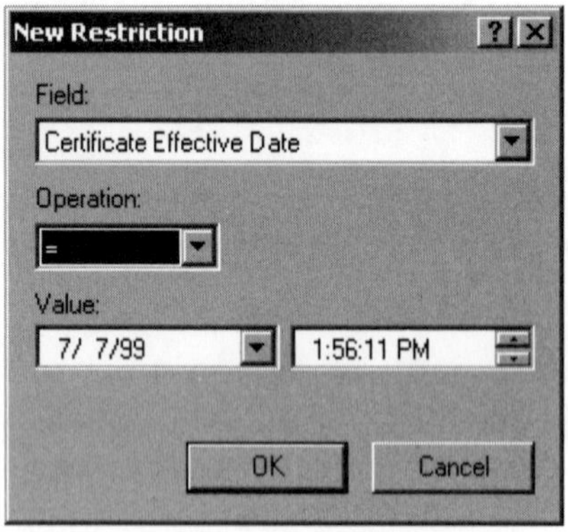

FIGURE 10.78 Displaying Restrictions

Starting and Stopping the Certificate Service

The Certificate service may be started and stopped from the **Certification Authority** snap-in. Open the **Certification Authority** snap-in tool. Right-click on the CA server node and select **All Tasks**. If the server is running, the **All Tasks** → **Stop Service** option is available (Figure 10.83, page 444). Otherwise, the **Start Service** option is selectable.

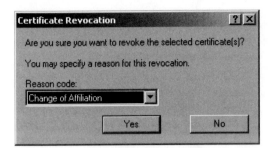

FIGURE 10.79 A Revocation Reason Code

NOTE   The **Certificate Authority** snap-in tool distinguishes status by color code and icon. A green checkmark is visible next to the CA server icon when the CA service is running and a red dot is visible when the service is stopped.

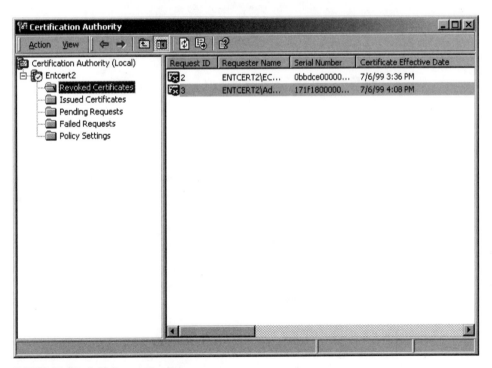

FIGURE 10.80 A CA Revocation List

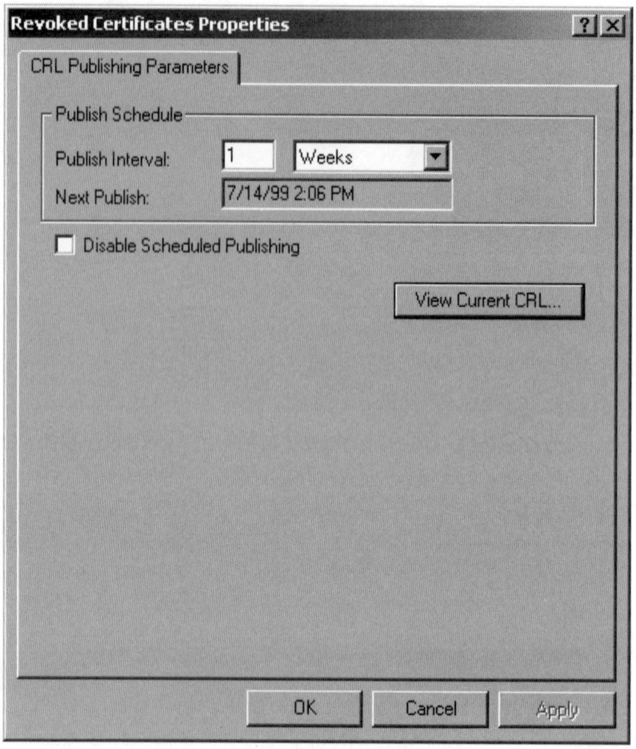

FIGURE 10.81 CRL Publishing Parameters

CERTIFICATE AUTHORITY PROPERTIES

CA properties are viewed from the **Certification Authority** MMC snap-in as well. Right-click the CA service node and select **Properties**. The Properties dialog appears for the Certification Server in which five tabs are displayed. **General** displays the CA name and description entered during creation or modification. The **Security settings** on General display the CSP and hash algorithm used with the CA certificate. The **View Certificate** button displays the CA's certificate via the **Certificate** dialog box, as discussed earlier. The following sections describe the remaining tabs.

The Policy Module Tab

The **Policy Module** tab (Figure 10.84) displays default policy settings for certificates issued by the CA. It sets default Certificate Revocation List distribution points, authority information access points, and the default actions the CA will

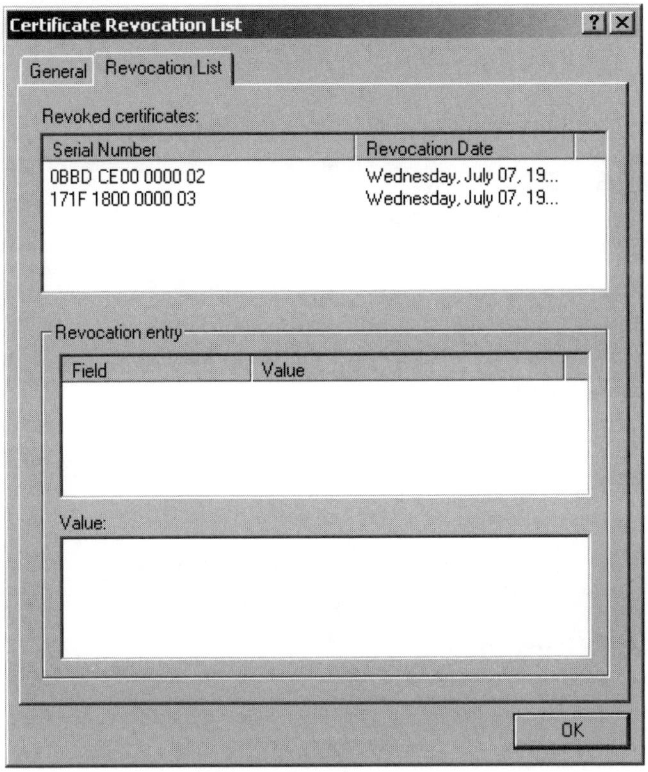

FIGURE 10.82 Revoked Certificates

take when receiving certificate requests. Requests can be denied, accepted, and queued for later authorization.

Policy Module also displays information about the current active policy (name, version, and copyright). Pressing its **Select** button allows the administrator to choose the active policy module from the list of those installed (Figure 10.85). Put new modules in the *%SystemRoot%\system32* directory and then use the rgsrv32 *modulename.dll* command to register new policies.

Pressing the **Configure** button from the **Policy Module** tab displays the **Default Action** tab. Only standalone CA servers have policy options here; enterprise CA servers will immediately issue or deny a certificate request based on user information retrieved from the Active Directory. Standalone CA servers usually hold off on issuing certificates until the administrator permits them to do so by selecting the "pending" option from the **Default Action** tab (Figure 10.86). The administrator must make an informed decision about the type of certificate a user may be issued.

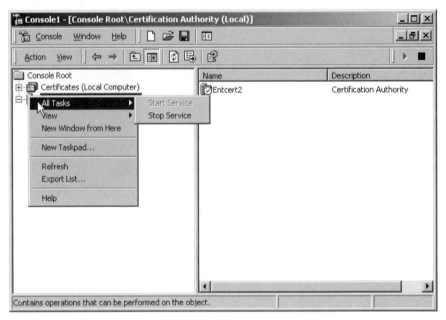

FIGURE 10.83 A Start/Stop CA

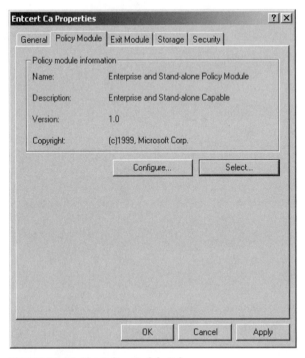

FIGURE 10.84 The Policy Module Tab

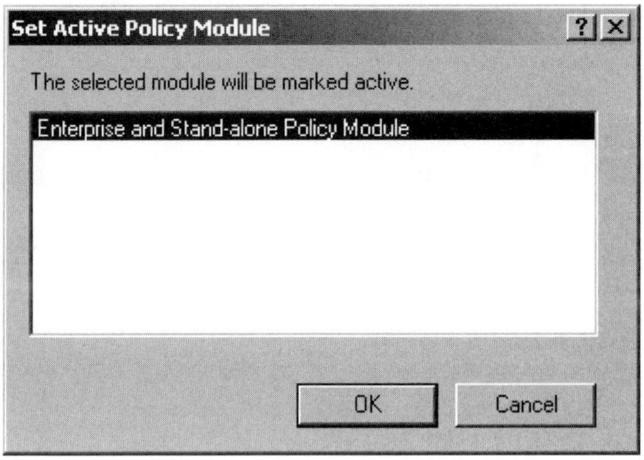

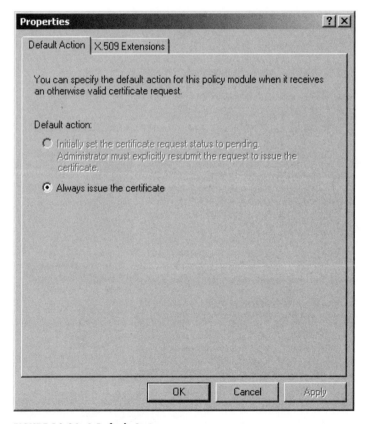

FIGURE 10.85 The Active Policy Module

FIGURE 10.86 A Default Action

Pressing the **X.509 Extensions** tab displays two more configuration items. **CRL Distribution Points** (HTTP, FTP, LDAP, and file addresses) are inserted by default into every issued certificate (Figure 10.87). These are URLs that can check for current Certification Revocation Lists (CRLs) to validate the certificate. The **Authority Information Access** list of URLs specifies where a certificate can be obtained for the CA that issued it. Someone verifying a certificate issued with this policy could search this list and retrieve a CA certificate to verify the certificate.

The Exit Module Tab

Exit Modules perform tasks and control actions taken after the certificate has been issued. This is in contrast to policy modules, which determine certificate content. These actions determine if the certificate can be published in the Active Directory and file system. They also determine where the Certificate Revocation List is published. The **Exit Module** tab (Figure 10.88) displays exit module details and allows the administrator to add, remove, or select the active exit module.

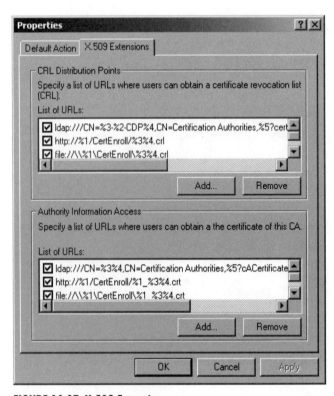

FIGURE 10.87 X.509 Extensions

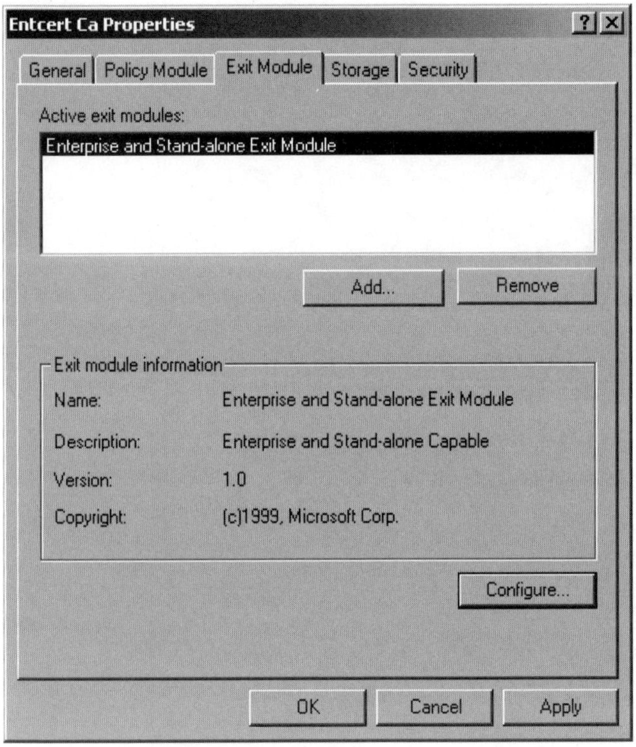

FIGURE 10.88 The Exit Module Tab

Pressing the **Configure** button displays the **Certificate Publication** tab (Figure 10.89) and determines if the CA server will allow publication to the Active Directory and file system. If publication is permitted, the client being issued the certificate must provide the location in the request. When an Active Directory is present, the default setting is to allow publication to it and restrict publication to a file system. The opposite is the case when an Active Directory is absent.

Storage and Security Tabs

The **Storage** tab specifies where the certification log is stored. This location is not modifiable on an enterprise CA server. The **Security** tab allows the assigning of permissions regarding the **Certificate Authority** snap-in.

CERTIFICATION AUTHORITY BACKUP

Without a current log of the issued and revoked certificates it is difficult to manage previously issued certificates. This means that the CA should be backed up on

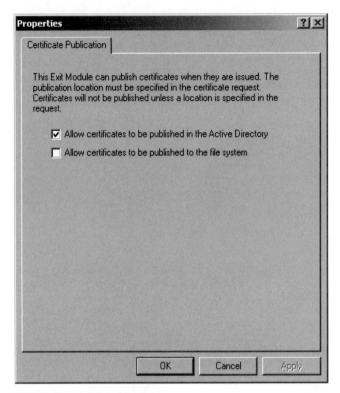

FIGURE 10.89 CRL Publication

a regular basis. The created backup file should be placed in a directory that will then be backed up by whatever backup system is in place.

NOTE   If you are using Windows Backup be sure to complete the CA backup and stop the CA service beforehand. Windows Backup may not function properly if the CA service is running.

---

1. Start the backup wizard by selecting the CA server from the **Certification Authority** snap-in and right-clicking the **All Tasks → Backup CA...** option to start the wizard (Figure 10.90).
2. Follow the wizard instructions, but pay close attention to what data types are backed up and where the log is stored (Figure 10.91).
3. Use a password to protect the backup file and the CA's private key.

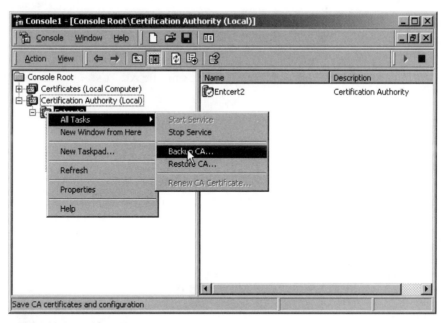

FIGURE 10.90 Backup CA

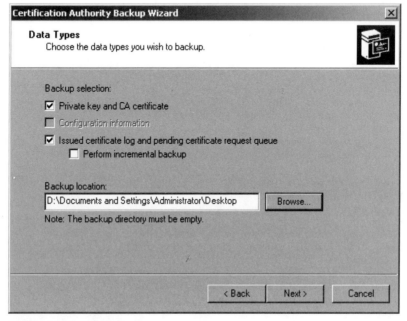

FIGURE 10.91 Data Types

Restoration of the backup is similarly started; however, the CA service must be stopped first.

1. Start the backup wizard by selecting the CA server from the **Certification Authority** snap-in and right-clicking the **All Tasks → Restore CA...** option.

2. Follow the wizard instructions and re-enter the password for the selected backup retrieval file.

POSTSCRIPT

Both Kerberos and the Public Key Infrastructure are integral parts of the Windows 2000 operating system. Kerberos provides domain-wide authentication to any service throughout the Windows 2000 domain and offers compatibility with many other operating systems. PKI enables secure communication, data storage, and universal authentication throughout Internet and extranet environments. These technologies lay the groundwork for IPSec, VPNs, secure Web transactions, e-mail communications, and centralized user account management.

Additional Security Issues and Solutions

The previous two chapters examined permissions, the Public Key Infrastructure, and user authentication as aspects of securing a Windows 2000 system or domain. Although these are the cornerstones for Windows 2000 security, there is a variety of other security issues and solutions to be discussed.

This chapter rounds out the discussion of Windows 2000 security. First we examine the snap-in tools that are available for security management. Then we look at how to secure the computer systems themselves primarily from potential internal abuses. Finally we turn our attention to securing the Windows 2000 environment from external intrusions over the network.

Security breaches compromise protocols, services, permission settings, readable network data, downloadable components, and e-mail messages. Practically every feature on the operating system can be used against it, which is why it must be secured against outside "crackers" or criminal hackers.

Protecting against malicious outside attack is only one aspect of a totally secure program. Authorized users are also the cause of purposeful or inadvertent data destruction or even system crashes. A proper framework must include control over hardware and file system access, data archival and restoration, and data transmission.

Security vulnerabilities can result in a number of crippling results. The user is denied service when a system is crashed, damaged, or taxed so that it cannot perform intended duties. Data corruption can cost both time and money. The invasion of privacy through improper sniffing or other forms of intrusion can result in the loss of confidential information. A common hacker practice known as spoofing permits an unauthorized user to pretend to be another person or service. Finally, physical security breaches can result in the theft of equipment or sensitive data. In this chapter we identify these issues in greater detail and suggest both commonsense and specific Windows 2000 solutions.

SECURITY POLICY

A security policy is an important element of the overall security of the computer or network being protected. In general, the more security that is applied to a system or network, the more inconvenient the system will be for users.

A security policy, as well as security procedures, help to define what you are trying to protect and how to protect it. Because of different goals, each type of industry or organization has different security needs. An e-commerce site needs a different security policy from that of an accounting firm or government agency. Before you begin securing your site, it is wise to see if a security policy has been established. If not, develop one.

Most technology decisions should be based on policy. To develop a security policy, take the following guidelines into consideration:

- In preparing a risk analysis, ask yourself, what am I trying to protect and from whom?
- Determine the probability of risk with a cost/benefit analysis of resource(s) protection.
- Determine who is responsible for protecting the resources.
- Define how you will respond during a security event.

Security policies should not be made in a vacuum, but should be approved and supported by persons with authority. To be effective, they should not be too difficult to implement. Once the security policy is in place, procedures and guidelines should be established to ensure that it can be monitored and enforced. The security policy snap-ins discussed later should be configured to meet the security goals and policy of the organizational unit, site, and domain structure, as the procedures they implement will affect how users do their work. Larger companies may have compartmentalized security that has different needs between sites, divisions, or departments.

There are some general considerations that will determine how security will be implemented and enforced. This list is by no means all-inclusive but is here to give examples of the questions that should be asked.

- Is there an Internet connection, and how can the users utilize it?
- How are disks or information shared?
- Is data backed up? If so, what and how often?
- Do the users know their responsibilities?

- Is remote access needed?
- How will you know if security has been compromised?
- Is there a firewall in place, and if so, what is permitted to go through it?

Once these questions have been answered, it is necessary to apply them to categories of effort. These questions can be broken down into the following general areas:

- *Confidentiality*. How will you protect information from being read by unauthorized sources? This includes consideration of technologies such as encryption, file permissions, and network sniffing.

- *Integrity*. How will you ensure that your data will not be deleted or modified, and, if it is, that you know the source? You must decide how to deal with file permissions, unsecure programs, digital signatures, and viruses.

- *Availability*. How will you ensure that your systems remain available? The plan must involve issues like denial of service, acceptable system use, and employment of redundant systems.

- *Recoverability*. How will you recover if you have been compromised? You will need to decide how best to utilize data backups, hard copies, and remote data stores.

- *Audit*. Will you be able to tell if a security event has happened? Use of log files, system auditing, event monitors, and alarms in guarding against abuse must be factored into the plan.

Implementing security can be a full-time job, and monitoring it and maintaining it can be an even larger time commitment. When designing security policies and procedures, it is important to consider the necessary resources that must be available to implement, monitor, and enforce them.

Security Policy Snap-Ins

The security tools for Windows 2000 do not introduce new conceptual or technological advancements to PKI, group policies, or the Active Directory, but instead offer a convenient and uniform way to distribute these features. The **Security Configuration and Analysis** and **Security Template** snap-ins are the two main components of the Microsoft Security Configuration Tool Set. They configure, analyze, and distribute a subset of the Security Settings portion of the Group Policy tree. These settings include

- *Account Policies*—include passwords, system lockouts, and Kerberos policy settings.
- *Local Policies*—include user rights and security events.

- *Event Log*—permits review of events that could show a compromise of security.
- *Restricted Groups*—provide added security for default Windows 2000 groups with predefined functions, such as the Administrators group.
- *System Services*—manage local system services security.
- *Registry*—set local Registry key data permissions.
- *File System*—set local file system permissions.

NOTE　The Security Template snap-in does not provide a direct means for viewing and modifying **Public Key Policies** and **IP Security Policies**. Rather these policies must be set or imported from the **Default Domain** snap-in → **Windows Settings** → **Security Settings** → **IP Securities Policies on Active Directory** or **IP Security Policies**, respectively.

　　It's also important to remember that the **Local/Remote Computer Policy** snap-in includes only the **Account Policies** and the **Local Policies** from the above list.

In addition to distributing consistent security configurations, the tools can analyze security settings and graphically display differences between current and intended settings.

USING SECURITY TEMPLATE SNAP-INS

Group policies are used to apply security templates to designated user and computer accounts. Local Computer Policies can also apply security templates, but only local settings and account policies are affected by them. Security templates make the system administrator's job easier by allowing her to create templates that may then be distributed using Group Policies across a site, domain, organization unit, user group, or even individual users. They are ASCII files with *.INF extensions that can be modified with a text editor. All security templates can be found in the *%SystemRoot%security\templates*.inf directory*.

CAUTION　It is possible to copy, paste, and otherwise modify the *.INF files directly as text files within a tool such as Notepad. However, this is not recommended. The **Security Template** snap-in should be used to create and modify Windows 2000 security templates. Copying part of a template within the Security Templates snap-in and pasting it into another template is less risky. Again, extreme caution should be applied.

The **Security Templates** snap-in as seen in Figure 11.1 comes with eleven predefined templates. These are divided into *default* templates and *incremental* templates.

The default templates, designed to establish a baseline configuration for the **Security Settings** group policy node, all begin with the word "basic" to denote the base-level foundation they provide. There are default templates for domain controllers (basicdc.inf), servers (basicsv.inf), and workstations (basicwk.inf) (Table 11.1).

The incremental templates (Table 11.2) are meant to overlay or "apply on top of" the current settings to provide additional security measures implied by their names.

When Windows 2000 is initially installed on a clean NTFS partition the local computer policy should be similar to the *basic*.inf* template corresponding to the installed operating system or the *setup security.inf* template. If the system is upgraded from Windows NT 4.0, no security settings are applied; the previous

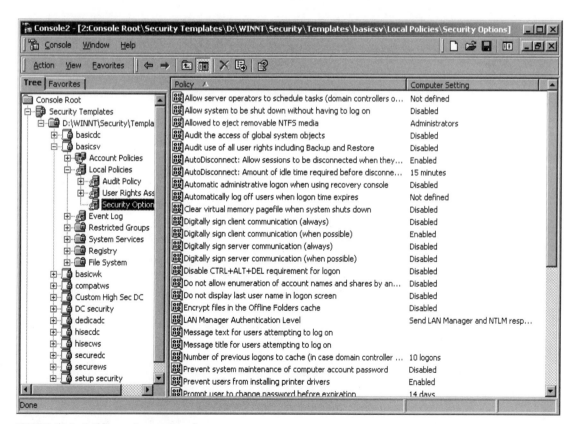

FIGURE 11.1 Building a Custom Template

TABLE 11.1 Default Security Templates

Default Template	Description
Basicdc.inf	For Windows 2000 domain controllers; sets Registry permissions, file permissions, Event Log policies, and the digitally signed server policy under Security Options.
Basicsv.inf	Designed for Windows 2000 servers; the only policy not modified is User Rights Assignments and Restricted Groups.
Basicwk.inf	Similar to the server template but intended for workstations.

TABLE 11.2 Incremental Security Templates

Incremental Template	Description
Compatws.inf	Contains the **Power Users** group without any members, which removes all users from that group. The Users group is granted more file system and Registry privileges so that Windows NT 4.0 and other legacy users may run applications on the server.
Ocfilesw.inf	Contains operating system file security support for workstations.
Ocfiless.inf	Contains operating system file security support for servers.
Notssid.inf	Removes Terminal Server user SIDs.
Securedc.inf	Imposes stricter Account Policies, Local Policies, and Event Log settings than the default settings. Digital signing and Secure channels are requested when possible. Down-level communication with Windows 9x/NT 4.0 is possible.
Securews.inf	Same as Securedc.inf except that all users are removed from the **Power Users** group with the **Restricted Groups** settings.
Hisecdc.inf	Enables Secure channel and digital signing for all communications. Disables NTLM and LM authentication (allows only Kerberos authentication) and all drivers must be signed. All communication is encrypted and authenticated at the highest level possible. Systems configured with this template will not be able to communicate with non-Windows 2000 systems (Windows 9x/NT 4.0).
Hisecws.inf	Same as Hisecdc.inf except that all users are removed from the **Power Users** group with the **Restricted Groups** settings.
Setup security.inf	Saves the original machine configuration after installation.

security settings from the legacy environment are not overwritten. The default or *basic*.inf* templates can be used to baseline the upgraded system or to baseline existing installations to match the suggested settings.

NOTE These templates modify Registry values in addition to setting permissions on the local Registry. There is nothing to stop someone with Read/Write permission from modifying the ASCII *.inf templates using an editor, and changing Registry parameters outside the scope of the **Security Settings**. That is why the templates must be protected from abuse.

BUILDING A CUSTOM TEMPLATE

The **Security Templates** snap-in is handy for viewing template settings, but its *true* purpose is to create custom templates. There are two methods for building a custom template: An existing template can be selected, modified, and then saved as another template; or a completely new template can be created.

Modifying an Existing Template

Creating a new template by using an existing one involves modifying the existing one and saving it under a different name. To do this, follow these steps:

1. Open the MMC **Security Templates** snap-in.
2. Right-click the desired template and select **Save As...** from the menu.
3. Enter a new template name and save.
4. Open the new template node and modify settings as needed.
5. Right-click the template node and select **Save** unless it is grayed out. In this case it is already saved.

Building a New Template

To create a new security template, take the following steps:

1. Open the MMC **Security Templates** snap-in.
2. Open **Security Templates** and right-click the templates directory icon.
3. Select **New Template...** from the menu.
4. Enter the file name for the template and open it.
5. Modify the template settings just as the Security Settings for Group Policy Objects (GPOs) are modified.
6. Right-click the template node and select **Save** unless it is grayed out. In this case it is already saved.

The Security Configuration and Analysis Tool

Analysis of security is a fundamental responsibility of the system administrator. The **Security Configuration and Analysis (SCA)** snap-in tool is designed to assist in this. Fine-tuning of security is accomplished through regular analysis.

The **Security Configuration and Analysis** snap-in tool is primarily used to analyze or compare the current computer settings to a personal database and thus view potential discrepancies in the current security landscape. It can also be used to configure the local system to match the personal database security settings and to layer templates and produce custom templates for later distribution. All of this is done preferably through a GPO.

Custom security templates are built by layering template upon template to produce security settings. For example, to configure a highly secure domain controller, the basicdc, securedc, and the hisecdc templates would all be applied to the server. Templates can be applied using GPOs, as we saw in the discussion of the **Security Settings** Extension. Or they can be applied with a personal settings database via the **Security Configuration and Analysis** tool. Importing security templates into GPOs is discussed in Chapter 8, Group Policies. Note that when GPOs import a template into Security Settings, the enabled settings overwrite previous configurations.

Security templates may be layered to configure high security status, for example, using the **Security Configuration and Analysis** tool to build a custom template that accumulates all settings from three separate templates. Using GPOs to layer templates and distribute **Security Settings** is the method of choice whenever the Active Directory is implemented, but for standalone systems the **SCA** should be used. The **Local Computer Policy** snap-in does not allow configuration of the **Event Log**, **Restricted Groups**, **System Services**, **Registry**, or **File System** policies.

USING THE SECURITY CONFIGURATION AND ANALYSIS SNAP-IN

There are distinct uses for the SCA snap-in, as its name implies: configuration and analysis. A quick examination on how to use each is appropriate.

Using SCA to Configure Security

Let's demonstrate how the **SCA** tool can be used to build a highly secure custom template for a domain controller. First the custom template is created and then the **SCA** tool is used to analyze or compare current computer settings with the template settings. Finally the custom template is used to manually configure the current computer settings. Again, *this last step is necessary only on systems without Active Directory support*. The following specific steps are invoked:

1. Add the **Security Configuration and Analysis** (**SCA**) tool to a custom console.

2. Right-click the **SCA** snap-in and select **Open database...** (Figure 11.2).

3. Enter the name *Custom High Sec DC.dbd* for the database and press **Open**.

4. Right-click the **SCA** snap-in and select **Import Template...**.

5. Choose the *setup security.inf* template and check the **Clear this database before importing** box and press **Open** (Figure 11.3).

Repeat this process for the *securedc.inf* and *hisecdc.inf* templates (but do not apply Step 5).

At this point you have successfully laid three templates on top of each other in an incremental fashion in the *Custom High Sec DC* database. This database must be exported to a template file to be later imported into a GPO. As a precaution, you must run an analysis on the database before you can export the new template.

1. Right-click the **SCA** snap-in and select **Analyze Computer Now...**.

2. Press **OK** to the *Error log file path:* dialog box.

3. Wait as the tool compares the current computer settings with the newly created ones.

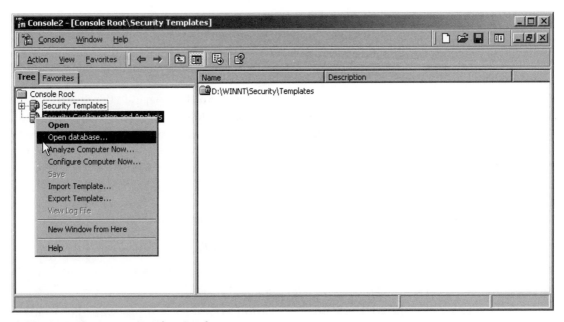

FIGURE 11.2 The Security Template Database

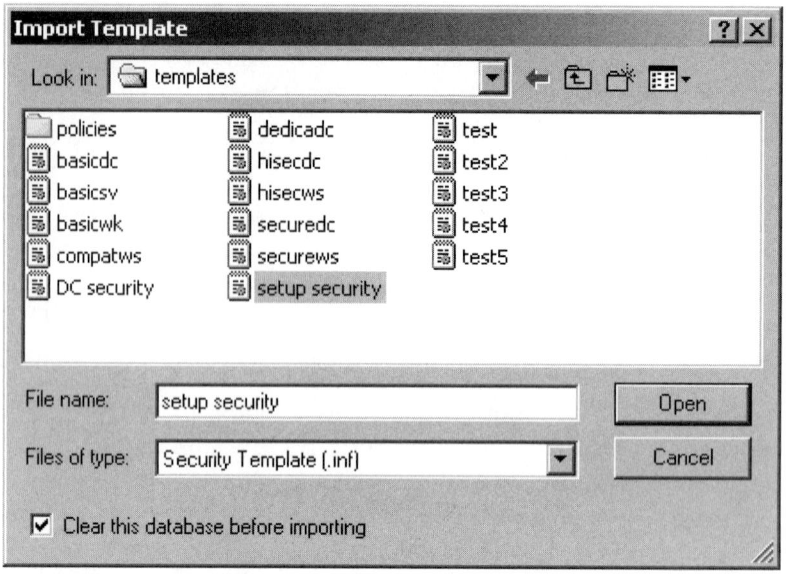

FIGURE 11.3 Import Templates

4. Verify the output of the log to make sure that everything is correct.

5. Right-click the **SCA** snap-in and select **Export Template…**.

6. Enter the name *Custom High Sec DC.inf* for the template name and press **Save**.

7. Right-click the **%SystemRoot%\Security\Templates** node below the **Security Templates** snap-in and select **Refresh**. The new template should be displayed among the standard templates.

Under the **Security Configuration and Analysis** snap-in the **Security Settings** nodes are displayed. Select the **Local Policies → Security Options** node. In the Details window the **Database Settings** are compared to the **Computer Settings**, as shown in Figure 11.4. Common policy settings are denoted with a green checkmark, and conflicting policy settings are denoted with a red *X*. If either the database policy or the computer setting is not defined, the policy is not marked.

To map the current database settings onto the local system:

1. Right-click the **SCA** snap-in and select **Configure Computer Now…**.

2. Press **OK** to the *You are about to configure this computer using…* dialog box.

3. Press **OK** to the *Error log file path:* dialog box.

4. Wait as the tool updates the current computer settings with the database settings.

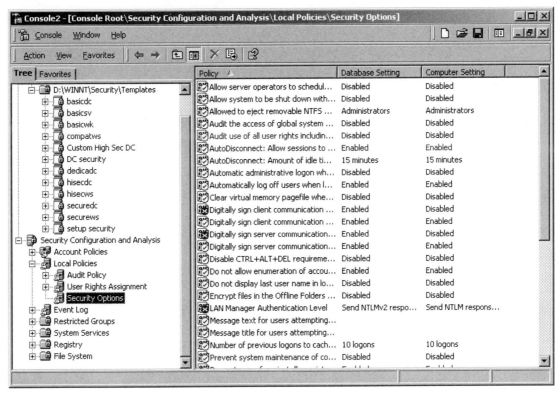

FIGURE 11.4 Security Options from the SCA Snap-In

The local system is now configured with the high-security settings. To put the system in its original state, reload the **setup security** template into a database and configure the system with the new database.

Analyzing Security

Security analysis involves several steps. The following should be invoked to conduct analysis:

1. Open the **Security Configuration and Analysis** snap-in.

2. Right-click **Security Configuration and Analysis** → click **Open database**.

3. Select an existing database, or create a new personal database by typing in a new file name → click **Open**.

4. Import one or more security templates by right-clicking **Security Configuration and Analysis** → **Open** the working database.

5. Select **Import Template**.

6. Select a template file and click **Open**.

7. Repeat the last step for every template that is to be merged into the database.

8. Perform a security analysis by right-clicking **Security Configuration and Analysis** → click **Analyze System Now**.

9. Click **OK** to use the default analysis log.

10. Review analysis results by clicking **Security Configuration and Analysis** → select the security **Lockout Policy** or **Password Policy**.

11. The right-hand window provides a number of columns, including **Attribute** for the analysis results, **Database Setting** for the security value, and **Analyzed System Setting** for the current security level. If a red *X* is displayed, inconsistencies exist between the current settings and the base configuration. A green checkmark is used to show consistency. If no icon appears, that attribute was not set and therefore was not analyzed.

12. Resolve any discrepancies revealed by analysis by accepting or changing some or all of the values flagged → select **Configure System Now**.

13. Repeat the import process and load multiple templates.

14. Once the templates are imported, select **Configure System Now**.

NOTE   The *secedit* command can be run from scripts to apply security settings to many computers. It can also be used to force the policy refresh throughout the domain.

NOTE   Security policies are applied with the same inheritance precedence as for any other policy. Windows 2000 follows the LSDOU model, in which inheritance order flows as follows: **Local Computer (L)** → **Site (S)** → **Domain (D)** → **Organizational Unit (OU)**.

WINDOWS 2000 SYSTEM LOCKDOWN

Securing the Windows 2000 system involves concentrating on a number of potential problem areas. These issues, which are internal to the enterprise and well within the scope of system administrator responsibility, include the following:

- User account security
- Proper password management

- Registry and file system lockdown
- Protection of network shares
- Trojan horses and virus control
- Environmental settings
- Removal of services that are not required
- RAS security
- Backup and restoration
- Physical security lockdown
- Dual-booting of multiple operating systems

User Account Security

A hacker's primary method of gaining unauthorized access is through user accounts. The system administrator is directly responsible for maintaining user account accountability and securing the enterprise against improper account usage. The three user accounts that can potentially be the most vulnerable are Administrator, Backup Operators, and Guest.

THE ADMINISTRATOR ACCOUNT

Providing an unauthorized user access to the Administrator account is comparable to giving away the keys to the castle. The Administrator account cannot be removed or locked out. Moreover, it permits an unlimited amount of logon attempts so that multiple logons cannot be used to intentionally deny the administrator access. Lastly, it allows a cracker plenty of opportunities to figure out the administrator's password. There are a number of precautions that can be implemented as a minimum safeguard against assaults, described in the following paragraphs.

The Administrator account should always be associated with a cryptic password that is generally too complicated to be remembered easily. This password should not be confused with the one used by the system administrator who belongs to the Administrators group. The use of the primary Administrator account logon should be limited to extreme situations. System administrators should always log on under their own account. As members of respective Administrators groups, they will be able to conduct appropriate support activity under that login. In theory, a hacker knows that there is always an Administrator account, but he or she is less likely to know the login name of individual members of the Administrators group.

Alternately, create a new account and add it to the Domain Admins global group. Only highly trusted system administrators should know its name and password. This account should be used for administrative duties. If each highly trusted administrator has her own account, a rogue administrator account can lock out the other accounts. However, an audit trail will more easily track individual patterns.

What makes a good password? It is easier to define a bad one. That would be your name or anyone's name, any word in the dictionary, your license plate, your phone number, or your social security number, all of which can be guessed by social engineering or can be quickly discovered via a cracking program. An example of a good password is a nonsense phrase—for example, "I like to sip soda in my sneakers." Use the first character of each word, mix some letters with numbers, and add punctuation. It now becomes Il2ss!mS, which is not too hard to remember and very difficult to guess or crack. Of course, this particular password is now bad, since it has been published.

The Domain Administrator account password should be written down and physically protected in a safe place, under lock and key. Again, it should be employed for emergency system restoration, not daily use. This password will be replicated to all domain controllers. It can also be retrieved if the administrator is unavailable or incapacitated for some reason.

The same strategy should be implemented for all local Administrator accounts as well. A different cryptic password should be assigned to all local Administrator accounts for a site and written down and stored in a safe place. If the physical security of one workstation is compromised, there is a chance the Local Administrator password can be recovered from the file system. The Domain Administrator account should remain protected.

NOTE   The suggestion to write down the Administrator account password and store it in a safe place is contrary to what a system administrator should tell a normal user. It is based on the assumption that the administrator will exercise extreme caution in securing it. However, a user should never write down his password, as it is simply too easy for someone to "eye" it in a normal work environment. Instead, since it will be used on a regular basis, the user should be required to mentally retain it. If for some reason the password is forgotten, the system administrator can reset it with little effort. As an added precaution, place the Administrator password in a sealed envelope. If the seal is broken, immediately change the password and reseal the envelope.

NOTE Passwords are used to generate a cryptographic key known as a hash. Even though only the hash of an account's password is stored in the KDC or SAM database, earlier hash algorithms are well known. This is particularly true for the down-level Windows NT 4.0 NTLMv1 hash algorithm. There are crack applications available to determine the account password through brute force. However, Kerberos and NTLMv2, supported on Windows NT 4.0 Service Pack 4 or greater, have much stronger hash-generating algorithms. In addition, disabling the Windows 2000 *Store password using reversible encryption for all users in domain* password policy will make reading the hash very difficult. This can be accomplished by opening the **Default Domain Policy** snap-in → select **Windows Settings → Security Settings → Account Policies → Password Policies**. Double-click on **Store password using reversible encryption** from the right panel. Within the dialog box, select to **Enable** or **Disable** and press **OK**. *One-way encryption is generally stronger. Therefore, we recommend that you disable this feature.*

BACKUP OPERATORS

The Default Domain Controllers Policy GPO gives both the Administrators and Backup Operators groups the right to *back up and restore files and directories* by default. This means that the Backup Operators can overwrite the file system regardless of assigned permissions. Two actions can be taken to minimize this problem:

- Use the Backup Operators group sparingly and assign only the most trusted persons to it.
- Remove these user right policies on all systems that do not require domain-level backup privileges.

GUEST ACCOUNT

The Guest account has significantly changed between Windows NT and Windows 2000. In Windows NT, it was a convenience to support Web servers and other applications that must run without user authentication. Thus, it had access to all objects with permissions assigned to the Everyone group, and as a result directories like *%SystemRoot%System32* were wide open to destruction from it. Windows 2000 has created a new built-in local group known as Authenticated Users, which is responsible for assigning permissions to users who previously belonged to Everyone. The Everyone group is specifically assigned to most objects with no permissions whatsoever. This has the effect of restricting Guest account privileges. To avoid the problems inherent in the Windows NT Guest account, use the Everyone group, which is disabled by default, very sparingly.

Password Policies

As previously underscored, passwords represent one of the most basic areas of potential security vulnerability. Since password policies can minimize abuses, we highly recommend establishing them.

DOMAIN PASSWORD POLICIES

Password lockdown is accomplished differently when working with domains and local system accounts. Password and account lockout policies should reflect the settings within the securews.inf (for secure workstations) and securedc.inf (for domain controllers) templates. Security templates are used to establish a standard set of policies that can be repeatedly used. For a quick visual inspection, the **Security Template** snap-in and **Default Domain Policy** snap-in can be used to rapidly compare template settings against those currently utilized, but a more in-depth comparison can be achieved with the **Security Configuration and Analysis** snap-in. Refer to Chapter 8, Group Policies, on utilizing and applying policies.

Table 11.3 outlines the password policies that are applicable to both domain and local computer passwords. To change or view domain password policies,

TABLE 11.3 Password Policy Options for Domains and Local Computers

Policy	Computer Setting	Description
Enforce Password History remembered	6 passwords remembered	User's previous 6 passwords are to prevent reuse.
Maximum Password Age	42 days	Password must be changed by the maximum age.
Minimum Password Length	8 characters	
Passwords Must Meet Password Filter Requirements	Enabled	Microsoft, third-party, or self-created password filter may be used.
Store Password Using Reversible Encryption for All Users in Domain	Disabled	
User Must Log On to Change the Password	Disabled	

open the MMC **Default Domain Policy** snap-in → select **Computer Configuration** → **Windows Settings** → **Account Policy**. Double-click on **Password Policy**. Select each of the listed policies and make the appropriate changes.

PASSWORD LOCKOUT POLICIES

Password lockout policies minimize a hacker's ability to repeatedly attempt to discover a logon name and password. They should be liberal enough to permit a user with "sloppy" typing skills to make several attempts at a successful logon but sufficiently tight to frustrate an attacker. There are three lockout policies (Table 11.4):

- *Account Lockout Duration*. This establishes the period of time in which the lockout will be enforced, after which the system is unlocked and new logon attempts will be recognized. A reasonable time is typically 30 minutes.
- *Account Lockout Threshold*. This establishes the number of unsuccessful logon attempts that will be permitted prior to a lockout. Although there will always be an authorized user who will repeatedly fail, five attempts is a reasonable number.
- *Reset Lockout Counter*. This resets the lockout attempt counter in the period designated. Again, 30 minutes is reasonable.

These policies are available from the MMC **Default Domain** snap-in → select **Computer Configuration** → select **Windows Settings** → select **Security Settings** → double-click on **Account Lockout Policy**. In order to modify the currently displayed settings, double-click on the target policy and make changes within the dialog box that appears.

LOCAL PASSWORD SETTINGS

If local user accounts are established, strict policies for local passwords should be set. The options available for local passwords mirror those of the domain password settings. They can be viewed and set from the **Security Configuration and Analysis** snap-in → select **Account Policy** → double-click on **Password Policy**.

TABLE 11.4 Lockout Policy Options

Account Policy	Computer Setting
Account Lockout Counter	5 invalid logon attempts
Account Lockout Duration	30 minutes
Reset Account Lockout Counter after 30 Minutes	30 minutes

They may also be viewed from the **Local Computer Policy** snap-in. Select from the listed policies and make the appropriate changes.

DETERMINING WHO SETS A PASSWORD

Windows 2000 configuration allows passwords to be established by either the end user or the system administrator. The system administrator typically selects the password when it is likely that the user's choice will be a weak one or if the sophistication of the end user may be minimal. The biggest problem with this scenario is that the system administrator is likely to create a password that is very difficult to remember, inclining the end user to write it down for easy reference. While the intent is to strengthen security, the moment a password is written down security is compromised.

The alternative approach is to have the end user set the password and enforce rules that make password creation very unique. Additionally, the user should be forced to change the password periodically.

PASSWORD FILTERING

One method of ensuring that the created password meets the level of complexity desired is password filters. A password may be filtered as suggested, but it must meet the complexity requirements policy. The password filter installed with Windows 2000 may be used or a custom filter may be applied. Installation is accomplished by modifying the HKEY_LOCAL_MACHINE\SYSTEM\CurrentControlSet\Control\Lsa Registry key and adding the *.dll file name to the string list. The *.dll filter should be placed in the %SYSTEMROOT%\SYSTEM32 folder.

OTHER USER ACCOUNT SECURITY OPTIONS

Windows 2000 provides many additional security restriction options for both domain and local users. Describing each of them would require dozens of pages of text, so, since they are fairly obvious, we will point you to them instead. To view and modify these options, open the **Default Domain** snap-in → select **Windows Settings** → select **Security Settings** → select **Local Policies** → select **Security Options**. Double-click the target policy and make appropriate changes in the dialog box that is displayed.

Registry and File System Lockdown

Registry and file system permissions are crucial to Windows 2000 security. Default security permissions can be viewed from the **Security Templates** snap-in. The *basicdc.inf, basicsv.inf,* and *basicwk.inf* templates are the only ones that modify **File System** and **Registry** group policy security settings. A GPO should be used to enforce these default templates and ensure that all users and services are covered by the secure file and Registry settings. These templates also reflect the default file and Registry permissions for all Windows 2000 installations and are considered secure. The other default templates in the Security Template snap-in are designed to cover other security policy areas.

In addition to manipulating the security templates to reflect the appropriate lockdown levels, four additional rules should be applied:

- Use NTFS and take advantage of Windows 2000 file/folder permissions, auditing, and file encryption.
- Do not place any sensitive information or system files on a FAT partition. There are no file/folder permissions for local access on a FAT file system.
- Remember that the file owner always maintains full control over the object. Even if the administrator denies the owner all permissions, the owner can still view and modify security settings.
- When auditing file systems, never neglect the file owner.

Trojan Horses and Viruses

One of the biggest security threats to your network is unauthorized scripts, applications, DLLs, applets, ActiveX, and any other code component that can run on the operating system. These components perform processes that can be destructive to system operation and data. The concept of the Trojan horse derives from the ancient tale of the battle of Troy and Greek soldiers being hidden within a giant wooden horse offered as a gift. That event created the saying "Beware of Greeks bearing gifts," but it might be better stated today as "Beware of geeks bearing unknown code." What might appear harmless could create significant losses.

Software components constructed by hostile individuals are generally imported through e-mail, FTP, or Web services, or are internally created and distributed within your network. Once a hostile component is strategically placed on a system, the "Trojan horse" waits to be executed by the user. All processes started within a user's session will run with that user's security token. Thus, when a user inadvertently runs a hostile component, the hostile assumes all of his rights and privileges. Additionally, the process will assign the user's default discretionary ACL to newly created objects, enabling it to create new elements with equal permission settings.

If a hostile individual is able to place the component on the user's machine in the first place, she obviously has some level of access (or the user downloaded the component from the Web). This security threat is also probably looking for a way to improve its current access rights, and the administrator's account is its most promising target.

There are a number of defensive stances you can employ against Trojan horses and viruses, including the following:

- Never run applications under the Administrator account.
- Use auditing and scripts to search for components in suspect directories.
- Ensure the environmental parameters are set correctly, as discussed in the next section.
- Don't run software from unknown sources, and use up-to-date antivirus software.

Environmental Path Settings

Path security is all too often overlooked. Most applications started from the command window and most applications started from the desktop use environmental parameters to determine common directory locations and system information. The *PATH* variable determines a logical search path direction through directories (or folders) to find a given component. If a hacker knows the exact location of a component, he can gain access to an object even without permission to the folder. This may take skill, but Chapter 8 discusses how to use absolute paths to override folder permissions. The system administrator should ensure that only the intended directories are included in the PATH variable. These variables can be viewed from the **Control Panel → System → Advanced** tab → **Environmental Variables...** button. They can also be viewed by typing `path` at the Command Prompt.

Environmental variables (illustrated in Figure 11.5) are applied in order from the following sources:

1. Autoexec.bat (tightly restrict access)—first modifies environmental parameters.
2. System environment—only administrators modify further parameters.
3. User environment—final modification to environmental parameters can be done by the user.

CURRENT WORKING DIRECTORY SECURITY RESOURCE

A misguided user could be the source of real problems stemming from within his or her current working directory. The default working directory is defined in the user's account properties and is otherwise known as the home directory. If a hacker has somehow broken into a user's account, some level of risk exists. The current working directory is searched in addition to the directories specified in the PATH variable. A cracker may place executables in the working directory that replace the intended system calls. Thus, if an application is run from a directory

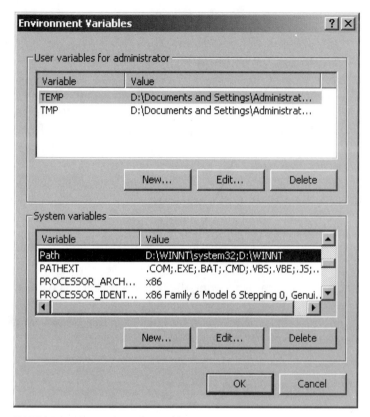

FIGURE 11.5 Environmental Variables

other than the system or program directory, a rewritten *.DLL impostor may be executed rather then the intended one. This *.DLL may perform the same tasks as the intended code in addition to providing the cracker access to the system at the user's privilege level. If this happens from an ordinary user's account, the resulting problems will ordinarily be restricted to that account. However, if it happens from an administrator's account, the entire system and perhaps the domain could be damaged. Obviously, this can lead to problems when users, and especially administrators, execute applications from directories that are not secure. To prevent working directory mishaps, the following commonsense steps should be enforced:

- Designate application directories and tightly configure permissions.
- Regularly search the system for *.DLL files that are not located in the %SystemRoot%, Program Files, or other designated application directories.
- Look for any type of executable created by unauthorized users.

EXTENSION MAPPING TO DISGUISE A FILE TYPE

Windows 2000 associates a file name extension with a particular application. When a file from **Explorer** or **My Computer** is opened, it is graphically displayed with the associated application's icon. Changing this mapping is very simple and can render the file nonexecutable. It is achieved by selecting it from the **Explorer** or **My Computer** window, selecting a file, right-clicking the **Properties** option, and pressing the **Change** button. This does not change the actual format of the file, but simply alters the **Open With** application list. The best defense is to encourage users to restrict their use of this facility.

A more serious problem can occur if the Registry is somehow violated. The HKEY_LOCAL_MACHINE\SOFTWARE\Classes key stores specific information on the application that is launched with each file extension. With *Regedit* or *Regedit32,* it is possible to re-map a plain text file (.txt) extension, for example, to any application available in the system. Let's assume that someone has loaded a malign program that removes all files in the current working directory. Further, through access to the Administrator account, the Registry had been changed so that all .txt extension files are mapped to this damaging program. The obvious effect is that the next time anyone launches a text file, all files in that current working directory will be lost. This is just another reason to guard against unauthorized Registry modification.

SPOOFING SHORTCUTS

Desktop shortcuts are used to streamline access to an application or file. If access is somehow granted to the shortcuts on a user's desktop, it is possible to change the properties and direct the shortcut to another file or application. In the case of a system administrator, a malicious internal user or hacker could direct a shortcut to a damaging virus or Trojan horse. While the administrator believes that he or she is executing a normal application, the shortcut is spoofing the reality of its redirection. This possibility again underscores the need for users not to leave their desktop unprotected.

Extraneous Services as a Security Threat

Common sense dictates that the more services available on a server, the greater the opportunities for possible attack. Thus, a minimalist approach to system administration can be a positive security action. Remove unneeded services and applications from all systems. For instance, some unused subsystems may not have any known security holes as yet but without careful monitoring may leave the system vulnerable.

In most environments, for example, the POSIX and OS/2 subsystems serve little or no value. (This statement does not apply if the Interix UNIX 95 environment is used in place of the standard POSIX subsystem.) However, because they communicate with the Windows 2000 Executive mode, they can create a program or command that does significant damage. Therefore, unless a clear requirement exists, remove the POSIX and OS/2 subsystems by removing the strings "OS/2" and "POSIX" from the Registry key using the Registry Editor. The modification should be made on the Registry tree level HKEY_LOCAL_MACHINE\System\CurrentControlSet\Control\Session Manager\Subsystems \Optional:

Backups and Restoration Security

An organization's philosophy on network security can vary greatly. Data integrity is not commonly viewed as a security issue, but maintaining system and data backup is fundamental. Securing valuable information through regular backups is the best defense against a natural disaster, a runaway virus, or a hack job. In Chapter 13 we elaborate on backup and restoration methods available in Windows 2000.

When implementing a backup policy, don't forget to also secure the backup media. For example, if you regularly back up critical data files and then tuck media away in an unsecured desk drawer, you are inviting theft. At a minimum, store backup media in a secure environment. It is also recommended that a second set of backup media be periodically archived in a secure remote location.

Physical Security

The importance of physical security cannot be understated, as it ranges from issues of outright theft of a system or key storage component to intervention with the boot drive during startup. Let's consider several common physical security threat scenarios.

THEFT OF SYSTEMS OR STORAGE MEDIA

At a minimum, efforts must be taken to physically lock down domain controllers and member servers. As powerful systems come packed in lighter and more portable footprints, the ability to take important services out the door without detection becomes increasingly easy.

Theft of critical media is just as easy. If unmonitored access is provided to a critical system like a domain controller, it is really no effort to open the cover and pull a hard drive. Your physical data is out the door and in the hands of a hacker in just a few minutes.

PHYSICAL ACCESS TO THE BOOT CD-ROM AND FLOPPY DRIVES

Let's consider another hardware-based scenario. Physical access to a floppy drive or CD-ROM on a domain controller or member server during the booting process invites intrusion. For the most malicious, it is obviously possible to use boot disks to completely erase all data or to get system access. With FAT-based Windows 2000 installations, the boot can also be used to gain direct access to files contained on the drive. All the invader has to do is abort the install process and revert to a DOS prompt. Even easier is simply booting directly from MS-DOS. Although native NTFS was designed to prevent intrusion, the same type of utilities that plagued Windows NT such as *ntdos.exe* will undoubtedly surface for Windows 2000.

General Physical Security Solutions

To prevent this type of serious damage, it is recommended that domain controllers and member servers be physically locked in a server room or, minimally, fit with locking devices. Also, use passwords to protect BIOS settings, which eliminate floppy and CD booting. If the BIOS password is not supplied, settings cannot be modified and thus attempts to boot floppies or CD-ROMs can be denied.

NOTE   Many CD-ROMs come with an auto-run function, which allows a virus to be executed or copied onto a hard drive without visibility. Turning off this feature is recommended. Using the Registry Editor, move to the HKEY_LOCAL_MACHINE\ SYSTEM\CurrentControllerSet\Services\CDROM key. Right-click on the **Autorun** REG_Word and select **Modify**. Set the value to **0**.

Another commonsense security action is placing critical systems and media in an environment that is not likely to experience water damage. For example, if a pipe breaks over the weekend that results in even a few inches of water, a floor-standing server could be damaged as well as its data.

Dual-Boot Environment Issues

Installing more than one bootable operating system on a machine can breach security. Even NTFS partitions are vulnerable to the Administrator account being accessed through a secondary operating system. If another operating system is booted, permissions set from the original are useless.

Auditing as a Line of Defense

The Windows 2000 audit trail is invaluable to the system administrator. For example, it can determine how a system crashed, how security was compromised, or how much disk space a user is consuming. Windows 2000 provides highly granular control over the events logged and the objects and services allowed to record events.

USING SECURITY AUDITING

The Windows 2000 auditing properties are viewed and modified through GPOs. The Audit policies found in the **Default Domain** snap-in under **Computer Configuration → Windows Settings → Security Settings → Local Policies → Audit Policies** determine what events are recorded in the Security Log. Standard events are shown is Figure 11.6.

The group policies found in the **Default Domain** snap-in under **Computer Configuration → Windows Settings → Security Settings → Event Log → Settings for Event Logs** (Figure 11.7) provide control over a number of proper-

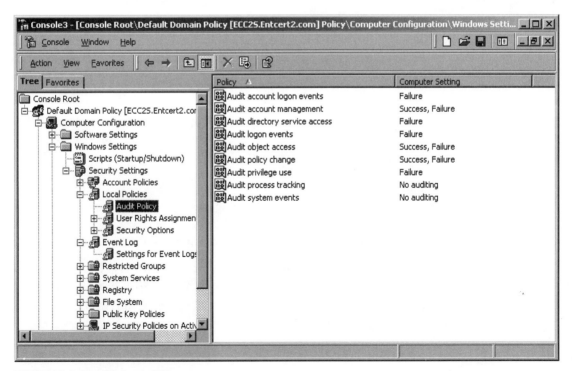

FIGURE 11.6 Possible Logged Events

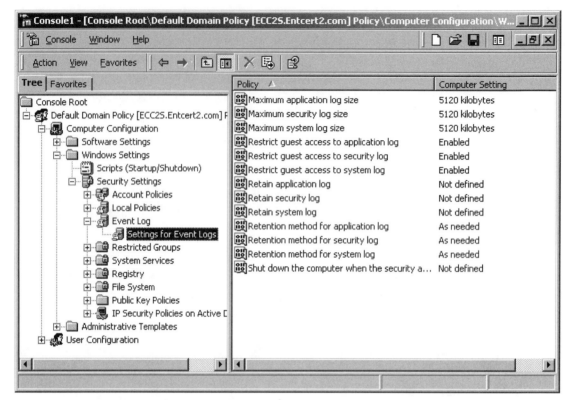

FIGURE 11.7 Settings for Event Logs

ties. This control includes how much disk space is dedicated to the logs, who can access them, how long they are retained, and the method for retaining them.

Event Log Retention

The retention method for a security log configures how the log is updated once it is full. If an overwrite option is not selected, the system will halt when the log is full, whereupon the administrator must take the following steps to enable the system:

1. From the **Start** menu select **Programs** → **Administrative Tools** → **Event Viewer** and save the current logs (if desired). **Clear All Events** from each.

2. Change the Registry key HKEY_LOCAL_MACHINE\SYSTEM\CurrentControlSet\Control\Lsa\crashonauditfail to 1.

3. Restart the system.

OFFLINE AUDITING POLICIES

Reviewing audit reports while offline may prove convenient in some administrative circumstances. Auditing policies for offline folders can be found in the **Default Domain** snap-in under **User Configuration** → **Administrative Templates** → **Network** → **Offline Files**. See Figure 11.8 for a list of options.

EVENT VIEWER USE

The Event Viewer gives the administrator access to six event logs. The Security Log displays successes and failures and classifies them into Object Access, Account Logon, Policy Change, Privilege Use, Directory Service Access, and Account Management categories (Figure 11.9).

The other logs have three types of records—Errors, Informative, and Warnings (Figure 11.10). The Application Log contains events logged from programs running on the system, including all exceptions raised. The System Log records events

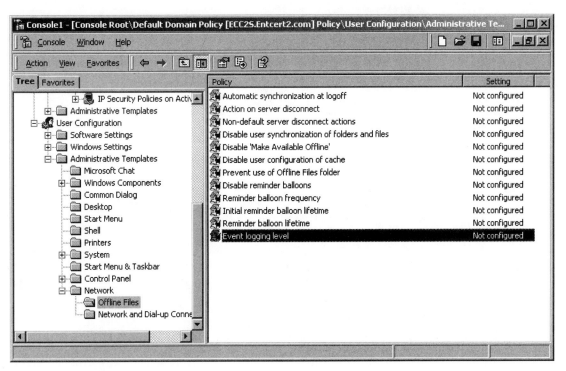

FIGURE 11.8 Offline Auditing Options

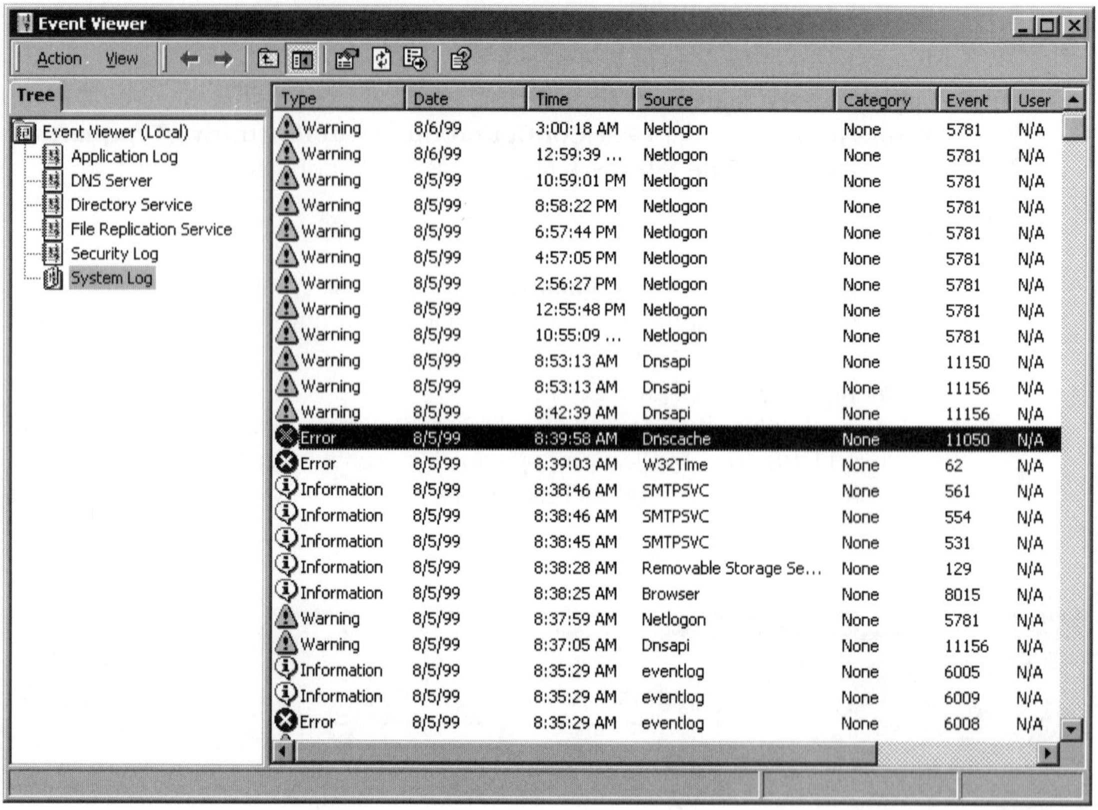

FIGURE 11.9 The Event Viewer Snap-In

raised by the Windows 2000 operating system (Figure 11.11). All users can view the System and Application Logs but only administrators can view the Security Log.

File, folder, printer, Active Directory, group policy, and other system objects have associated Access Control Lists (ACLs). Each ACL is composed of a Discretionary Access Control List (DACL) and a System Access Control List (SACL). The DACL details user and group access rights to an object (Figure 11.12, page 481); the SACL determines the users and groups that will be audited when attempting or performing access rights on the object (Figure 11.13, page 482).

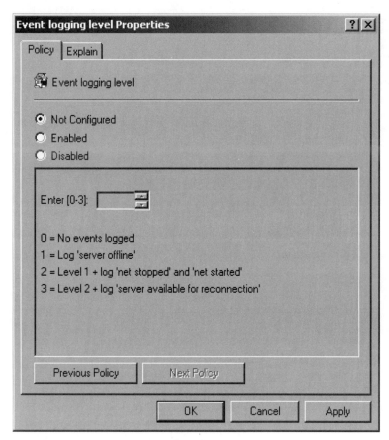

FIGURE 11.10 Event Logging Level Properties

GENERAL AUDITING PROCEDURES

The following steps should generally be observed when using Windows 2000 auditing:

1. Set the SACL on objects of interest to identify the group and user access events to monitor.

2. Set auditing policies to record the desired events.

3. Periodically view the logs and clear them out.

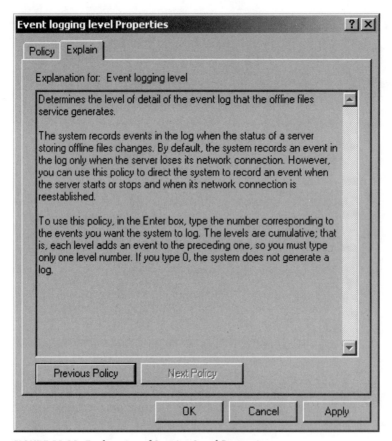

FIGURE 11.11 Explanation of Logging Level Properties

NOTE   As you establish your auditing strategy, remember that only NTFS files and folders may be audited.

AUDIT EVENTS THAT NEED THE MOST CAREFUL REVIEW

No system administrator can track and review all event items, but must restrict her attention to those of greatest potential importance. As a general rule, the following audit events are particularly helpful when tracking possible security threats:

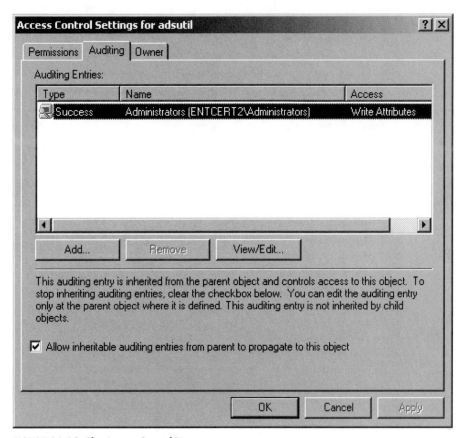

FIGURE 11.12 The Access Control List

- *Logon/Logoff*—provides information on logon failures and may indicate if a certain user account is under attack.
- *Account Management*—provides information on users who have sought rights to use administrative tools.
- *Startup/Shutdown*—shows who has attempted to invoke a shutdown command and also lists services that were not properly initiated during startup.
- *Policy Changes*—indicates what policy changes were attempted.
- *Privilege Use*—lists attempts to change permissions to objects.

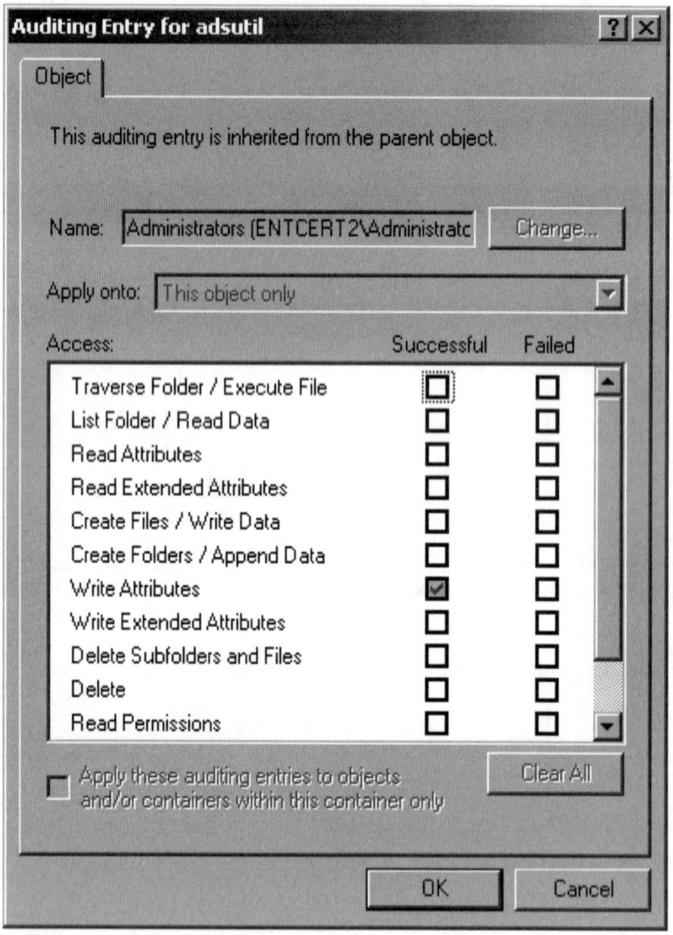

FIGURE 11.13 An Auditing Entry

NOTE   If a cracker breaks into the system, he will most certainly try to cover his tracks and erase the logs. To guard against this action and retain logs, provide remote logging of the above events to a secure log server that is in a safe place with only local logins, and have critical events printed out to a printer. This will keep the log files intact and help trace security problems.

SECURE NETWORK SERVICES AND ARCHITECTURE

Securing your domain internally is but one aspect of security. The system administrator must also be aware of network security issues. In this section, we explore the need to protect network shares, use firewalls, restrict RAS services, invoke IP security, and use other TCP/IP-based applications safely.

Protecting Network Shares

Network shares are an important part of the distributed computing environment, as they greatly enhance accessibility. However, they also represent a potential security weakness. To minimize problems associated with network shares, keep these administrative concepts in mind:

- The root share determines share permissions for all subdirectories. Subdirectories within a root share cannot be further restricted with share permissions, so NTFS permissions should be used for finer granular control.
- Share permissions only restrict network users (but not local users).
- Share names are visible to all users and should not reveal sensitive information or invite an attack.
- Hidden shares can be displayed using the *net share* command from the Command Prompt. They should be removed if not in use.

NOTE   One way to minimize the risk to hidden administrative shares is to remove them. Using the Registry Editor, set the Registry key HKEY_LOCAL_MACHINE\System\ CurrentControlSet\Services\LanManServer\Parameters to 0, which will disable hidden shares C$ and D$ (administrative shares).

However, if you are backing up files using these administrative shares, the 0 setting will prevent you from doing so.

Firewalls

In Internet communications, firewalls are normally established to buffer the intranet from outside attacks. Firewall functions are implemented on packet forwarding devices, which usually, but not always, have at least two interfaces. They can take the form of a dual-homed host with two interface cards or a piece of network gear known as a router.

A typical firewall configuration (Figure 11.14) consists of an external packet filtering firewall and a secondary firewall supporting the needed proxy services. The packet filtering rules are configured to allow external Internet users access to HTTP and FTP services on the company's Web and FTP servers or whatever ports you decide to let through, including SMTP or real audio. All other network and transport protocol packets not matching the packet filtering rules are dropped. Additional rule sets must be implemented to allow services such as DNS and SMTP to pass from the internal intranet through the packet filtering firewall to servers on the Internet. Servers located in the zone between the two firewalls, sometimes referred to as the Demilitarized Zone (DMZ), are given their own dedicated Ethernet segments. If one of them is compromised, a remotely installed network sniffer is prevented from monitoring traffic to the internal network. (This is really dependent on the firewall implementation.) The second firewall proxies Web and ftp services initiated by internal users to the Internet.

The firewall routes packets between interfaces performing packet filtering, stateful inspection, or proxy services. A review of each of these items is appropriate.

PACKET FILTERING

A packet filter is designed to restrict external connections to a limited set of services, protecting the internal network from the Internet. The firewall enforces rules for packet filtering. These rules typically filter on protocols, source ports, source addresses, destination ports and destination addresses, and allowed network interfaces a given address may use. They may also filter on whether the traffic is UDP or TCP. Packet rules define connection types that are accepted and

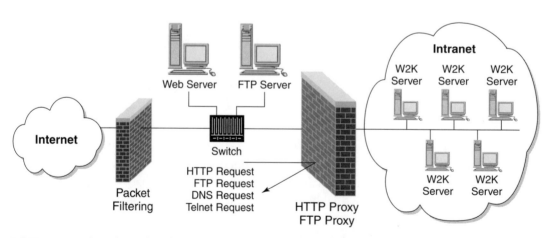

FIGURE 11.14 The Relationship of Firewalls to Intranets and the Internet

those that are rejected. For simplicity and security, it is probably best to establish rules for packets that will be accepted. Everything else is dropped and not forwarded.

Packet filtering occurs mostly at the network and transport protocol levels. If the NetBIOS service ports are not specifically enabled, traffic targeting the NetBIOS services will be blocked from Internet attacks. Attacks using IP source routing can also be stopped using packet filtering.

Packet Filtering Example

The rule set configuration shown in Table 11.5 allows external clients to access the internal Web server through the packet filtering router. The rule set allows inbound requests and outbound responses with IP addresses and TCP port settings, as shown in lines A and B in the table. It also allows internal intranet users to connect with external Web servers on the Internet. Packets with destination TCP port = 80 and return TCP port = random number above 1023 are considered inbound HTTP requests from Internet users (line A). In order for the internal Web server to respond to this client connection, the outbound destination TCP port = Random > 1023 and source TCP port = 80 (Line B) must be permitted. However, an Internet user attempting to connect to the intranet using an internal source IP address will not be permitted. Internal IP addresses are only forwarded from the internal to the external interface on the packet filter route.

NOTE   The foregoing is a general rule and is by no means absolute. Additionally, a filter may be applied to the incoming or outgoing interface and the ACK bits may be set. Since a cracker can make a request come from any port she wants, you must make sure that incoming requests either are to a specific IP address or were already established, by checking the ACK bit in the header.

TABLE 11.5 Filtering Example

Line	Source IP Address	Destination IP Address	Source TCP Port Number	Destination TCP Port Number	Description
A	Internet	Intranet	Random > 1023	80	Inbound request
B	Intranet	Internet	80	Random > 1023	Outbound response
C	Internet	Intranet	Random > 1023	80	Outbound request
D	Intranet	Internet	80	Random > 1023	Inbound response

TABLE 11.6 Other Windows 2000 Services for Implementing a Packet Filter

UDP Port Number	Description	TCP Port Number	Description
53	Domain Name Service (DNS)	20	FTP Server—data channel
69	Trivial File Transfer Protocol (TFTP)	21	FTP Server—control channel
137	NetBIOS Name Service	23	Telnet Server
138	NetBIOS Datagram Service	53	DNS Transfers
161	SNMP	80	Web Server—HTTP
		139	NetBIOS Session Service
		25	Simple Mail Transfer Protocol (SMTP)

A rule set similar to this example must be implemented for every network service that intends to communicate through the packet filter. Table 11.6 lists common network services and protocols that could take advantage of packet filtering.

Allowing TFTP, SNMP, or any of the NetBIOS services in from the Internet is not recommended. This of course will need to be based on policy, but these services are relatively insecure.

PROXY SERVICES

A proxy server is a popular way to give internal users access to the Internet without compromising external access. The proxy software runs on a host routing between the internal network and the Internet. The main idea is to allow internally initiated connections with the Internet while preventing any that are externally initiated. For example, after installing and configuring Microsoft Proxy Server 2.0 for HTTP, the internal users designate the HTTP proxy server in their Web browser. All external Web site requests are directed to it. The proxy receives HTTP URL requests and establishes its own connections with the destination websites. It then retrieves the data and relays it back to the correct internal client. This translation between internal Web client and external Web server can be transparent to the user. A proxy firewall requires client proxy and server proxy software specifically designed for each proxy service implemented to provide this transparency.

Both Netscape and Internet Explorer provide client proxy software for HTTP. Noncaching proxies degrade network performance but provide a secure firewall. We specifically mention noncaching because a caching server may actually respond much quicker if the answer is in the cache. The Microsoft Proxy Server also has an added caching feature. Commonly visited sites are stored on the proxy's local hard disk, preventing the need for Internet retrieval. Clients receive the pages faster and reduce the required Internet bandwidth. The proxy can also retrieve and refresh popular Web sites automatically without client requests.

STATEFUL INSPECTION

Stateful inspection offers an alternative way to provide internal users with connectivity to Internet resources while preventing external users from initiating inbound connections. As a user makes an outbound request to an external server, the stateful inspection firewall records details about it. The information tracked includes the source address, destination address, protocol, port number, and so forth, and it is evaluated for a certain period of time. When the destination service responds to the internal user, the packet is permitted to return through the firewall.

The firewall performs intelligent packet filtering without requiring the server and client software to support each network service. However, although stateful inspection offers better performance than the proxy model, it reveals internal IP addresses to the Internet. Several stateful inspection products hide internal IP addresses through address translation.

Web Security

When implementing a Web server, certain basic guidelines should be followed to protect against security breaches. A Web server allows users to download designated files and run CGI scripts, Active Server Pages, and server-side applets that are accessible to it. For this reason the server should not be able to access sensitive files that contain proprietary company information or files pertinent to system security.

Limit the Web server to a specific directory subtree and specifically dedicate a system to Web server duties (Windows 2000 uses %SystemRoot%Inetpub\wwwroot). Also, make sure that websites with password security do not place the password security file in a directory the server can read. The Web server should run as a very underprivileged user to limit its own access, with a privilege level just enough to perform required functions. It should have a firewall between it and the internal network, and no internal host should trust it through Windows 2000 domain trust relationships.

RESTRICTING SCRIPTS FROM EXTERNAL SOURCES

Since the Web server is permitted to run local components, all scripts, applets, and active components should be analyzed for unintended uses. Remember, these scripts can be run with freely chosen parameters from the outside, so any service that allows users to download scripts to the server should be carefully scrutinized. FTP users should not be able to download to the Web server's file system area. In fact, almost all services should be disabled on the Web server except for HTTP.

HTTP SECURITY

HTTP is an unencrypted protocol and will not prevent users from snooping or spoofing your Web server. The Secure HTTP protocol addresses these issues, but your Web clients must be familiar with your server to gain access. The Public Key Infrastructure discussed in Chapter 10 outlines how to use and configure the X.509 certificates and Certificate Authority.

IP Security

The Internet Protocol (IP) is the message delivery portion of the TCP/IP suite. It provides address and delivery of data packets. This is a "best-effort" delivery system that does not guarantee arrival of packets or that the information is properly sequenced. Thus, IP packets can be intercepted en route, reviewed, and even modified. The potential misuse is obvious. Let's take a second to examine some IP security issues.

IP spoofing can be a major threat. The IP address is ordinarily shown as plain text. The hacker can then direct the packet to the destination with altered information. The use of cryptographic technologies is the best defense against IP sniffing and spoofing.

Internet Browser Security

Downloadable objects accessible from the Internet open a gaping hole in network security because nontrusted components can be downloaded right through a firewall. The user must be educated and browsers must be configured to match your network's tolerance for active components and Java applets.

Any browser user may configure how his browser handles untrusted and trusted components. The Microsoft Internet Explorer v5 configures these options through the **Tools → Internet Options...** menu selection. Select the **Security** tab and press the **Custom Level...** button for the **Internet** zone. For the purpose of providing an example, we will examine both Java and ActiveX permissions.

RESTRICTING JAVA COMPONENTS

Internet Explorer v5.0 provides several ways to handle Java applets. Unsigned applets are without digital signatures to trusted certificate authorities. Thus, the user can disable, enable, or run the applet within the Java sandbox. If the sandbox is chosen, the user can individually configure all access rights to either the Enable or Disable setting. Signed applets with digital signatures from trusted authorities may choose the Enable, Disable, or Prompt option. If the Prompt option is selected the user must configure each access right to prompt, enable, or disable. The Prompt option will dialog the user whenever the access right is required for the applet in question.

Find the **Java permissions** and select **Custom**. Then press the **Java Custom Settings...** button. The attributes that can be modified are shown in Table 11.7. Again, browser permissions should be set at the same relative levels as those of the local server.

RESTRICTING ACTIVEX COMPONENTS

The ActiveX attributes require a Prompt, Enable, or Disable value for each security setting. ActiveX controls do not have the option of running within the sandbox and they have full control over the Win32 API. Therefore, you do not want users to run unsigned ActiveX controls. Period.

Find the **ActiveX permissions** and select **Custom**. Then press the **ActiveX Custom Settings...** button. The attributes that can be modified are shown in

TABLE 11.7 Java Permission Settings

Java Security Attribute	Unsigned Content (Run in sandbox)	Signed Content
Access to Files	Enable/Disable	Prompt/Enable/Disable
Access to Network Addresses	Enable/Disable	Prompt/Enable/Disable
Execute	Enable/Disable	Prompt/Enable/Disable
Dialogs	Enable/Disable	Prompt/Enable/Disable
System Information	Enable/Disable	Prompt/Enable/Disable
Printing	Enable/Disable	Prompt/Enable/Disable
Protected Scratch Space	Enable/Disable	Prompt/Enable/Disable
User Selected File Access	Enable/Disable	Prompt/Enable/Disable

TABLE 11.8 ActiveX Permission Settings

ActiveX Attribute	Option
Download Signed ActiveX Controls	Prompt/Enable/Disable
Download Unsigned ActiveX Controls	Prompt/Enable/Disable
Initialize and Script ActiveX Controls Not Marked Safe	Prompt/Enable/Disable
Run ActiveX Controls and Plug-Ins	Administrator approved/ Prompt/Enable/Disable
Script ActiveX Controls Marked Safe for Scripting	Prompt/Enable/Disable

Table 11.8. Again, browser permissions should be set at the same relative levels as those of the local server.

NOTE   The browser settings just discussed can be automatically assigned to users through a GPO. They are set from the **Default Domain** snap-in under **User Configuration → Windows Settings → Internet Explorer Maintenance → Security → Security Zones and Content Ratings**.

INTERNET CERTIFICATE MANAGEMENT

From the **Internet Options Content** tab, press the **Certificates...** button to display currently installed certificates for signing and encryption. See Chapter 10, Kerberos and the Public Key Infrastructure, for more information on local certificate stores.

Securing RAS Servers

The Remote Access Service (RAS) allows a connection across a phone dial-up so that a user can use resources like a printer in a remote location. Since these connections are made through unsecured telephone lines, many potential security breaches exist. This is particularly true if the RAS is provided a server that is not otherwise protected. A number of actions can be taken to protect the domain from potential RAS abuses, including these:

- RAS connections should only allow dial-in accounts to access the RAS server.
- The RAS server should have its own domain and maintain separate user accounts.

- There should be a one-way trust between the rest of the network and the RAS server. (Users can put data on the RAS server for remote access, but the server is buffered from the rest of the network.)
- Strong passwords to RAS accounts should be enforced.

Securing Electronic Mail

Electronic mail is the lifeblood of modern organizational communication. The ability to send and receive mail messages from external sources is a common requirement. As is the case with any information from external sources, e-mail presents a host of security problems, including

- *Flooding*. The e-mail server is hammered with a large number of messages, which can result in denial of service and system crash.
- *Spoofing*. The e-mail message has an incorrect sender name or address.
- *Viruses*. Application attachments may contain hostile macros (for example, the ActiveX-based Melissa).
- *Nonrepudiation*. The receiver needs to verify that the sender actually sent the message and the sender needs to verify that the receiver got the message.

PREVENTING E-MAIL SECURITY ABUSES

Packet filtering messages from sources that are known to flood is effective but reactionary, as the mail buffers and disk space can be monitored for excessive use. Spoofing and nonrepudiation are effectively combated with digital signatures.

Digital signatures are easily implemented from Outlook Express 5.0 via the **Tools → Options...** selection under the **Security** tab, where encryption and digitally signing can be configured for outgoing messages (Figures 11.15 and 11.16). The user and recipient must share a common certificate authority. For additional information see Chapter 10, Kerberos and the Public Key Infrastructure.

Virus attacks are difficult to filter out, especially when e-mail encryption is involved. Several virus scanners are available but are of limited effectiveness. If the scanner has an error and starts dropping all e-mail messages, regardless of viral content, the network and company can end up in a worse predicament than dealing with the virus. Denial of service is a serious downside to these tools, which means that careful monitoring and reaction time are key to successful implementation.

Other TCP/IP Security Issues

The TCP/IP networking suite provides a host of commonly used services and protocols. Each represents potential security vulnerability. The following is a sample

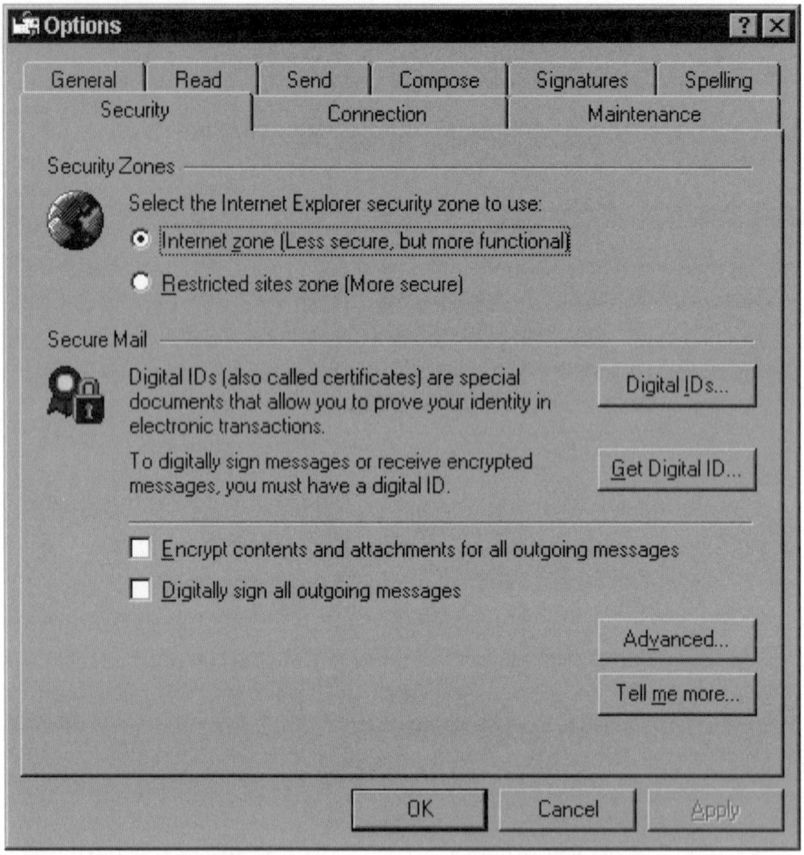

FIGURE 11.15 The Security Tab

of issues that could impact Windows 2000 environments using the following TCP/IP suite applications:

- *FTP*. The File Transfer Protocol is often used by anonymous user accounts that do not require password protection, which permits access to a system by virtually any user. Once inside, hackers can try to work their magic. To guard against this, set permissions to Read-Only and restrict directory access. (Or do not set up anonymous accounts at all unless you really need them.)

- *TFTP*. The Trivial File Transport Protocol is a relaxed version of *FTP,* in which generally any files can be transferred without a password—conceivably even system files such as the Windows 2000 Registry. We strongly recommend that TFTP be disabled by removing the *TFTPD* file. In Windows 2000 assure that the service is not enabled.

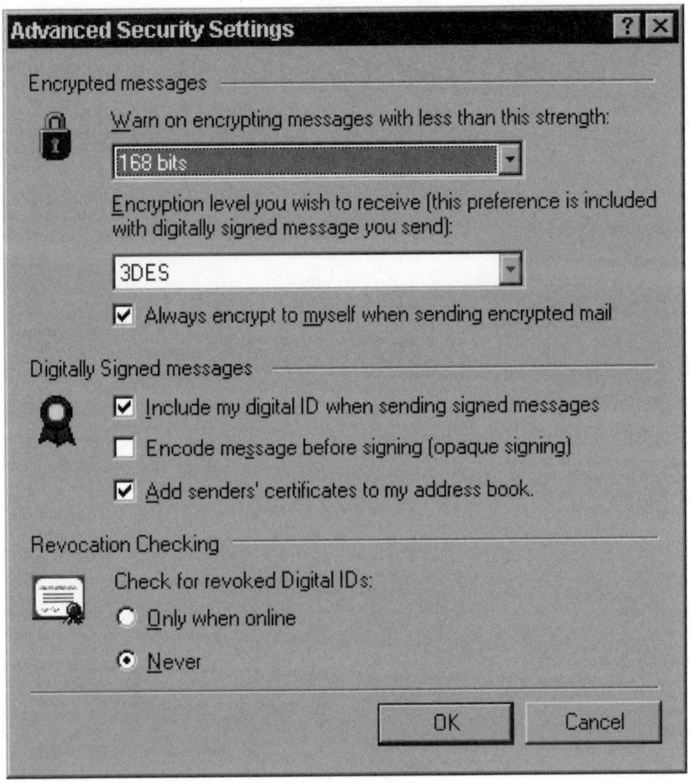

FIGURE 11.16 Advanced Security Settings

- *finger*. This utility outputs information about users on the system. Once a hacker has a list of user names, systematically discovering passwords becomes the game. This facility should also be disabled unless absolutely required.
- *DNS*. The Domain Naming Server includes vital network information. Protect yourself by segregating it. For example, two servers can be used with a firewall separating external Internet-required data from inside user account information. You may also want to set filters to allow DNS queries to go only to one specific DNS machine on the DMZ, and only allow zone transfers to and from your parent servers.
- *Telnet*. Telnet data is transmitted in plain text along with the user name and password. This makes Telnet a valuable tool in an internal environment, especially when attempting to view data on heterogeneous UNIX and Windows 2000 systems. However, outside a secured environment, the user must be aware that security breaches can occur with this open transmission.

THE END USER'S RESPONSIBILITY

Users have to take a certain amount of responsibility for the security of the computing environment, so it is reasonable for IT professionals to clearly articulate what is expected of them. When these expectations are not met, denial of privilege or restricted use can be invoked. This list represents some of the practices that system administrators should expect of end users:

- The selection of nonobvious passwords is the first line of defense. The user also should be periodically forced to change the password.
- The password must never be written down or revealed to associates.
- When leaving the work area, the user should be instructed to invoke a password-controlled screen saver or to log off. Log off must be enforced at the end of each work period.
- The user should be made aware of basic file and folder permissions parameters. This is particularly true if she moves or copies files. Additionally, the user should be aware of the implication of allowing another user to take ownership of a file.
- No user should import applications that are not specifically approved by the system administrator. This is one of the easiest ways to introduce viruses or Trojan horses.

POSTSCRIPT

There will always be a compromise between ease of use and network security. All operating systems and applications have a number of known system vulnerabilities whose exploitation is only a mouse click away even for novice users.

- Act on an aggressive security plan for network and system security.
- Plug security holes with the most current version of the operating system and service patches.
- Apply the same principle to all network services and client applications.
- Back up all system data and be able to reinstall operating and application components quickly.
- Outline and prioritize the resources needed to maintain a secure network.

Two additional sources should be tapped when administrating Windows 2000 security. First, keep abreast of regularly posted security update white papers and bulletins on Microsoft's website at *http://www.microsoft.com/security*. Additionally, check the website for security patches. As the hacker community goes forward, Microsoft will regularly post protective patches to prevent attacks.

NOTE   Install hot fixes to the operating system, IIS, Web servers, etc. Subscribe to the Microsoft Security alert mailing list.

Chapter 12

Networking Basics and Naming Services

This chapter is divided into two sections. The first part provides an overview of networking basics from 30,000 feet. It is written as a primer for readers who are not familiar with TCP/IP and related technologies; those experienced with networking may use it only as a quick reference. The second section examines naming services, including DNS and DHCP. It provides both theoretical and hands-on information that is vital to all Windows 2000 enterprises.

NETWORKING BASICS

Communication between network devices like computers assumes the existence of mutually understood protocols that comprise a set of rules and structural components. Computers must use a common protocol in order to communicate. Underlying communication in Windows 2000 enterprises is the default Transmission Control Protocol and Internet Protocol, otherwise known as TCP/IP.

Network Architecture

The Open Systems Interconnect (OSI) model defines network communication in a sequential and hierarchical fashion. As shown in Figure 12.1, it consists of seven layers, a brief explanation of which should provide a better understanding of its conceptual underpinnings. Protocols like TCP/IP embrace only a portion of the total conceptual model.

- *Physical layer*. The physical layer loosely refers to just about any characteristic of the hardware, such as signal voltages and cable and connector specifications.

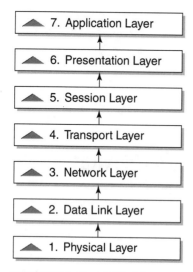

FIGURE 12.1 The OSI Model

It transmits and receives data in the raw bit form of 1s and 0s. Standards such as Ethernet 802.3, RS232C, and X.25 dictate the requirements of this layer.

- *Data link layer.* The data link layer changes the raw bit stream presented by the physical layer into data frames or blocks. TCP/IP typically assumes the use of other standards to specify the data link layer's characteristics.

- *Network layer.* The network layer is the first level in which TCP/IP directly relates to the OSI model. It is where the Internet Protocol (IP) manages communication between the application layer and the lower physical or data link layers. IP provides the Internet addressing scheme that defines a common structure or format for *datagrams*. These are packets of data that include information such as destination, type, source, and size. The Internet protocol defines how the datagrams are interpreted, as well as how data is routed between Internet networks and addresses, especially on segmented or subdivided networks.

- *Transport layer.* The transport layer communicates with the application layer. When errors are detected, it may request the re-transmission of bad or lost packets. IP traffic will typically use either the *Transmission Control Protocol (TCP)* or the *User Datagram Protocol (UDP)*. Each transport connection is identified by a port number.

- *Session layer.* The session layer refers to the connectivity and management of network applications. TCP/IP does not directly map this OSI layer.

- *Presentation layer*. The presentation layer establishes the data format prior to passing it along to the network application's interface. TCP/IP networks perform this task at the application layer.

- *Application layer*. The application layer processes data received or sent through the network.

A MODIFIED NETWORK MODEL

There is some debate as to how well TCP/IP maps to the OSI conceptual model. However, for the sake of a simple overview, it may be said that it does conceptually correspond (although not identically) to the OSI model with a four-layer hybrid model having an application layer, a transport layer, a network layer, and a physical/data link layer (Figure 12.2).

IP Addressing

The IP address is used to identify and address the network and devices or *nodes* such as servers, desktop computers, and routing devices. It consists of a 32-bit value that is separated into four octets. When data segments pass from the transport layer to the network layer, the IP protocol appends its own header information and the new grouping becomes an IP datagram (Figure 12.3). The most important fields in this datagram are the destination and the source addresses.

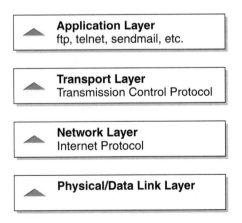

Application Layer
ftp, telnet, sendmail, etc.

Transport Layer
Transmission Control Protocol

Network Layer
Internet Protocol

Physical/Data Link Layer

FIGURE 12.2 Layers Used by the TCP/IP Model

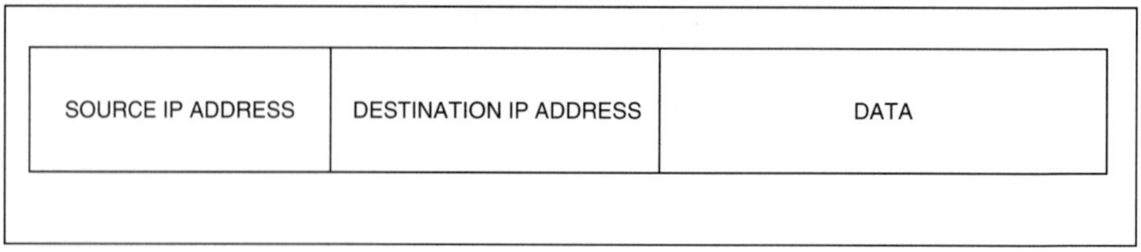

SOURCE IP ADDRESS	DESTINATION IP ADDRESS	DATA

FIGURE 12.3 The IP Datagram

DISSECTING IP ADDRESSING

There are three *classes* of IP addresses. An address class is determined by the following rules:

- *Class A*. In a Class A address the first number is in the range of 0–127, with the 0 value reserved for the default route and the 127 value reserved for identifying the local host. This means that only 126 (1–126) networks can be defined as Class A; the other bits in the address are used to assign specific node IP addresses. While the number of Class A networks is limited, and they are difficult to obtain, the number of nodes they can support is extensive. (x represents a fictitious decimal digit in the following tables.)

  Class A Address Example

8-bit Network Address	24-bit Host Address
1xx.	106.111.111

- *Class B*. A Class B address uses the first value range from 128–191 in the first byte. It also uses the second octal byte set for defining the network. The result is that there can be many more networks defined by Class B addresses. The remaining octal sets are used to assign specific node addresses.

  Class B Address Example

16-bit Network Address	16-bit Host Address
129.1xx.	111.111

- *Class C*. Class C addresses use the value range of 192–223 in the first byte, and the next two octal sets are used to define the network as well. With three octal sets defining networks, many more networks can be established and identified. However, since only one octal set is available to define the IP address of a specific node, the network is smaller, with a potential to provide up to 254 hosts or node addresses (the 0 value identifies the network and the 255 value is reserved for broadcasting).

Class C Address Example

24-bit Network Address	8-bit Host Address
192.1xx.111.	111

SUBNET MASKS

A subnet mask permits the division of a single IP address into multiple subnet-works. A subnet mask defines how the address space is divided between networks and hosts. It is a 32-bit binary number that designates which bits of the IP address are intended for the network and which determine the host. The network portion is identified by 1s, and the host by 0s. Thus, for the previously discussed Class A, B, and C addresses the following subnet masks would be used.

Class	Network Mask (Decimal)	Network Mask (Binary)
A	255.0.0.0	11111111 00000000 00000000 00000000
B	255.255.0.0	11111111 11111111 00000000 00000000
C	255.255.255.0	11111111 11111111 11111111 00000000

A Class C address could designate the first 24 bits as network space and the last 8 bits as host space on the network. Addressing at the data link layer is handled with Media Access Control (MAC) addresses. Discussing address frame delivery at the data link layer is beyond the scope of this book. However, once a packet is forwarded to the segment with the destination node, the data link media is responsible for frame delivery. In order for this to be accomplished, a node must map the destination IP address to the destination MAC address.

THE ADDRESS RESOLUTION PROTOCOL

A computer system or printer may establish connectivity via a serial port, phone line, interface card, or other device. However, most connectivity strategies for local area networks involve an interface card to one of the more popular media types, such as Ethernet, Token Ring, or FDDI, which implement elements from both the physical and data link layers of the OSI model. The interface card uses these hardware definitions and data link protocols to encapsulate network-level packets into media frames that are then delivered to a destination—another interface card.

Media Access Control (MAC) addresses identify and address the interface cards. Most consist of six hexadecimal numbers separated by colons (e.g., 00:53:45:00:00:00). The encapsulated network-level IP packet has its own addressing scheme that must then be mapped onto the MAC address in order to

communicate with systems via their interface cards. The Address Resolution Protocol (ARP) maps between MAC and IP addresses on the local network segment.

For example, if *Node A* desires to communicate with *Node B,* it must first map
Node B's IP address with its physical MAC address. Once the destination MAC
address is resolved, the data link layer is responsible for delivering the frame.
Node A broadcasts an ARP request, which contains the destination IP address, to
every node on the physical segment (Figure 12.4). Each node reads the request
and checks to see if the destination IP address matches its own. Only *Node B,*
owner of the destination IP address, returns an ARP reply to the source MAC
address. *Node A* retrieves the source MAC address from the ARP reply data link
frame and stores the IP-MAC address mapping in its ARP cache. This entry will
remain valid in the local volatile ARP cache for a predetermined period of time,
usually about 10 minutes. If the address mapping is validated with continued communication, the entry will be refreshed. Once *Node A* has *Node B*'s IP address and
corresponding MAC address, communication may be initiated with direct uni-cast
data link frames between the two.

NOTE   The contents of a system's ARP cache may be displayed by using `arp -a` at the
command line. The `ipconfig/?` command is very helpful for displaying and
configuring all aspects of the IP implementation on a system. See the Appendix or
Help pages for further information.

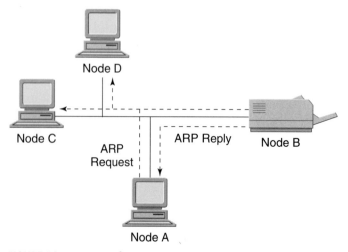

FIGURE 12.4 ARP Resolution

IP Routing

IP packets are forwarded between networks using specialized network equipment known as routers or by multi-homed hosts (i.e., systems with multiple network adapters) with routing software. Upon receiving a packet, the routing device determines which interface produces the quickest route to the destination IP address. The packet is then repackaged and sent out on the correct interface, which the router determines based on its *routing table*. This table is constructed with manually configured routes, or static routes, and routes obtained via communication with other routers.

Routers communicate these dynamically changing routes through the *Routing Information Protocol* (RIP), the *Open Shortest Path First* (OSPF) protocol, and others. Static routes are configured through the command line using the `route` command or through the **Routing and Remote Access** snap-in.

CLIENT-SIDE ROUTING CONFIGURATION

Three parameters are of particular interest when configuring a host for communication on a network. Double-click an interface from **Start** → **Settings** → **Network and Dial-up Connections**. Select the **Internet Protocol** (**TCP/IP**) and press the **Properties** button to see them (Figure 12.5):

- *IP address*—unique IP address assigned to the interface.
- *Subnet mask*—determines network and host portions of the IP address.
- *Default gateway*—IP address of network's router interface.

A client's IP address may be manually configured with a static IP address or assigned automatically via the Dynamic Host Configuration Protocol (DHCP) discussed later in the chapter. The subnet mask identifies the portion of the IP address pertaining to the network and host addresses, as discussed earlier, and is mapped against an outbound packet's destination IP address. If the packet is not bound for the local network segment, the client sends it to the default gateway. The gateway forwards the packet onto the destination network using routing tables, as discussed earlier.

NAMING SERVICES AND IP ASSIGNMENTS

Network naming services were developed to correlate numeric addresses best understood by computers and natural language names that are provided to the same network device. Windows 2000 embraces several of them. The Domain Name System (DNS) is an integral part of Windows 2000 and, especially, Active Directory implementations. It has evolved as the primary naming service for the

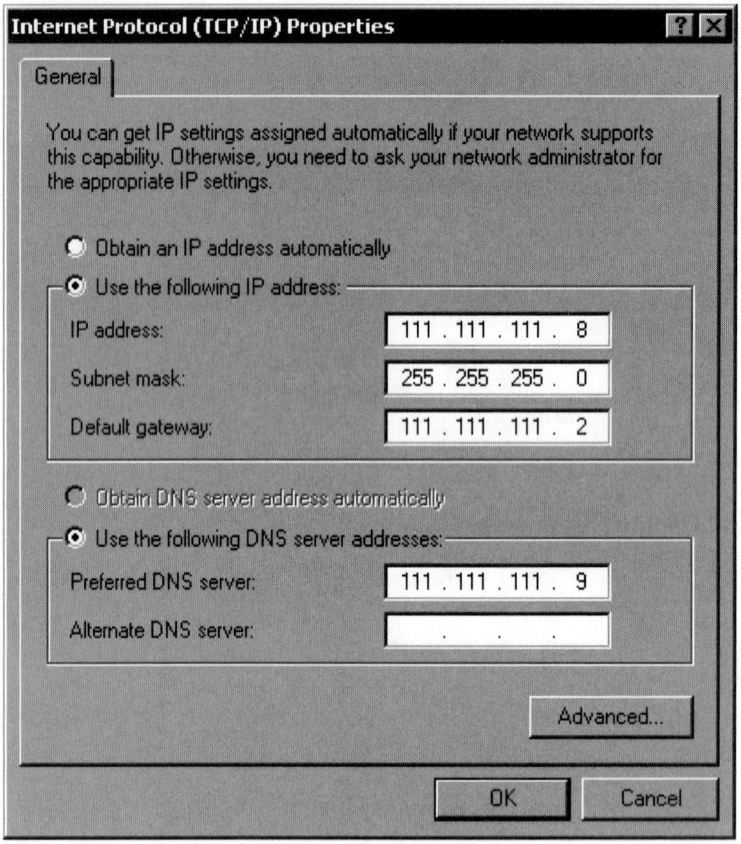

FIGURE 12.5 Internet Protocol Client Configuration

UNIX operating system and the Internet. Because of Microsoft's decision to make Windows 2000 Internet compatible, DNS has replaced the Windows Internet Name Service (WINS) as the default name resolution technology.

This section examines DNS and other naming services and related technologies, including DHCP and the Microsoft legacy WINS. DHCP dynamically assigns IP addresses. While technically not a naming service, it is very closely related when deploying networks.

Domain Name System Conventions

The role of DNS is to match a *Fully Qualified Domain Name* (FQDN) with its *IP address*. FQDNs are organized in a top-down fashion, forming a hierarchy from general to specific (Figure 12.6). This hierarchy is read from right to left and identifies a specific host in a subdomain. For example, the fully qualified host name *host.EntCert.com.* identifies *host* in the *EntCert* subdomain. The root domain, indicated by the period on the far right, is usually omitted from the FQDN for normal use, but is required for DNS configuration files. The *com* portion is, in this example, the highest subdomain under the root domain, indicating a commercially assigned name.

In our example (Figure 12.6), we have used a real company name and registered domain name of *EntCert.com*. Enterprise Certified is a private corporation that requested allocation of this subdomain name from the Network Information Center. The *host* portion is a host within the *EntCert* subdomain that is assigned an IP address for one of its network interfaces. This fully qualified host name can be used to reference this IP address by accessing a domain name server.

Understanding DNS

The DNS system is composed of clients and servers. DNS servers maintain forward and reverse records for their zones. The forward lookup zone is used to find the IP address of a host using an FQDN; the reverse lookup zone does just the opposite and uses an IP address to locate the subject's FQDN. A configured DNS client maintains the IP address of the DNS server for its zone. When the client attempts to resolve a fully qualified name it checks three sources:

- Local cache obtained from previous queries. These entries are valid for the Time To Live (TTL) period defined in the query response.

- *Lmhosts,* or host files containing host-name-to-address mappings that remain on the hard disk when the client is shut down.

- DNS server

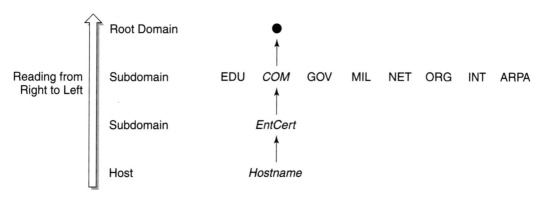

FIGURE 12.6 The DNS Hierarchy

Once the client has attempted to find a locally valid IP address for the sought after host name, it will query its DNS server. The server attempts to resolve the client's query using several strategies:

- If the query result is found in the local DNS zone, the server is supporting the host and can respond with an authoritative answer.
- If the result is not found in the local zone, the server references its local cache for a recent query containing the desired name mapping.
- If the local resources fail to provide the needed mapping, the DNS server will, depending on its configuration,

  –Perform a recursive search for client's query.

  –Forward the query to another DNS server to perform a recursive search.

  –Refer another DNS server to client's query and let the client perform a recursive search.

DNS RECURSION

A recursively configured DNS server accepts queries from a client and follows referrals, using the DNS hierarchy, to resolve the client's request. It does so by sending an iterative request to the root "." DNS server. (An *iterative* request instructs a server to provide a best guess or referral to another server when the query is not known.) The root server then refers the local DNS server to the next authoritative name server in the query's namespace. For example, in order to resolve the FQDN name *host.Entcert.com* from the "clientcompanydomain.com," the client company's local DNS server will query the "." root DNS server and be referred to the ".com." DNS server (Figure 12.7). Since a record exists for the ".com" server in the "." (root) server's database, its response is considered authoritative. The local DNS server queries the "com." DNS server and is referred to the "EntCert.com." DNS server. This server offers an authoritative query response and returns the *host.EntCert.com* name-to-IP-address mapping to the local DNS server. The client company's DNS server then returns the response to the client. The client uses the IP address to establish a connection with the remote server.

STANDARD VERSUS DIRECTORY INTEGRATED ZONES

The Windows 2000 DNS server may store zone information in two distinct formats: Active Directory integrated and standard zone format as a text file. Active Directory integrated is available when you install the DNS server along with the Active Directory. When this option is installed on a domain controller, the DNS information is updated between other DNS servers on domain controllers using the Active Directory's multi-master update techniques. Secondary zones (used with the standard

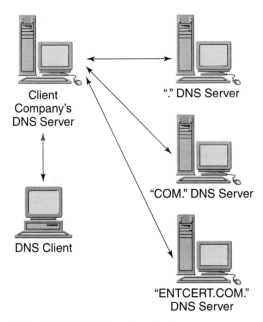

Client
Company's
DNS Server

"." DNS Server

DNS Client

"COM." DNS Server

"ENTCERT.COM."
DNS Server

FIGURE 12.7 DNS Name Resolution

zone format to back up DNS information and offload client queries) are supported but not required with Active Directory integrated DNS server zones. Any additional domain controllers installed with the Active Directory integrated DNS server will also act as a primary source for the zone.

In order to back up or offload client requests to one Active Directory integrated server, simply install an Active Directory integrated DNS server on another domain controller. Active Directory replication will ensure that the two servers have equivalent DNS records, so clients may contact any of the domain controllers and receive up-to-date DNS information. Additionally, the Active Directory integrated zones support ACLs to restrict access to the zone container so that a particular client can be prevented from performing dynamic updates. For more on dynamic updates see the DHCP section.

The standard zone format does not support ACLs and requires secondary zones to offload client queries and back up the DNS database. Secondary zones support their own replication strategy, as discussed in the coming sections. The standard zone is stored in a text file in the *%SystemRoot%\system32\dns* folder.

INSTALLATION WITH THE ACTIVE DIRECTORY

Active Directory installation, demonstrated in Chapter 7, requires DNS installation. This example picks up the DNS installation from there. The Active Directory may be fully installed without DNS on the server by referencing another DNS server in the domain. DNS may then be installed at a later date on such a domain controller using the **Configure Your Server** tool.

1. The first wizard configuration window requests the **Full DNS name for new domain:**. Enter a domain name and press the **Next>** button (Figure 12.8).

2. Enter the NetBIOS name for the domain (Figure 12.9). Press the **Next>** button.

3. Use the default **Database location:** and **Log location:** *%SystemRoot%\ NTDS*. Press the **Next>** button.

4. Choose the default **Shared System Volume** folder location *%System-Root%\SYSVOL* and press the **Next>** button.

5. Select **Yes, install and configure DNS on this computer** and press the **Next>** button.

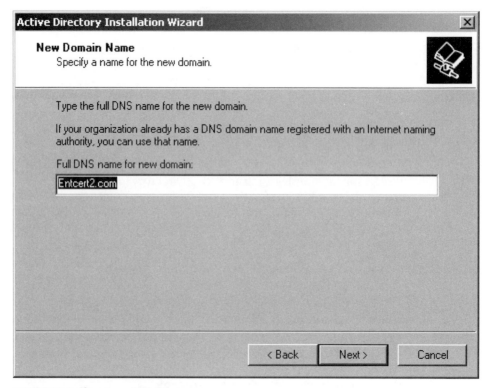

FIGURE 12.8 Choosing a DNS Name

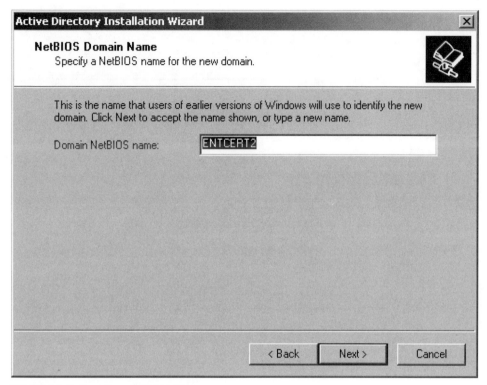

FIGURE 12.9 Choosing a NetBIOS Name

6. Select **Permissions compatible with pre-Windows 2000 servers** to support pre-Windows 2000 applications. Press the **Next>** button.

7. Select a password for the **Directory Services Restore Mode**. Press the **Next>** button.

8. Verify the summary screen and press the **Next>** button.

Once the Active Directory and DNS service have been installed, there are two modifications to make to the domain controller: adding an optional reverse lookup domain and configuring clients to target the new DNS server.

1. Start the DNS tool by selecting **Start → Programs → Administrative Tools → DNS**. Open the newly installed DNS server and view the **Forward** and **Reverse Lookup Zones**.

2. Ensure that the new server is found under the new domain name within the **Forward Lookup Zone**.

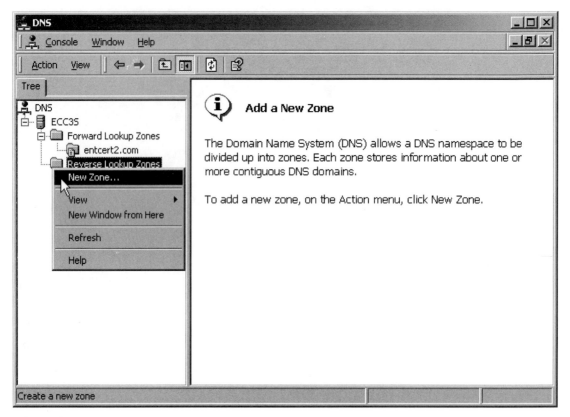

FIGURE 12.10 Creating a New Zone

3. Right-click the **Reverse Lookup Zone** and select **New Zone…** (Figure 12.10). The **New Zone Wizard** should start. Press the **Next>** button.

4. Select the **Active Directory-integrated** radio button. Choose this option so that DNS information will be replicated efficiently (only updating changes) and securely using Active Directory replication (Figure 12.11).

5. Enter the network address for the new zone (Figure 12.12) and press the **Next>** button.

6. Create the new zone by pressing the **Finish** button.

7. Go to the **DNS** tool and view the contents of the new **Reverse Lookup Zone**.

8. Right-click the new zone and select **New Pointer…**.

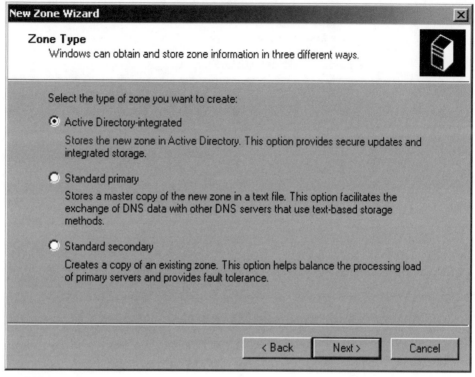

FIGURE 12.11 Zone Type

9. Enter the host portion of the IP address for the newly installed DNS server (Figure 12.13). Press the **Browse...** button and double-click the icons until you reach the new DNS server. Select the server and press the **OK** button.

The new reverse lookup zone should be configured with the new DNS server as the only member. Add new members to both the Forward and Reverse zones by right-clicking the **Forward Lookup Zone** domain folder and selecting **New Host...**. Check the **Create associated pointer (PTR) record** box to simultaneously create the reverse lookup entry (Figure 12.14, page 514). Once the host has been added to the DNS database the host's DNS client must be configured to target the new DNS server.

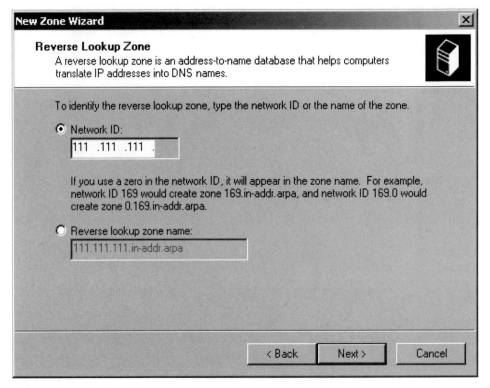

FIGURE 12.12 The Zone Address

CLIENT CONFIGURATION

1. From the new client host select **Start → Settings → Network and Dial-up-Connections** and right-click the interface to handle DNS requests.

2. Select **Properties → Internet Protocol (TCP/IP) → Properties** and enter the new DNS server's IP address in the **Preferred DNS server** field (Figure 12.15).

3. Test the reverse DNS lookup feature by opening a Command Prompt window and typing `nslookup hostname`.

The following should be returned:

```
Server: servername.domainname
Address: xxx.xxx.xxx.xxx

Name: hostname.domainname
Address: xxx.xxx.xxx.xxx
```

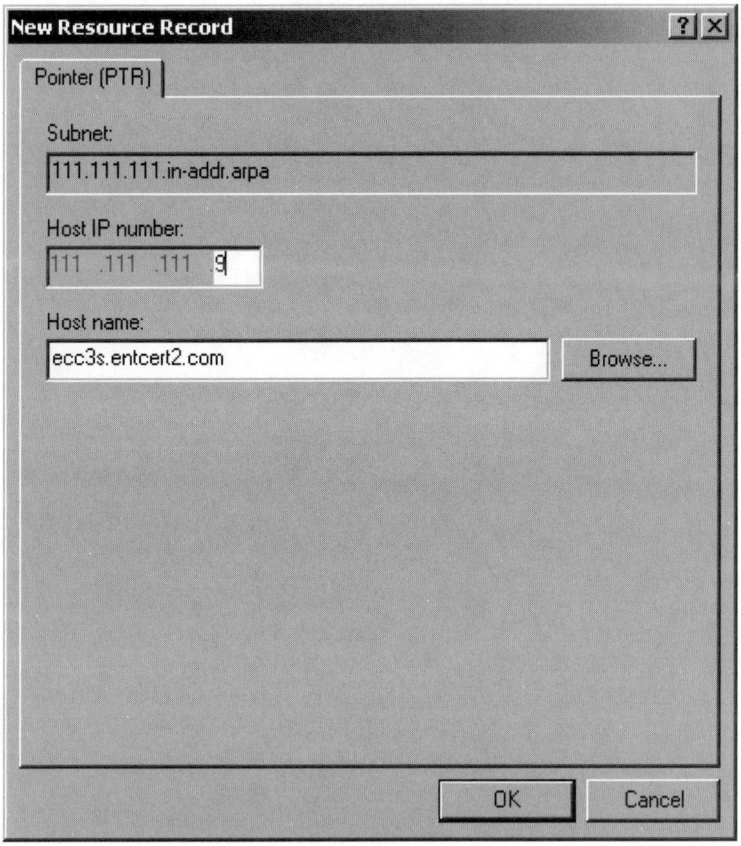

FIGURE 12.13 New Reverse Lookup Zone PTR Record

DNS ZONES AND FAULT TOLERANCE

When the first DNS server is installed to manage a namespace, it is configured as the primary DNS server for the domain. The namespace it maintains defines the server's responsibility. As subdomain names are added below a domain name, new zones may be created to maintain them. These new zones may be configured with new DNS servers to maintain each one's name-to-IP-address mapping information. For example, if the Enterprise Certified Corporation were to extend its namespace with new branches such as *Engineering* and *Marketing*, administration of the new branches could be delegated to new zones and respective servers. The *Engineering.EntCert.com* and *Marketing.EntCert.com* domain names could be used to define the two new zones, which would have their own databases to maintain IP addresses mapped in their namespaces (Figure 12.16).

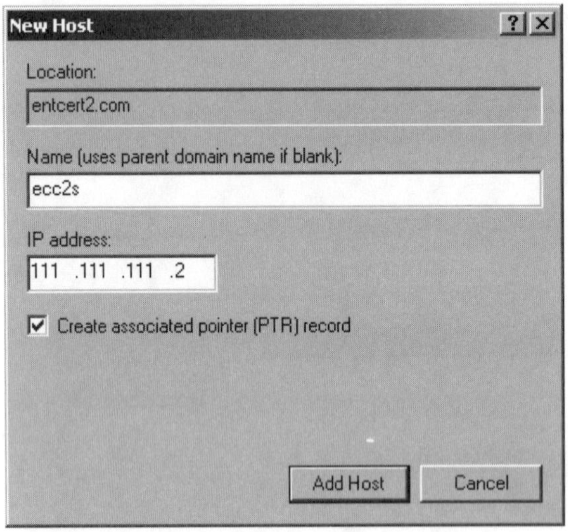

FIGURE 12.14 A New Host Record

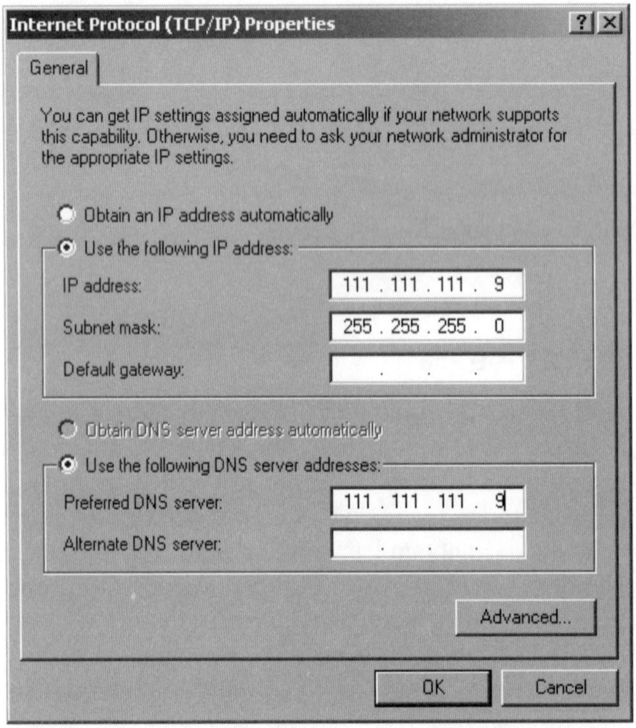

FIGURE 12.15 Choosing the DNS Server's IP Address

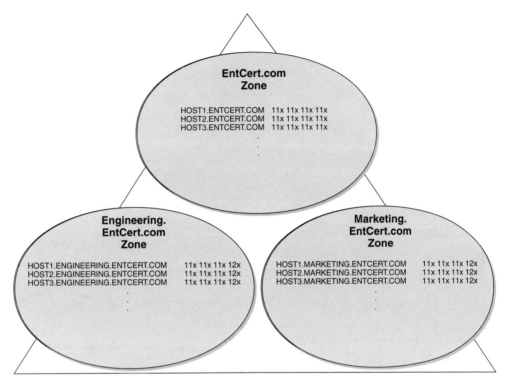

FIGURE 12.16 Individual DNS Zone Databases

Replication

Each zone may set up secondary servers to back up the primary server in the event of failure. The secondary server synchronizes its own DNS database by sending update requests to its master server, which may be the primary DNS server for the domain or another secondary server (Figure 12.17). The secondary server update request may be for either an incremental or an all-zones transfer. A brand-new secondary server will request an all-zones transfer to completely update its database. After initialization the secondary server initiates only incremental transfers, which only convey zone changes to the database, cutting down on network traffic and system resource use. A zone transfer is initiated for several reasons:

NOTE   This is only required when implementing standard zone DNS servers. Active Directory integrated zones are backed up when more than one DNS server exists in a zone. Multi-master replication between the Active Directory integrated DNS servers automatically supports updates between domain controllers and supports fault tolerance.

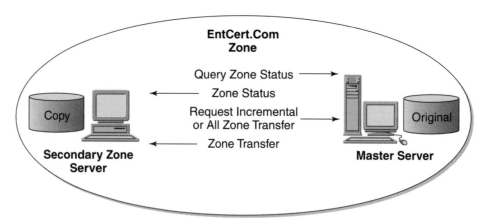

FIGURE 12.17 Replication within Zones

1. The secondary server's refresh timer expires (default one hour).
2. The master server notifies members of a zone change.
3. The secondary DNS service is started (either boot-up or installation).
4. A zone transfer is manually initiated from a DNS snap-in for a secondary server.

Secondary DNS Server Management

The secondary DNS server installation is similar to the primary installation. Here are the steps required:

1. Install the Windows 2000 DNS server from the **Start → Programs → Administrative Tools → Configure Your Server** tool. You will find it under the **Networking → DNS** pull-down menu. Start the **Windows Components Wizard** and select **Networking Services**. Press the **Details...** button to bring up subcomponents for networking services. Checkmark the **Domain Name System** (**DNS**) selection and press the **OK** button.

2. Once the Windows 2000 DNS server components have been installed, open the **DNS** snap-in tool from the new DNS server. Any other DNS server can be managed from one system's **DNS** snap-in by right-clicking the DNS node and selecting **Connect To Computer...**. Enter the name of the desired server to administrate and press the **OK** button. The new server should appear as a new node under the **DNS** node.

3. Right-click the **Forward Lookup Zones** node and select **New Zone...**. Press the **Next>** button to start the **New Zone Wizard**.

4. Select the **Standard secondary** radio button option and press the **Next>** button (Figure 12.18).

5. Select the **Forward Lookup zone** radio button option and press the **Next>** button.

6. Enter the name of the DNS zone the secondary server is supporting and press the **Next>** button.

7. Enter the IP address of the new secondary DNS server's master. A full DNS database transfer will be performed from the master server (Figure 12.19). Press the **Add** button and press the **Next>** button. Press the **Finish** button to complete the secondary zone creation.

The finished forward lookup zones defined on the master DNS server should be replicated on the secondary DNS server. The easiest visual way to identify the newly created secondary zone is to right-click on the new zone and select **Properties**. From the **General** tab the **Type:** field should read **Secondary** (Figure 12.20).

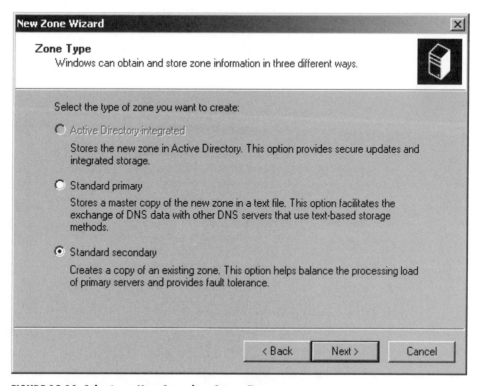

FIGURE 12.18 Selecting a New Secondary Server Zone

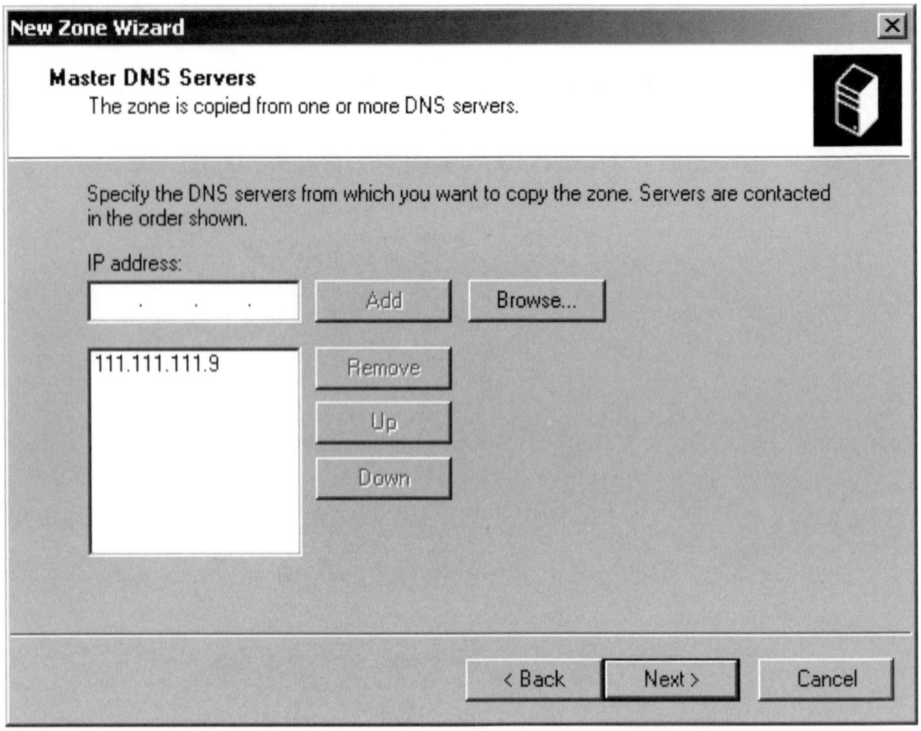

FIGURE 12.19 Configuring Master DNS Server(s) for a Secondary DNS Server

Notification

Secondary DNS servers must initiate the replication sequence to maintain current record sets. DNS notification, as defined by RFC 1996, allows master DNS servers to inform secondary servers that updates have been made to the current DNS database. Once the secondary servers receive this notification, they may request zone transfers. Notification is available to primary DNS servers and may be configured as follows:

1. Right-click on a primary zone and select **Properties**.
2. Select the **Zone Transfers** tab and press the **Notify...** button.
3. Ensure that the **Automatically notify** field is checkmarked.
4. Configure a notification list in either of the following ways (Figure 12.21):
   – Select the **Servers listed on the Name Servers** tab option and add servers requiring notification to the **Name Servers** tab.
   – Select **The following servers** option and add IP addresses to this local list.

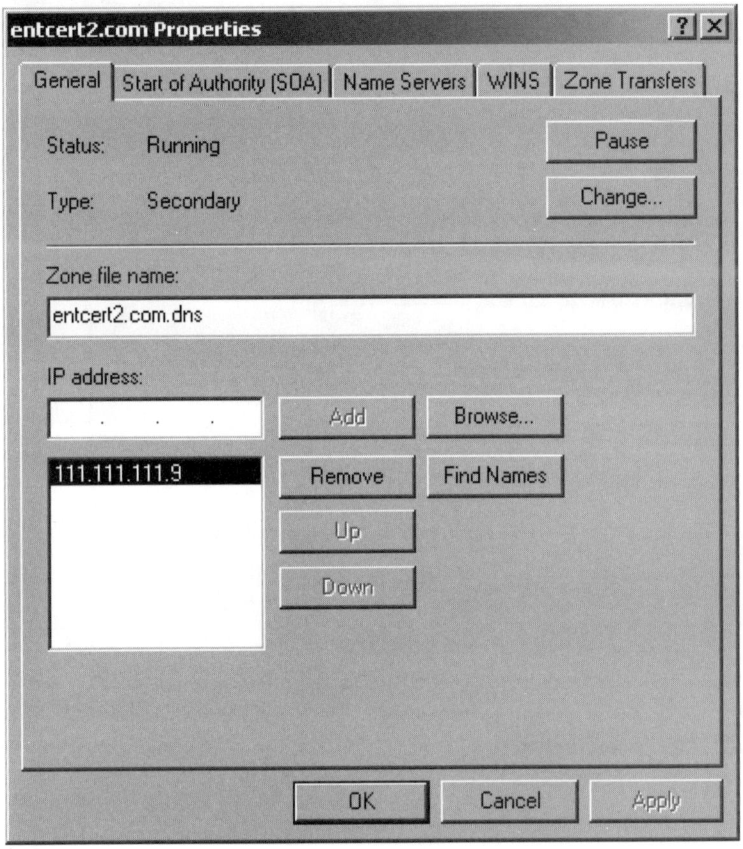

FIGURE 12.20 Forward Lookup Zone Properties

NOTE   Active Directory integrated zones do not require notification.

Both methods allow notifications to be designated to specific servers. The **Zone Transfers** tab (Figure 12.22) also permits zone transfer restrictions to limit which DNS servers may be allowed to request zone transfers. Not only will the specified servers receive notification of current record updates, but they also can be set as the only servers permitted to make transfer requests.

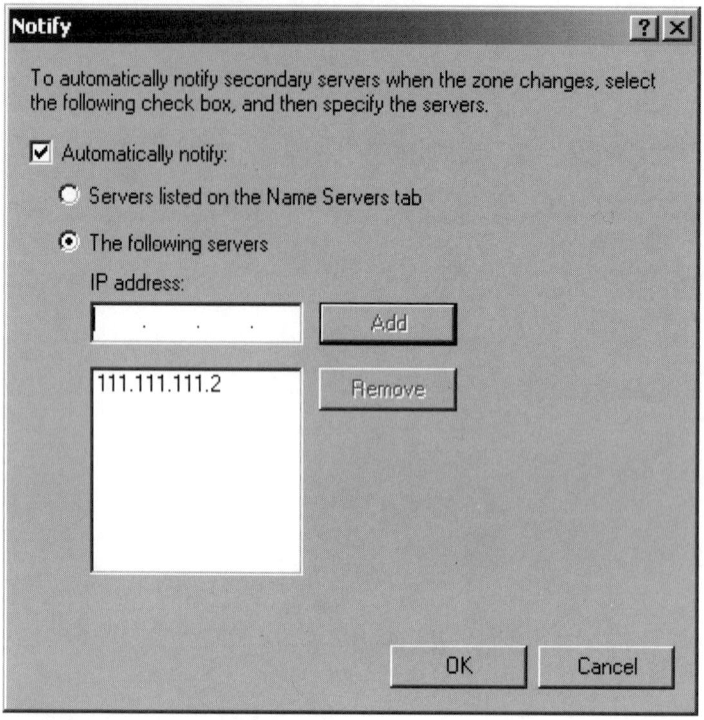

FIGURE 12.21 A Notification List

NOTE   To instigate a manual zone transfer at the secondary server, right-click the zone to transfer from the **DNS** snap-in and select **Transfer from master**.

FORWARDING

Because the recursive search creates network traffic and consumes system resources, forwarding allows one DNS server to forward name queries to another DNS server. Thus, a network may offload name resolution responsibility to a particular server or set of servers with high bandwidth to the Internet, limiting intensive searches over slow or expensive connections. When requests are forwarded to one server, the system's cache becomes more extensive, enhancing its ability to resolve name queries locally. Ideally a company's ISP can provide a target for the network's forwarding DNS name server and offload name query resolution to the Internet.

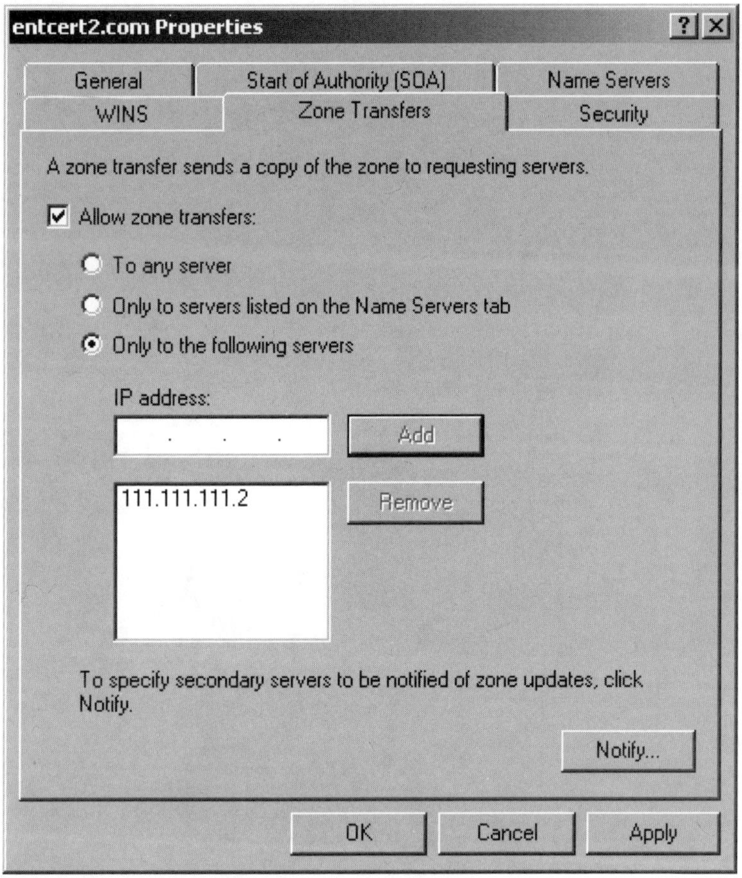

FIGURE 12.22 Restricting DNS Zone Transfers

To forward a DNS server's name queries to another server, follow these steps:

1. Right-click the DNS server node from the **DNS** snap-in and select **Properties**.

2. Select the **Forwarders** tab and checkmark the **Enable forwarders** box. Put the IP address of the designated forwarder in an IP address field and press the **Add** button (Figure 12.23).

The forward time-out specifies how long the DNS server will wait for a response from the designated forwarder. If this forwarder does not respond, the server will try the next one on the list. For a forwarder to be attempted more than once, its IP address must be entered in the list multiple times. Once this list has been

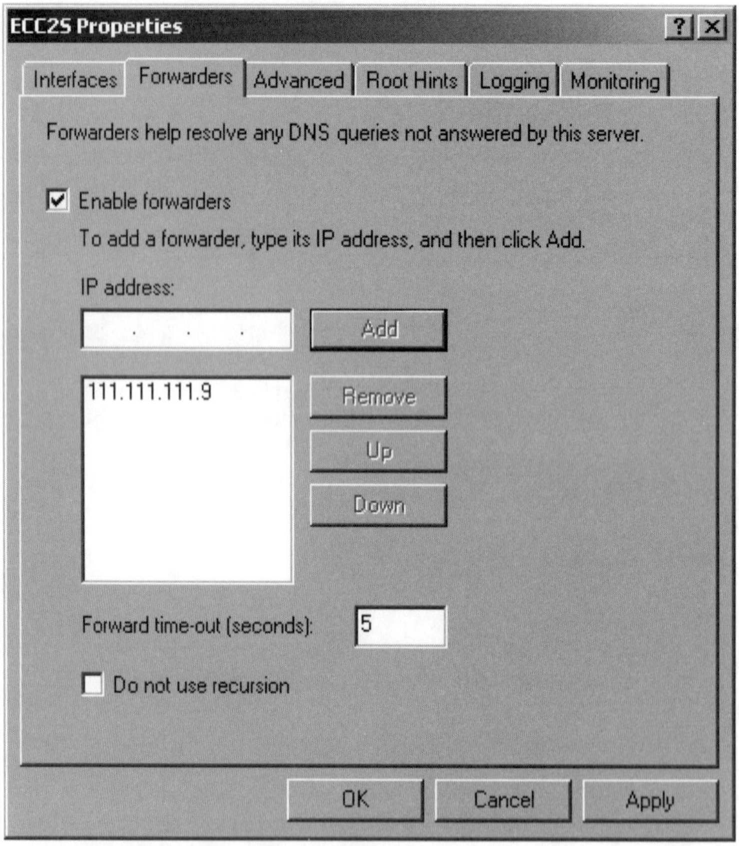

FIGURE 12.23 DNS Forwarder Properties

depleted, with no resolution, the server will attempt to resolve the query using recursion. To prevent this select the **Do not use recursion** field. The server returns a failed name query when the forwarder list is depleted.

SCAVENGING

The Windows 2000 DNS server can scavenge zones and remove outdated DNS records. By default this feature is disabled and may involve careful planning to ensure that valid resource records are not removed. Scavenging can eliminate incorrect resource records, save on disk space, and increase performance. It may be initiated manually or configured to run automatically. Statically configured resource records are configured by default to have a refresh time of zero, which removes them from the scavenging process. Dynamically configured resource records, established through DHCP, are configured with a non-zero timestamp that exposes them to scavenging.

NOTE   Configuring scavenging can be complex, so see the **Help** pages for further explanation before enabling it.

Initiating Manual Scavenging

Manually initiate scavenging by right-clicking the DNS server from the **DNS** snap-in and selecting the **Scavenge stale resource records** option to scavenge.

Initiating Automatic Scavenging

Configure automatic scavenging by following these steps:

1. Right-click the DNS server from the **DNS** snap-in and select **Properties**. Choose the **Advanced** tab and checkmark the **Enable automatic scavenging of stale records** box.

2. Scavenging must be enabled at the zone node in addition to the server node. Right-click the desired zone and select **Properties**. Select the **General** tab and press the **Aging...** button. Checkmark the **Scavenge stale resource records** box.

A DNS server is required for all Active Directory implementations. The mapping between FQDNs and their respective IP addresses can be in constant flux. Windows 2000 offers two DNS implementations, the Active Directory integrated and Standard zone DNS server, which both support dynamic DNS updates. The following section describes how these features can be fully maximized.

The Dynamic Host Configuration Protocol

The Dynamic Host Configuration Protocol (DHCP) provides a convenient and centralized method to configure and assign IP addresses on systems throughout the network. Once that is done the entire network may be configured to retrieve and renew these addresses whenever they boot to ensure correct IP configuration for the current network. This is especially useful for mobile users and dial-in clients. Let's look at some of the basic DHCP server installation and configuration issues.

SERVER-SIDE DHCP CONFIGURATIONS

To install the DHCP server, follow these steps:

1. Ensure that the DHCP server system is configured with a static IP address. Clients must be configured with a DHCP server address to obtain an IP address (and other information) when booting.

2. From the **Start → Administrative Tools → Configure Your Server** tool select the **Networking** pull-down menu and select **DHCP**.

3. Press the **Start Windows Components Wizard** button. Highlight the **Network Services** option and press the **Details...** button.

4. When the **Networking Services** Details window appears, checkmark the **Dynamic Host Configuration Protocol** (**DHCP**) box and press the **OK** button and the **Next>** button.

5. Bring up the DHCP tool by selecting **Start → Program → Administrative Tools → DHCP** (Figure 12.24).

DHCP Authorization

DHCP servers may be installed on domain controllers, member servers, or standalone servers. However, the first DHCP server must participate in the Active Directory and it must be a member server or domain controller. The Active Directory maintains a list of authorized DHCP servers, which a DHCP server participating in the domain can query. If the server finds itself in the list, it will provide DHCP services. If it does not, it will not initialize or provide services. A standalone server does not participate with the directory service and depends on the limited broadcast DHCP informational message on the local network to invoke responses from

FIGURE 12.24 The DHCP Snap-In

functional DHCP servers. These DHCP responses will contain the enterprise root for each DHCP server, which the standalone server queries to obtain the DHCP authorization list for the directory. If it finds its IP address in each list, it will proceed with initialization. Otherwise the service is stopped.

To authorize a DHCP server for the Active Directory, follow these steps:

1. Open the DHCP tool by adding the snap-in or select **Start** → **Programs** → **Administrative Tools** → **DHCP**.

2. Right-click the DHCP node and select **Manage authorized servers…**.

3. The **Manage Authorized Servers** dialog appears (Figure 12.25). Press the **Authorize** button and enter the DHCP server's DNS name or an IP address. Preferably enter the FQDN name or the **Name** field will remain empty. Press the **OK** button.

4. Answer **Yes** to the following dialogs. The DHCP server has been authorized for the domain.

Scopes and Classes

Once the DHCP server has been authorized for the domain, scopes must be created to define IP addresses and lease durations for its clients. The scope will be applied to all clients requesting dynamically assigned IP addresses within its subnet and will also determine several other client properties:

- Address range
- Address exclusion ranges

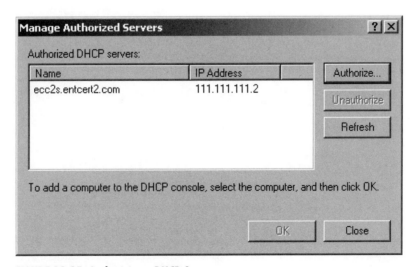

FIGURE 12.25 Authorizing a DHCP Server

- Lease duration
- DHCP options
- Reservations
- Classes

Let's look at these properties as we create a scope for the new DHCP server:

1. Right-click on the DHCP server within the **DHCP** snap-in and select **New Scope...**. The **New Scope Wizard** appears. Press the **Next>** button to start scope creation.

2. Enter a name and description for the new scope and press the **Next>** button.

3. Enter a contiguous address range for the new scope by entering a **Start IP address** and an **End IP address** (Figure 12.26). This address range defines the pool of available IP addresses for DHCP clients requesting them. Always assign the entire range of IP addresses to be used for the subnet and then use exclusion ranges to remove addresses from the available pool.

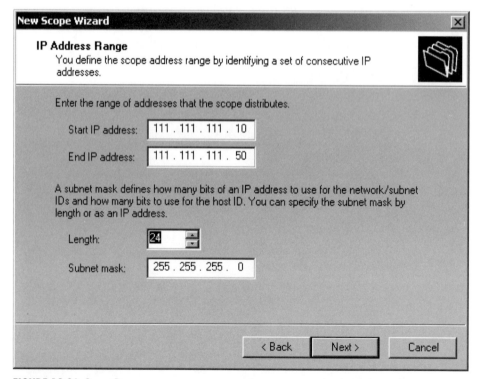

FIGURE 12.26 Scope Range

4. The subnet mask identifies which bits of the IP address identify the network or subnet address. If the subnet mask bits are contiguous, you may use the **Length:** field to define how many bits there are from left to right. Press the **Next>** button.

5. Add exclusion ranges to remove IP addresses from the available pool to lease DHCP clients. All IP addresses that have been statically configured for network interfaces should be excluded from the scope address range. Obviously, router addresses and the DHCP server's statically configured IP address should be excluded as well. Enter beginning and ending addresses and press the **Add** button to create an exclusion range (Figure 12.27). When finished press the **Next>** button.

6. Enter a time interval for the duration of a DHCP client's lease of the IP address before it expires. Laptop and remote clients that regularly move networks should be assigned shorter lease periods to free up available addresses sooner. More stable networks may benefit from longer lease periods (Figure 12.28).

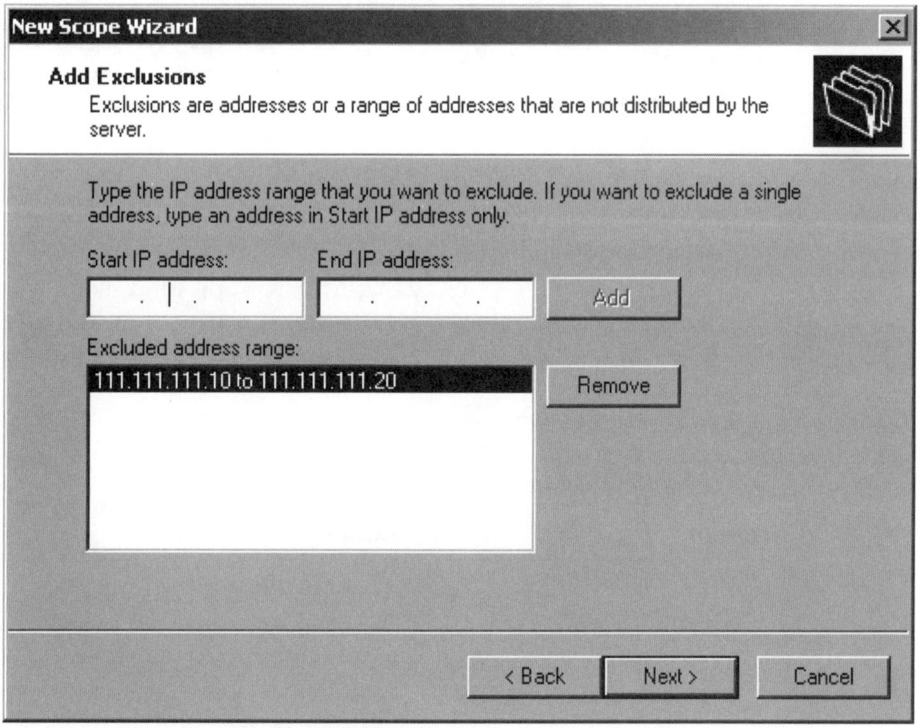

FIGURE 12.27 An Excluded Address Range

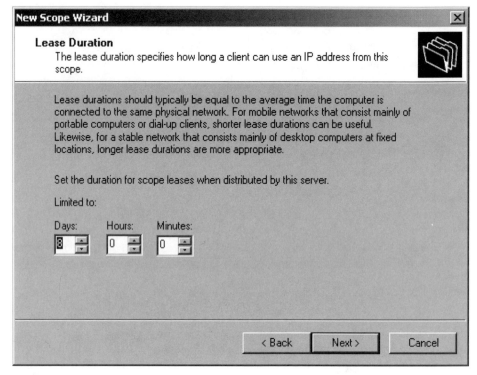

FIGURE 12.28 Lease Duration

7. The next wizard dialog allows you to configure DHCP options. Although many DHCP options are provided by the DHCP server and detailed in the DHCP standards document RFC 2132, five are supported by all Windows and MS-DOS client systems. Selecting the **Yes, I want to configure these options now** radio button permits configuration of the options listed in Table 12.1.

TABLE 12.1 DHCP Options

Option	Description
Router	List of available routers in order of preference
DNS Server	List of available DNS servers in order of preference
DNS Domain Name	Parent domain for client name resolution
WINS Server	List of available WINS servers in order of preference
NetBIOS Node Type	Mechanism for NetBIOS name resolution

8. Follow the next four screens and configure the DHCP options for clients leasing in the new scope.

9. When you reach the **Activate Scope** dialog windows (Figure 12.29) you may choose to activate the scope and start DHCP service for it. Press the **Finish** button on the last dialog to complete scope creation.

The **DHCP** tool should display the newly activated scope from under the server's node (Figure 12.30). The previously configured parameters may be further viewed and modified from here. Table 12.2 details the containers within a scope's node.

Each of the subcategories within the DHCP scope may be modified by right-clicking on the desired node and selecting an action. For example, the exclusion ranges are added to the address pool by right-clicking the **Address Pool** node and selecting **New Exclusion Range...**.

Reservations for clients are made by right-clicking **Reservations** and selecting **New Reservation...**. The **New Reservations** dialog appears and requests a

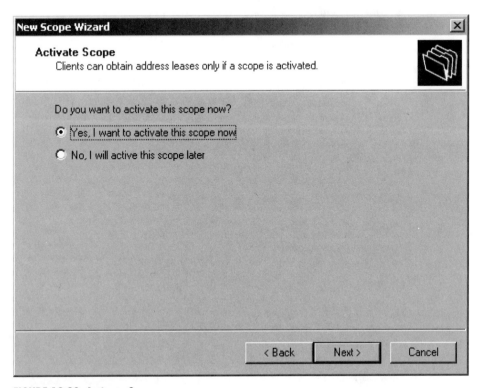

FIGURE 12.29 Activate Scope

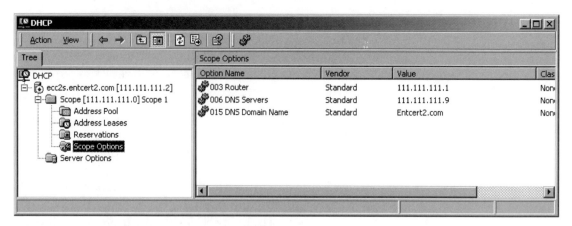

FIGURE 12.30 Scope Configuration from the DHCP Snap-In Tool

reservation name, IP address, and MAC address (Figure 12.31). The DHCP server may also selectively reserve IP addresses for DHCP, BOOTP, or both. When it receives a DHCP request message from a client with a source MAC address matching a reservation, it assigns the reserved IP address to the client's lease.

The DHCP options may be modified by right-clicking the **Scope Options** node and selecting **Configure Options…**. In the **General** tab of the **Scope Options** dialog box options with a checkmark will be sent to DHCP clients and may be configured by modifying their **Data entry** fields. The **Advanced** tab of the **Scope Options** dialog box presents several more opportunities to configure options for DHCP server clients (Figure 12.32).

TABLE 12.2 DHCP Configuration Options

Scope Configuration	Description
Address Pool	Displays address and exclusion ranges for the scope. Exclusion ranges may be added to and deleted from the scope.
Address Leases	Displays leases currently in use and their expiration dates.
Reservations	Reserves IP addresses for clients that require the same IP address every time they boot.
Scope Options	Display and modify DHCP options.

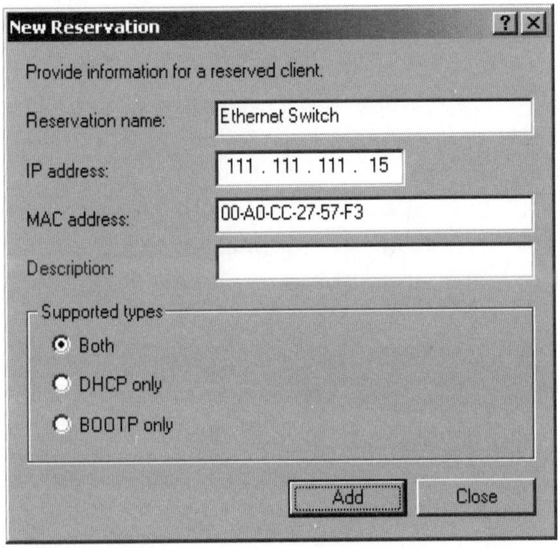

FIGURE 12.31 A Reserved IP Address

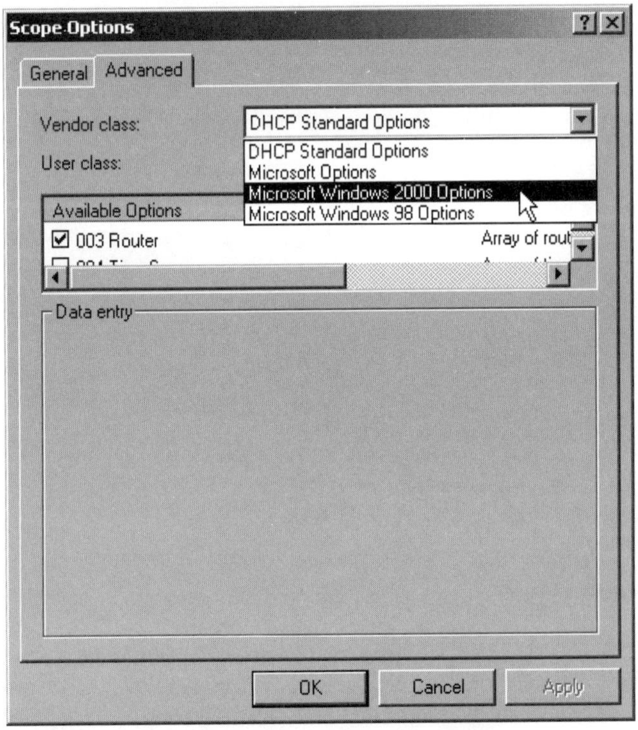

FIGURE 12.32 Advanced DHCP Option Configuration

VENDOR AND USER CLASSES

Vendor and user classes allow different DHCP options to be applied to different systems and users. The DHCP server will map the client's vendor class ID from the DHCP request message to the configured vendor class list. The administrator can customize DHCP options for each vendor class. The vendor ID is configured internally only in the DHCP client software and set by the software manufacturer. For example, the Microsoft Windows 98 vendor class is set on Windows 98 clients and may not be modified. The administrator may point all Windows 98 clients to a certain DNS server, using the vendor class to set the DNS server option.

NOTE   The Windows 2000 vendor class offers the following additional DHCP options to configure clients:

- Disable NetBIOS on a Windows 2000 client.
- Configure the system to release a DHCP lease upon shutdown.
- Define a default router metric for establishing the quickest and most reliable routes.

User classes, on the other hand, may be configured on the client using the *ipconfig* line command. From the **Command Prompt** on the client system, type

```
C:\>ipconfig /setclassid "Local Area Connection" "Second Floor Users"
```

The following should be displayed:

```
Windows 2000 IP Configuration
DHCP ClassId successfully modified for adapter "Local Area Connection"
```

When the DHCP server is sent the DHCP request message by the client, it will look for a user class identified by the "Second Floor Users" ASCII string.

To create the corresponding user class on the DHCP server:

1. Right-click on the corresponding DHCP server name from the **DHCP** snap-in. Select the **Define User Classes...** option.
2. The current user classes are displayed in the **DHCP User Classes** dialog box. Press the **Add...** button to reveal the **New Class** dialog box (Figure 12.33).
3. Enter a name and description for the new user class. Enter the user class ID as either a text string in the **ASCII:** field or a hexadecimal number in the **Binary:** field. Press the **OK** button.

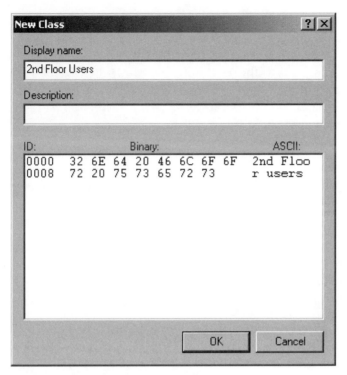

FIGURE 12.33 Creating a New User Class

4. The new User Class has been created. Right-click on the **Scope Options** node on the server with the new user class and select **Configure Options...**.

5. Select the **Advanced** tab and press the pull-down arrow for the **User Class:** field.

6. Select the new user class and check DHCP options under the **Available Options:** field and configure them using the **Data entry** field.

All clients requesting DHCP leases from this DHCP server, configured with the "Second Floor Users" class ID, will receive only DHCP options assigned to this user class.

SUPERSCOPES

The DHCP server must be configured and scoped with IP addresses for all subnets it intends to support. If a server receives a request from a subnet other than its pool of addresses, it cannot lease a meaningful IP address to the client. A DHCP server can be configured to support multiple logical IP networks within one physical subnet. In order to support multiple IP network ranges on the same Ethernet segment, a scope must be created for each network and then all scopes must be grouped together under one *superscope*. The superscope allows one or more scopes to be applied to the local network. Also, when DHCP relays or BOOTP relays are supported, their corresponding requests will be forwarded through IP layer switches and routers. Because the DHCP server will be receiving requests from other networks, superscopes will need to be configured.

To create a superscope, follow these steps:

1. Right-click on the DHCP server node from the **DHCP** snap-in and select **New Superscope…**. The **New Superscope Wizard** starts up. Press the **Next>** button.

2. Enter a name for the new superscope and press the **Next>** button.

3. Select the scopes to include in the new superscope from the **Available Scopes:** field. To select more than one scope, hold down the *Shift* key and click multiple scopes. Press the **Next>** button.

4. Press the **Finish** button to complete the wizard.

The new superscope, *Super Scope 1,* contains *Scope 1* and *Scope 2* and can now service clients requesting addresses for both networks 111.111.111 and 111.111.112 (Figure 12.34). See the Help pages for further superscope configurations.

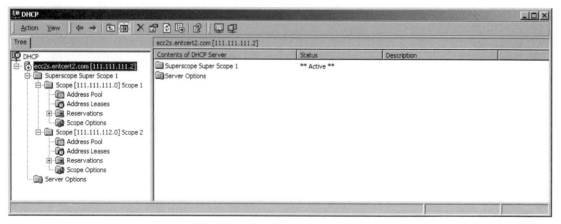

FIGURE 12.34 The Superscope Viewed from the DHCP Snap-In (Supporting Two Networks)

DHCP AND BOOTP RELAY AGENTS

Both DHCP and BOOTP clients use broadcast addressing to initiate contact with their corresponding server. Routers do not normally permit this broadcast traffic to traverse networks by default, which means that a DHCP/BOOTP server must be allocated for every network in the enterprise, unless routers are configured as DHCP/BOOTP Relay Agents. Most routers can be configured in accordance with RFC 1542 and forward DHCP and BOOTP packets between network interfaces. Another option is to configure a dual-homed Windows 2000 server with the DHCP Relay Agent. This server will then forward DHCP and BOOTP requests between the two networks. The DHCP Relay Agent must also be configured for dial-in/remote access clients. See the Remote Access section for details.

THE 80/20 RULE FOR FAULT TOLERANCE

Fault tolerance is most effectively handled by configuring two DHCP servers to lease IP addresses on a given network. One server is configured with 20 percent of the address range; the other is configured with the remaining 80 percent. For instance, to service the 111.111.111.0 network with two DHCP servers the first server would be scoped with 80 percent of the address range:

```
Scope range:   111.111.111.5 - 111.111.111.254
Excluding:     111.111.111.204 - 111.111.111.254
```

The second server would be scoped with 20 percent of the address range:

```
Scope range:   111.111.111.5 - 111.111.111.254
Excluding:     111.111.111.5 - 111.111.111.203
```

If one of the servers were to fail, the other could renew and issue leases for the network.

Another option is to configure a second, standby server the same as the currently active server. The scopes on the secondary server would remain inactive until the primary server failed. Then they could be manually activated to handle client requests.

CLIENT-SIDE CONFIGURATIONS

Configure DHCP on the Windows 2000 client system for a network or dial-up connection by Selecting **Start** → **Settings** → **Network and Dial-up Connections** → *connection name* and pressing the **Properties** button. Select **Internet Protocol (TCP/IP)** and press the **Properties** button. Select the **Obtain an IP address automatically** and the **Obtain DNS server address automatically** options (Figure 12.35).

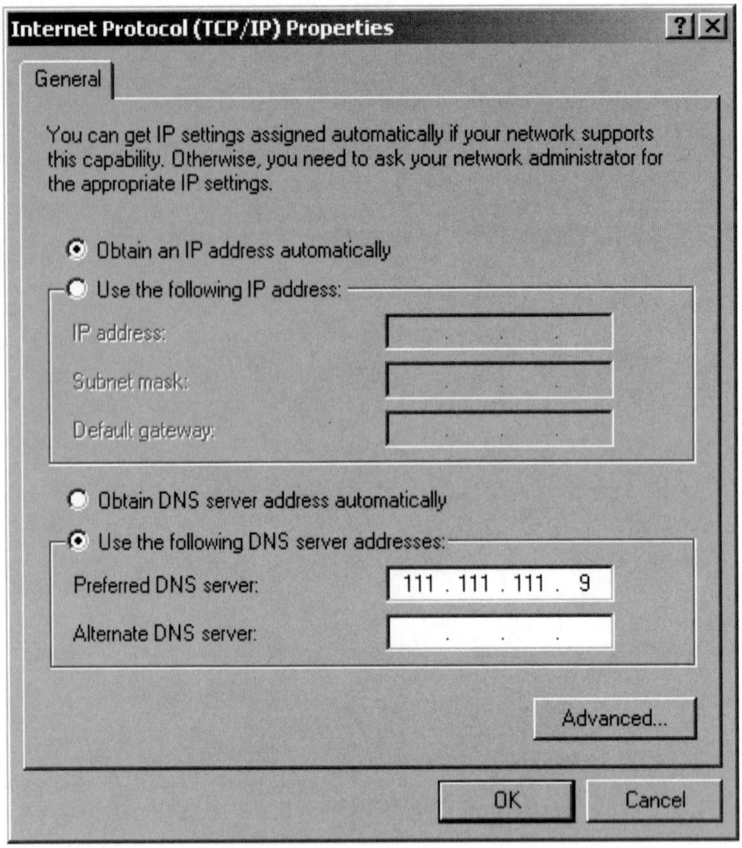

FIGURE 12.35 Configuring a Client for DHCP

Automatic Client Configuration

Windows 2000 DHCP clients automatically configure network interfaces when a DHCP server is unavailable. When a client boots up and cannot obtain a response from a DHCP server, it will be configured to boot with an IP address from the Microsoft Class B range 169.254.0.0 with the subnet 255.255.0.0. Automatic client configuration works well for small business and home networks. An ARP request will be used to test if another client on the network is using the selected IP address. If so, the client will continue to search for an available DHCP server every five minutes. When one is found, a new IP address is leased, with which the client silently reconfigures the interface. Automatic client configuration also comes into play when the client owns a validly leased IP address and cannot communicate with the DHCP server. The client will ping the default gateway assigned in the original lease. If the router responds, the client assumes it is on the same IP network, has not been moved, and continues to use the previously leased IP address. If no router responds to the request, the client assumes it has been moved off the network and chooses an IP address from the auto-configuration network range (169.254.0.0).

Client/Server Communication

To understand how DHCP works, it's important to discuss the basic message exchange between client and server. The client approaches the DHCP server according to two scenarios: (1) it is new to a network or its leased IP address has expired, or (2) it is renewing a currently leased IP address.

- In the first scenario (Figure 12.36), the client broadcasts a DHCP discovery message on the local segment/ring for a DHCP server. If the DHCP server responds with a DHCP offer message, the client obtains a new lease. If not, the client can auto-configure itself or continue to send DHCP server requests every five minutes. Eventually the client will receive the DHCP offer message and choose to accept the lease by returning a DHCP request to the server. The server sends the client a DHCP acknowledgment message to confirm the lease along with DHCP option configuration information.

- The second scenario involves DHCP renewal. The client usually waits until the IP address lease's lifetime is 50 percent spent. Then it attempts to renew the lease by sending a DHCP request to the server who issued the lease. If the client does not obtain a DHCP acknowledgment from the server, it waits until the lease time reaches the rebinding state. Once this occurs the client will attempt to renew its lease with any DHCP server on the network. Unless another server renews the lease, the client terminates the current IP address and then resorts to the first scenario and attempts to locate a DHCP server with the discovery message.

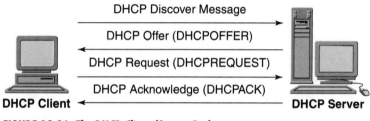

FIGURE 12.36 The DHCP Client/Server Exchange

DNS with DHCP

Domain DNS servers can be updated with dynamically leased IP addresses to support current name/IP address mapping. DHCP servers and clients have several strategies for implementing these DNS entry updates. Configuration on the DHCP client and server determines which one is used.

The Windows 2000 DHCP client supports the Client *Fully Qualified Domain Name* (FQDN) option when communicating with the DHCP server. This allows it to instruct the DHCP on how to handle dynamic DNS updates. The **Register this connection's address in DNS** option is the default for Windows 2000 clients. It is set through the **Local Area Connections Properties** → **TCP/IP** → **Properties** → **Advanced...** → **DNS** tab (Figure 12.37) and instructs the client to send a

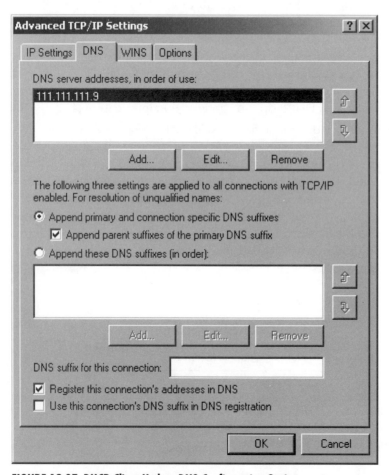

FIGURE 12.37 DHCP Client Update DNS Configuration Options

DNS update request to the primary domain DNS server. This update will contain only the client's forward lookup record ("A" record—hostname-to-IP mapping) update.

DHCP SERVER CONFIGURATION FOR DNS

The DHCP server is capable of updating both forward and reverse lookup zones on the DNS server for DHCP clients. Several DHCP server configuration options are accessible from the **DHCP** tool. To reach them, right-click the DHCP server node and select **Properties**. Then select the **DNS** tab to display dynamic DNS update properties (Figure 12.38).

To prevent the DHCP server from updating any DNS information, clear the **Automatically update DHCP client information in DNS**. Otherwise a choice

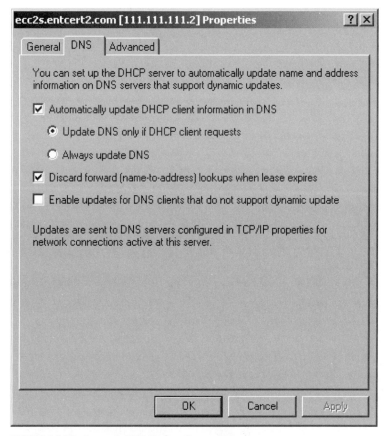

FIGURE 12.38 Dynamic DNS Update Properties

must be made between two options: If the **Update DNS only if DHCP client requests** option is selected, the DHCP will attempt to configure the DNS server according to the client's suggestion; the **Always update DNS** option will configure the DHCP server to always update both the forward and reverse lookup zones on behalf of the client.

Clients that do not support the client FQDN option (non–Windows 2000 DHCP clients) will not update the forward lookup zone and must rely on the DHCP server to handle the DNS update request. Selecting the **Enable updates for DNS clients that do not support dynamic updates** option will configure the DHCP server to do this. Selecting the **Discard forward (name-to-address) lookups when lease expires** checkbox instructs the DHCP server not to send updates for the forward (A) record when leases expire. However, the server will still update the reverse lookup zone as long as automatic DHCP updates are permitted.

NOTE   DHCP servers must be added to the DnsUpdateProxy security group to enable dynamic DNS update. This occurs when the DHCP server is authorized (see the DHCP Authorization section).

THE BACKUP AND RESTORE OPTIONS

If the currently active DHCP server were to crash, many IP addresses would still be leased out to network clients. DHCP server backup is paramount to smooth operation and will help prevent duplicate address leases that might occur without it. Use Windows 2000 Backup and Restore options or use the `netsh set databaserestore` flag to load a copy of the DHCP dbs from the default backup directory. Use logs to determine if the database is corrupt, indicated by JET errors. Initially try using the `Jetpack.exe` to repair the database. If this doesn't work, resort to backups. See the Help pages for moving a DHCP server database to another system.

BOOTP

The BOOTP protocol allows diskless clients to obtain IP addresses and boot image (executable code) locations to download software for operation. The image is then retrieved using the TFTP protocol. The BOOTP sequence is only performed when the client is rebooted. Dynamic BOOTP address assignment is now supported under Windows 2000. To enable this feature right-click a previously created *scope* node and select **Properties**. Select the **Advanced** tab and then the **BOOTP only** or the **Both** option to enable dynamic IP address assignment for both protocols (Figure 12.39). A separate lease duration period available for BOOTP clients

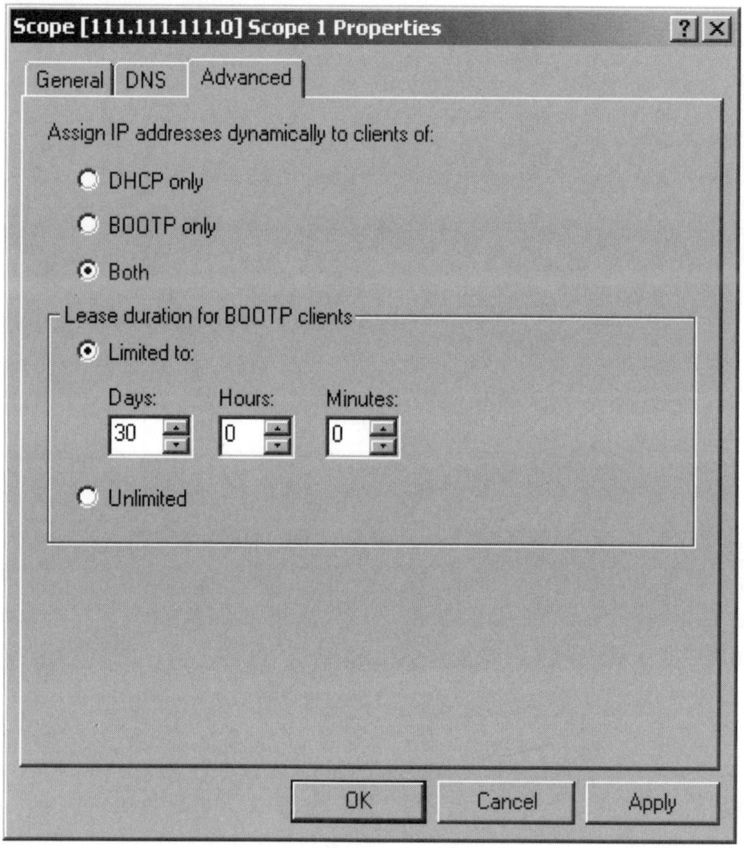

FIGURE 12.39 Scope Properties

is configurable under **Lease duration for BOOTP clients**. The same DHCP options discussed earlier are also sent to the BOOTP clients.

In addition to address assignment, BOOTP clients may request file information. This is accomplished in two steps. First, a reservation is established for a BOOTP client, tying the client's MAC address to a single IP address in the same way that DHCP clients reserve IP addresses. Right-click the **Reservations** node on the appropriate scope and select **New Reservation...**. Assign an IP address, name, and MAC address, and be sure to select the **Both** or **BOOTP only** option (Figure 12.40).

Second, an entry is defined in the **BOOTP Table** from the **DHCP** snap-in. Right-click on the **BOOTP Table** node and select **New Boot Image...**. Enter the image name, directory path, and DNS server name or IP address for the TFTP that hosts the client's boot image (Figure 12.41).

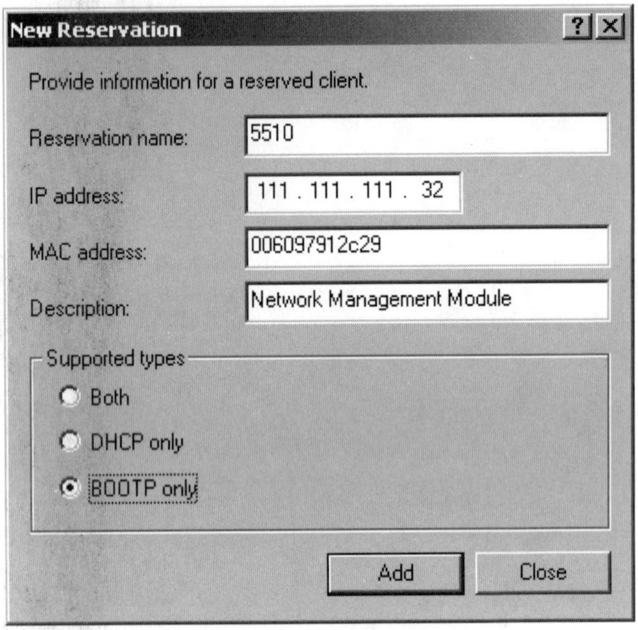

FIGURE 12.40 BOOTP Client IP Reservation

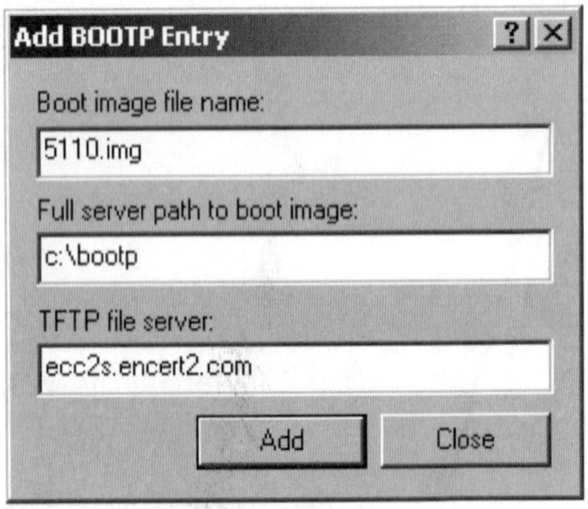

FIGURE 12.41 A BOOTP Table Entry

The BOOTP client communicates to the file server using the Trivial File Transfer Protocol (TFTP) to retrieve code and continue booting. Current client images can easily be distributed throughout the network using BOOTP.

WINS

The Microsoft implementation for the Windows Internet Name Service (WINS) provides services similar to those of the DNS server earlier discussed. The WINS server maps NetBIOS names to IP addresses. This is required for legacy systems that do not support the DNS FQDN format. The new WINS server supports dynamic updates for IP addresses assigned via the DHCP server. Also, it has no need for troublesome IP broadcasts for inter-network updates. WINS is not the preferred name server; DNS integration with the Active Directory is the primary name resolution model.

POSTSCRIPT

The first part of this chapter provided a view of networking protocols and models from a very high level. Hopefully, this conceptual view will give new system administrators a construct from which to work. The second part provided hands-on guides primarily for the installation, configuration, and management of DNS and DHCP. DNS and the Active Directory are closely connected; thus, the two should be viewed collectively in administering a Windows 2000 domain.

13

Virtual Private Networks and IP Security

Virtual Private Networks (VPNs) are rapidly becoming the method by which organizations with remote offices can utilize the Internet with relatively secure communications. IPSecurity (IPSec) secures intranets and is the primary method of securing L2TP tunnels, and it can also interoperate with tunneling devices that only support its tunneling standard.

Many of the technologies that underlie VPN and IPSec are covered in other chapters, and so we will not begin with a heavy dose of theory. Instead, most of this chapter provides a hands-on description of how these technologies are deployed.

In this chapter you will learn the concepts relating to VPN authentication, encryption, and tunneling. Examples are also provided for creating a Virtual Private Network. IPSec is then explored as both a complementary and alternative technology to VPN.

VIRTUAL PRIVATE NETWORKS

A Virtual Private Network is a connection between two communication endpoints that ensures privacy and authentication. A *tunnel* coupled with *encryption* creates a "virtual private network" between an organization's central network and its branch offices or dial-in users. Thus, these offices and dial-in users may interconnect through the Internet's infrastructure without being subject to unauthorized snooping and impersonation. VPN technology establishes a Wide Area Network (WAN) between sites that allows a user to log on to the network from one location and access company resources throughout the "virtual network." Connecting directly to the Internet through an ISP's point of presence (POP) is cheaper than leasing expensive dedicated circuits or making long-distance telephone calls, which is the reason for the VPN's increasing popularity.

The VPN connections discussed in this chapter are composed of three elements. A connection is considered a VPN when all three are correctly functioning.

- Authentication
- Encryption
- Tunneling

Authentication

Let's first introduce some basic strategies for authenticating users and computers when establishing VPNs. Not all tunneling protocols support every authentication protocol, but a general awareness will allow you to compare technologies for the best VPN solution.

Authentication protocols are designed to guarantee the identity of users and servers, as discussed in Chapter 10, Kerberos and the Public Key Infrastructure. The password is the basis for most implementations, but X.509 certificates are also used when establishing secure channels and IP Security. There is a difference between user authentication (both passwords and certificates) and machine authentication (usually certificates). Table 13.1 lists the authentication protocols supported by Windows 2000.

Role of Encryption

Encryption provides data confidentiality and forms the "black pipe" between tunnel endpoints. Once the tunnel has been formed, packets are encrypted and encapsulated within the tunnel protocol. Usually hidden within the encrypted portions of these packets is the original IP header information, which prevents eavesdroppers not only from reading the encrypted data but also from reading the packets' final destination. The destination tunnel endpoint IP address and other IP header information are the only pieces of information required to route a packet from one end of the tunnel to the other. Although there many implementations and levels of encryption, primarily IPSec and MPPE are used to encrypt tunnels with Windows 2000. (See Table 13.2.)

Tunnels

The tunnel is defined by two endpoints that communicate with each other through a tunneling protocol. One end of the tunnel encapsulates incoming traffic and routes it to the other end. This encapsulation process can occur at either

TABLE 13.1 Windows 2000 Authentication Protocols

Protocol	Description
Password Authentication Protocol (PAP)	A "last choice" authentication protocol used to authenticate older VPN clients. PAP sends the password in clear text and is not secure.
Shiva Password Authentication Protocol (SPAP)	Sends an encrypted password between Shiva LAN Rover and a Windows 2000 or Shiva client and Windows 2000 Server. Although more secure than PAP, it resends the same password encryption for a given password and is therefore susceptible to replay attack.
Challenge Handshake Authentication Protocol (CHAP)	Uses the MD-5 hash algorithm. Although not the same as MS-CHAP, Windows 2000 supports CHAP to interoperate with many other remote access vendors and operating systems.
Microsoft Challenge Handshake Authentication Protocol (MS-CHAP)	One-way authentication (*not* mutual) between client and server using RSA's MD-4/DES encryption. The single session key is generated based on the user's password and thus is the same for every session.
MS-CHAP Version 2	Provides mutual authentication between client and server using two session keys (one for transmitting and one for receiving) based on the user's password and a random string. Each authentication session uses different keys.
Extensible Authentication Protocol (EAP)	EAP-MD-5 CHAP—uses the Message Digest 5 similar to the CHAP protocol but only in EAP format. It uses user name password data and is not for Smart Card support but good for testing EAP authenticating systems; EAP-Transport Level Security (TLS)—used with Smart Cards and X.509 v3 certificates for mutual authentication between server and client.

TABLE 13.2 Windows 2000 Encryption Method

Method	Description
Encapsulated Security Payload (ESP)	Supports 40-bit DES, 56-bit DES, and 128-bit 3DES encryption standards. Authentication is also provided with either the MD-5 or SHA-1 integrity standards.
Microsoft Point-to-Point Encryption (MPPE)	Requires authentication with MS-CHAP or EAP and supports 40-bit encryption for international use and 128-bit encryption within the United States and Canada.

the second or third protocol layer as defined by the Open Systems Interconnections (OSI) model. Layer 2 protocols encapsulate at the data link layer and retain MAC-level addresses and frame information for different media types. Layer 3 protocols encapsulate packets from the network layer up. The Point-to-Point Tunneling Protocol (PPTP) and the Layer 2 Tunneling Protocol (L2TP) are layer 2 tunneling protocols, whereas IP Security implemented in tunnel mode is a Layer 3. Windows 2000 supports all three, but L2TP is the preferred implementation for Microsoft products.

The following discussion outlines these mutually exclusive protocols in relationship to VPN.

POINT-TO-POINT TUNNELING PROTOCOL

The *Point-to-Point Tunneling Protocol (PPTP)* is one way to create a VPN. PPTP relies on the *Point-to-Point Protocol (PPP)* to initially encapsulate an IP packet coming from a source at one end of the tunnel (Figure 13.1). *Microsoft Point-to-Point Encryption* (MPPE) can be used to encrypt the PPP payload information. MPPE is set up with keys passed using the MS-CHAP or EAP-TLS authentication methods.

The PPP header and payload are encapsulated into a Generic Routing Encapsulation (GRE) header and an IP header. The source IP address in the IP header corresponds to the tunnel server at the start of the tunnel, and the destination IP address corresponds to the tunnel server at the end (Figure 13.2).

LAYER 2 TUNNELING PROTOCOL

The use of the Layer 2 Tunneling Protocol (L2TP) is the preferred method of establishing a VPN in a Windows 2000 environment and also relies on the prepackaged PPP frame (Figure 13.3). L2TP encapsulates the PPP frame with an L2TP header and User Diagram Protocol (UDP) header.

L2TP over IPSec, as illustrated in Table 13.3, is the preferred method of encryption for the L2TP tunnel. An IPSec Encapsulating Security Payload (ESP)

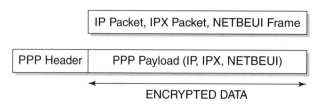

FIGURE 13.1 PPP Encapsulation

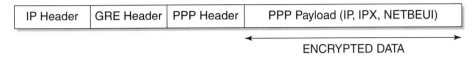

| IP Header | GRE Header | PPP Header | PPP Payload (IP, IPX, NETBEUI) |

ENCRYPTED DATA

FIGURE 13.2 PPTP Encapsulation

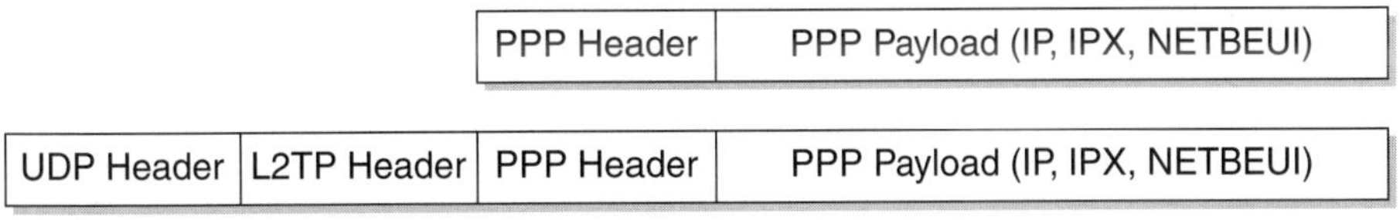

| PPP Header | PPP Payload (IP, IPX, NETBEUI) |

| UDP Header | L2TP Header | PPP Header | PPP Payload (IP, IPX, NETBEUI) |

FIGURE 13.3 L2TP Encapsulation

header and trailer encapsulate the L2TP payload for encryption and authentication (Figure 13.4). IPSec negotiates the transport level connection using computer certificates and the Internet Key Exchange (IKE) protocol, and once this is complete L2TP tunnel settings are used to establish the tunnel and authenticate the user. The IP header contains the tunnel endpoints for the source and destination IP addresses. The packet's true source and final destination are not visible to the Internet when encryption is enabled. L2TP over IPSec also offers data integrity and authentication without encryption through the use of digital signatures supported in Authentication Headers (AH).

TABLE 13.3 Tunneling Protocol Comparison

Capability	PPTP	L2TP/IPSEC	IPSEC Tunnel
Compression		X	
Tunnel Authentication		X	X
Encryption Method	MPPE	IPSec Transport	IPSec Transport
Transit Media Type Support between Tunnel Endpoints	IP	IP, X.25, Frame Relay, or ATM	IP
Datagram/Frame Types Supported between Client Endpoints	IP, IPX, or NetBEUI	IP, IPX, or NetBEUI	IP

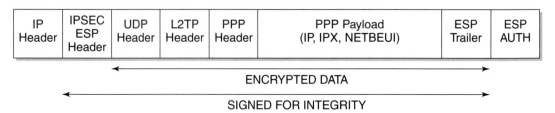

IP Header	IPSEC ESP Header	UDP Header	L2TP Header	PPP Header	PPP Payload (IP, IPX, NETBEUI)	ESP Trailer	ESP AUTH

ENCRYPTED DATA

SIGNED FOR INTEGRITY

FIGURE 13.4 IPSec Encapsulation and Encryption

NOTE   The current Windows 2000 implementation of L2TP does not support connections over X.25, Frame Relay, or ATM networks.

IPSEC TUNNELING

The IPSec tunnel operates at layer 3 and incorporates the IP packet and its contents. When L2TP and PPTP are not available on VPN servers or clients, it may be used for interoperability. IPSec provides two general modes of operation: Tunnel and Transport. Transport mode is discussed in the next section; Tunnel mode is discussed below.

Tunnel mode involves two configurations: ESP (Encapsulating Security Payload) (Figure 13.5) and AH (Authentication Headers) (Figure 13.6). ESP encapsulates IP packets for encryption and integrity. AH signs packets for integrity only. Both append a new IP header to the packet containing routing information between tunnel endpoints.

Comparison of Tunneling Methods

Some implementations of the three tunneling protocols might vary on different operating systems. As can be seen from Table 13.3, L2TP and IPSec offer the most favorable solution thanks to features inherited from both PPP encapsulation and the IPSec transport.

New IP Header	IPSEC ESP Header	Original IP Header	TCP/UDP Header	Payload (IP)	ESP Trailer	ESP AUTH

ENCRYPTED DATA

INTEGRITY VERIFICATION

FIGURE 13.5 ESP Tunnel Mode

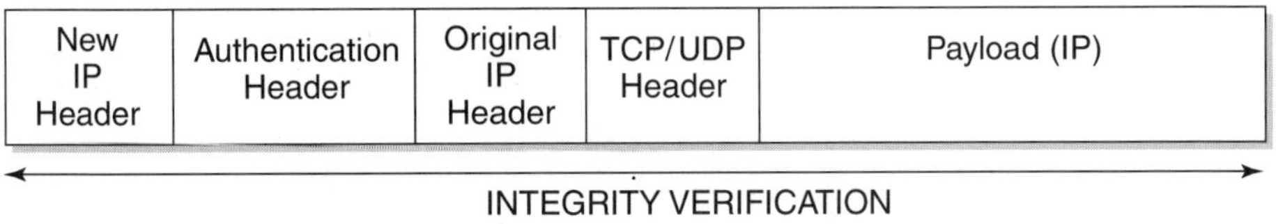

New IP Header
Authentication Header
Original IP Header
TCP/UDP Header
Payload (IP)
INTEGRITY VERIFICATION

FIGURE 13.6 AH Tunnel Mode

VPN Configurations

When designing a virtual private network, it is important to understand that there are two general VPN configurations:

- *Router-to-router*—Example: A branch office router is connected to corporate intranet.
- *Remote access*—Example: One dial-in client establishes a connection at the time of the call.

These are examined in the following sections.

ROUTER-TO-ROUTER

Branch office connections through a router-to-router VPN (Figure 13.7) can be configured to meet a wide range of organizational and physical requirements. For example, they may be *persistent* 24 hours a day or they may be established *on demand*. The nonpersistent router-to-router VPN may cut down on expensive long-distance phone or data connections, and establishing it is transparent to the user. Many users on both networks may use a VPN connection concurrently.

REMOTE ACCESS

The remote access VPN configuration is established when a single client dials in to either an ISP or a corporate Remote Access Server. The connection is then estab-

Network Resource
Tunnel
Internet
VPN Connection
User
Tunnel Server
Corporate Intranet
Tunnel Server
Branch Office Network

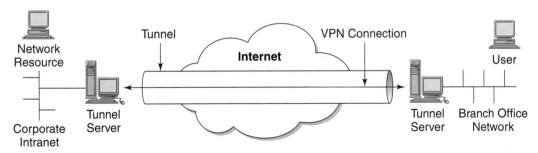

FIGURE 13.7 A Router-to-Router VPN Connection

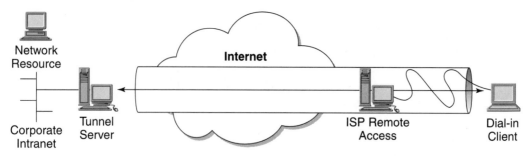

FIGURE 13.8 A VPN Connection Directly between a Client and the VPN Server

lished between the client and the Tunnel Server, but not before mutual authentication between them is established. Once the user is identified, Remote Access Policies determine the conditions for the VPN connection setup. If the client dials in to an ISP, the VPN connection remains with the corporate Tunnel Server and is transparent to the ISP (Figure 13.8).

VOLUNTARY AND COMPULSORY TUNNELS

The two methods for establishing a tunnel between the client and the corporate intranet are voluntary and compulsory. Remote access policy for individual users determines which method will be used. The voluntary tunnel is initiated by the individual VPN client workstation when accessing the corporate network. The compulsory tunnel is initiated by a VPN client server at the ISP when the user attempts to log on to the corporate network. Policies set on the corporate VPN server force users to set up this mandatory (required) tunnel and may exist on the corporate VPN server or corporate Internet Authentication Server (IAS), to be discussed in a later section.

VPN Architecture and Configuration

With a conceptual understanding of VPN, it is now appropriate to turn our attention to implementations associated with the previously discussed VPN configurations in greater detail. The three common VPN configurations are router-to-router persistent, router-to-router on demand, and remote access over the Internet. Here are the basic steps to implement them:

- Internet/intranet connection interface configuration
- Routing and remote access setup
- Certificates supporting IPSec

- Static routes
- Tunnel port configuration
- Tunnel filter configuration
- Remote Access Policy
- VPN client configuration

REMOTE ACCESS OVER THE INTERNET—EXAMPLE

To provide a better understanding of VPN implementation, the following example demonstrates how to configure a RAS server for VPN connections with individual clients. In this scenario, the client establishes a remote connection over an intranet or the Internet using a tunneling protocol and encryption mechanism as in Figure 13.4. She dials in to her ISP and establishes Internet connectivity. Remote access policies prevent a client connection unless a tunnel is established. The tunnel is therefore mandatory before intranet connectivity is permitted. The RAS will be configured to authenticate clients using L2TP over IPSec encryption. Once a client has been authenticated, and a VPN connection has been established, the RAS will forward data between the client and the intranet behind the server. This is known as configuring a RAS server for VPN.

Setting Up Internet and Intranet Interfaces on the VPN Server

The following provides a step-by-step review of VPN setup using sample IP addresses. (These *should not* be used in a real or test environment. Secure your own IP addresses and utilize them when simulating this example.) For this example, assign 111.111.111.2 and subnet mask 255.255.255.0 to the intranet interface. Then, assign IP address 111.111.112.2 with 255.255.255.0 subnet mask to the Internet interface (Figure 13.9).

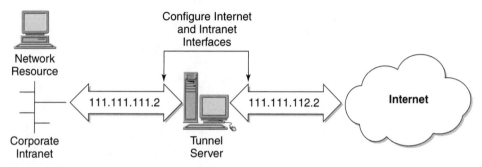

FIGURE 13.9 Configuring Interfaces

1. Select **Start** → **Settings** → **Network and Dial-up Connections** and double-click the intranet interface. Press the **Properties** button.

2. Select the **Internet Protocol** (**TCP/IP**) option and press the **Properties** button. Enter the IP address and subnet mask for the intranet interface.

3. Repeat this process for the Internet interface.

Setting Up Routing and Remote Access

To route between the Internet and the intranet, the **Routing and Remote Access Service** must be installed.

1. Select **Start** → **Programs** → **Administrative Tools** → **Routing and Remote Access**. Right-click the VPN server node and select **Configure and Enable Routing and Remote Access**. The **Routing and Remote Access Server Setup Wizard** starts. Press the **Next>** button.

2. Select the **Virtual private network (VPN) server** radio button and press the **Next>** button (Figure 13.10).

3. Ensure that the TCP/IP protocol is supported at the RAS server. Press the **Next>** Button (Figure 13.11).

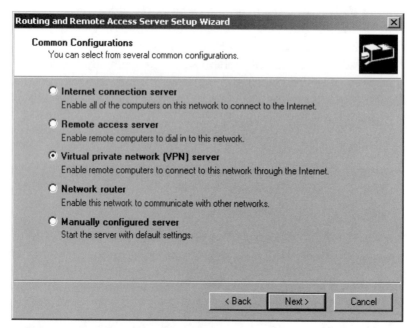

FIGURE 13.10 Common Configuration Options

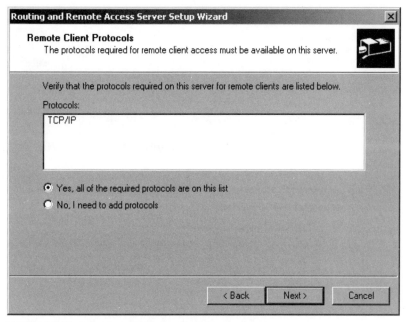

FIGURE 13.11 Selection of Remote Client Protocols

4. Select the interface that is attached to the Internet. This is the network from which the client is communicating (Figure 13.12). In this case that interface is 111.111.112.2. Press the **Next>** button.

5. Use DHCP to assign IP addresses to VPN clients by selecting **Automatically**. For this example, configure a pool of addresses for the RAS server to assign to clients using the **From a specified range of addresses** option (Figure 13.13). Press the **Next>** button.

6. Create a range of IP addresses to assign VPN clients by pressing the **New** button (Figure 13.14). Enter the **Start IP address** and **End IP address** to designate the new IP address range. Press the **OK** button. Press the **Next>** button.

7. The next dialog box involves the RADIUS service, which is discussed in another example. Here select the **No, I don't want to set up the server to use RADIUS now** (Figure 13.15). Press the **Next>** button.

8. Press the **Finish** button. The wizard may bring up some suggestions for your RAS installation.

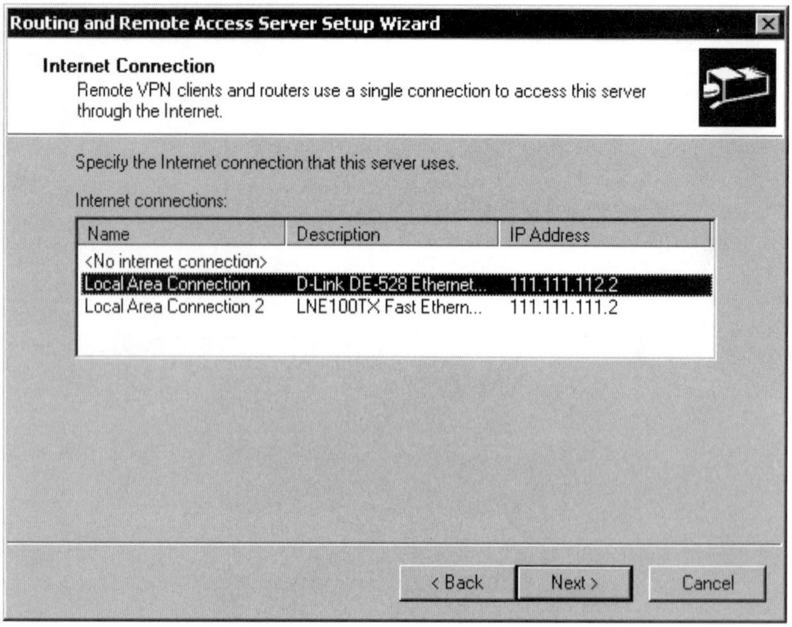

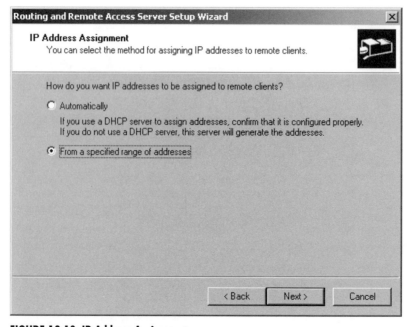

FIGURE 13.12 Network Selection

FIGURE 13.13 IP Address Assignment

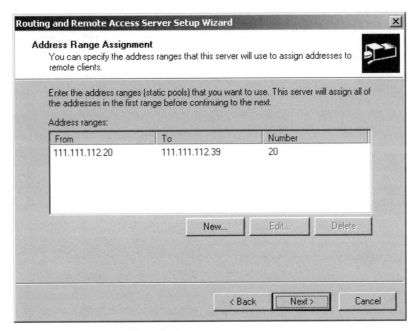

FIGURE 13.14 Address Range Assignment

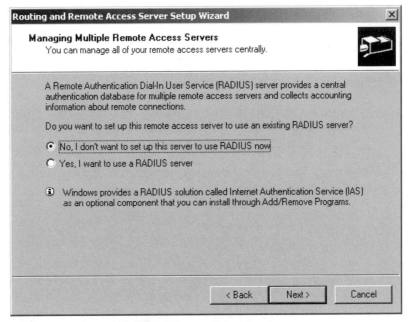

FIGURE 13.15 Managing Multiple Remote Access Services

Once the Routing and Remote Access server is up and running, there should be a green dot visible on the new server from the **Routing and Remote Access** snap-in. If you plan to dial directly in to the RAS (as well as access the server over the Internet through a LAN interface), make sure that the following options are enabled.

9. Right-click on the new server and select **Properties**. From the **General** tab ensure that the **Remote access server** option has a checkmark and that the **LAN and demand-dial routing** option is selected.

Applying Certificates for IPSEC

IP Security requires an X.509 version 3 certificate to be installed on all participating systems. Install an IPSec machine certificate from a trusted Certificate Authority. (See Chapter 11 for additional information.) We recommend using the **Certificate** snap-in to request an IPSec certificate. Right-click on the **Personal** store node and select **All Tasks** → **Request New Certificate...**. Follow the **Certificate Request Wizard** instructions. If the client is offsite, request a certificate from the Certificate Authority using the Web server Certificate Request Web pages. (Again, see Chapter 11.)

Configuring Static Routes

The RAS/VPN server may be configured with either routing protocols (such as the Routing Information Protocol (RIP) and Open Shortest Path First protocol (OSPF)) or static routes to direct traffic between the VPN client and the destination internal networks. For the sake of simplicity, we will examine how to configure RAS/VPN using static routes. All networks the VPN client wishes to communicate with must have a configured *route* in the table.

1. From the **Routing and Remote Access** snap-in right-click the **Routing and Remote Access** node → *Servername* node → **IP Routing** → **Static Routes** and select **New Static Route...**.

To forward external traffic destined for an internal network other than the 111.111.111.0 network (or your intranet network):

2. Select the intranet interface from the **Interface:** pull-down menu.
3. Enter the destination network and subnet mask. All IP packets destined for this network will now follow this new route.
4. Enter the router interface address responsible for forwarding the packet on to the destination network in the **Gateway** field. In this example a router has an interface on the 111.111.111.0 internal network. It is also capable of routing to the 111.111.113.0 network.

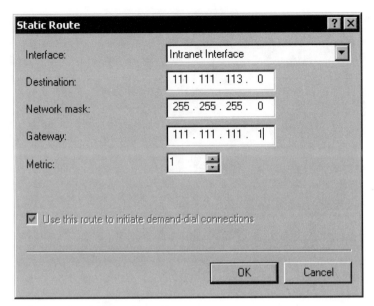

FIGURE 13.16 Adding a Static Route

5. A low metric number gives high preference to this route when multiple options for a destination network exist.

For instance, in order to route incoming packets from the 111.111.112.2 interface onto the 111.111.113.0 network, the entries shown in Figure 13.6 would be made. The Intranet interface address is 111.111.111.2.

Display the routes for the VPN server using the `route print` command from the Command Prompt (Figure 13.17) to verify the newly created route.

NOTE   If there is only one network at the corporate intranet or branch office, no static routes are required. RAS will forward packets between the two interfaces if all packets are destined for addresses on the local VPN network.

The routing table can also be displayed from the **Routing and Remote Access** snap-in by right-clicking the **Routing and Remote Access** node → *Servername* node → **IP Routing** node → **Static Routes** node and selecting **Show IP Routing Table...**. The full table is displayed for the routing and remote access server (Figure 13.18).

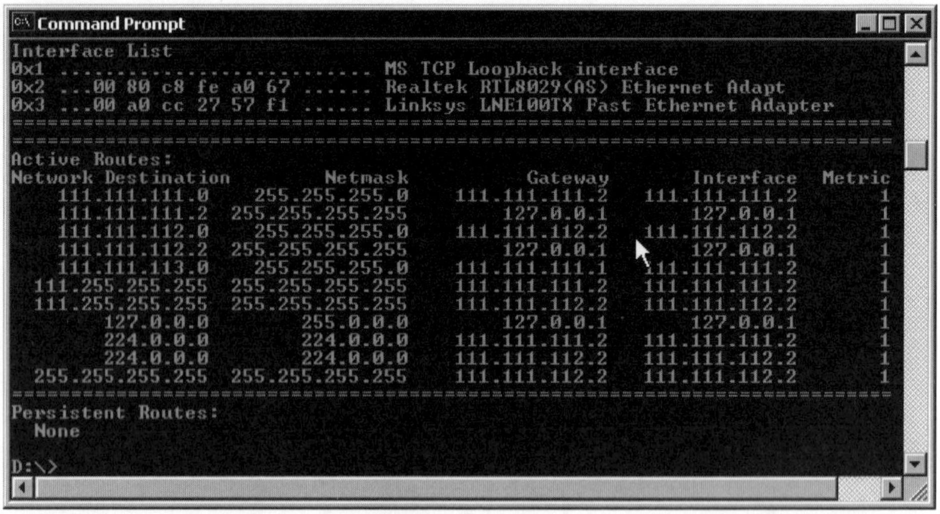

```
DOS  Command Prompt                                                    _ □ ✗
Interface List
0x1 ............................ MS TCP Loopback interface
0x2 ...00 80 c8 fe a0 67 ...... Realtek RTL8029(AS) Ethernet Adapt
0x3 ...00 a0 cc 27 57 f1 ...... Linksys LNE100TX Fast Ethernet Adapter
===================================================================
===================================================================
Active Routes:
Network Destination        Netmask          Gateway         Interface   Metric
      111.111.111.0    255.255.255.0    111.111.111.2    111.111.111.2      1
      111.111.111.2  255.255.255.255        127.0.0.1        127.0.0.1      1
      111.111.112.0    255.255.255.0    111.111.112.2    111.111.112.2      1
      111.111.112.2  255.255.255.255        127.0.0.1        127.0.0.1      1
      111.111.113.0    255.255.255.0    111.111.111.1    111.111.111.2      1
  111.255.255.255  255.255.255.255    111.111.111.2    111.111.111.2      1
  111.255.255.255  255.255.255.255    111.111.112.2    111.111.112.2      1
        127.0.0.0        255.0.0.0        127.0.0.1        127.0.0.1      1
        224.0.0.0        224.0.0.0    111.111.111.2    111.111.111.2      1
        224.0.0.0        224.0.0.0    111.111.112.2    111.111.112.2      1
  255.255.255.255  255.255.255.255    111.111.112.2    111.111.112.2      1
===================================================================
Persistent Routes:
  None

D:\>
```

FIGURE 13.17 Display of a Routing Table

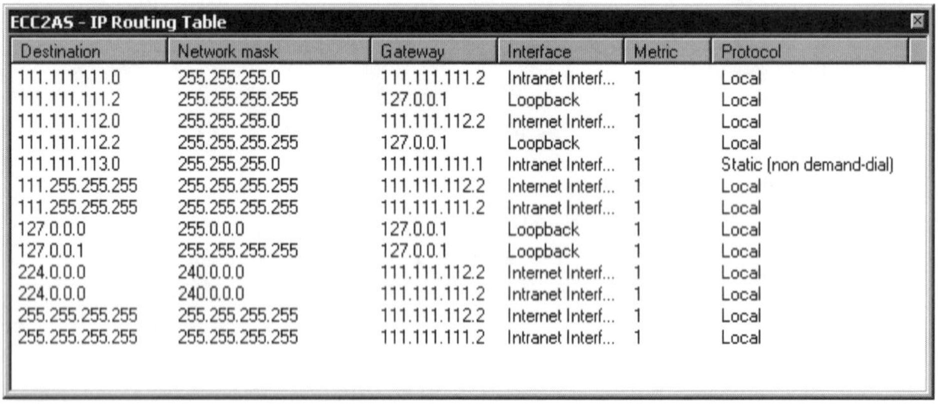

Destination	Network mask	Gateway	Interface	Metric	Protocol
111.111.111.0	255.255.255.0	111.111.111.2	Intranet Interf...	1	Local
111.111.111.2	255.255.255.255	127.0.0.1	Loopback	1	Local
111.111.112.0	255.255.255.0	111.111.112.2	Internet Interf...	1	Local
111.111.112.2	255.255.255.255	127.0.0.1	Loopback	1	Local
111.111.113.0	255.255.255.0	111.111.111.1	Intranet Interf...	1	Static (non demand-dial)
111.255.255.255	255.255.255.255	111.111.112.2	Internet Interf...	1	Local
111.255.255.255	255.255.255.255	111.111.111.2	Intranet Interf...	1	Local
127.0.0.0	255.0.0.0	127.0.0.1	Loopback	1	Local
127.0.0.1	255.255.255.255	127.0.0.1	Loopback	1	Local
224.0.0.0	240.0.0.0	111.111.112.2	Internet Interf...	1	Local
224.0.0.0	240.0.0.0	111.111.111.2	Intranet Interf...	1	Local
255.255.255.255	255.255.255.255	111.111.112.2	Internet Interf...	1	Local
255.255.255.255	255.255.255.255	111.111.111.2	Intranet Interf...	1	Local

ECC2AS – IP Routing Table

FIGURE 13.18 An IP Static Routing Table

Tunnel Ports

By default there are five PPTP and five L2TP ports defined for the RAS server. If you expect more than five concurrent VPN connections using L2TP, increase the number of L2TP ports by

1. Right-clicking the **Routing and Remote Access** node → *Servername* node → **Ports** node and selecting **Properties**. Select **WAN Miniport (L2TP)** and press the **Configure** button.
2. Increasing the **Maximum ports:** field and pressing **OK** (Figure 13.19).

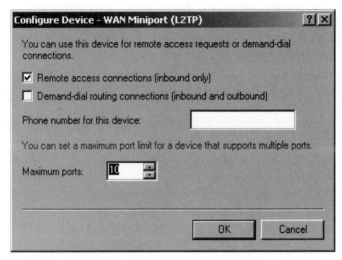

FIGURE 13.19 WAN Mini-Port Device Configuration

L2TP over IPSEC Filters

Tunnel filtering can be used to disable all other connection types. Filtering UDP port numbers and source and destination IP addresses is effective for eliminating connections for other services. Some protection is afforded the VPN server through inbound and outbound packet filtering. To configure L2TP input filters

1. Open the **Routing and Remote Access** node → *Servername* node → **IP Routing** node → **General** node, right-click the Internet interface from the Details windows and select **Properties**. The **General** tab displays properties for the external adapter.

2. Press the **Input Filters...** button. Press the **Add...** button.

3. Select the **Destination network** checkbox and enter the IP address of the internal interface. Enter 255.255.255.255 for the **Subnet mask:** field (Figure 13.20).

4. Select the **UDP** protocol from the **Protocol:** field pull-down menu.

5. Enter 500 for the **Source port:** field and 500 for the **Destination port:** field (Figure 13.20). Port 500 is used by the Internet Security Association and Key Management Protocol (ISAKMP) to authenticate keys and negotiate IPSec connections. (ISAKMP is also known as the Internet Key Exchange protocol.)

6. Repeat steps 2 through 5 with the **Source port:** and **Destination port:** fields set to 1701. Press the **OK** button. Port 1701 is reserved for L2TP communications.

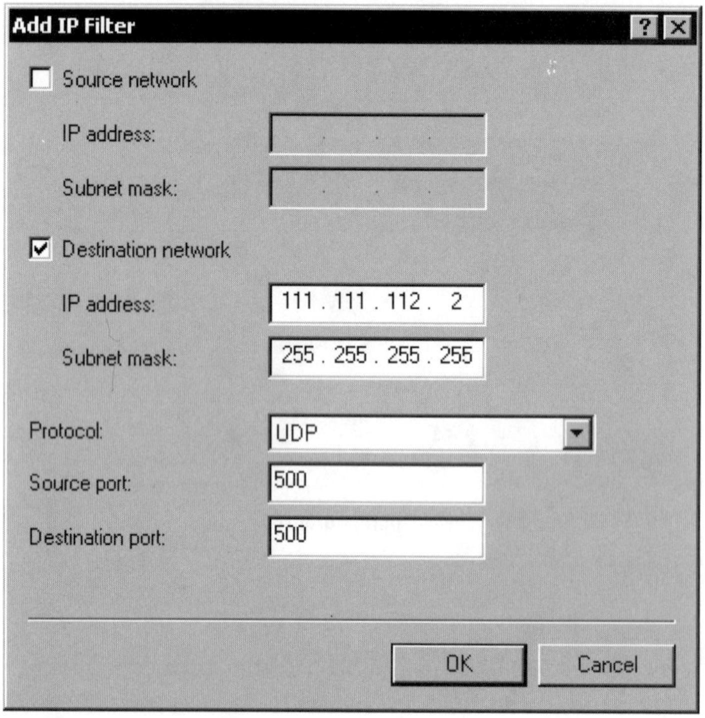

FIGURE 13.20 Add IP Filter

7. From the **Input Filters** dialog select the **Drop all packets except those that meet the criteria below** radio button. Press the **OK** button.

At this stage, it is necessary to add appropriate L2TP input and output filtering, as here:

8. From the ***Internet adapter's* Properties** dialog box press the **Output Filters...** button.

9. Press the **Add...** button and checkmark the **Source network** box.

10. Enter the IP address of the external interface in the **IP address:** field.

11. Enter 255.255.255.255 for the **Subnet mask:** field.

12. Enter 500 for the **Source port:** and **Destination port:** fields. Press the **OK** button.

13. Repeat steps 8 through 12 with source and destination port 1701.

14. Select the **Drop all packets except those that meet the criteria below** radio button. Press the **OK** button.

All four filters (two input and two output) should have been applied to the Internet adapter IP address, preventing all other connections from passing through the adapter. The intranet adapter (on the corporate network) will be unaffected by these filter settings, and thus internal systems will still be able to establish any type of connection with the VPN server.

Remote Access Policy

Remote access permissions are granted on a user-by-user basis through the **Dial-in** tab associated with each user account's properties. Right-click on a user from the **Active Directory Users and Computers** snap-in and select the **Dial-in** tab. Select the **Allow access** or **Deny access** as appropriate to assign VPN or Dial-in permissions (Figure 13.21).

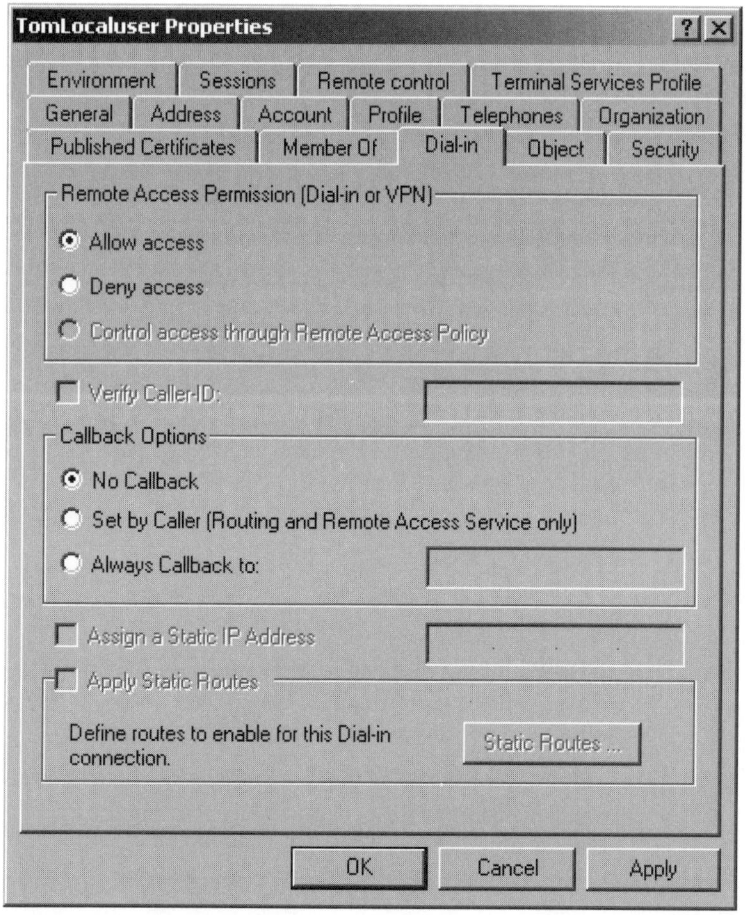

FIGURE 13.21 Dial-In Properties

Remote access policies provide conditions and a profile that clients must meet in order to access the server. To use one, select the **Allow access** option for each user account. (Native mode Windows 2000 systems have the **Control Access through Remote Access Policy** option instead of **Allow access**.) Once all the user accounts have been given remote access capability, additional policies are used to further restrict which users and connection types are permitted to access the server. Table 13.4 describes remote access policy attributes. A few examples will be discussed in the next procedural steps.

TABLE 13.4 Remote Policy Attributes

Attribute	Description	Wildcard (*)
Called-Station-Id	Text string that identifies the text string of the phone number the user dialed to establish this connection.	
Calling-Station-Id	Text string that represents the phone number from which the client is dialing.	
Client-Friendly-Name	Text string for a RADIUS client computer (IAS only).	X
Client-IP-Address	Text string identifying client computers' IP address (IAS only).	X
Client-Vendor	Vendor of the RADIUS proxy server (IAS only).	X
Day-And-Time-Restrictions	Time periods during the week when user may connect.	
Framed-Protocol	Identifies the framing protocol used. L2TP supports multiple frame types such as Frame Relay, X.25, Serial Line Internet Protocol (SLIP), and PPP.	X
NAS-Identifier	Text string that identifies the NAS with which the client is establishing the "front end" of the tunnel for VPN access (IAS only).	
NAS-IP-Address	Text string identifying IP address of the NAS with which the client is establishing the "front end" of the tunnel for VPN access (IAS only).	X
NAS-Port-Type	Media type the caller is using, such as ISDN or phone line.	
Service-Type	Type of connection the user is attempting to establish (PPP, telnet).	X
Tunnel-Type	Tunnel protocols permitted.	
Windows-Group	Windows 2000 security group memberships that may be denied or permitted access to the RAS.	

Setting remote policies is the next step to be undertaken to support RAS client utilization. Follow these steps to create one:

1. From the **Routing and Remote Access** snap-in select the **Routing and Remote Access** node → *Servername* node → **Remote Access Policies**. Right-click the **Remote Access Policies** node and select **New Remote Access Policy**.

2. Enter something like *VPN Policy* for the policy name. Press the **Next>** button.

   Select several conditions in the following steps:

3. Press the **Add** button. Select the **Windows-Groups** attribute and press the **Add...** button (Figure 13.22). The Windows-Groups condition identifies security group membership required to meet the policy.

4. Press the **Add...** button in the **Groups** dialog box and select security groups to govern remote access privileges. Press the **OK** button. Press the **OK** button.

5. Press the **Add...** button. Select **NAS-Port-Type** and press the **Add...** button. From the available NAS port types select **Virtual (VPN)** and press the **Add>>** button. Press the **OK** button.

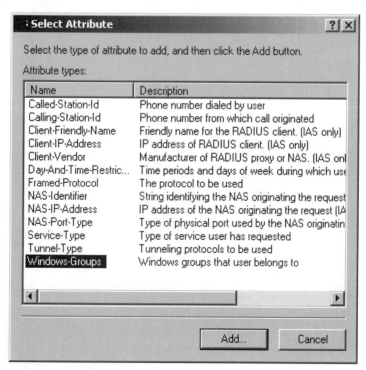

FIGURE 13.22 Remote Policy Attributes

6. Press the **Add...** button. Select the **Tunnel-Type** condition and press the **Add...** button. Select the L2TP protocol and press the **Add>>** button. Press the **OK** button.

7. Press the **Next>** button.

8. Select the **Grant remote access permission** option to allow users who meet this policy's requirements to have remote access privileges. Press the **Next>** button.

9. Press the **Edit Profile...** button to modify profile settings for *VPN Policy*. Select the **Authentication** tab. Smart Card authentication is configurable from here. Both MS-CHAP v2 and MS-CHAP should be enabled (Figure 13.23).

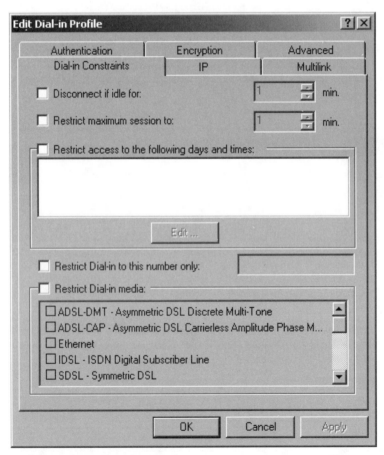

FIGURE 13.23 Profile Properties

10. The **Encryption** tab offers the following selections:

    –*Basic*—40-bit DES encryption

    –*Strong*—56-bit DES encryption

    –*Strongest*—3DES encryption (encrypts each data block using between one and three different keys with the DES algorithm—this is only for North American VPN clients)

11. Press the **OK** button. Press the **Finish** button. If any other default policies exist, remove them. This will eliminate conflicts that may occur with previously established RAS policies.

Remote Access Client Configuration

For the client to dial in to a VPN, specific steps must be taken to configure its remote access. From the client computer, create a local dial-in connection:

1. Start the **Network Connection Wizard** by selecting **Start → Settings → Network and Dial-up Connections**. Double-click the **Make New Connection** icon to start the wizard. Press the **Next>** button.

2. Select the **Dial-up to the Internet** option and create a dial-up connection. This will provide the client Internet connectivity via its local ISP POP.

The next step involves connecting to the VPN. Create a second connection using the **Network Connection Wizard**. Make it a VPN connection to be invoked after the dial-in connection is established:

3. Start the **Network Connection Wizard** by selecting **Start → Settings → Network and Dial-up Connections**. Double-click the **Make New Connection** icon to start the wizard. Press the **Next>** button.

4. Select the **Connect to a private network through the Internet** option (Figure 13.24). Press the **Next>** button.

5. Select **Automatically dial this initial connection** and select the previously created dial-in connection to invoke the dial-up when this new VPN connection is established. If you plan to access the Internet through a LAN interface, select the **Do not dial the initial connection**. You may also select this option and dial up to the Internet manually. Press the **Next>** button.

6. Enter the IP address of the VPN server's external interface. Press the **Next>** button.

7. Select whether all users on the system will be able to use the VPN connection. Press the **Next>** button.

8. Decide whether or not to **Enable Internet Connection Sharing for this connection**. Also choose whether on-demand dialing will be permitted. On-

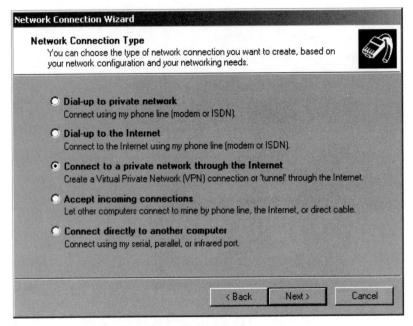

FIGURE 13.24 Setting Up a Client VPN Connection

demand dialing will instruct this VPN to establish the tunnel when other users request access to the resource. Press the **Next>** button. Press the **Finish** button.

Once the VPN client's dial-in and VPN network connections are created, the client system is ready to establish a VPN tunnel. The user need only start the dial-in connection first and then the VPN connection. If the VPN connection has been selected to automatically dial the dial-in connection, it alone need be invoked. The same is true if the VPN server is available through a LAN interface (Figure 13.25).

Routing and Remote Access Server Management

The **Routing and Remote Access** snap-in can perform several functions. To control the server's behavior, right-click the RAS server and select **Start**, **Stop**, **Pause**, **Resume**, or **Restart**.

VIEWING REMOTE ACCESS CLIENTS

To properly manage this environment, it is important to have a facility for easy viewing of current remote access clients. Right-click on *servername* → **Remote Access Clients**, select the desired client from the Details window, and choose

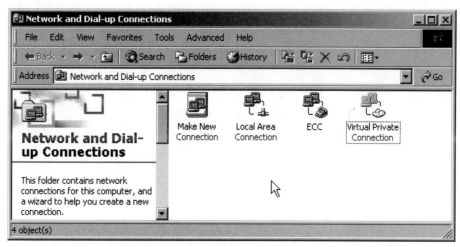

FIGURE 13.25 A Client VPN Connection

Status—see statistics, errors, and network information (Figure 13.26).

Disconnect—disconnect a client from the VPN server.

Send Message—send a text message to a single client.

Send to All—send text message to all remote clients.

Internet Authentication Service and RADIUS

The *Internet Authentication Service (IAS)* enables centralized authentication, authorization, and auditing for remote clients. Once the client has been authorized with the centralized account manager a VPN connection may be established according to the user's account policies. This is accomplished through the *Remote Authentication Dial-In User Service (RADIUS),* which enables the ISP's *Points Of Presence (POPs)* to authenticate dial-in and VPN clients on one IAS server for the corporation. User account profiles are maintained in one location, not on every VPN server the local network supports. Once the IAS server on the local corporate network has verified the user's credentials the POP can establish a VPN connection with a local VPN server.

The general architecture of IAS has the following components (Figure 13.27):

1. The mobile remote client connects to a nearby ISP's POP using a modem connection and any one of the supported authentication methods discussed at the beginning of the Virtual Private Networks section. The user's realm name is either provided at the connection login in the form *username @realm* or provided by the Connection Manager automatically. This name is easier to handle if it corresponds to the corporation's Active Directory user account realm name (this is discussed later in an example).

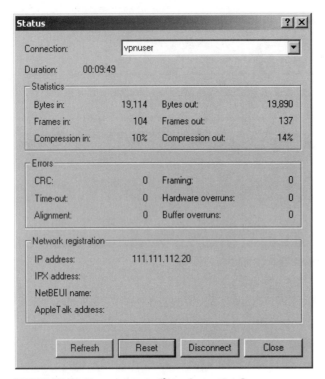

FIGURE 13.26 Remote Access Client Connection Status

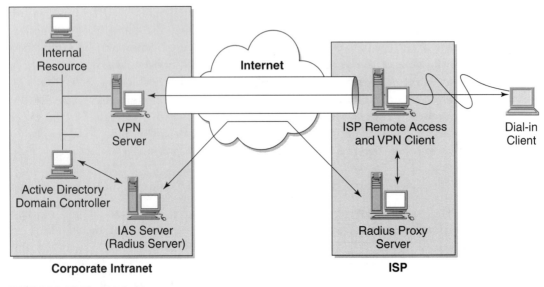

FIGURE 13.27 The IAS Architecture

2. The ISP dial-in server (soon to be a VPN client with user's corporate network) forwards the RADIUS request to the RADIUS server configured as a proxy.

3. The proxy sends a RADIUS request to the RADIUS server at the corporate site.

4. The RADIUS server verifies the user's credentials in the Active Directory and checks the user's applicable remote access policies.

5. The RADIUS proxy relays the user's connection request to the VPN client at the ISP. The VPN client at the ISP then initiates a tunnel with the VPN server at the corporate site.

NOTE   The VPN connection is entirely separate from the RADIUS authentication process. The RADIUS server at the corporate site is configured with the **Internet Authentication Service** snap-in tool. RADIUS clients are added to the RADIUS server's client list, where logging and accounting properties can be configured. Remote Access policies and profiles are modified in the same fashion as they are for VPNs. The main difference between the VPN scenarios and the IAS architecture is the method of authentication chosen from the **Routing and Remote Access** snap-in tool.

Firewalls must be configured to forward RADIUS UDP communications and permit remote connections with the IAS server. This is usually accomplished by putting the IAS server in a Demilitarized Zone (DMZ) to provide both Internet access and limited intranet exposure.

The RADIUS architecture permits all user requests throughout the Internet to be forwarded to one or more IAS servers maintained and administered from the corporate intranet. In this way remote access policies can be managed in a central location. ISPs forward requests to the local intranet verifying a user's remote access policy. Remote user accounts can be managed from the corporate intranet without the need to constantly update accounts with different ISPs.

IAS INSTALLATION

The IAS installation is not automatic during standard installation. The following steps should be followed to install IAS on a Windows 2000 server:

1. From the **Control Panel** start **Add/Remove Programs** and select **Add/Remove Windows Components**.

2. From **Windows Components** select **Networking Services** and press the **Details...** button. Checkmark the **Internet Authentication Service** option and press the **OK** button. Press the **Next>** button. Press the **Finish** button.

3. From the **Internet Authentication Service** snap-in right-click the **Internet Authentication Service** node and select **Properties**. The following tabs are available:

- The **Service** tab configures the logging of accepted or rejected authentication requests.

- The **RADIUS** tab identifies UDP ports required for IAS to provide authentication and accounting services through a firewall (Figure 13.28).

- The **Realms** tab translates user realms in authentication requests to Active Directory or Kerberos realm names. If a user logs in to his ISP as *joeuser@ispname.com*, this tab can translate his authentication request into *joeuser@corporatename.com*. Obviously, maintaining a large realm name mapping list can become quite tedious.

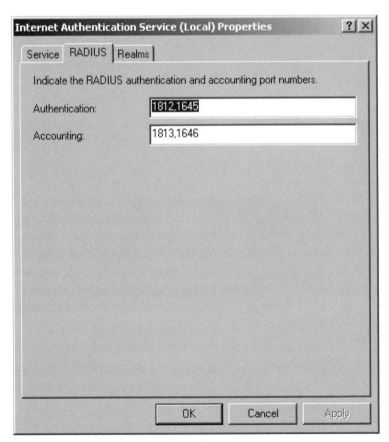

FIGURE 13.28 Authentication and Accounting UDP Ports

4. Right-click the **Clients** node and select **New Client**. A client will usually be an Internet POP supported by an ISP. Enter a client name. Press the **Next>** button. Specify an IP address or DNS name for the client. Select **Client-Vendor:** identifying the client's RADIUS implementation from the pull-down menu. To take advantage of vendor-specific attributes, select the correct vendor for the RADIUS client. If this is not known, select **RADIUS-standard**. Otherwise, if the RADIUS client is running **Routing and Remote Access**, select the **Microsoft** option.

5. Enter a shared secret to encrypt communication between the RADIUS client and server. Press the **Finish** button.

IAS Remote Access Policy

Remote access policies for IAS must be established. Follow these steps to do this:

1. Right-click the **Remote Access Policy** node and select **New Remote Access Policy**. Enter a name for the new policy such as *IAS VPN Client Policy*. Press the **Next>** button.

2. Press the **Add...** button to modify conditions. The same attributes for VPN remote access configuration are also available for the IAS RAS policy. Select the **Windows-Groups** option and press the **Add...** button. Press the **Add...** button again and select a Windows 2000 security group. Client users must have membership in this group to meet this access policy. Press the **OK** button. Press the **Next>** button.

3. Select the **Grant remote access permission** option. Press the **Next>** button.

4. Press the **Edit Profile...** button and specify Encryption, Authentication, and IP Packet Filters just as in the VPN Remote Access example.

5. Press **OK** and **Finish**.

6. If any other default policies exist, remove them. This will eliminate conflicts that may occur with previously established RAS policies.

Registering the IAS Server with the Active Directory

To make IAS available throughout the enterprise, it is necessary to register it with the Active Directory. The following steps will do this:

1. From the **Active Directory Users and Computers** snap-in select the Users container.

2. Right-click the **RAS and IAS Servers** group and add the new IAS server to the group.

RADIUS Client Configuration

The Network Access Server (NAS) handling the client's dial-in connection also supports the RADIUS client software and configuration. The following example demonstrates configuration of a RADIUS client/RAS server running Windows 2000 Routing and Remote Access.

1. From the **Routing and Remote Access** snap-in right-click the **Routing and Remote Access** node and select *Servername* node. Select **Properties** and proceed to the **Security** tab.

2. Select **RADIUS Authentication** under **Authentication provider:** and press the **Authentication Methods** button. Ensure that the MS-CHAP v2 and MS-CHAP authentication protocols are selected (Figure 13.29). Press the **Add...** button. Enter the RADIUS server name or IP address and enter the shared secret by pressing the **Change...** button.

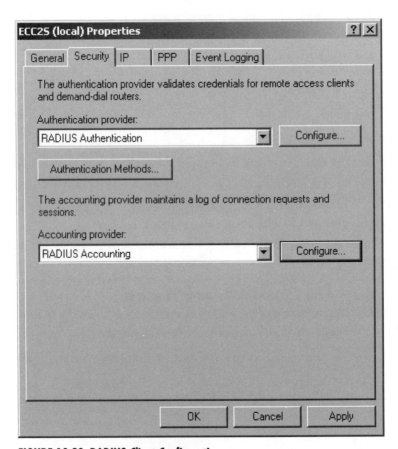

FIGURE 13.29 RADIUS Client Configuration

3. Select **RADIUS Accounting** under **Accounting provider:** and press the **Configure...** button. Press the **Configuration** button and repeat step 9 for RADIUS accounting.

4. Stop and restart the Routing and Remote Access service to make sure the new settings take effect.

5. Set up a remote access client as in the Remote Access Client Configuration section (page 567) and verify client connectivity and RADIUS configuration settings.

RADIUS ACCOUNT LOGGING

RADIUS records authentication and accounting requests made from the RADIUS client. This information can be used to track billing and account activity. To select the types of requests to be logged in to the RADIUS log file

1. From the **Internet Authentication Service** snap-in tool select the **Remote Access Logging** node. Right-click the local log file and select **Properties**.

2. From the settings tab three logging characteristics are available (Figure 13.30).

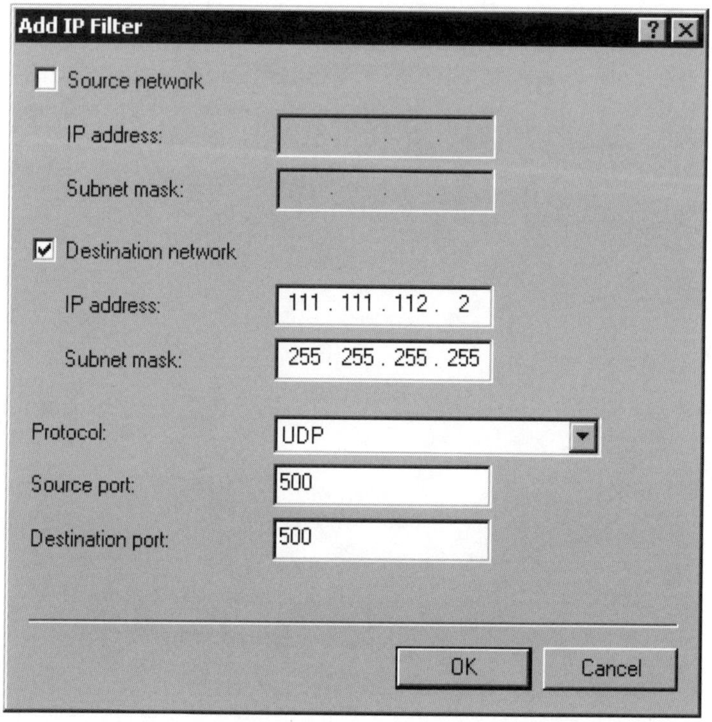

FIGURE 13.30 RADIUS Logging Options

RADIUS PROXY SERVERS

Radius proxy servers are configured at ISPs to forward communications with the desired IAS server. An ISP can configure a proxy server with all the needed IAS server information and can point RAS servers to it. This eliminates the need to configure every RAS server with current RADIUS server information.

IP SECURITY

IP Security (IPSec) was developed by the Internet Engineering Task Force (IETF) to enable IP authentication, encryption, and data integrity. IPSec services use the Public Key Infrastructure (PKI) to share secret keys over the network and establish secure communication sessions. Once established, the connections are transparent to users and applications. In the section on Virtual Private Networks, IPSec Tunnel mode was discussed and IPSec Transport mode was implemented using L2TP over IPSec. Here we will see that when applying IP Security to your internal network, routing and network conditions may alleviate the need for a tunnel, in which case IPSec may be implemented in Transport mode. Transport mode has no specified tunnel endpoints, and traffic flows between source and destination hosts without encapsulation or redirection. Group policies applied to Active Directory containers dictate the traffic type that is encrypted and signed either with Encrypted Security Payload (ESP) or by Authentication Header (AH) IPSec drivers. Packets are encrypted on the way out and decrypted on the way in, independent of TCP/IP stack processing (Figure 13.31).

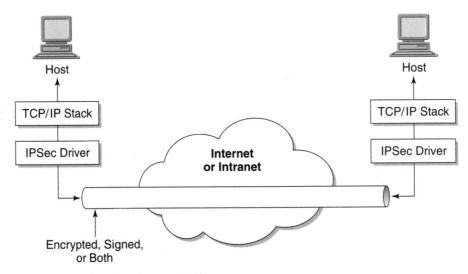

FIGURE 13.31 The IPSec Transport Mode

TABLE 13.5 Windows 2000 IPSec Technologies

Technology	Standard Implementations
Shared Secret Keys/Negotiation	Internet Key Exchange (IKE) for Windows 2000
Digital Signatures	Hash Message Authentication Code (HMAC)
	Hash Message Authentication Message Digest function 95 (HMAC-MD-5)
	Hash Message Authentication Secure Hash Algorithm (HMAC-SHA)
ESP Encryption	3DES, 56-bit DES, 40-bit DES

Individual IPSec packets use a standard format involving an Authentication Header (AH) and an Encapsulated Security Payload (ESP). The AH contains authentication information using digital signatures, and the message body is encrypted in the ESP to prevent data snooping. Table 13.5 lists some of the industry standards used with the Windows 2000 IPSec implementation.

Understanding IPSec Policies

IP Security policies can be assigned to either local computers or Active Directory containers to determine the security services a system will use when communicating with other systems. Some systems may require a higher level of security than others. For this reason IPSec policies allow the administrator granular control over the security protocols accepted at individual machines.

SETTING IPSEC POLICIES

IPSec policies are located in the Group Policy tree under **Computer Configuration → Windows Settings → Security Settings → IP Security Policies on Active Directory**. The default policies are defined as follows and may be assigned to any GPO.

- **Secure Server (require security)**—accepts initial unsecured communications but *requires* clients to establish IPSec using a security method acknowledged by it.

- **Server (request security)**—accepts unsecured communications but *requests* that clients establish IPSec using a security method acknowledged by it. This policy allows for unsecured communication if the other system is not IPSec enabled.

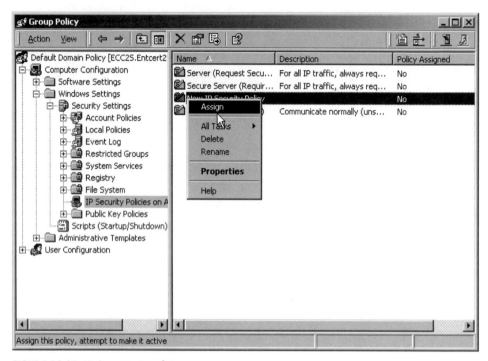

FIGURE 13.32 IP Security Templates

- **Client (respond only)**—should be assigned to computers that are secure within the intranet. When communication is initiated with other computers IPSec is not presented. However, if the remote computer requests secure communications, this policy is acknowledged.

To assign a security policy to a GPO, right-click the policy and select **Assign**. The **Policy Assigned** column should read **Yes** and all other policies should read **No** (Figure 13.32).

Creating a New IPSec Policy

Creating a new security policy involves right-clicking on the **IP Security Policies** from a selected GPO tree and selecting **Create IP Security Policy** (Figure 13.33). The **IP Security Policy Wizard** appears.

The creation process is straightforward, but a couple of concepts should be kept in mind. First, the default response rule, which is a part of every security policy, must be deactivated by the administrator if so desired (this can be done later). This filter enables the system to establish secure communication when other rules fail. Second, an authentication method needs to be established (Figure 13.34).

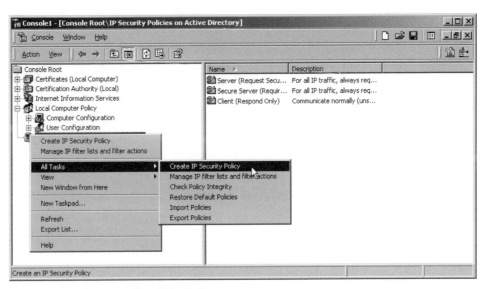

FIGURE 13.33 Creating a New IPSec Policy

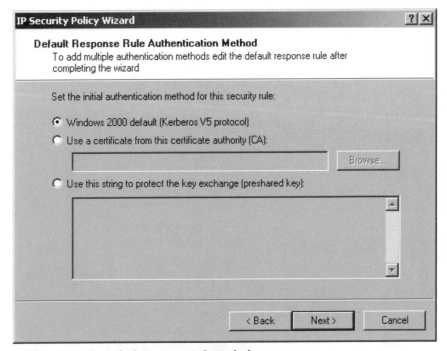

FIGURE 13.34 The Default Response Rule Method

AUTHENTICATION METHODS

The system administrator's ability to view security policies is a critical operating system requirement. View policy rules by right-clicking **Properties** for an **IP Security Policy** (Figure 13.35), selecting a filter, and then pressing the **Edit...** button.

The **Authentication Methods** tab presents the chosen method of authentication. Press the **Edit...** button to display the three methods IPSec uses (Figure 13.36).

- *Kerberos Version 5*—the default authentication method for clients who are part of a trusted Windows 2000 domain. The client does not need to be running Windows 2000.

- *Public Key Certificate*—used for non-Kerberos-enabled clients and for extranet and Internet access. The client and server must share a trusted CA to use certificate authentication.

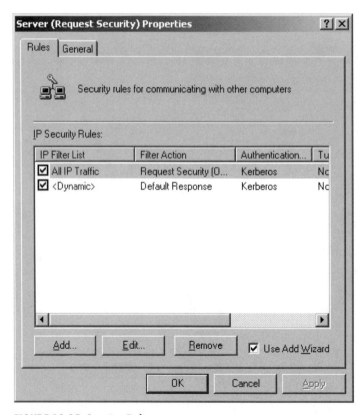

FIGURE 13.35 Security Rules

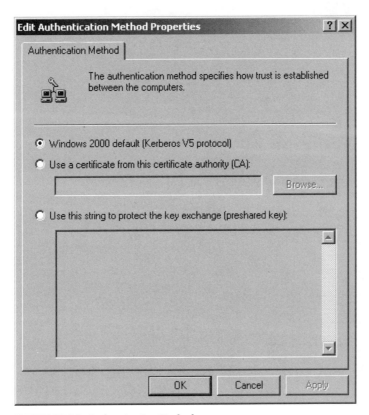

FIGURE 13.36 Authentication Method

- *Preshared Key*—requires a key to be shared between the client and server using an out-of-band method (telephone, snail mail, etc.) and manually configured on both systems. The shared string is used only for authentication purposes, not for data encryption.

TUNNEL SETTINGS

The **Tunnel Setting** tab allows the administrator to enter the destination or endpoint for an IPSec tunnel. Although we are not discussing tunneling here, this is where IPSec tunneling would be enabled. Windows 2000 is equipped with Layer 2 Tunneling Protocol (L2TP), which is preferred over IPSec as a tunneling implementation. IPSec should be used only for interoperability with systems that do not support PPTP or L2TP. The default selection **This rule does not specify an Ipsec tunnel** should be set to use L2TP (Figure 13.37).

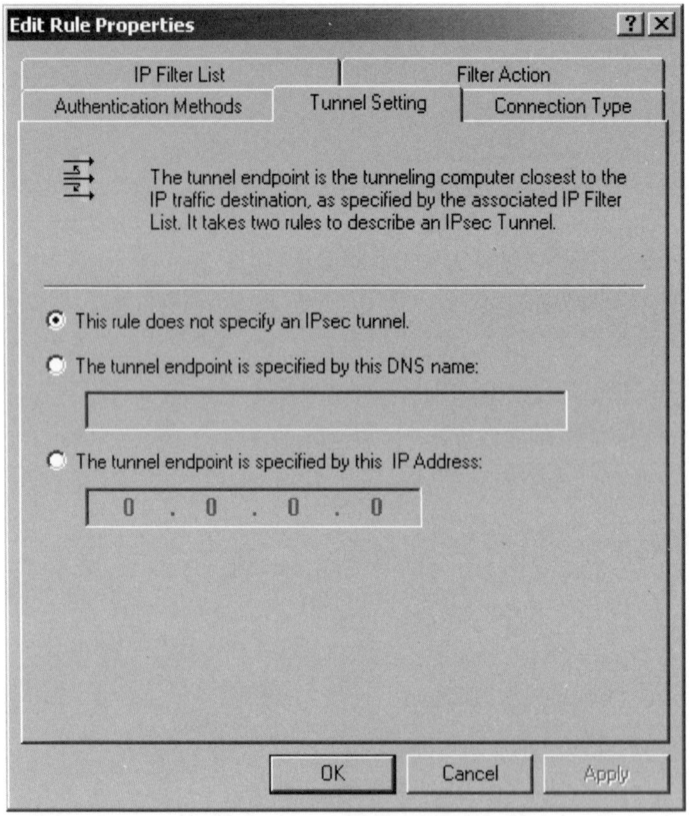

FIGURE 13.37 Editing a Rule Policy for Tunneling

CONNECTION TYPE

The **Connection Type** tab enables the user to select the type of connection to be utilized. The three choices are all network connections, LAN connections only, or remote access connections only (Figure 13.38). **Connection Type** allows the security policy to be limited to a couple of network connects. The local area network refers to the local adapter card, and the remote access option applies to *both* dial-in and VPN connections. Make sure to enable **Remote access** directly or through the **All network connections** selection when using this policy with tunneling.

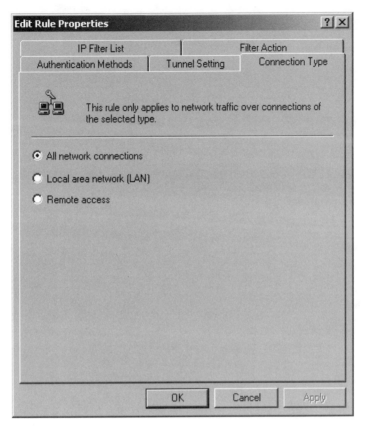

FIGURE 13.38 Connection Types

IP FILTERS

The **IP Filter List** tab enables selection of default filters and the ability to add new ones. These filters define IP addresses and subnets to which the IPSec rule will apply (Figure 13.39).

From the **IP Filter List** tab press the **Add...** button and follow the wizard instructions to add a new filter to the rule. Press the **Edit...** button to modify a current one. Press the next **Edit...** button to display filter properties (Figure 13.40). The **Source address:** and **Destination address:** fields on the **Address** tab for the IP filter each list five methods for setting filters on the address. Security policies implemented on a successful source/destination address match are determined by the filter actions to be discussed next.

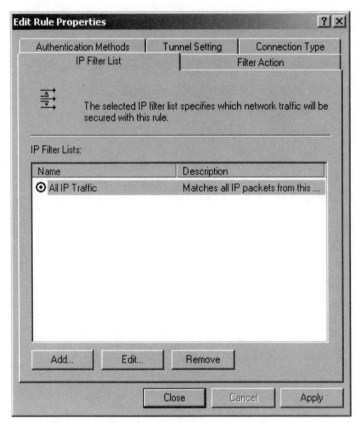

FIGURE 13.39 A Rule Policy for IP Filters

An IP packet will match the filter chosen if both its source and destination addresses match the filter's source and destination address ranges. These can be a particular address or a range of addresses.

- *My IP address.* The IP address of the system to which the rule has been applied. If My IP is the filter's source address, the rule is applied to all outgoing IP packets sent to the addresses specified in the filter's destination address. On the other hand, if it is the filter's destination address, the rule is applied to all incoming IP packets sent from the addresses specified in the filter's source address.

- *Any IP address.* Any IP value in the source or destination address of the IP packet will match this filter field.

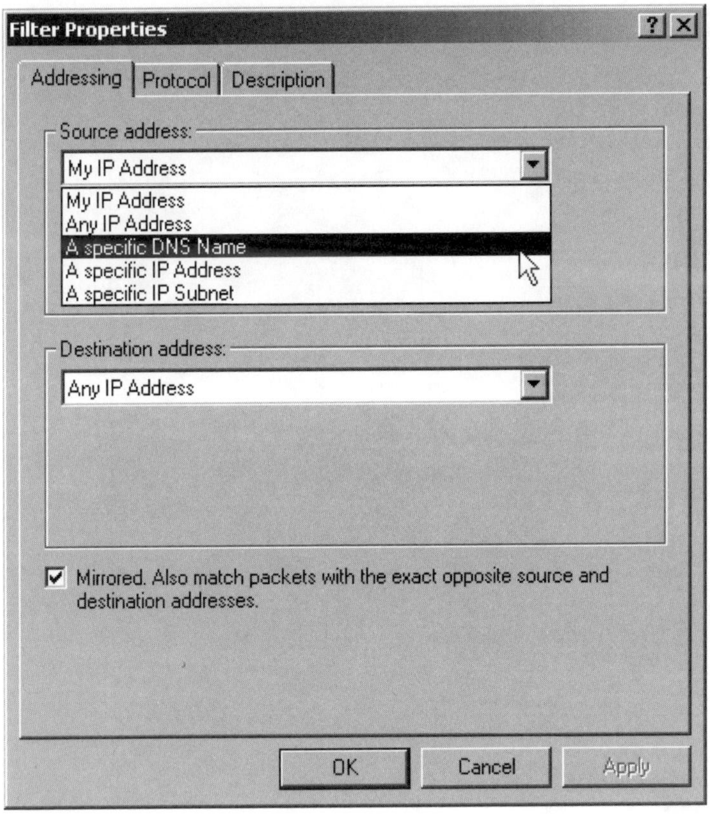

FIGURE 13.40 Filter Properties

- *A specific DNS name*. A DNS name is resolved to an IP address and compared with the source or the destination IP address field in the IP packet.
- *A specific IP address*. The entered IP address is compared with the source or destination IP address field in the IP packet.
- *A specific IP subnet*. An IP address range specified by subnet is compared with the source or destination IP address in the IP packet.

Checkmark the **Mirrored** box to create a reverse version of the current filter. This enables the rule to be applied to both inbound and outbound IP packets. **Mirrored** should not be used for IPSec tunneling rules. A tunneling filter specifies the tunnel destination IP address required to set up the IPSec tunnel.

The **Protocol** tab reveals transport layer protocols and port specifications for advanced protocol filtering (Figure 13.41). The **Description** tab allows detailed explanation and filter naming.

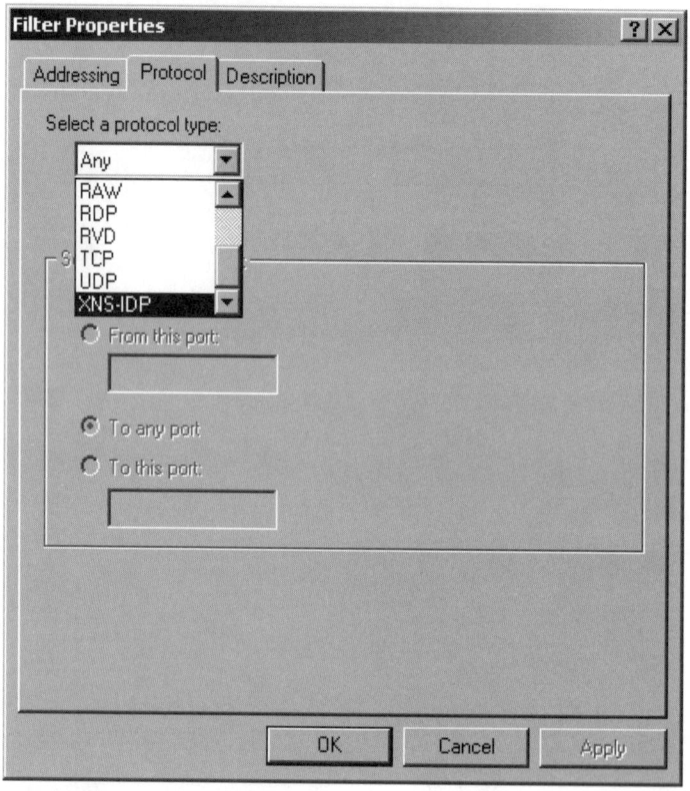

FIGURE 13.41 Filter Property Protocols

IP FILTER ACTIONS

Filter actions determine if and how the rule will negotiate for secure connections and the security methods to be used. From the **Filter Action** tab press the **Add...** button and follow the wizard instructions to add a new filter action. Select a filter action to modify and press the **Edit...** button (Figure 13.42). This brings up the **Security Methods** tab.

The **Security Methods** tab (Figure 13.43) has several options to configure. The first three work as follows:

- *Permit*. The rule will refuse to negotiate IP security and ignore all incoming secure communications. Only plain text nonsecured communication will be permitted.

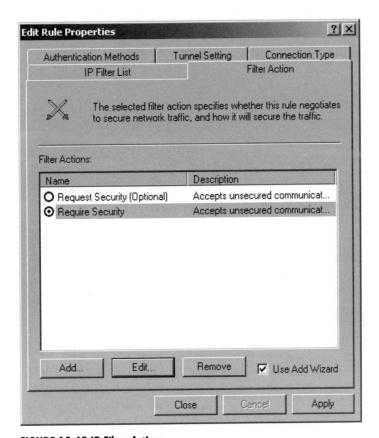

FIGURE 13.42 IP Filter Actions

- *Block.* All communications that meet the filter's requirements are blocked. There is no IP secure communication and no plain text communication.
- *Negotiate Security.* Communications that match a rule filter undergo IP security negotiation. Security methods are tried in descending order as listed under the **Security Method Preference order**.

The security properties options for a connection are

- *Accept unsecured communication, but always respond using IPSec.* This option will allow a client to initiate a plain text communication session but will immediately request that the client agree on a security method. If the client and server cannot establish a secure connection, communication will be terminated.

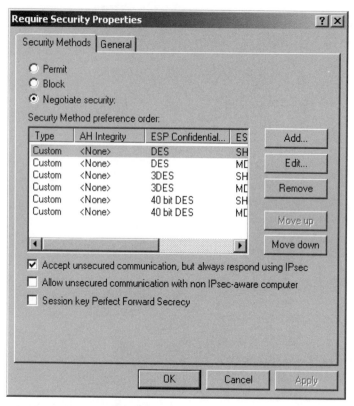

FIGURE 13.43 Security Methods

- *Allow unsecured communication with a non-IPsec-aware computer.* This option will first request negotiation for secure communication, but will disable IP security for clients that do not support IPSec. IPSec security is not required for this rule.

- *Session key perfect forward secrecy.* A new master key will need to be regenerated before a session key is obtained.

Press the **Edit** button to modify advanced features for security methods (Figure 13.44).

Selecting custom settings and pressing the **Settings** button (Figure 13.45) will display available custom IP security settings. Specific algorithms for data integrity (AH), encryption (ESP), and session key lifetime are configurable.

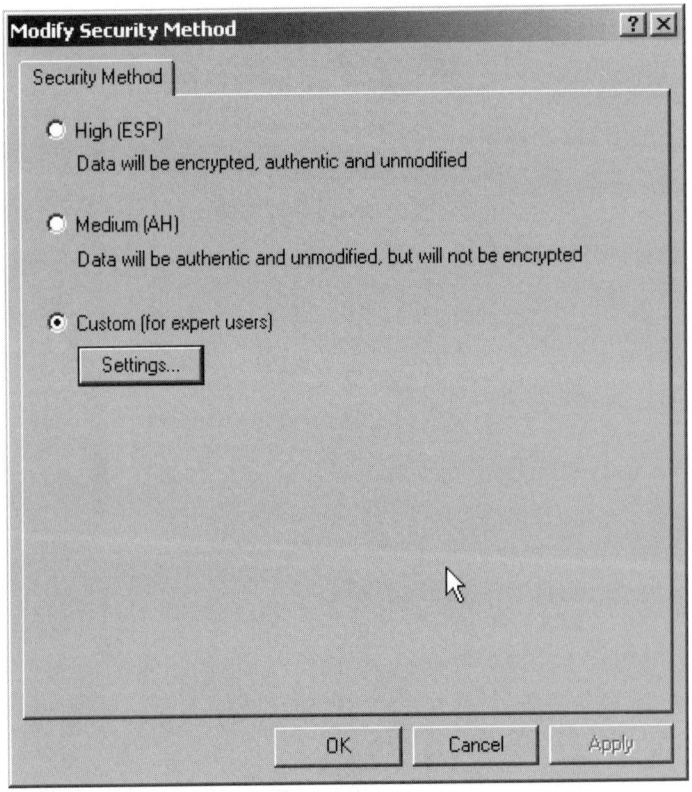

FIGURE 13.44 Modify Security Method

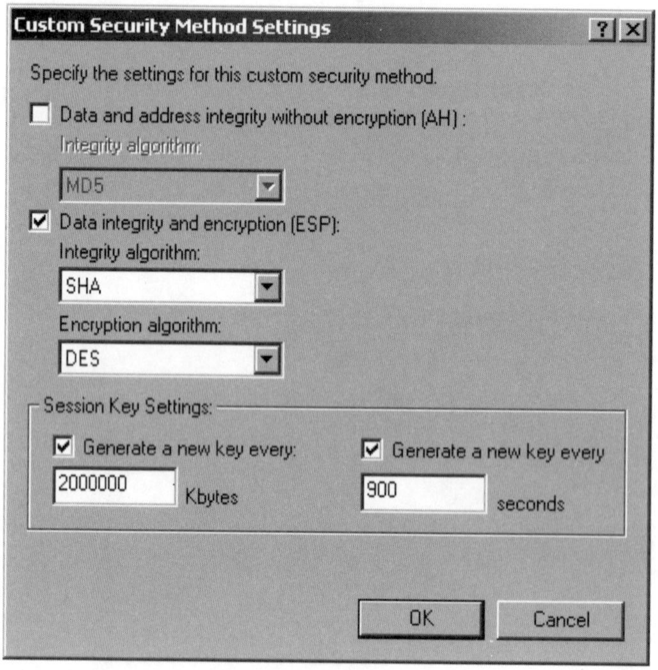

FIGURE 13.45 Custom Security Methods

POSTSCRIPT

This chapter provided a practical overview of VPN and IPSec. As the examples illustrated, these technologies can be used together, or IPSec can be configured as a replacement to VPN. We discussed these technologies by example rather than abstract theory, as your own environment will likely be different from the examples provided. However, when broadly applied the steps covered here should provide a reasonable approach to deploying VPN and IPSec.

Chapter 14

Disk Management, Backup and Restoration, and Disaster Recovery

This chapter examines Windows 2000 disk management, backup and restore technologies, and disaster recovery, which are all important system administrator functions. Failure to develop and enforce programs that implement them can result in significant damage to an IT organization. This is preventive medicine. Disk management, data restoration, and disaster recovery become important when the unexpected occurs. Unfortunately, this area of administration is often treated as an afterthought, although it should always be regarded as a primary activity.

Upon completion of this chapter, you should have knowledge of the following topics:

- Disk management, management tools, and storage types
- Striped, mirrored, and RAID-5 volumes
- Disk fragmentation
- Storage libraries
- Back-up and restore policies and methods
- Disaster recovery

DISK MANAGEMENT

In this section we examine disk storage types, partitions, and volumes, as well as NTFS disk-related features. The techniques explored include striping, mirroring, spanning, and RAID-5. We also look at disk quotas, compression, and defragmentation, along with remote storage, libraries, and tape/disk management.

NTFS and FAT/FAT32 Disk Management

NTFS and FAT/FAT32 file systems provide different features and levels of support with respect to disk management. NTFS is the preferred file system because of its expanded functionality. FAT/FAT32 is recommended on a partition only to get access to other Microsoft operating systems like MS-DOS or Windows 95/98. Otherwise, NTFS should be used because of the following features not available under FAT/FAT32:

- Compression
- Dynamic volume configuration
- Remote storage
- Disk quotas
- Mount points
- Encryption

Disk Management Tools

Windows 2000 provides a number of snap-in tools that can be added to the Microsoft Management Console. Some are grouped together for more convenient system administration. Table 14.1 lists the standard functions available within each of the snap-ins.

TABLE 14.1 Disk Management Snap-In Tools

Snap-In and Function Location	Function
Local Computer Policy → Computer Configuration → System → Disk Quota	Sets policies for disk quotas on a local machine.
Default Domain → Computer Configuration → System → Disk Quota	Sets policies for disk quotas on a local machine.
Computer Management → Storage	Accesses Disk Management, Disk Fragmenter, Logical Drives, and Removal Storage tools.
Standalone Disk Management	Primary disk management tool.
Standalone Disk Fragmenter	Disk fragmentation.
Windows 2000 Support Tools → Tools → Disk Probe	Optional Resource Kit tools that permit examination and editing of disk sectors.
Standalone Removal Storage	Manages removal storage.
Hardware Wizard (available through Control Panel)	Adds/removes storage media.

Disk Storage Types

Windows 2000 utilizes the **Disk Management** snap-in tool to view, administer, and migrate to disk storage types, partitions, and volumes.

Two disk storage types known as *basic* and *dynamic* are supported. The underlying difference between the two is the use of partitions versus volumes for disk management. Both are physical disks, but the basic type contains partitions, extended partitions, logical drivers, and an assortment of static volumes, whereas the dynamic type does not use partitions but dynamically manages volumes and provides advanced storage options, as discussed later.

Partitions are divisions of physical space on the same disk. Volumes can consist of one or more disks or portions of them and must be of the same storage type. Windows 2000 initially installs the operating system using a basic disk format. While the basic format works well, an upgrade to a dynamic disk is required to create spanned, striped, mirrored, or RAID-5 volumes.

UPGRADING A BASIC DISK TO A DYNAMIC DISK

The actual process of upgrading a disk to dynamic storage is very straightforward. However, several rules can impact this transformation, including the following:

- In cases where a volume crosses multiple disks, all related disks must be upgraded.
- Any operating system other than Windows 2000 located on a partition or volume will be rendered inoperable.
- Removable media cannot be upgraded.
- A basic disk with the boot partition cannot be upgraded; instead, it becomes a simple boot volume after the system is restarted.
- When a boot partition is upgraded to a simple volume, it can be used to mirror a volume on another disk for redundancy.

The following steps should be taken to upgrade a disk from basic to dynamic:

- Open the **Disk Management** snap-in.
- Right-click the target basic disk, click **Upgrade to Dynamic Disk**, and follow the remaining steps as prompted.

CAUTION   This upgrade cannot be reversed without serious impact. The only way to return to partitions is to delete all dynamic volumes, so make sure you back up all information on the volumes first. Then use the **Revert To Basic Disk** command by repeating the procedure outlined in the previous example.

MANAGING PARTITIONS AND BASIC STORAGE

Basic storage provides backward compatibility with Windows NT 4.0 disk schemes. In an upgrade to Windows 2000, it is established on the existing partition. Existing Windows NT 4.0 volumes can also be preserved using the **Disk Management** tool.

NOTE

While it was possible to create striped and mirrored disk sets under Windows NT Server 4.0, this is not the case with a Windows 2000 basic disk. Existing striped and mirrored volumes will be recognized after a Windows 2000 upgrade, but you will be restricted to repairing and deleting them. Creating new fault tolerance is reserved for dynamic disk volumes.

Windows 2000 basic disks can consist of up to four partitions on a physical drive, and extended partitions larger than 2 GB can be created, as can logical drives. This is done in the same fashion as on Windows NT Server 4.0, except that restarting the computer system is no longer necessary.

Partition Management

The **Disk Management** snap-in tool supports four primary basic partition and volume administration actions. The following summarizes how to accomplish the partition management tasks:

- *Formatting a partition.* This is done through the **Disk Management** tool → **All Tasks** → **Format**. Although not recommended, you can use the **Quick** format to format the disk; however, **Quick** does not scan the disk for bad sectors, and when formatting, all data on the partition is lost.

- *Designating the partition as active.* From the **Disk Management** tool, right-click on the target partition and select the active (or primary) partition.

- *Assigning drive letters.* Open the **Disk Management** tool, right-click on the partition, select **Change Drive Letter or Path**, and make the designation. Up to 26 letters can be assigned, with drives A and B being reserved for floppy disks.

- *Deleting a partition.* From the **Disk Management** tool, right-click on the partition to be removed and select **Delete Partition**. Remember, this will destroy all the data on the partition.

MANAGING VOLUMES

Dynamic disk simple volumes cannot include partitions or logical drives. They are used strictly for Windows 2000, not Windows 95/98/NT or MS-DOS. Despite these restrictions, the dynamic disk system offers many advantages, including the ability to utilize spanned, striped, and mirrored volumes and RAID-5, and support of compression. A brief examination of each of these technologies should underscore dynamic disk volumes' inherent flexibility.

NTFS Compression

Compression of files and folders is an excellent way to use available disk space efficiently. Although physical disk costs per storage unit continue to fall, it is still appropriate to use compression, especially for archival information.

NTFS file and folder compression is achieved by right-clicking on the object from within **Explorer**, selecting **Properties**, and then selecting **Advanced**. As shown in Figure 14.1, the **Advanced Attributes** dialog box permits you to select **Compress contents to save disk space**, and the confirmation window then permits you to apply the compression only to the current folder or to all subfolders with a checkmark as appropriate. A file or folder can be uncompressed by

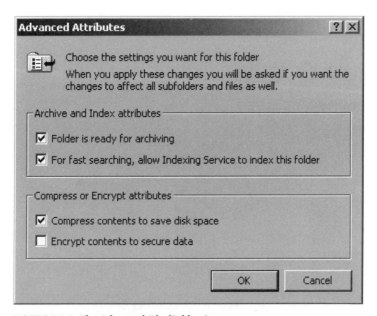

FIGURE 14.1 The Advanced File/Folder Screen

removing the checkmark. (You can also assign index attributes and encrypt the connects by selecting the appropriate item in this same dialog box.) Compression ratios are generally higher for files such as those created by Word or Excel than for bitmap or graphic files. Applications are usually already optimized for size and generally result in minimal compression.

When moving and copying compressed files or folders within or between NTFS volumes, the compression state remains; however, when copying or moving an NTFS compressed file or folder to a FAT file system, the compression is lost and the file/folder returns to its normal size. Remember, compression is not supported in the FAT file system.

Spanned Volumes

Spanned volume technology is a method of combining free space on 1 to 32 physical disks into a single volume, with the available space on each of the spanned disks of varying size. Storage is accomplished by filling the space on one disk and logically moving to each subsequent spanned disk as more data storage is added. This involves the concatenation of data from one disk to another (Figure 14.2).

CAUTION   While spanned disks provide greater efficiency, they have two significant downsides. First, fault tolerance is not supported. Second, if one of the disks fails in a spanned disk volume, the entire volume fails. The only protection for this type of disaster is regular backups.

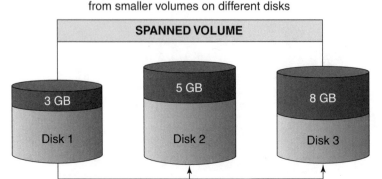

FIGURE 14.2 A Single 16GB Spanned Volume Created from Smaller Volumes on Different Disks

Creating a Spanned Volume.   Spanned volumes are created from dynamic disks with the **Disk Management** tool with the following steps:

1. Open the **Disk Management** snap-in tool.

2. Right-click the unallocated volume to be spanned from the dynamic disks, then click **Create Volume**.

3. The **Create Volume** wizard appears. Click **Next**, then click **Spanned Volume**, and then follow the remaining instructions.

Extending a Spanned Volume.   A spanned volume is extended through the **Disk Management** snap-in tool. First, the computer system must recognize the space on available disks. To make sure this is properly calculated, select the **Action** pull-down menu and select **Rescan Disks**. To actually expand the volume, right-click on the spanned volume, select **Extend Volume**, and then follow the remaining instructions.

Managing Striped Volumes

Striped volumes are similar to spanned volumes in that both permit the utilization of available space on up to 32 disks. However, unlike spanned volumes, which sequentially store data on disks, the striped logical volume distributes the information simultaneously across all of the disks within it. Individual striped volumes are divided into fixed and ordered blocks. Because of this architecture, they have faster I/O.

A failure of a single disk will result in the loss of data on the entire logical striped volume. As discussed later, RAID-5 offers a fault-tolerant version of striped volumes.

A striped volume is created by following these steps:

1. Open the **Disk Management** snap-in.

2. Right-click unallocated space for the dynamic disks, then click **Create Volume**.

3. The **Create Volume** wizard appears. Click **Next**, click **Striped Volume**, and then follow the remaining instructions.

Managing Mirrored Volumes

A mirrored volume does exactly as its name implies by duplicating data on multiple physical disks. This fault-tolerant technology is highly recommended for mission-critical data stores. If one of the disks fails, the other disk continues to operate as normal without any data loss (Figure 14.3).

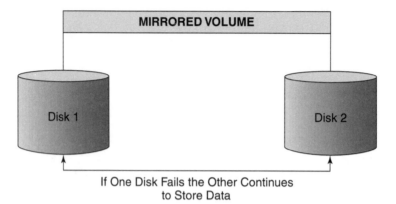

FIGURE 14.3 **A Mirrored Volume Containing Duplicate Data**

Mirrored volumes generally perform better than RAID-5 (discussed in the next section). Moreover, there is no loss of performance when one volume fails. A disadvantage is that mirrored volumes' use of the physical disk is less efficient. They require a minimum of two disks whereas RAID-5 requires three.

Mirrored volumes are created with the **Disk Management** tool from dynamic disks by following these steps:

1. Open the **Disk Management** snap-in tool.

2. Right-click the unallocated volume to be mirrored from the dynamic disks, and then click **Create Volume**.

3. The **Create Volume** wizard appears. Click **Next**, then **Mirrored Volume**, and follow the remaining instructions.

If one of the disks fails and you want to create another mirror, you must manually *break* the original mirror by using the **Disk Management** tool. The new mirror is created as in the above walk-through.

Managing RAID-5 Volumes

Known as a striped volume with parity under Windows NT, RAID-5 in Windows 2000 is a fault-tolerant volume across three or more disks, two of which duplicate the data while the third stores the parity information. If a portion of a disk fails, it can be reconstructed from the data and the parity of the remaining disks. In environments where disk reading is intense, this form of fault tolerance should be considered. It is generally a better solution than mirrored volumes, which require a very high redundancy.

RAID-5 can be viewed as a compromise between full redundancy and disk utilization. Remember, mirroring is used for redundancy, striping for greater speed;

thus parity is the middle ground, providing single-bit protection for striped data. Generally, RAID-5 is used when some level of protection is desired but full mirroring is not cost justified.

RAID-5 volumes are created with the **Disk Management** tool from dynamic disks by following these steps:

1. Open the **Disk Management** snap-in tool.

2. Right-click the unallocated volume from the dynamic disks; and then click **Create Volume**.

3. The **Create Volume** wizard appears. Click **Next**, click **RAID-5 Volume**, and then follow the instructions.

The Disk Management Snap-In Tool

In the previous section, the **Disk Management** snap-in tool was explored as a way to administer spanned, striped, mirrored, and RAID-5 disk configurations, but it has additional functions. For this reason it is appropriate to step back for a moment and review this tool in more generic terms.

The Disk Management tool can be added as a standalone Microsoft Management Console (MMC) snap-in. It is also available as part of the **Computer Management** snap-in or the **Start → Programs → Administrative** tool. As shown in Figure 14.4, Disk Management is divided into sections that detail various aspects of the system's storage devices. Hard drives, removable disks, CD-ROMs, and other devices are shown with current status and statistics. In the event that the system administrator doubts that this information is current, or if a new device was just added, **Rescan Disks** from the **Action** menu can perform a reevaluation.

In Figure 14.4 the primary partition is a dark blue banner and the logical drive is a lighter blue. Extended partitions (not shown) are green.

Each partition, volume, or logical drive has its own unique properties. These properties can be viewed or modified by right-clicking on the desired partition, volume, or logical drive and selecting **Properties**. The Local Disk Properties dialog is divided into several sections as shown in Figure 14.5.

DISK PROPERTIES OPTIONS AVAILABLE UNDER NTFS

The Disk Management tool options are different for NTFS and FAT/FAT32 file systems. Properties Tabs for NTFS perform the administrative tasks listed here:

- *General*. In addition to providing basic utilization statistics, the administrator can compress the drive, allow the **Indexing Service** to index the disk for fast file searches, and clean up the disk by pressing the **Disk Cleanup** button.

- *Tools*. These tools support error checking, backup, and disk defragmentation.

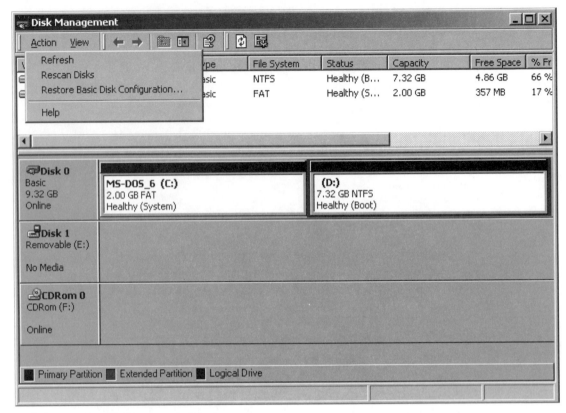

FIGURE 14.4 The Disk Management Snap-In

- *Hardware*. This tab identifies storage devices. Via the **Properties** button, new device drivers can be added through the respective dialog box.
- *Sharing*. This tab lists the current sharing status in addition to permissions and caching. New shares with associated permissions levels can also be created.
- *Web Sharing*. This tab establishes whether the disk can be shared on the Web. By default, sharing is not allowed. Web sharing is not available on Windows 2000 Professional.
- *Quota*. This tab enables quota management as discussed in a later section.
- *Security*. This tab establishes which users and groups have access to the disk at various permissions levels.

DISK PROPERTIES OPTIONS UNDER FAT/FAT32

The options available for FAT/FAT32 are more limited than those for NTFS. Its Properties tabs perform administrative tasks as follows (Figure 14.6):

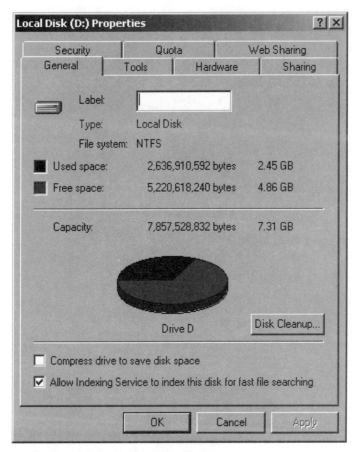

FIGURE 14.5 NTFS Disk Properties Management

- *General*. In addition to providing basic utilization statistics, the administrator can elect to compress the drive or allow the **Indexing Service** to index the disk for fast file searches.
- *Tools*. These tools support error checking, backup, and disk defragmentation.
- *Hardware*. This tab lists the identified storage devices. The **Properties** button allows new device drivers to be added through the respective dialog box.
- *Sharing*. This tab lists the current sharing status in addition to permissions and caching. New shares with associated permissions levels can also be created.
- *Web Sharing*. This tab establishes whether the disk can be shared on the Web. No sharing is the default.

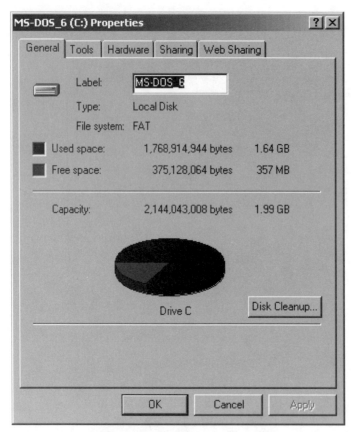

FIGURE 14.6 FAT Disk Properties Management

DISK QUOTAS

Disk quotas are used to control unbridled storage of data. They can be applied on an individual or system-wide basis, and permit the system administrator to limit the amount of space allocated for storage of information on a given volume. Quotas are generally recommended. A user is notified when she approaches the maximum allowable disk space level, at which point she can delete any unwanted files. Alternatively, the user can request additional space for archiving files to backup media. In any case, greater control over disk space utilization is achieved.

Applying Disk Quotas to All Users

Most system administrators will initially set the same disk quotas for all system users. As illustrated in the next section, individual users or groups can then receive a unique quota as needed. Applying the same set of disk quotas for all users in a local system is achieved by following these steps:

1. Open **My Computer** and right-click on the volume (for example, drive D). Select **Properties**.

2. Select the **Quotas** tab. Check **Enable quota management**.

3. Complete the form as appropriate.

The Quotas tab (Figure 14.7) requires four decisions: first, whether quota management is to be enforced; second, whether or not to deny additional space if the quota is exceeded; third, the level at which the quota amount and warning must be set; and finally, the type of event logging required.

NOTE   Most system administrators will not expressly deny the use of additional space. To deny a user the ability to save a file can result in hostility and the possible loss of data. As an alternative, the system administrator should use the event logging facility to determine where potential abuse is occurring and then contact the user about disk use. Most users will take appropriate action. If a user continues to abuse privileges, then the more radical step of denial can be taken.

Applying disk quota policies to an entire domain is similar. Open the **Default Domain** snap-in for the target domain, select **Computer Configuration**, select **Administrative Templates**, select **Disk Quotas**, and configure each of the policies in the right-hand panel.

Applying Disk Quotas to Individual Users

As with most things, there are exceptions to disk quotas. Once a global standard is set, it is possible to set limits for individuals or groups. Individual quotas are set by pressing the **Quota Entries** button in the **Quota** tab as shown in Figure 14.8. The **Quota Entries for Drive** is then displayed. Select the **Quota** pull-down menu and then choose **New Quota**. Add the users and groups to which you want to apply individual quotas. In the dialog box, select the disk quota constraints to be applied.

DISK FRAGMENTATION MANAGEMENT

Saved data is stored in the first available location on the physical drive. To make a drive its most efficient, a file can be broken up and stored in a number of locations—a process known as "fragmenting." This process ordinarily does not compromise file integrity because the parts are indexed for reassembly. However, when a large number of files are fragmented, indexing can impact performance. In this case reconstructing a file may require several reads of the hard drive to find all of the fragments. To correct fragmentation performance losses, a method known as "defragmentation" is provided to periodically "reorganize" the disk drive to gather the fragments together.

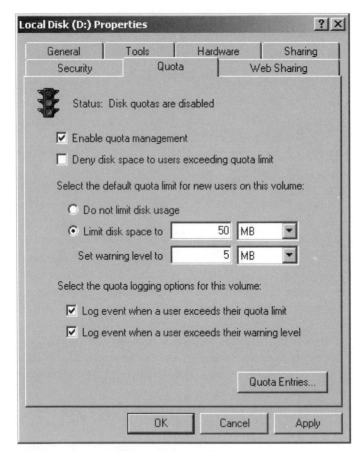

FIGURE 14.7 The Disk Quota Properties Tab

Analyzing and Defragmenting a Drive

Defragmentation first collects information about the physical drive and the fragmented files. It then rewrites the disk to rejoin fragmented files in continuous blocks. The analysis and defragmentation of a drive is accomplished with the **Disk Defragmenter** snap-in tool (Figure 14.9) as follows:

1. Open the **Disk Defragmenter** snap-in tool.
2. Select the **Analyze** button for the target volume.
3. After the analysis is complete, Windows 2000 will prompt you if defragmentation is appropriate. Select **Defragment**.

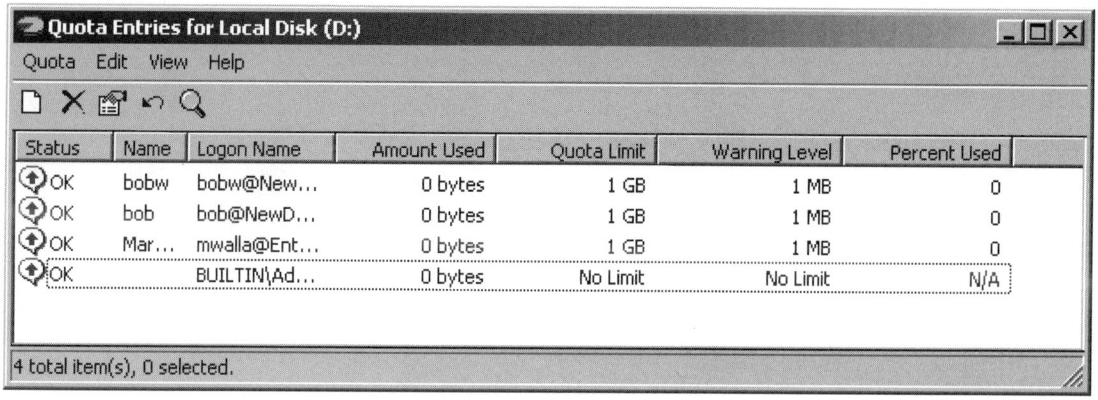

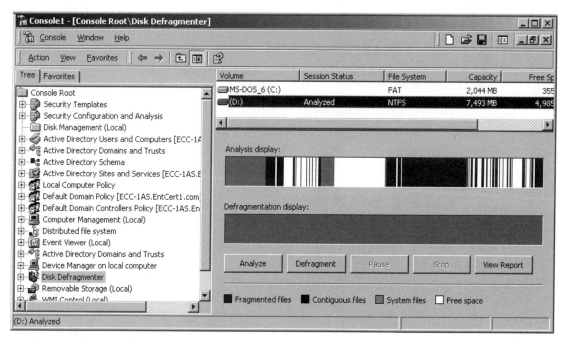

FIGURE 14.8 Quota Entries

FIGURE 14.9 The Disk Defragmenter Snap-In Tool

Removable Media and Library Management

The **Removable Media** snap-in tool assists in the identification, modification, and management of removable media libraries and devices like ZIP drives, CD-ROMs, and DVDs. As shown in Figure 14.10, it is divided between the administra-

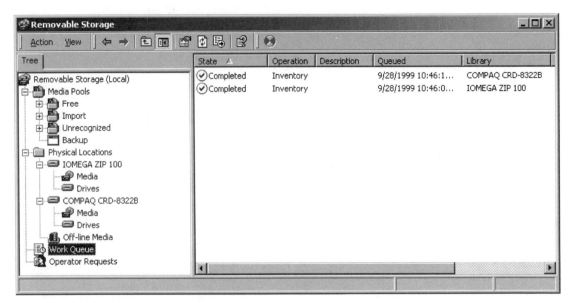

FIGURE 14.10 The Removable Media Snap-In Tool

tion of Media Pools, Physical Locations, Work Queue, and Operator Requests. The tool also permits the insertion and rejection of robotic library media. The **Removable Storage** tool supports the creation of media inventories, properties viewing, and mounting/dismounting.

WORKING WITH LIBRARIES

In the context of this discussion, a library is the combination of storage media and devices that permit the reading and writing of a given removable medium. The type of media can vary widely. For example, in more sophisticated systems, a transport mechanism known as a robotic library (also called a tape or disc changer or jukebox) is used to locate and mount a piece of media into the read or read/write device. Depending on the robotic library's features, many other items can be managed with the **Removable Media** tool. The use of such devices is generally manufacturer dependent, so consult the user or administrative manuals for the device.

A much simpler type of library is the single media device that is not automatically loaded or changed, such as a CD-ROM, DVD player, or ZIP drive. The following examples are based on the use of such a simple, standalone library.

Enabling or Disabling a Library

The enabling or disabling of a library involves a few simple steps, as follows:

1. Open the **Removable Storage** snap-in tool.

2. Open the **Physical Locations** console tree.

3. Right-click on the library component and select **Properties**.

4. From the **General** tab verify that the **Enable library** check is selected in order to enable this library, or remove the check to disable it.

Changing the Media Type

Change the media type for a library as follows:

1. Open the **Removable Storage** snap-in tool.

2. Open the **Physical Locations** console tree.

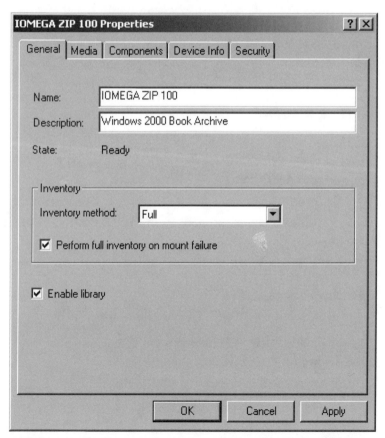

FIGURE 14.11 The Library Properties General Tab with a Library Enabled

3. Right-click on the library component and select **Properties**.

4. From the **Media** tab select **Change**.

5. From the **Change Media Types** dialog add or remove the media types as desired.

Initiating a Library Inventory

To create an inventory for the library, take the following steps:

1. Open the **Removable Storage** snap-in tool.

2. Open the **Physical Locations** console tree.

3. Right-click on the library component and select **Inventory**.

WORKING WITH MEDIA POOLS

A media pool is any compilation of disks or tapes with the same administrative properties. Multiple media pools can be supported, but they must all be of the same type—disks and tapes cannot be mixed. More than one media pool constitutes a library, which can include media pools of different type and property settings. Since common properties are applied to a media pool, they can also be addressed with multiple libraries (Figure 14.12).

Creating a New Media Pool

New media pools are created by following these steps:

1. Open the **Removable Storage** snap-in tool.

2. Right-click on **Media Pools** and select **Create Media Pool**.

3. From the **General** tab complete the **Name** and **Description** textboxes.

4. From the **General** tab select media from the **Contains media of type** pull-down menu.

5. From the **General** tab set the Allocation/Deallocation policy desired.

Deleting an Application Media Pool

Application media pools are deleted by following these steps:

1. Open the **Removable Storage** snap-in tool.

2. Open the **Media Pools** console tree.

3. Click the target media pool and select **Delete**.

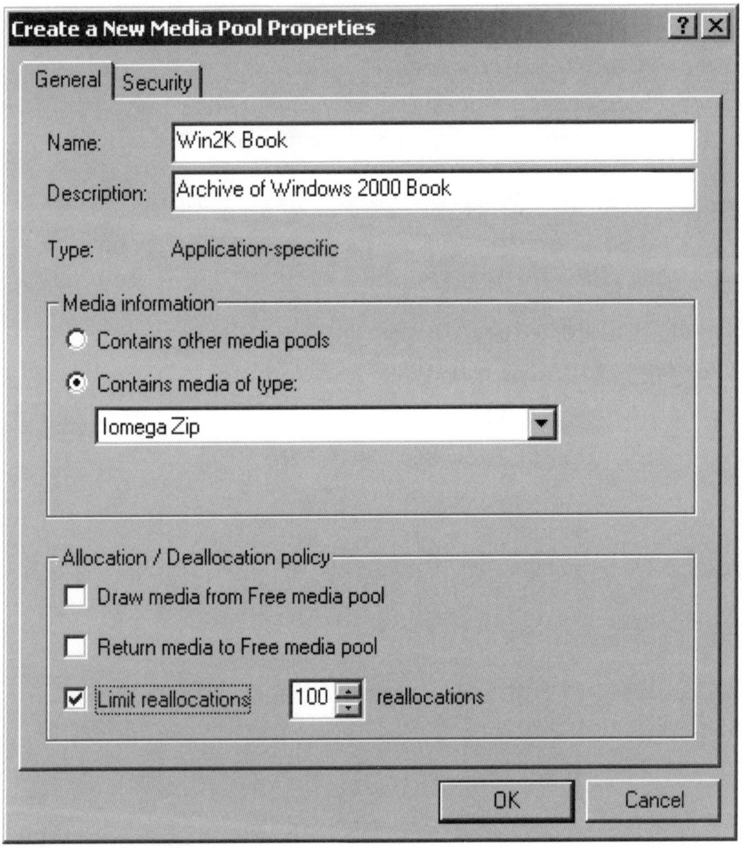

FIGURE 14.12 Creating a New Media Pool

Moving Media to Another Media Pool

To move media to another media pool, take the following steps. Remember that the media type and administrative properties of the pool to be moved must be the same as those of the target media pool.

1. Open the **Removable Storage** snap-in tool.

2. Open the **Media Pools** console tree.

3. Click on **Physical Locations** and select the desired application library. Select **Media**.

4. From the right-hand Details pane, drag and drop the tape or disk to the target media pool.

OPERATOR REQUEST MANAGEMENT

The Removal Storage tool permits management of certain operator requests. The options include how to respond to requests, deleting requests from the log, canceling pending operations, and altering the mount order.

Responding to Operator Requests

Operator requests are stored for about an hour after they have been processed. To instruct Windows 2000 on responding to them, follow these steps:

1. Open the **Removable Storage** snap-in tool.
2. Open the **Operator Requests** console tree.
3. From the right-hand Details panel, right-click the target request.
4. To enforce the request select **Complete**.
5. To disregard the request select **Refuse**.

Canceling a Pending Operations Request

If a request for a medium is incorrectly made or inappropriately timed, it can be canceled as follows:

1. Open the **Removable Storage** snap-in tool.
2. Open the **Work Queue** console tree.
3. Right-click on the request to be canceled and click **Cancel Request** (or **Delete**).

Changing the Mount Order of a Work Queue

Windows 2000 makes it easy to change the order in which tapes or disks are mounted. Follow these steps to change the mount order:

1. Open the **Removable Storage** snap-in tool.
2. From the Details panel right-click on the mount operation and click **Re-order Mounts**.
3. Through the **Change Mount Order** select the medium and move it to the beginning or end or to another location.

SECURING REMOVABLE STORAGE

The **Removable Storage** snap-in affords ways of determining which users have permission to use removal media and associated devices. The system administrator can add, modify, or delete users and their respective permissions by selecting the **Securities** tab of the media or device **Properties**. Refer to Chapter 9 for additional information regarding general permissions settings.

Remote Storage

The remote storage facility automatically archives the least used files to another device when available space on the local partition or volume becomes tight. Remote storage occurs only when local disk space is required. When the file is needed again, it is retrieved and saved locally.

Remote storage is often maintained on removable storage libraries but always in the same media pool. This means that only the same media types with identical administrative properties can be remotely stored. Optical disks are not supported for remote storage. Also note that retrieval of remotely stored files is only as fast as the storage device. Thus, if it is necessary to robotically find, mount, and read a tape, for example, the user can anticipate a low to moderate delay.

Remote storage is not automatically installed with the operating system but through the Windows 2000 Setup. After installation it is necessary to verify that a sufficiently large and free media pool exists that is formatted for Windows 2000 NTFS.

The administrator establishes the rules and criteria for remote storage, and only those files that meet these specific policies will be eligible for movement. The **Remote Storage** tool provides a list of default inclusion and exclusion settings for files, which can also be removed or modified. Use the **Remote Storage** snap-in tool to manage file rules and associated tasks.

BACKUP AND RESTORATION

Backup strategies are based on the effective requirements to restore data. Restoration can range from periodic retrieval of archived information to a full-scale recovery from disaster.

BACKUP STRATEGY BASICS

A backup strategy requires an understanding of the types of backup available along with their methods and applicable rules. Windows 2000 backup should be planned according to these considerations, among others:

- *Frequency of backup*. This varies according to nature of the data. Mission-critical data should be backed up at least daily. Less critical data can be scheduled for backup over the weekend.

- *Archival media*. Depending on the amount of information to be backed up, data can be archived on a variety of media. Capacity must be determined beforehand.

- *Files/folders selection*. The administrator needs to have a plan for the backup of critical system files (like the Active Directory or the Registry), mission-critical files, and ordinary data files. The files and folders to be backed up must be selected first.

- *Network and local backup*. The plan must include where the backup is to be archived. Obviously, remote backups assume the availability of a fast and reliable network connection. Security over the remote connection is also a consideration.

- *Secure storage of backup media*. The archival plan must include securing media from theft, damage, or unauthorized review.

AVAILABLE BACKUP TYPES

There are four basic Windows 2000 backup schemes. Each has its strengths. In most IT environments, all four types are employed at different times, and they can be combined as well. In some backup schemes when a file changes, a marker is set to flag the change. This marker is known as an archive attribute. A backup will clear the marker.

- *Daily*. Selected file and folder backup is performed daily but only for files that were changed during that day. Markers are not reset in daily backups.

- *Incremental*. Only selected files and folders that have set markers are sent for backup. The marker is then cleared so that future incremental backups do not include them. Incremental backups can be scheduled at any time.

- *Copy*. All selected files and folders are archived without clearing markers.

- *Normal*. All selected files and folders are backed up and their existing markers cleared. Normal backup does not rely on markers but backs up all selected files or folders.

WHO CAN BACK UP

The Administrators, Backup Operators, and Server Operators groups have authority to back up and restore all files of a local computer. Domain Administrator and Domain Backup Operators can perform domain-wide backups.

Individual users can back up their own files and folders as well as those in which they have Read, Read & Execute, Modify, or Full Control permissions. File and folder restoration by a user requires Write, Modify, or Full Control permissions.

CAUTION   Allowing a normal user with mere Read permission to back up any file or folder creates potential security risks. For example, such a file could be backed up and spirited out of the organization. It is therefore advised that these rights be restricted. Confine backup only to the owner of the file and the Administrator or Backup Operator. This restriction should be set in the **Backup Job Information** dialog box.

Managing Backups with NTBACKUP

The backup tool is invoked from either the **Start** → **Accessories** → **Backup** menu or the command line *ntbackup* utility available through **Command Prompt** or **Start** → **Run**. The Backup and Restore Wizard is shown in Figure 14.13.

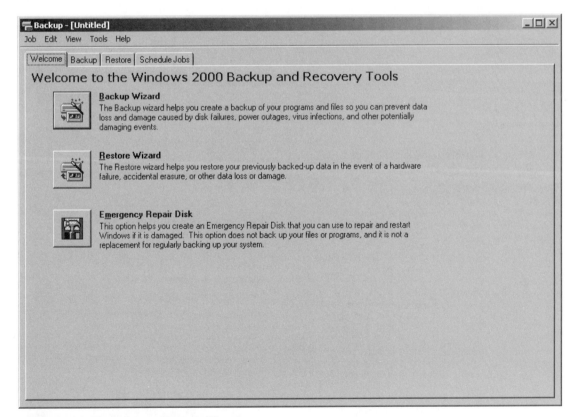

FIGURE 14.13 The Backup and Restore Wizard

The Backup Wizard walks you through the standard backup decisions, the first of which is presented in the initial dialog box. The first option is to back up everything on the system; the second is the selection of specific files and folders; and the third is to back up *System State* data. Selecting any of these options opens up other options.

Let's select the option to back up selected files, drives, or network data, which invokes a dialog box that permits selection of the items to be backed up, as shown in Figure 14.14.

The next option is to determine where the data will be saved. Use the **Browse** button to navigate to the chosen local or network location and then select to finish the backup. The **Advanced** button fine-tunes this process. As Figure 14.15 shows, you can select the type of backup, and subsequent dialog boxes allow you to append information such as the name of the archived volume and the date and time it is to be backed up.

The time for the backup is selected through the **Schedule** tab (Figure 14.16). Double-click on the date. The **Backup Wizard** is then launched to define the scope and type of backup as just reviewed.

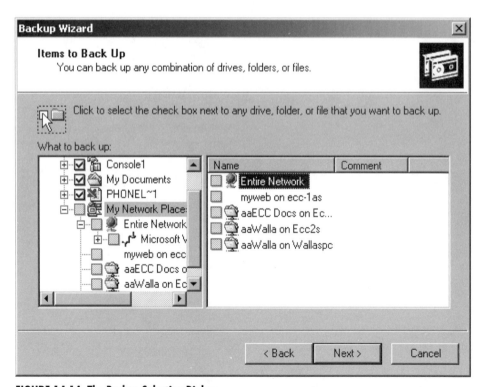

FIGURE 14.14 The Backup Selection Dialog

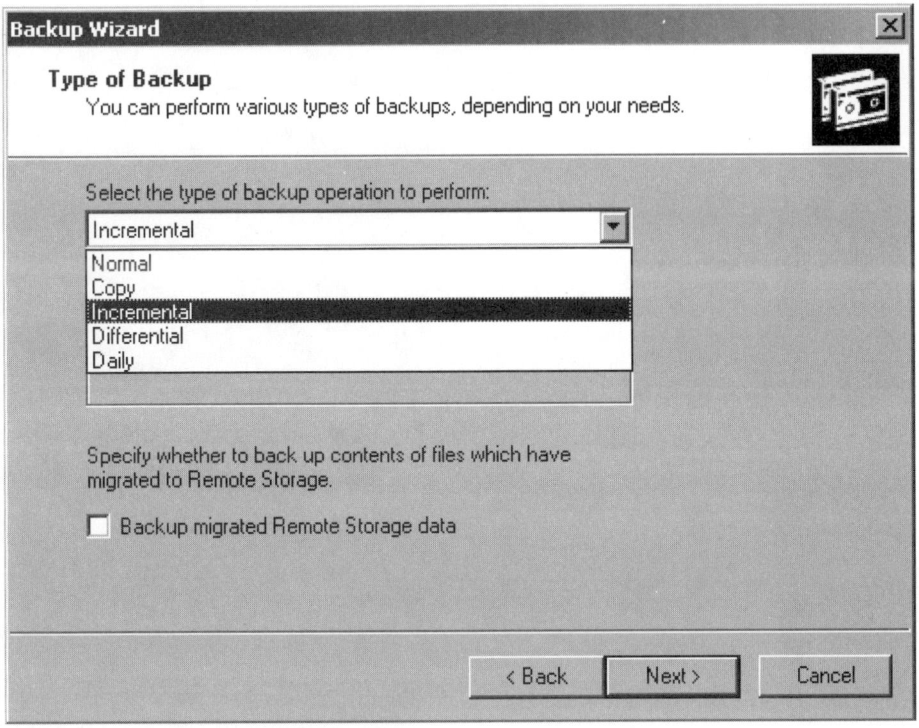

FIGURE 14.15 Selecting the Type of Backup

Changing Default Backup Options

The *ntbackup* tool provides a number of options that fit the organization's backup needs. From the *ntbackup* application select **Tools** and then **Options**. Make the appropriate changes in any of the following tabs:

- General backup rules and reporting methods
- Restore rules
- Default backup types as discussed previously
- Backup log default settings
- Exclusionary rules for backup and restore

Restoration Basics

Restoration is used primarily to recover lost or damaged data. For this reason, maintaining accurate records on backups can save valuable time. With proper records, it is possible to apply only the incremental or daily backup containing the

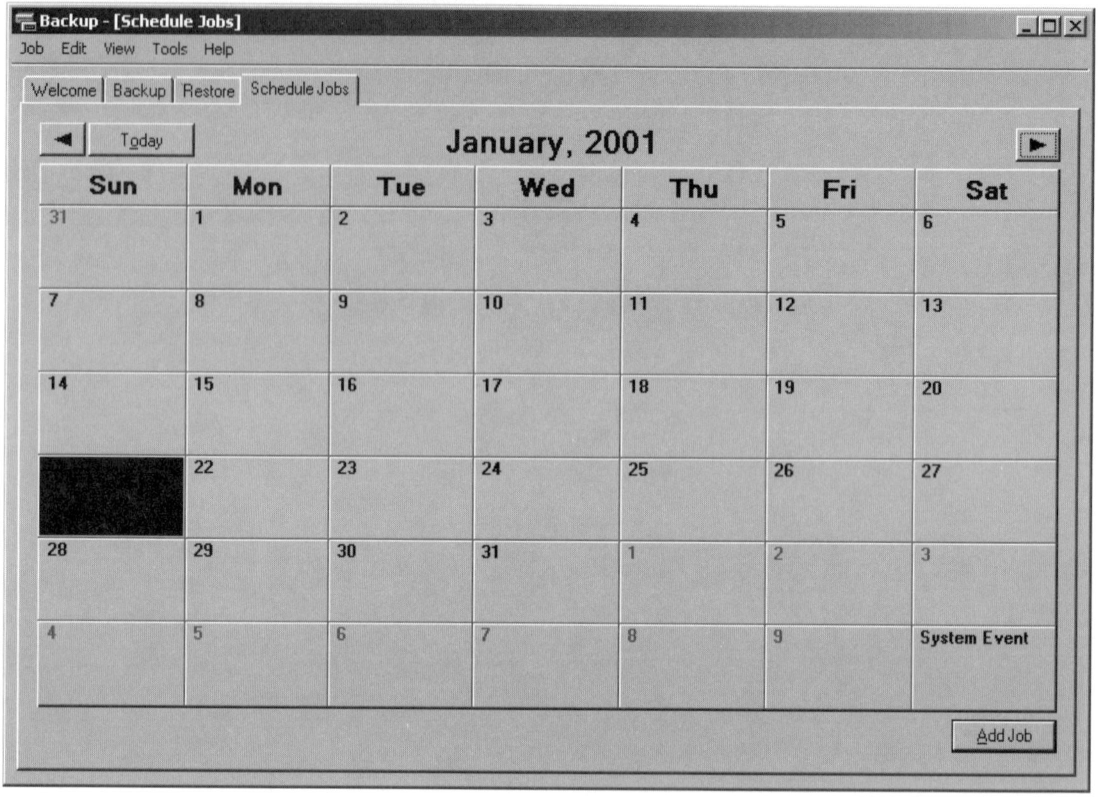

FIGURE 14.16 Backup Scheduling

lost or damaged data. If more radical restoration is required, begin with the last normal backup and then apply incremental backup sequentially until full restoration is achieved.

How to Restore

The process of restoration is carried out by the Restore Wizard, which is available from the *ntbackup* application or the **Start → Accessories → Backup** menu (Figure 14.17). This Wizard requires you to identify the media and files or folders to be restored according to the following basic procedure:

1. Open the *ntbackup* application and select **Restore Wizard** (Figure 14.18). Select **Next**.

2. Select the file, folder, or drive to be restored (expand if necessary as you would open subtrees in **Explorer**). Press **Next**.

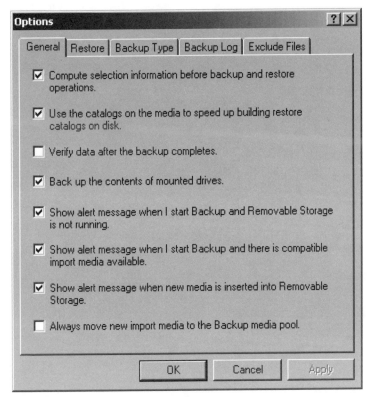

FIGURE 14.17 Backup and Restore Options

3. The next prompt allows you to restore the file in the original location, an alternative location, or a single folder (Figure 14.19). Select the location and press **Next**.

4. The next set of choices allows you to choose how the restored files will be written. The three choices provided are shown in Figure 14.20. Select the option desired and press **Next**.

Other dialog boxes may open depending on the options selected. To complete the restoration, press **Finish** on the final Restore Wizard dialog box.

NOTE It is generally advisable to restore files and folders initially in a temporary directory that can be used for testing, which will indicate if the backup data is corrupt or the media are damaged. Testing safeguards against writing corrupted backup data over current data.

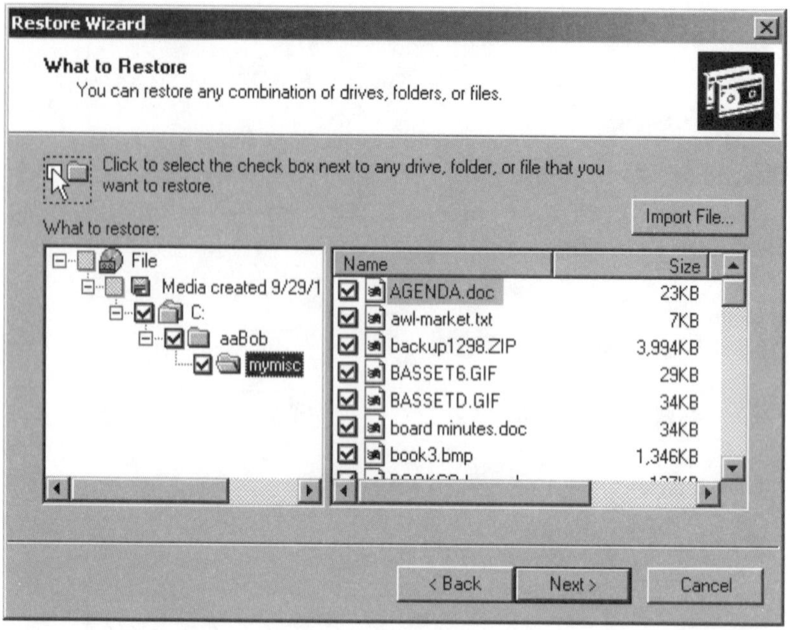

FIGURE 14.18 Selecting Files/Folders for Restoration

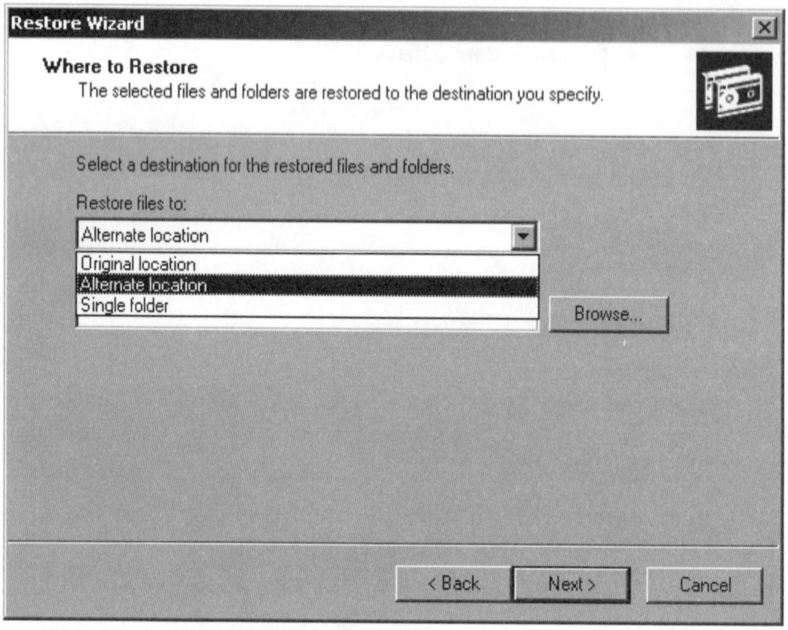

FIGURE 14.19 Selecting the Restoration Location

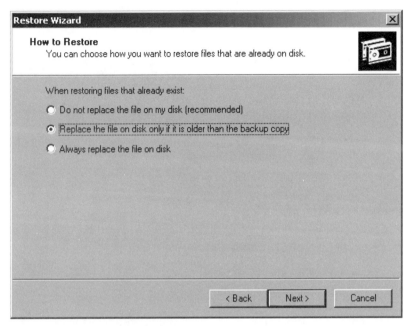

FIGURE 14.20 Writing Restored Files

USING BATCH RESTORATION

The *ntbackup* utility can be employed in a command line mode to create batch backups, as the following examples illustrate.

Creating a Normal Batch Backup

A normal batch backup is created by typing a command line statement similar to the one that follows from the **Start** → **Run** menu or the **Command Prompt**:

```
ntbackup backup \\ECC-1\c$ /m normal /j " My Current Job 1" /p "Backup"
/n "Command Backup 1" /d " My Command Line Backup Test " /v:yes /r:yes
/l:s /rs:yes /hc:on
```

A brief description of the command line follows:

- *Ntbackup backup*—instructs the utility that it is using backup mode.
- *\\ECC-1\c$*—identifies a remote share known as ECC-1.
- */m normal*—sets the backup type to normal.
- */j "My Current Job 1"*—the name of the backup.
- */p "Backup"*—requests that a media poll be used.

- */n "Command Backup 1"*—identifies the name of the tape or disk in the media pool.
- */d "My Command Line Backup Test"*—describes the backup.
- */v: yes*—provides verification of when the backup is completed.
- */r:yes*—restricts access to the owner and/or administrator.
- */l:s*—the log will show a summary statement only.
- */rs:yes*—remote storage data will also be backed up (not recommended because of the time required).
- */hc:on*—hardware compression is enabled.

Performing a Batch Copy Backup

A batch copy backup involves a simple command line statement from the **Start →
Run** menu or the **Command Prompt**:

```
ntbackup backup c:\ /j "Copy Job 1" /a /t "Command Line Example 1" /m copy
```

A brief description of the command line follows:

- *ntbackup backup*—instructs the utility that it is using backup mode.
- *\\ECC-\c$*—identifies a remote share known as ECC-1.
- *c:\ /j "Copy Job 1"*—identifies the name of the backup for drive c:.
- */t /a "Command Line Example"*—appends the backup to a tape named a "Command Line Example."
- */m copy*—sets the type of backup to the copy type.

AUTHORITATIVE RESTORATION

Authoritative restoration is useful when System State data such as that associated with the Active Directory, domain controllers, or the Registry must be restored. As a default, Windows 2000 backup is done in a nonauthoritative mode. Since objects are stored with a sequential identification number, a nonauthoritative restore will not overwrite an object with a more recent number. Instead, it regards the archived data simply as old. If the Active Directory or Registry has been damaged or corrupted in some fashion, the System State data cannot be restored unless an authoritative override is applied.

The *ntdsutil* shipped with the Windows 2000 Resource Kit permits you to mark those objects that need to be authoritatively restored. Update sequence names are changed to a higher level, which allows the substitution of the object. Where multiple domain controllers exist, this new number will be treated as an update and replicated throughout the domain. The ntdsutil must be run *after* the System State data has been restored and *before* the system is restarted.

DISASTER MANAGEMENT

IT disasters can come in many forms—floods, fires, earthquakes, tidal waves, and war are some dramatic examples. More common, less dramatic disasters involve the loss of a boot sector, accidental removal of operating system files, power supply interruption, hard drive crashes, or theft of equipment.

Automatic System Recovery

When a system loses its boot sector, critical operating system files, or other data vital to base-level function, the login processes must be restored. Thus, the first thing automatic system recovery (ASR) does is restore this configuration information as partition structure and file system type. Windows 2000 system files are restored with the appropriate hierarchy. The Windows 2000 Ntldr and Ntdetect .com files are rebuilt if necessary. Once this is complete, system login is possible. Then ASR attempts to recover user and auxiliary system files.

CREATING AN ASR SAVESET

To use this important recovery technology, an ASR Saveset must be created as follows:

1. Open the **Backup and Restore Wizard** from the **Start** → **Accessories** → **Backup** menu or the *ntbackup* command line utility.
2. Select the **Automated System Recovery and Preparation** wizard.
3. Select the destination for the ASR Saveset—usually a CD-ROM or diskette set.
4. Press **Finish**.

If you must attempt to repair a nonbootable system, boot from the ASR Saveset diskettes or CD-ROM you created as discussed above. The screens lead you though a logical set of steps. At one stage you must decide to conduct either a fast repair, which automatically attempts to repair items, or a manual repair, which gives you direct control over the process. Unless you are very sophisticated, we recommend the use of the fast repair so that standard approaches are uniformly applied.

Manual Recovery with the Advanced Options Menu

Advanced Options is an alternate boot menu that is invoked by pressing F8 during the initial boot sequence. It provides several alternative approaches to the repair or recovery of a Windows 2000 system, as follows:

- *Safe Mode*. The Safe Mode executes a minimal version of Windows 2000 and runs essential services only. You can run it as the default with explorer.exe enabled, with basic networking, or with the Command Prompt (cmd.exe is loaded instead of explorer.exe). Local applications can be run in Safe Mode, but the screen resolution will be 640x480 and 16 colors by default. Use this mode as it was used in earlier versions of Windows NT and Windows 9x to manually repair problems.

- *Enable Boot Logging*. If this option is selected, it will create a file called ntbt-log.txt that records all boot-related activity. The file is stored at the beginning of the system root directory and can be reviewed if boot sequence issues, such as bad drivers, occur.

- *Enable VGA Mode*. This was part of the normal boot menu in Windows NT. It is in the Advanced Options menu in Windows 2000 because it is not something that would be regularly selected. Use this option primarily to correct video display options set during a normal session that somehow render the display output unreadable. Once new sets have been set, you can reboot the system.

- *LastKnownGood Configuration*. Windows 2000 stores a new copy of a system's configuration. Copies of previous configurations are numbered sequentially and stored, and the LastKnownGood Configuration is then applied if the current configuration is faulty. Chapter 3 discusses using the Registry Editor to view and modify Registry entries. However, there is no need to use the Registry Editor to apply the LastKnownGood Configuration. When this option is selected from the Advanced Menu, follow the commands presented and note all warnings. This process will reverse all nonsecurity-related configuration items.

The Command-Line Recovery Console

Another alternative in recovery is the command line-based **Recovery Console**, which can be used in either normal or Safe Mode environments. The first time the Command Prompt is invoked it will initially install the Recovery Console, but the Windows 2000 CD-ROM must be present. To install the Recovery Console, type the following from the Command Prompt or Run menu:

```
<cd designation>:\i386\win32 /cmdcons
```

The Recovery Console is a character-based environment that looks very much like MS-DOS. It permits you to perform a great many command line tasks, including starting and stopping services. A complete list of Recovery Console functions is obtained by typing *help* <press ENTER>. Typing *exit* <press ENTER> terminates the Recovery Console and reboots the system.

Because it provides direct control, the Recovery Console is probably the preferred method of experienced system administrators. Commands can be selected as needed by the administrator without the intervention of Wizards or any other actions that are not visible.

Emergency Repair Disk

The creation of an emergency repair disk (ERD) is a prudent action for any system administrator. While highly unlikely, it is possible for critical Windows 2000 files to be lost or corrupted. The ERD can be used to restart the system so that these files can be restored. The ERD is created through the Backup utility by copying the following hidden system files to a formatted floppy disk:

- Ntldr
- Ntdetect.com
- Ntbootdd.sys
- Boot.ini

Fault Tolerance for Disaster Protection

Fault-tolerant systems are an important first line of defense in protecting data from system failures. As discussed earlier, RAID-5 and mirrored environments are two methods that are well supported by Windows 2000. In Chapter 17 we examine a more expensive but extremely viable fault-tolerant approach known as system clustering. Refer to these sections for additional information on how to apply fault tolerance to your disaster recovery plan.

Uninterrupted Power Supply Management

Power failures happen in any jurisdiction, and, along with power spikes and lightning, can destroy sensitive electronic equipment. This is why a relatively small investment can help avert disaster. An uninterrupted power supply (UPS) provides sufficient power to permit you to gracefully shut down Windows 2000 systems in a power failure and provides guards against electrical storms and power spikes. The analysis of UPS systems by make and model is outside the scope of this book, but we recommend them. Their configuration is through the **Control Panel** → **Power Options** → **UPS** tab.

POSTSCRIPT

Disk management, backup, restoration, and disaster recovery are critical system administrator responsibilities. This chapter centered strictly on the maintenance of homogeneous Windows 2000 environments, but in mixed environments many other considerations exist. For example, if you want to gain access to files on a UNIX system, a number of third-party utilities can be applied to mount such disks. Two are NFS and Samba, which should be investigated by system administrators working in mixed environments. An abundance of information about products that support these technologies is available on the Internet.

Terminal Services

Terminal Services is Microsoft's answer to thin client technology. In many ways, it mirrors environments that relied on server-based computing and the use of terminals for data input. While a common computer paradigm for many operating systems like UNIX, Terminal Services is Microsoft's first real venture into traditional multi-user support.

When installing Terminal Services, you are prompted to select either application server functions or administrative support. Both function sets can be installed sequentially on the same server. However, a server can perform only applications *or* administrative functions at one time. This chapter examines both sets of Terminal Services functions.

CONCEPTUAL REVIEW

Terminal Services is a significant departure from the default Windows 2000 environment. In all other discussions in this book we have assumed that the user is operating from a self-contained computer system. Otherwise known as a fat client, this system type is responsible for application processing, local storage, and management of the Win32 user interface.

By contrast, Terminal Services uses a thin client. Although the local computer might have storage and a resident operating system, all processing is remotely performed on the server. The Windows 2000 Terminal Services passes the Win32 user interface to the thin client, where it is locally displayed. As keystrokes and mouse clicks are entered, they are sent back to the server for interruption and execution, after which the server refreshes the thin client's local "terminal" screen. The default

Windows 2000 environment is a decentralized multi-console environment, but Terminal Services provides server-based multiple user capabilities (see Figure 15.1).

The Terminal Server operates with either Windows 2000 workgroups or domains (see Figure 15.2). Users of thin client systems must be authenticated, and as such their privileges are defined by Windows 2000 group policies. Users of thin

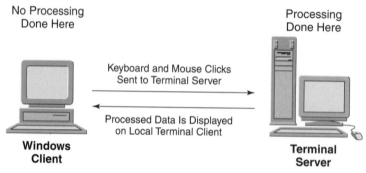

FIGURE 15.1 The Terminal Server–Thin Client Relationship

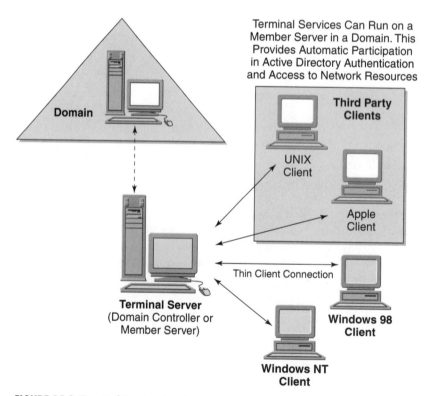

FIGURE 15.2 Terminal Services in a Domain Environment

client terminals are not unlike their fat client counterparts except for some system configuration and hardware availability differences. Windows 2000 Terminal Services supplies terminal clients for Microsoft Windows environments only. Client support for other operating system environments must be obtained from third-party vendors.

INSTALLING TERMINAL SERVICES

Installation of Terminal Services is extremely straightforward, with the Administrative and Application server functions installed in separate actions. The **Windows Components Wizard** for **Terminal Services Setup** asks you to choose either

- *Remote administration mode*. This allows an administrator to remotely manage the server.
- *Application server mode*. This allows users to remotely run applications from the server.

Select the desired setup mode and press **Next** (see Figure 15.3).

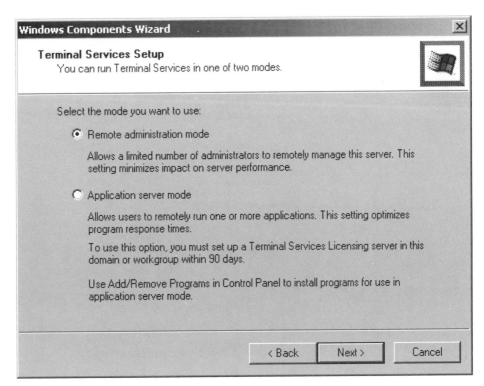

FIGURE 15.3 Terminal Services Setup

The installation process gathers information and writes appropriate files locally. When the process is complete, select the **Finish** button when prompted. Then restart the system so that the installation can take effect.

Sizing Terminal Services Systems

Sizing a system for Terminal Services is not an exact science, given that the applications that will run on the server and the demands placed on the system by individual users can vary radically. If the typical user maintains a single session and runs a single medium-level memory-dependent application, plan on an allocation of 4–8 MB of additional RAM per user above the base 64MB Terminal Services system requirement. (This calculation does not include the base memory requirement for the operating system.) However, be prepared for the amount of RAM to increase with added demands. A system administrator must monitor the performance of the server and make adjustments to available memory, the number of users, or application types.

The architecture of the applications can also impact performance. Wherever possible, 32-bit software should be utilized. Windows 16-bit programs that generally date back to the days of Windows 3.11 must be processed through the *Windows on Windows (WOW)* operating system layer, which translates application processes and therefore requires additional system resources.

As for network or asynchronous computer adapters such as an RS323 serial port, use the highest-performance hardware available. While down-level adapters can generally be employed, interrupts and data flow speed may be significantly impacted.

Disk access is the final major consideration. Since multiple users will be seeking stored information at the same time, speed of throughput is critical. Generally, Fast SCSI or SCSI-2 drives are recommended. IDE, ESDI, and ST-506 drives have lower throughput.

Enabling and Disabling Terminal Services

Terminal Services can be toggled off and on, but because of its potential impact on installed applications, this is generally not recommended. Still, there may be times when Terminal Services on a particular server may be necessary, such as for security or system performance. By default, Terminal Services are enabled. To disable Terminal Services without de-installing the software, follow these steps:

1. Launch the **Control Panel** and select **Add/Remove programs**.
2. Select the **Add/Remove Windows Components**.
3. From the **Windows Components Wizard** dialog, highlight **Terminal Services**.

4. Select the **Details** button and remove the checkmark from **Terminal Services**.

5. Press **OK**.

Terminal Services can be re-enabled by following the steps above but adding the checkmark in the Terminal Services dialog box.

Installing Applications for Use with Terminal Services

Although Microsoft has tested the compatibility of Terminal Services with many popular commercial software packages, such as its own Office 97/2000, Corel Office, and Lotus SmartSuite, not all applications will run in this environment. When in doubt, check with the third-party software vendor for compatibility and special installation or configuration requirements.

Applications should be installed *after* Terminal Server installation, and they must be set up to work with it. Installation is either through the standard **Control Panel** → **Add/Remove Programs** wizard or via the command line. When using the **Add/Remove Programs** wizard, select the **Change User Option** and click **All users *being* with common applications settings** for universal access or **Install applications setting for this user only**. To install using the **Command Prompt**, type *change user /install* and press **ENTER**. Then run the application's setup program. Type *change user /execute* and press **ENTER** to complete the installation. If available, run the post-installation script as discussed in the next paragraph.

Applications installed prior to Terminal Services will normally need to be either re-installed or properly configured. For example, we installed Office 2000 before Terminal Services on a member server. When we then attempted to launch Office 2000, the warning message shown in Figure 15.4 was displayed. In this case,

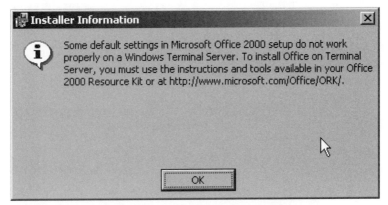

FIGURE 15.4 The Terminal Services Installation Warning Message

a download of configuration information was necessary. In most other cases, the only changes required are to run a post-installation script located in *\WINNT \Application Compatibility Scripts\Install*. Refer to that directory for available compatibility scripts and to the Microsoft website for updates.

NOTE   To work, an application should store per-user data in the HKEY_CURRENT_USER Registry key. Unfortunately, many applications store information such as default color or screen size settings in HKEY_CURRENT_MACHINE key, which means that users cannot customize preferences. However, unless this is hard-coded into the application, the installation script for the specific application can often be modified to correct this problem. Even so, when modifying installation scripts, be sure to test the application prior to any deployment.

CONFIGURING TERMINAL SERVICES

The **Terminal Services Configuration** tool is available from the **Start** menu → **Programs** → **Administrative Tools** or as a **Microsoft Management Console** (MMC) snap-in. These tools support the administration of Terminal Services **Connections** and **Settings**.

Configuring Connections

Terminal Services **Connections** support the link between the server and client session settings. Its **Properties** are the critical component in determining how and where Terminal Services can be used. The **Terminal Services Configuration** snap-in tool modifies RDP-TCP properties, including the users and groups allowed to use these services (see Figure 15.5).

Terminal services utilize a TCP/IP connection through TCP port 3389 for Microsoft Windows access—specifically, the *Remote Desktop Protocol* stack (RDP-TCP).

NOTE   Third-party vendor Citrix provides a Terminal Services connection to Apple Macintosh, UNIX, and MS-DOS workstations and terminals. It utilizes its own ICA protocol on clients to connect through asynchronous communications, IPX/SPX, NetBIOS, and TCP/IP. For specific information on integrating Citrix's MetaFrame and WinFrame technology visit the Citrix website at *www.citrix.com*.

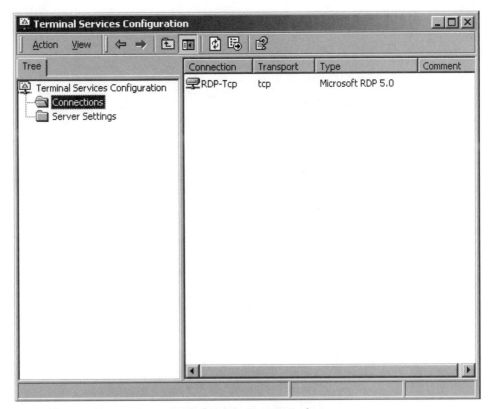

FIGURE 15.5 The Terminal Services Configuration Snap-In Tool

RDP-TCP configuration is accomplished through a series of **Properties** tabs, each of which provides options that deserve independent consideration. The **Properties** dialog box is displayed by right-clicking **RDP-Tcp** and selecting **Properties**.

GENERAL SETTINGS

The **General** tab (Figure 15.6) identifies the Microsoft RDP version level and the transport used, with TCP as the default. It also allows the system administrator to add comments about this particular installation.

The most important configuration option available from the **General** tab is the encryption level for data transport. Data encryption is one-directional from the client to the server and must coincide with the server's defined encryption level— that is, low, medium, or high. Data transmitted from the server is not protected by encryption to the client.

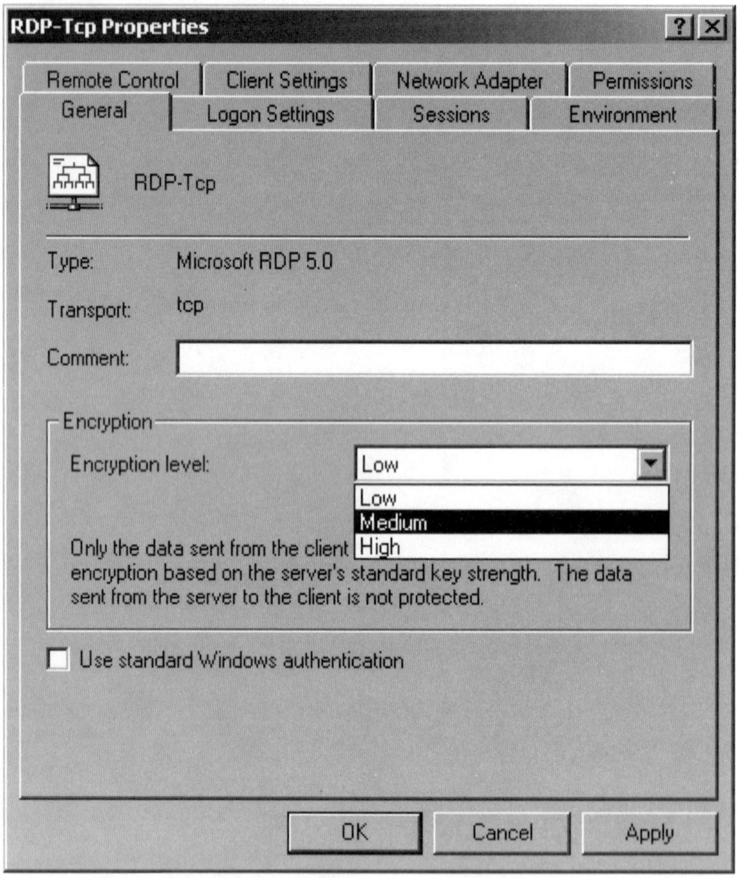

FIGURE 15.6 The General Settings Tab

Standard Windows user authentication is confirmed by checking the last option on the **General** tab screen.

REMOTE CONTROL OPTIONS

The **Remote Control** tab (Figure 15.7) establishes how the user can gain access and the level of control to be granted. It is a particularly important setting for a system administrator as it permits control over and observation of a user's session. **Remote Control** is used to select the level of control desired. The first two options retain the user's default settings on remote control or negate the function; the third one establishes the right to **View the session** and/or **Interact with the session**. If the **Require user's permission** box is checked, the message box will be displayed on the user's desktop when control is attempted, so that the user can grant or deny access.

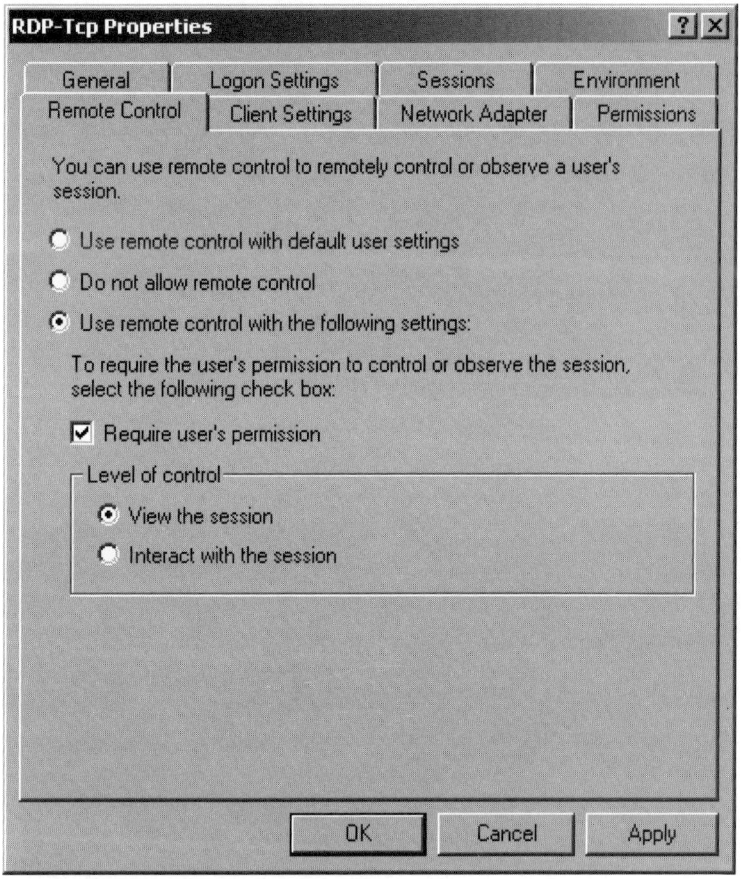

FIGURE 15.7 The Remote Control Tab

An organizational policy should be considered as to the proper utilization of this function, since the ability to control and observe a user's session obviously has both positive and negative ramifications. When a user encounters a problem, it is a system administration blessing to be able to remotely view and correct it; however, this also creates concern over eavesdropping and confidentiality.

Remote control is defined differently for domain users and local users. For domain users, follow these steps: From the **Active Directory Users Accounts and Computers** snap-in, select the domain, select **Users**, select the target user, right-click on the user and choice properties, select the **Remote Control** tab, and make the desired changes. For local users, use the **Computer Management (Local)** snap-in, select **System Tools**, select **Local Users and Groups**, right-click on the user, select **Properties**, and select the **Remote Control** tab.

CLIENT SETTINGS FOR REMOTE CONTROL

The **Client Settings** tab enables and disables a number of client-side items. The Connection options (1) connect local drives; (2) connect the local printer; and (3) set the local printer as the default device for applications executed by the user. In essence, these settings direct the respective devices to the terminal user's local environment. As shown in Figure 15.8, the six mapping options can be disabled by a checkmark.

NETWORK ADAPTER SETTINGS

The **Network Adapter** tab (Figure 15.9) performs two functions. First, it permits the selection of the adapters that have been found to be compatible for the net-

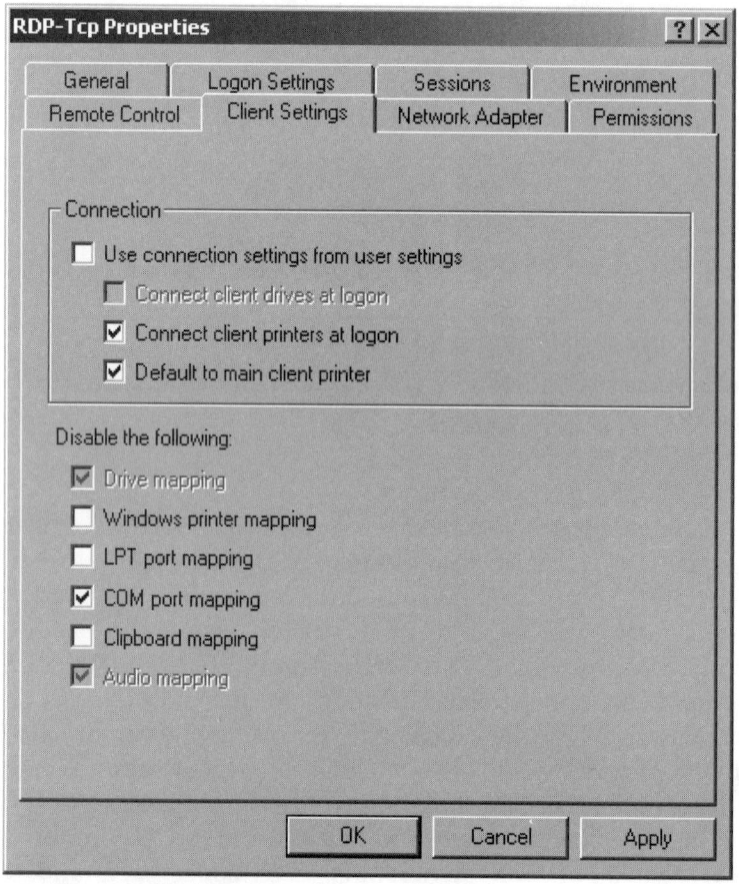

FIGURE 15.8 The Client Settings Tab

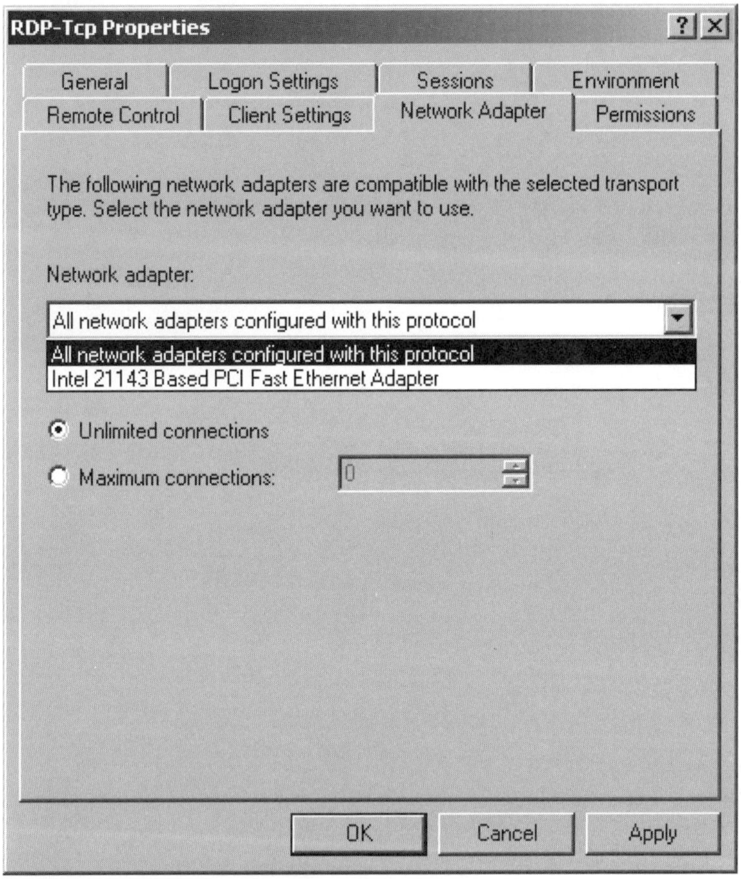

FIGURE 15.9 The Network Adapter Tab

work, with the default setting *All network adapters configured with this protocol*. Second, it establishes the number of allowable connections. If **Unlimited connections** is selected, there is no limit to the number of connections allowed to the Terminal Server. If **Maximum connections** is selected, a number for the upper limit for concurrent connections must be entered. This option is generally recommended because system performance can be seriously affected by too many connections. Once system capacity is properly sized, setting an upper limit will reduce the possibility of system overload.

PERMISSIONS

The Terminal Services **Permissions** tab (Figure 15.10) defines which users and groups have rights to assume **Full Control**, **User Access**, and **Guest Access**. By

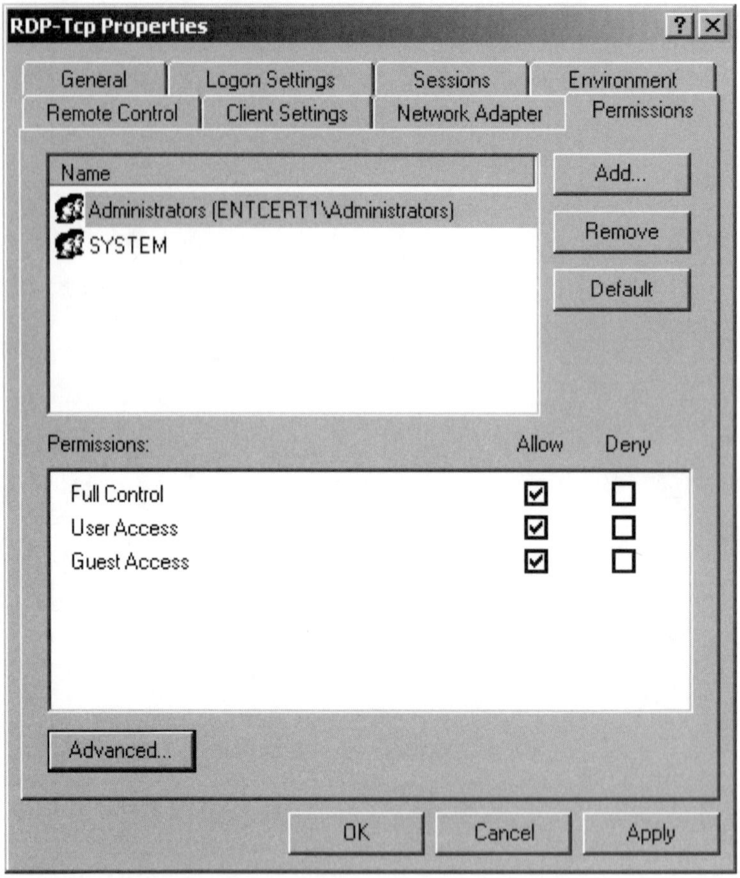

FIGURE 15.10 The Permissions Tab

default, the *Administrator* and *System* groups are allowed all three. This tab is employed to delegate authority to other users or groups for Terminal Server management.

As with other **Permissions** properties dialog boxes, additional users and groups are included by selecting the **Add** button and deleted with the **Remove** button. The **Advanced** button is used to apply special permissions. (See Chapter 10, Permissions, for more information about managing this Permissions tab.)

LOGON SETTINGS

The **Logon Settings** tab (Figure 15.11) permits the use of either client-provided or administrator-defined logon information. If the latter option is selected, complete the text boxes for user name, domain, password, and confirmed password.

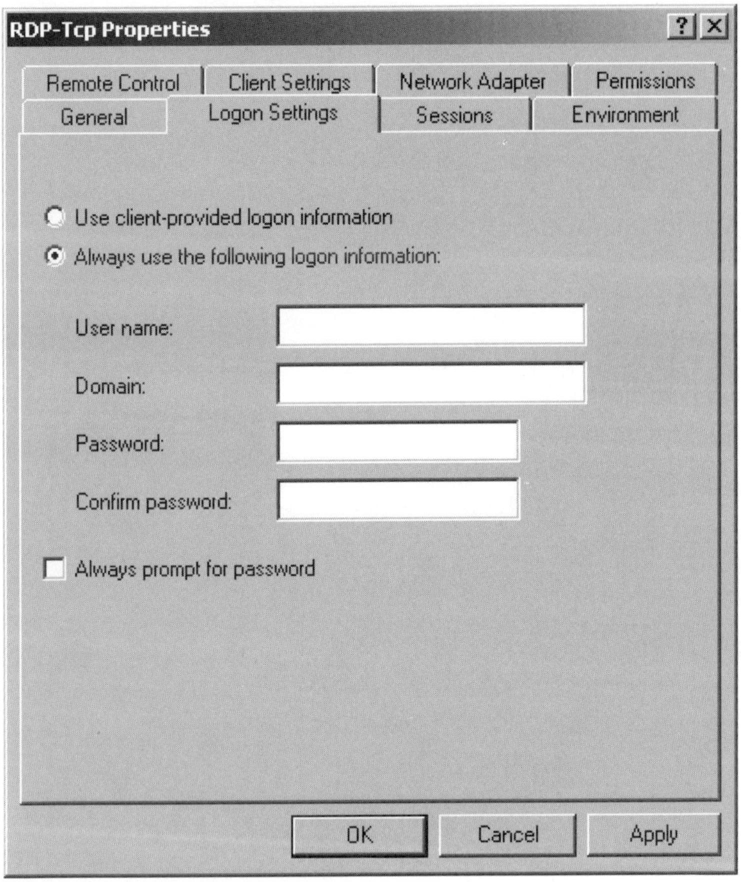

FIGURE 15.11 The Logon Settings Tab

SESSIONS OPTIONS

The **Sessions** tab (Figure 15.12) establishes parameters around the time a client can remain idle, the maximum length of a session, and whether that same client can reconnect. One of the benefits of Terminal Services is that a user can disconnect without terminating the session. Providing that the parameters are set to enable this function and time period, he can reconnect as the same or a different client exactly where he left off.

ENVIRONMENT SETTINGS

The **Environment** tab (Figure 15.13) permits the user to utilize an individual profile or overrides these settings with those established in this dialog box. In many environments, only certain applications need be initiated. For example, in a

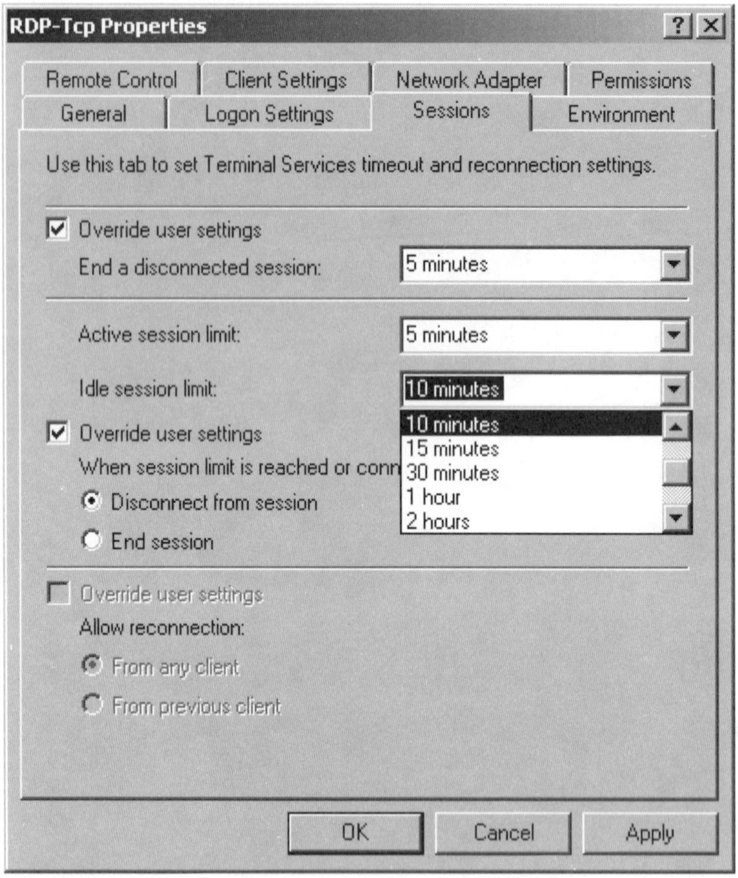

FIGURE 15.12 The Sessions Tab

customer service environment, a set of knowledge-based Help applications may be all that is necessary. In such a case, check the **Override settings** and designate the program path and file name.

Terminal Services Server Settings

The **Server Settings** determine how Terminal Services is applied (Figure 15.14). The five default settings are

- *Terminal server mode*—defines whether the server is in application or administrative mode.

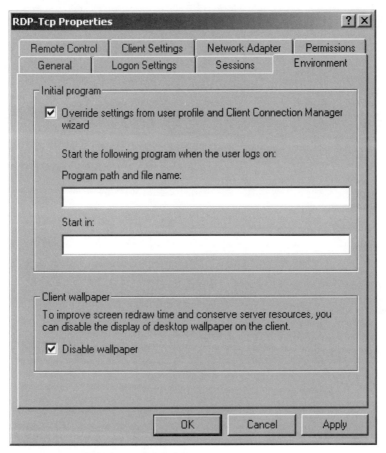

FIGURE 15.13 The Environment Tab

- *Delete temporary folders on exit*—determines how temporary folders are treated on exit.
- *Use temporary folders per session*—determines where temporary folders are created during a session.
- *Internet Connector licensing*—defines whether a license for Internet access is enabled.
- *Active Desktop*—defines whether the Microsoft Active Desktop environment is enabled or disabled.

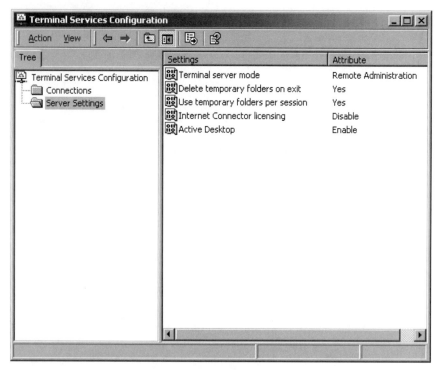

FIGURE 15.14 Server Settings

CONNECTION MANAGEMENT

The Terminal Services **Connection Manager Administration Kit** builds a common profile for client/server connectivity so that system administrators and users can establish connections to one or more servers. On the client side, the client Connection Manager creates default settings that can be distributed to users.

This section outlines the steps required to configure and manage connections.

Using the Connection Manager Wizard

The **Connection Manager Administration Kit Wizard** is available from the **Start** menu → **Programs** → **Administrative Tools**. Figure 15.15 shows the initial Wizard screen. The first option is employed to either create a new service profile or utilize an existing one. The second option is typically used when a configuration utilized for another terminal server can be repetitively applied to achieve standardization. We will step through the process to **Create a new service profile**.

1. The **Service and File Names** dialog box appears. In the first text box, type the name of your services, such as the company or division. In the second text box, type the name of the service profile folder. This can be a maximum of eight characters.

2. The **Merged Service Profile** appears and provides the opportunity to couple existing profiles in this new one. Press the **Add** button to display and select existing profiles. Press the **Delete** button to remove those previously selected.

3. The next dialog box allows you to provide support information for the user. Type the appropriate data in the text box (Figure 15.16).

4. The next dialog box permits the naming of a specific realm as shown in Figure 15.17. Utilize this facility to separate this realm from other terminal servers.

5. The **Dial-Up Network Entries** dialog box appears next. Use the **Add** button to select dial-up numbers from the phone book. The entries must match those in the preexisting phone book.

FIGURE 15.15 The Initial Wizard Screen

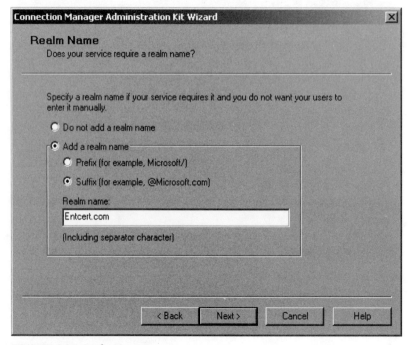

FIGURE 15.16 The Support Information Dialog Box

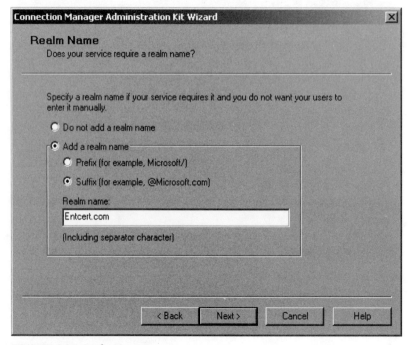

FIGURE 15.17 Realm Naming

6. **VPN Support** can be selected within the next dialog box. For additional information on VPN, consult Chapter 13.

7. The next dialog box permits you to select among three **Connection Actions**. The specific options are listed in Figure 15.18. Select any of the items appropriate to your installation.

8. The **Pre-Connect Actions** dialog permits selected programs to be executed prior to the user connection. Use the **Add** button to designate the applications. Their order can be changed with the **Move Up** and **Move Down** buttons.

9. The **Post-Connect Actions** dialog permits selected applications to be run immediately upon user connection (Figure 15.19). Use the **Add** button to designate the applications (these can include downloads and clean-up scripts). Change their order with the **Move Up** and **Move Down** buttons.

10. The **Disconnect Actions** dialog button permits selected programs to be run immediately after disconnection. This is particular useful for clean-up scripts such as those for clearing temporary directories.

11. The **Logon Bitmap** dialog permits adjustments for different display pixel counts. Select the pixel matrix that best fits the client displays.

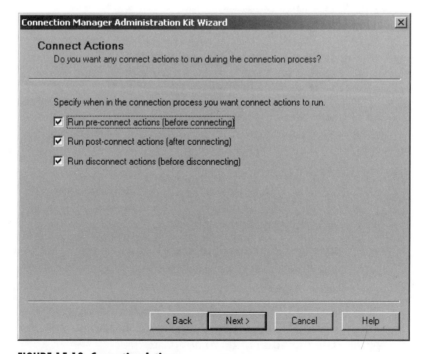

FIGURE 15.18 Connection Actions

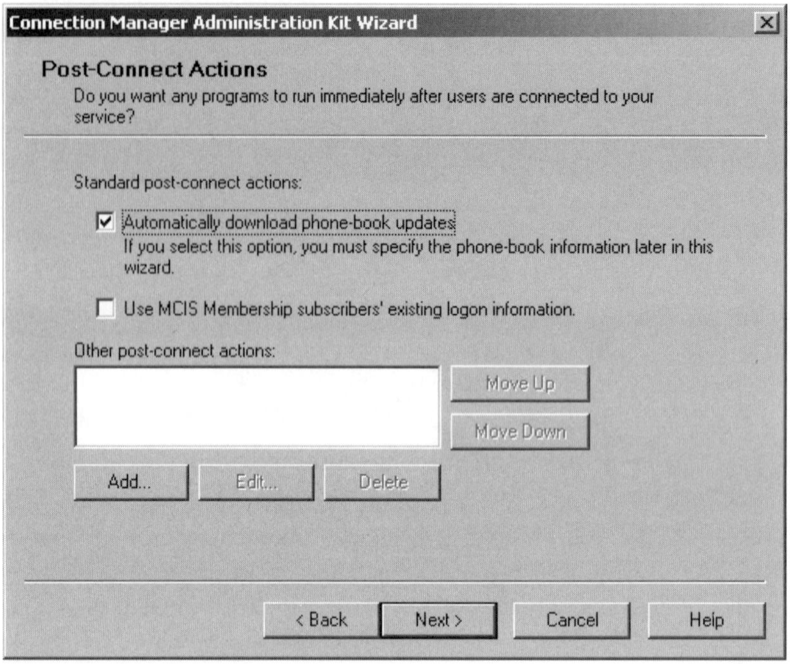

FIGURE 15.19 The Post-Connect Actions Dialog

12. The **Phone Book** dialog permits the inclusion of phone listings as part of the service profile. If this is desired, use the **Browse** button to select a preexisting phone book.

13. The **Phone Book Update** dialog determines how phone book updates are to be provided and displayed. Enter the name of the phone book to be downloaded and/or the Connection Point Services server as shown in Figure 15.20.

14. The **Icons** dialog box permits the selection of either the default icon size or a different one.

15. The **Help File** dialog permits the selection of default or customized Help files. Use the **Browse** button to select preexisting custom Help.

16. The **Connection Manager Software** dialog box permits inclusion of version 1.2 of the software.

17. The **License Agreement** dialog provides for the inclusion of license agreements the users must accept prior to installation and use.

18. The **Additional Files** dialog permits other files to be included in the service profile. Use the **Add** button to designate them.

19. Press the **Finish** button to complete the connection configuration process.

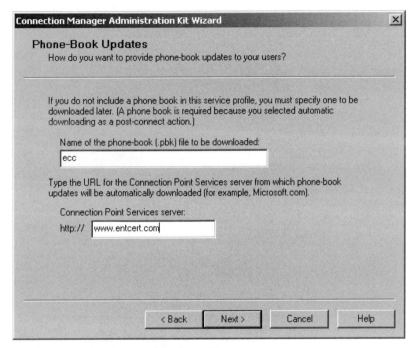

FIGURE 15.20 The Phone Book Update Dialog Box

TERMINAL SERVICES ADMINISTRATION

The Terminal Server allows the administrator to remotely monitor servers, sessions, users, and processes, and supports the centralized deployment of applications, disk management, and device access. It also allows the administrator to manage the applications available to users, logon privileges, and security.

Administrative Tools

Terminal Services offers a number of system administrative tools. With the exception of the **Services Configuration** and **Connections Manager** snap-ins, discussed earlier, the following tools will be explored in this section:

- Terminal Services Manager
- The Active Directory Users and Computers snap-in and the Local Users and Groups snap-in
- Task Manager additions
- Client Creator

- Client Connection Manager
- Common Commands

TERMINAL SERVICES MANAGER

Terminal Services Manager (Figure 15.21) is used to view and administer users, active sessions, and processes on terminal servers anywhere on the network. It is available from the **Start** menu → **Administrative Tools** → **Terminal Services Manager**.

The **Actions** menu invokes the ability to connect and disconnect sessions. Users and sessions as well as processes can be displayed by drilling down the administrative tree. Processes can be terminated at this stage.

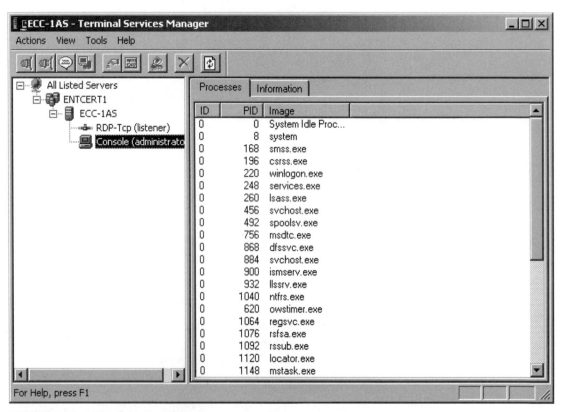

FIGURE 15.21 Terminal Services Manager

ACTIVE DIRECTORY USERS AND COMPUTERS SNAP-IN AND THE LOCAL USERS AND GROUPS SNAP-IN

Depending on the environment, the **Active Directory Users and Computers** snap-in or the **Local Users and Groups** snap-in establishes individual user Terminal Services settings. From the respective snap-in, select the local computer or domain, select **Users**, right-click on the target user, and select **Properties**. As four of the **Properties** tabs are important to Terminal Services, let's briefly examine them:

- *Remote Access*—establishes the settings for individual user access to Terminal Services. Figure 15.22 shows the available Remote Access options.

- *Terminal Services Profiles*—establishes the path and file name of Terminal Services profiles for an individual user (see Figure 15.23).

- *Sessions*—regulates the amount of flexibility granted to an individual user with regard to session length and reconnection options. Refer to Figure 15.24 for a description of Sessions options.

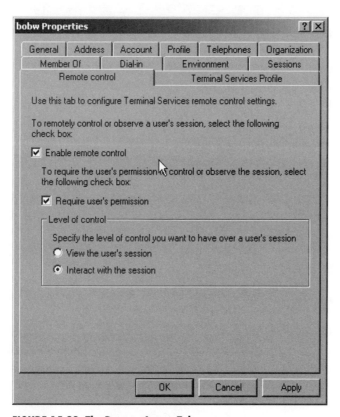

FIGURE 15.22 The Remote Access Tab

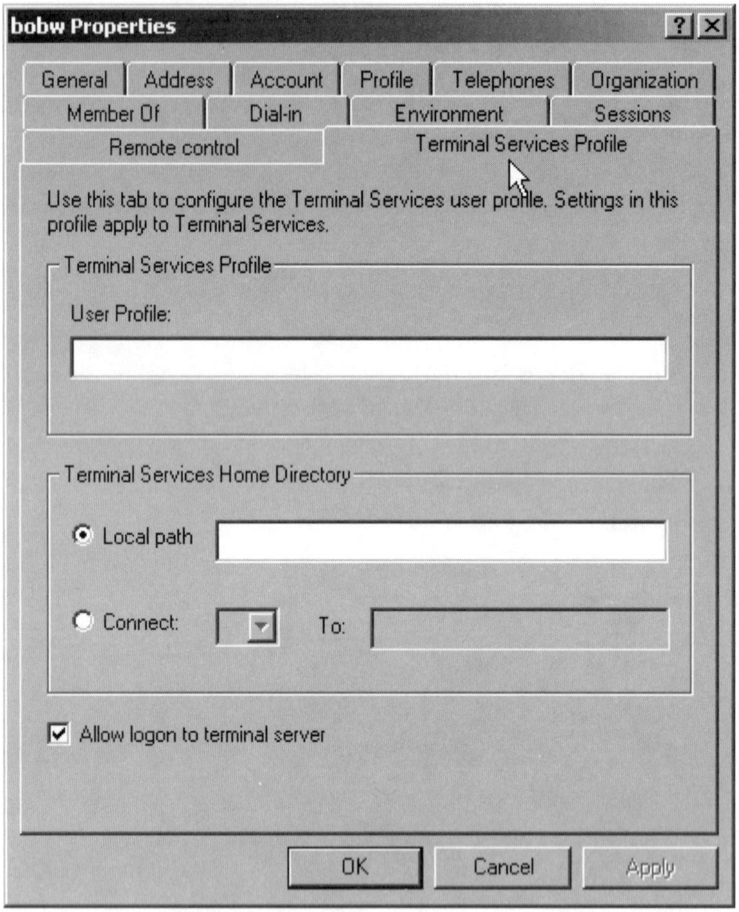

FIGURE 15.23 Terminal Services

- *Environment*—determines which applications are to be launched at logon. The client's local disk drives and printer can be made available under Terminal Services–supported applications.

TASK MANAGER ADDITIONS

The **Task Manager** also monitors and administrates Terminal Services. Two additional fields have been added to it in Windows 2000. These are used to view processes and to terminate them as required. The Task Manager is available by pressing **Ctrl-Alt-Del** and selecting **Task Manager**.

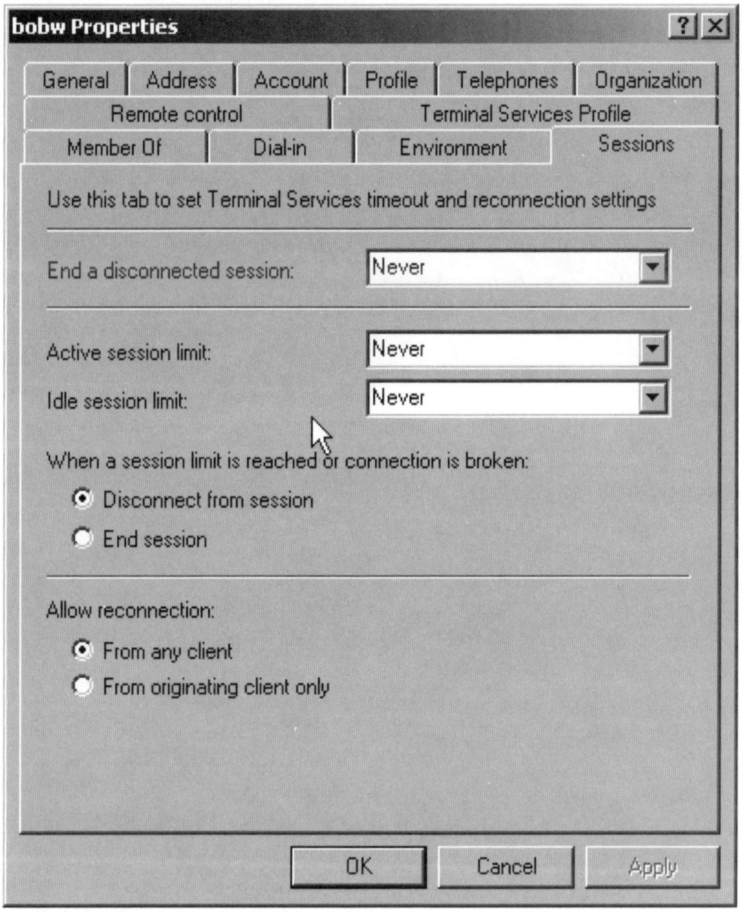

FIGURE 15.24 The Sessions Tab

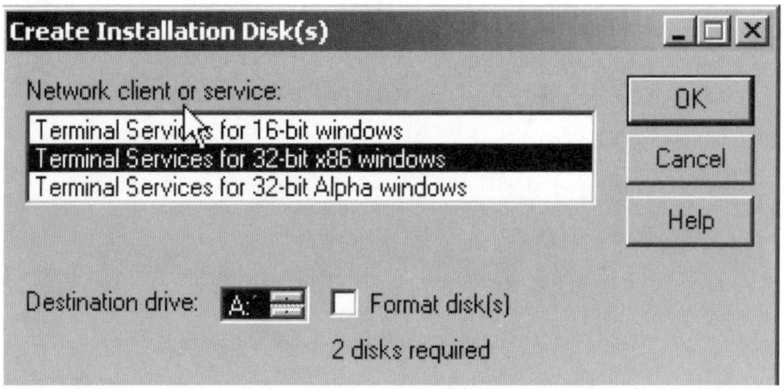

FIGURE 15.25 The Terminal Services Client Creator

CLIENT CREATOR AND INSTALLATION

The **Terminal Services Client Creator**, available from the **Start** menu →
Administrative Tools, creates either 16-bit or 32-bit client software (see Figure
15.25 on the preceding page). The creation process requires four formatted
diskettes for each client type. It is fully automated except for the replacement of
diskettes when prompted.

    Terminal Services Client Creator creates a set of installation diskettes. To
install either the 16-bit or 32-bit version, simply execute the setup command
loaded on diskette 1 on the client machine. Insert each of the other diskettes
when prompted.

COMMAND LINE PROGRAMS

Terminal Services provides a number of command line functions, shown in the following list. They may be executed from the **Command Prompt** or via the *Run*
option available from the Start menu.

- *Change logon*—temporarily disables Terminal Service logons.
- *Change port*—shifts the COM port mappings required by MS-DOS programs.
- *Change user*—executes changes to the .ini policies file mapping for a current
  user.
- *Cprofile*—deletes individual files linked to a user's profiles.
- *Dbgtrace*—enables or disables debug traces.
- *Flattemp*—enables or disables temporary directories.
- *Logoff*—terminates the client session.
- *Msg*—sends messages to a user or multiple users.
- *Query process*—outputs process information on Terminal Services.
- *Query session*—displays Terminal Services session data.
- *Query termserver*—outputs a list of network terminal servers.
- *Register*—registers an application with execution characteristics.
- *Reset session*—deletes a session and re-establishes a connection.
- *Shadow*—remotely monitors and controls a user's session.
- *Tscon*—connects to other Terminal Server sessions.
- *Tsdiscon*—disconnects a user's Terminal Services session.
- *Tskill*—kills a Terminal Services session.
- *Tsprof*—copies an existing user's configuration and modifies the profile path.
- *Tsshutdn*—shuts down the Terminal Services server.

TERMINAL SERVICES FROM A USER'S PERSPECTIVE

The Microsoft implementation of Terminal Services provides application server support on even minimally configured Windows-based personal computers—for example, old 8086-class machines running Windows 3.1. Using add-on software from third-party vendors, Windows 2000 applications can also be displayed and used from UNIX, Apple Macintosh, Java, and MS-DOS platforms. This ability to run applications such as Office 2000 using existing hardware equipment, and thus preserve previous hardware investments through the purchase of Terminal Server licenses, can be very attractive.

With Terminal Services the users of thin clients can immediately utilize Windows 2000 applications while maintaining their current and familiar environment. If the server is properly sized, the response time between a keystroke or mouse click and a displayed result should be transparent to them. This response time is predicated on persistent caching.

A user can roam between thin clients with Terminal Services and not have to log off. Instead, she need only disconnect the session and then, when she returns to the terminal or to another thin client system, merely log back in to the same session. The user can also maintain multiple concurrent sessions from one or more clients and run several tasks at the same time. Moreover, she can easily cut and paste between terminal sessions. The cut and paste facility is also supported between the local computer and the Terminal Server session.

Finally, printers that are currently operational on the local client can be recognized through Windows 2000 Terminal Services.

User Launching

Users of Windows 3.11 launch Terminal Services from the **Control Panel**, double-clicking **TSClient**. For all other Windows versions, use the **Start** menu, select **Programs**, and select **Terminal Services Client**.

To disconnect the **Terminal Services Client** without ending the session, select the **Start** menu, then choose **Disconnect**. The user can then reconnect where he left off. To end the session, select the **Start** menu and click on **Shut Down**. From the **Shut Down Windows** dialog box select **Log Off** and confirm with **OK**.

A number of shortcuts can be used while in a Terminal Services session to streamline operations. These are listed in Table 15.1.

TABLE 15.1 Terminal Server Shortcut Keys

Shortcut Keys	Description
ALT+PAGE UP	Switches between programs going right to left.
ALT+PAGE DOWN	Switches between programs going left to right.
ALT+INSERT	Moves though programs in the order they were launched.
ALT+HOME	Displays the Start menu.
CTRL+ALT+BREAK	Switches the client between a full screen and an active window.
ALT+DELETE	Displays the Windows popup menu.

POSTSCRIPT

Terminal Services offers a thin client architecture that permits the retrofitting of existing, less powerful computer systems. For an administrator, it also permits remote management for any server in the network. If only for that reason, Terminal Services should be a very popular add-on. In conjunction with other thin client technologies, such as a Web- or Java-based implementation, Terminal Services adds a broader dimension of the Windows 2000 enterprise.

Chapter 16

Internet Information Services

As a fully integrated Web, SMTP, NNTP, and FTP server, Internet Information Services (IIS) is an integral part of Windows 2000. Indeed, since IIS is integrated at the operating system level, it is difficult to discuss Windows 2000 without major reference to it.

Many of IIS's technological foundations are covered in other chapters, including key integration with the Active Directory, security, and remote networking. For that reason, this chapter will center on its functional aspects, specifically,

- Concepts and features
- Basic administration
- The Simple Mail Transfer Protocol server
- The Network News Transfer Protocol server
- The File Transfer Protocol server

OVERVIEW

Internet Information Services incorporates some of the most advanced Web technologies in a single integrated set of functions. For the system administrator IIS offers Web security, data and process reliability, Web-based application development, and management tools. A brief examination of these features should help put IIS functionality into perspective.

IIS Security Features

The IIS application suite relies on and is integrated with Windows 2000 security schemes. It also relies on additional Internet standard security features. This section reviews IIS security from a high level; for additional information about Windows 2000 security and authentication, refer to Chapters 8 through 10.

IIS SECURITY MECHANISMS

IIS security works in parallel with Windows 2000 operating system security in that the range of mechanisms includes access control, authentication, encryption, certificates, and system auditing. These are briefly examined in the following list:

- *Access control.* Access control simply oversees how a user who has been granted access to the IIS server can utilize resources. NTFS permissions are still applied to system resources as with any other Windows 2000 activity, but IIS also uses HTTP 1.0 and 1.1 Web security specifications. In particular, WebDAV (described in greater detail later) permits navigation through files and directories. With WebDAV commands, also known as *verbs,* authorized users can edit, delete, and add files and directories.

- *Authentication.* IIS 5.0 employs several forms of user name and password authentication.

  –Anonymous Authentication utilizes the IUSR_*computername* user account, to which special permissions should be applied if appropriate to avoid any user gaining access to the public content of the website or FTP site. When enabled, IIS always authenticates a user through this account first.

  –Basic FTP Authentication utilizes the user name and password associated with a specific Windows 2000 user account on the system. Its major downside is that passwords are transmitted without encryption and can be captured, exposing Windows 2000 user accounts to security breaches.

  –Kerberos v5 authentication is ideally suited for intranets in Windows 2000 environments. However, since it does not work in conjunction with HTTP Proxy services, it may have significant limitations on the Internet.

- *Encryption.* Encryption scrambles information at one end of the communication and deciphers it at the verified receiving end. It is commonly used for financial and banking transactions such as credit card number transmission. Encryption is based on the Secure Sockets Layer (SSL 3.0) protocol and its extension, Server-Gated Cryptography. In the United States or Canada, IIS encryption can use a minimum size 128-bit session key rather than the 48-bit or 56-bit DES standard used in other parts of the world.

- *Certificates*. Certificates are digital documents used in the authentication process. They are always required when encrypted data is sent over an SSL 3.0 connection. A certificate is created through Microsoft's Certificate Authority, discussed in Chapter 11, or obtained from third-party certificate grantors.
- *Services Auditing*. Monitoring the IIS services for irregular activities is an important security safeguard. Auditing uses logs to detect activities that violate file and directory policies. Either Windows 2000 standard auditing features or IIS 5.0 configured logs can be employed and are generated through the **Audit Policies** or **Internet Information Services** snap-in tool.

IIS INTERNET SECURITY TECHNOLOGIES

In addition to security features employed by the Windows 2000 operating system itself such as Kerberos version 5, IIS's Web-specific security schemes include

- *Basic Authentication*—derived from the HTTP 1.0 specification and the most widely used Web-based method for matching user names and passwords for access purposes. A password is sent in Base64 encoded format, but it is not encrypted, which means that in unsecured environments it can be captured by a sniffer. For this reason, Basic Authentication provides only marginal Web security. Its major advantage is that most Web browsers support this HTTP 1.0 standard.
- *Digest Authentication*—based on the W3C (World Wide Web consortium) standards for HTTP 1.1. Digest Authentication extends Basic Authentication by utilizing a one-way hash (or message digest) for password interpretation. The password is not decipherable from the hash, which prevents password capture in an unsecure environment. Only advanced browsers like Internet Explorer 5.0 or above can receive data using this technology; older browsers are returned an error message.
- Certificate-based Web transactions using *PKCS#7/PKCS#10* protocols are also supported by IIS. When used with IIS certification functions, PKCS#7 establishes encryption formats for data like digital signatures. PKCS#10 determines the request format for certificates.
- *Fortezza*—a U.S. government cryptographic standard used for authentication, nonrepudiation, access control, and systems security.
- *Secure Sockets Layer (SSL 3.0)*—utilizes certification authorities and is one of the most widely used methods on the Web to ensure authentication and message integrity.
- *Server-Gated Cryptography (SGC)*—primarily utilized by banking and financial institutions over the Internet.

- *Transport Layer Security (TLS)*—extends SSL by providing cryptographic authentication. Its API framework permits the writing of TLS-enabled applications.

Applying these standards within an IIS environment is covered in the Properties section. IIS also supports three security-related wizards:

- *Certificate* leads the administrator through the creation and establishment of life cycles for a certificate.

- *Certificate Trust Lists (CTL)* constructs a list of trusted certificate authorities for a directory.

- *Permissions* consolidates authentication and NTFS permissions for website and FTP access.

IIS Data and Process Reliability

With its better performance and reliability, IIS 5.0 has overcome the shortcomings of Microsoft's IIS 4.0. This section outlines some of the features that have been added to this version to enhance performance options and stability.

- *Process Management*. When shared resources are utilized, unstable elements can impact the environment. For example, as a default, Web services are run in the *inetinfo.exe* process space, which ensures the fastest performance but may allow a misbehaving application to disable the IIS server. In previous versions, services could also be directed for separate process execution to *DLL-Host.exe,* which was generally used for the highest priority application and can still be employed in the current version. However, IIS 5.0 adds a third option that permits a pool of applications to utilize *DLLHost.exe* pooled processes. The disadvantage of pooled processes is that if one of the applications fails, all the others die. The advantage is that even in the event of failure, the IIS server will continue to run unaffected. As discussed later in the **Home Directory** and **Virtual Directory** properties discussions, the administrator can direct applications to use isolated or pooled processes by selecting **High** or **Medium Application Protection**.

- *Socket Pooling*. A socket consists of a default node (computer) address and a port number, such as the server's IP address Internet Web TCP number 80. IIS 5.0 permits the pooling of sockets so that more sites can be bound to the same IP address and share the same port number.

- *Process and Bandwidth Throttling*. When running multiple sites on the same server, it may be appropriate to limit processes, CPU usage, and bandwidth. This is equally true when multiple applications are running on the IIS server.

Process and **Bandwidth Throttling** allows the system administrator to set these limits, and over time it can be used to obtain maximum system performance. Process accounting should also be employed to measure CPU utilization or to determine if an application or script is using a disproportionate amount of resources.

- *Site Hosting Scalability*. Scalability is achieved by permitting multiple websites to share an IP address. Multiple sites can be hosted within IIS by appending port numbers to the same IP address or by adding IP addresses to the same server. In the first case, the port number is appended to the end of the IP address, such as 111.111.111.111:80 or 111.111.111.111:140. Individuals share the same IP address but are connected through different ports. An alternative to ports is to use headers to distinguish between sites on the same IP address and computer and resolve domain names to that address. Multiple IP addresses are bound to a single network interface card or multiple cards on the same system. Once it arrives at the server, the header determines which site is to be contacted. The simplicity of this alternative can be very attractive because it makes maintaining multiple IP addresses or port tables unnecessary. However, it cannot be used in conjunction with SSL and other encryption environments because the header information will not be readable.

- *Clustering for IIS*. For mission-critical Web and FTP environments, clustering (discussed in Chapter 17) should certainly be considered. With clustering, when one node (server) has services or hardware problems, a second system assumes the activities in the failover process. This type of redundancy, although more costly, can provide significantly greater reliability. Also to be considered is the use of a mirrored or RAID-5 disk system as discussed in Chapter 14.

- *Dfs for Web File Systems*. The physical distribution of files across a network has always been a major problem. Windows 2000's distributed file system (Dfs) is easily adaptable to a Web-based environment, allowing the client browser to be used for resource access throughout the network.

The Web Application Environment

A centerpiece of IIS support for application sharing and development is Web Distributed Authoring and Versioning (WebDAV). This is an extension to the HTTP 1.1 specification used for publishing and manipulating Web documents. By setting WebDAV properties and permissions, different Windows 2000 clients can have different levels of access such as Read/Write or Read-Only.

Application development for IIS utilizes Active Server Pages (ASP) as the preferred Web medium. Although development issues are outside our scope, we note the ASP helps integrate HTML, scripts (including Java and VScript), and COM components.

IIS Management Components

Later in this chapter we will explore how to specifically apply administrative tools to the management of IIS. Here we provide a brief overview of IIS management tools and techniques, including

- *Command line script administration.* Much traditional Web administration is UNIX based and by definition heavily reliant on command line utilities and scripts. Acknowledging this, Microsoft has made at least a partial effort to permit UNIX-type administrative interaction. For example, the Cscript.exe command can invoke Visual Basic scripts. Other commands allow the use of CGI, Perl, and other scripts.

- *Internet Information Services snap-in centralized administration.* A replacement for the older Internet Services Manager, the **Internet Information Services** snap-in is an integrated tool for creating, modifying, and managing IIS components and properties, which is explored later in the chapter. Its Remote administration is made possible through Terminal Services.

- *Delegation to website operators.* One of the strengths of Windows 2000 is the ability to delegate certain administrative responsibilities. **Web Site Operators** is an administrative group that has authority over IIS functions. Its responsibility can be very extensive or site specific, which can be very valuable in environments with multiple sites on the same server. A website operator for a specific site can be granted full control over it but have no authority over other sites.

- *Custom Error Messaging.* The system administrator's burden can be greatly reduced through the use of instructive error messages. IIS employs the HTTP 1.1 error messaging scheme to handle standardized problems. Use of this facility and the errors it handles are dealt with later.

UNDERSTANDING THE IIS WEB SERVER

IIS includes a robust Web server designed to host both internal intranets and public Internet sites. It works closely with many development tools such as Microsoft's FrontPage.

Administering IIS Web Services

In this section we explore the major administrative aspects associated with host Web services under IIS. One of the best methods of illustrating the ease of IIS operation is to create and configure a website.

CREATING A WEBSITE USING IIS

Here we assume that Web pages have already been created with a product such as FrontPage and are ready to be loaded on the Web server for intranet or Internet exposure. Follow these steps to create the site itself:

1. Open the **Internet Information Services** snap-in.
2. Right-click on **Default Web Server**, select **New**, and then **Site**. The initial Web Site Creation Wizard screen is displayed as in Figure 16.1.
3. In the **Web Site Description Dialog** box input a description of the site.
4. In the **Address and Port Settings Dialog** box (Figure 16.2), enter **the IP address to use**, the **TCP port**, the **Host Header for this site**, and the **SSL port**. The header is a website description. An ISP that is hosting a number of websites on the same server, for example, might make the header the name of each organization.
5. In the **Web Site Directory Location** dialog box, enter the path or use the **Browse** button to locate the directory containing the Web pages.
6. In the **Web Site Access Permissions** dialog box (Figure 16.3), check the types of access to be allowed, including **Read**, **Run Scripts**, **Execute**, **Write**, and **Browse**.
7. Click **Finish** to complete the creation process.

FIGURE 16.1 The Web Site Creation Wizard

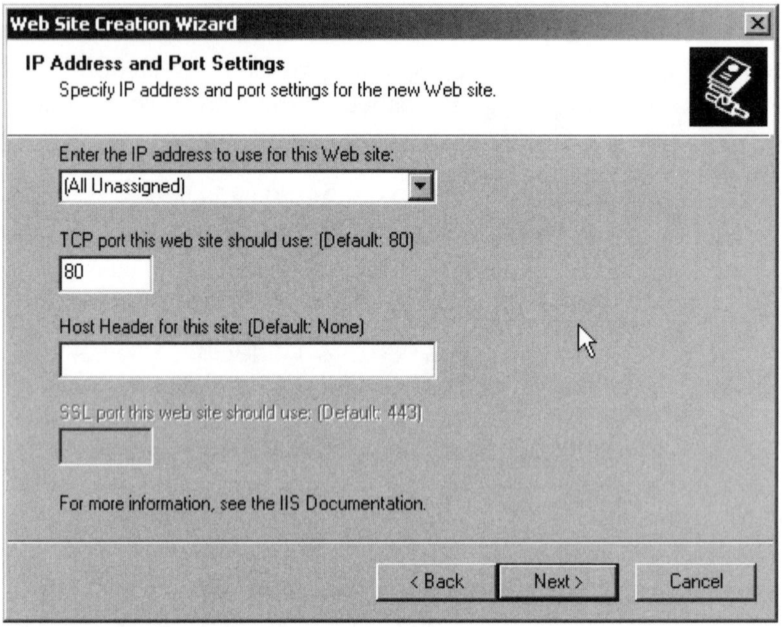

FIGURE 16.2 The IP Address and Port Settings Dialog Box

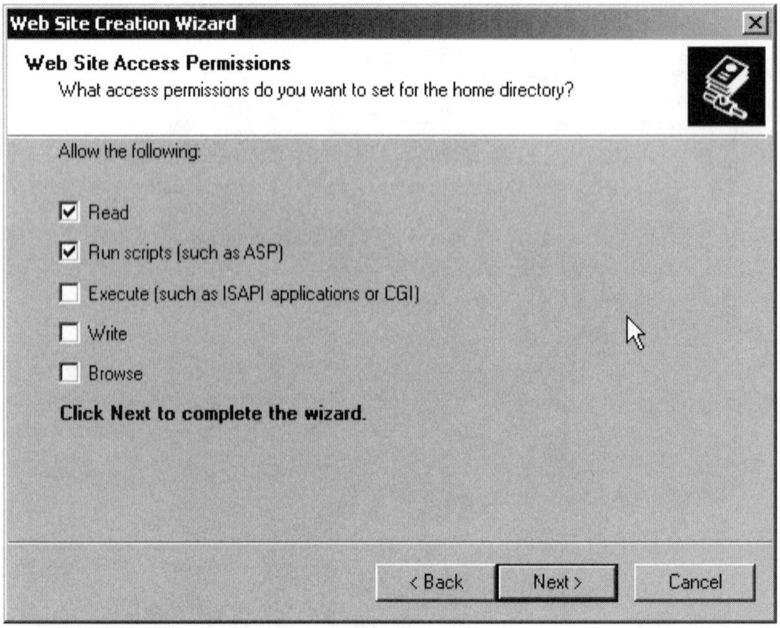

FIGURE 16.3 Web Site Access Permissions

BASIC WEBSITE ADMINISTRATION

Basic website administration can be illustrated by a walk-through of some of the
activities available from the **Internet Information Services** snap-in.

Opening or Exploring Components and Browse

To view the component parts of a website, use either of the methods described in
these steps:

1. Open the **Internet Information Services** snap-in.

2. Right-click on the desired website and select **Open** or **Explore**.

3. Either the **My Computer** view or the **Explorer** view of the contents will be displayed. To browse a website from the **Internet Information Services** snap-in,
   follow the steps above, except the last. Here select **Browse** (see Figure 16.4).

FIGURE 16.4 An Example of a Browsed Website

Using the Website Permissions Wizard

Permissions for a site are set by the Permissions Wizard as follows:

1. Open the **Internet Information Services** snap-in.

2. Right-click on the desired website, select **All Tasks**, and select **Permissions Wizard**.

3. In the first dialog box, select either that the permissions should be inherited from a parent website or virtual directory or that new permissions be established. If you select the default-inherited permissions, a confirmation box as shown in Figure 16.5 lists the settings. If this is satisfactory, select **Next**, and then **Finish** to complete the task. Select **Cancel** and repeat the process if other permissions that are not represented by that parent website or virtual directory need to be set.

4. If new or different permissions are required, **select new permission from a template**. Two standard templates are available. The **Public Web Site** option allows all users to browse static and dynamic content. The **Secure**

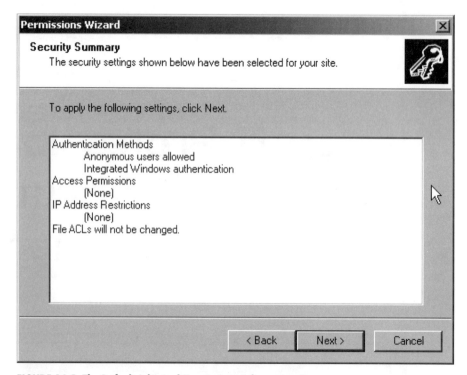

FIGURE 16.5 The Default Inherited Permissions Information Box

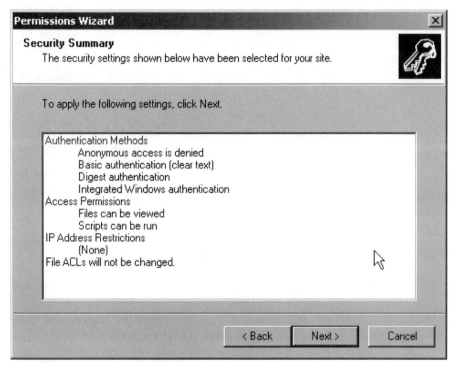

FIGURE 16.6 Secure Site Default Permissions

Web Site option allows only users with a Windows 2000 account to do so. If this is satisfactory, select **Next** and then **Finish** to complete the task (see Figure 16.6).

Configuring Web Extensions

The **Web Site Extensions Configuration Wizard** walks the system administrator through the following steps:

1. Open the **Internet Information Services** snap-in.

2. Right-click on the desired website, select **All Tasks**, and select **Configure Server Extensions**.

3. Move from the introductory Wizard page to the second dialog box by selecting **Next**. Enter the name of the database and password and select **Next** again.

4. In the **Create Windows Group** dialog box, check the **Create Local Machine Groups** if you want local, specific website access. Figure 16.7 out-

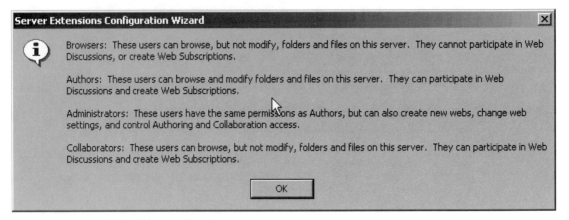

Server Extensions Configuration Wizard   ☒

Browsers: These users can browse, but not modify, folders and files on this server. They cannot participate in Web Discussions, or create Web Subscriptions.

Authors: These users can browse and modify folders and files on this server. They can participate in Web Discussions and create Web Subscriptions.

Administrators: These users have the same permissions as Authors, but can also create new webs, change web settings, and control Authoring and Collaboration access.

Collaborators: These users can browse, but not modify, folders and files on this server. They can participate in Web Discussions and create Web Subscriptions.

OK

FIGURE 16.7 Extended Web Server User Groups

lines the group types and rights. These groups must also be added to Windows 2000 accounts if they are using the **User Manager**.

5. In the next dialog box, establish **Access Control** by completing the appropriate text boxes and drop-down menus. Make the desired selections and press **Next**.

6. **Mail Configuration** can be completed in the next dialog box. You can also select not to configure basic website mail at this time. If you select mail configuration, input the appropriate information in the dialog boxes. When complete or if the second option is selected, press **Next**.

7. The Confirmation of Settings window is displayed. Press **Finish** if the settings are satisfactory.

CONFIGURING WEBSITE PROPERTIES

Website properties can be set on the site and individual page/directory level. Most are configured through the **Properties** tabs, which are explored in this section. Open the **Internet Information Services** snap-in, right-click on the desired website, and select **Properties**.

Setting Website Properties

The **Web Site** tab (Figure 16.8) provides a text box for inputting the site description, desired IP address, and designated port. Connections can also be set to unlimited or to a specific limit on this tab. Selecting the **Advanced** button allows an extensive set of logging configurations to be established.

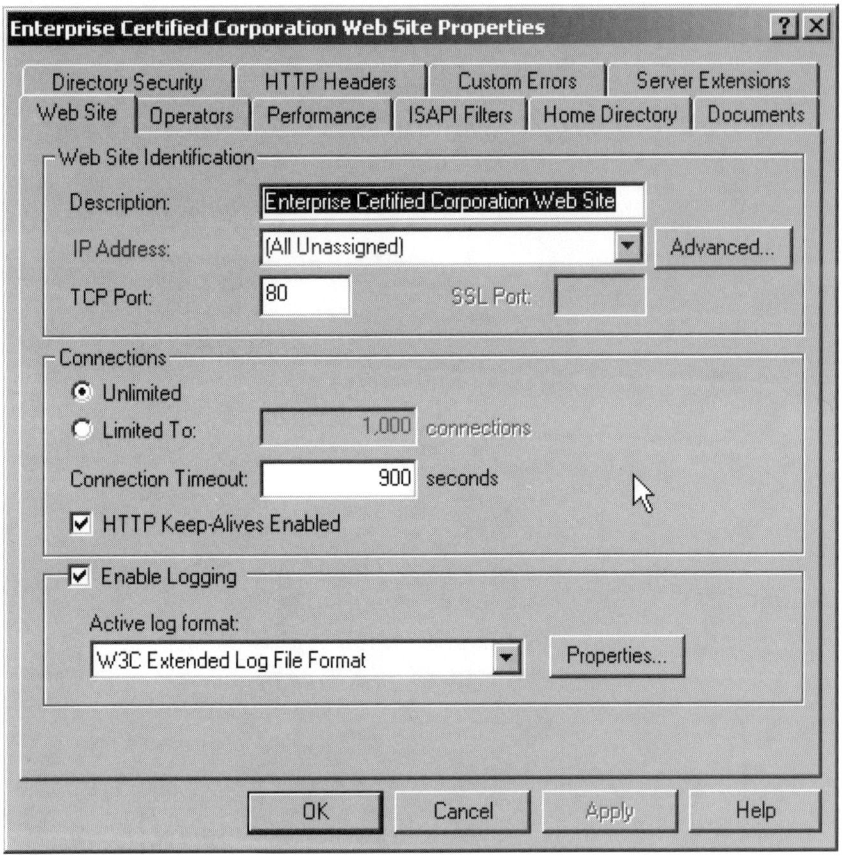

FIGURE 16.8 General Website Properties

Setting IIS Operators
The **Web Site Operators** tab (Figure 16.9) delegates authority over a website to specific users and user groups. The **Add** button adds users and groups; the **Remove** button deletes them.

Setting IIS Performance Properties
The **Performance Properties** tab (Figure 16.10) is used to set process and bandwidth throttling. In the appropriate box, set the throttling level to establish appropriate limits. *Process throttling* is based on a kilobyte-per-second limitation level. *CPU throttling* is based upon the maximum allowable percentage of CPU resources. The number of anticipated hits measures overall performance based on expected activities.

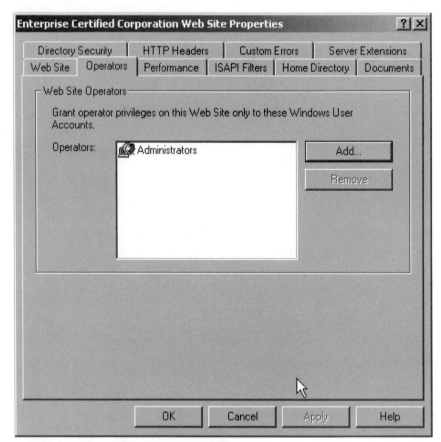

FIGURE 16.9 Properties Set Operator Privileges

Setting Execution Filters

Internet Services API **ISAPI Filters** can be applied to expand or limit functions and resources (Figure 16.11). Use the **Add**, **Remove**, and **Disable** buttons as appropriate on filters.

Managing the IIS Home Directory

The IIS home directory can be on a local computer, at a shared location on a remote computer, or on a redirected URL system. This is determined by the **Home Directory** tab, shown in Figure 16.12, which also establishes series of permissions and other properties.

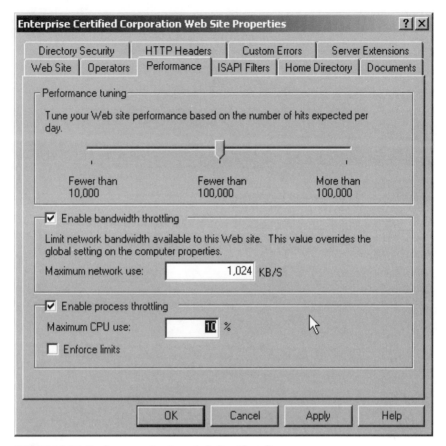

FIGURE 16.10 Performance Settings, Including Throttling

Enabling Default Documents

Access to a website's home page is based on the establishment of a default page.
The **Documents** tab, displayed in Figure 16.13, defines the acceptable name of
default pages as well as footer information for the entire website.

Setting the Directory or File Security

Directory Security, shown in Figure 16.14, is perhaps the most important of all
of the tabs, as it permits the editing of anonymous account access and authentication and defines the IP address and domain restrictions. Through the **Edit** button, access is granted or denied. Secure communication configuration can be set
through the **Certificate Wizard**, which is launched by pressing the **Server Certificate** button.

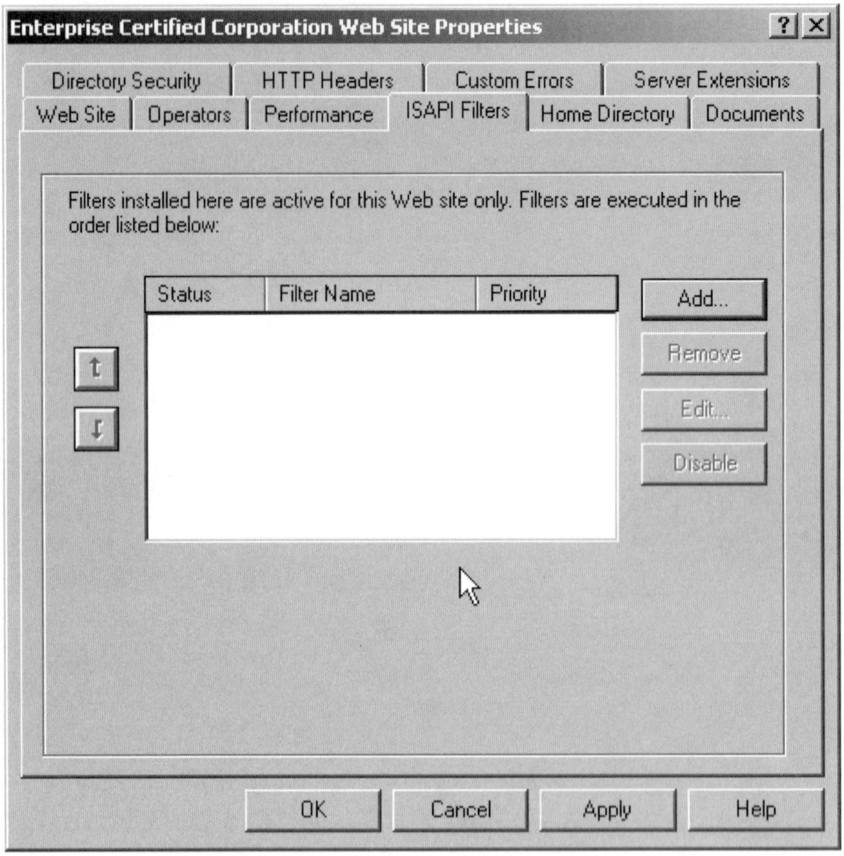

FIGURE 16.11 An ISAPI Filters List

The **Anonymous access and authentication control** panel deserves special examination, since anytime access to a server is permitted without a password, a system administrator should take heed. When the **Edit** button is selected the **Authentication Methods** dialog box is displayed. This is where anonymous account security can be defined and edited as shown in Figure 16.15.

Setting Content Expiration, HTTP Headers, Ratings, and MIME
The HTTP Headers tab (Figure 16.16) permits the configuration of a number of important website features. The first part enables content expiration. If it is checked, information posted to the site can be marked for automatic removal, which obviously ensures a more timely website. The second part permits HTTP headers to be added, edited, and removed.

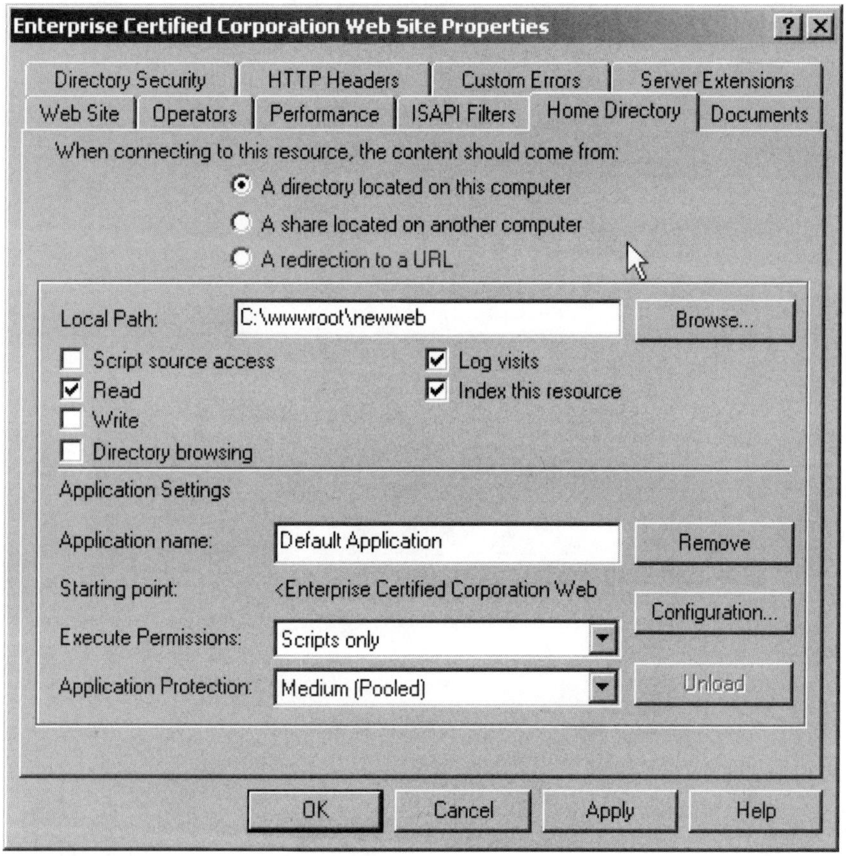

FIGURE 16.12 Home Directory Properties

Headers are used on multi-site Web servers sharing a single IP address to distinguish one site from another. They can be used with the self-regulating rating system of the Recreational Software Advisor Council (RSAC) to rate sites containing adult material, for example, and to warn underage visitors prior to entering them.

The third part of this tab establishes MIME file types supported by the Web server.

Customizing Error Messages

The **Custom Errors** tab (Figure 16.17, page 672) lists the default set of error messages established by HTTP 1.1 specifications. The **Edit Properties** button permits these messages to be redefined. Each message is directed to a specific HTML file. If further clarification is required, these files should be modified.

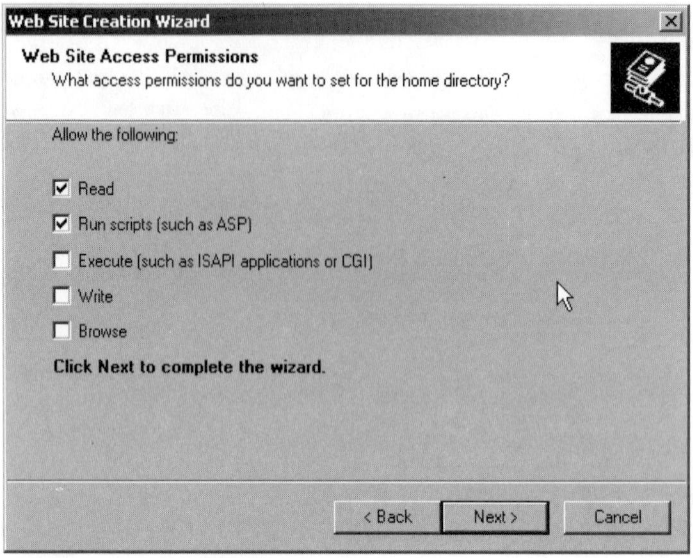

FIGURE 16.13 A Default Documents List

FIGURE 16.14 Web Directory Security Properties

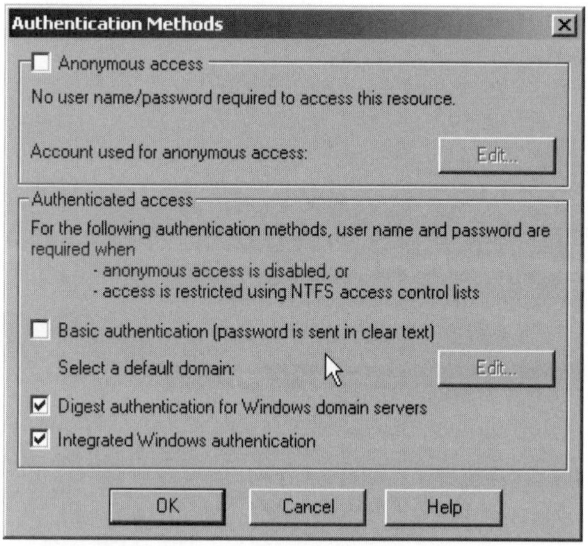

FIGURE 16.15 Authentication Subtab Options

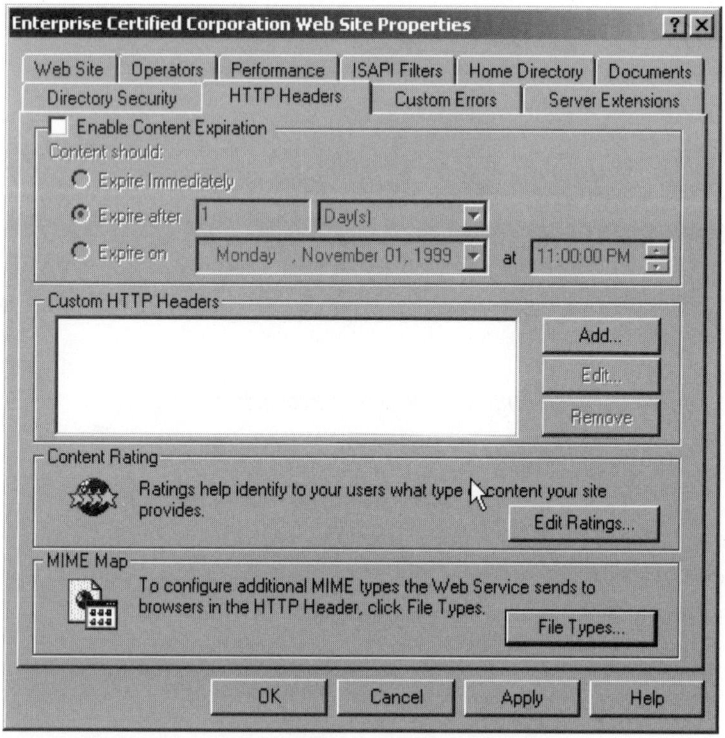

FIGURE 16.16 Web Headers, Rating, and the MIME Map

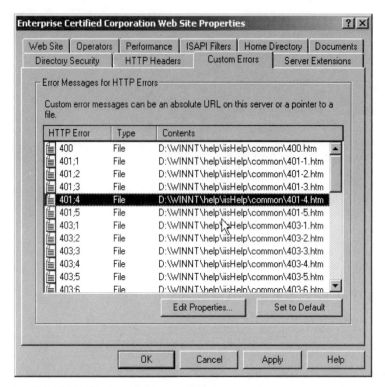

FIGURE 16.17 The Error Message Catalog

Configuring Server Extensions

The **Server Extensions** tab (Figure 16.18) permits the viewing of installed add-ons such as FrontPage Server Extensions. The FrontPage snap-in is used to edit and manipulate those specific extensions.

Setting Individual Web Page and Directory Properties

Properties for individual Web pages can be set by right-clicking on the target document and selecting **Properties**. This will display four tabs, as shown in Figure 16.19. The **File Security**, **HTTP Headers**, and **Custom Errors** tabs are largely the same as previously described. The **File** tab designates the file or the source for redirection, the local path, and basic permissions.

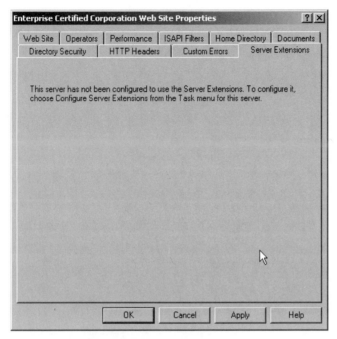

FIGURE 16.18 The Web Server Extensions Tab

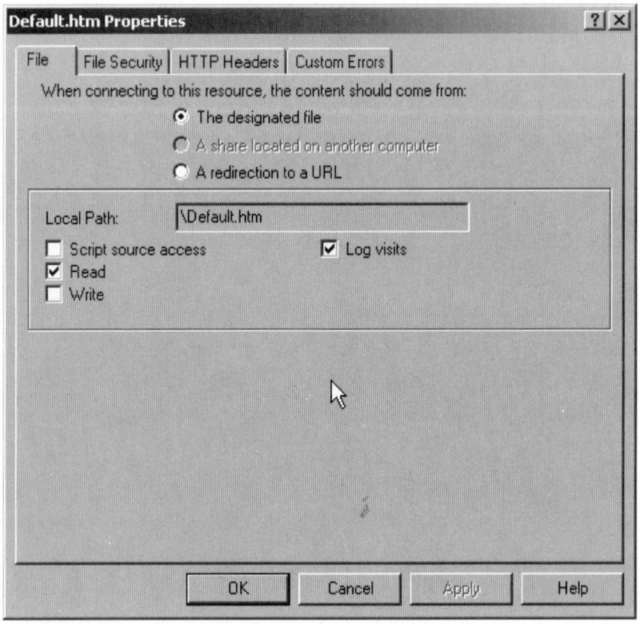

FIGURE 16.19 Default.htm Properties

WORKING WITH THE SMTP SERVER

The Simple Mail Transfer Protocol (SMTP) has become the industry standard Internet protocol for electronic mail. The specifications are established in RFC 821 and 822. Commonly used on UNIX and Linux environments, it is now integrally connected to mail products like Microsoft Exchange. SMTP Services in IIS provides administrative options for setting routing and message delivery and for governing mail security. It can support hundreds of client mail connections.

Start SMTP Services by right-clicking the **SMTP** virtual service from the **Internet Information Services** snap-in and selecting **Start**. Temporarily suspend and terminate it by selecting **Pause** or **Stop**. Multiple SMTP Virtual Servers can be established using IIS.

SMTP Properties

SMTP is primarily configured through a series of properties settings. To gain access to the six configuration tabs, right-click on the target **SMTP Virtual Server** and select **Properties**.

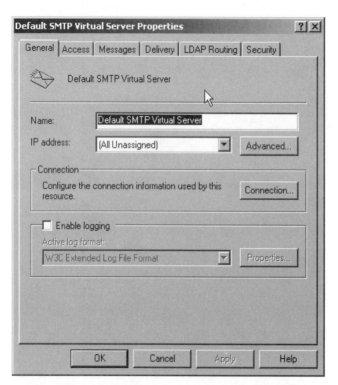

FIGURE 16.20 The SMTP Virtual Server Properties General Tab

In environments that use Microsoft Exchange Server, the documentation on specific procedures for that environment explain how to connect SMTP services. Once connected, products like *sendmail,* which is widely used in UNIX and other operating system environments, can flow transparently.

GENERAL SMTP SETTINGS

The **General** tab (Figure 16.20) permits the setting of the SMTP Virtual Server name, IP addresses, incoming and outgoing message size (through the **Connection** button), and *administrative logging administration.*

SETTING SMTP AUTHENTICATION, SECURITY, AND PERMISSIONS

The **Access** tab (Figure 16.21), which deserves special system administrator consideration, has four potentially important settings. First, the level of anonymous access is set through the **Authentication** button. Second, under the Secure Communications section the **Certificate** button launches the **Certification Wizard** and the **Communication** button defines how the certificate is to be used. The Connection Control section grants or denies access depending on IP addresses or

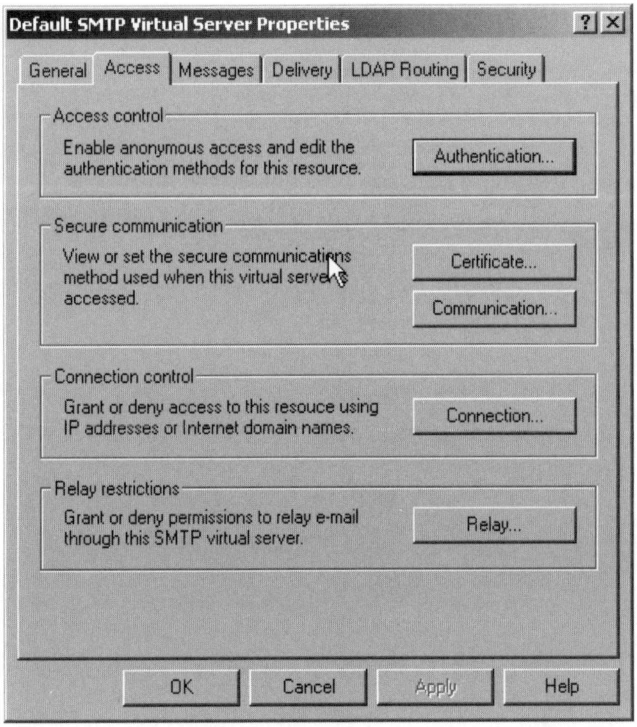

FIGURE 16.21 The SMTP Access Tab

domain names. Finally, the **Relay** button establishes permission to relay e-mail through the SMTP virtual service.

REGULATING SMTP DELIVERY

Delivery options are established with the **Delivery** tab for both outbound and local messages (Figure 16.22). For outbound messages, the system administrator can set the number of retries and intervals for them. For local messages, notification and expiration time periods can be established. The **Outbound Security** button defines the type of authentication to be utilized. The **Advanced** button permits configuration of such communication-specific settings as the maximum number of hops allowable to deliver the mail.

CONFIGURING SMTP LDAP ROUTING

The **LDAP Routing** tab (Figure 16.23) specifies the identity and properties of the directory services server. This is where mail client data and mailboxes are stored. Just like the Windows 2000 Active Directory, the SMTP virtual server uses the *Lightweight Directory Access Protocol* (LDAP) to communicate with directory services.

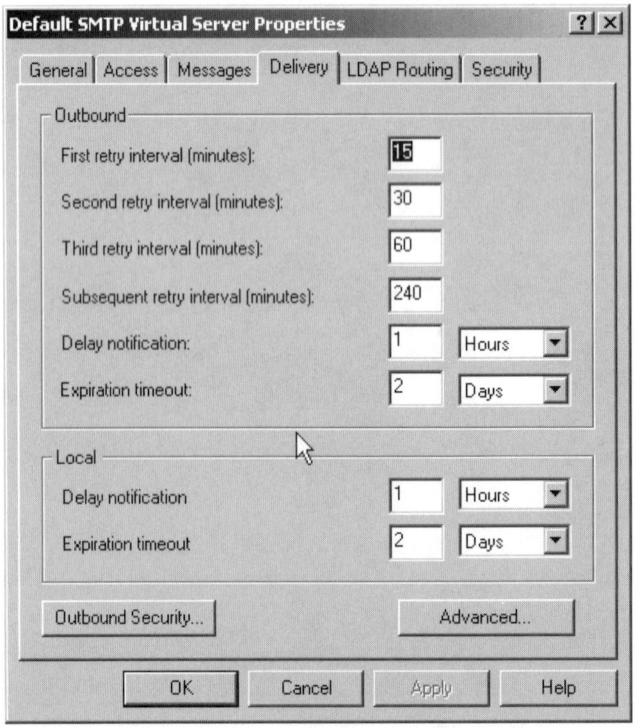

FIGURE 16.22 The SMTP Delivery Tab

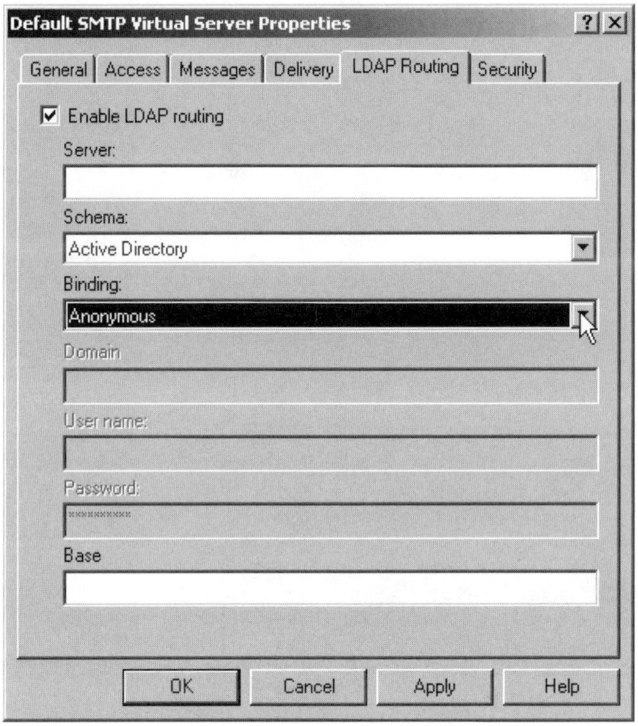

FIGURE 16.23 The SMTP LDAP Tab

SMTP "consults" with an LDAP server to resolve senders and recipients. Once the **Enable LDAP routing** option is checked, specific LDAP related configuration can be set for the server, schema, domain, network bindings, user name, and password.

SETTING SMTP OPERATOR SECURITY

The **LDAP Routing** tab (Figure 16.24) works like any other Windows 2000 security operations property setting. Use the **Add** button to increase the users or groups that have permission to administer the SMTP virtual server and the **Remove** button to delete them.

SETTING SMTP MESSAGE LIMITS

The **Messages** tab (Figure 16.25) is used to set limits on file size, length of the mail session, number of messages per connection, number of recipients, and path to where bad mail should be delivered.

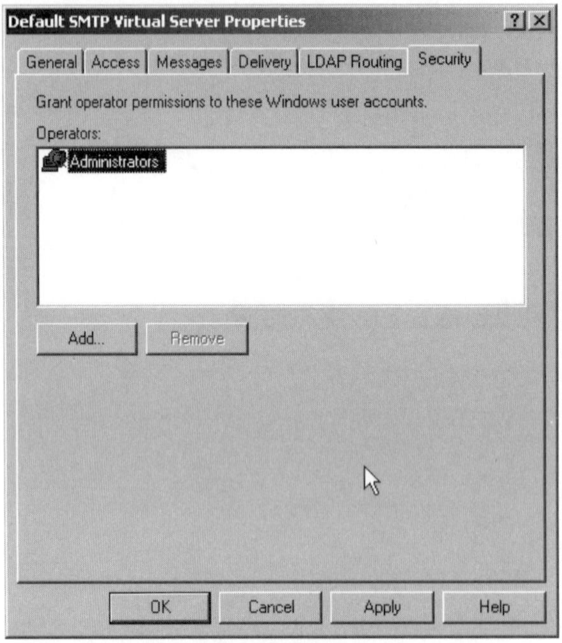

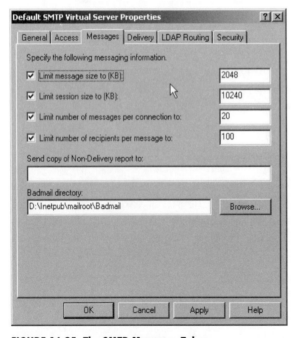

FIGURE 16.24 The SMTP Security Tab

FIGURE 16.25 The SMTP Messages Tab

UNDERSTANDING THE NNTP SERVER

The ability to post and receive messages on a bulletin board is becoming increasingly important in communications. IIS facilitates this through its Network News Transfer Protocol (NNTP). Newsgroup communication can be established and administered through the **Internet Information Services** snap-in. The system administrator can **Start**, **Stop**, or **Pause** it by right-clicking on the target NNTP server and selecting the desired option. Additional NNTP Virtual Servers are created by right-clicking on **NNTP**, selecting **New**, selecting **Virtual Server**, and entering the appropriate data in the associated dialog boxes (see Figure 16.26).

Under the NNTP console tree, policies can be set for newsgroups, expiration, virtual directories, and current sessions. NNTP Virtual Server configuration is carried out by right-clicking on the desired NNTP server, selecting **Properties**, and then sequentially configuring from the four available tabs.

The NNTP **General** tab (Figure 16.27) is used to establish the virtual server's name, IP-assigned addresses, connection options, and enabled logging. The other three tabs are essentially the same as those for SMTP, which were discussed in the previous sections and so needn't be discussed here. They are illustrated in Figures 16.28 through 16.30.

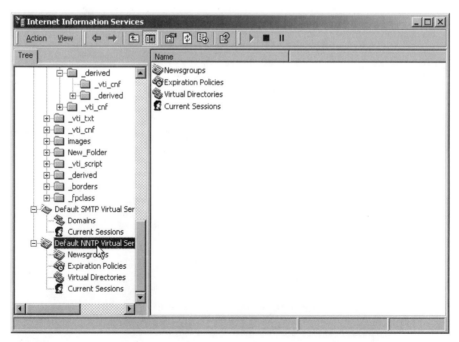

FIGURE 16.26 The IIS Snap-In tool with Default NNTP Administration Tree Options

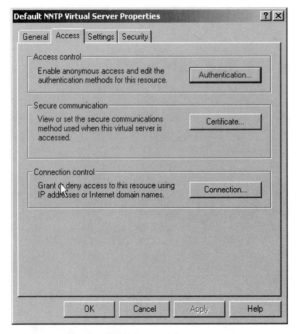

FIGURE 16.27 The NNTP General Tab

FIGURE 16.28 The NNTP Access Tab

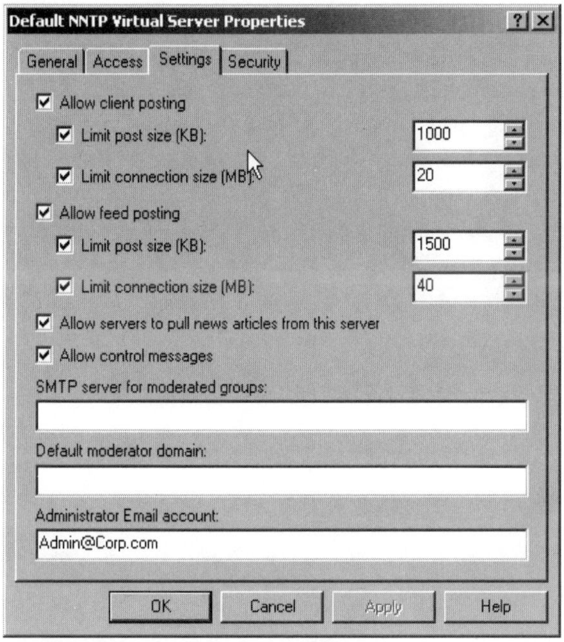

FIGURE 16.29 The NNTP Settings Tab

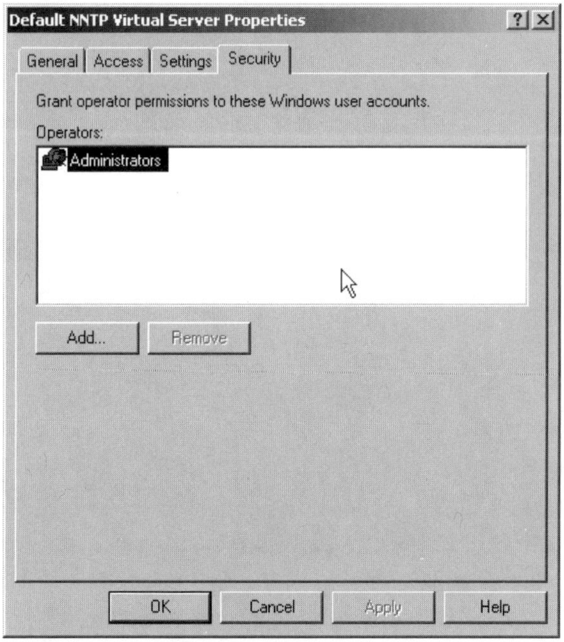

FIGURE 16.30 The NNTP Security Tab

UNDERSTANDING THE FTP SERVER

The file transfer protocol (FTP), one of the mainstays of the TCP/IP application suite, is a way to move files in UNIX environments. The FTP Service offered by IIS provides industry standard document transfer facilities, with which the system administrator can **Start**, **Stop**, or **Pause** FTP services by right-clicking on the target FTP server and selecting the desired option. Additional FTP Services are invoked by right-clicking on **FTP**, selecting **New**, selecting **Virtual Directory** or **Site**, and entering the appropriate data in the associated dialog boxes. To configure FTP, right-click on the target FTP site and select **Properties**. A brief description of the six Properties tabs follows.

FTP Properties

ESTABLISHING GENERAL FTP SITE CONFIGURATION

The **FTP Site** tab (Figure 16.31) is used to configure general specifications such as description, assigned IP address, TCP number, connection limitations, and enabled logging format.

ESTABLISHING BASIC FTP SECURITY

The **Security Accounts** tab (Figure 16.32) resolves two important security issues. First, it is used to determine whether anonymous accounts will be allowed. If so, the user account name utilized for anonymous logons must be specified, which by default is IUSR_*computername*. If the **Allow anonymous connections** box is checked, users will not be required to submit passwords to gain access to the FTP site. If **allow IIS to control password** is selected, password protection is applied.

The second function of this tab is to establish which users or groups have administrative privileges. By default, the Administrator group has Full Control. Other groups can be added or deleted with the **Add** or **Delete** button.

The **Messages** tab (Figure 16.33) provides a "user friendly" face to the FTP site. An introductory or exit greeting can be added via this tab.

ESTABLISHING THE FTP HOME DIRECTORY AND SECURITY

Figures 16.34 and 16.35 illustrate how FTP home directory properties and directory security are established. The **Home Directory** properties tab provides both location information and UNIX or MS-DOS directory style. The **Directory Security** tab designates what IP address subnet masks are granted or denied access.

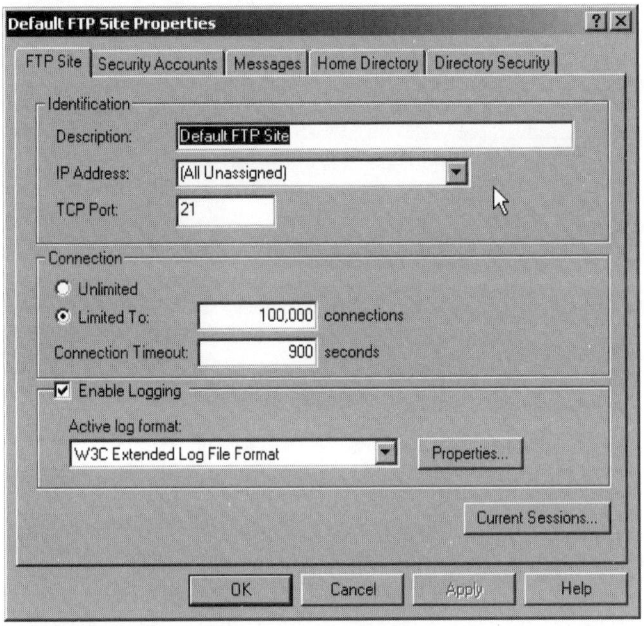

FIGURE 16.31 The FTP Site General Tab

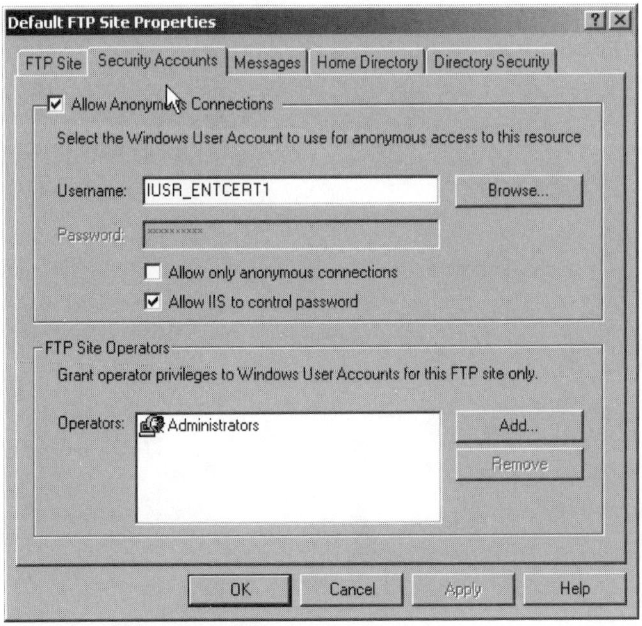

FIGURE 16.32 The FTP Security Account Tab

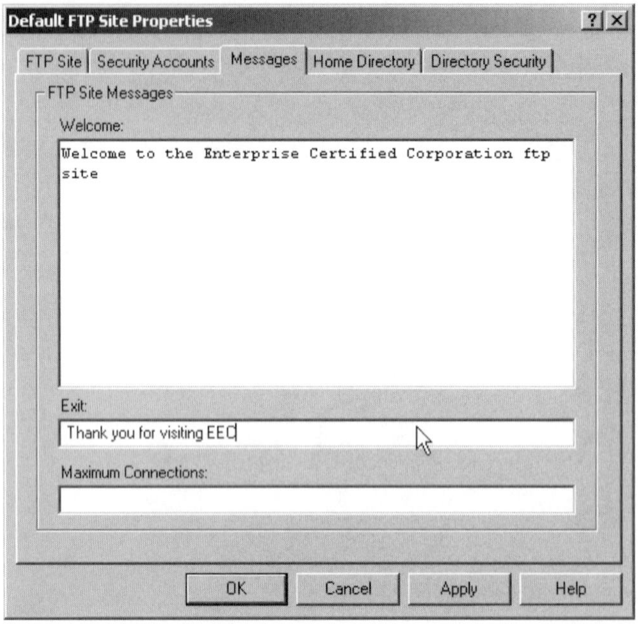

FIGURE 16.33 The FTP Messages Tab

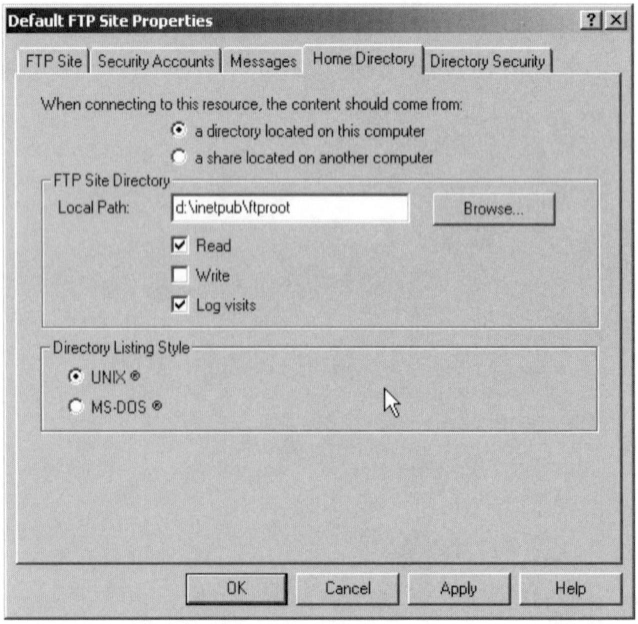

FIGURE 16.34 The FTP Home Directory Tab

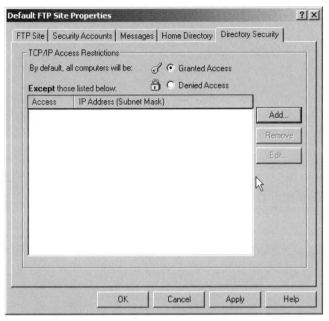

FIGURE 16.35 The FTP Directory Security Tab

POSTSCRIPT

This chapter reviewed the functionality and basic administration of Microsoft Internet Information Services. IIS is fully integrated with Windows 2000 on the operating system level. It also embraces many important Web standards. With consolidated central and remote administration, IIS should be widely embraced by Web operators and Windows 2000 system administrators.

Cluster, Indexing, Message Queuing, SMS, and WSH

This chapter examines several advanced features, each of which plays a potentially important role within a Windows 2000 enterprise.

- *Clustering* provides high availability for critical services and applications by maintaining two joined servers (or nodes); if one of the nodes or subcomponents fails, the other assumes functional responsibility. This chapter provides a conceptual view of Windows 2000 clustering technology and base-level administrative information.

- *Windows 2000 Index Services* builds local and remote disk drive index catalogs.

- *Microsoft Message Queuing Service (MSMQ)* is an inter-application communication system and development tool. It is analogous to electronic mail except that it involves communication between system queues rather than between users.

- *System Management Server 2.0 (SMS)* is part of the BackOffice product family and not one of the core Windows 2000 operating system components. Nevertheless, the tools available via SMS can significantly improve system administration, especially in larger enterprises.

- *Windows Scripting Host (WSH 2.0).*

UNDERSTANDING CLUSTER SERVICES

Clustering involves linking two servers (known as nodes) that share a common disk drive(s) and configured clustering software. All configuration and resource data is stored on the shared storage devices, and the nodes are networked through independent interconnects that ensure reliable communication. They are grouped together under a common name. Since all nodes are aware of what is being processed locally and on sister nodes, a single group name is used to manage the cluster as a whole.

Within the Windows 2000 clustering implementation, there are two forms of software. *Clustering software* manages intercommunications between the nodes; *Cluster Services* manages internode activities. The **Resource Monitor** checks on the viability of cluster communications and the health of the nodes. The **Cluster Administrator** views, configures, and modifies cluster operations and is invoked through the **Start** menu → **Administrative Tools** → **Cluster Administrator** or by invoking **cluster** from the **Command Prompt**.

As a node goes online, it searches for other nodes to join by polling the designated internal network. In this way all nodes are notified of the new node's existence. If other nodes cannot be found on a preexisting cluster, the new node takes control of the *quorum resources* residing on the shared disk that contains state and configuration data. It will theoretically receive current information, since Cluster Services maintains the latest copy of the quorum resource database. The quorum-capable resource selected to maintain the configuration data is necessary for the cluster's recovery as this data contains all of the changes applied to the cluster database. The quorum resource is generally accessible to other cluster resources so that any cluster node will have access to database changes. If the node is the first to be placed in the cluster, it will automatically create the quorum resources database, which can be shared as other nodes come online.

Failover and Failback

Every node is aware of when another node goes offline or returns to service. When one of the clustered servers fails, its processes are transferred to another member node. This process is known as *failover*. When the failed node comes back online, the workload is transferred back to it in a process known as *failback* (see Figure 17.1).

While every node is aware of the activities of all the others, each performs specialized functions while online to balance processing loads. The administrator collects cluster resources into groups and assigns group activities to particular nodes. If a node fails, the affected group functions are transferred to an operational node until the failed node can be brought back online. Every group contains a priority list of which node should execute its functions. Group functions can only be owned by one server at any given time. Although they ordinarily comprise related objects, this is not a requirement. However, where resources are dependent upon one another, they must reside in the same group.

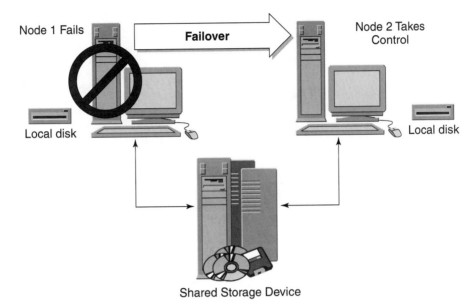

Node 1 Fails

Failover

Node 2 Takes Control

Local disk

Local disk

Shared Storage Device

FIGURE 17.1 Basic Cluster Failover

Clusters can perform a number of general or special functions, but are most often established as file, print, application, and Web servers. These can take the form of physical or "virtual" servers. A virtual server is a special group type that acts ordinarily as a server. However, its functions will failover just like those of any other cluster group. Although virtual servers have a network name and an IP address like any physical server, failover capabilities make its resources available even when the system fails. Clusters are also commonly created as high-availability file servers, printer servers, Web servers, and application servers (Figure 17.2).

Cluster Network Concerns

Clusters are dependent on the ability to reliably communicate between nodes. Therefore, they will utilize any privately available network to locate and communicate with their nodes. For reasons of security and reliability, clusters do not use networks that are configured for public use.

Nodes that are unable to communicate are said to be *partitioned*. When this occurs, Cluster Services shuts down all but one node in order to ensure data consistency.

A problem can arise if each node has only one network adapter. If an adapter on one of the nodes fails, that node will be unable to communicate with the others, and thus all nodes will automatically attempt to take control of quorum resources.

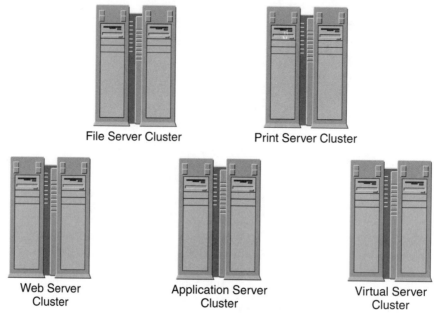

File Server Cluster

Print Server Cluster

Web Server
Cluster

Application Server
Cluster

Virtual Server
Cluster

FIGURE 17.2 Common Generic and Specialized Cluster Uses

Should the node with the failed adapter take control, all cluster resources will be out of reach by clients dependent on them. For that reason there should be more than one network adapter to provide added redundancy.

Traffic is another clear issue that arises with having only one network adapter available on cluster nodes. The single adapter must handle node-to-node traffic and also cluster-to-client systems traffic. Thus, a multi-homed environment is recommended so that all traffic can be appropriately routed.

The Cluster Database

The cluster database is maintained on every node and housed in the Windows 2000 Registry. All updates are globally distributed to all nodes in the cluster through periodic checks to ensure consistent data. As discussed earlier, the *quorum resource* database creates a recovery log so that configuration and state data can be used in case of massive failures.

In addition to configuration information, the cluster database contains data about cluster objects and properties. A cluster object can be a group of functions that have been gathered together to run on a designated node, for example. Cluster objects also include internal network data, network adapters and interfaces, node resources, and cluster resources such as shared storage devices.

Basic Cluster Planning

A number of commonsense steps should be taken during the cluster planning phase. Since the primary purpose of a cluster is to provide redundancy, risk assessment is one of them. The system administrator must minimize any area of potential failure while ensuring that a redundant system will perform in the event of a node failure. The following sections describe key planning issues that should be resolved prior to the deployment of Windows 2000 clusters.

APPLICATION SELECTION

The selection of applications to be hosted on a cluster represents one aspect of planning. This requires that a number of criteria be met by an application before it can be used in a cluster environment, since not all applications have been written to the API and so are not cluster aware. Nevertheless, many applications that are non-aware can function in a cluster if they meet the following basic requirements:

- Storage of the application data must be flexible and configurable. That is, in order to ensure failover of data, it is necessary to direct storage to the shared cluster disks.

- The application must be able to retry and recover connection in the event of temporary network disconnections.

- The application must utilize TCP/IP. Applications that are aware of DCOM, named pipes, or RPC in concert with TCP/IP will have greater reliability.

NOTE   Applications written solely to support NetBEUI or IPX are not candidates for Windows 2000 clusters.

GROUPING AND CAPACITY ISSUES

Cluster capacity is often determined by how applications and functions are grouped and assigned to particular nodes. All cluster-qualified applications must be examined in terms of resource requirements and dependencies, and all those with mutual dependencies should be grouped together. (The Dependency Walker discussed in Chapter 2 can be used to determine application dependencies.) Groups of applications should then be assigned to nodes to achieve a relative workload balance. All nodes must have sufficient disk space for the applications and sufficiently fast CPU capacity and memory. Remember, all nodes must be identically configured in terms of hardware capacity.

Nodes must belong to the same domain either as domain controllers or member servers. Cluster nodes that are also domain controllers require additional system capacity, since they can be heavily burdened by authentication and replication services in large networked environments.

NETWORK ISSUES

Clusters are connected through one or more independent physical networks, also known as interconnects. It is strongly recommended that there be at least two PCI bus-based interfaces, and prior to the cluster software installation, the nodes must be interconnected using TCP/IP for all interfaces. No routers can be used to connect nodes; they must be directly connected and assigned IP addresses on the same network. DHCP can be used to lease IP addresses, but if a lease expires and the DHCP is unavailable, connectivity can be interrupted or an automatic failover can occur. If DHCP is to be used, obtain a permanently leased IP address.

Hubs can be utilized. The hub between nodes should create a dedicated segment for the interconnect, which has no other systems connected to it.

Once the nodes are interconnected, the clustering software can be installed. The communications that occur between cluster nodes are known as heartbeats and primarily involve keeping track of node states. If an irregular heartbeat is detected from a cluster partner, the process of failover begins.

REQUIRED DOMAIN ACCOUNTS

Computer accounts must be established for each of the nodes before Cluster Services installation, and they must be in the same domain. An account should become a member of the local **Administrators** group, but if the nodes are configured as domain controllers, it becomes a member of the **Domain Administrators** group. The **Change password on next Logon** property should also be disabled.

POTENTIAL POINTS OF FAILURE

Clustering assumes reliability of hardware and interconnectivity, so the system administrator has a responsibility to reduce the number of potential failure points. As discussed in Chapter 14, Disk Management, Windows 2000 supports both disk mirrors and RAID-5 striping with parity. It is strongly recommended that nodes be built with multiple network interfaces in case an adapter fails and that disk redundancy be implemented. A UPS system is also highly recommended.

Cluster Administration

Clusters are managed through the use of a number of tools and utilities. The **Application Configuration Wizard** manages cluster-serviced software. The

Cluster Administrator tool, automatically installed on all nodes with Cluster Services, views cluster configurations and manages failover activities. The **cluster.exe** utility provides command line support.

THE APPLICATION CONFIGURATION WIZARD

The **Application Configuration Wizard** configures software for clusters. It helps to define dependencies and sets failover/failback policies, and it creates a virtual server to run the applications. The virtual server will need an IP address in order to run applications. You should reserve the IP address before running the Applications Configuration Wizard.

UNDERSTANDING DEFAULT GROUPS

The **Cluster Administrator** tool is used to view *cluster* and *disk* groups, which contain default settings and resources for generic clusters and failover. The cluster group attributes contain the information necessary for network connectivity. This information—a name and IP address that applies to the entire cluster—is entered during Cluster Services setup. The cluster group should never be deleted, renamed, or modified. If changes must be made, do it through the disk group.

Each shared storage disk has its resources identified through the disk group. Also a part of this group is the physical disk resource data. It is possible to add IP address resources and the network name resource. The latter can then be renamed to distinguish its function.

FAILOVER ADMINISTRATION

Failover occurs when either the entire node or a node resource fails. In this case the **Cluster Administrator** tool is notified. Resource failures do not always bring down the entire node and may just cause group failovers. Unfortunately, group failures are more difficult to detect. The Cluster Administrator should be employed to periodically check group ownerships to determine if a failover has occurred, as even minor failovers can cause performance degradation and decrease resource availability. It should also be regularly used to review cluster states and make appropriate corrections.

USING THE CLUSTER.EXE COMMAND LINE UTILITY

Many administrative tasks can be accomplished using the **cluster.exe** utility from the **Command Prompt** or **Start** menu → **Run**. The syntax is shown here, with the cluster name being an optional component:

```
Cluster [cluster name] /option
```

These are the cluster.exe command options:

- */rename: new name*—renames the client.
- */version*—displays the version number for Cluster Services.
- */quorumresource: resource name [/path:path] [maxlogsize:maximum size in kilobytes]*—changes the name of the quorum resource and its location and log size.
- */list: domain name*—lists the cluster in the named domain.
- */?*—provides more cluster.exe syntax information.

The following are the cluster.exec functions that can be used for administration:

- *Cluster [name] Node [name] /option*—locates the option information for the specified node. Options include status, pause, resume, evict (or remove node), listinterfaces, privproperties (private properties), properties, and help.
- *Cluster [name] Group [name] /option*—permits viewing and managing of cluster groups. The options include status, create, delete, rename, moveto, online, offline, properties, privproperties, listowners, setowners, and help.
- *Cluster [name] Network [name] /option*—permits the management of cluster networks. Options include status, properties, privproperties, rename, and listinterfaces.
- *Cluster [name] Netinterfaces [name] /option*—supports the management of the network interfaces. The options include status, properties, and privproperties.
- *Cluster [name] Resources [name] /option*—administers cluster resources. The options include status, create, delete, rename, addowner, removeowner, listowner, moveto, properties, privproperties, online, fail, offline, listdependencies, removedependencies, and help.

Setting Cluster Properties

Cluster configuration can be changed by altering the settings within the selected cluster's **File** menu → **Properties** dialog box.

Group properties are viewed and modified from the **State** option, which also allows the node that currently owns the group to be viewed. The State option is used to change the Name, Description, and Preferred owner properties.

Failover policy and **failback policy** are set by selecting their respective tabs and making appropriate changes. The number of times a group can failover during a given period is established by the **Failover** tab. If a group failover occurs more often than the amount set in the policy, Cluster Services takes the resource offline until it can be fixed. The default policy is not to have this function occur automatically. However, in some cases it may be appropriate to have an automatic failback after so many hours.

The **Properties** dialog box is used to check and modify other settings, including

- *Resource dependencies*. A great number of dependencies will impact clusters. For example, DHCP, File share, ISS Server Instance, Message Queuing Services, WINS Services, and Print spoolers are all dependent on the availability of the physical disk or storage device. Many are also dependent on network name and IP address availability.
- *Network settings*. This option is used to view and change the network name, description, state, IP address, and address mask, as well as to enable or disable the network cluster. If enabled, the communication types can be set as client-to-cluster and/or node-to-node.
- *Advanced settings*. This option is used to determine whether the resource is to be restarted or allowed to fail. If the latter, the **Affect the group** box must be checked. Then a **Threshold**—the number of times a restart is attempted within a defined **Period** of time—must be defined. When that threshold is exceeded during that period, failover occurs. It will not occur if the **Affect the group** option is not checked.

Postscript

This section provided a conceptual and administrative overview of Windows 2000 clustering technology, with shared disk clustering at its center. Much information needs to be gathered before deploying a cluster. Moreover, the technology is shifting. Thus, it is highly recommended that a system administrator download the latest Microsoft white papers on clusters prior to installing and deploying Cluster Services.

INDEX SERVICES

Windows 2000 **Index Services** builds an index catalog from local and remote disk drives that contains information about document contents and properties. Like a regular index, this catalog includes all words that will help a user locate data. Typically, 15 to 30 percent of the contents of a document are cataloged. The rest are held in an exception list and include common nouns, verbs, articles, prepositions, and other words deemed not appropriate to finding data.

Document properties cataloged include creation date, author name, and size in characters. Each document type treats properties differently, requiring that some be generated automatically and others entered manually. This is the case with products like Microsoft Office. Meta tags found in HTML files must be stored in the property cache in order for HTML properties to be indexed.

The indexing process involves *scanning* documents, either on a full or an incremental basis. When indexing is run for a first time, all documents in the selected directory or directories are scanned for the catalog. A new full scan can be created at any time using the **Indexing Services** snap-in, selecting **Directories**, right-clicking on the desired directory, selecting **All Tasks**, and choosing **Full Scan** (Figure 17.3). Manual incremental scans are initiated in the same manner except, of course, for the final selection. Automatic incremental scans are conducted each time Indexing Services is started, and when a document is modified Indexing Services is notified that it requires rescanning. Incremental scans index only new or modified documents.

The full process invoked by Indexing Services has a number of distinct steps. First, it identifies the type of file involved and then loads the appropriate document filter. A filter merely reflects the document's structure. Word processors from different vendors, for example, have different structures, and the filters strip away encoded structural information from the content itself. They also determine the international language in which the document is written and parse the information into individual words. At that point the exception list of verbs, common nouns, articles, and prepositions for the international language is applied, and those on it are dropped from the process. Every international language supported

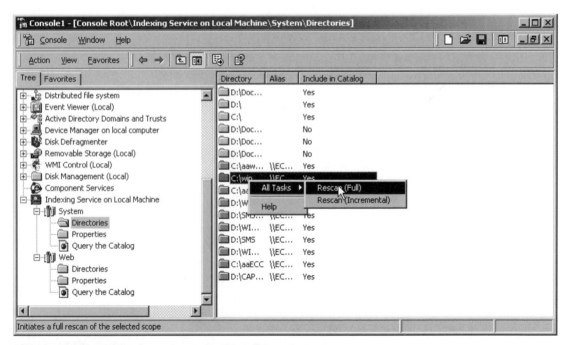

FIGURE 17.3 The MMC Indexing Service Snap-In Full Scan Option

by Windows 2000 has an individual exception list. All words that remain are placed in the index. Properties are also collected and stored in the properties cache.

NOTE   In terms of security, users will only be able to view those files for which they have permission on NTFS partitions. Catalogs saved on a FAT system will be visible to all users. Encrypted documents are never indexed.

Using Index Services to Find Data

Indexed information can be found in one of two ways. The one best known by users is **Start** menu → **Search** function, discussed in Chapter 4. Any of the found items can be opened by highlighting the target item and double-clicking on it.

The second method of locating content is the Index Services query form, which locates content and data output according to several criteria. Figure 17.4

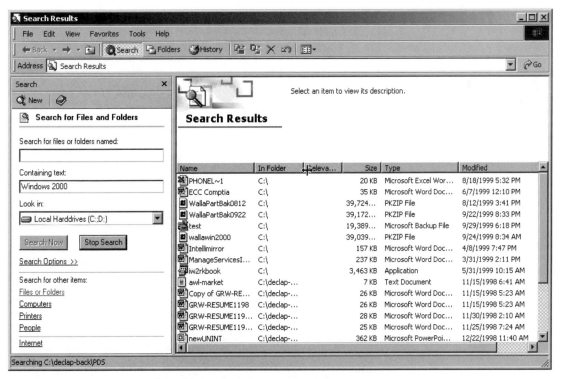

FIGURE 17.4 Content Location from the Search Dialog

shows a simple query and its results. Note that the query provides direct hot links to each found item. To open one of the files, simply double-click on it (see Figure 17.5).

Indexing Service Sizing

As with any other Windows 2000 service, indexing large numbers of documents increases the pressure on the host server. The complexity and rapidity of queries also dictates system requirements. For less than 100,000 documents, 64 to 128 MB of storage memory should be sufficient. However, for 500,000 documents, the memory demands can easily exceed 256 MB. The system administrator should monitor memory demands periodically and routinely add memory as the number and complexity of queries shift upward. CPU speed also impacts indexing effi-

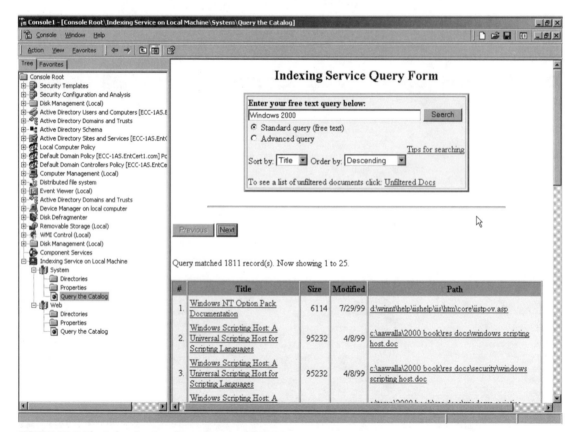

FIGURE 17.5 The Index Services Query Form and Output

ciency, as does available disk space. As a general rule, allocate an additional 30 percent for disk storage for all documents saved on a FAT system. Catalogs on NTFS require about 15 percent of the disk space used by the indexed documents.

Indexing Services Query Language

A query is simply a structure string of data that narrows the scope of a given search. Its syntax is very precise and generally takes the form

```
[Mode] [property name] [query_text] [attribute=value] query_text [/mode]
```

The *mode* is optional and defines the type of query, including free text, phrase, relational, and regular expressions (regex). *Free text* is the default if *mode* is not utilized. Short-form inquires use the @ symbol for phrase mode, # for regular expressions, and *$* for free text. Long-form queries use curly braces to define the type. For example, the long form for a query about a title is *{prop name=title};* the short form is *#name #title*.

Index Services recognizes over 40 property types that can be queried. These include creation time, time last accessed, physical path, number of characters, and document author. Refer to the Windows 2000 Help menu for a full list of query properties.

RULES AND OPERATORS

Index Services requires adherence to several query rules, within which standard query operators can be applied. The following rules are applicable to all Index Services queries:

- Queries are not case sensitive.
- A number of special characters must be enclosed in quotation marks (' '). They are *& @ $ # ^ ( ) |.* (How these characters can be applied is covered later.)
- Two forms of date and time queries are recognized: *yyyy/mm/dd hh:mm:ss* and *yyyy-mm-dd hh:mm:ss.*
- No words in the exception list can be utilized. Remember, these include verbs, common nouns, articles, and pronouns.
- Numeric values can be hexadecimals or decimals.

Available Operators

Industry standard operators can be applied to queries. The following describes them and how they are applied. This is not a comprehensive treatment; the Help menu provides additional information.

- *Contains and Equals*. The **contains** operator is employed to find specific words or phrases. For example, if you want to find the phrase "all basset hounds are cool," use the short form *@DocTitle "all basset hounds are cool"* or the long form *{phrase name=DocTitle} Contains {phrase}all basset hounds are cool{/phase}{/prop}*. The **equals** operator specifies an exact equivalent condition. The short form is *@DocTitle = "all basset hounds are cool"*, which finds documents with that exact phrase.

- *Boolean*. Boolean operators use conditions that are strung together by *AND (&)*, *OR (|)*, *NOT (&!)*, and *NEAR (~)*. For example, to find documents containing the words "basset hound" and "cool," use *"basset hound & cool"* or *"basset hound and cool."* (Don't forget the quote marks.) The order of precedence for Booleans is NOT, AND or NEAR, and OR.

- *Free text*. Free text is the default operator. The words or phrases are entered without further filtering.

- *Phrase*. In a phrase query the quotation in the short form is *basset hounds are cool*. In the long form, the *{phrase}* tag is in the form *{phrase} basset hounds are cool {/phrase}*.

- *Wildcards*. Wildcards are used for very simple pattern matching using the asterisk or question mark. The asterisk with the letters *b*, *a*, and *s*, *bas**, results in findings such as "basset," "basket," "bass," and many others. The short form of the query is *@filename = bas**.

- *Regular Expression pattern matching*. Regular expressions are used commonly in statistical and other forms of analysis. If you are unfamiliar with regular expressions, refer to the Help pages.

- *Alternate Word Forms*. These are often called fuzzy or imprecise queries and are of two types. The first finds all words with common prefixes, and the short form simply uses the wildcard asterisk. The second type involves alternate forms of the word, such as "come" and "came." Here the long form for the *inflected* operator is *{Generate method=inflect} come {/Generate}*.

- *Relational*. These permit you to set parameters that include constraints such as *less than (<)*, *less than or equal to (<=)*, *equal to (=)*, *greater than or equal to (>=)*, *greater than (>)*, and *not equal to (| =)*.

- *Vector Space Queries*. In the vector space model common in information retrieval the order can be separated by a comma—*basset, hound,* and a ranking can be applied to set the priority of the query match. In this case, ranking *basset [20], hound [4]* places a greater importance on the word "hound."

- *Term Weighting Queries*. This operator assigns a relative value to each of the words being queried. The syntax is *{weight} word,* and a value between 0.0

and 1.0 is assigned. For example, a query on *basset hounds are cool* might be weighted with this structure: *{weight value = .300}basset AND {weight value=.600} hound AND {weight value=.100}cool*. In this example, "hound" has a much heavier weight than "cool."

Common Indexing Server Administrative Tasks

Index Services is one of the simplest Windows 2000 applications to administer. In this section, we will review only some of the common administrative tasks; the complete task scope is fairly obvious when exploring the **Indexing Services** MMC snap-in or the **Computer Management** snap-in → **Server Applications and Services** → **Indexing Services**. Both provide the same set of options and can be used interchangeably, but for the sake of simplicity we will reference the **Indexing Services** snap-in the following examples.

Launch **Indexing Services** by opening the **Indexing Services** snap-in, clicking the **Action** menu, and selecting **Start**. To pause or stop Indexing Services, follow the same steps, but select **Pause** or **Stop** as appropriate.

CREATING A CATALOG

The creation of an Index Services catalog requires the following steps:

1. Open the **Indexing Services** snap-in.
2. Select the **Action** menu, click **New**, and select **Catalog**.
3. From the **Add Catalog** dialog box, type the name of catalog and enter the location. Use the **Browse** button to navigate to the desired location (Figure 17.6).
4. Click **OK** to complete the process.

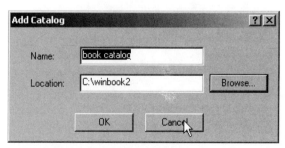

FIGURE 17.6 The Add Catalog Dialog Box

ADDING OR EXCLUDING A DIRECTORY TO THE CATALOG

To add or exclude an Index Services directory to the catalog, follow these steps:

1. Open the **Indexing Services** snap-in.
2. Open the **Systems** tree console and click the **Directories** folder.
3. Select the **Action** menu, click **New**, and select **Directory**.
4. From the **Add Directory** dialog box, type the name of the catalog and enter the location. Use the **Browse** button to navigate to the desired location. Enter an alias name for the directory in the **Alias (UNC)** text box (Figure 17.7).
5. If this is a remote directory, add an authorized user name and password in the appropriate text boxes.
6. To include the directory, select **YES**; to exclude the directory, select **NO**.
7. Click **OK** to complete the process.

The removal of a directory from a catalog is accomplished by loading the **Index Services** snap-in, double-clicking on the target catalog, double-clicking on the **Directories** folder, highlighting the target directory, pressing the **Action** menu, and selecting **Delete**.

ADDING, EDITING, AND REMOVING PROPERTIES

In the properties cache adding, editing, and removing properties, follow these steps:

1. Open the **Indexing Services** snap-in.
2. Double-click the target catalog.
3. Click **Properties** from the catalog console tree.

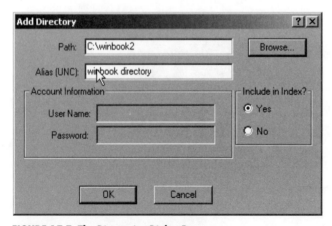

FIGURE 17.7 The Directories Dialog Box

4. From the right-hand Details window move to the **Property Set** column and select the property ID to add to the cache.

5. Click the **Action** menu and select **Properties**.

6. From within the **Properties** dialog box, checkmark the **Cached** option and select the data type appropriate for the property from the **Datatype** list. Set the size in bytes for the property in the **Size** box.

To remove the properties, follow the above process except the last step and simply remove the checkmark on the **Cached** option. Edit properties by following the previous steps and making appropriate changes.

Postscript

The **Indexing Service** snap-in does not have to be installed for a typical user to find things using the **Start** menu → **Search** function. However, with the service in place, searches can be more detailed, accurate, and efficient. Remember, the primary function of Index Services is to catalog document content and properties for fast retrieval.

MESSAGE QUEUING SERVICES

Microsoft Message Queuing (MSMQ) gives system administrators the ability to manage a communications infrastructure. MSMQ is also of great interest to software developers who want to build message-queuing-aware applications. Such applications go by several industry names, including message queuing, message-oriented middleware (MOM), and store-and-forward software. Unlike e-mail, which passes messages between people, message queuing passes messages between applications.

A queue is a temporary storage environment that buffers data transmission until an appointed time or until the recipient is available. This allows communication regardless of the state of the receiving computer and even if the system is offline. MSMQ communications remain in the queue until the receiving application is available to accept it (unless other parameters are set to discharge the message after a defined number of attempts or a period of time).

NOTE   The developmental aspect of MSMQ is outside the scope of Windows 2000 administration. Those interested in developing message queuing applications should obtain the MSMQ Software Development Kit.

NOTE

Cross-platform connectivity to IBM MQSeries versions 2 and 5 is provided with the optional SMQ-MQSeries Bridge available from the Microsoft SNA Server version 4 Service Pack 2 or later. The Bridge was purchased from Level8 Systems and was commercially known as FalconMQ Bridge.

Concepts

Several concepts must be understood prior to installing and deploying MSMQ. Messages, queues, network topology, and routing are explored in this section.

UNDERSTANDING MESSAGES

MSMQ messages have two primary parts. The body is either binary or text information readable by the receiving application which can be encrypted. It also contains specific properties, including the message ID and those required by the application. The maximum size of a message is 4 megabytes.

Normal messages are regular communications between applications delivered from public, private, journal, dead letter, or transactions queues. *Report messages* are generally sent as tests or for route tracking. *Response messages* are confirmations from the receiving application and are often invoked by the MQPing function. Finally, *acknowledgment messages* confirm the receipt or failure of a normal message from the receiving application to the sending computer's administrative queue.

Messages are delivered via an express or a recoverable method. *Express message* delivery takes place within the queues stored in the RAM and is the fastest and most efficient method. However, express messages are lost when MSMQ service is shut down or, if MSMQ is run on a cluster, during a failover. *Recoverable messages* are written to disk until delivery can be achieved. This method is slower but safer.

UNDERSTANDING QUEUES

The queue is the base structure used by MSMQ to store and transmit messages. Different queues perform different functions, as follows:

- *Administration*. These are established by the sending application and simply provide acknowledgments from sent messages.
- *Public*. These are available to any computer within an enterprise. Their properties are published by the Active Directory and replicated to domain controllers.

- *Private*. These are used only by MSMQ applications that have knowledge of the format and path to the queue. They are not known by or published to the Active Directory.

- *Dead-letter*. These hold messages that cannot be delivered or that exceed the time specified for delivery.

- *Response*. These hold response messages sent from the receiving application to the sender.

- *Report*. These simply report the route taken by a message.

- *System*. These combine other queues to conduct system communication and cannot be deleted.

- *Journal*. These copy messages to ensure delivery. Journal messages can be saved to disk on the source or target computer.

UNDERSTANDING NETWORK TOPOLOGY FOR MSMQ

As the basis for its network topology MSMQ utilizes the Windows 2000 site. This site definition is created by the Windows 2000 Active Directory, which means that the site topologies for both the Active Directory and MSMQ are identical. (For information about site structure, refer to Chapters 5 and 6.) With specific regard to MSMQ, it is essential that the intrasite network be permanent and that sufficient bandwidth exist to support the anticipated volume of messages. For intersite messages, multiple MSMQs are commonly configured for redundancy. However, since multiple MSMQ servers can dramatically increase network traffic, it is recommended that at least one MSMQ server be installed for each site or subnet.

Routing links are used to communicate messages between sites by MSMQ services when one or more MSMQ servers is used. To view and modify MSMQ data on the Active Directory, the MSMQ must be installed on a domain controller. Message queuing services are configured to store and forward messages and provide dynamic routing. MSMQ can be configured to route messages between sites using either IP- or IPX-based networks, but the respective MSMQ server must also be configured for that network routing protocol. Moreover, name resolution is required for MSMQ configured for IPX, which can be provided by a Novell server. Lacking a Novell server, the Service Advertising Protocol (SAP) Agent must be installed.

CAUTION   When using IPX with multiple adapters the computers must be configured with a unique internal network number. This is required to ensure the proper operation of remote procedure calls (RPCs) over IPX. Zero is not an acceptable network number.

Independent MSMQ clients cannot immediately store and forward message queues. Other than this limitation, they can send and receive messages in a manner similar to the MSMQ server. The client MSMQ generates local messages and sends them when a connection to the receiving computer or application is available. If the system is offline, it will store the messages until connectivity is restored.

The dependent MSMQ client is similar to the independent client except that it uses synchronous communications, which makes it dependent on its server to perform the MSMQ functions.

Understanding Message Routing

If a direct connection cannot be established, MSMQ uses routing to deliver messages and accept acknowledgments. That is, it hops from computer to computer until the destination is found. These hops are measured by MSMQ to facilitate future communication. MSMQ attempts to provide the least costly link route, but if the most direct route is not available, it will utilize any route available to complete the delivery.

In large organizations where message volumes are substantial, it is wise to consider creating specialized MSMQ servers to handle traffic. *In-routing servers* manage messages within a site; *out-routing servers* move messages across wide-bandwidth networks and control the message flow. Clients should be generally configured to employ multiple in-routing and out-routing servers in order to minimize message transmission failure.

Routing is generally predicated on the availability of links and their relative costs. Once multiple links are established, MSMQ attempts to route to the least costly link based upon costs input during the configuration process. These costs are usually derived from throughput divided by the actual cost of the connection, which provides a relative number of megabits or kilobits per second of message transfer per monetary unit. From this a link value can be calculated and compared to other values.

Routing links use MSMQ servers to route messages. One or more MSMQ servers must be assigned to routing links.

When utilizing a firewall with MSMQ, a PPTP-based secure communication channel should be established. This is usually RCP ports 2103 and 2105, although the MQPing uses UDP port 3527. Three basic modes can be set in a firewall environment. First, messages can be sent only through TCP port 1801 for independent client computer access. Second, messages can be sent and Active Directory access allowed using TCP port 1801 and RPC port 135 and 2101. Third, messages can be sent and read with Active Directory access. Here, in addition to the ports allowed in the second mode, RCP port 2105 can be used to allow remote clients to receive queues from the internal MSMQ server.

CREATING A ROUTING LINK

The creation of a routing link for MSMQ is accomplished via these steps:

1. Open the **Active Directory Sites and Services** snap-in.
2. Open the console tree and right-click on **MsmqServices**.
3. Select **New**.
4. Select **MSMQ Routing Link**.
5. From the dialog box, select the two sites to be linked by scrolling through the **Site 1** and **Site 2** options menus.
6. Assign a relative cost (positive value) for the link in the **MSMQ Link Cost** text box.

CHANGING ROUTING SERVERS FOR A ROUTING LINK

To change the routing server of a routing link for MSMQ, follow these steps:

1. Open the **Active Directory Sites and Services** snap-in.
2. Open the console tree and right-click on **MsmqServices**.
3. Right-click on the target link and select **Properties**.
4. Within the **Site Gates** tab → select **Site Servers** and click on **Add**.

   To remove a routing server, simply repeat all the steps above except step 4. Here select **Remove** rather than **Add**.

CREATING A COST FOR A ROUTING LINK

Follow these steps to create a cost for an MSMQ routing link:

1. Open the **Active Directory Sites and Services** snap-in.
2. Open the console tree and right-click on **MsmqServices**.
3. Select **Properties**.
4. Within the **General** tab insert the cost in the **Link Cost** text box.

CHANGING THE ROUTING SERVER FOR INDEPENDENT CLIENTS

To change the routing server for independent MSMQ clients, perform the following steps:

1. Open the **Active Directory Users and Computers** snap-in.
2. Open the **View** menu and select **Users, Groups, and Computers** as containers.

3. Open the **View** menu and select **Advanced Features**.

4. From the console tree, select **MSMQ**.

5. Right-click **msmq** and select **Properties**.

6. Select the **Routing** tab. Within **In Routing Servers** scroll and select up to three servers or *none* to remove in-routing servers.

Out-routing servers are changed by the same method as above except for the last step, in which **Out Routing Servers** is selected.

TESTING CONNECTIVITY USING MQPing

Test connectivity using MQPing with the following steps:

1. Open the **Active Directory Users and Computers** snap-in.

2. Open the **View** menu and select **Users, Groups, and Computers** as containers.

3. Open the **View** menu and select **Advanced Features**.

4. From the console tree, select **MSMQ**.

5. Right click **msmq** and select **Properties**.

6. Select the **Diagnostics** tab and click **MQPing**.

Installing Message Queuing Services

The installation process begins with an analysis of hardware and network requirements. Once these items are mapped out and available, the actual installation of MSMQ can begin.

PRE-INSTALLATION HARDWARE CONSIDERATIONS

One of the keys to efficient message queuing is appropriately sized and configured hardware. Hard disk drives, memory, processors, and network adapters all play a role.

The number and size of hard drives dedicated to MSMQ servers are important because of the requirement to save to disk-recoverable queues, journals, and logs. With this amount of constant writing to disk, seek times can cause a slowing of message delivery, so using only a single hard drive is not advised. With two disk drives the messages should go to one disk and the logs to the other. Microsoft recommends as the optimum disk configuration five hard disk drives for storing MSMQ messages, the message log file, transaction logs, virtual memory paging, and application data files.

NOTE   The **Start** menu → **Administrative Tools** → **Performance Monitor** can be utilized to view the **Avg. Disk Queue Length** counter. If the queue length exceeds 0.6, adding additional disks is probably warranted.

Sizing a disk is also important. Recoverable messages are allocated 4 KB or 250 messages per megabit. Express messages are stored only if virtual memory is not available and need about one-fourth the amount of storage space that recoverable messages require. If the server runs out of memory, paging will occur and demand additional disk space.

As suggested before, system memory should be sufficient to minimize paging, but sizing can be difficult. The receiving server may have enough RAM or disk space to store messages only until the associated application is started. Sending computers have a similar problem with accumulation of messages if the network or receiving system is down. Ideally, systems will be configured with sufficient memory to accommodate peak message loads. For example, Microsoft estimates the average message size as 150 bytes and the average header size as 1 kilobyte, for a total of 1,150 bytes. Assuming that the maximum number of messages expected through an MSMQ is 50,000, that number would be multiplied by 1,150 bytes, meaning that a minimum 57.5 MB should be added.

The speed of both the CPU and network adapters has obvious impacts on message queuing. Use the fastest economically feasible CPU for MSMQ servers and multiple fast network adapters to enhance message throughput.

INSTALLATION CONSIDERATIONS

Installation of MSMQ can take several steps. First, the Message Queuing servers must be installed. During this process, it is necessary to determine whether or not routing support will be enabled. Then independent and dependent clients are installed. This is automatic for existing message queuing clients. If appropriate, MSMQ Exchange connectors are applied. In a domain environment, both Active Directory and RCP must be operational. For each site, MSMQ must be installed on a domain controller before it is installed on member services or clients within the site.

The actual installation involves these steps: **Start** menu → **Administrative Tools** → **Configure Your Server**. From the dialog box select **Advanced** → **Message Queuing**. The options afforded by the installation wizard are fairly obvious. For specific questions, refer to the Help menu (see Figure 17.8).

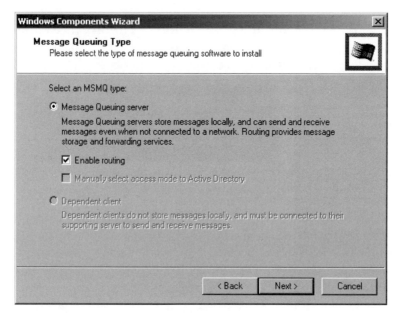

FIGURE 17.8 A Sample Installation Wizard Screen

CAUTION   If you are migrating from an existing Windows NT MSMQ server, you must resolve numerous incompatibilities and other issues, many of which can be handled by the MSMQ Migration Tool wizard. (Previous versions used a MQIS controller server.) The migration tool, which should be run on the MQIS controller and all other MSMQ client computers, transfers the topology and other information to the Active Directory.

Among the differences that should be noted when upgrading from Windows NT are these:

- There is no longer an MSMQ-specific database (MQIS) requirement to use the SQL Server to store information such as the network topology.
- There are no MSMQ-specific sites.
- There is no MSMQ-specific enterprise designation.

CAUTION   MSMQ servers can be clustered. If this is desired, group them together first and then assign them to a specific node. The major downside to clustering is that messages resident on the node will be lost in the event of a failover.

Administrative Tools for Message Queuing Services

The primary MSMQ administrative tools are integrated in the **Active Directory Users and Computers**, **Active Directory Sites and Services**, and **Computer Management** snap-ins. The first two tools are used to administer MSMQ in an enterprise setting, whereas **Computer Management** does this for the local computer or workgroup. These tools replace the standalone **MSMQ Explorer** used in Windows NT, which is still required for the administration of down-level MSMQ servers that have not been updated to Windows 2000.

The **Active Directory Users and Computers** snap-in creates and sets properties of public and private queues, views message properties, and views MSMQ computers with their properties. The properties that can be set and viewed include Admin queue name, format and length, arrived time, authentication, class, delivery mode, encryption options, hash algorithm, message ID, priority, sender ID, sent time, size, and source computer GUID and path.

The **Active Directory Sites and Services** snap-in views, creates, and sets properties for routing links. It can also create and set foreign computer properties and sites. The **Computer Management** snap-in views and removes local messages, and views and creates public and private queues and their properties.

FINDING AN MSMQ SYSTEM

An MSMQ computer can be located using the following steps:

1. Open the **Active Directory Users and Computers** snap-in.
2. Open the **View** menu and select **Users, Groups, and Computers** as containers.
3. Open the **View** menu and select **Advanced Features**.
4. From the console tree, select the target domain and select **Computers**.
5. Sequentially click on each computer to see if an MSMQ folder exists.

SETTING A COMPUTER MESSAGE STORAGE SIZE

The message storage size on a computer can be determined as follows:

1. Open the **Active Directory Users and Computers** snap-in.
2. Open the **View** menu and select **Users, Groups, and Computers** as containers.
3. Open the **View** menu and select **Advanced Features**.
4. From the console tree, select **MSMQ**.
5. Right-click **msmq** and select **Properties**.
6. Select the **General** tab. Within the **Storage limits** box check the **Limit message storage to (KB)** option.
7. Enter the total number of maximum kilobytes available for a message.

LIMITING JOURNAL STORAGE SIZE

The journal storage size on a computer can be determined with the following steps:

1. Open the **Active Directory Users and Computers** snap-in.
2. Open the **View** menu and select **Users, Groups, and Computers** as containers.
3. Open the **View** menu and select **Advanced Features**.
4. From the console tree, select **MSMQ**.
5. Right-click **msmq** and select **Properties**.
6. Select the **General** tab. Within the **Storage limits** box check the **Limit journal storage to (KB)** option.
7. Enter the total number of maximum kilobytes available for the journal.

FINDING A QUEUE

To find a queue, take the following steps:

1. Open the **Active Directory Users and Computers** snap-in.
2. Open the **View** menu and select **Users, Groups, and Computers** as containers.
3. Open the **View** menu and select **Advanced Features**.
4. Open the console tree and right-click on **Computers** or **Domain Controllers**. Select **Find**.
5. Within the **Find MSMQ Queue** tab type the appropriate data in the **Label** or **Type ID** text box. Select **Find Now**.

DELETING A QUEUE

Delete a queue this way:

1. Open the **Active Directory Users and Computers** snap-in.
2. Open the **View** menu and select **Users, Groups, and Computers** as containers.
3. Open the **View** menu and select **Advanced Features**.
4. Open the console tree and right-click on the target queue. Select **Delete**.
5. Select **YES** to confirm the deletion.

ENABLING OR DISABLING JOURNALS

To enable or disable journaling, take the following steps:

1. Open the **Active Directory Users and Computers** snap-in.
2. Open the **View** menu and select **Users, Groups, and Computers** as containers.
3. Open the **View** menu and select **Advanced Features**.

4. Open the console tree, right-click on the target queue, and select **Properties**.

5. Select the **General** tab. In the **Journal** section select the **Enable** checkbox.

To disable journaling, follow all of the above steps except step 5. There, remove the check mark for **Enable**.

VIEWING MESSAGE PROPERTIES

View message properties according to the following steps:

1. Open the **Active Directory Users and Computers** snap-in.

2. Open the **View** menu and select **Users, Groups, and Computers** as containers.

3. Open the **View** menu and select **Advanced Features**.

4. Open the console tree, right-click **Queue messages**, and right-click on the target message in the Details pane. Select **Properties**.

5. Sequentially review the properties by moving between the available tabs.

PURGING ALL MESSAGES

Purge all messages as follows:

1. Open the **Active Directory Users and Computers** snap-in.

2. Open the **View** menu and select **Users, Groups, and Computers** as containers.

3. Open the **View** menu and select **Advanced Features**.

4. Open the console tree. Right-click **Queue messages**, right-click **All tasks**, and select **Purge**.

5. Select **Yes** to confirm the deletion of all messages.

MSMQ Security Issues and Management

MSMQ relies on the security features of Windows 2000, including Access Control Lists (ACLs), encryption, and authentication. Queues, messages, computers, and routing links are all treated by the ACL as objects with associated permissions. The **Everyone** group is granted **Write** permission to queues by default. **Read** permissions allow the user to receive and view messages for a queue. Only the **Administrator** group has **Full Control** over all local MSMQ messages, logs, and queues by default.

The **Active Directory Users and Computers** snap-in with the **MSMQConfiguration** object is used to set permissions. First, however, there are a number of security-related issues that must be considered, as follows:

- *Service account*. MSMQ can be executed through the local system account or a specific user account. For greater security, use a specific user account created for MSMQ management.

- *Guest account*. The Guest account on Windows 2000 is displayed by default. However, it must be enabled to communicate messages between Windows 2000 Active Directory domains and Windows 2000 workgroups or Windows NT 4.0 MSMQ. Alternately, you can create a user account from those systems with **Read** permission to the Active Directory. This might be preferable to opening the **Guest** account to anonymous access.

- *Message authentication*. Message authentication is not the default setting. Therefore, ensure that the sender of a message is authenticated with digital signatures. While this provides a greater level of security, it may slow down the delivery process. Consider this trade-off before using authentication.

- *MSMQ server authentication*. MSMQ server certificates are granted to authenticate communication with MSMQ clients. Although optional, if installed, Server Authentication will be used by both MSMQ servers and the Internet Information Services (IIS) for secure HTTP-S Web data exchange.

- *MSMQ encryption*. Message encryption is not used by default. Nevertheless, it is possible to encode and decode messages using the Microsoft CryptoAPI in conjunction with the Microsoft Base Cryptographic Service *Provide,* version 2.0 or higher. CryptoAPI must be installed on any MSMQ system that sends and receives messages. The U.S. version utilizes 128-bit encryption whereas international versions do not. The downside of encryption is the reduced speed of message communication because of the requirement to create symmetric keys, encrypt the message with a public key of the receiving system, and use the receiving computer's private key to decrypt the message.

- *Auditing*. The auditing feature permits an administrator to review users attempting to access the MSMQ server. Through analysis of the success and failure logs, attempts by unauthorized users are more likely to be detected.

SETTING PERMISSIONS FOR A COMPUTER OR QUEUE

To set the permissions for a computer or queue, do the following:

1. Open the **Active Directory Users and Computers** snap-in.
2. Open the **View** menu and select **Users, Groups, and Computers** as containers.
3. Open the console tree and highlight the computer or queue.
4. Right-click **msmq** and select **Properties**.
5. Select the **Security** tab and select the desired permissions for the computer or queue.

CHANGING OWNERSHIP OF A COMPUTER OR QUEUE

Set the permissions for a computer or queue as follows:

1. Open the **Active Directory Users and Computers** snap-in.
2. Open the **View** menu and select **Users, Groups, and Computers** as containers.
3. Open the console tree and highlight the computer or queue.
4. Right-click **msmq** and select **Properties**.
5. Select the **Security** tab and select **Advanced**.
6. Select the **Owner** tab. Within the **Change Owner to** box select the new user or group.
7. Select **OK**.

SETTING DEFAULT SECURITY FOR MSMQ STORAGE FILES

MSMQ storage of message, log, and transaction files is usually in the *Winnt\ System32\MSMQ\Storage* folder. To set default security for these files, perform the following:

1. Open **Windows Explorer** and navigate to the storage directory.
2. Right-click on the storage directory and select **Properties**.
3. Within the **Permissions** option, under **Allow**, select **Full Control**.
4. Within the **Name** box select all users and groups that do not have access to the MSMQ directory. Select **Remove**.

SETTING UP COMPUTER OR QUEUE AUDITING

To set the permissions for a computer or queue, take the following steps:

1. Open the **Active Directory Users and Computers** snap-in.
2. Open the **View** menu and select **Users, Groups, or Computers** as containers.
3. Open the console tree and highlight the computer or queue.
4. Right-click **msmq** and select **Properties**.
5. Select the **Security** tab and select **Advanced**.
6. Select the **Auditing** tab and select **Add**.
7. Within the **Select Users, Group or Computer** dialog box click the user or group to audit in the **Name** option. Select **OK**.
8. Within the **Auditing Entry** for the **msmq** dialog box select all objects to audit in the **Apply onto** option. In the **Access** option select the desired settings.

AUDITING A ROUTING LINK

To audit access to a routing link, do the following:

1. Open the **Active Directory Users and Computers** snap-in.
2. Open the **View** menu and select **Users, Groups, and Computers** as containers.
3. Open the console tree and highlight the computer or queue.
4. Right-click **msmq**, select the routing link, and select **Properties**.
5. Select the **Security** tab and select **Advanced**.
6. Select the **Auditing** tab. Within the **Access Control Settings** for the **msmq** dialog box select **Add**.
7. Within the **Select Users, Group or Computer** dialog box click the user or group to audit in the **Name** option. Select **OK**.
8. Within the **Auditing Entry** for the **msmq** dialog box select all objects to audit in the **Apply onto** option. In the **Access** option select the desired settings.

Postscript

Since MSMQ is interweaved with networking, the Active Directory, and other computer management topics, we chose not to replicate much of that information here but instead provided a summary view of this application. When installing and deploying MSMQ, refer to the latest release notes and appropriate sections in this book.

MSMQ can be used to connect with Exchange Server. Additional information on this feature is available from online Help.

SYSTEM MANAGEMENT SERVER

System Management Server (SMS) 2.0 is one of the most important add-on products of the BackOffice family. It is not part of the core Windows 2000 operating system, but some of its features can be very valuable in deployment and administration. Since SMS is an optional component, we will merely provide a review of its key features rather than more in-depth "how to" instructions. Despite its summary treatment here, however, SMS should be seriously considered for relatively large and complex enterprises.

The five primary SMS features that can be effectively utilized in the administration of Windows 2000 enterprises are

- Software and hardware inventory gathering and management
- Software installation and distribution
- Remote tools
- Software metering
- Network diagnostics

(A sixth component measures Y2K compliance. Hopefully, this is no longer an issue for readers of this book.)

System Management Server 2.0 depends on Microsoft SQL Server 6.5 or 7.0 (or later) to store and manage SMS data. SQL Server is available as an independent database or as an integrated part of the BackOffice family. While SMS can be licensed independently or as part of the BackOffice suite, you must still calculate the use and cost of a local or remote SQL Server installation.

System Management Server 2.0 supports administrative snap-ins to the Microsoft Management Console (MMC). SMS service pack 2 must be employed.

Software and Hardware Inventory

In Chapter 4 we underscored the importance of inventorying hardware and software as part of Windows 2000 planning and deployment. SMS can streamline this necessary step by automatically collecting software and hardware data and creating a dynamic inventory database. Moreover, it permits filtering of information so that both global and very granular inventories can be maintained. Through the use of SMS, specific software versions can be obtained, which permits rapid evaluation of enterprise upgrade status. For example, the hardware inventory evaluates system components according to processor manufacturer, revision levels, and type.

Software Installation and Distribution

The problems associated with centralized software installation and distribution to a remote computer or groups of computers are greatly reduced by SMS because it automates and schedules installation for minimal impact on the end user. Through the use of SMS's software inventory features, it is possible to create what is known as *collector groups*. The system administrator should use these to gather together systems with the same processor, user group, or existing software, and then, with this information in hand, apply specific software upgrades to define collector groups automatically. In this way the inventory database is automatically updated.

The SMS installer creates application-specific scripts to support this distribution process. Physical distribution can be direct to the client disk or through the posting of the application to a Web or FTP site.

Remote Administrative Tools

Using SMS, the system administrator can gain access to a remote client system and display the contents locally. By seeing exactly what is displayed on the user's end, the administrator can troubleshoot system problems. Moreover, an interactive chat feature permits the administrator and end user to discuss potential problems on screen. Client computer commands and applications can be executed with *Remote Execute*. *Remote Boot* restarts the client computer.

Software Metering

The software-monitoring feature is used primarily to manage licenses and identify unsupported or unregistered packages. Monitoring concurrent software usage throughout an enterprise makes it easy to determine if too many or too few licenses exist for a given software title. The monitoring tool is set to access and restrict use of applications by the individual user, user group, computer, quota, or license. Mobile users can also use it to check software licenses when not connected to the network.

Network Diagnostics

SMS extends Windows 2000 network administrative and monitoring with its network discover and trace functions. These provide a framework of the network structure in a dynamic enterprise environment by discovering and tracing network devices. By using SMS a network topology map can be easily generated.

The Network Monitor is used primarily to troubleshoot a network by capturing packets or frames and "sniffing" them. The information revealed is then displayed and filtered. The system administrator can edit specific network packets (see Figure 17.9).

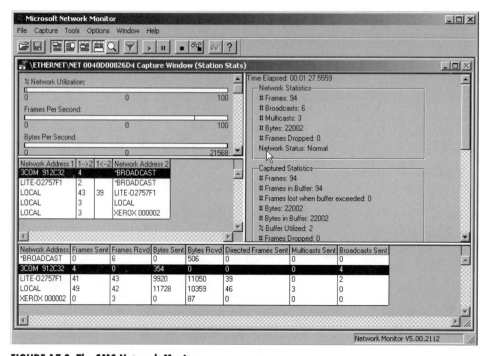

FIGURE 17.9 The SMS Network Monitor

Windows Scripting Host (WSH) **719**

WINDOWS SCRIPTING HOST

Windows Scripting Host (WSH 2.0) is a language independent scripting engine used to automate administrative tasks, such as controlling network connections. WSH supports Windows 2000, Windows NT, and Windows 9x environments. The earlier version of WSH only supported Microsoft languages, such as Visual Basic VBScripts and Jscript. Microsoft and third parties are now providing Windows Scripting Host version 2.0 with an augmented list of scripts to support other environments, including Visual Basic, Java, HTML, Perl, and XML. Previously, only Windows native scripts such as the MS-DOS command language were supported.

NOTE An abundance of scripts is available on the Internet and from specialized programming books. We have included only a few scripts here because they tend to be enterprise or task specific. Instead, we provide an overview of WSH that should give you sufficient information to host your own scripts.

For readers who would like to create scripts, we recommend the Microsoft Windows Scripting Host Programmer's Reference site. A number of sample scripts can be downloaded from *http://www.microsoft.com/scripting*.

Using WSH to Run Scripts

There is both a Windows version and a command line version of WSH. The Windows version (wscript.exe) provides the standard GUI interface to set properties. The command line version (cscript.exe) utilizes switches to do this. Either version can be launched from the Command Prompt or by drag and drop.

RUNNING WSCRIPT.EXE

Scripts can be launched within the Windows environment in several ways. From within Windows Explorer, simply double-click on the icon identified as a script, as shown in Figure 17.10. Alternately, from the **Start → Run** command line or the **Command Prompt**, enter the name of the script and press **OK** or **ENTER**, respectively, as shown in Figure 17.11.

Setting Properties for the Wscript.exe Environment
Two properties can be set for a Wscript.exe launched script. From **Windows Explorer** → right-click on the target script and select **Properties**, where you will see two tabs available for scripts residing on a FAT/FAT 32 partition and four avail-

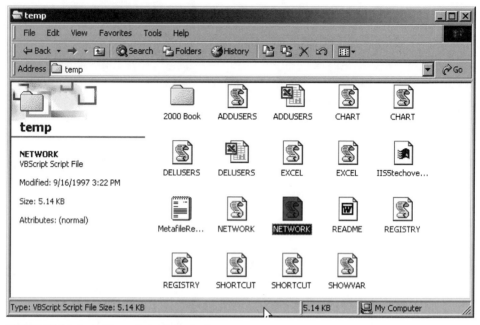

FIGURE 17.10 Launching a Script from Explorer

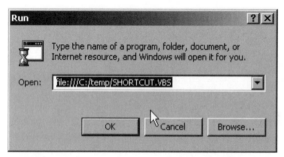

FIGURE 17.11 Launching a Script from the Run Command Line

able for NTFS—common to both are the General and Script tabs. From the **General** tab you can set the basic attribute for the script read or hidden. From the **Script** tab you can automatically stop the script after the specified (*nn*) number of seconds, and you can display a logo banner. The two additional NTFS partition tabs are **Security** for setting user permissions and **Summary** as shown in Figure 17.12.

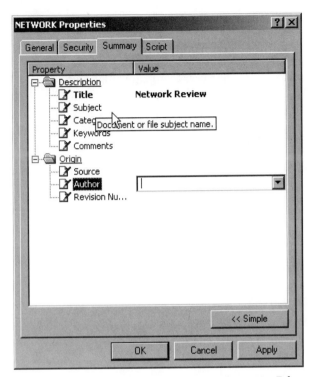

FIGURE 17.12 The NTFS Partition Summary Properties Tab

When properties are set on a script, a text file with the .wsh extension is created as a control file for the script's settings. The .wsh file uses the same name as the script itself and can also be used to launch the script in the manner just described.

RUNNING CSCRIPT.EXE

The command line version of WSH is launched from the Command Prompt. It uses the following syntax:

```
Cscript [script name] [host options] [script options]
```

The only required item is the script name. The host options enable or disable WSH options. The script options are passed directly to the script and are preceded by a single slash (/).

TABLE 17.1 Cscript.exe Host Parameters

Option	Description
//I	The default setting; permits interactive prompts and the display of errors.
//B	Batch mode; suppresses command displays and user prompts.
//D	Enables the debugger.
//E:engine	Specifies the specific script language engine.
//Job:xxx	Specifies a specific batch script to execute.
//T:nn	Enables a time-out on script execution after (nn) seconds.
//logo	The default; displays a logo banner.
//nolog	Suppresses the logo banner.
//H:C script or //H:W script	Registers which version of WSH is the default—C for cscript, W for wscript.
//S	Saves the command line options.
/?	Displays command usage.

EXAMPLE WSH SCRIPTS

Example 1: Programming with the Windows Scripting Host (WSH) allows direct access to the Active Directory via Active Directory Services Interface (ADSI).

```
'Display Objects in the Engineering Organizational Unit
Set ou = GetObject ("LDAP://OU=Engineering,DC=Entcert1,DC=Com")
For each obj in ou
    WScript.Echo obj.Name
Next
```

Example 2: Properties relating to the Scripting Engine and executing script are accessible through script and argument properties.

```
'Display Script Properties
wscript.Echo Wscript.Application
wscript.Echo Wscript.Arguments(0)

WScript.Echo Wscript.FullName
WScript.Echo Wscript.Name
WScript.Echo Wscript.Path
WScript.Echo Wscript.ScriptFullName
WScript.Echo Wscript.ScriptName
WScript.Echo Wscript.Version
```

```
' Display script argument properties
WScript.Echo Wscript.arguments.Count
WScript.Echo Wscript.arguments.length
WScript.Echo Wscript.arguments.Item
```

Example 3: Environmental parameters from four different environments are accessible by setting the environment context.

```
'Create shell object
Set WshShell = Wscript.CreateObject("Wscript.Shell")

' Set variables environmental variable access
' of system, User, Volatile, process
Set SystemEnvironment = WshShell.Environment("System")
Set UserEnvironment = WshShell.Environment("User")
Set VolatileEnvironment = WshShell.Environment("Volatile")
Set ProcessEnvironment = WshShell.Environment("Process")

' Display example parameters from each environment set
wscript.Echo SystemEnvironment("PATH")
wscript.Echo UserEnvironment("PROMPT")
wscript.Echo VolatileEnvironment("OS")
wscript.Echo ProcessEnvironment("PROCESSOR_ARCHITECTURE")
```

Example 4: Advanced dialog window capabilities are available and based on Win32 user interface programming. The Registry may be read and modified through shell methods.

```
' Registry reading and writing
Set WshShell = Wscript.CreateObject("Wscript.Shell")

' Simple Popup window
WshShell.Popup "Test Popup Window"

' Popup Window with advanced options following Win32 conventions
WshShell.Popup "Test Popup Window",10, "SysAdmin Tool", 4

' Read from the systems registry
str = WshShell.RegRead ("HKCU\Environment\TEMP")

WshShell.Popup str
```

Example 5: The network functions allow drives and printers to be mapped to users and systems throughout the network.

```
' Network methods can be used to add and remove printers and network
drives.
Set WshNetwork = Wscript.CreateObject("Wscript.Network")

' Print out computer name
Wscript.echo WshNetwork.ComputerName
```

```
'Add a printer
WshNetwork.AddPrinterConnection "Laser"."\\ecc3s\HP Printer"

'Map a network drive
WshNetwork.MapNetWorkDrive "M:","\\ecc3s\aaECC"

'Display Username and domain
Wscript.echo WshNetwork.Username
Wscript.echo WshNetwork.UserDomain
```

Example 6: Shortcuts may be added to the desktop and assigned properties.

```
' Shortcut properties allow the modification of a shortcut's
arguments, Description
' Hotkey, Iconlocation, TargetPath,WindowStyle and WorkingDirectory.
'

Set WshShell = Wscript.CreateObject("Wscript.WshShell")
strFavoritespath = WshShell.SpecialFolders("My Documents")
Set NewShortcut = WshShell.CreateShortcut(strFavoritespath &
"\short.lnk)
NewShortcut.TargetPath = "path to application here"
NewShortcut.Save
```

POSTSCRIPT

This chapter discussed the concepts and base-level use of five relatively unrelated services. Since these services will not be universally applied by system administrators as other Windows 2000 features are, we provided only a summary, not a comprehensive review. If you will be employing these technologies, we hope this chapter has provided the foundation necessary to do so. Utilize the release notes and online Help available with these products to fill in the necessary details.

Appendix: Windows 2000 Commands and Utilities

This appendix is designed as a reference tool for users and system administrators. It defines and discusses a number of procedures and commands with options that are used in the day-to-day operation of a Windows 2000 system. These commands and utilities are listed alphabetically in the index. Here they have been broken down into several categories as follows:

- Backup
- Batch
- Comparison
- Compression
- Display
- File management
- File manipulation
- Miscellaneous
- Networking
- Ownership
- Print
- Search
- Security options
- System management
- Resource Kit support tools

We distinguish between procedures and commands in this way:

- Procedures are methods for accomplishing a task using the Windows 2000 graphical interface.
- Commands are executed within the **Command Prompt**, which invokes the Virtual DOS Machine (VDM).

In some cases, we provide both procedures and commands to give the system administrator a broader view of the capabilities of Windows 2000.

Within Windows 2000 two methods are available to review the file hierarchy: one using the My Computer icon and its accompanying windows and the other using Windows 2000 Explorer. We have chosen to focus primarily on Windows 2000 Explorer, which is accessed via **Start → Programs → Accessories → Windows 2000 Explorer**. Procedures that can be completed using the My Computer windows will be referenced as appropriate. The command prompt is accessed via **Start → Programs → Accessories → Command Prompt**. In this mode, Windows 2000 is not case sensitive, so commands and their parameters and options may be entered in either lower or upper case. Here lower case is used as a matter of style. In addition, Windows 2000 has a series of what are referred to as "net commands." These assist the system administrator in maintaining the network and are distributed among the other sections where appropriate.

The following syntax conventions are used in the Appendix:

- Command names are lower case.
- *Lowercase italic* represents variables that must be replaced in the command. For example, *filename* must be replaced with the actual file name on which the command will operate.
- [Brackets] surround optional parameters.
- {Braces} surround a list of items, options, or parameters from which one must be chosen.
- The pipe symbol (|) separates options from which one must be chosen. In this case, it works like an "or"—that is, one or the other.

Navigating the Command Prompt is very similar to working within a "dumb terminal" environment. Keystrokes are generally intepreted individually. Special shortcuts known as *doskeys* facilitate navigation. The following lists those most commonly used:

- *UP ARROW*—recalls the command used before.
- *DOWN ARROW*—recalls the command used after.
- *PAGE UP*—recalls the oldest command used in the session.

- *PAGE DOWN*—recalls the most recent command used.
- *LEFT ARROW*—moves the insertion point back one character.
- *RIGHT ARROW*—moves the insertion point forward one character.
- *CTRL-LEFT ARROW*—moves the insertion point back one word.
- *CTRL-RIGHT ARROW*—moves the insertion point forward one word.
- *HOME*—moves the insertion point to the beginning of the line.
- *END*—moves the insertion point to the end of the line.
- *ESC*—clears the command.
- *F1*—copies one character from the same column in the template.
- *F2*—searches forward in the template for the next key typed after it is pressed.
- *F3*—copies the remainder of the template to the command line.
- *F4*—deletes characters from the current insertion point position up to the character specified.
- *F5*—copies the template into the current command line.
- *F6*—places an end-of-file character (CTRL-Z) at the current point.
- *F7*—displays all commands for this program stored in memory in a popup box.
- *F8*—displays all commands in the history buffer that start with the characters in the current command.
- *F9*—prompts for a history buffer command number, then displays the command.

For more detail on a particular command or procedure, please refer to Windows 2000 **Help**, which can be accessed from the **Start** menu or from the window in which you are working.

BACKUP COMMANDS

Chapter 14 examined the recommended backup and restoration methods for Windows 2000. However, in mixed environments a command line approach may also be warranted, in which a user can back up data to tape, floppy, and hard disk. Windows NT commands such as *backup* and *restore* are no longer fully supported. The *Ntrestore* utility can be used either to launch the graphical backup tools or in a command line mode.

Using ntbackup on the Command Line

The *ntbackup* utility can be used within the Command Prompt or within a batch file to achieve the same results as with the graphical backup. It has several different formats, but the primary syntax is

```
ntbackup backup path [options]
```

The *backup* parameter must be included except for the other variations of the syntax shown in Table A.1. The *path* parameter should contain the path or paths of the directories to be copied to the backup tape. Table A.1 identifies the *options* available for the command. They can be entered in any sequence.

To erase a tape, enter the following command:

```
ntbackup /nopoll
```

No other options are available with the */nopoll* switch. This format requires user input and cannot be used in a batch file.

TABLE A.1 ntbackup Options

Option	Qualifier	Description
/a		Appends the data to the end of an existing backup tape. The default option is to "replace" the data on the tape with the new backup.
/b		Backs up the Registry from the local system.
/d	"*text*"	Enters the description for the backup set between the quotes in place of the variable *text*.
/e		Includes exceptions only in the backup log. The default is to create a full detail backup log.
/hc:on		Turns on hardware compression. Not valid if the /a option is used.
/hc:off		Turns off hardware compression. Not valid if the /a option is used.
/l	"*filename*"	Creates a log file as *filename*. The path can be included as part of *filename*.
/r		Restricts access to the data on the backup tape to members of the Administrators group and the Backup Operators group. Must not be used with the /a option.
/t	type	Specifies the backup *type*, where *type* can be one of the following values: copy, daily, differential, incremental, normal.
/tape:*n*		Identifies the number of the tape drive to use, where *n* can be a value from 0 through 9. This option is necessary only if there is more than one tape drive on the system.
/v		Verifies the data after it has been backed up.

To eject a tape, the following syntax may be used:

```
ntbackup eject /tape:n
```

The /tape:*n* option is necessary only if there is more than one tape drive installed on the system. The variable *n* can be a value from 0 through 9 and designates which tape drive should eject the tape.

EXAMPLE NTBACKUP COMMAND

Enter the following command to back up and verify the C: drive, including the local Registry. This restricts access to the Administrators and Backup Operators groups with a full detail log of the backup in the file C:\winnt\backup.log.

```
ntbackup backup c: /b/r/l "c:\winnt\backup.log"
```

BATCH COMMANDS

Batch commands or programs are also commonly known as batch files. They are essentially simplified scripts that support the execution routine or repetitive tasks. A batch program is written as a text file with one or more command lines that are executed sequentially from top to bottom. They are identified by either a .bat or .cmd extension.

All Windows 2000 commands and many applications can be executed from a batch file. To provide greater flexibility, a number of conditional parameters, shown in Table A.2, can be set.

TABLE A.2 Batch File Conditional Commands

Option	Description
call	Permits the execution of another batch program without terminating the parent program.
echo	Turns the display of command action on or off as the batch file is executed. Can also be used to output a message to the screen—for example, "One moment please while searching …"
endlocal	Ends the *setlocal* command described below.
for	Executes a specific command for every file in a set of files. Can also be run directly from the Command Prompt.
goto	Directs Windows 2000 to process the line in the batch file that is specified.

(continued)

TABLE A.2 (*continued*)

Option	Description
if	Processes a command when the specified condition is true; ignored when the condition is not met. The conditions of *not* and *else* can also be used in combination as part of this option.
pause	Temporarily suspends the batch file until the user takes an action such as hitting a key to confirm an action.
rem	Short for remarks that can be added to the batch file for referencing. These are programming notes that are not executed.
setlocal	Permits the establishment of new localization variables. The localization is retained until the *endlocal* option resets the environment.
Shift	Modifies the position of parameters in a batch program and permits the stringing
| *(pipe)*	together of multiple commands on the same line.
>	Outputs command results to the directed point.
()	Groups commands together.
||	Executes either the first or next command.
&&	Executes the first command AND, if successful, executes the next one.

COMPARISON COMMANDS

Within a Windows environment, a user can compare two files visually by displaying each in a separate window. While graphically based file comparisons can be executed within applications that are installed on Windows 2000, two utilities available within the base system are executed from the command line. Two commands that compare files are *fc* and *comp*.

fc Command

The *fc* command enables a user to compare two files and display the differences, where both are in either an ASCII or a binary format. The syntax is

```
fc [options] file1 file2
```

The files *file1* and *file2* can be just a file name, a path with a file name, or a drive, path, and file name in the format *drive:path\ filename*. In addition, they can contain the wildcard characters * and ?. When using a wildcard character in *file1,* the *fc* command will compare each file found to *file2*. In other words, it compares many to one. When using a wildcard character in *file2*, the command will compare *file1* to a file with a corresponding name in *file2*'s location. Examples using the wildcard characters are given in Table A.3.

TABLE A.3 fc Options

Option	Description
/a	Used only for ASCII comparisons and provides the output display in abbreviated form. Only the first and last lines of each set of differences are displayed.
/b	Does a compare of binary files. This option is automatically the default for files with .EXE, .COM, .SYS, .OBJ, .LIB, and .BIN extensions. The files are compared by byte, and differences are output in the format *xxxxxxxx: yy zz,* where *xxxxxxxx* is the address of the bytes being compared in hexadecimal; *yy* is the contents of the byte from *file1*; and *zz* is the contents of the byte from *file2*.
/c	Ignores the distinctions between upper and lower case.
/l	Does a compare of ASCII files. This is considered the default for all files except those mentioned in the /b option above. The comparison is executed line by line and the differences are output in the following format: the name of *file1,* then the lines of *file1* that differ from *file2,* the first line that matches between the two files, the name of *file2,* the lines of *file2* that differ from *file1,* the first line that matches between the two files. After a difference is found, the command tries to resynchronize the two files.
/lb*n*	Sets the size of the internal line buffer to *n*. The default size is 100 lines. If the number of consecutive differences is greater than *n,* the command terminates.
/n	Displays the line numbers; used only for ASCII files.
/t	Does not treat tabs as spaces. The default is to treat tabs as spaces.
/w	Treats consecutive tabs/spaces as one space. Does not compare tabs/spaces at the beginning and end of a line.
/*nnnn*	Considers the file to be resynchronized when *nnnn* number of consecutive lines match; otherwise, matching lines are displayed as differences. The default value for *nnnn* is 2.

FC COMMAND EXAMPLES

To compare two binary files with the names *test.exe* and *test1.exe,* the command can be entered as

```
fc /b test.exe test1.exe
```

or

```
fc test.exe test1.exe
```

Both formats are acceptable because a file with an *.exe* extension is assumed to be binary by default.

To compare the files *autoexec.bat, autoold.bat,* and *autoex3.bat* to the file *newauto.bat,* enter the following:

```
fc auto*.bat newauto.bat
```

Suppose that a system administrator needs to compare some test result .tst files in the C:/test directory with files of the same name in test directory named bob on the D: drive. He enters

```
fc c:/test/*.tst d:/bob/test/*.tst
```

comp Command

Another comparison command available through the command line is *comp,* which compares the content of files by byte. Output consists of error messages of the format

```
Compare error at OFFSET xxxxxxxx = yy = zz
```

where *xxxxxxxx* is the memory address of the differing bytes, *yy* is the contents of the bytes in *file1,* and *zz* is the contents of the bytes in *file2.* The addresses and contents are in hexadecimal format unless an option is specified to display them in decimal or character format.

The syntax of the *comp* command is

```
comp [file1] [file2] [options]
```

The *file1* and *file2* can be the names of two files, including as necessary the drive designation and the directory path. The wildcard characters * and ? can be used to compare multiple files. Options are listed in Table A.4.

EXAMPLE comp COMMAND

To compare the first 15 lines of the files *newtest.log* and *oldtest.log*, displaying the line numbers where the differences occur, enter the following:

```
comp newtest.log oldtest.log /n=15 /l
```

TABLE A.4 comp Options

Option	Description
/a	Displays the differences between the files in character format.
/d	Displays the differences between the files in decimal format instead of hexadecimal.
/l	Displays the line number of the differences instead of the number of the byte offset.
/n=*num*	Compares the first *num* lines of both files, particularly when two files are different sizes.
/c	Ignores upper and lower case distinctions.

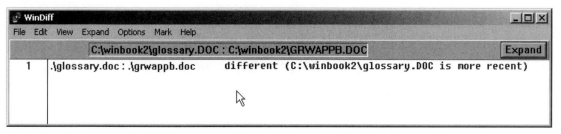

FIGURE A.1 The Windows 2000 Resource Kit WinDiff

WinDiff

Windows 2000 Support Tools provides a graphical tool that compares two files as shown in Figure A.1.

COMPRESSION COMMANDS

Each file within the Windows 2000 NTFS file system contains a compression attribute that identifies either that the file should be stored as compressed or is already compressed. It is recommended for large files that are used infrequently. When this attribute is selected, files are automatically compressed when they are saved and decompressed when accessed for use. (Remember that this compression technology is not available with the FAT file system.)

The compression attribute can be set from within the My Computer windows or through Windows 2000 Explorer. From Explorer, select the file you wish to view or set the compression attribute. Next, select from the menu bar **File → Properties**. Within the Properties window select the **General** tab if not already displayed. Within the **General** tab select **Advanced**. In the **Attributes** section box click the Compressed checkbox to compress or decompress a file.

As an alternative to the menu bar, you can right-click the file and, from the menu that displays, select **Properties**.

compact Command

The *compact* command allows the user to set or display the compression attribute on NTFS files from the command line. Its syntax is

```
compact [options] [filename]
```

The *filename* parameter can actually be the name of a file or a directory. In a directory the compression attribute indicates that any new files added to it will automatically have their compression attributes set and thereby be compressed.

This does not change the compression attribute for files that already exist in the directory. For them, wildcard characters can be used as part of the *file* parameter.

If no options are used or no file names are entered, the compression attribute for the current directory is displayed. See options list in Table A.5.

compact COMMAND

To set the compression attribute on the directory *ellen\oldfiles* as well as any of its subdirectories, enter the following:

```
compact /c /s c:\ellen\oldfiles
```

To remove the compression attribute from the directory *d:\bob\contracts*, enter

```
compact /u d:\bob\contracts
```

Remember, the above command will only remove the attribute from the directory and will not affect any of the files and subdirectories currently in the directory *bob\contracts*.

expand COMMAND

The *expand* command is used to decompress one or more files as well as to retrieve files from a distribution disk. Its syntax is

```
expand [-r] source [destination]
```

TABLE A.5 compact Options

Option	Qualifier	Description
/c		Compresses the named file(s).
/u		Decompresses the named file(s).
/s	:directory	Compresses or decompresses all subdirectories for the *directory* identified. The :*directory* qualifier is optional. The default is the current directory.
/i		Ignores any errors that occur.
/a		Displays hidden or system files. These will be omitted by default.
/f		Forces *filename* to be compressed or decompressed. The main use for this option occurs when a file was only partially compressed or decompressed and the system administrator needs to complete the task.

Table A.6 lists the options for the expand command.

TABLE A.6 expand Options

Option	Qualifier	Description
-d		Displays a list of files in the source volume.
-f:	filename	Specifies a file.
-r		Renames the expanded file.

DISPLAY COMMANDS

The display commands display the contents of files, the properties of files, lists of files, and Help files. They also organize displays into a sequence the user desires. This section will describe the procedures and commands available.

Displaying the Contents of Files

Windows 2000 primarily uses installed applications for file viewing. The Windows 2000 Registry maintains a list of installed applications and attempts to match file extensions to appropriate software so that the file can be viewed in its native format. When you double-click on a file within Windows 2000 Explorer, the file opens within the application. If the file type is unknown, the **Open With** window is displayed, allowing you to select the application that should be used to open the file.

The WordPad applications that are part of the base Windows 2000 system allow the user to display and create text or ASCII files. These applications are accessed by selecting **Start → Programs → Accessories → WordPad**.

From the command line, two commands are available for displaying files: *more* and *type*. The *more* command displays long files one screenful at a time; the *type* command just displays the entire contents of a file and is usually used for short files only.

cls COMMAND

The *cls* command is used to clear the Command Prompt screen.

more COMMAND

The *more* command displays long text files from within the Command Prompt window one screen at a time. Its basic syntax is

```
more [options] [file(s)]
```

Options for the more command are listed in Table A.7.

TABLE A.7 more Options

Option	Description
/e	Enables the "extended" features that allow the user to control how the file is displayed by entering commands whenever the "—More—" prompt displays. These commands are identified in Table A.8.
/p	Expands any form-feed characters.
/s	Consolidates multiple blank lines into one blank line.
/tn	Substitutes n spaces for each tab.
+n	Starts displaying the first file in the *file(s)* list at line n.

The *file(s)* parameter is not necessary when data is passed to the *more* command from another command using the pipe symbol (|). If it is used, it can be in the format of one or more file names, including the drive designation and path if necessary.

If the /e switch is used, the commands in Table A.8 may be used whenever the "—More—" prompt displays.

type COMMAND

The *type* command simply displays the contents of one or more files and is similar to the UNIX *cat* command. Its syntax is

```
type file(s)
```

TABLE A.8 more Commands

Command	Description
Space Bar	Displays the next page of text.
<ENTER> Key	Displays the next line of text.
f	Displays the next file in the *file(s)* list.
p*n*	Displays the next n lines.
s*n*	Skips n lines.
?	Displays the commands that are acceptable at the "—More—" prompt. In other words, the Help function.
=	Displays the line number.
q	Quits.

The *file(s)* parameter can consist of just the file names entered with the drive designation and path name if necessary. Multiple files in the *file(s)* list are separated by spaces. When entering a file name, remember to enclose it in quotes if it contains spaces itself.

Displaying Attributes and Properties of Files and Folders

Windows 2000 provides graphical and Command Prompt methods of displaying the file and directory hierarchy of a system and its network. The graphical methods are available through the My Computer windows, Windows 2000 Explorer, and the *My Network Places. My Network Places,* accessible either from its desktop icon or through Explorer, allows the user to display network files and directories.

This section will describe the file and folder views available through Windows 2000 Explorer as well as the *dir* command that is available at the Command Prompt.

DISPLAYING FILE PROPERTIES USING WINDOWS 2000 EXPLORER

In Windows 2000 Explorer, the left pane of the Primary window (Figure A.2) shows the top level of the hierarchy for the Desktop. Here directories have file folder

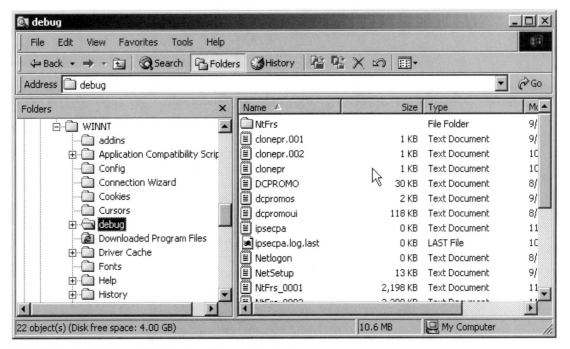

FIGURE A.2 The Windows 2000 Explorer Primary Window

icons and are referred to as folders. To view the subdirectories, left-click on the box containing a plus sign. When the subdirectories are displayed, the plus will become a minus. To display both the files and subdirectories of a particular folder, select the folder by clicking on it with the mouse. The folder contents will appear in the right pane.

To view detailed information about each file in the **Contents of** pane, select **View → Details** from the menu bar. This detailed information includes the name of the file, its size in bytes, its type, the date it was last modified, and the attributes associated with it, which can be Archive (A), Read-Only (R), Hidden (H), System (S), or Compressed (C) (Compressed will only display on NTFS file systems).

Note that by default certain file types are omitted (or hidden) from the Explorer hierarchical display, such as system (.SYS) and application extension (.DLL). To automatically show all files or to view a list of the hidden file types, select **Tools → Folder Options → View**. Then select **Show all files**.

Files in the **Contents of** pane can be sorted for viewing by name, type, size, or date. To change this display sequence, select **View → Arrange Icons** from the menu bar and choose the desired sort order.

There are two ways to view the properties and attributes of a particular folder. After selecting a file or folder in the **Contents of** pane, do the following:

1. Right-click or select **File** from the menu bar.
2. Select **Properties**.
3. Within the Properties window, select the **General** tab.

Figure A.3 displays the General tab for a file using the FAT file system. If the NTFS file system were used, an Advanced Attributes option would also be displayed.

dir COMMAND

The *dir* command is available from the Command Prompt and gives the user the ability to display file and directory properties and attributes via the command line. Its default output display includes the volume label and serial number of the disk, a listing of the current or selected directory, the total number of files listed, the total size of the files listed, and the amount of disk space remaining. The listing for each file or directory includes its size in bytes as well as the date and time it was last modified. The file extension, if any, is displayed following the file name.

An example of a portion of the *dir* command output is shown in Figure A.4. Its syntax is

```
dir [file(s)] [options]
```

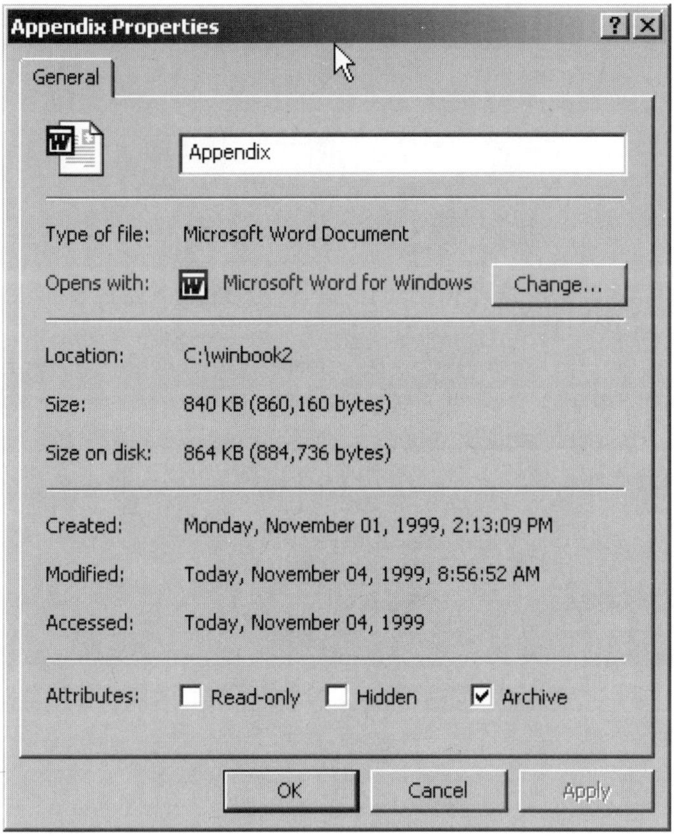

FIGURE A.3 File Properties

Neither *file(s)* nor *options* is required. Without these parameters the *dir* command will simply display the default information for the current directory. The *file(s)* parameter can be one or more file names or directories. Its format can be just the file or directory name or the drive designation and path as well, using the standard syntax *drive:path\filename*; the wildcard characters * and ? may also be used (unlike early versions of DOS that require *.*). Separate multiple filenames with spaces, commas, or semicolons.

Windows 2000 allows a user to create his own default results for the *dir* command through the *dircmd* environment variable. To set the default switches to be automatically executed whenever *dir* is entered at the command line, enter the following:

```
set dircmd=options
```

```
┌──────────────────────────────────────────────────────────────────────────┐
│ ⚏ Command Prompt                                                 _ □ ×     │
├──────────────────────────────────────────────────────────────────────────┤
│D:\>dir /w                                                          ▲       │
│ Volume in drive D has no label.                                            │
│ Volume Serial Number is 0CE1-1FAE                                          │
│                                                                            │
│ Directory of D:\                                                           │
│                                                                            │
│[2000 Book]               [Acrobat3]              bookdraft.ZIP             │
│[Documents and Settings] [Inetpub]                ldif.log                  │
│ldif.log.0                LOG_FILE_NAME            [MSSQL7]                  │
│[Office51]                [PerfLogs]               [PKWARE]                  │
│[Program Files]           schupgr.log             [SMS]                     │
│[SMSDATA]                 SMSSETUP.LOG             [star]                    │
│[temp]                    verifier                [walla]                   │
│WHATSNEW.TXT              [WINNT]                                            │
│              8 File(s)       23,306,037 bytes                              │
│             15 Dir(s)     4,291,547,136 bytes free                         │
│                                                                            │
│D:\>dir                                                                     │
│ Volume in drive D has no label.                                            │
│ Volume Serial Number is 0CE1-1FAE                                          │
│                                                                            │
│ Directory of D:\                                                           │
│                                                                            │
│10/12/1999   03:11p    <DIR>         2000 Book                              │
│08/01/1999   06:58p    <DIR>         Acrobat3                               │
│11/01/1999   04:12p        22,913,183 bookdraft.ZIP                         │
│10/13/1999   06:56p    <DIR>         Documents and Settings                 │
│10/23/1999   02:55p    <DIR>         Inetpub                                │
│09/21/1999   09:20a         3,656 ldif.log                                  │
│09/21/1999   09:20a         3,656 ldif.log.0                        ▼       │
└──────────────────────────────────────────────────────────────────────────┘
```

FIGURE A.4 Directory Listing

where *options* are any of the switches identified in Table A.9, which are considered the default until they are reset or Windows 2000 is restarted. To override the default for a single command, enter a minus sign before the switch. For example, if the user enters the command *set dircmd=/n* and wants to see the shorter, wide listing for a directory that contains a large number of files, he enters *dir /-n/w*. Refer to the *set* command for more information regarding setting, overriding, and clearing environment variables.

dir Command Examples

For recursive listings, enter the following while in the root directory:

```
dir /s/n/o/p
```

This command produces a long alphabetical listing of all files, directories, and subdirectories, pausing at the end of each full screen of information. The directories display first, then the files.

To display files in the current directory that have both the Hidden and System attributes, enter the following:

```
dir /ahs
```

TABLE A.9 dir Options

Option	Qualifier	Description
/a	:attributes	Displays only those files that match the *attributes* listed. The default (which is without the /a switch) displays all files except those with the Hidden or System attribute set. The *attributes* qualifier is optional; when not used, the *dir* /a command will display all files, even hidden and system. The colon (:) is optional as well. Multiple attributes may be entered in any order as long as there are no spaces between them, but only files that match all of the attributes will be displayed. A minus sign in front of the attribute will display all files that do not match that attribute. Acceptable values are *a* (files that have the Archive or Backup attribute set), *-a* (files that do not have the Archive attribute set), *d* (directories only), *-d* (files only, no directories), *h* (hidden files), *-h* (files that are not hidden), *r* (read-only files), *-r* (files that are not read-only), *s* (system files), *-s* (nonsystem files).
/b		Prohibits display of any heading or summary information. Do not use in conjunction with the /w option.
/d		Displays the files/directories in columns, sorting by columns.
/l		Displays any unsorted files/directories in lower case letters.
/n		Displays the following information for each file/directory: date and time last modified, whether the file is a directory, the size of the file, the name of the file or directory. This is the default format for the *dir* command. If the user wants the file names to display on the left, enter this option as /-n.
/o	:order	Displays the files sorted in the order given. The default (without the /o switch) is to display the files/directories in the order stored. Using the /o switch without any order specified will display the directories sorted alphabetically, then the files sorted alphabetically. The colon (:) is optional. Values for *order* may be entered in any order and combination as long as there are no spaces between them, but the sort order will be defined by the order of the values, such that the first order value will be the primary sort key, the next one the secondary sort key, and so on. Acceptable values are *d* (sort in ascending order by date and time, oldest first), *-d* (sort in descending order by date and time, newest first), *e* (sort alphabetically by file extension), *-e* (sort in reverse alphabetical order by file extension), *g* (display with directories grouped before files), *-g* (display with directories grouped after files), *n* (sort alphabetically by file or directory name), *-n* (sort in reverse alphabetical order by name), *s* (sort in ascending order by size, smallest first), *-s* (sort in descending order by size, largest first).

(continued)

TABLE A.9 dir Options (*continued*)

Option	Qualifier	Description
/q		Pauses after each full screen of data
/p		Displays only one screen at a time. Any key can be pressed to display the next screen.
/s		Displays all occurrences of the file name given in the directory specified as well as its subdirectories. Obviously, this option requires the *file(s)* parameter.
/t	:time	Displays the selected *time* for each file, where *time* can be *c* for the creation time, *a* for the time the file was last accessed, or *w* for the time the file was last written. When used in conjunction with the */od* or */o-d,* it identifies the time field that is used for sorting.
/w		Displays the directory contents in wide format, which contains up to five columns of file/directory names.
/x		Displays the MS-DOS names for the files before the Windows 2000 names. Remember that Windows 2000 allows longer file names than the MS-DOS 8/3 character limit. The format of the display is similar to that of the */n* option.
/4		Displays four-digit years

or

```
dir /a:hs
```

To simply display all files with a .doc extension in the current directory and its sub-directories, enter the following:

```
dir *.doc /s
```

echo Command

The *echo* command is used primarily in batch files to either enable or disable the command echoing feature or to display a message to the screen. Its syntax is

```
echo [options]
```

Using *echo* without *options* will display whether the echo feature is turned on or off. See Table A.10 for options.

TABLE A.10 echo Options

Option	Description
On	Turns the echo feature on. In other words, displays (or echos) each command as it is executed.
Off	Turns the echo feature off. Typing *echo off* on the command line removes the prompt from screen.
Message	Displays the *message* on the screen. This command is usually used in batch files following an *echo off* command.
. (period)	Displays a blank line. The syntax for this option is *echo.* with no spaces between the word echo and the period.

Displaying Help

Windows 2000 provides both graphical and command line methods of displaying Help documentation to the user. The graphical version is accessed from the Start menu by choosing **Start → Help**. The window **Help Topics: Windows 2000 Help** that appears displays three tabs:

- *Contents* displays a table of contents of available Help categories. Double-clicking on the Book icon for a particular entry displays subtopics.
- *Index* provides an alphabetical index of Help topics. The user can select one from the list or enter a portion of a topic to locate it more quickly.
- *Search* enables the user to search the online documentation for any references to the word(s) or phrase entered. An example search on the Active Directory is shown in Figure A.5.

help COMMAND

Through the command line the *help* command can be used to display Help information about Windows 2000 commands except *net* commands. The syntax is

```
help [command]
```

The parameter *command* is the name of the command for which you wish information. Omitting *command* creates a display of each available command along with a brief description.

As an alternative to typing *help* and then the command name, the user can use the */?* switch after the command. For example, *dir /?* and *help dir* will both produce the same Help information.

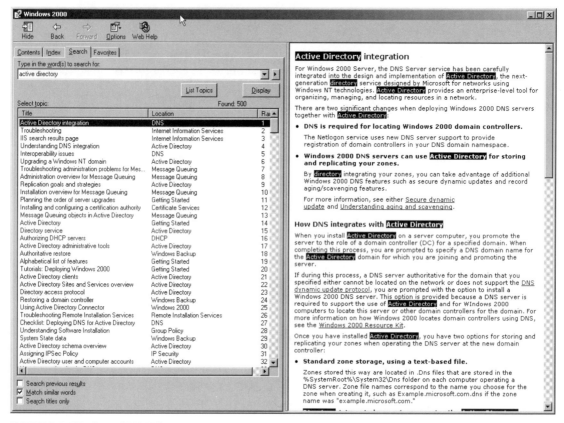

FIGURE A.5 Windows 2000 Help

net help COMMAND

The *net help* command provides Help information for the Windows 2000 *net* commands. It has two acceptable formats:

```
net help [command]
```

and

```
net command {/help | /?}
```

The *command* parameter can contain one of three values:

- A *net* command, such as *net account, net start, net user,* etc.
- The word *services,* which provides a list a network services the user executing the command can start.
- The word *syntax,* which provides information on interpreting the syntax used within the net Help documentation.

net helpmsg COMMAND

The *net helpmsg* command provides the user with more information regarding a net error message. The syntax is

```
net helpmsg number
```

The *number* parameter is the number of the net error message. Net error messages are displayed in the following way:

```
NET ####: Message
```

where *####* is the number included in the *net helpmsg* command.

FILE MANAGEMENT COMMANDS

The file management commands and procedures allow a user to create, remove, copy, move, and rename files and directories. These tasks may be completed using graphical methods in Windows 2000 Explorer or My Computer windows. My Network Places windows will permit some of these actions for resources shared across the network, provided that the user has the permission to execute them. Windows 2000 Explorer is the application we use for most examples.

Displaying Path Names

While in Windows 2000 Explorer, a user can view the full path name of his current location by selecting **View** from the menu bar and then selecting **Options** → **View**. Within the View tab, select the option **Display the full path in the title bar**, which is the default setting.

If you want to determine the current directory while at the Command Prompt, enter *cd* and press **ENTER**.

Creating and Removing Folders

Windows 2000 provides both command line and graphical procedures for creating and removing directories or folders. This section will discuss both.

CREATING FOLDERS

New folders can be created through Windows 2000 Explorer and My Computer windows using the same procedure. To create a folder (or directory) from Windows 2000 Explorer, follow this procedure:

1. Select the folder that will contain the new directory.
2. Select **File** from the menu bar.

3. Select **New**.

4. Select **Folder**.

5. Within the **Contents of** pane the New Folder icon will appear at the bottom of the file list. Enter the name of the new folder at this point.

mkdir Command

The *mkdir* command enables the user to create a directory from the command line. Another name for it is *md,* and its syntax is

```
mkdir directory-name
```

or

```
md directory-name
```

The *directory-name* parameter is the name of the folder (or directory) you wish to create. The drive designation may be included here as well as a path should you wish to create a subdirectory. Suppose, for example, that the current directory is the root directory on the *C:* drive and you want to create the folder *budget* in the *year2000* directory on the *D:* drive. To do this without moving from the current location, enter

```
mkdir d:\year2000\budget
```

REMOVING FOLDERS

Windows 2000 provides several ways to remove folders through either Windows 2000 Explorer or the My Computer windows. Removing a folder places it in the Recycle Bin where it can still be accessed. Only when the Recycle Bin is cleared are folders permanently removed from the system.

The simplest way to remove a folder is to select it and then press **Delete**. A confirmation message similar to the following will display: "Are you sure you want to remove the folder and move all its contents to the Recycle Bin?" to which you must respond by selecting **Yes** or **No**.

Another way to remove a folder using Windows 2000 Explorer follows:

1. Select the folder.

2. Select **File** from the menu bar.

3. Select **Delete**.

Step 2 is not necessary if you select the folder by right-clicking on it. Doing so displays a menu that also contains the Delete option.

As an alternative, you can select the folder and then, while holding down the left mouse button, drag the folder to the Recycle Bin icon and release the button.

If you want the folder to be permanently removed from the system, hold down the <Shift> key while dragging the folder to the Recycle Bin.

rmdir Command

The *rmdir* command, also known as *rd*, deletes the given directory (or folder). The syntax is

```
rmdir directory-name [/s]
```

or

```
rd directory-name [/s]
```

The *directory-name* parameter is the name of the directory or folder you wish to delete. It can contain both the drive designation and the path name if necessary.

The */s* switch is optional and enables any files and subdirectories contained within the folder to be deleted as well. If it is not used, the directory must be empty of any files before it can be removed.

Moving between Folders

Moving between folders within Windows 2000 is as simple as selecting a different folder with the mouse, which you can do in Windows 2000 Explorer either in the **All Folders** or the **Contents of** pane. Within My Computer windows, just click on the icon representing the folder or the folder name.

chdir COMMAND

The *chdir* command, also known as *cd*, enables the user to display the name of the current directory as well as to change to a different directory. The syntax is

```
chdir [/d] [[drive:]directory-name]
```

or

```
cd [/d] [[drive:]directory-name]
```

The parameters */d* and *drive:directory-name* are optional. If neither is entered, the *chdir* command will display the name of the current directory, including the drive designation.

The */d* switch changes the current drive designation. The *drive:directory-name* parameter identifies the new drive and directory. The drive designation is entered only when necessary. Using a double period (..) in place of the directory name will change the directory from the current one to its parent.

Creating and Removing Files

This section provides procedures and commands for creating and removing files within Windows 2000.

CREATING FILES

Files are usually created within Windows 2000 via an installed application, such as Notepad or WordPad. From within Windows 2000 Explorer and the My Computer windows, selecting **File** → **New** will provide a list of the file types you can create based upon the applications installed on your system. In addition, the MS-DOS editor, *edlin,* is available from the Command Prompt. The *vi* editor is also shipped with Windows 2000.

REMOVING FILES

The procedure for removing files is the same as that for removing folders. The simplest method is to select it and then press **Delete**. To do so using Windows 2000 Explorer:

1. Select the file.
2. Select **File** from the menu bar.
3. Select **Delete**.

Step 2 is not necessary if you select the file using the right mouse button. Right-clicking will display a menu that also contains the Delete option.

As an alternative, you can select the file and drag it to the Recycle Bin icon. If you want the file permanently removed from the system, hold the <Shift> key down while dragging it to the Recycle Bin or simultaneously press the <Shift> and <Delete> keys.

To select multiple files for deletion, hold down the <Ctrl> key while selecting the files with the mouse and then drag them to the Recycle Bin.

del and erase Commands

The *del* command deletes or erases files from the system. Another name for this command is *erase,* and its syntax is

```
del file(s) [options]
```

or

```
erase file(s) [options]
```

The *file(s)* parameter identifies the files to be removed from the system and can contain the drive designation and the directory path in the format *drive:path\file*. More than one file can be deleted using the same *del* command by separating the multiple file names with spaces, commas, or semicolons.

The wildcard characters * and ? can be used when specifying files to be deleted. It is important that these be used with care to reduce the risk of deleting critical files. See Table A.11 for options.

TABLE A.11 del Options

Option	Qualifier	Description
/a	:attributes	Deletes files that match the given attributes: r for Read-Only, h for Hidden, s for System, a for Archive. A minus (–) sign may be used in front of any of the above options to identify files that do not match the given attribute.
/f		Forces Read-Only files to be deleted.
/p		Requires the user to confirm whether a file should or should not be deleted by displaying the following prompt: file, Delete (Y/N)? Y will delete the file, N will not. (To abort the delete command altogether, enter a Ctrl-C.)
/q		Does not prompt for confirmation. This is the default option.
/s		Deletes the files listed from not only the current directory but also from the subdirectories.

Copying and Moving Files

The copy procedure creates a duplicate of the original file in another location so that more than one copy exists. The move procedure places the original file in another location without making a duplicate of it.

Windows 2000 provides both graphical and command line methods for copying and moving files. The graphical method using the Windows 2000 Explorer application provides the user multiple ways to copy and move such as menus and drag and drop. In addition, it enables a user to copy and move files within and between disks, or across the network. The following sections discuss both the graphical and command line procedures for these tasks.

COPYING FILES

To copy a file using the drag and drop method within Windows 2000 Explorer:

1. Display the file in the **Contents of** pane.
2. Make sure that the destination directory is visible in the **All Folders** pane. (Or start another copy of Explorer and display the destination directory in the **Contents of** pane.)
3. Select the file you wish to copy.
4. Hold down the <Ctrl> key and drag the file to its destination.

For multiple files, hold down the <Ctrl> key while selecting.

To use the menu bar in Windows 2000 Explorer to copy files:

1. Select the files.
2. Select **Edit → Copy** or press **<Ctrl>C**.
3. Select the destination directory.
4. Select **Edit → Paste** or press **<Ctrl>V**.

Selecting the files with the right mouse button also displays a menu that contains the Copy menu command.

Copying an executable file (one that has a .exe or .com extension) may create a shortcut—that is, a link to the executable that gives the user an alternative way of executing the program. Shortcuts are often dragged and dropped to the main screen so that the user can bypass the menus.

copy Command

The *copy* command copies the source file or files to the destination defined. It can also be used to combine the contents of files. The syntax is

```
copy [/a|/b] source-file [/a|/b] dest-file [/a|/b] [options]
```

The *source-file* is the name of the file to be copied. It can be just the file name, it can include the drive designation and the directory path as necessary, or it can be an actual device.

The *dest-file* is the name of the destination file but can be extended to include the drive designation and the directory path or it can be a device name such as COM1 or LPT1. If this parameter is omitted, a file with the same name, creation date, and time is created in the current directory and on the current drive. If a file with that name already exists, an error is displayed.

The parameter [/a|/b] indicates whether the file is ASCII (/a switch) or binary (/b switch). The default value is binary when copying and ASCII when combining. When the [/a|/b] switch is entered before the *source-file,* all items that follow use that flag until a different [/a|/b] switch is entered. This new switch applies to the *source-file* that immediately precedes it as well as to any *source-files* that follow it. Placement of the /a or /b after the *source-file* or the *dest-file* results in different copy procedures, as explained in Table A.12.

When the *dest-file* is a device, the /b switch should be used so that special control characters are copied to it as data. If the /a switch is used in this instance, the ASCII copy might cause those control characters to be interpreted, providing unpredictable results.

Two additional options are available, indicated in the syntax line as *options,* and are defined in Table A.13.

TABLE A.12 copy Options

Option	Used after the source-file	Used after the dest-file
/a	Copies all data in the file up to the first end-of-file character. The end-of-file character is not copied. The data is considered to be in ASCII format.	Adds an end-of-file character to the end of the *dest-file* as the last character.
/b	Copies all data in the file including the end-of-file character. The data is considered to be in binary format.	Does not add an end-of-file character to the end of the *dest-file*.

TABLE A.13 copy Options

Option	Description
/n	Uses the MS-DOS file name format of *filename.ext* when copying files with longer names.
/v	Verifies each file copied. If an error occurs, a message is displayed. This switch causes the *copy* command to execute more slowly.
/y	Suppresses the prompt to overwrite an existing file.
/z	Copies networked files so that they are in restart mode.

- copy command examples. To copy the file *budget.xls,* which exists on the C: drive, to the directory *d:\financial\year2000,* enter the following:

```
copy budget.xls d:\financial\year2000
```

If you want to copy an ASCII file up to the first end-of-file character and output it to a file with the end-of-file character added, enter

```
copy demo.txt /a newdemo.txt /a
```

- Combining files with the copy command. To instruct the *copy* command to combine files, enter multiple *source-files* separated by plus signs. Remember that the default file type is considered ASCII when combining files. For binary files, you must enter the /b switch. The syntax for combining files is

```
copy [/a|/b] source-file1 [+ source-file2 [/a|/b] [+ source-file...]]
dest-file [/a|/b] options
```

Wildcard characters can also be used to designate multiple files to be combined.

A special use of the plus sign parameter allows the user to update the date and time of the file to the current date and time without changing the file contents. The syntax is

```
copy [/a|/b] source-file+ ,,
```

- copy command examples using the Combining Option. Suppose that a department manager wants to combine all of her employees' monthly status reports for April into one file. She enters

```
copy grwapr.rpt + ebgapr.rpt + eegapr.rpt April.rpt
```

If all of the above files were in the same directory, a variation of this command could be entered:

```
copy *apr.rpt April.rpt
```

xcopy Command

The *xcopy* command is more comprehensive than the *copy* command, as it allows the user to copy not only files and directories but also subdirectories. The syntax is

```
xcopy source-file [dest-file] [options]
```

The *source-file* parameter represents the names of the files to be copied and their locations. It must include either a drive designation or a directory path.

The *dest-file* parameter is the destination of the files to be copied and may include the file name as well as the drive designation and the directory path as necessary. It is optional, and if not included, the *source-files* are copied to the current drive and directory. The destination files automatically have the archive attribute set.

- xcopy command example. To copy the directory *budget* and all of its files and subdirectories to the *year2000* directory, creating a directory named *budget* at the same time, enter

```
xcopy \budget \year2000 /i/s/e
```

The */i* switch will create a directory named *budget* under this directory, copying both files and subdirectories; the */e* switch will ensure that empty subdirectories get copied as well. See Table A.14 for options.

TABLE A.14 xcopy Options

Option	Qualifier	Description
/a		Copies only those *source-files* with the Archive attribute set. Using this switch does not cause the Archive attribute to change.
/d	:date	Copies only those files with a modification date the same as or after the *:date* qualifier, which is in the format of MM-DD-YY. The *:date* qualifier is optional; if it is not used, only those files that are more recent than any existing destination files are copied.
/e		Must be used with the /s and /t options and allows empty subdirectories to be copied as well as those containing files.
/exclude	:filename	Excludes from copying the files contained in *filename*. *Filename* is a file that can contain one pattern per line without the use of wildcard characters. A file is not copied when any portion of the *source-file* parameter matches a line in *filename*.
/i		Creates a directory called *dest-file,* if the *source-file* contains wildcards or if the *source-file* is a directory and if *dest-file* does not exist. Then copies all *source-files* to the *dest-file* directory. When not set, the *xcopy* command prompts the user to identify the *dest-file* as a file (F) or a directory (D).
/k		Copies the *source-files* without changing the Read-Only attribute. Automatically removes the Read-Only attribute whenever this option is *not* used.
/n		Copies files using the short file name format of *filename.ext*. This is required when copying files to a system that can only handle shorter file names.
/p		Displays a confirmation prompt prior to creating the destination file.
/q		Does not display messages.
/r		Enables the command to copy over read-only files.
/s		Copies both directories and subdirectories, except empty ones. When omitted, subdirectories are not copied.
/t		Does not copy files under subdirectories but only the subdirectories themselves. Must be used with the /e switch to copy empty subdirectories.
/u		The update option. When used, it will only copy files that already exist at the destination, thereby updating them.
/v		Verifies each new file.
/w		Displays a message requiring the user to press any key to start the copy process.
/x		Copies file auditing settings.
/y /-y		Suppresses prompting before overwriting a file; -y forces the prompt.
/z		Copies files over the network in restartable mode.

MOVING FILES

To move a file using the drag and drop method within Windows 2000 Explorer

1. Display the file in the **Contents of** pane.
2. Make sure that the destination directory is visible in the **All Folders** pane. (Or start another copy of Explorer and display the destination directory in the **Contents of** pane.)
3. Select the file you wish to move.
4. Drag the file to its new destination if it is on the same disk as its current location. Otherwise, hold down the <Shift> key while dragging the file to force the move. If the <Shift> key is not held down, the file will be copied, not moved.

Remember, to select multiple files, hold down the <Ctrl> key while selecting. To use the menu bar in Windows 2000 Explorer to do this

1. Select the files.
2. Select **Edit → Cut** or press <Ctrl>X.
3. Select the destination directory.
4. Select **Edit → Paste** or press <Ctrl>V.

move Command

The *move* command actually moves files, from one directory to another so that they no longer exist in their original location. The syntax is

```
move source-file(s) dest-file
```

The *source-file(s)* parameter indicates the files that you wish to move. It can be just the file name or it can include the drive designation and directory as necessary. Wildcard characters can be used to move multiple files.

The *dest-file* parameter represents the new location. It too can be a new file name or it can include a new drive designation or new directory path as necessary. Wildcard characters can be used here as well, such as when you need to change the extension of a number of files.

RENAMING FILES OR FOLDERS

To rename a file using Windows 2000 Explorer:

1. Select the file or folder.
2. From the menu bar select **File → Rename**.
3. Enter the new name for the file or folder.

or

1. Select the file or folder by right-clicking to display a menu.

2. Select **Rename**.

3. Enter the new name for the file or folder.

rename *Command*

The *rename,* or *ren,* command permits changing the name of a file or directory without changing its location. In other words, file names cannot be changed across drives or directories with this command. For that you need the *copy* or *move* command. The syntax for both formats of *rename* is

```
rename oldfile newfile
```

or

```
ren oldfile newfile
```

The *oldfile* parameter is the name of the file you wish to change and may include the drive designation and directory path. The *newfile* parameter is the new name for the file and may not include a drive or path. If a file already exists with the *newfile* name, an error will be displayed. Wildcard characters can be used in both *oldfile* and *newfile*.

Determining File Type

Windows 2000 Explorer will automatically attempt to identify a file type, which is displayed in the Type column of the **Contents of** pane as long as a detailed view is selected (**View → Details**). Another method of displaying the file type is to select **File → Properties → General**. You can also select the file with the right mouse button and then select **Properties → General**.

FILE MANIPULATION COMMANDS

Several commands may be entered at the Command Prompt that allow the manipulation of files, such as *attrib, copy,* and *sort*. *Attrib* permits the user to change file attributes; *copy* permits the user to combine files; and *sort* sorts data. The *attrib* and *sort* commands are discussed below; *copy* was discussed in the File Management Commands section.

assoc Command

The *assoc* command displays and changes the file name extension that is associated with a file type or application. The syntax it uses is

```
assoc [.ext[=[filetype]]]
```

To view the associated extension of file type .doc

Type `assoc .doc`

attrib Command

The *attrib* command allows the user to either display or change a file's attributes, that is, Archive, Hidden, Read-Only, Compressed, and System (Compressed is only available on NTFS file systems and cannot be altered using this command). The syntax is

```
attrib [attributes] filename [/s]
```

Neither the *attributes* parameter nor the */s* switch is entered to display the attributes associated with a particular file. Instead, the syntax is *attrib filename*. The *filename* parameter is the name of the file with the drive designation and path included where necessary. The */s* switch is used when setting or changing attributes and instructs the command to change not only the files in the current directory but also those in the subdirectories. As with most commands, the wildcard characters * and ? may be used to designate multiple files to change.

Table A.15 identifies the acceptable values for the *attributes* parameter. More than one attribute can be set within a single command, but if the system or hidden attribute is set, it must be removed before any other attribute can be modified.

attrib COMMAND EXAMPLE

To add the Archive attribute to all the files in the current directory, enter

```
attrib +a *.*
```

sort Command

The *sort* command sorts the input data and outputs the result to the screen, a file, or a device. It also accepts input from another command, from a file, or from data entered on the terminal screen. The syntax of *sort* can be one of the following:

```
sort options < infilename > outfilename
command | sort options > outfilename
```

TABLE A.15 Attribute Values

Attribute	Description
+a	Adds the Archive attribute.
-a	Removes the Archive attribute.
+h	Adds the Hidden attribute.
-h	Removes the Hidden attribute.
+r	Adds the Read-Only attribute.
-r	Removes the Read-Only attribute.
+s	Adds the System attribute.
-s	Removes the System attribute.

The *infilename* parameter is the name of the file containing the data to be sorted. The drive designation and directory path may be entered as necessary. The *outfilename* parameter is the name of the file containing the sorted data. Once again, the drive designation and directory path may be entered if needed. The *command* parameter is a command whose output will be sorted by *sort*. Two options are available as shown in Table A.16.

If the *command* or *infilename* parameters are omitted, the *sort* command will take input as the user enters it on the screen until a Ctrl-Z <Enter> sequence is encountered. If the *outfilename* parameter is omitted, the sorted data will display on the screen.

TABLE A.16 sort Options

Option	Description
/+n	Sorts the data based on the character in column *n*. The default sort is based on the character in column 1.
/r	Executes a reverse sort either in reverse alphabetical or reverse numerical order.

MISCELLANEOUS COMMANDS

The following set of commands do not fit neatly into a broader category, so we have placed them in a miscellaneous grouping simply for editorial convenience.

cacls Command

The *cacls* command line utility displays and modifies file Access Control Lists (ACL). See Table A.17 for options. The syntax is

```
cacls filename [/option] [permissions]
```

Converting to NTFS

While Windows 2000 can run on FAT and FAT32 file systems, there are many advantages to using NTFS. You do not have to reinstall the operating system to change a file system to NTFS, but once you do, you cannot change it back.

convert COMMAND

The *convert* command will change an existing FAT or FAT32 file system volume to NTFS. The current active drive cannot be converted during the present session with *convert* but only at the next system reboot. The syntax is

```
convert [drive:] /fs:ntfs [/v]
```

TABLE A.17 cacls Options

Option	Qualifier	Description
/e		Edits the ACL rather than replaces it.
/c		Makes changes even if errors are found.
/g	*User:perm*	Grants special rights to the specified user.
/t		Changes the ACL in the defined files and all subdirectories.
n		No permission.
r		Read permission.
c		Change or Write permission.
f		Full Control permission.
/r	*User*	Revokes the rights of a specified user.
/p	*User*	Replaces the permissions of specified users with new ones.

Setting and Displaying Date and Time

To display the current date, move the cursor to the time display in the bottom right corner of the task bar. To modify this date, double-click on the time to bring up the **Date/Time Properties** window (Figure A.6). Within the Date/Time tab, you can change the current date as well as view a calendar for the month and year selected. You can also modify the time from this window. An alternate way of displaying the **Date/Time Properties** window is by selecting **Start → Settings → Control Panel → Date/Time**.

To change the format of a date or time display, select **Start → Settings → Control Panel → Regional Settings**. Once in the **Regional Settings Properties** window, select either the **Date** or the **Time** tab as appropriate. Within these tabs, you can, for example, change the time format to a 24-hour clock or change the date to the format yy/mm/dd. Another method of displaying the date and time is by selecting **Start → Programs → Accessories → Clock**.

The command line also offers options to assist in displaying and changing the date and time. These are discussed below.

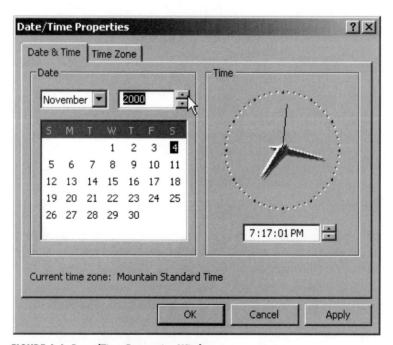

FIGURE A.6 Date/Time Properties Window

date COMMAND

The *date* command allows the user to either display or change the date. The syntax is

```
date [mm-dd-yy]
```

If the *mm-dd-yy* parameter is omitted, the current system date is displayed. If not, the date is set to the value you enter. Acceptable values for the month, or *mm,* parameter are 1 through 12; for the day, or *dd,* parameter, 1 through 31. The year, or *yy,* parameter can be 80 through 99 or 1980 through 2099. If you prefer dashes separating the month, day, and year, parameters can be replaced with either a period (.) or a slash (/).

time COMMAND

The *time* command allows the user to either display or change the system time. The syntax is

```
time [hrs:[min[:sec[.hun]]]] [AP]
```

When no parameters are entered, the current system time is displayed, which you can change if necessary. If you do not enter a new time, just press the <Enter> key. If you do, use the syntax identified in Table A.18.

net time COMMAND

The *net time* command allows a user to synchronize the time across the network between her current system and another domain (or computer). It also allows her to display the time for any system on the network. The syntax is

```
net time [\\computername | /domain[:domainname]] [/set]
```

TABLE A.18 time Options

Option	Description
hrs	Enters the hour in either regular or 24-hour format. Acceptable values are 0 through 23.
min	Enters the minutes, ranging from 0 through 59.
sec	Enters the seconds, ranging from 0 through 59.
.hun	Enters the hundredths of a second, ranging from 0 through 99.
AP	Enters A for A.M. or P for P.M. This field is not necessary if the 24-hour format is used.

When no parameters are given, the *net time* command will display the time from the time server system. The */set* parameter is optional and required only when you want to change the time. If omitted, the time on the system named is displayed; if used, the time on the current system is synchronized with the time on the system named.

The *computername* or the /domain:*domainname* identifies the system for which to display the time or the system with which the current system's time is synchronized. The *domainname* portion of the /domain:*domainname* parameter is optional.

Logging in as Another User

To log in as another user, you must first access the **Windows 2000 Security** window by pressing **Ctrl-Alt-Del**. This window displays who you are currently logged in as, the name of the current domain, and the date and time of login. Select the **Logoff** button to log off as this user.

Chat Mode

The Windows 2000 *winchat* application allows users to converse with each other. It is accessed by typing *winchat* from the Command Prompt. To initiate a conversation, select **Conversation → Dial** from the menu bar. In the **Select Computer** window that appears, either enter the name of the computer of the person you want to chat with or select one from the list.

When you receive a chat message, a **Chat** button will display on the task bar. To respond to the message, click the **Chat** button and select **Conversation → Answer**.

While researching some problems we were having with this utility, we discovered Microsoft's NetMeeting software, which enables communication over the Internet or an intranet. The Windows 2000 version has the Internet phone feature along with multi-user data conferencing, which allows for application sharing, an electronic white board, a text-based chat facility, and binary file transfer.

net name COMMAND

The *net name* command adds, deletes, or displays names that are authorized to receive messages. These names are used only for messaging and must be unique throughout the network. Windows 2000 acknowledges three types of names here: computer, user, and messaging. To execute the *net name* command, the Messenger service must be running. The syntax is

```
net name [name [/action]]
```

Executing the *net name* command without any parameters will display a list of all names that can accept messages on this computer. The *name* parameter is the unique name authorized to receive messages and can be 15 characters in length. Acceptable values for the /*action* parameter are /*add* or /*delete,* which instructs the command to add or delete the messaging name entered. The /*action* parameter is optional, with /*add* as the default.

net name Command Example

To add the messaging name techsupport to the computer, enter one of the following commands:

```
net name techsupport /add
```

or

```
net name techsupport
```

net send COMMAND

The *net send* command works in conjunction with the Messenger service and enables you to send messages on the network to users, computers, and messaging names. Only users connected to the network and running the Messenger service will receive them. The syntax for *net send* is

```
net send destination message
```

The *message* parameter contains the message that will be delivered, which should be in quotes if it contains special characters, such as a slash. A message can hold up to 128 characters.

The values for the *destination* parameter are described in Table A.19. This parameter is required and must contain one of these values.

TABLE A.19 net send Options for the destination Parameter

Option	Qualifier	Description
*		Sends the message to all names in the user's group.
/*domain*	:*domainname*	Sends the message to all names in either the current domain or the domain or workgroup given by the :*domainname* parameter.
name		Enters the user name, the computer name, or the messaging name of the recipient of the message. Names that include space characters should be enclosed in quotes.
/*users*		Sends the message to all users connected to the server.

NETWORKING COMMANDS

In this section, we review some of the networking commands and procedures that are available on Windows 2000, and we discuss how to connect to a system via modem and determine and set the system host name.

Each net command is identified here but its detailed description may actually appear in another section. When this is the case, we reference that section.

arp Command

The *arp* (Address Resolution Protocol) command displays and changes the IP to an Ethernet (or Token Ring) physical address translation table. The syntax for *arp* is

```
arp -option inet_addr eth_addr [if_addr]
```

The *inet_addr* is the Internet address; the *eth_addr* is the Ethernet address; and the *if_addr* is the address translation table to be modified for the Internet address of the network interface. See Table A.20 for options.

HyperTerminal

The HyperTerminal application is bundled with Windows 2000 and enables a user to dial out to another computer via modem. It is accessed by selecting **Start** → **Programs** → **Accessories** → **HyperTerminal**.

TABLE A.20 arp Options

Option	Description
/-a	Displays all ARP entries in the current protocol data. When the *inet_addr* is specified, the specific IP and physical address are displayed.
/-g	Performs the same function as *–a*.
/-N	Displays the specified *if_addr network* interface.
/-d	Deletes the *inet_addr* host. All hosts can be deleted by using the wildcard with *inet_addr*.
/-s	Associates the Internet address with the physical address (presented as 6 hexadecimal bytes separated by hyphens).

Take the following steps to set up and connect to a remote location:

1. In the **Connect Description** window, enter the name of the connection you wish to make, such as "Microsoft BBS."

2. Select **OK** to display the **Connect To** window. Enter the appropriate information in the **Country Code**, **Area Code**, **Phone #**, and **Connect Using** fields to identify the number you wish to call using which modem installed on the system.

3. After entering the phone number and modifying any other field, the **Connect** window displays (Figure A.7) here change the phone number as well as the configuration of the local modem, including baud rate, data bits, and parity via the **Modify** button.

4. Select the **Dialing Properties** button to define the location from which to dial including any dialing prefixes to access an outside line or to turn off call waiting.

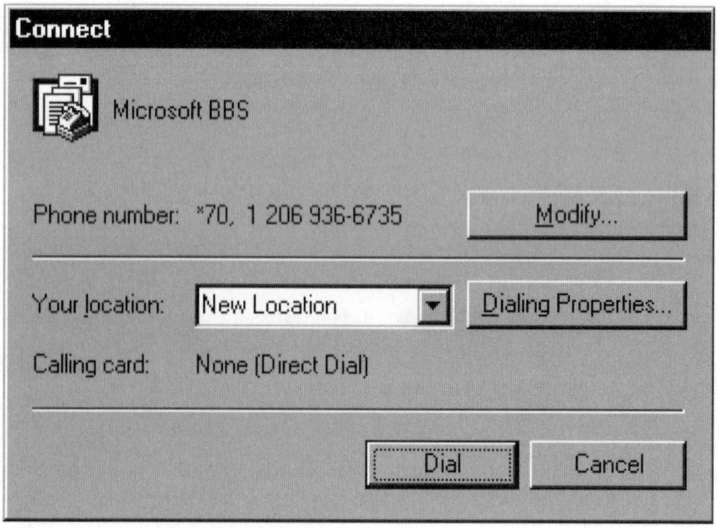

FIGURE A.7 The Connect Window

5. Select the **Dial** button to display the status of the modem, such as disconnected.

6. Select **Dial Now** to initiate the connection process.

To transfer files between systems, select **Transfer** from the menu bar; then **Send File** to send a file or **Receive File** to receive one. Within each of these options, the transfer protocol can be selected. To terminate a session, select the Disconnect icon from the toolbar or select **Call** → **Disconnect** from the menu bar.

ftp and tftp Commands

The file transfer protocol (*FTP*) command enables a user to transfer files between systems that have *FTP* installed and running. See Table A.21 for options list. Its syntax is

```
ftp [options] [hostname]
```

The *hostname* is the name or IP address of the remote system. When given, *FTP* establishes a connection with that system. Otherwise, it goes into command mode waiting for the user to enter a command. A list of the available *FTP* com-

TABLE A.21 ftp Options

Option	Qualifier	Description
-d		Turns on the debugging option, which displays all *FTP* commands that are passed between the systems.
-g		Turns off file name "globbing," which means that wildcard characters are not expanded.
-I		Turns off interactive prompting, which means that *FTP* will automatically execute a given command for all file names entered.
-n		Does not allow auto-login when the initial connection is made. Instead, the user must log on to the remote system.
-s	:filename	The *filename* qualifier is the name of a file that contains *FTP* commands that are executed immediately upon connection. Do not include any spaces in this parameter.
-v		Does not display responses from the remote system.
-w	:size	Changes the size of the transfer buffer to *size*. The default is 4096.

mands can be retrieved by entering *help* at this point. Given the number of commands available, we do not discuss them here but recommend that you refer to Windows 2000 Help.

The trivial file transfer protocol (TFTP) is a nonsecure version of FTP. Its use is generally not recommended, and it should not be enabled.

hostname Command

The host name is the name of a device that is on the network, which can be the computer name. In Windows 2000 it can be displayed from the Command Prompt by entering *hostname*. To identify the computer's full name and domain, open the **Control Panel**, select **System Properties**, and select the **Network Identification** tab.

ipconfig Command

TCP/IP network configuration values are displayed by the *ipconfig* diagnostic command. These are the DNS suffix, IP address, subnet mask, and default gateway. When the */all* option is utilized, much additional information is output, including the host name, node type, adapter physical address, and more. The syntax used is

```
ipconfig [/all] [/renew] [/release]
```

The *ipconfig* command is of great value when running DHCP, as it permits the identification of DHCP-configured TCP/IP values. The */renew* option reaffirms the current DHCP values. The */release* option disables the related TCP/IP configuration values.

ipxroute Command

The *ipxroute* command permits the viewing and modification of routing table data employed by the IPX protocol, which uses different options than those for source routing. The *ipxroute* syntax for IPX is

```
ipxroute servers [type=x]
ipxroute stats [/show] [/clear]
ipxroute table
```

The syntax for source routing is

```
ipxroute board=n
ipxroute config
```

TABLE A.22 Nbtstat Options

Option	Qualifier	Description
-a	*remotename*	Lists the remote computer's name table.
-A	*IP address*	Lists the remote computer's address.
-c		Lists the NetBIOS cache including the IP addresses.
-n		Lists the NetBIOS registration by type.
-R		Loads the lmhost file after deleting the NetBIOS cache.
-r		Lists WINS name resolution statistics.
-S		Lists client and server connections. For remote computers, these are listed by IP address.
-s		Lists client and server connections and converts IP addresses to names.

nbtstat Command

The *nbtstat* command is a diagnostic tool that displays current TCP/IP data and connections using NetBIOS over TCP/IP (NBT). See Table A.22 for an options list. The syntax is

```
nbtstat [- a remotename] [-A IP address] [-c] [-n] [-R] [-r] [-S] [-s]
[interval]
```

netstat Command

The *netstat* command displays protocol statistics and current TCP/IP connection information. See Table A.23 for an options list. The syntax is

```
netstat [options]
```

Without any options used the output includes

- *Proto*—the protocol used by the connection, such as TCP/IP.
- *Local Address*—either the IP address or host name of the local system as well as the connection's port number displayed as name:port. An asterisk displays in the port field if it hasn't been established yet.
- *Foreign Address*—displays either the IP address or the host name of the remote system as well as the port number, displayed as name:port.
- *State*—the state of the TCP/IP connection. Some examples are CLOSED, ESTABLISHED, and LAST_ACK.

TABLE A.23 netstat Options

Option	Qualifier	Description
-a		Displays the status of all connections and listening ports.
-e		Displays Ethernet statistics.
interval		Displays statistics after each interval, where interval is the number of seconds between capturing statistics. To terminate the display, enter a Ctrl-C. This option should be the last one on the command line.
-n		Displays addresses numerically—for example, the IP address instead of the host name.
-p	protocol	Displays the connections for the protocol given. Acceptable values are tcp and udp. If the -s option is also used, icmp or ip are also acceptable values.
-r		Displays the network routing tables.
-s		Displays protocol statistics for tcp, ucp, icmp, and ip. To reduce the number of protocols displayed, use this in conjunction with the -p option.

nslookup Command

The *nslookup* command provides data from the Domain Name System (DNS) server(s) both interactively and noninteractively. It also supports over a dozen subcommands. With *nslookup* the IP address of host can be identified or a reverse lookup performed. The syntax is

```
nlslookup [-subcommand] [IP address]
```

ping Command

The *ping* command is used to test and verify network connections by sending ICMP (Internet Control Message Protocol) data packets to a remote computer and waiting for a reply. By default four packets are transmitted and validated when received. See Table A.24 for an options list. The syntax of this command is

```
ping [options] hostname(s)
```

The *hostname(s)* is the remote computer whose network connections you wish to test. It may contain either the host name itself or the IP address.

TABLE A.24 ping Options

Option	Qualifier	Description
-a		Converts numerical addresses to their corresponding host names.
-f		Includes a flag in the data packet that instructs the gateways not to fragment the data.
-i	time	Sets the Time To Live field in the echo request packet to *time,* where *time* can be a value from 0 to 255.
-j	list	Routes the data packets through up to 9 host names contained in *list.* This option allows loose source routing, which means that intermediate gateways may separate consecutive hosts. It cannot be used in conjunction with the -*k* option.
-k	list	Routes the data packets through up to 9 host names contained in *list.* This option allows strict source routing, which means that intermediate gateways may not separate consecutive hosts. It cannot be used in conjunction with the -*j* option.
-l	length	Sends echo packets containing the amount of data specified by *length.* The default is 32 bytes; the maximum is 65,527.
-n	count	Defines the number of packets (*count*) transmitted before terminating the *ping* command. Zero is the default, where ping keeps running until receiving an interrupt signal.
-r	count	Sends the echo request directly to the host, bypassing routing tables.
-t		Only for multicast addresses, sets the Time To Live field in the echo request packet (datagram) or *TTL,* where *TTL* is a value from 0 to 255. The Time to Live field defines the maximum number of systems through which the packet can be sent. For example, a *TTL* of 0 limits the datagram to the local system. A *TTL* of 1 (the default) limits the transmission to systems directly connected to the default interface address (or the address specified by the -*i* option)
-v	type	Displays other packets received in addition to the echo request packets.
-w	time	Defines the timeout interval in milliseconds.

pathping Command

The *pathping* tool combines *ping* and *tracert* plus additional information. The statistics it provides allow network router or link problems to be identified. *Pathping*

TABLE A.25 pathping Options

Option	Qualifer	Description
-n		Does not resolve host names.
-m	maximum_hops	Sets the maximum number of hops.
-g		Lists hosts within the intermediate gateways.
-p	period	Specifies the milliseconds to wait between consequent pings; the default is 250.
-n	num_queries	Specifies the number of queries to each computer; the default is 100.
-w	timeout	Specifies the milliseconds to wait for a response; the default is 3000 (or 3 seconds).

forwards packets to routers and then computes the results based on returned packets for each network hop. See Table A.25 for an options list. Its syntax is

```
pathping [-n] [-h maximum_hops] [-g host-list] [-p period] [-q
num_queries] [-w timeout] target_name
```

rcp Command

The *rcp* command copies files between networked machines including UNIX systems. It must be initiated by Windows 2000, and other systems must be running rshd, the remote shell daemon, and have the rcp utility installed. See Table A.26 for a list of options. The syntax for this command is

```
rcp [options] host.user:srcfile(s) host.user:dest-file
```

The *host.user:srcfile(s)* parameter is the name of the file to be copied to another system. It breaks down as follows:

- *host*—the name of the source computer system. It is required only if the source system is different from the system from which the command was executed, or if a specific user name must be entered. The host can be either the host name or the IP address.

- *user*—the login name of the user whose files are being copied. It is required when the host is entered as an IP address and when copying files that belong to another user.

- *srcfile*—the name of the file being copied. It may contain the entire path if necessary to locate the file if it is not in the current directory or in the user's login directory when *host.user* is used.

TABLE A.26 rcp Options

Option	Description
-a	Copies files in ASCII mode. This is the default.
-b	Copies files in binary mode.
-h	Copies files that have the Hidden attribute set. By default, these files are not copied even if they are specifically requested.
-r	Copies the contents of a directory and its subdirectories. This is considered a recursive copy. Both the *source-file* and the *dest-file* should be directories.

The parameter *host.user:dest-file* is the name of the destination file or directory to which the file is copied. If more that one *srcfile* is listed, *dest-file* must be a directory. The *host.user* portion identifies the remote system as well as the login name of the destination system. If the *host.user:dest-file* parameter is omitted, the local system is considered the default.

For the *rcp* command to be successful with UNIX systems, the *.rhosts* file must exist in the user's home directory on the remote computer. This file contains the host name of the local system as well as the user's name. It is recommended that the host name of the local system also be included in the remote system's */etc/hosts* or */etc/hosts.equiv* file.

route Command

The *route* command is used to manage and manipulate network routing tables under TCP/IP environments. See Table A.27 for an options list. Its syntax is

```
route [-f] [-p] [command [destination] [mask subnetmask] [gateway]
[metric costmetric]]
```

The *-f* parameter option clears all gateway routing tables. The *-p* parameter option is employed in conjunction with the *add* command to create a persistent route across boots of the system. (By default, routes are not preserved between system boots.)

Other parameters used with the *route* command are

- *destination*—determines the computer to send *command*.
- mask *subnetmask*—identifies a subnet mask to be associated with this route entry; the default is 255.255.255.255.

TABLE A.27 route Commands

Command	Description
Add	Adds a route.
Print	Prints a route.
Delete	Deletes a route.
Change	Changes the current route.

- *gateway*—identifies the gateway.
- metric *costmetric*—specifies an integer cost metric (from 1 to 9999) used in calculating the fastest, most reliable, and/or least expensive routes.

rsh Command

When the rsh service is running, the *rsh* command permits a user to execute commands on a remote system. See Table A.28 for an options list. The syntax is

```
rsh hostname [options] command
```

The *hostname* parameter is the name of the system on which you wish to run a command. The *command* parameter contains the command to be run on the remote system.

When the *rsh* command is run from a Windows 2000 Server, the primary domain controller must be available to validate the name of the user currently logged in. Also, to access a remote UNIX system, an *.rhosts* file should exist in the user's home directory. This file contains both the host names and the login names of computers and users who have access to this remote system.

TABLE A.28 rsh Options

Option	Qualifier	Description
-l	*user*	Logon to the remote computer uses the name represented by *user*. When not used, logon is the user executing the *rsh* command.
-n		Redirects the input to NULL.

Telnet

Using telnet enables a user to connect to and communicate with another system using that system's own protocol. To access telnet within Windows 2000, select **Start** → **Programs** → **Accessories** → **telnet**. To connect to a remote system

1. Select **Connect** from the menu bar.

2. Select **Remote System**.

3. Within the **Connect** window, select or enter the **Host Name**, **Port**, and **TermType** (terminal emulation type).

4. Select **Connect**.

From the **Terminal** menu, select **Preferences** to define default preferences such as cursor type, terminal emulation, and fonts.

From the Command Prompt, simply type *telnet* to launch the telnet window; however, it is important to understand that this is a telnet client only. To accept telnet sessions from other systems, you must install the telnet Server, which is included on the Windows 2000 Resource Kit.

net Commands

Windows 2000 provides a series of commands, known as net commands, that may be executed from the Prompt or within batch files. Many of them may be performed through the graphical interface, but users sometimes prefer to use the command line interface instead.

All of the net commands are identified here with at least a brief description. When necessary, we have referenced the section where a more detailed definition may be found.

The common options available for all net commands are described in Table A.29.

TABLE A.29 Common net Command Options

Option	Description
/no	Automatically responds to any prompt the *net* command issues with a "no." An alternative format is */n*.
/yes	Automatically responds to any prompt the *net* command issues with a "yes." An alternative format is */n*.

net accounts COMMAND

The *net accounts* command allows authorized users to update the user accounts database. In addition, it facilitates modifications to the password and logon requirements for all users. For *net accounts* to execute properly, the Net Logon service must be running on the system containing the accounts you wish to change. See Table A.30 for an options list. The syntax is

```
net accounts [options]
```

TABLE A.30 net accounts Options

Option	Qualifier	Description
/forcelogoff	*:minutes*	Defines the number of *minutes* a user has before the system automatically logs him off after the expiration of either the account or login time. The variable *minutes* can be numeric or the value "no." The value "no" is the default and does not allow a forced logoff. When a numeric value is entered for *minutes,* a warning is sent to the user.
/minpwlen	*:length*	Defines the minimum password *length* for a user account password. Acceptable values are 0–14, with 6 being the default.
maxpwage	*:days*	Defines the maximum *days* that a password is valid. Acceptable values for *days* are 1–49, 710, and "unlimited," which means that the password does not expire. The value used here must be greater than that defined for the */minpwage* option.
/minpwage	*:days*	Defines the minimum number of *days* that must pass before a user can change his password. Acceptable values are 0–49 and 710, with 0 as the default, which means that no limitations are set.
/uniquepw	*:number*	Defines the *number* of password changes that must occur before a password can be reused. Acceptable values are 0–8, with 5 as the default.
/domain		Updates the user accounts database based on the parameters given for the primary domain controller of the current domain. Omitting this parameter updates the database on the current system.
/sync		Can only be used with the */domain* option. It synchronizes the user account database. When executed from the primary domain controller, all backup domain controllers are synchronized. When executed from a backup domain controller, the backup is synchronized with the primary.

When *net accounts* is run without any options, the current settings for password, logon limitations, and domain information are displayed.

net accounts Command Examples

To synchronize the user account databases on all member servers, enter

```
net accounts /sync
```

If you are currently using a Windows 2000 workstation and want to set the minimum password length to 10 characters for the domain to which the workstation is connected, enter

```
net accounts /minpwlen:10 /domain
```

net computer COMMAND

The *net computer* command enables the user to add or delete computers from the domain database. These modifications are automatically forwarded to the primary domain controller. *net computer* can only be executed from a server. Its syntax is

```
net computer \\computername option
```

The *\\computername* parameter is the name of the computer to add to or delete. The *option* parameter can contain one of two options: */add* to add the computer name to the domain; and */del* to delete the computer name from the domain.

net computer Command Example

To delete the computer \\incy from the domain, enter the following:

```
net computer \\incy /del
```

net config COMMAND

Executing the *net config* command without any parameters displays the services that are both configurable and running. With the appropriate parameters and options, this command enables a system administrator to permanently change the settings for a running service.

Two variations of *net config* are *net config server* and *net config workstation*. Both are discussed below.

TABLE A.31 net config server Options

Option	Qualifier	Description
/autodisconnect	*:time*	Sets the maximum amount of *time* that a user's login session can be idle before it is automatically disconnected. Acceptable values are −1–65535 minutes, with 15 minutes the default. Setting *time* to −1 instructs the service to never disconnect an idle user.
/hidden	*:{yes	no}*	Determines whether the computer name of the server will display on the lists of servers depending on whether yes or no is entered as the qualifier. The default is no.
/srvcomment	*:"text"*	Defines a message that can be displayed in many Windows 2000 windows as well as with the *net view* command. The qualifier *text* can be 48 characters long. The quotation marks are required.

net config server Command

The *net config server* command either displays or modifies the settings of the Server service while the service is running. Any changes are permanent. See Table A.31 for an options list. The syntax of this command is

```
net config server [options]
```

Executing the *net config server* command without any options will display the current settings for the Server service. The following is an example of the output display:

```
Server Name                        \\incy
Server Comment
Software version                   Windows 2000
Server is active on                NetBT_NDISLoop1 (204c4f4f5020)
NetBT_NDISLoop1 (204c4f4f5020)
Server hidden                      No
Maximum Logged On Users            Unlimited
Maximum open files per session     2048
Idle session time (min)            15
The command completed successfully.
```

net config server Command Example
To disconnect users after 30 minutes of idle time, enter the following command:

```
net config server /autodisconnect:30
```

net config workstation Command
The *net config workstation* command either displays or permanently modifies the settings of the Workstation service while the service is running. See Table A.32 for an options list. The command syntax is

```
net config workstation [options]
```

Executing the *net config workstation* command without any options will display the current settings for the Workstation service on the local computer. The following is an example of the output display:

```
Computer name                      \\incy
User name                          Administrator
Workstation active on              NetBT_NDISLoop1 (204C4F4F5020)
Software version                   Windows 2000
Workstation domain                 BOOK
Logon domain                       BOOK
COM Open Timeout (sec)             3600
COM Send Count (byte)              16
COM Send Timeout (msec)            250
The command completed successfully.
```

TABLE A.32 net config workstation Options

Option	Qualifier	Description
/charcount	:bytes	Sets the number of *bytes* of data to be collected prior to sending them to a communications device. Acceptable values are 0–65535, with 16 bytes the default.
/chartime	:msec	Sets the number of milliseconds (*msec*) for collecting data prior to sending it to a communications device. Acceptable values for *msec* are 0–65,535,000 milliseconds, with 250 milliseconds as the default.
/charwait	:sec	Specifies the number of seconds (*sec*) to wait for a communications device to become available. Acceptable values are 0–65535 seconds, with 3600 seconds the default.

If both the */charcount:bytes* and */chartime:msec* options are used, Windows 2000 sends data to a communication device based upon whichever parameter is fulfilled first.

net continue COMMAND

The *net continue* command reactivates a service that has been suspended by the *net pause* command, without canceling a user's connection. The syntax is

```
net continue service
```

Acceptable values for the service parameter for standard services follow. Other services may be acceptable depending on what is installed on the system.

- FTP publishing service
- lpdsvc
- Net logon
- Network dde
- network dde dsdm
- lm security support provider
- remoteboot (at the Windows 2000 Server level only)
- remote access server
- Schedule
- Server
- Simple TCP/IP services
- Workstation

net file COMMAND

The ability to share files between computer systems and users is at the heart of a networked system. These shared files can be periodically left open or locked to prohibit access. The *net file* command enables the user to display both the names of any open shared file and the number of locks on it. In addition, it can close shared files and remove file locks. The syntax for *net file* is

```
net file [options]
```

When used without any options, the command displays a listing of all shared open files on the server as well as the number of locks each file has. The two possible options are shown in Table A.33.

TABLE A.33 net file Options

Option	Description
id	Enters the identification number of the file, which is found in the first column of the net file listing that displays all open files.
/close	Must be used in conjunction with the *id* option. It closes the file represented by the identification number, *id*.

net group COMMAND

The *net group* command permits the addition, display, or modification of global groups on Windows 2000 Server domains and can only be run from these domains. Users who work together or who have the same requirements for system use are usually classified as members of the same group.

It is important to remember that the *net group* command deals with *global* groups. In essence, this means that group members can only be from the domain in which the group was created, but they can be assigned privileges anywhere in the network as long as there is a trust relationship among domains.

There are three syntax formats for this command:

```
net group [options]
net group groupname [options]
net group groupname user(s) [options]
```

When the *net group* command is executed without any options, the display will include the name of the server as well as the name of each group on it. When the group name is displayed, it is preceded by an asterisk, which assists the user in differentiating group from user names when both are displayed.

net group Command Examples

To display all the users in the group sales1, enter

```
net group sales1
```

To add a comment to the record for this group, enter

```
net group sales1 /comment:"Direct Sales Personnel"
```

To add a group called sales2 and include a comment, enter

```
net group sales2 /add /comment:"Indirect Sales Personnel"
```

TABLE A.34 net group Options

Option	Qualifier	Description
groupname	/comment: *"text"* or /*action*	Enters the name of the group (*groupname*) to add, modify, or delete. When used without any qualifiers (*net group groupname*), users within that group are displayed. When used with just the qualifier /comment:*"text"*, the comment, *text,* is added to the existing *groupname* entered, where *text* can be 48 characters long and must be enclosed in quotes. The */action* qualifier either adds the *groupname* as new or deletes it. Acceptable values for */action* are /*add* or /*delete*. When using the /*add* qualifier, the /*comment:"text"* option can be used as well as in the format: *net group groupname /add /comment:"text"*.
user(s)	/*action*	Lists the *user(s)* to be added to or deleted from *groupname* based upon the *action* given. Acceptable values for */action* are /*add* or /*delete*. If more than one user is entered, separate them with a space character.
/*domain*		Can be used with any of the syntax formats and is necessary only when executing the command from a workstation that is a member of a Windows 2000 Server domain. The option causes the *net group* command to execute on the primary domain controller of the current domain. The default (without this option) is to execute the command for the local computer.

To delete the user gregh from sales1 and add the user to sales2, enter

```
net group sales1 gregh /delete
net group sales2 gregh /add
```

net localgroup COMMAND

The *net localgroup* command enables the addition, deletion, or modification of local groups. Remember that a local group can contain users from the domain in which it was created as well as global users and global groups from other domains that have a trust relationship with that domain. One difference between a local group and a global group is that the former can only be assigned privileges in its own domain, whereas the latter can be assigned privileges in trusted domains. See Table A.35 for an options list.

The three syntax formats for the *net localgroup* command are

```
net localgroup [options]
net localgroup groupname [options]
net localgroup groupname name(s) [options]
```

When the *net localgroup* command is executed without any options, the display will include the name of the server as well as the name of each local group on it.

net localgroup Command Examples

To display all the users in the group tech1, enter

```
net localgroup tech1
```

To add a comment to the record for tech1, enter

```
net localgroup tech1 /comment:"Primary Tech Support Team"
```

TABLE A.35 net localgroup Options

Option	Qualifier	Description
groupname	*/comment:"text"* or */action*	Enters the name of the local group (*groupname*) to add, modify, or delete. When used without any qualifiers (*net localgroup groupname*), the users and global groups within the local group *groupname* are displayed. When used with just the qualifier */comment:"text"*, the comment, *text,* is added to the existing *groupname* entered, where *text* can be 48 characters long and must be enclosed in quotes. The */action* qualifier either adds the *groupname* as new or deletes it. Acceptable values are */add* or */delete*. When using the */add* qualifier, the */comment:"text"* option can be used as well as in the format *net localgroup groupname /add /comment:"text"*.
name(s)	*/action*	Lists the *name(s)* to be added to or deleted from *groupname* based upon the *action* given. Acceptable values include either local users or users on trusted domains or global groups. If more than one name is entered, separate them with a space. Acceptable values are */add* or */delete*.
/domain		Can be used with any of the syntax formats and is necessary only when executing the command from a workstation that is a member of a Windows 2000 Server domain. The option causes the *net localgroup* command to execute on the primary domain controller of the current domain. The default (without this option) is to execute the command for the local computer.

To add a group called tech2 and include a comment, enter

```
net localgroup tech2 /add /comment:"Secondary Tech Support Team"
```

To add the names nancyd and phill from the helpdesk domain and global group sales2, respectively, to the tech2 local group, enter

```
net localgroup tech2 nancyd helpdesk\phill sales2 /add
```

net help COMMAND

The *net help* command provides help for the Windows 2000 net commands by listing all of the commands or by providing detailed information on a requested one. This command is discussed in more detail in the Display Commands section.

net helpmsg COMMAND

The *net helpmsg* command displays an explanation for the requested Windows 2000 error message. This command is discussed in more detail in the Display Commands section.

net name COMMAND

The *net name* command adds, deletes, or displays names that are authorized to receive messages. These names are used only for messaging and must be unique throughout the network. In Windows 2000 three types of names—computer, user, and messaging—are set up by *net name*. In order to execute this command, the Messenger service must be running. For more information please refer to the Miscellaneous Commands section.

net pause COMMAND

The *net pause* command is used to suspend a Windows 2000 service or resource. Pausing a service instead of stopping it enables current users to continue working while prohibiting new users from gaining access. System administrators will sometimes do this in order to warn users and give them an opportunity to finish what they are doing. The *net continue* command reactivates a service that has been paused. Its syntax is

```
net pause service
```

The *service* parameter is required and can be one of the following standard services. Other services may also be available depending on the configuration of your system.

- File server for Macintosh (at the Windows 2000 Server level only)
- FTP publishing service

- lpdsvc
- Net logon
- Network dde
- Network dde dsdm
- lm security support provider
- remoteboot (at the Windows 2000 Server level only)
- Remote access server
- Schedule
- Server
- Simple TCP/IP services
- Workstation

net print COMMAND

The *net print* command displays information about both printer queues and printer jobs. Print jobs can also be deleted, put on hold, or reactivated. This command is described in more detail in the Print Commands section.

net send COMMAND

The *net send* command uses the Messenger service to send messages to users, computers, and messaging names set up on the network. It is described in more detail in the Miscellaneous Commands section.

net session COMMAND

The *net session* command provides a listing of the current sessions between the local computer and its clients, and it enables an administrator to disconnect them. A session between the client and the server is established when a user contacts a server from a client computer and successfully logs on.

The syntax for *net session* is

```
net session [\\computername] [/delete]
```

The *net session* command can only be executed from a server. When run without any parameters, its display will contain the following information regarding each session on the local computer: computer name, user name, client type, number of open files, and idle time.

The *computername* parameter is the name of the computer for which you wish to list sessions. If specified, the user name, computer name, guest logon, client type, session time, idle time, and a listing of all the shared resources connected to the user are displayed. The shared resource list includes the share name, the type of resource, and the number of open files.

The /delete parameter is used to disconnect a session with the *computer-name* given. If the *computername* parameter is not used, /delete will disconnect all sessions associated with the server.

net share COMMAND

The *net share* command displays, creates, or deletes shared resources. Once created, a shared resource is available immediately and remains shared until it is deleted. See Table A.36 for an options list. There are three syntax formats for this command:

```
net share sharename [options]
net share sharename=drive:path [options]
net share {sharename | drive:path } /delete
```

When *net share* is executed without any options or parameters, it displays the share name, the device name or path, and a comment field for all shared resources on the local system.

The *sharename* parameter contains the name by which the network refers to the shared resource. The command *net share sharename* displays the share name, path, remark, maximum number of users, and users connected to the share.

TABLE A.36 net share Options

Option	Description
/delete	Stops sharing the resource identified by either *sharename* or *drive:path*.
/users:*number*	Sets the maximum number of users that can access a shared resource at the same time to *number*. This option cannot be used in conjunction with /*unlimited*.
/unlimited	Allows an unlimited number of users to access a shared resource simultaneously. This option cannot be used in conjunction with /*users:number*.
/remark:"*text*"	Defines a comment, *text,* to be associated with the shared resource. Surround the text of the comment with quotes.

To establish a directory share, use the parameter *sharename=drive:path,* where *sharename* is the network name for the directory and *drive:path* is the absolute path of the directory being shared. Remember to enclose the *drive:path* in quotes if there is a space in the directory name.

net share Command Examples

To share the directory c:\customers with the name *contacts,* limit the access to a maximum of 15 users, and include a comment, enter the following:

```
net share contacts:c:\customers /user:15 /remark:"Contact Information"
```

To remove the share when the shared resource is no longer needed

```
net share taskforce /delete
```

net statistics COMMAND

The *net statistics* command, also known as *net stats service,* displays network statistics information for either the Workstation or the Server service. The syntax is

```
net statistics [service]
```

Running *net statistics* without specifying a service will display a list of the services that are running and for which there are statistics. Acceptable values for the *service* parameter are the words "Workstation" and "Server" (not the actual name of the server or workstation).

Running *net statistics server* displays the following statistics for the local server:

- Number of sessions started, timed-out, or terminated due to an error
- Number of kilobytes sent and received
- Average response time
- Number of system errors and permission and password violations
- Number of files and communication devices accessed
- Number of print jobs spooled
- Number of times the memory buffer was exceeded

Running *net statistics workstation* displays the following statistics for the local workstation:

- Number of bytes and Server Message Blocks (SMB) received and transmitted
- Number of read and write operations
- Number of failed read and write operations
- Number of network errors

- Number of successful and failed connections to shared resources
- Number of reconnections to shared resources
- Number of sessions started, failed, and disconnected
- Number of failed operations
- Total use count and the total failed use count

net start COMMAND

The *net start* command either displays services that are currently running or starts a new service. The syntax is

```
net start service
```

Executing *net start* without the *service* parameter will provide a list of the services currently running. The *service* parameter is the name of the service you wish to start. (If that name contains more than one word, be sure to enclose it in quotes.) Table A.37 identifies the Windows 2000 services that may be started with this command along with a brief description.

net stop COMMAND

The *net stop* command stops the Windows 2000 service named. The syntax is

```
net stop service
```

Executing *net stop* without the service parameters will display a list of the valid services. The service parameter can be any of the standard services listed in Table A.37 as well as any services that were additionally installed on your system.

net time COMMAND

The *net time* command allows the user to synchronize the time across the network between the current system and another domain (or computer). It also allows the user to display the time for any system on the network. This command is described in more detail in the Miscellaneous Commands section.

net use COMMAND

The *net use* command either connects or disconnects a computer and a shared resource and displays shared resources currently connected to a computer. It has several syntax formats:

```
net use [devicename] [\\computername\sharename[\volume]] [password]
[/user:[domainname\]username] [[/delete] | [persistent:{yes | no}]]
net use devicename [/home[password]] [/delete:{yes | no}]
net use [persistent:{yes | no}]
```

TABLE A.37 Windows 2000 Services

Service	Description
Alerter	Enables alert messages to be sent to specific users and users connected to the server. Must be used in conjunction with the Messenger service.
Client Service for NetWare	Available only on Windows 2000 Workstation when Client service for NetWare has been installed. Starts the Client service for NetWare.
ClipBook Server	Enables cutting and pasting over the network.
Computer Browser	Enables computers to be browsed over the network and the computer starting the service to be browsed by other computers on the network. The alternative command is *net start browser*.
DHCP Client	Allows IP addresses to be retrieved from a DHCP (Dynamic Host Configuration Protocol) server.
Directory Replicator	Ensures that designated files are the same on all requested servers. These files and servers must be set up prior to starting this service. The alternative command is *net start replicator*.
Eventlog	Logs any type of system, security, or application event that requires a notification to be sent to users. This service cannot be stopped or paused and must be running to use the Event Viewer.
File Server for Macintosh	Allows file sharing with Macintosh computers and is only available on Windows 2000 servers.
FTP Publishing Service	Available only if the Internet Information server is installed.
Gateway Service for NetWare	Available only if the Gateway Service for NetWare is installed.
Lpdsvc	Enables UNIX clients to print via a printer connected to a Windows 2000 computer and is available only if the TCP/IP protocol has been installed.
Messenger	Enables a computer to receive messages.
Microsoft DHCP Server	Provides network clients with IP addresses and is available only on Windows 2000 servers and if both TCP/IP and the DHCP server have been installed. The alternative command is *net start dhcpserver*.
Net Logon	Verifies requests to log on and controls copies of the user accounts database in the domain. This service is started on all servers in a domain that use a copy of the domain's user accounts database. The alternative command is *net start netlogon*.
Network DDE	Starts the Network Dynamic Data Exchange service.
Network DDE DSDM	Starts the Network Dynamic Data Exchange Share Database Manager service.
Network Monitor Agent	Enables remote monitoring of a client machine's network communication.
LM Security Support Provider	Available only if the LM Security Support Provider is installed.

(continued)

TABLE A.37 Windows 2000 Services (*continued*)

Service	Description
Print Server for Macintosh	Enables printing from Macintosh computers and is available only on Windows 2000 servers.
Remoteboot	Permits networked computers to load the operating system from the server and is available only on Windows 2000 servers.
Remote Access Connection Manager	Allows remote access to the network through a dial-up connection and is available only if the Remote Access service is installed.
Remote Access ISNSAP Service	Available only if the Remote Access service is installed.
Remote Access Server	Available only if the Remote Access service is installed.
Remote Procedure Call (RPC) Locator	Allows applications to use the Microsoft RPC name service and manages the RPC name service database.
Remote Procedure Call (RPC) Service	Allows applications to use dynamic endpoints and manages the endpoint map database.
Schedule	Enables use of the *at* command to start programs at a specified time.
Server	Enables a computer to share resources on the network, such as files and printers, and provides RPC support.
Simple TCP/IP Services	Activates the TCP/IP services of Character Generator, Daytime, Discard, Echo, and Quote of the Day and is available only if TCP/IP and the simple TCP/IP service are installed.
SNMP	Enables a server to report its status to the SNMP (Simple Network Management Protocol) management system and is available only if both the TCP/IP and SNMP protocols are installed.
Spooler	Starts the spooler service.
TCP/IP NetBIOS Helper	Enables NetBIOS over the TCP/IP service and is available only if TCP/IP is installed.
UPS	Manages an uninterruptible power supply (UPS) that is connected to the computer.
Windows Internet Name Service	Enables the mapping of computer names to TCP/IP addresses for networked client systems and is available only on Windows 2000 Servers.
Workstation	Enables a computer to connect to and communicate with network resources.

Executing *net use* without any options will produce a display of all currently connected shared resources.

Table A.38 defines the options that are valid for use in all syntax formats of the *net use* command.

Another syntax format of the *net use* command is *net use persistent{yes | no}*. When *yes* is used, all current connections will be reestablished at subsequent logins. When *no* is entered, no subsequent connections will be saved and therefore will not be reestablished at subsequent logins.

net use Command Examples

To disconnect from the printer designated by LPT2:, enter

```
net use lpt2: /delete
```

To connect to the shared resource g:\Sales\Contacts as the user bosco, enter

```
net use g:\Sales\Contracts * /user:bosco
```

The asterisk forces a password to be entered at a prompt before allowing the connection to occur.

net user COMMAND

The *net user* command allows an administrator to perform many of the user management tasks from the command line or Command Prompt. It adds, modifies, and deletes user accounts, and it displays information about a specific user account or lists all user accounts on the system. Executing this command at a Windows 2000 Server will update the user accounts database on the primary domain controller. That data is then replicated to the backup domain controllers.

There are three syntax formats for this command:

```
net user [username [password]] [options] [/domain]
net user username password /add [options] [/domain]
net user username [/delete] [/domain]
```

Without any parameters or options, *net user* will display a listing of the user accounts set up for the current system. With only the *username* parameter it will display information specific to that user account. The display contains such information as the expiration date of the account, password-related information like expiration dates, the name of the user's logon script and profile, the user's home directory, the date of the last login, and the name of the account's local and global

TABLE A.38 net use Options

Option	Qualifier	Description
devicename		Enters the name of the device to be connected or disconnected. Acceptable values are D: through Z: for disk drives, LPT1: through LPT3: for printers, or an asterisk (*) to assign the next available device designation. Executing the command *net use devicename* displays information about the connection made to the shared resource, *devicename*.
computername\ *sharename*	*volume*	Enters the name of the computer that controls the shared resource for *computername,* which can be no longer than 15 characters, or for the shared resource for *sharename*. The *volume* qualifier contains the name of a volume on a NetWare server and can only be used if either Client Services for NetWare or Gateway Services for NetWare is installed.
password		Enters the password necessary to access the shared resource. Using an asterisk (*) in place of the password forces a prompt for the password, which is often preferred since the password is not visible on the screen when it is entered in response to the prompt. This option can only be used after the *computername**sharename* option.
/user:*name*		Makes the connection using the user, *name,* instead of the currently logged on user. A domain different from the current one can be specified as part of *name* (/user:*domainname**name*).
/*delete*		Disconnects the connection to the shared resource and removes it from the list of persistent connections. This option cannot be used in conjunction with /*persistent*.
/persistent:{*yes* | *no*}		Identifies whether a connection is persistent or not. Entering *yes* {*yes* | *no*} saves each connection made as a persistent connection so that it can be reestablished at each login. Entering *no* {*yes* | *no*} stops saving the current connection and all future connections so that only existing connections will be reestablished at the next login. The current persistent setting remains the default until it is changed. Once a connection is considered persistent, it can only be removed from the recurring list with the /*delete* option.
/*home*		Connects the user to his home directory.

groups. Tables A.39 and A.40 define the parameters and the options available for *net user*.

net user Command Examples

The following command sets up a user named emilyg, prompting for a password. This user is permitted to log in Monday through Friday from 8:00 A.M. to 6:00 P.M. from the workstations named incy, sales, techsupp, and mktg.

```
net user bosco * /add /times:M-F,08:00-18:00
/workstations:incy,sales,techsupp,mktg
```

To delete the user bosco from the system, enter

```
net user bosco /delete
```

To deactivate user bosco rather than delete him altogether, enter

```
net user bosco /active:no
```

TABLE A.39 net user Parameters

Option	Description
username	Enters the name of the user account to be added, changed, deleted, or displayed. A *username* can contain a maximum of 20 characters.
password	Either sets up a password for a new account or changes the password for an existing account. The password can consist of a maximum of 14 characters and must conform to the password specifications defined by the *net accounts* command. Entering an asterisk (*) instead of the actual password forces a prompt for the password, which in this instance will not be displayed on the screen while it is entered.
/domain	Specifies the command be executed on the primary domain controller of the current system's domain. This parameter should be used only from Windows 2000 workstations that are members of a Windows 2000 Server domain.
/add	Adds the user name to the user accounts database. The *password* parameter is required with this function.
/delete	Deletes the user name from the user accounts database.

TABLE A.40 net user Options

Option	Description
/active:{yes | no}	Enters *yes* to activate the user account or *no* to disable it and thus prohibit the user from accessing the server. The default is *yes*.
/comment:"*text*"	Enters a comment up to a maximum of 48 characters for *text*.
/countrycode:*nnn*	Enters the numeric value for the operating system country code for *nnn* in order to display the user's help and error messages in a different language. Zero signifies the default.
/expires:*date*	Enters the *date* the account will expire. Acceptable values are *never* (the account will never expire) or a date in the default format defined by the country code. Examples of date formats are mm/dd/yy, dd,mm,yyyy, mm,dd,yy. The month can be either numeric or alphabetic; the year can be 2 or 4 digits. Either slashes or commas can be used to separate the components of the date.
/fullname:"*name*"	Enters the user's full name for the variable *name*.
/homedir:*path*	Enters the path for the user's home directory for the variable *path*. The path specified must already exist.
/homedirreq:{yes | no}	Enters *yes* to specify that a home directory is required or *no* if not.
/passwordchg:{yes | no}	Enters *yes* to identify whether a user can change his password or *no* if not. The default is yes.
/passwordreq:{yes | no}	Enters *yes* to require a password for a user or *no* otherwise. The default is yes.
/profilepath:*path*	Enters the pathname for the user's logon profile for *path*.
/scriptpath:*path*	Enters the pathname of the user's logon script for *path*.
/times:*time*	Enters the times of day that a user can log on to the system. Acceptable values include all (a user can always log on), a space or blank (a user can never log on), and days and times in the format day, hour. Days are the days of the week either spelled out or abbreviated as M, T, W, Th, F, Sa, Su; time can be either in 12- or 24-hour format. When 12-hour format is used, use A.M. or P.M., am, pm, a.m., or p.m. to designate. Days and times are separated with commas. If multiple days and times are listed, they are separated with semicolons. There should be no spaces. For example, /times:M,8am-5pm;T,12pm-8pm;W,13:00-17:00.
/usercomment:"*text*"	Enters a comment for the variable *text*.
/workstations:*name(s)*	Substitutes for *name* a list of workstations from which a user can access the network. A maximum of eight workstations can be listed, separated by commas. An asterisk (*) allows the user to log on to the network from any computer.

net view COMMAND

The *net view* command displays the resources being shared on the computer. Depending on the parameters selected, the output is a listing of computers in the current domain or a listing of all domains in the network. The syntax can be one of the following:

```
net view \\computername
net view /domain:domainname
```

Entering *net view* without parameters will produce a list of all computers on the network. Specifying a computer name for the *computername* parameter will produce a listing of all resources that are shared with that computer. Using the /domain:*domainname* parameter and specifying a particular *domainname* will produce a listing of all resources shared with the computer in the named domain. Omitting the *domainname* will produce a listing of all domains in the network.

A special format of this command will display all the servers available on a NetWare network:

```
net view /network:nw
```

PRINT COMMANDS

Within Windows 2000 a printer can be attached to the local system or to the network. This section outlines the steps necessary to create a printer, send files to print, determine the status of a print job, manage printer operations, and define printer properties.

Creating a Printer

Here creating a printer means installing it so that it is accessible to both users and applications. Windows 2000 simplifies this process with the Add Printer Wizard, which can be accessed in three ways:

- From the **My Computer** icon, double-click the **Printers** folder.
- Select **Start** → **Settings** → **Control Panel**, then double-click the **Printers** folder.
- Select **Start** → **Settings** → **Printers**.

Printers can be created as local or as remote. To create a local printer, from the Add Printer Wizard

1. Select the **My Computer** button and click **Next**.
2. Choose the port the printer is connected to from the **Available Ports** list; then click **Next**.

3. Choose the manufacturer and printer from the lists provided; click **Next**. (Before clicking Next you may select the **Have Disk** button in order to install the printer driver at this point. If a printer driver is necessary, you will have an opportunity to install it later as well.)

4. Enter a name for the printer that your users will understand and recognize. You may also designate whether this printer will be considered the default for the system. Select **Next**.

5. If the printer is to be shared over the network, select **Shared** and either accept the shared printer name displayed or enter one that you prefer. Remember, if this printer is to be available to MS-DOS and Windows 3.x users, be sure the name is consistent with their file-naming restrictions of eight characters before a period and three characters after (filename.ext).

6. If sharing the printer over the network, select the operating systems that will be accessing it. Select **Next**.

7. Select **Yes** to print a test page; **No** to bypass it.

8. Select **Finish** to complete the installation.

9. At this point, the wizard may request that you insert the media that contains the print drivers for the operating systems that you selected. Just follow the instructions on the screen.

Creating a remote printer is often referred to as "connecting to a network printer." This printer can be new or it may have already been installed elsewhere on the network. To create a remote printer, access the Add Printer Wizard and follow the steps below.

1. Select **Network Printer Server**; click **Next**.

2. The **Connect to Printer** window displays. From the **Shared Printers** list, choose the network printer to which you wish to connect, then select **OK**.

3. Select **Finish** to complete the installation.

Sending Files to Print

To ensure that a file is printed correctly, we recommend using the print facility provided by the application that created the file. From within a Windows-based application, select the Printer icon to send a file to the default printer. To select a specific printer, select **File** → **Print** from the menu bar.

Files recognized by Windows 2000 can be dragged and dropped onto the icon for the desired printer. To accomplish this, select **Start** → **Settings** → **Printers** to display the printer icons. Then, using either Windows 2000 Explorer or the My

Computer windows, select a file and drag it to the appropriate icon in the **Printers** window; release the mouse button to drop it.

lpr COMMAND

The *lpr* command enables a user to print to a computer that is running the LPD server. Thus, a Windows 2000 user can print to a UNIX printer. The syntax is

```
lpr -Sserver -Pprinter [options] filename
```

Enter for *filename* the name of the file to be printed. All other parameters and options are described in Table A.41.

print COMMAND

The *print* command enables the user to print a text file in the background. The syntax is

```
print [/d:device] filename(s)
```

Executing *print* without any options or parameters will display a list of the files currently in the print queue.

The first parameter, /d:*device,* is optional and designates the name of the print device. Acceptable values are LPT1, LPT2, and LPT3 for parallel ports; COM1, COM2, COM3, and COM4 for serial ports; and *servername**sharename* for a network printer where *servername* is the name of the server and *sharename* is the

TABLE A.41 lpr Options

Option	Qualifier	Description
-S	*server*	Enters the name of the computer where the printer is attached for the variable *server*. This is a required parameter.
-P	*printer*	Enters the name of the printer in place of the variable *printer*. This is a required parameter.
-C	*class*	Enters the *class* of the print jobs in order to list the contents of the banner page. This is an optional parameter.
-J	*jobname*	Enters the name of this print job in place of the variable *jobname*.
-O	*option*	Describes the type of file to be printed. The default is a text file. A lower case *l* is entered to signify a binary file, such as a PostScript file. In this case the option is *–Ol*.

name of the shared printer resource. The default value for /d:*device* is PRN, which is the same as LPT1, the first parallel port.

The *filename(s)* parameter is optional and should include the name of the file or files to be printed. Multiple file names are separated by a space. If necessary, a drive designation and pathname may be entered in the format *drive:path\ filename*.

As a note of interest, PostScript files require the *copy*, not the *print*, command. For example, *copy file.ps lpt1:* prints a PostScript file on LPT1.

Print Status

To determine the status of files in the print queue, select **Start → Settings → Printers** and double-click on the appropriate printer. A status window for that printer will display containing the following information for each print job currently printing or waiting to print:

- *Document name*—at a minimum the name of the file being printed and possibly the name of the application that created the file.
- *Status*—if nothing displays in this field, the file is waiting to print; otherwise, the status messages printing, spooling, paused, or deleting are displayed.
- *Owner*—the logon name of the owner of the document.
- *Pages*—the number of pages in the document.
- *Size*—the size of the document in bytes.
- *Submitted*—the date and time the print request was submitted.
- *Port*—the port where the printer is connected.

lpq COMMAND

The *lpq* command displays status information for a print queue on a host computer running the LPD server. The syntax is

```
lpq -Sserver -Pprinter [-l]
```

TABLE A.42 lpq Options

Option	Qualifier	Description
-S	server	Enters the name of the computer with the printer attached for the qualifier *server*. This is a required parameter.
-P	printer	Enters the name of the *printer* to identify the queue for which to display status information. This parameter is required.
-l		Included only when a detailed status report is desired.

net print COMMAND

The *net print* command displays information about printer queues and printer jobs. It also deletes, suspends, or reactivates print jobs. *Net print* has two formats, the first of which is

```
net print \\computername\sharename
```

This format displays, for each print queue, name, number of jobs, and status. For each job in the queue, it displays user name, job number, size, and status. Table A.43 defines the parameters.

The second format is

```
net print [\\computername] job# [options]
```

This format either displays information about a specific job number or enables you to control network print jobs. The *computername* parameter is optional and should contain the name of the computer sharing the printer queue. The *job#* parameter is required and should contain the number of the print job in question. This number is part of the print queue listing that can be displayed using the *net print* *computername* command. The options are described in Table A.44.

net print COMMAND EXAMPLES

To display all print jobs in the marketing print queue on the computer incy, enter

```
net print \\incy\marketing
```

TABLE A.43 net print Parameters

Option	Description
computername	Enters the name of the computer sharing the print queue.
sharename	Enters the name of the specific print queue. This parameter is optional; when not entered, the *net print* *computername* command displays all print queues on this computer.

TABLE A.44 net print Options

Option	Description
/*delete*	Deletes *job#* from the printer queue.
/*hold*	Puts a hold on a *job#* that is waiting in the print queue so that it will not print but stays in the print queue until it is released or deleted.
/*release*	Releases a *job#* that has been put on hold.

To delete print job 12 from that computer, enter

```
net print \\incy 12 /delete
```

Managing Printer Operations

Once a document is in the print queue, several operations can be executed to pause and resume printing, restart documents from the beginning, and cancel documents.

PAUSING AND RESUMING A PRINTER

Pausing a printer stops printing but permits files to be accepted into the print queue. To pause a printer

1. Select **Start** → **Settings** → **Printers**.
2. Double-click the icon for the desired printer.
3. From the selected printer's window, select **Printer** → **Pause Printing**; the title bar will display "Paused."

   To resume printing, select **Printer** → **Pause Printing** from the printer's window.

PAUSING AND RESUMING PRINTING

To suspend printing

1. Select the desired document from the printer's window.
2. From the menu bar, select **Document** → **Pause**; the status column for the document will display "Paused."

   To resume printing

1. Select the paused document from the printer's window.
2. From the menu bar, select **Document** → **Resume**.

RESTARTING AND CANCELING A DOCUMENT

To restart the printing of a document from the beginning

1. Select the document to be restarted from the printer's window.
2. From the menu bar, select **Document** → **Restart**.

   To remove a document from the print queue (i.e., cancel it)

1. Select the document to be canceled from the printer's window.
2. From the menu bar, select **Document** → **Cancel**.

Defining Printer Properties

In order to define or change the default behavior of a printer, the printer properties must be modified. To do this, first select **Start** → **Settings** → **Printers** and right-click the desired printer icon. From the menu that displays, select **Properties**. Another way is to double-click on the desired printer icon to display the printer's window and then, from the menu bar, select **Printer** → **Properties**.

The Properties window contains six tabs. A brief description of each follows.

- *General*—contains comments and printer location information. It also enables you to configure a separator page or a print processor, or to print a test page.
- *Ports*—enables the addition, deletion, and configuration of ports. It can be used to create a printer pool that consists of more than one printer device of the same type connected to the same print server.
- *Scheduling*—defines when the printer is available for printing. It also has options to configure the spooler operation, such as whether to start the printing of the document before it is completely spooled.
- *Sharing*—defines whether a printer is shared over the network.
- *Security*—defines or displays parameters for permissions, auditing, and ownership.
- *Device Settings*—displays a hierarchical list of the printer's hardware features and allows them to be changed based upon the content of the printer driver.

LPD Service

The LPD Service (lpdsvc), referred to as the TCP/IP Print Service within Windows 2000, enables Windows 2000 printers to print jobs from remote clients such as UNIX systems. As part of the Resource Kit, it is installed as follows: Select **Start** → **Settings** → **Control Panel** → **Network** → **Services**. Within the **Services** window, select **Add**. From the Network Service list, select **Microsoft TCP/IP Printing**, then select **OK**. At this point follow the instructions on the screen, including inserting the Windows 2000 Server Resource Kit CD-ROM so that additional files may be installed. Once the files have been installed, restart the computer.

To start the LPD Service, select **Start** → **Settings** → **Control Panel** → **Services**. From the list, select **TCP/IP Print Server**, then click **Start**.

SEARCH COMMANDS

Windows 2000 provides commands for locating files and folders as well as a specific string of text within files. This section covers some of them.

TABLE A.45 find Options

Option	Description
/c	Outputs a count of the lines matching the string instead of the lines themselves. This option should not be used in conjunction with the /n option.
/i	Ignores differences between upper and lowercase when trying to match the string.
/n	Includes the line number of the matched line when displaying it.
/v	Displays the lines that do *not* match the string. If used in conjunction with the /c option, displays the number of lines that did *not* match the string.

find Command

The *find* command searches for a specified string of text in one or more files and displays any matches. The syntax is

```
find [options] "string" filename(s)
```

The *"string"* parameter is required and consists of the string of text that you wish to match. As in the above syntax example, the string must be enclosed in quotes and must be found in files in its entirety. It cannot be interrupted with a carriage return.

The *filename(s)* parameter is the name of one or more files to be searched, with the drive designation and path name included if necessary. Multiple file names should be separated by a space, and cannot be designated with wildcard characters. In place of a file name, the *find* command can accept input from the keyboard, from another command via a pipe, or from a file via a redirection command (<).

The *options* available for the *find* command are defined in Table A.45.

find COMMAND EXAMPLES

Enter the following to find all files on a disk that contain the word "auto":

```
dir c:\ /s | find /i "auto"
```

findstr Command

The *findstr* command is a more comprehensive search mechanism than *find*, as it will match a string of text exactly or use regular expressions to match a pattern of text. Regular expressions use both metacharacters and actual characters to define the search pattern. Table A.46 describes acceptable metacharacters, which can be used singly or in combination.

The syntax for *findstr* is

```
findstr [options] strings file(s)
```

The *strings* parameter contains the text the command is searching for in the file(s) listed. If there is more than one string of text, they must be separated with spaces. If the string itself has spaces, the */c:string* option must be used as described in Table A.47.

The *file(s)* parameter contains the name of the file(s) that will be searched and can use wildcard characters such as * and ? to designate multiple files. For example, to search all files in a particular directory, enter *.*. If necessary, this parameter can include the drive designation and the path in addition to the file name.

By default *findstr* will display the lines of the *file(s)* that match the specified *string*. This display may vary based upon the options selected, which are described in Table A.47.

TABLE A.46 Metacharacters

Character	Description
. *(period)*	Wildcard. Will match any character.
*	Repeat. Will find zero or more occurrences of the previous character or class.
^	Beginning of the line.
$	End of the line.
[*class*]	Matches any one character (*class*) enclosed in the brackets. For example, [abc] will match one of the characters a, b, or c.
[^*class*]	Matches any character (*class*) not enclosed in the brackets. For example, [^abc] will match any character except a, b, or c.
[*range*]	Will match any character within the *range,* where *range* is in the format of x-y. To match any character in the range m–p, enter [m-p].
\x	Represents the metacharacter, *x,* literally. For example, to match $ enter \$.
\<*xyz*	Matches *xyz* at the beginning of a word.
xyz\>	Matches *xyz* at the end of a word.
\<*xyz*\>	Finds anything containing the letters *xyz*.
.*	Matches any string of characters.

TABLE A.47 findstr Options

Option	Qualifier	Description
/b		Matches the string pattern if it is at the beginning of a line.
/e		Matches the string pattern if it is at the end of a line.
/l		Interprets the strings literally. In other words, it does not use metacharacters.
/c	:"*string*"	Matches the entire text defined by *string* literally. Use this option to find a string consisting of two or more words separated by spaces.
/r		Interprets metacharacters in search strings as regular expressions. This option is the default unless the /l option is included.
/s		Searches the current directory and its subdirectories for matching files.
/i		Ignores upper and lower case distinctions.
/x		Displays lines that match exactly.
/v		Displays only those lines that do not contain a match.
/n		Displays the line number before each line that matches.
/m		Displays only the file name of the file that contains a match.
/o		Displays the seek offset before each line that contains a match.
/g	:*filename*	*filename* is the name of the file that contains the search strings.
/f	:*filename*	*filename* is the name of the file that contains the file names to be searched.

findstr Command Examples

Suppose a user is looking for a particular email message with the subject "Mary's Retirement Party." To search all of her saved email messages, even those in subdirectories, and display the file name that contains the message, she enters

```
findstr /s /i /m /c:"Mary's Retirement Party" *.*
```

Now suppose a user wants to display the numbers of the lines that contain the acronym "GOSIP" in the govt.txt file. He enters

```
findstr /n GOSIP govt.txt
```

SYSTEM MANAGEMENT COMMANDS

System management commands help the system administrator keep the system running smoothly on a day-to-day basis. They include disk management, process management, password management, user and group management, and service management.

Disk Management

System administrators must keep track of how disks are being utilized and how they are performing so that they can maintain them and add new ones if necessary. Windows 2000 provides both graphical and command line functions that assist in these tasks. The graphical disk management facilities were discussed in Chapter 14, Disk Management. Here we describe their command line counterparts.

chkdsk COMMAND

The *chkdsk* command can be used by the Administrators group and provides the status of the disk as well as a list of errors. The command's options allow these errors to be corrected. For errors to be displayed and corrected accurately, the drive being checked should be locked; this means that no files are open and in use. If the drive is not locked, *chkdsk* offers the user the option of automatically executing the command at the next reboot. In this instance, any errors are automatically corrected.

The syntax for *chkdsk* is

```
chkdsk [drive:][[path\]filename] [options]
```

Running *chkdsk* without any parameters or options displays a status report for the current disk drive. The *drive:* parameter is the letter designation for the drive you want checked. For FAT file system volumes, a *path\filename* parameter can

TABLE A.48 chkdsk Options

Option	Description
/f	Fixes the errors found on the disk. The disk must be locked; if not, it will be checked at the next reboot.
/v	Displays the name of each file as it is checked.
/r	Identifies any bad sectors, then tries to recover any readable information.

TABLE A.49 chkntfs Parameters

Option	Description
/c	Checks the specified volume at boot time.
/d	Resets the default settings, except the countdown time for checking.
/t	Sets the countdown time for scheduled checking.
/x	Does not check the specified volumes.

be entered to designate one or more files to be checked for fragmentation. Wild-card characters can be used to specify multiple files.

chkntfs COMMAND

The *chkntfs* command determines when or if automatic system checking is to occur on FAT, FAT32, or NTFS volumes when the computer boots. It is launched from the Command Prompt with the following syntax:

```
chkntfs [/t[:time]] [/d][/x] [/c] volume: [...]
```

For example,

```
chkntfs /d
```

restores the default settings, and

```
chkntfs /x c: d: e:
```

excludes the c, d, and e volumes from checking.

diskperf COMMAND

The *diskperf* command starts and stops the system disk performance counters. It works in conjunction with the Performance Monitor (**Start → Programs → Administrative Tools → Performance Monitor**), and its syntax is

```
diskperf [-y[e] | -n] [\\computername]
```

When *diskperf* is executed without any parameters, it displays whether the disk performance counters have been activated. The other options are described in Table A.50.

Process Management

Process management governs the running of processes and applications on the local system. It includes such tasks as scheduling programs, terminating applica-

TABLE A.50 diskperf Options

Option	Qualifier	Description
-*y*	*e*	Flags the disk performance counters to start the next time the system is rebooted. These counters continue to collect data until they are turned off using the -*n* option. Use the *e* qualifier only to measure the performance of the drives in a striped disk set. To revert to the standard performance measurements, execute the command again with just the -*y* option.
-*n*		Stops gathering the disk performance information after the next reboot.
computername		Enters the name of the computer on which to start or stop the disk performance counters. When the -*y* or -*n* parameters are omitted, this option displays whether the performance counters have been activated for the specified computer.

tions and processes, displaying active applications and processes, and monitoring the performance of processes and the local system.

at COMMAND

The *at* command works in conjunction with the Schedule service and enables commands and programs to be executed in the background at a predefined date and time. The user executing *at* should be a member of the Administrators group on the local system. (The Schedule service is started by selecting **Start** → **Settings** → **Control Panel** → **Services**. In the **Services** window, select **Schedule** and hit the Start button.)

The two syntax formats for the *at* command are

```
at [\\computername] [[id] [/delete [/yes]]]
at [\\computername] time [/interactive] [/every:date | /next:date]
"command"
```

When *at* is executed without any options, it performs two functions. First it displays a list of the scheduled commands with their status, identification number, and day and time to be executed. Second, it synchronizes the scheduler with the system clock to ensure that the commands will be executed at the proper time, especially after the system clock has been adjusted.

Both required and optional parameters are described in Table A.51.

TABLE A.51 at Parameters

Option	Description
computername	Enters the name of the remote system on which to schedule the command. The default (without the parameter) is the local system.
id	Enters the identification number of the scheduled command that is displayed when the *at* command is run without parameters. To display information specific to this particular job number, enter the command *at id*.
/*delete*	Deletes the scheduled command represented by *id* or deletes all scheduled commands on the computer. Use the /*yes* parameter in conjunction with /*delete* to automatically respond "yes" to any prompts that /*delete* provides.
time	Enters the time a command is to run using the format of hours:minutes, where acceptable values are 00:00 through 23:59. The hours must be in 24-hour format.
/*interactive*	Permits the scheduled command to interact with a logged on user's desktop while the command is running. Use this option only when you know that a user will be logged on. It is not a good idea to use it when scheduling off-hours backups.
/every:*date*	Executes the scheduled command on every specified day of the week (M, T, W, Th, F, S, Su) or specified days of the month (1 through 31). Separate multiple date entries with commas. The default is the current date.
/next:*date*	Executes the scheduled command on the next specified day of the week (M, T, W, Th, F, S, Su) or next specified days of the month (1 through 31). Separate multiple date entries with commas. The default is the current date.
"*command*"	Enters the command to be run at the scheduled day and time, where *command* is a Windows 2000 command, a program (files with extensions .exe or .com), or a batch program (files with extensions .bat or .cmd). All types of commands except those with an .exe extension should be preceded by *cmd /c*. Use only absolute pathnames when path names are required. When specifying remote computers, use the *computername\sharename* designation rather than the assigned remote drive letter. Enclose the command in quotes.

Since the *at* command runs in the background, it is a good idea to redirect its results to a file using the redirection symbol (>).

at Command Examples

To display the network statistics for the server every Monday, Wednesday, and Friday at 10:00 A.M., enter the following:

```
at 10:00 /every:M,W,F "net statistics server > srvrstat"
```

The srvrstat file will be placed in the system's root directory.

To delete a scheduled job, first determine the ID number by running the *at* command without any options. If, say, the ID number is 3, enter the following

```
at 3 /delete
```

TASK MANAGER

The Task Manager enables a user to display and control the processes and applications running on the local system. It also allows the user to monitor the system performance.

To access the Task Manager, right-click in an open area of the the task bar and select this application. The task bar displays at the bottom of the screen by default and displays the **Start menu** button as well as a list of the open windows on the desktop.

There are three tabs within the Task Manager: Applications, Processes, and Performance. Each of these will be discussed briefly.

Applications

The Applications tab displays the name and status of any applications currently running on the local computer. It offers three functions: ending a task, switching to a task, and starting a new task.

Ending a task is the same as terminating an application. To do it

1. Select the application you wish to terminate.
2. Click on the **End Task** button

As an alternative to selecting a task from the task bar, the Task Manager can switch to another task in this way:

1. Select the application you wish to switch to.
2. Click on the **Switch To** button.

Rather than starting a task from the desktop or from the Start menu, the Task Manager can start a new program as follows:

1. Select the **New Task** button.
2. Enter the name of the new task or select **Browse** and browse through the available programs to select one.

Processes

The Processes tab offers information about the processes currently running on the local system. The default information for each process includes name, ID number, CPU and CPU time, and memory usage. To display additional or different information, select **View** → **Select Columns** from the menu bar.

To end, or kill, a process, first select it and then click the **End Process** button at the bottom of the window. Or right-click the process and select **End Process** from the menu that displays. Also see the **Process View** and **kill.exe** options described in the Resource Kit Support Tool section.

To change the priority for a process, right-click on the process. From the menu that displays, select **Set Priority**, and then choose Realtime, High, Normal, or Low.

Performance

The Performance tab allows the user to monitor the performance of the local computer. Information, displayed numerically or graphically, includes CPU usage and history; memory usage and history; total number of threads, handles, and processes; and physical and kernel memory.

Windows 2000 also provides a configurable Performance Monitor that can be accessed by selecting **Start → Programs → Administrative Tools → Performance**.

Other System Management Tools

This section briefly discusses other system management tools that are of interest to administrators and users.

LOGGING OFF OF THE SYSTEM

To log off of the system, press **Ctrl-Alt-Del** to display the **Windows 2000 Security** window. Then select the **Logoff** button. You can log in again as the same or as a different user.

SHUTTING DOWN THE SYSTEM

There are two ways to shut down the system: Select **Start → Shutdown** or select **Shutdown** from the **Windows 2000 Security** window, which is accessed via **Ctrl-Alt-Del**.

ENVIRONMENT VARIABLES

There are times when a user or an administrator must define or change system environment variables, such as default paths, and temporary directories. To do this, select **Start → Settings → Control Panel → System**, and within the **System Properties** window select the **Environment** tab. Only administrators may change **System Variables**, but users or administrators may change **User Variables**.

To change a variable, select it and it will display in the **Variable** and **Value** fields at the bottom of the screen. Make whatever changes are necessary, and then select **Set**.

To add a variable, just enter its name and value in the appropriate fields and then select **Set**.

To delete an environment variable, select it and then select **Delete**. In all cases, select **OK** to exit the window. Changes made to system variables are effective the next time the computer is restarted. Changes made to user variables are effective the next time the user logs on to the computer.

RESOURCE KIT SUPPORT TOOLS

The Resource Kit provides a variety of Support Tools that can aid in system administration activities. As they are optional, we provide only an overview of each. Please note that their inclusion or exclusion in the Resource Kit is subject to change. Unless otherwise noted, these tools are launched from the **Command Prompt** or the **Start** → **Run** menu. They are described in alphabetical order.

acldiag.exe—ACL Diagnostics

This tool troubleshoots issues associated with Active Directory permissions associated with object access control lists. It reads ACL security attributes and outputs the results in either text or tab-delimited format for review with a text editor or spreadsheet. The command syntax is as follows:

```
acldiag "ObjectDN" [/chkdeleg] [/fixdeleg] [/geteffective:{User | Group}]
[/schema] [/skip] [/tdo]
```

ObjectDN refers to the distinguished name of the object and must be included in quote marks. Other *acldiag.exe* required and optional parameters are described in Table A.52.

TABLE A.52 acldiag Parameters

Option	Description
/chkdeleg	Checks the security on the object to view delegation templates currently in use by the Delegation of Control wizard in the Active Directory Users and Computers snap-in.
/fixdeleg	Fixes any applied delegations by the Delegation of Control wizard.
/geteffective: {user | group}	Outputs effective permissions of the specified user or group in a text-readable format. The wildcard (*) for *user* or *group* prints the effective rights of all users and groups in the ACL.
/schema	Verifies if the object's security includes schema defaults.
/skip	Suppresses security descriptions.
/tdo	Outputs in tab-delimited format for use in databases or spreadsheets.

adsiedit.msc—ADSI Editor

The ADSI development tool is described in Chapter 5.

apcompat.exe—Application Compatibility Tool

The Application compatibility tool determines if a specified application can be used in a Windows 2000 environment. It is described in Chapter 2.

apmstat.exe—Advanced Power Management Status

This tool provides the status of Advanced Power Management (APM) features and is primarily intended to support older notebook computers. The Advanced Configuration and Power Interface (ACPI) is the default power management scheme for Windows 2000.

The syntax for *apmstat.exe* is

```
Admstat [-v]
```

where -v is used to output the verbose version.

clonepr.dll—Clone Principal

This tool moves users from Windows NT to Windows 2000 and is particularly helpful when incremental movement is desired. It also provides an emergency fallback to the older Windows NT policies if Windows 2000 fails during the migration period. *Clonepr.dll* must be run on the destination Windows 2000 domain controller, on which objects are duplicated (not moved) from the Windows NT domain controller. It can only be applied within a domain. While *clonepr.dll* does not recognize the user's password, it works in connection with the *Movetree* support tool, which does retain the password.

The following files are required to use the Clone Principal.

- *Clonepr.dll*—A COM object to support ClonePrincipal operations.
- *Clonegg.vbs*—A sample script to clone Global groups in a domain.
- *Cloneggu.vbs*—A sample script to clone all the Global groups and users.
- *Clonelg.vbs*—A sample script to clone all the Local groups in a domain.
- *Clonepr.vbs*—A sample script to clone a single security principal.
- *Sidhist.vbs*—A sample script to add the SID of a source account to the SID History of a destination account.

For more information on the Clone Principal refer to the *ClonePrincipal User Guide (clonepr.doc)* shipped with the Resource Kit.

dcdiag.exe—Domain Controller Diagnostic Tool

This utility analyzes domain controllers and identifies abnormal behavior in the system. It is used in the review of domain controller problems such as connectivity, replication, topology, logon rights, domain controller locator, intersite state, and trust verification.

The *dcdiag.exe* syntax is

```
dcdiag /s:DomainController [/n:NamingContext] [/u:Domain\Username
/p:{* | Password | ""}] [{/a | /e}] [{/q | /v}] [/i] [/f:LogFile]
[/ferr:ErrLog] [/c [/skip:Test]] [/test:Test] [{/h | /?}]
```

TABLE A.53 dcdiag Parameters

Option	Description
/n:*NamingContext*	Defines the type of naming—NetBIOS, DNS, or Distinguished Name.
/s:*DomainController*	Utilizes the home service.
/u:*Domain\Username* /p:{* | *Password* | ""}	Employs the *Domain\Username* credentials and binds with the password, where "" is a null password and * prompts for a password.
/a	Tests all site servers.
/e	Tests all servers enterprise-wide and overrides /a.
/q	Prints out messages in quiet mode.
/v	Prints information in verbose or extended mode.
/f:*logfile*	Redirects the output to a specified log file.
/ferr:*Errlog*	Redirects only fatal errors to a designated error log.
/c	Runs a comprehensive (all) tests .. /skip is also used it will ignore those tests that are specified.
/skip:*test*	Skips the specified test.
/test:*test*	Runs only the test specified. The following tests are valid: *Connectivity*—tests if the domain controller is DNS registered and has connectivity. *Replications*—checks for timely domain controller replication. *Topology*—checks that the topology is connected for all domain controllers. *CutoffServers*—checks for any down replication domain controller. *NetLogons*—checks for appropriate replication logon privileges. *LocatorGetDc*—checks each domain controller promoting its capabilities. *Intersite*—checks for failures that would prevent intersite replication. *RolesHeld*—checks that global role-holders can be located and responding. *RidManager*—checks to see if RID master is accessible with information. *MachineAccount*—checks if the machine account has the proper information. *Services*—checks if appropriate domain controller services are running. *OutboundSecureChannels*—checks that secure channels exist. *ObjectsReplicated*—checks for replication of machine account and DSA objects.
{/h | /?}	Displays the proper syntax options within the Command Prompt.

depend.exe—Dependency Walker

The Dependency Walker is launched from the Command Prompt by invoking *depend.exe*. It is used to ascertain dependencies for applications and DLLs and is discussed in Chapter 2.

dfsutil.exe—Distributed File System Utility

This tool permits the Command Prompt to query the Distributed File System (Dfs). It is used for Dfs root maintenance and troubleshooting, and helps remove metadata left after removal of a domain-level Dfs root.

The syntax for *Dfsutil.exe* is

```
Dfsutil [option(s)]
```

TABLE A.54 Dfsutil.exe Parameters

Option	Description
/list:*Domain* [/dcname:*DcName*]	Outputs the Dfs in the domains that are fully qualified, with the Active Directory domain name defining a specific domain controller.
/view:*dfsname**dfsshare* [/dcname:*DcName*] [/level:*Level*]	Displays the metadata in *dfsname**dfsshare* and dumps the Active Directory-based Partition Knowledge Table (PKT) that shows the Dfs tree for each computer directory and site location. The |**more** pipe command can be used. The */dcname* option defines a specific domain controller and */level* specifies the level of viewing material, with the highest providing greater detail.
/verify:*dfsname**dfsshare* [/dcname:*DcName*] [/level:*Level*]	Verifies metadata in *dfnsame**dfshare*. The */dcname* option defines a specific domain controller and */level* specifies the level of viewing material, with the highest providing greater detail.
/reinit:*ServerName*	Reestablishes or refreshes the Dfs server name.
/whatis:*ServerName*	Displays the type of the specified server.
/dfsalt:*UNCPath*	Resolves the UNC path for the server.
/clean:ServerName	Removes the Dfs designation within the registry of the defined server.
/dclist:*Domain*	Lists all the domain controllers in the defined domain.
/trusts:*Domain*	Lists the trust relationships of the specified domains.
/pktinfo [/dfs] [/level:*Level*]	Shows the Partition Kit Table for the designated Dfs.
/pktflush[:*EntryToFlush*]	Removes or flushes Partition Kit Table entries.
/spcinfo [/all]	Outputs the SPC information—the */all* switch outputs all the data.
/spcflush[:*EntrytoFlush*]	Removes or flushes the SPC data.

dnscmd.exe—DNS Troubleshooting Tool

This administrative tool is used to view and diagnosis DNS settings and properties of DNS servers, zones, and resource records. The syntax is

```
dnscmd ServerName Command [Command Parameters]
```

TABLE A.55 dnscmd.exe Parameters

Option	Description
ServerName	Specifies the server to be managed.
IP address	Specifies the IP address.
Command	Defines the command desired from the following options:
	/Info—provides DNS server properties.
	/Config—resets server or zone configuration.
	/Statistics—provides server statistics data.
	/ClearCache—clears the cache for a DNS server.
	/WriteBackFile—writes back all data for the specified zone.
	/StartScavenging—initiates server scavenging.
	/ResetListenAddresses—resets/selects server IP address(es).
	/ResetForwarders—resets/selects and forwards IP address(es).
	/EnumZone—enumerates zones on the DNS server.
	/ZoneInfo—displays zone data.
	/ZoneAdd—creates a new zone.
	/ZoneDelete—deletes a specified zone.
	/ZonePause—pauses the specified zone.
	/ZoneResumes—resumes the specified zone.
	/ZoneReload—reloads the specified zone from its database.
	/ZoneWriteBack—writes back the specified zone to the file.
	/ZoneRefresh—forces a refresh of the secondary zone.
	/ZoneUpdateFromDs—updates the specified DS integrated zone by data from DS.
	/ZoneResetType—changes a type of the specified zone.
	/ZoneResetSecondaries—sets/resets a notify list for the specified zone.
	/ZoneResetScavengeServers—resets scavenging servers for a zone.
	/EnumRecords—enumerate records at a name.
	/RecordAdd—creates a record in the specified zone on the DNS server.
	/RecordDelete—deletes a record from the specified zone on the DNS server.
	/NodeDelete—deletes all records at a name from the specified zone, RootHints, or Cache at the specified DNS server.
	/Restart—restarts the DNS server.
	/AgeAllRecords—forces timestamping and aging on a zone.

TABLE A.56 dsacls.exe Parameters

Option	Description
/a	Outputs permissions, ownership, and auditing data.
/d	Denies permissions for the specified user or group.
/g	Grants permissions for the specific user or group.
/i:{c | o | i | p}	Specifies the inheritance—**p** = propagate inheritable permissions one level only; **s** = subobjects only; **t** = this object and subobjects.
/n	Replaces the object permissions.
/p	Sets the object as protected (**y** = yes) or not (**n** = no). Lacking the **/p** option, the current protection flag is preserved.
/r	Removes the security permissions for specified user or group.
/s	Restores the security permissions for the specified user or group.
/t	Restores the security permissions for the object tree.
/?	Output to syntax options.

dsacls.exe—dsacls

This tool is used to manage Access Control Lists. It permits the manipulation of security attributes for Active Directory objects and serves as a command line alternative to the Active Directory snap-in tools.

The *dsacls.exe* command syntax is as follows:

```
dsacls object [/a] [/d {user | group}:permissions [...]] [/g {user |
group}:permissions [...]] [/i:{p | s | t}] [/n] [/p:{y | n}] [/r {user
| group} [...]] [/s [/t]] [/?]
```

dsastat.exe—dsastat

This tool compares naming contexts on domain controllers and detects differences. In the case of a Global Catalog it compares two directory trees within the same or different domains, gathering capacity statistics that include megabytes per server, objects per server, megabytes per object class, and attribute comparisons for replicated objects.

The syntax for *dsastat.exe* is

```
dsastat [/?] [-loglevel:option] [-output:option] [-f:filename] [-
s:servername[portnumber][;servername[portnumber];...]] [-t:option] [-
sort:option] [-p:entrynumber] [-b:searchpath] [-filter:ldapfilter]
[-gcattrs:option[;option;...]]
```

TABLE A.57 dsastat.exe Parameters

Option	Description
/?	Displays the syntax options.
-loglevel:option	Establishes the extent of logging performed during execution. The valid *option* values are INFO (default), TRACE, and DEBUG.
-output:option	Sets where the output of DsaStat is displayed. The valid *option* values are SCREEN (default), FILE, or BOTH.
-f:filename	Sets the name for the initialization file to use for parameters if not user-specified
-s:servername[portnumber][;servername[portnumber]]	Sets the name of servers to be compared, separated by a semicolon. The server name can include the IP port number. The default port number is the default LDAP port (389).
-t:option	Determines if a full or statistical comparison is to be made. The option TRUE is for statistical; FALSE is for a complete content comparison.
-sort:option	Determines if the GUID is to be used as the sorting basis. The option TRUE will sort by GUID; FALSE will not.
-p:entrynumber	Sets the page size for ldap-search from 1–999, with 54 as the default.
-filter:ldapfilter	Sets the LDAP filter used in the LDAP search operation. The default is "(objectclass=*)".
-b:searchpath	Uses the Distinguished Name as the basis of comparison and allows reviews of all subtrees.
-gcattrs:option[;option;...]	Specifies attributes to be returned for the search.

dskprobe.exe—Disk Probe

The *dskprobe.exe* command launches the graphical Disk Probe application discussed in Chapter 14.

dumpchk.exe—Dump Check

This is a debugging tool used to review crash and other system dumps. Its syntax is as follows:

```
dumpchk [-v] [-p] [-c] [-x] [-e] [-y] [-?] CrashDumpFile
```

TABLE A.58 dumpchk.exe Parameters

Option	Description
-e	Performs a dump examination.
-c	Validates the dump file.
-v	Outputs in verbose mode.
-x	Performs extra dump file examination.
-y	Sets the path to the symbols file.

filever.exe—File Version Verification

This is a command line utility employed to verify the version level of an .exe of .dll file. The syntax is as follows:

```
filever [/s] [/v] [/e] [/x] [/b] [/a] [/d] [[drive:][path][filename]]
```

gflags.exe—Global Flags

The *gflags* command launches a graphical application used by system administrators and developers to edit NTGlobalFlag. This command is used to modify the current flags for the kernel or the global Registry.

CAUTION   Modifying global flags is not advised except by the most experienced developer or system administrator. Consult with Microsoft Professional Services when doing this, as flag changes that are inappropriately applied can damage your system.

TABLE A.59 dumpchk.exe Parameters

Option	Description
/a	Does not display attributes.
/b	Outputs a bare format with directories.
/d	Does not display time and date.
/e	Lists executable components only.
/s	Shows all directories and subdirectories.
/v	Uses verbose mode.
/x	Generates a short name for even now non-8.3-based names.

TABLE A.60 gflag.exe Parameters

Option	Description
-i	Operates on the specified image.
-I	Launches the command line for a specified flag.
-r	Displays Registry settings.
-k	Operates on the kernel settings.

The syntax used for *gflags* is

```
gflag [-r [flag [maxdepth]] [-k [flag]] [-i ImageFileName [flag]] [-l
flag commandline...]
```

The global flag abbreviations are

- *kst*—create kernel mode stack trace database.
- *ust*—Create user mode stack trace database
- *dic*—debug Initial Command.
- *dwl*—debug WINLOGON.
- *dhc*—disable Heap Coalesce on Free.
- *ddp*—disable kernel mode DbgPrint output.
- *dps*—disable paging of kernel stacks.
- *dpd*—disable protected DLL verification.
- *ece*—enable Close Exception.
- *d32*—enable Win32 Subsystem debugging.
- *eel*—enable Exception Logging.
- *hat*—enable Heap API Call Tracing.
- *hfc*—enable heap free checking.
- *hpc*—enable heap parameter checking.
- *htg*—enable heap tagging.
- *htd*—enable Heap Tagging by DLL.
- *htc*—enable heap tail checking.
- *hvc*—enable heap validation on call.
- *ksl*—enable loading of kernel debugger symbols.
- *eot*—enable Object Handle Type Tagging.
- *pfc*—enable pool free checking.
- *ptg*—enable pool tagging.
- *ptc*—enable pool tail checking.

- *otl*—maintain a list of objects for each type.
- *hpa*—place heap allocations at ends of pages.
- *sls*—Show Loader Snaps.
- *soe*—Stop On Exception.
- *shg*—Stop on Hung GUI.
- *idp*—unused.

kill.exe—Task Killing Utility

This command line utility is employed to terminate one or more processes, using the Process identification number (PID) to recognize them. See the Tlist.exe to view the tasks.

The syntax for the *kill.exe* utility is

```
kill [/f] {process_id | pattern}
```

The */f* option forces termination.

ksetup.exe—Kerberos Client Configuration

KSetup is a command line tool that configures Windows 2000 Server or Professional clients used by an MIT Kerberos server. The Windows 2000 client employs a Kerberos realm (instead of a Windows 2000 domain), which establishes a single signon to the Key Distribution Center (KDC) and a local Windows 2000 client account.

The syntax for *ksetup.exe* is as follows:

```
ksetup [/SetRealm DnsDomainName] [/MapUser Principal Account] [/AddKdc
RealmName KdcName] [/DelKdc RealmName KdcName] [/AddKpasswd Realmname
KpasswdName] [/DelKpasswd Realmname KpasswdName] [/Server Servername]
[/SetComputerPassword Password] [/Domain DomainName] [/ChangePassword
OldPasswd NewPasswd][/?][/Help]
```

ktpass.exe—Kerberos Tab Key Setup

The command line *ktpass.exe* is a configuration utility that creates Kerberos keytab Ktpass files. It generates a mapping of password and account names for UNIX services that utilize Windows 2000 KDCs. Along with the Trustdom.exe utility, they establish Kerberos interoperability by creating a shared key between UNIX and Windows 2000 Kerberos services.

The syntax for *ktpass.exe* is

```
ktpass /out filename /princ username [/mapuser] [/in filename]
[/crpyto type] [/ptype type] [/keyno keynum] [/?]
```

TABLE A.61 ksetup.exe Parameters

Option	Description
/AddKdc Realmname Kdcname	Adds the Kpasswd server address for a realm.
/ChangePassword OldPasswd NewPasswd	Changes a logged-on user's password via Kpassword.
/DelKdc RealmName KdcName	Deletes instance(s) of the KDC address for the realm.
/DelKpasswd Realmname KpasswdName	Deletes the Kpasswd server address for a realm.
/Domain DnsDomainName	Uses the current domain if no domain name is set.
/MapUser KerbName LocalName	Maps the name of a Kerberos principal and an account (* = any/all).
/SetComputerPassword Passwd	Sets the local computer password.
/SetRealm DnsDomainName	Establishes /SetRealm DnsDomainName.
/Server servername	Sets the target Windows 2000 server that will be changed.

TABLE A.62 ktpass.exe Parameters

Option	Description
/crypto [DES-CBC-CRC | DES-CBC-MD5]	Establishes the cryptographic type—DES-CBC-CRC is the default.
/DesOnly	Establishes the use of DES only.
/in	The keytab to digest or read.
/kvno	The key version number—the default is 1.
/mapOp	The mapping attribute—add: add value (default) or set: set value.
/mapuser	Maps the user of the Kerberos principal to a local account; this is done by default.
/out	Sets the name of the Krb5 keytable file. This keytable file is transferred to the UNIX system and then merged with (or replaces) the /etc/krb5/keytab.
/pass	Sets password for the principle. The wildcard * prompts for the password.
/princ	Inputs the principal name in the form user@REALM, for example, "example" or "host/unix.com".
/ptype [KRB5_NT_PRINCIPAL | KRB5_NT_SRV_INST | KRB5_NT_SRV_HST]	Specifies the principal type: KRB5_NT_PRINCIPAL for the general type and the name of the principal is recommended; KRB5_NT_SRV_INST for user service instance; or KRB5_NT_SRV_HST for host service instance.

ldp.exe—LDAP Tool

The *Ldp.exe* tool launches a graphical utility for performing LDAP (Lightweight Directory Access Protocol) functions. These functions include connect, bind, search, modify, add, and delete against any LDAP-compatible directory, such as the Active Directory.

memsnap.exe—Memory Profiling Tool

The *memsnap.exe* utility is used to capture information about the memory utilized by active processes. This data is dumped to a log. The syntax of *memsnap.exe* is as follows:

```
memsnap [-t] [-g] [-?] [logfile]
```

The *-t* option adds tags for Greenwich mean time (GMT), date, and computer name. The *-g* option adds GDI and USER resource counts.

movetree.exe—Movetree Object Manager

The command line *movetree.exe* interfaces with the Active Directory Object Manager (MoveTree) that allows the movement of Active Directory objects such as domains within a tree or organizational units. When organizational units are moved, the linked grouped policies remain intact. Universal groups are moved intact during a movetree.exe operation, whereas local and domain global groups are not moved at all with this utility. Other objects that can not be moved with movetree include

- System objects that identified by the objectClass as systemOnly
- Configuration or schema naming contexts objects
- Special container objects in the domain including Builtin, ForeignSecurity-Principal, System, and LostAndFound
- Domain controllers
- Objects with the same name as an object that exists in the target domain

The syntax for the *movetree.exe* utility is

```
movetree {/start | /startnocheck | /continue | /check} /s SrcDSA /d
DstDSA /sdn SrcDN /ddn DstDN [/u [Domain\]Username /p Password]
[/verbose] [{/? | /help}]
```

TABLE A.63 movetree.exe Parameters

Option	Description
/check	Performs a test of MoveTree before actually moving. The reports provide an opportunity to correct noted errors.
/continue	Continues to the move effort even after it is paused or a network failure occurs.
/d Destination DSA	Sets the fully qualified primary DNS name of the destination server.
/ddn DestinationDN	Sets the full distinguished name for the destination server subtree.
/s SrcDSA	Sets the DNS of the source server.
/sdn SrcDN	Sets the full distinguished name for the source server subtree.
/start	Starts the MoveTree operation with the /check option.
/startnocheck	Starts without the /check option.
/u [Domain\]Username /p Password	Launches MoveTree with the specified user and password account.
/verbose	Uses the verbose mode.

msinfo32.exe—MS System Information Tool

The *msinfo32.exe* utility gathers system configuration data including hardware, software, and other system components. It is used to rapidly gather data necessary to resolve system conflicts or other problems.

The syntax for *msinfo32.exe* is as follows:

```
msinfo32 [/?] [/report filename] [/s filename] [/info filename]
[/computer computername] [/categories +|- category name(s)]
```

TABLE A.64 msinfo32.exe Parameters

Option	Description
/computer computername	Establishes the computer to be analyzed.
/categories +|-categoryname(s)	Sets the category of data to be retrieved for the output report.
/report filename	Saves the report in the specified text file.
/s filename	Saves the report in a System Information file.

netdiag.exe—Network Connectivity Tester

The *netdiag.exe* command line diagnostic tool identifies network connectivity problems and tests network client connectivity. Its syntax is

```
netdiag [/q] [/v] [/l] [/debug] [/d:DomainName] [/fix] [/DcAccountEnum]
        [/test:testname] [/skip:testname]
```

TABLE A.65 netdiag.exe Parameters

Option	Description
/d:DomainName	Locates the specified domain.
/debug	Place in debug mode and output more data that even the verbose mode.
/DcAccountEnum	Enumerates domain controller accounts.
/fix	Fixes any identified minor problems automatically.
/l	Outputs results to the netdiag.log log file.
/q	Uses quiet mode and outputs errors only.
/skip:TestName	Skips the named test among those listed below:
	• *Autonet*—Automatic Private IP Addressing (APIPA) address test
	• *Bindings*—bindings test
	• *Browser*—redirect and browser test
	• *DcList*—domain controller list test
	• *DefGw*—default gateway test
	• *DNS*—DNS test
	• *DsGetDc*—domain controller discovery test
	• *IpConfig*—IP address configuration test
	• *IpLoopBk*—IP address loopback ping test
	• *IPX*—IPX test
	• *Kerberos*—Kerberos test
	• *Ldap*—LDAP test
	• *Modem*—modem diagnostics test
	• *NbtNm*—NetBT name test
	• *Netstat*—netstat information test
	• *Netware*—netware test
	• *Route*—routing table test
	• *Trust*—trust relationship test
	• *WAN*—WAN configuration test
	• *WINS*—WINS service test
	• *Winsock*—Winsock test
/test:TestName	Performs the specified test. The optional tests are the same as those listed in the /*skip* option.
/v	Outputs in verbose mode.

netdom.exe—Domain Manager

The *netdom.exe* command line utility manages domains and trust relationships. It can be used to join Windows 2000 domains to either a Windows NT or Windows 2000 domain and to create one-way explicit trusts. Relationships can be viewed and displayed.

The syntax for the *netdom.exe* utility is as follows:

```
netdom command object [/D:domain] [options]
```

NOTE
This command should be used only by the most knowledgeable system administrator. We recommend that the graphical Active Directory snap-in tools be utilized while gaining familiarity with Windows 2000 domains. The options available for this utility are expansive. If you use it, refer to the published information supplied for the Netdom Resource Kit Support Tool.

nltest.exe—Network Domain Test

The *nltest.exe* utility identifies domain controllers and trust relationships. It can also be used to force a shutdown and to synchronize Windows NT 4.0 user accounts. The syntax is as follows:

```
nltest [option] ...
```

pmon.exe—Process Monitor

The *pmon.exe* command launches the Process Monitor, which examines processes to identify problems like memory leaks. Chapter 2 has more information on process monitoring.

pviewer.exe—Process Viewer

The *pviewer.exe* command launches the Process Viewer. It is used to view processes and identify problems such as memory leaks. See Chapter 2 for more information on process monitoring.

TABLE A.66 nltest.exe Parameters

Option	Description
/SERVER:ServerName	Directs nltest to a specified remote computer.
/QUERY	Verifies the health of the named *Servername* domain controller.
/REPL	Forces a partial replication on the local system or the *Servername*.
/SYNC	Forces a full replication on the local system or the *Servername*.
/SC_QUERY:DomainName	Verifies the secure channel.
/SC_RESET:DomainName	Resets the secure channel between Windows 2000 computers.
/DCLIST:DomainName	Lists all domain controllers—Windows 2000, PDC, and BDC.
/TRANSPORT_NOTIFY	Notifies of a new transport.
/USER:UserName	Displays user account attributes.
/LOGON_QUERY	Outputs the cumulative number of logon attempts.
/PARENTDOMAIN	Identifies the parent domain.
/BDC_QUERY:DomainName	Identifies all domain BDCs and their current state of replication.
/SHUTDOWN:Reason [Seconds]	Shuts down in the specified time period.
/SHUTDOWN_ABORT	Aborts the shutdown command.

repadmin.exe—Replication Diagnosis Tool

The *repadmin.exe* command line utility permits the administrator to view the replication topology (also called RepsFrom and RepsTo) from each domain controller and can be used to manually create the replication topology. The syntax is as follows:

```
repadmin command arguments [/u:[domain\]user /pw:{password|*}]
```

Here *command* represents one of the commands listed in Table A.67, and *arguments* specifies the *command*'s arguments.

TABLE A.67 repadmin.exe Parameters

Option	Description
/u:[domain\]user	Sets an optional user as the administrator.
/pw:{password|}*	Sets the password for the alternate administrator set with the */u* option.
/sync name-context Destination_DSA Source_ DSA_UUID [/force] [/async] [/full] [/addref] [/allsources]	Starts the replication with following options: • /force—overrides the normal replication schedule. • /async—starts the replication but does not wait for [/full] [/addref] the replication event to complete. • /full—forces a full replication of all objects.
/showreps [Naming_Context] [DSA [Source_DSA_UUID]] [/verbose] [/unreplicated] [/nocache]	Outputs the replication partners.
/showmeta Object_DN [DSA] [/nocache]	Shows the metadata for Active Directory objects.
/?	Outputs all optional commands.

replmon.exe—Replication Monitor

The *replmon.exe* command launches the graphical Replication Monitor snap-in tool, which provides a view of Active Directory replication status and topology. It can also be used to force replication, as discussed in Chapter 6.

rsdiag.exe—Remote Storage Diagnosis Tool

The *rsdiag.exe* command line utility is used to view diagnostic information about jobs, managed NTFS volumes, removable media, and other remote storage data. The syntax is

```
rsdiag [/c jobname] [/d filetype fullpath&filename] [/e errorcode]
[/i] [/j [jobname]] [/m] [/r [/f]] [/s] [/t] [/v [driveletter]] [/x
queuedrecall] [/w fullpath&filename]
```

TABLE A.68 rsdiag.exe Parameters

Option	Description
/c *jobname*	Cancels the specified job.
/d *filetype fullpath&filename*	Converts the database to a text file. The file type identifies the source file type from among the following (*fullpath&filename* must include the full path):
	• **e**—Engine database
	• **f**—File System Agent database
	• **a**—File System Agent collection
	• **n**—Engine collection
	• **s**—Subsystem collection
/i	Identifies the version data.
/j *[jobname]*	Specifies the job to be output. If not specified, all jobs are output.
/m	Displays the volumes that can be managed.
/s	Outputs physical storage information.
/t	Loads the trace files.
/v *[driveletter]*	Displays extended information about the specified drive.

sdcheck.exe—Security Descriptor Check Utility

The *sdcheck.exe* command line tool outputs the security descriptor for any Active Directory object stored. This descriptor contains the object's ACL.

The syntax for sdcheck.exe utility is as follows:

```
sdcheck Server Object [-dumpSD] [-dumpAll] [-debug] [[-domain:
DomainName] - user: UserName -password: Password] [/?]
```

TABLE A.69 sdcheck.exe Parameters

Option	Description
-dumpSD	Outputs the security descriptor of the specified object only.
-dumpSD	Outputs the security descriptor of the object and its parents.
-domain: DomainName	Specifies the domain for the object.
-user: UserName	Specifies a user other than the one currently logged.
-password: Password	Identifies the password for the specified user.

TABLE A.70 sidwalk.exe Parameters

Option	Description
/l file	Creates a converter file as named.
/f [path]	Scans all directories unless the path is set, then only the subtree directories are scanned.
/g	Scans local groups.
/p	Scans shared printers.
/r	Scans the Registry.
/s	Scan all shares.
/t	Performs a test or dry run.

sidwalk.exe—SID Walk

The *sidwalk.exe* command line utility takes a mapping file as input and scans its ACLs in the Registry, file system, file and print shares, and local group membership. The mapping file can be used for Sidwalk conversion on multiple computers.

The syntax for this utility is as follows:

```
sidwalk profile_file [profile_file …] [/t] [/f [path]] [/r] [/s] [/p]
[/g] [/l file] [/?]
```

snmputilg.exe—SNMP Utility Tool

The *snmputilg.exe* command invokes the graphical SNMP Utility Tool and is used in conjunction with the older SNMP Browser Tools (*snmputil.exe*.) to manage SNMP network elements.

TABLE A.71 tlist.exe Parameters

Option	Description
-m pattern	Lists all processes with associated DLLs.
-p processname	Outputs the PID for the specified process.
-s	Outputs the services associated with a process.
-t	Outputs a process tree.

tlist.exe—Task List Viewer

The *tlist.exe* command line utility lists currently executing processes (tasks) and outputs information such as the process identification number (PID) and process name. Its syntax is

```
tlist [pid] [pattern] [-m pattern] [-p processname] [-s] [-t]
```

POSTSCRIPT

This Appendix provided an overview of the most frequently used utilities available under Windows 2000. Our selection was based on feedback from system administrators who reviewed early versions of the book. A special note of appreciation is made to Ellen Beck Gardner for her help in compiling the command descriptions.

Glossary

ACE (Access Control Entry)   An ACE is an entry in the Access Control List (ACL) that includes a security ID (SID) and an access rights list. When the SID is matched, access or denial rights are granted.

ACL (Access Control List)   An object's owner has discretionary access control over how access is allowed or disallowed. Each object has an ACL for this purpose that comprises Access Control Entries (ACE). Also known as the Discretionary Access Control List (DACL), the ACL is the portion of the security descriptor that enforces permissions associated with an object. (The other components of the security descriptor are the object's Creator (otherwise known as the Owner), Group (a POSIX compliance element that relates to the "primary group"), and the SACL (System Access Control List) that regulates auditing.)

Account lockout   Based on the lockout security policy, a user will be denied access (or locked out) after a predefined number of failed logon attempts. The period in which the lockout remains is also set in the lockout security policy.

ACPI (Advanced Configuration and Power Interface)   ACPI is an industry power management specification used by Windows 2000 Plug and Play hardware management.

Active Directory   The Active Directory comprises the advanced directory services shipped with Windows 2000 Server versions. Chapters 5 and 6 discuss Active Directory concepts and utilization.

ADSI (Active Directory Service Interface)   ADSI is an API that permits applications on Windows 9x, Windows NT, and Windows 2000 to interface with networked directory services.

Active partition   The active partition is the partition from which the operating system starts and must be the primary partition on a basic disk. On Windows 2000-only systems the active partition can also be the system volume. On systems where Windows 2000 is dual-booted with earlier Microsoft operating systems, all start-up files for both operating systems must reside on the active partition.

ACS (Admission Control Service)   The ACS is part of the Quality of Service (QoS) network management feature and defines who shares shared network resources and how they are used. It also regulates subnet bandwidth.

ActiveX   ActiveX is an umbrella term for Microsoft technologies that permit applications developers to create Web interactive content.

Adapter card   Also known as a network card, the adapter card is a printed circuit board or hardware chipset that permits network connections between computers.

address   An address is a DNS resource record that maps the name to an IP address.

Address classes   Three levels of address classes exist based upon IP numbers: A, B, and C. For additional information, see Chapter 12.

Address pool   An address pool contains the scoped addresses available for license by a DHCP Server.

Address Resolution Protocol (ARP)   As part of the TCP/IP suite, ARP provides resolution between IP and MAC addresses.

Administrator   As defined by Windows 2000, an administrator is a member of the Administrators group, with full control over a specific computer or domain.

Agent   An agent is a computer or network device that runs SNMP (the Simple Network Management Protocol) and provides information about its location and configuration.

API (Application Programming Interface)   An API is a routine that can be called by an application to carry out requests of other applications or the operating system. An example is the display handling routines available from the Win32 API.

APIPA (Automatic Private IP Addressing)   A feature of Windows 2000 and Windows 98, APIPA automatically assigns an IP address from 169.254.0.0 to 169.254.254.254 (with a subnet of 255.255.255.0) if a static IP was not set or when DCHP is unavailable.

AppleTalk   AppleTalk is the default network protocol for Apple Macintosh computer systems. Windows 2000 Server provides connectivity to AppleTalk clients.

Asymmetric encryption   Asymmetric encryption utilizes mathematically related public and private encryption keys. The private key remains confidential; the public key is passed out freely. To encrypt a message, a sender uses the receiver's public key. The receiver can then decrypt the message with the corresponding private key. The use of public key exchanges is known as asymmetric encryption.

Asynchronous communication   In asynchronous communication data is sent and received at irregular intervals. Start and stop bits are used to signal when each character has been received.

ATM (asynchronous transfer mode)   ATM is a communication protocol that transmits fixed-length 53-byte packets. It is generally viewed as a rapid method of data communication.

Attribute   In terms of files, an attribute defines if the file is read-only, archival, encrypted, or compressed. In terms of Active Directory schema, the attribute defines the features of the object class.

Auditing   Auditing is a means of tracking the activities of system and user behavior. Windows 2000 supports a wide range of auditing options.

Authentication   Authentication is the process of matching a user's logon name and password against Windows 2000 security files. It is carried out on the local system for standalone computers. For network logon, it is conducted by an Active Directory domain controller.

Authoritative restore   This is a form of object resolution used by the Backup tool in which specified objects are replaced.

AXFR (full zone transfer)   AXFR is a common query used by DNS to synchronize changed zone transfer data.

Backup media pool   The backup media pool is defined by the Backup tool and consists of hardware devices dedicated to storage.

Backup Operators   Backup Operators is a predefined user group. Members have authority to perform backup of data regardless of the object's attribute.

Bandwidth   Bandwidth in digital communications terms is defined by a bits-per-second (bps) transfer rate. Within an analog communications environment it is seen as a range between high and low frequencies.

Basic disk   The basic disk is the hard drive that contains the primary partition, extended partitions, and logical drives. It can also access MS-DOS.

Basic volume   A basic volume is a storage method used by Windows NT 4.0 or earlier.

Batch program   A batch program is a form of a text-based (ASCII) script that invokes other applications or batch programs. It uses the extension .CMD or .BAT.

BDC (Backup Domain Controller)   The BDC is used by Windows NT Server 4.0 or earlier as a subordinate domain controller to the Primary Domain Controller. It contains read-only copies of information such as the domain's security account manager (SAM). It is used in a Windows 2000 domain when the domain is configured in mixed mode.

BIND (Berkeley Internet Name Domain)   BIND is a version of DNS ported to most variants of UNIX.

BIOS (basic input/output system)   The BIOS is used in personal computers to check hardware, for basic operating system startup, and to initiate data communications. It is stored in Read-Only Memory (ROM).

bit (binary digit)   Expressed as a 1 or 0 to designate true or false, the bit is the smallest unit of information utilized by personal computers.

bits per second (bps)   Bps is a measure of communication speed based on character transfer. A character is defined as 8 bits. In a typical asynchronous environment, an additional start and stop bit is added.

Boot   Booting is the process of starting or resetting a computer operating system.

Boot files   Boot files are required to initiate a Windows 2000 operating system including Ntldr and Ntdetect.com.

Boot logging   The boot logging process occurs automatically with system startup and saves information regarding boot activities. It is stored in the root directory as an ASCII file called Ntldr.txt.

Boot partition   The boot partition is the location of Windows 2000 operating system and support files. It has to be located in the same partition used for initial booting that contains Ntldr and Ntdetect.com.

BOOTP (Bootstrap Protocol)   BOOTP is part of the TCP/IP used by diskless workstations or devices like network printers.

Browser   A browser is an application that interprets HTTP communications and displays HTML output from the Internet or an intranet.

Built-in groups   Built-in groups are shipped by default with Windows 2000 to incorporate a standard set of rights. These groups are provided so that rights can be easily applied to user accounts.

CA (Certification Authority)   The CA establishes and verifies public keys. See Chapter 10 for additional information about the public key infrastructure and Microsoft's implementation of CA.

Cache   A cache is a local store of data commonly used by programs like DNS.

Callback number   A callback number is defined by the end user or the administrator as the number the server will call to connect with a remote client. It is often used for roaming users who want to limit hotel toll costs while connected to the home office server.

Canonical name   The canonical name is an object's distinguished name but is output without LDAP attribute tags like DC= or CN=.

CAPI (CryptoAPI)   CAPI is used to develop applications that can take advantage of encryption and digital signatures.

CDE (Common Desktop Environment)   CDE is an integrated graphical desktop environment.

CDFS (Compact Disk File System)   The CDFS is a protected mode file system used for CD-ROM storage and access.

Certificate   A certificate binds an encryption key with encrypted data. Certificates are digitally signed by certificate authorities.

Certificate trust list (CTL)   The CTL is a listing of certificate authorities the system administrator considers appropriate and safe for the particular environment.

CGI (Common Gateway Interface)   The CGI takes the form of a server-based script that initiates services. It is commonly used in association with Web services.

Child domain   A child domain is part of a domain hierarchical tree. It shares the same domain namespace, Global Catalog, and schema with all other domains in the tree. If the child domain is called "sales" within the EntCert.com domain, its name is sales.EntCert.com.

Child object   A child object is nested within a parent object.

Client   A client is any system connected to or requesting services from another computer. That other computer is known as a server. At any given time, a computer can be a client or a server.

Cluster   Cluster is a group of computers that together share a work load and perform redundant fault tolerance. If a member of a cluster fails, another member will assume the work load in a process know as failover.

Cluster Services   The Cluster Services software component manages cluster functions.

Cluster-aware application   Not all applications are designed to work within a cluster environment. Cluster-aware applications must conform to the cluster API. For additional information, see Chapter 17.

COM (Component Object Model)   The Component Object Model is programming model that permits object interoperability and reusability. COM components theoretically can be utilized by different applications and within varied operating system environments. Microsoft's Object Linking & Embedding (OLE) and ActiveX are based on COM. DCOM (Distributed Component Object Model) is the network variant of COM.

Command Prompt   The Command Prompt provides a character-based window in which supported MS-DOS utilities and certain scripts such as batch files are run.

Common groups   Common groups make up the listing from the Start menu that is common to all users.

Communication port   Also known as the serial port, the communication port permits single-bit asynchronous data transmission.

Community name   The community name is used to group SNMP devices.

Compact Disk File System (CDFS)   CDFS is a 32-bit protected mode file system used for compact disks.

Computer account   Created by the domain administrator, the computer account identifies a unique computer within the domain.

CPU time   CPU time is the total processor time in seconds used by a process.

CPU usage   CPU usage is shown in the Task Manager and indicates the percentage of CPU utilization.

CRC (cyclical redundancy check)   CRC checks for errors in data transmission. Each transmission includes data and extra (redundant) error-checking values. CRC is used by communications protocols such as XMODEM and Kermit.

Cryptographic Service Provider (CSP)   CSP is code that performs authentication, encoding, and encryption services. It creates and destroys keys and their utilization. Windows-based applications gain access through the CryptoAPI.

DACL (Discretionary Access Control List)   The DACL is part of an object's security descriptor and defines who has permission to use, or is specifically denied access to, an object.

DDE (dynamic data exchange)   This is a Microsoft implementation of Inter-Process Communication (IPC) that permits DDE-enabled applications to share data.

Device driver   A device driver is code that communicates between Windows 2000 and hardware such as a modem, network card, or printer. Without it a device is not recognized by Windows 2000. The Hardware Compatibility List (HCL) lists device drivers shipped with Windows 2000. Other drivers must be obtained from the hardware manufacturer.

Device Manager   Interfacing within the Executive, or kernel, mode of Windows 2000, the Device Manager is an administrative tool used to control computer devices. It lists device properties and performs updates and further configuration.

Dfs link   The Dfs link is from the Dfs root to shared folders or other Dfs roots.

Dfs (distributed file system)   Dfs links shared folders located on different servers into a single namespace, permitting transparent access to shared folders regardless of their location on the network.

Dfs root   The Dfs root is simply a container for Dfs files and links.

DHCP (Dynamic Host Configuration Protocol)   DHCP is an industry standard networking protocol that provides TCP/IP-based networks the ability to dynamically assign Internet Protocol (IP) addresses and eliminate address conflicts for the defined IP number range.

Dial-up connection   A dial-up connection permits communication from a computer or network through telephone exchanges. It can be made through a modem, ISDN line, or X.25 network.

Differential backup   This is a backup of all files that have been added or modified since the last scheduled full or incremental backup. It does not set the Archival attribute, thereby marking the files as having been backed up.

Digital signature   The digital signature binds the identity of a user to a file or object.

Digital Signature Standard (DSS)   DSS uses the Digital Signature Algorithm (DSA) as its signature algorithm and SHA-1 as its message hash algorithm. DSA is a public-key cipher used to create digital signatures. It is not employed for data encryption.

Directory   A directory is listing of people, places, and things. A phone book is a common example.

Directory partition   The Active Directory has three partitions that are really directory subtrees, each of which has a separate replication schedule. The three partitions are the schema, the configuration, and actual objects.

Directory replication   The Active Directory utilizes a multi-master replication model in which all domain controllers have read/write capacity and communicate changes to their peers through defined policies.

Directory Service   The Directory Service manages elements within the directory and permits users to locate objects based on definitions known as attributes.

Disk mirroring   Mirroring permits the creation of a duplicate or mirrored version of a disk. Mirrored volumes must reside on different disks. In the event of a disk failure, access is obtained to the mirrored volume.

Distinguished name   The Windows 2000 Active Directory utilizes a distinguished name to identify an object. See Chapter 5 on naming conventions.

DLL (dynamic linked library)   The dynamic linked library consists of executable routines whose specific functions can be called by applications. As a specific function is needed, the application will locate and execute the .DLL file required. DLLs are reusable.

DNS (Domain Name System)   An industry standard service that works with TCP/IP networks, DNS is a hierarchical name service for host computers and is used as a foundation technology by the Active Directory. DNS lists host names and IP addresses so that a computer can be located in either fashion.

DNS Dynamic Update Protocol   This is an enhanced version of DNS that permits the dynamic registration of hosts.

Domain   The Active Directory manages a hierarchical infrastructure of networked computers with the domain as the foundation. A *domain* comprises computer systems and network resources that share a common logical security boundary and can store over 17 terabytes within the Active Directory database store. While a domain can cross physical locations, it maintains its own security policies and security relationships with other domains. Domains are sometimes created to define functional boundaries such as an administrative unit (e.g. marketing versus engineering). They are also viewed as groupings of resources or servers that utilize a common domain name known as a namespace.

Domain controller   A domain controller is a server containing a copy of the Active Directory. All domain controllers are peers and maintain replicated versions of the Active Directory for their domains. The domain controller plays an important role in both the logical and physical structure of the Active Directory. It organizes all the domain's object data in a logical and hierarchical data store. It also authenticates users, provides responses to queries about network objects, and replicates directory services. The physical structure provides the means to transmit this data through well-connected sites.

Domain local group   The domain local group is a security or distribution group. It may contain universal groups, global groups, and accounts from any domain in the domain tree or forest.

Domain model   The Active Directory domain model involves connection of one or more domains into hierarchical trust relationships. Domain trees and forests are created as part of this model. Also included are subadministrative structures known as organizational units.

Domain name and namespace   The domain name is used by DNS to identify a computer, host, or network device. It is made up of a preface identifier (like "EntCert" or "Microsoft") and a suffix (like "com," "gov," "net," etc.) separated by a dot. The namespace is the database structure used by DNS for names.

Domain naming master   One of the several operations masters, this domain controller is responsible for adding and removing domain controllers from the forest.

Domain tree   When multiple domains share a common schema, security trust relationships, and a Global Catalog, a *domain tree* is created, defined by a common and contiguous namespace. For example, all domains with the ending namespace of *EntCert.com* belong to the *EntCert* domain tree. A domain tree is formed through the expansion of child domains like *Sales.EntCert.com* or *Research. EntCert.com*. In this example, the *root domain* is *EntCert.com*.

EFS (Encrypting File System)   EFS is an extension to NTFS and permits users to secure files through encryption.

Emergency Repair Disk (ERD)   Created by the Backup utility, the ERD contains Windows 2000 system data, including configuration information.

Event   Any significant activity or process that requires logging for documentation.

Event Log service   This is a documentation service that organizes a variety of events into lists that describe them and underscores whether they are normal or abnormal.

Explicit permissions   These are permissions that are automatically set on an object or those that are set by the object's owner.

Extensible Authentication Protocol (EAP)   EAP is an extension of the Point-to-Point Protocol (PPP) providing remote user access authentication. Authentication schemes supported by EAP include dial-up using Kerberos V5, one-time passwords, and public key authentication using smart cards and certificates. EAP can be used with dial-up, PPTP, and L2TP clients. It offers security against brute-force or dictionary attacks and greater protection against password guessing than other authentication methods, such as CHAP.

Failback   Used in clustering environments, failback is the process of reestablishing cluster node responsibilities when the original failure has been corrected.

Failover   Used in clustering environments, failover is the process of handing over responsibility to another node when a failure occurs.

FAT (File Allocation Table)   FAT is a legacy file system used in MS-DOS and earlier versions of Windows. While supported by Windows 2000, it has many limitations, especially regarding security and storage.

FAT32   FAT32 is an extension of FAT introduced with Windows 98. While supported in Windows 2000, it is still regarded as a legacy file system that limits many operating system features.

Fault tolerance   Fault tolerance ensures data integrity in the event of hardware failures. This is most closely associated with clustering.

File Transfer Protocol (FTP)   FTP is used in TCP/IP networks to transmit files across the network.

Firewall   A firewall usually includes a combination of software and hardware used to secure a computer or enterprise from unauthorized external access.

Forest   Trust relationships can be formed between domain trees with different namespaces, thus creating a domain forest. Forests allow the formation of an enterprise with different domain names such as *EntCert.com* and *unint.com*. All trees within the forest share a number of common attributes, including a Global

Catalog, configuration, and schema. A forest simply is a reference point between trees and does not have its own name.

Forward lookup   This is the DNS name locator using the friendly name (as opposed to the IP address).

Fragmentation   As data is stored on a disk, files may be divided and located in a number of physical locations. As files are so distributed, the disk is said to be fragmented. Unless defragmentation programs are run, this can cause system performance loss.

Gateway   A gateway connects dissimilar networks and transmits the data.

Global Catalog   The Global Catalog (GC) is designed for two primary functions. First, it is a domain controller that stores object data and manages queries on locating objects according to their most common attributes. Second, it provides data that permits network logon. In single-domain-controller environments the Active Directory and the GC reside on the same server.

Global group   The global group is used to organize users within the domain.

Group   A group is a collection of users, computers, and other groups. It is the method by which rights and other characteristics can be assigned to multiple users.

Group memberships   Users are members of one or more groups and derive rights from group membership.

Group Policy   The Group Policy is an administrative mechanism for defining and managing how objects may be utilized by users and computers.

Group Policy Object (GPO)   The GPO is a collection of Group Policy settings.

Guest account   This is an account for users who do not have a regular user account.

GUID (Global unique identifier)   The GUID identifies a device or component through the use of a 16-byte value.

HAL (Hardware Abstraction Layer)   HAL is a layer of code that separates the hardware interface from the kernel and Executive Services.

Hash   Also known as a message digest, the hash is a one-way mathematical function (hash algorithm) that is applied to data to secure it.

Hive   The hive is a portion of the Registry that appears as a file on the hard disk. It is edited by the Registry Editor.

Home directory   The home directory is accessible by a user for the storage and manipulation of her files. Every user has a home directory, whose default location can be set by the administrator.

HTML (Hypertext Markup Language)   HTML is a text-based markup language interpret by Web browsers to format and output file contents.

HTTP (Hypertext Transfer Protocol) HTTP is the protocol used to transfer information on the World Wide Web.

IAS (Internet Authentication Service) IAS is used to provide security and authentication for dial-in connections.

IIS (Internet Information Services) IIS maintains and configures Internet services. It includes Web, Network News Transfer Protocol (NNTP), file transfer protocol (FTP) and Simple Mail Transfer Protocol (SMTP) services.

Incremental backup An incremental backup stores only those files that are new or that have been modified since the last full backup and marks them as having been backed up.

Indexing Service This is an advanced search facility that indexes data for more rapid location.

.inf This is the file extension for device drivers.

Infrastructure Master One of the operations masters, this domain controller manages group-to-user references as changes within group membership occur. This data is then replicated to the other domain controllers.

Inheritance Inheritance is the method of passing permissions or attributes from parent to child.

IP (Internet Protocol) IP is the messenger protocol within the TCP/IP suite. It is responsible for addressing and sending TCP packets.

IP address The IP address is a unique, logical set of numbers identifying each host computer or node in a TCP/IP network. It is a 32-bit number divided into four decimal numbers from 0 to 255, with the numbers separated by periods. An example of an IP address is 111.111.111.111.

KCC (Knowledge Consistency Checker) The KCC is used to create and manage site topology for Active Directory replication.

Kerberos This MIT-developed authentication protocol is used by Windows 2000 to verify a user's encrypted password so that he can achieve logon rights.

KDC (Key Distribution Center) The KDC is a distributed network service that supplies session tickets and temporary session keys used by Kerberos.

Kernel Windows 2000 uses a nonconfigurable microkernel that provides basic operating system functions.

Kernel mode The operating system operates in the kernel mode (also known as the Executive mode) and the User mode. The kernel mode manages such services as security, I/O, device drives, and HAL—that is, generally those things that are not directly involved with users or the Win32 subsystem.

L2TP (Layer 2 Tunneling Protocol) L2TP is an industry standard tunneling protocol.

LAN (local area network)   A LAN is defined by a relatively small area in which the communications network connects a group of computers, printers, and other devices.

LDAP (Lightweight Directory Access Protocol)   LDAP is used by the Active Directory to locate objects within a Windows 2000 domain. As an industry standard, it also permits some directory service interoperability.

Line Printer Daemon (LPD)   LPD is a service that accepts print jobs.

Line Printer Remote (LPR)   LPR is a service used to support remote printer jobs from clients.

Local account   Local accounts are created for users who want access only to the local computer. The Active Directory is not aware of local accounts, and network logon cannot occur through a local account.

Local computer   The local computer is one that is not part of a domain.

Local group   A local group is used to assign permissions to local users for the specific computer in which the group resides.

Logon   Logon is the process in which the user provides a logon name and password that is then passed to Windows 2000 for authentication. Logon scripts are read to provide unique user environments.

Master File Table (MFT)   The MFT is the first file on an NTFS volume and contains information about folders and files on that volume.

MBR (Master Boot Record)   The booting process starts by initiating the MBR data structure. If this sector is corrupted, booting will not occur.

Member server   A member server is any computer that runs Windows 2000 Server or above but is not a domain controller.

Message Queuing   Messages between applications can be queued and distributed across the network even to systems that may be offline. Message Queuing provides guaranteed message delivery and priority-based messaging.

Microsoft Management Console (MMC)   The MMC provides administrative tools with a consistent interface. An administrator can create one or more MMCs and add to it the administrative tools desired. An MMC can also be distributed to other administrators.

Mirror set   A mirror set is a fully redundant copy of data. This provides fault tolerance.

Mixed mode   A mixed mode environment exists when domain-level domain controllers have not be promoted to the Active Directory and still run the Windows 2000 MMC (Microsoft Management Console).

MS-DOS   This is the original Microsoft operating system. Many of its utilities are available on Windows 2000 and are accessible from the Command Prompt.

MS-CHAP (Challenge Handshake Authentication Protocol) This is a Microsoft-centric authenticator for remote dial-in access.

Multi-master replication Multi-master replication replaces the Windows NT replication model in which a Primary Domain Controller (PDC) writes updates to Backup Domain Controllers (BDC). With Windows 2000, all domain controllers have read and write capability so that they all share the same data.

Multiple boot Windows 2000 permits system configuration so that more than one operating system can be booted from the computer. For example, for reasons of legacy application support, it may be necessary to configure a system with both MS-DOS and Windows 2000 boot capability. Multiple boots present some potential security risks and are not highly recommended.

Named pipe This is the name for dedicated shared memory between two processes used for exchanging data.

Namespace A namespace is defined by conventions such as the Domain Name System (DNS), Fully Qualified Domain Name (FQDN), distinguished names (DN), or Domain Name System (DNS), or User Principle Names (UPN)s used by the Active Directory to locate Users, hosts, and objects throughout the domain.

Native mode In native mode all domain controllers are running Windows 2000 Server and have been converted from mixed mode. Windows NT 4.0 BDCs are no longer allowed to participate in Active Directory replication or to perform administrative functions.

Network adapter The network adapter is a hardware circuit board that interfaces between the computer system and the shared network media. Each network interface card, supporting the TCP/IP protocol suite, must obtain its own unique IP address to communicate with other interface cards on the network.

Network card driver A network card driver allows the protocol driver to communicate with the network adapter card. A driver is programmed with vendor- and model-specific hardware requirements for each type of card. This driver must be found from among the Windows 2000 drivers or retrieved from the network adapter's vendor.

NNTP (Network News Transfer Protocol) NNTP is a subset of the TCP/IP suite that allows clients to read and post news messages to a newssite. This allows readers to follow conversation threads.

Node A node may be a member of a server cluster or a device with one or more network interfaces connected to a network.

Nonauthoritative restore A Windows 2000 domain controller reconfigured with a nonauthoritative restore from a directory backup will be overwritten by Active Directory information replicated from domain controllers currently operating in the domain. The restored directory is not given the same priority as current domain controller information.

Noncontainer object   This is an object that may not contain another object— for example, a leaf object, such as a file.

Nonpaged memory   Sections of the computer's RAM that may not be paged to disk are nonpaged. Data stored in them is always available for quick read and write operations.

Nontransitive trust   This is either a one-way or a two-way trust that does not support transitivity. If A trusts B and B trusts C, then A does not trust C.

Normal backup   In a normal backup the archive attribute is set on all files that have been backed up. Incremental backups then back up files that have been updated since the last normal backup.

NS (Name Server) resource record   This record identifies authoritative DNS name servers for a domain.

Nslookup   This is a DNS client command line tool for testing the DNS lookup functionality.

NTFS   NTFS is the most advanced file system for Windows 2000-supported special file/folder permissions, auditing, file encryption, and large volumes.

NTLM   NTLM is the authentication mechanism for Windows NT and down-level versions of Windows. It is supported in Windows 2000 to authorize these earlier systems.

Object   Object is an instantiation of a class definition. Typical objects include files and folders. In the Active Directory, user accounts, computers, and containers are all examples of objects. An object such as a user account has associated attributes like name, telephone, and title.

ODBC   Open Database Connectivity is based on the Call Level Interface (CLI) for implementing common Structured Query Language (SQL) statements when access is desired for different database implementations.

Offline   A cluster server node is offline when it is inactive or shutdown.

OLE   In Object Linking and Embedding technology, portions of documents, spreadsheets, or graphics are either linked to another document or embedded and copied. Linking objects allows changes to an object to be reflected in the link. Embedding or copying the object creates two separate objects, and changes in one object will not be reflected in the other.

On-disk catalog   This is a list of files and folders that have been backed up using the Backup utility on the local drive.

On-media catalog   This is a list of files and folders that have been backed up, using the Backup utility, to another medium other than the local drive.

One-way trust   In a one-way trust relationship one domain trusts another, but the second domain does not trust the first. This type of trust is nontransitive.

Online   A Cluster Server node is online when it is active or running.

Operations Master   Unique roles that are performed by a single domain controller, as discussed in Chapter 5.

Operator   The operator is used to make string matches and comparisons when performing searches.

Organizational unit (OU)   An OU is a subcategory within a domain used to provide more granular control over the application of Group Policies and the delegation of administrative authority.

Orphan   This is a crashed or failed volume within a RAID-5 configuration.

Orphan file   This is a briefcase file not related to any other file on the system.

Owner   An Owner is a user who may change permissions on an object regardless of its current permission settings.

Packet   A collection of binary data used to communicate information over networks is referred to as a packet. The packet definition is limited to the network layer (OSI layer 3) and above. Data link layer information is considered frame information.

Packet header   The header contains the source, destination, and size information for data contained in the packet.

Page fault   When a process cannot find needed memory from RAM and must retrieve a memory paged to the disk, a hard page fault occurs. When a process cannot access needed memory from RAM because another process is the memory, a soft page fault occurs.

Paged pool   This is the amount of virtual memory allocated to a process.

Paging file   This is a hidden file on the hard disk that stores paged data. Paging file information is accessed when a hard page fault occurs. RAM and paging files make up the virtual memory space.

Parent domain   A parent is the domain above a given domain in the domain hierarchy.

Parent object   A parent is an object that contains a given object.

Partition   A physical disk may be broken up into as many as four partitions that appear to be separate disk drives to the user.

Partition boot sector   The partition boot sector contains information necessary to read disks and load the operating system during system startup.

Password   A password is a unique string that may be up to 14 characters in length for Windows 2000 user accounts.

Password Authentication Protocol (PAP)   This is a primitive remote access authentication protocol that communicates passwords in plain text.

Path   A disk volume, folders, and a file name ordered to identify a particular file or folder in the directory hierarchy together form a path. Domain names and host names may also be used to identify objects—for example, *Entcert.com*\ *Documents**username**Address Book*.

PDC emulator master   This is the designated Windows 2000 domain controller that handles PDC responsibilities for down versions of Windows NT and handles all Group Policy modifications and updates.

Peak Memory Usage   This is the highest amount of memory consumed by a process since starting.

Pel   also known as a pixel, a pel is the smallest controllable video screen component.

Per Seat Licensing   In this type of licensing, each client is given a license to access a given server, and all licensed clients may access the serve at once.

Per Server Licensing   This type of licensing dedicates licenses to a given number of clients. Any client may use an available license, but no more then the number of client licenses may access the server at the same time.

Permission   Permissions are assigned to users and security groups and govern access privileges and actions that may be performed on an object.

PID (process identifier)   see *process identifier*.

PIF (program information file)   The PIF contains information to assist the operating system when starting MS-DOS applications.

Ping   A ping is a command line utility used to verify IP connectivity to a given IP address.

Pixel   see *pel*.

Plug and Play   This facility automatically detects hardware components so that the correct driver may be loaded for further communication with the device.

Point of presence (POP)   Post Office Protocol.

Point-to-Point Protocol (PPP)   The PPP is designed to provide serial encapsulation of IP/IPX/AppleTalk protocols over remote access connections.

Point-to-Point Tunneling Protocol (PPTP)   PPTP supports two endpoints of a tunnel, allowing encapsulated data to travel between them. Encryption and authentication supported by the tunneling protocol create a Virtual Private Network (VPN) through the tunnel to give users secure access to corporate networks over the Internet or an intranet.

Pointer (PTR) resource record   A PTR record permits the reverse mapping of an IP address to a host name. PTR records can be found in reverse lookup zones.

Policy   Group Policies determine the look and feel of the desktop environment, user profile locations, application availability, security settings, and logon/logoff scripts.

POP (point of presence)   POP is the closest Internet remote access point for a traveling user that permits the use of a local telephone number. Once the user dials in to an ISP's POP, she may then establish access to her corporate network without long-distance phone charges.

Port   Hardware ports usually consist of serial (COM) ports, parallel (LPT) ports, Universal Serial Bus (USB) ports, and any other communication port on the computer.

Port ID   A port ID usually refers to a communication protocol's port number used by the service. For example, HTTP servers usually listen for communication on TCP port 80.

Port rule   A port rule determines the action taken when traffic attempts to send or receive on a given port.

POSIX   The Portable Operating System Interface for Computing Environments comprises a set of standards drafted by the Institute of Electrical and Electronic Engineers (IEEE) that define various aspects of an operating system, including programming interface, security, networking, and graphical interface. Programs that adhere to the POSIX standard can be easily ported from one system to another.

Predefined key   This is the section or category of the Registry accessible through the Registry Editor.

Primary Domain Controller (PDC)   The PDC contains the writeable version of the user accounts database for Windows NT 4.0 domains and down-level versions. Only a PDC may exist for a Windows NT 4.0 domain. BDCs contain read-only versions of the database.

Primary partition   Up to four primary partitions may be created on a disk and act as a reference point for booting the system.

Print job   This comprises the queued data for printing and associated print format commands.

Print server   This is the computer assigned to handle print jobs for a printer or set of printers.

Print spooler   The spooler is the application on a print server that handles print jobs and distributes them to corresponding printers.

Printer   This is any device that transfers electronic data to paper or film media.

Printer driver   The printer driver allows the operating system to interface with a particular printer designated by a vendor and printer model.

Printer fonts   These are text fonts contained in nonvolatile memory on a printer. The printer is capable of printing only these font types.

Printer permissions   These are access permissions for a particular printer.

Printing pool   A pool contains one or more printers attached to a print server that are assigned print jobs based on current load.

Private key   A private key's owned by a user or computer and is not accessible to any other party. It has a corresponding public key that may be used to decrypt data encrypted by the private key. The public key can also be used to encrypt data that can only be decrypted by the private key.

Process   A process is any application or program started within Windows 2000 that has associated dynamic memory, static memory, and program memory space. Threads may also be created within the process's memory space.

Process identifier (PID)   The PID is a unique number identifying a process easily accessible from the Task Manager.

Protocol   A protocol is a standard for interpreting data sent and received between one process and another. Some protocols, such as the Internet Protocol (IP), allow routing over the Internet, and some, such as the Transfer Control Protocol (TCP), guarantee packet delivery via a connection.

Public key   A public key is owned by a user or computer and is accessible other parties. It has a corresponding private key that may be used to decrypt data encrypted by the public key. It can also be used to encrypt data that can only be decrypted by the private key.

Public Key Cryptography   This is an asymmetric key technology using private and public keys to exchange information.

Public Key Infrastructure (PKI)   The PKI consists of methods and strategies for distributing public and private keys for secure communication, authentication, and integrity.

Quality of Service (QoS)   The QoS attempts to guarantee bandwidth and delivery of Internet Protocol (IP) packets using protocols implemented by Windows 2000.

Query   A query contains the criteria for a search using Index Services.

Queue   A queue is a buffer or list of items waiting to be processed.

Quota limit   The quota limit restricts the amount of disk space a user may consume.

RAID-5   RAID-5 is a fault-tolerant strategy implemented by Windows 2000 using three or more dynamic volumes to protect data. Parity information is stored along with protected data across several disks. When one disk fails, the data may be reconstructed from what's left of it and the parity information.

Random-Access Memory (RAM)   RAM is the volatile memory used by the system's microprocessor that is lost when the computer loses power or is turned off. It provides the fastest memory accesses (Reads/Writes) available to the system.

Read-Only Memory (ROM)   ROM is the nonvolatile memory that is not lost when the system's power is turned off and is not modified frequently or quickly. Most ROM is not modifiable by the system.

Recovery agent   A recovery agent is a user account that is provided a recovery key for decrypting files using the Encrypted File System (EFS). Usually this is the Administrator account.

Recovery Console   The Recovery Console is started from the Windows 2000 recovery disks or directly from the Command Prompt using the Winnt32.exe / cmdcons command. It allows basic disk access, format ability, and some repair abilities.

Recycle Bin   The Recycle Bin acts as temporary storage for deleted files and folders. Once it has been emptied, data is lost and disk space is freed.

Redundant Array of Independent Disks (RAID)   RAID categorizes six levels of disk fault tolerance (0–5). Windows 2000 implements striping (0), mirroring (1), and Raid-5 (5). See *RAID-5*.

Registered file type   This is a file type recognized by the system.

Registry   The registry contains application and operating system configuration information and may be viewed and modified using the regedit.exe command.

Registry boot   The Windows 2000 DNS server has a couple of boot options: Registry settings and boots with settings contained in the text file.

Registry size limit (RSL)   The RSL limits the amount of space an application may consume when modifying a Registry hive.

Relative distinguished name   This is a subset of an object's full distinguished name, usually the CN, or common name, portion.

Relative ID   This is an identification number that relates back to a specific domain controller. A domain controller requests relative IDs from the relative ID master. A combination of the domain ID and retrieved relative IDs forms a security ID, which is then assigned to uniquely identify users, security groups, and computers within the domain.

Relative ID master   One domain controller, the master, is assigned the responsibility to generate relative IDs for all domain controllers within the domain. See *relative ID*.

Relative name   The host name portion of the Fully Qualified Domain Name used in DNS naming. For example, in *ahost@domainname.com* the relative name is *ahost*.

Remote access   Remote access is that to users outside the intranet via dial-in access or network interfaces attached to the Internet.

Remote Access Server (RAS)   The RAS is a system configured to accept remote access.

Remote administration   This is administration of system settings without local logon.

Remote Authentication Dial-In User Service (RADIUS)   RADIUS is used by many ISPs to authenticate, authorize, and provide accounting for users accessing their corporate intranets using tunneling protocols.

Remote computer   A remote computer is not available for a local logon.

Remote Procedure Call (RPC)   RPC is a message-passing facility that allows a distributed application to call services from other computers in the computer.

Replication   One of the core functions of Active Directory domain controllers is to replicate data to provide redundancy and object availability. A multi-master replication screen is used so that all domain controllers have the same information and read/write capability.

Replication topology   In replication topology information is shared between pairs of domain controllers. The KCC automatically generates the topology within a site. An administrator establishes replication between sites.

Root   The root is defined as the highest level of the structure. For example, the first domain created is the root domain.

Router   A router is a network server designed to support connectivity and inter-operability. It analyzes network addresses in a packet and then passes the packet along. Routers make packet forwarding decisions.

RR (resource record)   Resource records are defined by RFC 1035 and utilized by DNS. They associate addresses to other data.

RSA   The default for Microsoft Windows, RSA is a public and private key algorithm utilization.

SACL (System Access Control List)   The SACL is a partial list of an object's security descriptor. It defines which events are to be audited per user or group.

Safe mode   As part of the option menu system accessed by pressing F8 during the initial boot phase of a system, Safe mode loads Windows 2000 with minimal services. It provides an environment in which a system that will not normally boot can be corrected and repaired. Safe mode can be launched in its default manner, within the Command Prompt, or with networking services.

SAM (Security Account Manager)   SAM is a protected subsystem of Windows 2000 and Windows NT that maintains the Security Account Manager database. The Active Directory supplants SAM in domain environments.

Schema   The *schema* is simply a framework of definitions that establishes the type of objects available to the Active Directory. The definitions are divided into *object classes* and *attributes*. Attributes are divided into two types: those that *must* exist and those that *may* exist. For example, the schema defines a user object class as having the user's name as a required attribute and the user's physical location or job description as an optional attribute. Attributes help distinguish an object from other objects. They are defined to include the Object Name, Object Identifier (OID), Syntax, and optional information.

Schema master   As one of the operations masters, the schema master is a domain controller that manages schema changes and replicates them to other domain controllers.

Scope   The scope is a range of IP address available for assignment by DHCP.

Script   A script is a program that executes a series of instructions. The Windows Scripts Hosting facility permits the launching of a variety of scripts. Batch programs (with .bat or .cmd extensions) are scripts.

Secure Hash Algorithm (SHA-1)   SHA-1 is a message digest hash that creates a 160-bit hash value.

Secure Multipurpose Internet Mail Extensions (S/MIME)   S/MIME is a secure extension to the industry standard mail protocol.

Secure Sockets Layer (SSL)   SSL is a protocol for securing network communication using public and private keys.

Security descriptor   The security descriptor is a set of data attached to an object. It specifies the permissions granted to users and groups and defines the security events to be audited.

Security group   A security group is anything that can be listed in the DACL that provides or defines permissions.

Security ID (SID)   The SID is an unique identifying number of a user or other network object.

Server Message Block   SMB is file-sharing protocol to allow networked computers to access files that reside remotely.

Service (SRV) resource record   SRV is resource record employed in a zone to register and locate TCP/IP services.

Shared folder   Shared folders permit other defined users to access files on a remote system.

Simple Mail Transfer Protocol (SMTP)   SMTP is used on the Internet to transfer mail. It can relay mail across transport service environments.

Simple Network Management Protocol (SNMP)   SNMP is a TCP/IP-based network management protocol that transports information and commands between management programs. The SNMP agent sends status data. SNMP defines the form and meaning of the messages exchanged.

Site   The physical network structure of the Active Directory is based on a unit know as a *site*. The role of the administrator is to design sites that ensure the greatest network performance. A *site* comprises one or more Internet Protocol (IP) subnets that are tied together by high-speed, reliable connections.

Smart Card   The smart card is a credit-card-size device that contains public/private key information and other data.

Snap-in   A snap-in is an application that is added to the Microsoft Management Console and conforms to its standard API.

Socket   A socket is a bidirectional pipe for incoming and outgoing data between networked computers.

Spanned volume   In a spanned volume data is stored across multiple volumes. If one of the disks in the volume fails, all the data is lost.

Special access permissions   These are custom permissions available under NTFS.

Static routes   These are permanent routing network tables.

Stripe set   The stripe set permits the storage of identical partitions on different disks.

Stripe set with parity   This extends basic stripe sets to allow for fault tolerance.

Subkey   Within the Windows 2000 Registry structure, the subkey is simply a child key within a key.

Subnet mask   This is a 32-bit value that distinguishes the TCP/IP network ID portion of the IP address from the host ID portion. TCP/IP hosts use the subnet mask to determine whether a destination host is located on a local or remote network.

System partition   The system partition contains the configuration files necessary to boot Windows 2000.

System State   System State is the portion of the backup that archives the system configuration used for emergency recovery.

SYSVOL   SYSVOL is a shared directory that stores the server's copy of the public files, which are replicated among all domain controllers.

TAPI (Telephony API)   Telephony API is an applications programming interface that allows data/fax/voice calls by programs including HyperTerminal, Dial-up Networking, Phone Dialer, and other communications.

TCP/IP (Transmission Control Protocol/Internet Protocol)   TCP/IP is one of the most commonly used networking protocols on the Internet. It includes a suite of applications and standards for inter-computer communication and conventions for connecting networks and routing traffic.

Telnet   Telnet is a terminal emulation protocol widely used on the Internet.

Terminal Services   Terminal Services supports traditional multi-user environments for Windows 2000. An application run on a server can be displayed and interfaced from a client computer. Microsoft supplies Terminal Services for its Windows products. Terminal Services for other environments like UNIX or Macintosh are available from third-party vendors.

TFTP (Trivial File Transfer Protocol)   TFTP is a nonsecure TCP/IP file transfer protocol. Its use is general discouraged.

TGS (Ticket-Granting Service)   Part of the public key infrastructure, TGS is a service that authorizes the granting of certificates.

TGT (Ticket to Get Tickets)   The TGT is issued to obtain a security certificate.

Thread   A threat is a type of object within a process that executes the program instructions. Multiple threads permit the running of concurrent operations within a process.

Topology   The topology defines the relationships among domains, sites, and network devices.

Transitive trust   A transitive trust is a two-way trust relationship established between domain trees and forests. Assuming a user has permission, a transitive trust relationship permits access to objects anywhere in the tree or forest.

Trojan horse   A Trojan horse is generally viewed as a program that appears to perform one function but executes other functions, generally to the detriment of the user or computer system.

Trust relationship   All domains in a tree or forest automatically establish two-way trust relationships. In addition, explicit one-way trusts can be established between a single domain with another single domain. A trust relationship allows users and global groups from another user accounts database to be used. With trust relationships, a user who has only one user account in one domain can potentially access the entire network.

UNC (Universal Naming Convention)   The UNC is a convention for naming files and other resources beginning with two backslashes (\\).

URL (Uniform Resource Locator)   The URL uniquely identifies a location on the Internet. A URL for a World Wide Web site is preceded with *http://* and can contain more detail, such as the name of a page of hypertext, usually identified by a suffix of *.html* or *.htm*.

User account   The user account contains all of the properties of a user, including a unique name and password.

User profile   The user profile is file that defines the configuration data for a user, including desktop settings, persistent network connections, and application settings.

User rights   User rights indicate the activities a user is permitted to perform. Many user rights are established through membership in security and distribution groups.

User rights policy   These policies are security settings that underscore user rights.

Virtual DOS machine (VDM)   The VDM is invoked when MS-DOS commands or utilities are invoked.

Virtual memory   Virtual memory is used on a temporary basis to execute programs and processes.

Virtual Private Network (VPN)   A VPN is an extended private network that involves authentication and encryption of data across public networks.

Volume   A volume is a partition on a disk that operates as if it were a separate physical disk.

WAN (wide area network)   A wide area network is typically defined as a geographically separated communications network.

Windows Internet Name Service (WINS)   WINS is a service that maps computer names to IP addresses. It is used by earlier versions of Windows and will be supplanted by Windows 2000 use of DNS and DHCP.

Workgroup   A workgroup is a collection of Windows 2000 and other computers that are interconnected but do not belong to a domain.

X.500   X.500 is a set of standards defining a distributed directory service. The standards are developed and supported by the International Standards Organization (ISO).

Zone   A zone is a subtree of the DNS database. It is administered as a single DNS server. This administrative unit can consist of a single domain or child domains.

Index

Addison-Wesley Professional

How to Register Your Book

Register this Book

Visit: **http://www.aw.com/cseng/register**
Enter the ISBN*
Then you will receive:

- Notices and reminders about upcoming author appearances, tradeshows, and online chats with special guests
- Advanced notice of forthcoming editions of your book
- Book recommendations
- Notification about special contests and promotions throughout the year

*The ISBN can be found on the copyright page of the book

Visit our Web site

http://www.aw.com/cseng

When you think you've read enough, there's always more content for you at Addison-Wesley's web site. Our web site contains a directory of complete product information including:

- Chapters
- Exclusive author interviews
- Links to authors' pages
- Tables of contents
- Source code

You can also discover what tradeshows and conferences Addison-Wesley will be attending, read what others are saying about our titles, and find out where and when you can meet our authors and have them sign your book.

We encourage you to patronize the many fine retailers who stock Addison-Wesley titles. Visit our online directory to find stores near you.

Contact Us via Email

cepubprof@awl.com
Ask general questions about our books.
Sign up for our electronic mailing lists.
Submit corrections for our web site.

cepubeditors@awl.com
Submit a book proposal.
Send errata for a book.

cepubpublicity@awl.com
Request a review copy for a member of the media interested in reviewing new titles.

registration@awl.com
Request information about book registration.

Addison-Wesley Professional

One Jacob Way, Reading, Massachusetts 01867 USA
TEL 781-944-3700 • FAX 781-942-3076